Great Writing

■

Great Writing:

A Reader for Writers

■

Second Edition

Harvey S. Wiener
Adelphi University

Nora Eisenberg
CUNY—LaGuardia Community College

Boston, Massachusetts   Burr Ridge, Illinois   Dubuque, Iowa
Madison, Wisconsin   New York, New York   San Francisco, California
St. Louis, Missouri

McGraw-Hill

*A Division of The **McGraw·Hill** Companies*

GREAT WRITING: A READER FOR WRITERS

This book is printed on acid-free paper.

1 2 3 4 5 7 8 9 0 DOC/DOC 9 0 9 8 7

ISBN 0-07-070190-3

Editorial director: *Phillip A. Butcher*
Sponsoring editor: *Tim Julet*
Marketing manager: *Lesley Denton*
Project manager: *Christina Thornton-Villagomez*
Production supervisor: *Lori Koetters*
Designer: *Larry J. Cope*
Compositor: *Shepherd Incorporated*
Typeface: *10/12 Times Roman*
Printer: *R. R. Donnelley*

Library of Congress Cataloging-in-Publication Data

Great writing: a reader for writers/ [compiled by] Harvey S. Wiener,
   Nora Eisenberg. —2nd ed.
      p. cm.
   ISBN 0-07-070190-3 (alk. paper)
   1. College readers. 2. English language—Rhetoric. 3. Report
writing—Problems, exercises, etc. I. Wiener, Harvey S.
II. Eisenberg, Nora, 1946-
PE1417.G67 1997
808'.0427—dc21   97-7538

http://www.mhcollege.com

About the Authors

Harvey S. Wiener is Vice Provost for Academic Affairs at Adelphi University. He was founding president of the Council of Writing Program Administrators. Dr. Wiener is the author of many books on reading and writing for college students and their teachers, including *The Writing Room* (Oxford, 1981). He has served as chair of the Teaching of Writing Division of the Modern Language Association and as a member of the Executive Committee of the Conference on College Composition and Communication. Dr. Wiener has taught at every level of education from elementary school to graduate school. A Phi Beta Kappa graduate of Brooklyn College, he holds a Ph.D. in Renaissance literature from Fordham University. Dr. Wiener has won grants from the National Endowment for the Humanities, the Fund for the Improvement of Postsecondary Education, and the Exxon Education Foundation.

Nora Eisenberg is a professor of English at LaGuardia Community College of the City University of New York, where she teaches courses in composition, creative writing, and literature, and is senior mentor in the Dissertation Program. Dr. Eisenberg holds a Ph.D. from Columbia University and has taught at Brooklyn College, Stanford University, and Georgetown University. She has published numerous articles on Virginia Woolf and is the coauthor with Harvey Wiener of *Stepping Stones: A Course in Basic Writing* (Random House, 1985). Dr. Eisenberg is also a fiction writer; her short stories have appeared in such journals as the *Voice Literary Supplement* and *Partisan Review*.

Contents

Chapter Three
EXEMPLIFICATION

Chapter Four
PROCESS

Chapter Eight
DEFINITION

Chapter Nine
ARGUMENTATION AND PERSUASION

Acknowledgments   595

Thematic Contents

Language and Writing

Family

Love and Loss

Education, Science, and Culture

Death, Illness, and Mortality

Race, Gender, and Ethnicity

Work, Professions, and Money

Nature

Preface

We believe in a number of important principles about learning to write, and these principles inform this book and establish its content, approach, and format.

We believe first in the primacy of text and in the enduring authority, intelligence, and joy in great writing. When aspiring writers read great writing carefully and attentively, they come closer to producing exceptional writing themselves. Aiming for contemporaneity, too many anthologies for writers avoid great writing; they may offer readable, serviceable samples, but they rarely show our language at its very best or address the great intellectual issues of our civilization. To use readings as guides for writing—as exercises in form, as explorations of style, as laboratories for the growth of ideas in words and sentences—students must read the very best our culture has to offer. Shakespeare, Swift, Virginia Woolf, Cather, Plato, Conrad, Orwell, John Stuart Mill, Poe, Emerson, Emily Brontë, E. B. White, Langston Hughes, Didion, Keats, James Joyce, Thoreau, great writers of our civilization, help provide the models that teach the writer's craft.

With a title like *Great Writing* we know that we are going out on a limb, and we want to admit at the outset that our selections unabashedly proclaim our own subjective judgments, tastes, and prejudices. An experienced reader could grumble about our exclusions or could question some of the pieces or authors we chose to include. Still, we strove to make selections that many educated readers would identify as important writing by great figures. You will recognize most of the authors and many of the selections. Our goal was always to choose the most clearly written, the most elegantly and intelligently reasoned, the most sensitive and thought-provoking pieces that suited the rhetorical strategies we believe best organize a course of study. We aimed for ethnic, geographical, and sexual diversity among our authors, and we tried to balance long pieces with short ones, humorous pieces with serious ones, and intense pieces with relaxed ones. We chose excerpts as rarely as possible, yet could not always avoid them when we drew from novels, or long essays. Where excerpts appear, we have explained the context so that what precedes or follows the selection is always clear. Of course, our wish is that students will like so much of what they read here that they will choose to read or reread on their own the full-length works—all of *Huckleberry Finn, Native Son, Wuthering Heights,* and *Walden,* to name a few.

We also believe that poets, dramatists, novelists, and short story writers have as much to teach about writing essays as do nonfiction writers. Certainly in regard to description, narration, imagery, style, tone, characterization, symbol, point of view, satire, irony, dialogue, diction, coherence, allusion, and analogy—basic terms that readers and writers use to talk about their efforts—our collection of poems, short stories, and scenes from novels and plays can speak to beginning writers and can teach them. To exclude poetry, fiction, and dramatic literature from a reader is to risk a loss of exposure to great minds at a critical point in a student's growth.

More than offering great ideas and brilliant style, poets, fiction writers, and playwrights grapple with the same kinds of rhetorical principles that many people have too long insisted are the purview of essayists alone. Surely Marvell in "To His Coy Mistress" worked through the familiar conventions of argument and persuasion that face any writer who chooses to take a position and to win supporters. Certainly Carson McCullers in "A Tree. A Rock. A Cloud." faced the same need for clarity and personalized meaning, the same confusions of denotation and connotation, the same impulse to establish new lexical validity that any writer faces in attempting an important definition. This is not to say, of course, that we are challenging the rightful place of the expository essay in a program for developing writers; rather, we aim to complement that place by establishing for it a larger context that includes great writing in any genre. In fact, you will find many outstanding essays in this book.

Exploring the writer's craft through a consideration of rhetorical patterns is a useful way to study writing. We have chosen to organize this book by means of traditional rhetorical categories: description, narration, exemplification, process analysis, comparison, classification, causation, definition, and argumentation. Our choice of selections demonstrates our conviction that elements of writing in all genres rely upon these categories. Every chapter contains poetry, fiction, essays, and occasionally drama—all within familiar rhetorical contexts. We're not offering these examples as pure or absolute models of their type, however. Sometimes the rhetorical strategy is a dominant mode in the selection and is easy to recognize. At other times the strategy may be more subtle. A single paragraph or two, even a couple of sentences, may demonstrate some particularly striking application of a rhetorical principle. Sometimes more than one strategy—say, description and narration, causality and process, or definition, illustration and argumentation—may work hand in hand.

The value in practicing rhetorical patterns is that they point the way to a range of available options for writers. We agree with many critics of rhetorically organized readers—it's the rare writer who chooses a rhetorical strategy and then sets out to fill it with ideas. No one says, "Today I'm going to write a classification essay." Ideas always come first for writers, and as these ideas develop, writers pay attention to audience, purpose, language, style, and all the varied, complex factors that help make an essay successful. Still, as ideas develop, writers cannot help but benefit from knowing rhetorical options and using them creatively and intelligently. Thus, if a writer wanted to develop an essay about the Civil War, a knowledge of cause-and-effect strategies would help him or her present clearly a sense of why the war began; a knowledge of descriptive strategies would help breathe life into a Union hospital scene; a knowledge of comparison and contrast strategies would help in a consideration of the relative strengths of the North and the South. The writer would not have to exclude one strategy for the other: Powerful writing often relies upon a number of different rhetorical patterns within a single essay. Again, the key is choices. Learning to write within rhetorical contexts expands a writer's choices and, no matter what the assignment, improves dramatically the possible approaches to writing.

We have made significant revisions for this new edition, adding outstanding pieces of great writing to an already noteworthy collection. Drawing from a wide range of cultures and ethnic backgrounds, we continue to offer challenging essays, stories, poems, and plays. Louise Erdrich, Franz Kafka, Judith Ortiz Cofer, Gwendolyn Brooks, Joan Didion, Anton Chekhov, Albert Camus, Alice Walker, Ruth Prawer Jhabvala—these and other renowned writers add fresh voices to the chorus of talent in *Great Writing*. Also new to this edition are "Summing Up" sections at the end of each chapter's introduction. Students will find the summary lists useful as reviews of the rhetorical strategy at hand. In crystalizing the main points, "Summing Up" will help guide students' thoughtful reading and writing throughout the book. We also have added a section at the end of each chapter called "Crossover," which taps students' critical thinking skills by asking them to consider linkages among selections that raise similar issues, themes, and ideas.

We want to thank our friends and colleagues who encouraged us to develop this text and who read proposals and early drafts. Don McQuade and Bob Atwan listened to early versions of our thoughts. John Wright saw the goals of our project immediately and gave us the support and energy we needed to carry it through. Elizabeth McMahan (Illinois State University), Lee Jacobus (University of Connecticut), and Gratia Murphey (Youngstown State University) did a thorough, thoughtful job of critiquing an early manuscript. Tim Julet at McGraw-Hill guided *Great Writing* to, and through, production with affection, respect, and care. To all the people who helped us along, including our families, we are deeply in debt.

Harvey S. Wiener
Nora Eisenberg

INTRODUCTION:
THE WRITING
PROCESS

All public writing—whether fiction, nonfiction, drama, or poetry—is the end-point of a creative process made permanent by language. Understanding the process of writing, that is, how a piece develops from start to finish, is an essential feature of learning how to write. Yet without digging in diaries, personal journals, biographies, or letters, when we read what great writers have written, we do not see any of that process. We see only a final product. The routes of access to it—the false starts, the wrong turns, the winding roadways—are not open to our inspection as we read.

If they share anything, though, great writers share an elaborate and often agonizing commitment to process. To produce a page of writing they follow a series of irregular, often undefinable steps that, despite some similarities, may differ from task to task and from writer to writer. If this seems paradoxical—writers doing the same thing differently—it is nonetheless true. The steps are different, are taken in no certain sequence, and vary dramatically; yet every writer follows some steps that take him or her from an emerging idea to a piece of finished prose or poetry. Of course, we can rarely arrive at a fully satisfactory response to the age-old question that attentive readers will ask, often incredulously, about the writer of a wonderful essay or story or poem: "How did she do that?" Still, by considering the ways writers get to where they want to go, we can uncover new paths to our own final products.

All writers begin with thinking. They may use pen, pencil, typewriter, or computer to pin down tentatively that thinking in language, before making any permanent commitment to an idea with polished, well-crafted sentences. A vague notion about your subject is frequently your only starting point, but you want to sharpen this notion in your own mind before trying to develop it fully in a draft. The point here is that writing even a first draft is an effort you should usually make *after* the idea starts to take its course. The various stages of thinking and writing in advance of a draft are called *prewriting*. Thus, you might prewrite by jotting ideas on a small slip of paper or writing a list of questions or a very rough outline that you'll subject to frequent revision. Some writers who have trouble generating ideas on a subject will try free association. They make a list of everything that enters their minds about the topic, or they write nonstop for a set time period. In either case, they censor nothing. These are useful strategies for bringing unconscious thoughts and ideas to the surface. Looking the list over, a writer can see just how he or she is thinking, can group together related ideas that appear on different parts of the page, or can identify some feature of the topic that limits it and makes it more clearly focused than before. To tease this feature out even further, a writer might try list making, outlining, or free association again and again.

You can nurture an emerging idea by holding it up to someone else's thinking. What have others written about the topic? What do trusted people—a friend, a professor, a parent—believe about the issues? Has a recent television documentary or radio talk show addressed them? Ezra Pound, the great twentieth-century poet who along with T. S. Eliot and a number of others helped usher in the modern age of literature, called poets "the antennae of the race." We extend that neat label to all writers. Put out your antennae, consider how the world is thinking about your concerns, write about them freshly and with your own special insights. And don't hesitate to share your drafts as *drafts* with any sound thinker who will read what you've written. Pound tore apart Eliot's early drafts of *The Wasteland* and with trenchant commentary helped bring great poetry to birth.

By the time the first draft appears, then, a writer has already taken a number of definable steps. These steps may be recursive (writers go back and forth form their questions to their outlines to their drafts) and in no logical order; and many writers skip some steps altogether or replace them with other steps. One thing for sure, though, is that the trail leading to the draft, and the draft itself, are pretty messy affairs. You can always tell how intense the prewriting effort was from the scratch-outs, erasures, insertions, and loops and arrows on a page. A tidy early draft is probably a bad one. You've got to be struggling with word choice, syntax, emphasis, rhythm, and so many other issues that your page is often a battlefield of as many dead words as living ones to take up the charge. Don't aim for neatness. Slash foggy thinking. Snip imprecise words. Trim wordy sentences. Changing words and ideas while you write and after you write is absolutely vital for an emerging creative effort. Look at some of the changes that Virginia Woolf makes in a draft of the first three paragraphs of her brilliant novel *Mrs. Dalloway:*

Mrs Dalloway said she would buy the flowers herself.

For Lucy had her work cut ~~of~~ out for her. The doors would be taken off their hinges; Rumpelmayers men were coming. And then, thought Clarissa, what a day! What ~~an ecstasy!~~ a ~~miracle!~~ ~~ecstasy!~~ lark! What a plunge! For so it had always seemed to her, when, with a little squeak of the hinges which she could hear now, she had burst open the French windows ~~as and stepped out on to the terrace at Bourton~~, and plunged at Bourton ~~into the terrace~~ into the open air. ~~Like waves, like~~ How fresh, how calm, stiller than this of course, ~~and~~ the air was in the early morning; rooks cawing, dogs barking; ~~and the~~ ——, ~~which naturally one lost later~~ ~~and then, rooks cawing, dogs barking; and and with it all~~— but Peter Walsh ~~she would say she~~ like the flap of a wave; like the kiss of a wave; ~~for~~—chill and sharp and yet, (for a girl of eighteen as she was then) ~~how~~ . ~~and~~ a ~~little~~ solemn, ~~yes, solemn.~~ Peter Walsh would say—whatever Peter Walsh did say—~~when he found when he found her~~ "Musing among the vegetables?" Wasn't that it? Peter who didn't know a rose from a cauliflower, and "preferred men to cabbages." She "I prefer men to cabbages." He must have said it at breakfast, for her to be thinking of it on the terrace, in a morning, ~~and then going she had out on to the terrace~~, and she had gone on to the terrace, as she done over and over again, ~~with to escape, to look, to think it over, what Peter said and how the morning looked~~ and stood there, just for a moment, and felt as she could not feel now, ~~at her age~~, that something tremendous was about to happen, but ~~that~~ and so stood, and so looked, at the flowers, at the trees, and wondered why, then, ~~that~~ this young man, whom they hardly knew, should begin like that, to Aunt Helena of all people, at breakfast. ~~Not to like flowers!~~ It was very like him. And he would be back from India one of these days, June or July, she forgot which, ~~and to be perfectly~~ honest she ~~had for she never could not read~~ his letters; they were awfully dry; it was his sayings one remembered, his big pocket knife, his eyes; his ~~charm too~~; and his grumpiness; and ~~when~~ millions of things ~~were~~ had utterly vanished, a few ~~sayin~~things. like this. ~~which brought back to her that~~ about cabbages.*

And that's not all by any means. The final draft shows many changes from the earlier efforts as she struggles to root abstract concepts in sensory diction:

> Mrs. Dalloway said she would buy the flowers herself.
>
> For Lucy had her work cut out for her. The doors would be taken off their hinges; Rumpelmayer's men were coming. And then, thought Clarissa Dalloway, what a morning—fresh as if issued to children on a beach.
>
> What a lark! What a plunge! For so it had always seemed to her, when, with a little squeak of the hinges, which she could hear now, she had burst open the French windows and plunged at Bourton into the open air. How fresh, how calm, stiller than this of course, the air was in the early morning; like the flap of a wave; the kiss of a wave; chill and sharp and yet (for a girl of eighteen as she then was) solemn, feeling as she did, standing there at the open window, that something awful was about to happen; looking at the flowers, at the trees with the smoke winding off them and the rooks rising, falling; standing and looking until Peter Walsh said, "Musing among the vegetables?"—was that it?—"I prefer men to cauliflowers"—was that it? He must have said it at breakfast one morning when she had gone out on to the terrace—Peter Walsh. He would be back from India one of these days, June or July, she forgot which, for his letters were awfully dull; it was his sayings one remembered; his eyes, his pocket-knife, his smile, his grumpiness and, when millions of things had utterly vanished—how strange it was!—a few sayings like this about cabbages.

One only can imagine the emotional energy, the intellectual vigor, the agony of creation at play here as these early paragraphs develop. But there is joy, too, in the process, an excitement of discovery, self-awareness, and pride as the words and sentences finally say what Woolf wants them to say. She reports that joy while writing her book; she reports plunging "deep into the richest strata of my mind. I can write, & write & write now: The happiest feeling in the world." As you write, you too will move from states of frustration and despair to states of exhilaration; that is all part of the roller coaster a writer will ride to a finished draft.

Among your most important concerns as you shape your drafts into efforts you'll want to make public is whether your thoughts cohere and whether they are unified. *Unity* and *coherence* are two of the most important aims writers can have for anything they write. Your writing is coherent if one idea leads smoothly and logically to the next. Your writing is unified if each idea relates clearly to your main point and to the other ideas you've presented. Transitional devices, repetitions, a constant focus on your thesis—these can help you produce unified, coherent writing. As you read the selections in this text, pay particular attention to the way great writers achieve the same goals you're after.

---

*These paragraphs are reproduced from Wallace Hildicks' *Word for Word* (New York: Norton, 1965).

One of the surest beacons to unity and coherence in an essay (and most of your college writing, as you probably know, will focus on the expository essay) is a carefully wrought *thesis statement.* What is a thesis? Simply put, a thesis is the main point you wish to make, and like much else in your writing, your thesis will evolve as you develop your drafts. But the thesis is more than just a statement of topic: It represents a conviction that you have about that topic. Thus, the most useful kind of thesis is one that states your topic and your opinion or attitude toward it as well. When James Thurber writes, in "Courtship through the Ages" (see Chapter Three), "For the past ten million years nature has been busily inventing ways to make the male attractive to the female, but the whole business of courtship, from the marine annelids up to man, still lumbers heavily along, like a complicated musical comedy," you know both his topic, *that for ten million years nature has tried ways to make the male attractive to the female* and his opinion about the topic, *that courtship after ten million years still trudges along clumsily.* In many cases your thesis will declare a generalization that the rest of your essay will develop with specifics. When Langston Hughes opens "Salvation" (see Chapter Two) with "I was saved from sin when I was going on thirteen" he establishes the general theme of the selection. Throughout the piece, Hughes supports his assertion with concrete detail. Although not all writers will state a thesis in their essays, allowing readers on occasion to infer it for the pleasure of arriving at the knowledge on their own, any writer must be able to state the thesis of her or his writing; and it's always a near-perfect check on the essay itself to use the thesis as a touchstone for determining whether or not you've actually achieved what you set out to do. Students writing to fulfill course requirements find it very productive to include a thesis in their essays.

If you do include a thesis, you'll generally make it the centerpiece of your *introduction*—the first paragraph or two of your written effort. A good introduction aims for one result only: To grab the readers' attention and make it worth their while to read on. Introductions generally are not troublesome: Yes, you must consider issues of length, tone, and style, issues important throughout your writing, but once you have a thesis in mind, you should find that, without any high drama or overwrought writing, the introduction will emerge from that thesis as you set the stage for your topic. Tell a story; explain why the topic is important; give background information; ask questions to stimulate the reader's interest; state contradictory arguments to the one you will propose—you have many options for developing an original introduction.

Your essay will take shape along the rhetorical lines explored in *Great Writing,* and, as you'll see in each chapter, we try to help you link what you've read with what you're trying to write so that each paper flowers on its own from your unique ideas, the rhetorical context, and the selections we have presented. Thesis statements and introductions, of course, cut across the various essays you'll have to write—as does the *conclusion* of your paper. A good conclusion does more than just sum up the main point of your essay. Don't accept the maxim of tiresome instruction in conclusion writing: "Just restate the thesis." True, in complex essays, it's often a good idea to remind the reader of what you had planned to do when you started and how you have achieved your intentions. But merely telling your readers that you have told them what you said you were going to tell them at the outset—this is tedious and pointless. Use the opportunity of a concluding paragraph or two to set a new frame of reference for your topic. Make a generalization built on what you've asserted in the essay. State any views that oppose your own, in an effort to acquaint the reader with a spectrum of insights about the subject. Refute those who disagree with your position. Propose a solution to a problem that you have uncovered. The last words the readers sees of your writing are its conclusion, and it's well worth the effort to come up with something fresh and powerful.

We've structured the chapters in this book and the questioning apparatus to reflect important principles we believe in: a commitment to great writing; enthusiasm for fiction, nonfiction, poetry, and drama as models that developing writers must study; a belief in rhetorical strategies as important and useful approaches to writing exercises; and strong support for attention to the writing process as a means for learning the writer's craft.

First, read the introduction to each chapter. Each introduction provides an overview of the rhetorical strategy at hand by defining it and by placing it in the larger context of human thought and expression. In this section we try to point out what you should be looking for in the essays, poems, plays, and stories you will read that will help you with your own writing. The introduction considers the reading selections that follow and calls attention to readers' expectations for the rhetorical mode. In addition, the introduction treats the general issues you must attend to as a writer practicing a particular rhetorical technique. In every chapter the section entitled Purpose and Audience focuses on these major elements in writing. Finally, in the section entitled Process, we try to help you think about how to produce your own writing in the mode we are exploring. Here we make suggestions about steps to take and pitfalls to avoid.

Once you finish the chapter introductions and turn to the selections themselves, you'll find a headnote before each selection. The first paragraph of the headnote provides biographical information on the writer, and the second paragraph provides any important information you might need to know about the selection in order to help you understand or appreciate it better. Study questions appear after each selection. The first group of questions asks you to test your literal understanding of the piece; the next group focuses your attention on the language, form, and structure that help make the piece great; and the final group offers ideas for writing that grow out of what you've read.

"A good book," John Milton wrote in the *Aereopogitica* (1644), "is the precious life-blood of a master-spirit, embalmed and treasured up on purpose to a life beyond life." We bring you many of those master spirits in *Great Writing* and wish only that their grand efforts help you develop your own craft and spur you to continue perfecting it.

SUMMING UP: THE WRITING PROCESS

- Think about your subject before you begin to write.

- Use prewriting—the stages of thinking and writing in advance of a draft—to sharpen your tentative thoughts on a topic: Prewriting may include jotting ideas, producing a list of questions, using free association, or making a rough outline.

- Consider what others think or have thought about your subject: Read what others have written; talk to friends; review a film.

- Share your drafts with readers you trust.

- As you revise, slash foggy thinking, cut imprecise words, and trim wordy sentences.

- Observe *unity* and *coherence* as you write. *Unity* means that each idea relates to your main point and the other ideas. *Coherence* means that one idea leads smoothly and logically to the next.

- Produce a thesis that states your main point and your attitude or opinion toward it.

- Transitions, repetitions, and a constant focus on your thesis help you achieve unity and coherence.

- Invent an introduction that draws the reader's attention to the topic.

- Produce a conclusion that goes beyond the mere restatement of your thesis.

Chapter One

■

DESCRIPTION

In a famous and frequently quoted line, Joseph Conrad, one of the great novelists in the English language, asserts the preeminent role of description in the writer's craft. "My task which I am trying to achieve," he writes in the Preface to *The Nigger of the Narcissus* (1897), "is, by the power of the written word to make you hear, to make you feel—it is before all, to make you *see*. That—and no more, and it is everything."

The senses are the stock in trade for any writer, but particularly for the writer of description. The French novelist George Sand wrote to her friend Flaubert, "I believe that art needs a palette overflowing with colour, soft or violent according to the subject of the painting; that the artist is an instrument on which everything must play before he can play on others." To bring readers to sense what they themselves sense, writers turn to the language of the senses, to words that convey sight, sound, smell, taste, and touch. What, in fact, other than an image—a sketch, a photograph, a painting, a film sequence, a cluster of sentences—immediately links the mind of the creator of the image with the mind of the observer? In any kind of writing an image can create a sudden and immediate illumination that pages and pages of prose that lack sensory detail rarely achieve.

READING DESCRIPTION

Readers of description acknowledge the power of the image, the phrase or sentence that provides an indelible sensation in language. The image may appeal to the sense of sight with colors and with actions portrayed by energetic verbs. In a poem in this chapter, Tennyson writes of the eagle on a mountain, who "ringed with the azure world," "clasps the crag with crooked hands," and with that picture, the poet fixes the majesty of the great bird in our minds forever. The image may appeal to the sense of sound with one of the multitude of English words that name sounds (onomatopoeia like *ring, whoosh, buzz,* and *roar*) or that describe them (*loud, groaning, shattering, hoarse*). The image may appeal to the sense of touch (*soft, wet, rough*), to the sense of smell (*acrid, perfumed, dusty*), to the sense of taste (*bitter, lemony, sweet*). Often a single image or a combination of images appeals to many senses. Conrad himself was a master of sensory diction. This brief passage opening Chapter Three of *Lord Jim* is only one of hundreds like it alive in color, action, sound, and touch.

> A marvellous stillness pervaded the world, and the stars, together with the serenity of their rays, seemed to shed upon the earth the assurance of everlasting security. The young moon recurved, and shining low in the west, was like a slender shaving thrown up from a bard of gold, and the Arabian Sea, smooth and cool to the eye like a sheet of ice, extended its perfect level to the perfect circle of a dark horizon. The propeller turned without a check, as though its beat had been part of the scheme of a safe universe; and on each side of the *Patna* two deep folds of water, permanent and somber on the unwrinkled shimmer, enclosed within their straight and diverging ridges a few white swirls of foam bursting in a low hiss, a few wavelets, a few ripples, a few undulations that, left behind, agitated the surface of the sea for an

instant after the passage of the ship, subsided splashing gently, calmed down at last into the circular stillness of water and sky with the black speck of the moving hull remaining everlastingly in its centre.

Conrad does make us hear and feel, and above all see. We hear the hissing foam and the gentle splash as the ship passes; we feel the smooth, cool, Arabian sea and the marvelous stillness of the moment; we see the reflecting moon in the dark, the somber folds of water, the ripples and the undulations of the waves. It is Conrad's genius, of course, his photographic eye, as Galsworthy calls it, that records the scene and shapes it for his readers. But his language helps establish some general features to look for as we read description. First, the main goal of description is clarity, and toward that end the writer uses what Flaubert calls *le seul mot juste,* the single correct word. Notice the specificity of Conrad's nouns to signify the texture of the sea's surface—*ridges, swirls, foam, wavelets, ripples, undulations.* Specific words like these as opposed to a more general word like *waves,* for example, compel readers to see exactly what Conrad wants them to see. His modifiers sharpen the meaning of the nouns but do not overwhelm them. Only a fifth of the words in this passage are adjectives. Great writers resist using modifiers when specific nouns can create a clearer picture than any describing words could. Similarly, verbs show remarkable precision here, with minimal help from adverbs: *recurved, thrown up, turned, agitated, subsided, calmed.*

Among the nouns and verbs, you will notice a preponderance of concrete as opposed to abstract words. Conrad does not totally avoid language apart from perceivable experience—"everlasting security" and "safe universe" are abstractions certainly—but his description hangs more upon concrete images like the passage of the ship through the water than upon these theoretical words and concepts. A writer's purpose may demand a higher degree of abstraction than Conrad allows here, but more often than not the descriptive passage relies heavily upon concrete sensory diction. Concrete words make descriptions clear and easy to see in the imagination.

Memorable, accurate description relies on selectivity of detail, perhaps the most difficult goal for the writer. In observing anything, we are bombarded with sensory impressions, hundreds of them, that register on our minds. In recreating an object, a person, or a scene, what does the writer leave in? What does the writer leave out? Including everything is never the intention; we readers would be overwhelmed and would have no clue to what makes the scene special. The intention is to include only indispensable detail. Paul Claudel, a twentieth-century French writer, insists quite correctly that "nothing unessential is the first condition of art." Leaving out is as important as putting in. When we read, we look for the economy of expression and the originality of thought that immediately make an object clear, sharp, and alive. Being original and conveying that originality at just the right level of detail are part of the genius of the writer and contribute to our judgments about the quality of a piece of prose or poetry.

In reaching for the clear and indelible image, writers often turn to figurative devices. Figurative devices compare. By likening one object in a description to some other object, writers can bring an immediately sharp, visual quality to a scene. With Conrad's unusual simile of the moon shining low in the west "like a slender shaving thrown up from a bar of gold" the comparison between the moon and a sliver of gold makes us see this moon as we have seen no other. Similes, metaphors, and personification (and other figures) are powerful descriptive tools, and you should be aware of them as you read.

With description, as with all other writing, readers are right to ask themselves what is the point of the writer's efforts to provide intense sensory details. A travel brochure or a catalogue can afford indulgent particulars, that is, description for its own sake, but serious writers always have a higher purpose than merely describing. In fiction, descriptive details set a scene, limn a character, provide a delectable insight that serves the larger purpose of the piece. In a descriptive essay, a thesis should emerge if the writer does not state one precisely; in other words, you should know why the writer is showing you the picture on which he or she has focused. When Kazin opens his piece with "In Brownsville tenements the kitchen is always the largest room and the center of the household," you can bet that the descriptive details throughout will support that point. Similarly, in E. B. White's essay "Once More to the Lake," you know from the very first paragraph why the writer intends to marshal descriptive details for his readers: The thesis here is very clear, and you could state it easily in your own words.

You should also note a writer's efforts to *show* you a scene, not just to tell you about it. Showing means drawing pictures; telling means offering judgments. Telling readers, for example, that a face is beautiful is very much different from showing details of the face so that readers infer its beauty. Critical readers like to draw their own conclusions, and writers can never be sure when they provide judgments that readers will see what the writer sees; in fact, without supporting details, how many people could agree on what a beautiful face was? No descriptive writer avoids judgments entirely, and as in every other case in writing, audience and purpose dictate the degree to which a writer will adhere to any principle, even one as sound as "show—don't tell." Even Conrad provides judgments—note how he starts his paragraph with a generalization that *tells* us about the scene: "A marvellous stillness pervaded the world, and the stars, together with the serenity of their rays, seemed to shed upon the earth the assurance of everlasting security." Yet we are not left to take Conrad's word for it. Every sentence after that judgment supports and enhances it, so that we are helpless to conclude anything other than "marvellous stillness" pervading the world he draws. In description the balance always tips in favor of details that show rather than tell. Similarly, Momaday's description of Rainy Mountain balances skillfully rich natural details of the scene with his judgments of it. As you read selections in this chapter—selections like Tennyson's "The Eagle," E. B. White's "Once More to the Lake," and O'Brien's "My Mother's Mother"—you will experience what writers of description always strive for: concrete, sensory language that brings a person, an object, a scene immediately to life.

WRITING DESCRIPTION

Description will find its way into much of your writing as a means of supporting your ideas with detail. In papers that narrate, compare and contrast, explain a process, or argue, for example, concrete sensory images will help you make a point with clarity and force. In this chapter, however, we ask you to use description as the dominant mode of your writing so that you can practice a range of strategies that will make your writing clear and original in execution whenever you need to call upon your descriptive powers.

PURPOSE AND AUDIENCE

As you choose your topics for description, you must consider your reasons for writing and the people you intend to read your work. A thesis statement can help you immeasurably here: Indicate what you plan to describe and, by stating your opinion or attitude about the topic, you can convey a general sense of purpose.

Textbooks often distinguish between *subjective* and *objective* description, and you would choose one or the other of these as a strategy, depending upon your purpose and your audience. True, an individual writer's personal perceptions are embedded in the details he or she offers to the reader, and it is therefore hard to make a strong case for an absolute distinction between subjective and objective description. Still, the distinction is worthwhile. Objective descriptions are technical; the details the writer uses are impersonal, at a distance, independent of the perceiving mind. Scientific writing relies on such objective description in one sense so that experiments are replicable. The size and shape of a vein in a dogfish shark dissected in a tray, the color and odor of chemicals in a test tube, the texture of a lesion on human skin—nonsubjective descriptions of these sensory observations help students validate their views as part of a large community of observers who record the details in similar language. Of course, the quality of even the most "objective" observation depends upon the observer and his or her past experience, ability to see and to hear, and talent for recognizing those details worth noting and those worth ignoring. Francis Bacon, the clarion of modern science, acknowledged the difficulties of sensory observation in science: "The subtlety of nature," he writes in *The Great Instauration* (1620), is "greater many times over than the subtlety of the senses and understanding." And he called repeatedly for aids to the sense: "Neither the naked hand nor the understanding left to itself can effect much. It is by instruments and helps that the work is done, which are as much wanted for the understanding as for the hand."

It is not so clear-cut or simple, then, to achieve objective writing. Yet despite difficulties, objective description has its uses, and in areas other than the pure sciences. As we said before, a writer's purpose and the reaction of the audience may demand that he or she keep opinions, impressions, or subjective responses out of the prose. Thus, in describing a bedroom of a nursing home for a report on the aging, your writing would be detached: You would show what you observed, not your reactions to your observations. You'd measure the bed, and, focusing on impressions of sights, you'd measure the length of the window, you'd name the colors of the walls and the ceiling, you'd identify by name and with sensory detail the various pieces of equipment around the room. You'd use language that means just what it says, not language rich in associations and accrued meanings. Certainly, in an objective description you'd avoid stating your opinions: You might think the color of the walls a sickly green, the bed stand dilapidated, the blankets worn and tattered, but none of those impressions should slip into your prose.

If on the other hand, your purposes in writing were to show the deplorable conditions you saw in a nursing home to an audience unfamiliar with those conditions, you'd choose a much more subjective approach, allowing your personal attitudes and impressions to guide your selection of words and to shape your construction of images. You'd want people to know how you felt about the scene. You'd select words whose connotations you'd weighed carefully so that readers had precisely the impression you had. You'd be sensitive to shades of meaning. In the simile of the moon and the bar of gold that we commented on earlier, note how Conrad emphasizes the wonderful placid beauty of the moment on the sea with carefully chosen words like *marvellous, stillness, serenity, slender, smooth,* and *cool.* (Try substituting synonyms for some of these words in the image— *astonishing* for *marvellous, quiet* for *stillness, peacefulness* for *serenity, thin* for *slender, unbroken* for *smooth, moderately cold* for *cool*—to see how they alter the impact of the original.) Note, too, the sound of the words to the ear, the repetition of the word *perfect,* the *s* or *sh* sound at the start of six words in the simile, the three coordinated structures with the word *and.* None of these is accidental. Especially in a subjective description, your words have the potential to compel your reader to see with your eyes, to hear with your ears, to touch with your fingers. All the selections in this chapter are examples of subjective descriptions, and you will see in them the care writers exercise in locating *le seul mot juste.*

PROCESS

To help focus your description, you want to spend some time thinking about purpose and audience. Just what point will you make by means of your description? What is the overriding impression you wish to create? What will your readers expect to learn from the details you present? Freewriting or brainstorming will help you think on paper about those questions. Conversations with friends who can help you answer some of these questions now will be useful. Once you have selected a subject for description, think about how you will bring it to life. If you choose something that you can visit before you write or that you can observe as you write—a quiet football field, say, or a child at play with her red wagon, or a taco on a paper plate—so much the better. Make lists of sensory images that contribute to the overall effect you are trying to convey; you might even group them in columns—"what I saw," "what I heard," "what I felt," and so on. Don't aim for completeness. You'll have to select carefully among your many sense impressions for those that give the best glimpse of the nature of your subject. If you choose a subject out of your memory of experiences, find some quiet place where you can concentrate and try to imagine your subject in the full richness of its details: the colors, actions, sounds, and smells you associate with it. Listing your sense impressions will be very helpful here too.

When you're ready to write a draft, consider what your thesis is (what you will describe and how you feel about the subject) and how you will arrange the details in your paper. Where do you, the observer, stand in relation to the object? Will you show it to the reader from a fixed position, presenting details spatially from left to right, front to back, top to bottom? Or will you move with the reader as you describe the features of your subject? Will you present details according to importance, building from the least to the most significant? In a subjective description of a ward in a nursing home, for example, you might tour its contents from your entry point at the door, showing what you see and hear as you take the reader around or across the room. But if your interest is to show the run-down conditions of the place, you might show instead the minor inconveniences first, like its threadbare sheets and curtains, peeling paint, and exposed pipes, and then move to what you consider more serious features of neglect, like lumpy beds, dirty floors, broken nightstands. If you're adventurous, you might trust to an impressionistic portrait, allowing your imagination freedom to both create and organize details. Though this is a tricky and difficult plan to follow, it can some-times produce a very interesting piece of writing.

Don't ever think of your draft as writing cut in stone. Put down as much as you can in your early efforts, but plan to revise carefully to achieve the goals of accurate description. Revise, edit, rewrite: In producing a public copy of your paper, you must pay attention to these steps that all writers take whenever they write.

Tolstoy writes: "To evoke in oneself a feeling one has once experienced, then by means of movement, lines, colors, sounds, or forms expressed in words, so to transmit that feeling that others experience the same feeling—this is the activity of art." You can carry that activity forward as you write your descriptive paper.

SUMMING UP: DESCRIPTION

Reading Description

- Look for imagery, the writer's appeal to the five senses.
- Determine the writer's thesis: What point is the writer trying to make through the description?
- Consider the use of precise nouns and verbs as part of the writer's goal of clarity and originality of expression.
- Pay attention to economy of expression: Why does the writer leave out some details and include others?
- Look for figurative expressions, that is, vivid comparisons such as simile, metaphor, and personification.

- Think about how the writer shows you the scene as opposed to telling you about it.

Writing Description

- Considering audience and purpose, distinguish between subjective and objective description.
- Determine the overall impression you wish to create in your description.
- Produce a thesis to identify your topic for description and your attitude toward that topic.
- Do freewriting and (or) brainstorming.
- Produce sensory images to portray your selected subject through concrete details.
- Determine how to arrange the details.
- Produce a draft and revise it.
- Edit your draft and rewrite further as needed.

The Last of the Kiowas

N. Scott Momaday

Born in 1934 of Kiowa and Cherokee descent, N. Scott Momaday now teaches at the University of Arizona. He has been awarded an Academy of American Poets prize and a Guggenheim fellowship.

Momaday says that he writes about "the memories of blood." He is widely respected as an innovator of written forms, and his work is often poetic, autobiographical, and historical, all in service of a central theme. The following selection, from his autobiography, *The Way to Rainy Mountain,* combines myth, history, and personal recollection to tell the story of Momaday's grandmother and the story of the Kiowa tribe.

A single knoll rises out of the plain in Oklahoma, north and west of 1 the Wichita Range. For my people, the Kiowas, it is an old landmark, and they gave it the name Rainy Mountain. The hardest weather in the world is there. Winter brings blizzards, hot tornadic winds arise in the spring, and in summer the prairie is an anvil's edge. The grass turns brittle and brown, and it cracks beneath your feet. There are green belts along the rivers and creeks, linear groves of hickory and pecan, willow and witch hazel. At a distance in July or August the steaming foliage seems almost to writhe in fire. Great green and yellow grasshoppers are everywhere in the tall grass, popping up like corn to sting the flesh, and tortoises crawl about on the red earth, going nowhere in the plenty of time. Loneliness is an aspect of the land. All things in the plain are isolate; there is no confusion of objects in the eye, but *one* hill or *one* tree or *one* man. To look upon that landscape in the early morning, with the sun at your back, is to lose the sense of proportion. Your imagination comes to life, and this, you think, is where Creation was begun.

I returned to Rainy Mountain in July. My grandmother had died in the 2 spring, and I waited to be at her grave. She had lived to be very old and at last infirm. Her only living daughter was with her when she died, and I was told that in death her face was that of a child.

I like to think of her as a child. When she was born, the Kiowas were liv- 3 ing the last great moment of their history. For more than a hundred years they had controlled the open range from the Smoky Hill River to the Red, from the headwaters of the Canadian to the fork of the Arkansas and Cimarron. In alliance with the Comanches, they had ruled the whole of the southern Plains. War was their sacred business, and they were among the finest horsemen the world has ever known. But warfare for the Kiowas was preeminently a matter of disposition rather than of survival, and they never understood the grim, unrelenting advance of the U.S. Cavalry. When at last, divided and ill-provisioned, they were driven onto the Staked Plains in the cold rains of autumn, they fell into panic. In Palo

Duro Canyon they abandoned their crucial stores to pillage and had nothing then but their lives. In order to save themselves, they surrendered to the soldiers at Fort Sill and were imprisoned in the old stone corral that now stands as a military museum. My grandmother was spared the humiliation of those high gray walls by eight or ten years, but she must have known from birth the affliction of defeat, the dark brooding of old warriors.

Her name was Aho, and she belonged to the last culture to evolve in North 4 America. Her forebears came down from the high country in western Montana nearly three centuries ago. They were a mountain people, a mysterious tribe of hunters whose language has never been positively classified in any major group. In the late seventeenth century they began a long migration to the south and east. It was a journey toward the dawn, and it led to a golden age. Along the way the Kiowas were befriended by the Crows, who gave them the culture and religion of the Plains. They acquired horses, and their ancient nomadic spirit was suddenly free of the ground. They acquired Tai-me, the sacred Sun Dance doll, from that moment the object and symbol of their worship, and so shared in the divinity of the sun. Not least, they acquired the sense of destiny, therefore courage and pride. When they entered upon the southern Plains they had been transformed. No longer were they slaves to the simple necessity of survival; they were a lordly and dangerous society of fighters and thieves, hunters and priests of the sun. According to their origin myth, they entered the world through a hollow log. From one point of view, their migration was the fruit of an old prophecy, for indeed they emerged from a sunless world.

Although my grandmother lived out her long life in the shadow of Rainy 5 Mountain, the immense landscape of the continental interior lay like memory in her blood. She could tell of the Crows, whom she had never seen, and of the Black Hills, where she had never been. I wanted to see in reality what she had seen more perfectly in the mind's eye, and traveled fifteen hundred miles to begin my pilgrimage.

Yellowstone, it seemed to me, was the top of the world, a region of deep 6 lakes and dark timber, canyons and waterfalls. But, beautiful as it is, one might have the sense of confinement there. The skyline in all directions is close at hand, the high wall of the woods and deep cleavages of shade. There is a perfect freedom in the mountains, but it belongs to the eagle and the elk, the badger and the bear. The Kiowas reckoned their stature by the distance they could see, and they were bent and blind in the wilderness.

Descending eastward, the highland meadows are a stairway to the plain. In 7 July the inland slope of the Rockies is luxuriant with flax and buckwheat, stonecrop amid larkspur. The earth unfolds and the limit of the land recedes. Clusters of trees, and animals grazing far in the distance, cause the vision to reach away and wonder to build upon the mind. The sun follows a longer course in the day, and the sky is immense beyond all comparison. The great billowing clouds that sail upon it are shadows that move upon the grain like water, dividing light. Farther down, in the land of the Crows and Blackfeet, the plain is yellow. Sweet clover takes hold of the hills and bends upon itself to cover and seal the soil. There the Kiowas paused on their way; they had come to the place where they must change their lives. The sun is at home on the plains. Precisely there does it have the certain character of a god. When the Kiowas came to the land of the Crows, they could see the dark lees of the hills at dawn across the Bighorn River, the profusion of light on the grain shelves, the oldest deity ranging after the solstices. Not yet would they veer southward to the caldron of the land that lay below; they must wean their blood from the northern winter and hold the mountains a while longer in their view. They bore Tai-me in procession to the east.

A dark mist lay over the Black Hills, and the land was like iron. At the top 8 of a ridge I caught sight of Devil's Tower upthrust against the gray sky as if in the birth of time the core of the earth had broken through its crust and the motion of the world was begun. There are things in nature that engender an awful quiet in the heart of man; Devil's Tower is one of them. Two centuries ago, because they could not do otherwise, the Kiowas made a legend at the base of the rock. My grandmother said:

> Eight children were there at play, seven sisters and their brother. Suddenly the boy was struck dumb; he trembled and began to run upon his hands and feet. His fingers became claws, and his body was covered with fur. Directly there was a bear where the boy had been. The sisters were terrified; they ran, and the bear after them. They came to the stump of a great tree, and the tree spoke to them. It bade them climb upon it, and as they did so it began to rise into the air. The bear came to kill them, but they were just beyond its reach. It reared against the tree and scored the bark all around with its claws. The seven sisters were borne into the sky, and they became the stars of the Big Dipper.

From that moment, and so long as the legend lives, the Kiowas have kinsmen in the night sky. Whatever they were in the mountains, they could be no more. However tenuous their well-being, however much they had suffered and would suffer again, they had found a way out of the wilderness.

My grandmother had a reverence for the sun, a holy regard that now is all 9 but gone out of mankind. There was a wariness in her, and an ancient awe. She was a Christian in her later years, but she had come a long way about, and she never forgot her birthright. As a child she had been to the Sun Dances; she had taken part in those annual rites, and by them she had learned the restoration of her people in the presence of Tai-me. She was about seven when the last Kiowa Sun Dance was held in 1887 on the Washita River above Rainy Mountain Creek. The buffalo were gone. In order to consummate the ancient sacrifice—to impale the head of a buffalo bull upon the medicine tree—a delegation of old men journeyed into Texas, there to beg and barter for an animal from the Goodnight herd. She was ten when the Kiowas came together for the last time as a living Sun Dance culture. They could find no buffalo; they had to hang an old hide from the sacred tree. Before the dance could begin, a company of soldiers rode out from Fort Sill under orders to disperse the tribe. Forbidden without cause the essential act of their faith, having seen the wild herds slaughtered and left to rot upon the ground, the Kiowas backed away forever from the medicine tree. That was July 20, 1890, at the great bend of the Washita. My grandmother was there. Without bitterness, and for as long as she lived, she bore a vision of deicide.

Now that I can have her only in memory, I see my grandmother in the sev- [10] eral postures that were peculiar to her: standing at the wood stove on a winter morning and turning meat in a great iron skillet; sitting at the south window, bent above her beadwork, and afterwards, when her vision failed, looking down for a long time into the fold of her hands; going out upon a cane, very slowly as she did when the weight of age came upon her; praying. I remember her most often at prayer. She made long, rambling prayers out of suffering and hope, having seen many things. I was never sure that I had the right to hear, so exclusive were they of all mere custom and company. The last time I saw her she prayed standing by the side of her bed at night, naked to the waist, the light of a kerosene lamp moving upon her dark skin. Her long, black hair, always drawn and braided in the day, lay upon her shoulders and against her breasts like a shawl. I do not speak Kiowa, and I never understood her prayers, but there was something inherently sad in the sound, some merest hesitation upon the syllabics of sorrow. She began in a high and descending pitch, exhausting her breath to silence; then again and again—and always the same intensity of effort, of something that is, and is not, like urgency in the human voice. Transported so in the dancing light among the shadows of her room, she seemed beyond the reach of time. But that was illusion; I think I knew then that I should not see her again.

Houses are like sentinels in the plain, old keepers of the weather watch. [11] There, in a very little while, wood takes on the appearance of great age. All colors wear soon away in the wind and rain, and then the wood is burned gray and the grain appears and the nails turn red with rust. The windowpanes are black and opaque; you imagine there is nothing within, and indeed there are many ghosts, bones given up to the land. They stand here and there against the sky, and you approach them for a longer time than you expect. They belong in the distance; it is their domain.

Once there was a lot of sound in my grandmother's house, a lot of coming [12] and going, feasting and talk. The summers there were full of excitement and reunion. The Kiowas are a summer people; they abide the cold and keep to themselves, but when the season turns and the land becomes warm and vital they cannot hold still; an old love of going returns upon them. The aged visitors who came to my grandmother's house when I was a child were made of lean and leather, and they bore themselves upright. They wore great black hats and bright ample shirts that shook in the wind. They rubbed fat upon their hair and wound their braids with strips of colored cloth. Some of them painted their faces and carried the scars of old and cherished enmities. They were an old council of warlords, come to remind and be reminded of who they were. Their wives and daughters served them well. The women might indulge themselves; gossip was at once the mark and compensation of their servitude. They made loud and elaborate talk among themselves, full of jest and gesture, flight and false alarm. They went abroad in fringed and flowered shawls, bright beadwork and German silver. They were at home in the kitchen, and they prepared meals that were banquets.

There were frequent prayer meetings, and great nocturnal feasts. When I [13] was a child I played with my cousins outside, where the lamplight fell upon the ground and the singing of the old people rose up around us and carried away into the darkness. There were a lot of good things to eat, a lot of laughter and surprise. And afterwards, when the quiet returned, I lay down with my grandmother and could hear the frogs away by the river and feel the motion of the air.

Now there is a funeral silence in the rooms, the endless wake of some final 14 word. The walls have closed in upon my grandmother's house. When I returned to it in mourning, I saw for the first time in my life how small it was. It was late at night, and there was a white moon, nearly full. I sat for a long time on the stone steps by the kitchen door. From there I could see out across the land; I could see the long row of trees by the creek, the low light upon the rolling plains, and the stars of the Big Dipper. Once I looked at the moon and caught sight of a strange thing. A cricket had perched upon the handrail, only a few inches away from me. My line of vision was such that the creature filled the moon like a fossil. It had gone there, I thought, to live and die, for there, of all places, was its small definition made whole and eternal. A warm wind rose up and purled like the longing within me.

The next morning I awoke at dawn and went out on the dirt road to Rainy 15 Mountain. It was already hot, and the grasshoppers began to fill the air. Still, it was early in the morning, and the birds sang out of the shadows. The long yellow grass on the mountain shone in the bright light, and a scissortail hied above the land. There, where it ought to be, at the end of a long and legendary way, was my grandmother's grave. Here and there on the dark stones were ancestral names. Looking back once, I saw the mountain and came away.

Meaning and Idea

1. What is the main idea of Momaday's essay? How do his descriptions and elaborations make his theme more effective?

2. It seems that Aho, Momaday's grandmother, is "The Last of the Kiowas," but somehow the reader also feels that Momaday himself is the person referred to in the title. How does the writer create this impression?

3. Momaday calls the cricket he sees on the handrail a *fossil*. Is it? How is this brief description evocative of the theme in the selection? What other passages seem *thematic* in this way?

Language, Form, Structure

1. Do you find Momaday's descriptive language effective? Even if you did not know the exact meaning of words he used, did you feel that they still conveyed something? Emotion? Atmosphere?

2. Identify the transition points in the essay where Momaday moves back and forth between describing Aho's world, his own memory of Aho and his own actions around Rainy Mountain, or other literal, topographic descriptions. How do the transitions contribute to the unity and coherence of the selection?

3. Define the following words and use each in a sentence, being sure to incorporate the same definition as the one used by the writer: knoll; writhe; infirm; preeminently; disposition; stature; caldron; reverence; sentinels; abide; ample; nocturnal.

Ideas for Writing

1. Use paragraph 10, beginning "Now that I can have her only in memory," as the model for an essay about a memorable relative or friend. Describe the person "in the several postures that were peculiar to her" or him. Use concrete sensory detail to bring your description to life.

2. Visit an environment you associate with a certain person. A park, a museum, or a part of your city or town would be a good choice. Wander around and keep a journal of your thoughts about the various places you go to. Use this material as a foundation for an essay in which you describe the environment, the person, and your relationship to that person.

3. Reread "The Last of the Kiowas." How and why is the description within the essay so effective? Why does the essay seem so *thematic?*

Once More to the Lake

E. B. White

Elwyn Brooks White was born in Mount Vernon, New York, in 1899. After graduating from Cornell University, he worked as a reporter, and in 1926, he joined the staff of *The New Yorker*. His delightful and insightful contributions to that magazine in great part helped set its past and present tone. White was a versatile writer whose descriptions have delighted readers of all ages. In addition to his *New Yorker* writing, his legacy includes *One Man's Meat* (1942), *Here Is New York* (1949), *Charlotte's Web* (1952), and the collected *Essays of E. B. White* (1977).

Taken from White's *Essays,* this reflective description of a scene first visited some thirty-seven years in the past amply supports President John Kennedy's evaluation of White as "an essayist whose concise comment on men and places has revealed to yet another age the vigor of the English sentence." His strongly subjective, yet precise, descriptions help bridge the gaps between the actual, physical changes he sees in the place and the emotional, perceptual changes he feels.

AUGUST 1941

*O*ne summer, along about 1904, my father rented a camp on a lake in Maine and took us all there for the month of August. We all got ringworm from some kittens and had to rub Pond's Extract on our arms and legs night and morning, and my father rolled over in a canoe with all his clothes on; but outside of that the vacation was a success and from then on none of us ever thought there was any place in the world like that lake in Maine. We returned summer after summer—always on August 1 for one month. I have since become a salt-water man, but sometimes in summer there are days when the restlessness of the tides and the fearful cold of the sea water and the incessant wind that blows across the afternoon and into the evening make me wish for the placidity of a lake in the woods. A few weeks ago this feeling got so strong I bought myself a couple of bass hooks and a spinner and returned to the lake where we used to go, for a week's fishing and to revisit old haunts.

I took along my son, who had never had any fresh water up his nose and who had seen lily pads only from train windows. On the journey over to the lake I began to wonder what it would be like. I wondered how time would have marred this unique, this holy spot—the coves and streams, the hills that the sun set behind, the camps and the paths behind the camps. I was sure that the tarred road would have found it out, and I wondered in what other ways it would be desolated. It is strange how much you can remember about places like that once you allow your mind to return into the grooves that lead back. You remember one thing, and that suddenly reminds you of another thing. I guess I remembered clearest of all the early mornings, when the lake was cool and motionless, remembered how the bedroom smelled of the lumber it was made of and of the wet woods whose scent entered through the screen. The partitions in the camp were thin and did not extend clear to the top of the rooms, and as I was always the first up I would dress softly so as not to wake the others, and sneak out into the sweet outdoors and start out in the canoe, keeping close along the shore in the long shadows of the pines. I remembered being very careful never to rub my paddle against the gunwale for fear of disturbing the stillness of the cathedral.

The lake had never been what you would call a wild lake. There were cot- ₃ tages sprinkled around the shores, and it was in farming country although the shores of the lake were quite heavily wooded. Some of the cottages were owned by nearby farmers, and you would live at the shore and eat your meals at the farm-house. That's what our family did. But although it wasn't wild, it was a fairly large and undisturbed lake and there were places in it that, to a child at least, seemed infinitely remote and primeval.

I was right about the tar: it led to within half a mile of the shore. But when I ₄ got back there, with my boy, and we settled into a camp near a farmhouse and into the kind of summertime I had known, I could tell that it was going to be pretty much the same as it had been before—I knew it, lying in bed the first morning smelling the bedroom and hearing the boy sneak quietly out and go off along the shore in a boat. I began to sustain the illusion that he was I, and therefore, by simple transpo-sition, that I was my father. This sensation persisted, kept cropping up all the time we were there. It was not an entirely new feeling, but in this setting it grew much stronger. I seemed to be living a dual existence. I would be in the middle of some simple act, I would be picking up a bait box or laying down a table fork, or I would be saying something and suddenly it would be not I but my father who was saying the words or making the gesture. It gave me a creepy sensation.

We went fishing the first morning. I felt the same damp moss covering the ₅ worms in the bait can, and saw the dragonfly alight on the tip of my rod as it hov-ered a few inches from the surface of the water. It was the arrival of this fly that convinced me beyond any doubt that everything was as it always had been, that the years were a mirage and that there had been no years. The small waves were the same, chucking the rowboat under the chin as we fished at anchor, and the boat was the same boat, the same color green and the ribs broken in the same places, and under the floorboards the same fresh water leavings and débris—the dead helgramite, the wisps of moss, the rusty discarded fishhook, the dried blood from yesterday's catch. We stared silently at the tips of our rods, at the dragon-flies that came and went. I lowered the tip of mine into the water, tentatively, pen-sively dislodging the fly, which darted two feet away, poised, darted two feet back, and came to rest again a little farther up the rod. There had been no years between the ducking of this dragonfly and the other one—the one that was part of memory. I looked at the boy, who was silently watching his fly, and it was my hands that held his rod, my eyes watching. I felt dizzy and didn't know which rod I was at the end of.

We caught two bass, hauling them in briskly as though they were mackerel, ₆ pulling them over the side of the boat in a businesslike manner without any landing net, and stunning them with a blow on the back of the head. When we got back for a swim before lunch, the lake was exactly where we had left it, the same number of inches from the dock, and there was only the merest suggestion of a breeze. This seemed an utterly enchanted sea, this lake you could leave to its own devices for a few hours and come back to, and find that it had not stirred, this constant and trustworthy body of water. In the shallows, the dark, water-soaked sticks and twigs, smooth and old, were undulating in clusters on the bottom against the clean ribbed sand, and the track of the mussel was plain. A school of minnows swam by, each minnow with its small individual shadow, doubling the attendance, so clear and sharp in the sunlight. Some of the other campers were in swimming, along the shore, one of them with a cake of soap, and the water felt thin and clear and unsubstantial. Over the years there had been this person with the cake of soap, this cultist, and here he was. There had been no years.

Up to the farmhouse to dinner through the teeming dusty field, the road 7 under our sneakers was only a two-track road. The middle track was missing, the one with the marks of the hooves and the splotches of dried, flaky manure. There had always been three tracks to choose from in choosing which track to walk in; now the choice was narrowed down to two. For a moment I missed terribly the middle alternative. But the way led past the tennis court, and something about the way it lay there in the sun reassured me; the tape had loosened along the backline, the alleys were green with plantains and other weeds, and the net (installed in June and removed in September) sagged in the dry noon, and the whole place steamed with midday heat and hunger and emptiness. There was a choice of pie for dessert, and one was blueberry and one was apple, and the waitresses were the same country girls, there having been no passage of time, only the illusion of it as in a dropped curtain—the waitresses were still fifteen; their hair had been washed, that was the only difference—they had been to the movies and seen the pretty girls with the clean hair.

Summertime, oh, summertime, pattern of life indelible with fade-proof 8 lake, the wood unshatterable, the pasture with the sweetfern and the juniper forever and ever, summer without end; this was the background, and the life along the shore was the design, the cottages with their innocent and tranquil design, their tiny docks with the flagpole and the American flag floating against the white clouds in the blue sky, the little paths over the roots of the trees leading from camp to camp and the paths leading back to the outhouses and the can of lime for sprinkling, and at the souvenir counters at the store the miniature birch-bark canoes and the postcards that showed things looking a little better than they looked. This was the American family at play, escaping the city heat, wondering whether the newcomers in the camp at the head of the cove were "common" or "nice," wondering whether it was true that the people who drove up for Sunday dinner at the farmhouse were turned away because there wasn't enough chicken.

It seemed to me, as I kept remembering all this, that those times and those 9 summers had been infinitely precious and worth saving. There had been jollity and peace and goodness. The arriving (at the beginning of August) had been so big a business in itself, at the railway station the farm wagon drawn up, the first smell of the pine-laden air, the first glimpse of the smiling farmer, and the great importance of the trunks and your father's enormous authority in such matters, and the feel of the wagon under you for the long ten-mile haul, and at the top of the last long hill catching the first view of the lake after eleven months of not seeing this cherished body of water. The shouts and cries of the other campers when they saw you, and the trunks to be unpacked, to give up their rich burden. (Arriving was less exciting nowadays, when you sneaked up in your car and parked it under a tree near the camp and took out the bags and in five minutes it was all over, no fuss, no loud wonderful fuss about trunks.)

Peace and goodness and jollity. The only thing that was wrong now, really, 10 was the sound of the place, an unfamiliar nervous sound of the outboard motors. This was the note that jarred, the one thing that would sometimes break the illusion and set the years moving. In those other summertimes all motors were inboard; and when they were at a little distance, the noise they made was a sedative, an ingredient of summer sleep. They were one-cylinder and two-cylinder engines, and some were make-and-break and some were jump-spark, but they all made a sleepy sound across the lake. The one-lungers throbbed and fluttered, and the twin-cylinder ones purred and purred, and that was a quiet sound, too. But now the campers all had outboards. In the daytime, in the hot mornings, these motors made a petulant, irritable sound; at night in the still evening when the afterglow lit the water, they whined about one's ears like mosquitoes. My boy loved our rented outboard, and his great desire was to achieve single-handed mastery over it, and authority, and he soon learned the trick of choking it a little (but not too much), and the adjustment of the needle valve. Watching him I would remember the things you could do with the old one-cylinder engine with the heavy flywheel, how you could have it eating out of your hand if you got really close to it spiritually. Motorboats in those days didn't have clutches, and you would make a landing by shutting off the motor at the proper time and coasting in with a dead rudder. But there was a way of reversing them, if you learned the trick, by cutting the switch and putting it on again exactly on the final dying revolution of the flywheel, so that it would kick back against compression and begin reversing. Approaching a dock in a strong following breeze, it was difficult to slow up sufficiently by the ordinary coasting method, and if a boy felt he had complete mastery over his motor, he was tempted to keep it running beyond its time and then reverse it a few feet from the dock. It took a cool nerve, because if you threw the switch a twentieth of a second too soon you would catch the flywheel when it still had speed enough to go up past center, and the boat would leap ahead, charging bull-fashion at the dock.

We had a good week at the camp. The bass were biting well and the sun 11 shone endlessly, day after day. We would be tired at night and lie down in the accumulated heat of the little bedrooms after the long hot day and the breeze would stir almost imperceptibly outside and the smell of the swamp drift in through the rusty screens. Sleep would come easily and in the morning the red squirrel would be on the roof, tapping out his gay routine. I kept remembering everything, lying in bed in the mornings—the small steamboat that had a long rounded stern like the lip of a Ubangi, and how quietly she ran on the moonlight sails, when the older boys played their mandolins and the girls sang and we ate doughnuts dipped in sugar, and how sweet the music was on the water in the shining night, and what it had felt like to think about girls then. After breakfast we would go up to the store and the things were in the same place—the minnows in a bottle, the plugs and spinners disarranged and pawed over by the youngsters from the boys' camp, the Fig Newtons and the Beeman's gum. Outside, the road was tarred and cars stood in front of the store. Inside, all was just as it had always been, except there was more Coca-Cola and not so much Moxie and root beer and birch beer and sarsaparilla. We would walk out with the bottle of pop apiece and sometimes the pop would backfire up our noses and hurt. We explored the streams, quietly, where the turtles slid off the sunny logs and dug their way into the soft bottom; and we lay on the town wharf and fed worms to the tame bass. Everywhere we went I had trouble making out which was I, the one walking at my side, the one walking in my pants.

One afternoon while we were at that lake a thunderstorm came up. It was   12
like the revival of an old melodrama that I had seen long ago with childish awe. The second-act climax of the drama of the electrical disturbance over a lake in America had not changed in any important respect. This was the big scene, still the big scene. The whole thing was so familiar, the first feeling of oppression and heat and a general air around camp of not wanting to go very far away. In midafternoon (it was all the same) a curious darkening of the sky, and a lull in everything that had made life tick; and then the way the boats suddenly swung the other way at their moorings with the coming of a breeze out of the new quarter, and the premonitory rumble. Then the kettle drum, then the snare, then the bass drum and cymbals, then crackling light against the dark, and the gods grinning and licking their chops in the hills. Afterward the calm, the rain steadily rustling in the calm lake, the return of light and hope and spirits, and the campers running out in joy and relief to go swimming in the rain, their bright cries perpetuating the deathless joke about how they were getting simply drenched, and the children screaming with delight at the new sensation of bathing in the rain, and the joke about getting drenched linking the generations in a strong indestructible chain. And the comedian who waded in carrying an umbrella.

When the others went swimming my son said he was going in, too. He   13
pulled his dripping trunks from the line where they had hung all through the shower and wrung them out. Languidly, and with no thought of going in, I watched him, his hard little body, skinny and bare, saw him wince slightly as he pulled up around his vitals the small, soggy, icy garment. As he buckled the swollen belt, suddenly my groin felt the chill of death.

Meaning and Idea

1. Why does White go to the lake? When was he at the lake before? Whom does he bring with him now? With whom did he go to the lake on his earlier visits?

2. During what season do the visits take place? Describe the weather during White's return.

3. White's essay traces things that have changed at the lake and things that have not changed over the years. Identify what seems not to have changed. Identify the changes that White notes. Why do you think White devotes a paragraph to the change in motor boats? What effect do the new outboard motors have on White's feeling of the years not passing? Why?

4. What understanding does he develop from his trip to the lake as an adult?

Language, Form, Structure

1. In paragraph one White writes that he returned to the lake "for a week's fishing and to revisit old haunts." What are the denotations and connotations of the word *haunt*? In what way is "haunt" central to the essay?

2. What illusion does White try to sustain (paragraph 4)? Why is the illusion "creepy" (paragraph 4)? How successful is White in maintaining his illusion? Relate the last line to the rest of the essay.

3. List the images in the essay that most effectively render White's sense of sameness. What senses does White call upon in these images? Which images do you find most compelling?

4. White's use of language invites attention. He refers to his son as "my son" and "my boy." But sometimes he calls him simply "the boy" (paragraphs 4 and 5). What effect does he achieve with this phrasing? How does this choice of words relate to the essay's meaning? White makes use of a simile in his discussion of the storm (paragraph 12). To what event or events does he compare the storm? Do you feel the simile contributes to the essay's meanings about time and change? Why?

5. In this essay about time, White makes use of temporal organization. Consider the sequence of time from paragraph to paragraph and within each paragraph. How does White's organizational pattern add to the essay's ideas?

Ideas for Writing

1. Write a paragraph in which you describe a favorite place—a room, a park, a street, a corner. Choose details that convey the place's special features and qualities. Organize your description spatially, moving from one direction to another.

2. Write an essay in which you describe a place that strongly impressed you in childhood, either positively or negatively. Choose details that make the reader feel the place and its atmosphere.

3. Write a paragraph in which you discuss White's language. What phrases most impressed you? What in them seemed special?

CROSSOVER ▄▄▄▄▄▄▄▄▄▄▄▄▄▄▄▄▄▄▄▄▄▄▄▄▄▄

1. Judith Ortiz Cofer in "The Witch's Husband" and Edna O'Brien in "My Mother's Mother" both write about the influence of a grandmother on the narrator's sensibilities. What seems most memorable about each grandmother? Write an essay exploring each writer's assertion about her grandmother along with your own insight into your own grandmother's (or grandfather's) life and influence on you or others.

Wuthering Heights

Emily Brontë

Born on July 30, 1818, in Yorkshire, as the fifth child of the Reverend and Mrs. Patrick Brontë, Emily Brontë attended Roe Head School with her sister Charlotte (author of *Jane Eyre*). Brontë worked as a governess and studied in Brussels, hoping to open a school in Haworth, where the Brontë family lived. In 1846, Emily, Charlotte, and their sister Anne published a collection of their poems under the pseudonyms Currer, Ellis, and Acton Bell. Ellis Bell is the author named for the 1847 edition of *Wuthering Heights*. (In the same year Emily Brontë's sisters published novels too, Charlotte's *Jane Eyre* and Anne's *Agnes Grey*.) Emily Brontë died of consumption at the age of 30.

Although *Wuthering Heights* is in the form of a journal written by the narrator Mr. Lockwood, the novel provides more than personal thoughts, speculations, and fantasy. Here we read a history of a household society, strange certainly, but so vividly described as to occupy a permanent place in western literature. In this first chapter Brontë pays careful attention to details of place and of people's actions to create a clear picture of some of the characters who dominate the book.

CHAPTER 1

*1*801—I have just returned from a visit to my landlord—the solitary   1
neighbour that I shall be troubled with. This is certainly a beautiful country! In all England, I do not believe that I could have fixed on a situation so completely removed from the stir of society. A perfect misanthropist's Heaven—and Mr. Heathcliff and I are such a suitable pair to divide the desolation between us. A capital fellow! He little imagined how my heart warmed towards him when I beheld his black eyes withdraw so suspiciously under their brows, as I rode up, and when his fingers sheltered themselves, with a jealous resolution, still further in his waistcoat, as I announced my name.

"Mr. Heathcliff?" I said.   2

A nod was the answer.   3

"Mr. Lockwood your new tenant, sir—I do myself the honour of calling as   4
soon as possible, after my arrival, to express the hope that I have not inconvenienced you by my perseverance in soliciting the occupation of Thrushcross Grange: I heard, yesterday, you had had some thoughts—"

"Thrushcross Grange is my own, sir," he interrupted wincing, "I should not   5
allow any one to inconvenience me, if I could hinder it—walk in!"

The "walk in," was uttered with closed teeth and expressed the sentiment,   6
"Go to the Deuce!" even the gate over which he leant manifested no sympathizing movement to the words; and I think that circumstance determined me to accept the invitation: I felt interested in a man who seemed more exaggeratedly reserved than myself.

When he saw my horse's breast fairly pushing the barrier, he did pull out   7
his hand to unchain it, and then sullenly preceded me up the causeway, calling, as
we entered the court:

"Joseph, take Mr. Lockwood's horse; and bring up some wine."   8

"Here we have the whole establishment of domestics, I suppose," was the   9
reflection, suggested by this compound order. "No wonder the grass grows up
between the flags, and cattle are the only hedge-cutters."

Joseph was an elderly, nay, an old man, very old, perhaps, though hale and   10
sinewy.

"The Lord help us!" he soliloquised in an undertone of peevish displeasure,   11
while relieving me of my horse: looking, meantime, in my face so sourly that I
charitably conjectured he must have need of divine aid to digest his dinner, and
his pious ejaculation had no reference to my unexpected advent.

Wuthering Heights is the name of Mr. Heathcliff's dwelling. "Wuthering"   12
being a significant provincial adjective, descriptive of the atmospheric tumult to
which its station is exposed, in stormy weather. Pure, bracing ventilation they
must have up there, at all times, indeed: one may guess the power of the north
wind, blowing over the edge, by the excessive slant of a few, stunted firs at the
end of the house; and by a range of gaunt thorns all stretching their limbs one
way, as if craving alms of the sun. Happily, the architect had foresight to build it
strong: the narrow windows are deeply set in the wall; and the corners defended
with large jutting stones.

Before passing the threshold, I paused to admire a quantity of grotesque   13
carving lavished over the front, and especially about the principal door, above
which, among a wilderness of crumbling griffins, and shameless little boys, I
detected the date "1500," and the name "Hareton Earnshaw." I would have made
a few comments, and requested a short history of the place, from the surly owner,
but his attitude at the door appeared to demand my speedy entrance, or complete
departure, and I had no desire to aggravate his impatience, previous to inspecting
the penetralium.

One step brought us into the family sitting-room, without any introductory   14
lobby, or passage: they call it here "the house" preeminently. It includes kitchen,
and parlor, generally, but I believe at Wuthering Heights, the kitchen is forced to
retreat altogether, into another quarter, at least I distinguished a chatter of
tongues, and a clatter of culinary utensils, deep within; and I observed no signs
of roasting, boiling, or baking, about the huge fire-place; nor any glitter of copper saucepans and tin cullenders on the walls. One end, indeed, reflected splen-
didly both light and heat, from ranks of immense pewter dishes; interspersed with
silver jugs, and tankards, towering row after row, in a vast oak dresser, to the very
roof. The latter had never been under-drawn, its entire anatomy lay bare to an
inquiring eye, except where a frame of wood laden with oatcakes, and clusters of
legs of beef, mutton and ham, concealed it. Above the chimney were sundry vil-
lanous old guns, and a couple of horse-pistols, and, by way of ornament, three
gaudily painted canisters disposed along its ledge. The floor was of smooth, white
stone: the chairs, high-backed, primitive structures, painted green: one or two

heavy black ones lurking in the shade. In an arch, under the dresser, reposed a huge, liver-coloured bitch pointer surrounded by a swarm of squealing puppies, and other dogs, haunted other recesses.

The apartment, and furniture would have been nothing extraordinary as belonging to a homely, northern farmer with a stubborn countenance, and stalwart limbs, set out to advantage in knee-breeches, and gaiters. Such an individual, seated in his arm-chair, his mug of ale frothing on the round table before him, is to be seen in any circuit of five or six miles among these hills, if you go at the right time, after dinner. But, Mr. Heathcliff forms a singular contrast to his abode and style of living. He is a dark skinned gypsy, in aspect, in dress, and manners, a gentleman, that is, as much a gentleman as many a country squire: rather slovenly, perhaps, yet not looking amiss, with his negligence, because he has an erect and handsome figure—and rather morose—possibly, some people might suspect him of a degree of under-bred pride—I have a sympathetic chord within that tells me it is nothing of the sort; I know, by instinct, his reserve springs from an aversion to showy displays of feeling—to manifestations of mutual kindliness. He'll love and hate, equally under cover, and esteem it a species of impertinence, to be loved or hated again—No, I'm running on too fast—I bestow my own attributes over liberally on him. Mr. Heathcliff may have entirely dissimilar reasons for keeping his hand out of the way, when he meets a would be acquaintance, to those which actuate me. Let me hope my constitution is almost peculiar: my dear mother used to say I should never have a comfortable home, and only last summer, I proved myself perfectly unworthy of one. [15]

While enjoying a month of fine weather at the sea-coast, I was thrown into the company of a most fascinating creature, a real goddess, in my eyes, as long as she took no notice of me. I "never told my love" vocally; still, if looks have language, the merest idiot might have guessed I was over head and ears: she understood me, at last, and looked a return—the sweetest of all imaginable looks—and what did I do? I confess it with shame—shrunk icily into myself, like a snail, at every glance retired colder and farther; till, finally, the poor innocent was led to doubt her own senses, and, overwhelmed with confusion at her supposed mistake, persuaded her mamma to decamp. [16]

By this curious turn of disposition I have gained the reputation of deliberate heartlessness, how undeserved, I alone can appreciate. [17]

I took a seat at the end of the hearthstone opposite that towards which my landlord advanced, and filled up an interval of silence by attempting to caress the canine mother, who had left her nursery, and was sneaking wolfishly to the back of my legs, her lip curled up, and her white teeth watering for a snatch. [18]

My caress provoked a long, guttural gnarl. [19]

"You'd better let the dog alone," growled Mr. Heathcliff, in unison, checking fiercer demonstrations with a punch of his foot. "She's not accustomed to be spoiled—not kept for a pet." [20]

Then, striding to a side-door, he shouted again. [21]

"Joseph!" [22]

Joseph mumbled indistinctly in the depths of the cellar; but, gave no inti- ₂₃ mation of ascending; so, his master dived down to him, leaving me *vis-à-vis* the ruffianly bitch, and a pair of grim, shaggy sheep dogs, who shared with her a jealous guardianship over all my movements.

Not anxious to come in contact with their fangs, I sat still—but, imagining ₂₄ they would scarcely understand tacit insults, I unfortunately indulged in winking and making faces at the trio, and some turn of my physiognomy so irritated madam, that she suddenly broke into a fury, and leapt on my knees. I flung her back, and hastened to interpose the table between us. This proceeding roused the whole hive. Half-a-dozen four-footed fiends, of various sizes, and ages, issued from hidden dens to the common centre. I felt my heels, and coat-laps peculiar subjects of assault; and, parrying off the larger combatants, as effectually as I could, with the poker, I was constrained to demand, aloud, assistance from some of the household, in re-establishing peace.

Mr. Heathcliff and his man climbed the cellar steps with vexatious phlegm. ₂₅ I don't think they moved one second faster than usual, though the hearth was an absolute tempest of worrying and yelping.

Happily, an inhabitant of the kitchen made more dispatch; a lusty dame, ₂₆ with tucked up gown, bare arms, and fire-flushed cheeks, rushed into the midst of us flourishing a fryingpan; and used that weapon, and her tongue to such purpose, that the storm subsided magically, and she only remained, heaving like a sea after a high wind, when her master entered on the scene.

"What the devil is the matter?" he asked, eyeing me in a manner that I could ₂₇ ill endure after this inhospitable treatment.

"What the devil, indeed!" I muttered. "The herd of possessed swine could ₂₈ have had no worse spirits in them than those animals of yours, sir. You might as well leave a stranger with a brood of tigers!"

"They wont meddle with persons who touch nothing," he remarked, putting ₂₉ the bottle before me, and restoring the displaced table. "The dogs do right to be vigilant. Take a glass of wine?"

"No, thank you." ₃₀

"Not bitten, are you?" ₃₁

"If I had been, I would have set my signet on the biter." ₃₂

Heathcliff's countenance relaxed into a grin. ₃₃

"Come, come," he said, "you are flurried, Mr. Lockwood. Here take a little ₃₄ wine. Guests are so exceedingly rare in this house that I and my dogs, I am willing to own, hardly know how to receive them. Your health, sir!"

I bowed and returned the pledge; beginning to perceive that it would be ₃₅ foolish to sit sulking for the misbehaviour of a pack of curs: besides, I felt loath to yield the fellow further amusement, at my expense; since his humour took that turn.

He—probably swayed by prudential considerations of the folly of offend- ₃₆ ing a good tenant—relaxed, a little, in the laconic style of chipping of his pronouns, and auxiliary verbs; and introduced, what he supposed would be a subject of interest to me, a discourse on the advantages and disadvantages of my present place of retirement.

I found him very intelligent on the topics we touched; and, before I went 37 home, I was encouraged so far as to volunteer another visit, tomorrow.

He evidently wished no repetition of my intrusion. I shall go, notwith- 38 standing. It is astonishing how sociable I feel myself compared with him.

Meaning and Idea

1. Why has Lockwood chosen to live in Thrushcross Grange? Why has he come to visit Heathcliff? What impression does Brontë give us of Heathcliff? Of Joseph? Describe each of these men in your own words.

2. What impression does Brontë create of the narrator Lockwood? Why does he see himself as having the reputation of "deliberate heartlessness"? How do Lockwood and Heathcliff compare in temperament? How does Lockwood feel toward Heathcliff? What is the meaning of the last sentence?

3. Describe the outside and the family sitting room of "Wuthering Heights," Heathcliff's dwelling. Why does Lockwood not ask for a history of the place? Why is "Wuthering Heights" an appropriate name for it?

Language, Form, Structure

1. What is Brontë's purpose in the first chapter of her novel *Wuthering Heights?* In an essay you might expect a thesis to state the main idea of the piece, but not in a novel, certainly. What, however, is the point of this chapter? Write a sentence in which you state the main idea as precisely as you can.

2. Brontë provides a series of outstanding descriptions here—of the house, of Heathcliff and Joseph, of the dogs, of the "lusty dame" from the kitchen. What details stand out particularly? Where does Brontë appeal to the senses of sight, sound, and touch? What does she achieve by using specific words like *jugs* and *tankards* (instead of *vessels,* say) or *beef, mutton,* and *ham* (instead of *meat*)? In the description of the dwelling, what impression do the details of the scene seem to be creating?

3. Make a list of images that describe actions in this chapter. How appropriate are the words Brontë selects to the impressions she wishes us to have of the characters? How does the sentence that first describes Heathcliff's actions (paragraph 1, sentence 6) serve to establish his character? What is the effect of an image like "Mr. Heathcliff and his man climbed the cellar steps with vexatious phlegm"? How does the spoken conversation of the men help establish their characters?

4. Reread the paragraph in which the dogs assault Lockwood. Which sensory details make their actions particularly clear and vivid to you? Why does Brontë dwell at such length on the dogs?

5. Use a dictionary to check meanings for any of the following words that you do not know: desolation; perseverance; sullenly; hale; sinewy; peevish; pious; sundry; stalwart; singular; slovenly; morose; aversion; impertinence; decamp; *vis-à-vis;* physiognomy; prudential.

Ideas for Writing

1. Write a paragraph description of a room in your house or in some other house that you know well. Concentrate on rich sensory details of color, action, sound, smell, and touch.

2. Write an essay in which you describe someone in the setting of his or her home or apartment. Use sharp sensory details to paint a picture of the person and the scene. Try to make the details revolve about a single impression you want to give of the person or place. Perhaps, like Brontë, you might wish to show a kind of hostile moroseness; or you might wish to show cheerfulness, neatness, friendliness, indifference, or some other quality.

3. Write a paragraph in which you comment on Brontë's skills as a writer of description. How effective are the images she creates? What patterns, if any, do you discover?

Wind and Silver

Amy Lowell

Amy Lowell (1874–1925) was a leader among the group of British and American poets called *imagists* in the early part of this century. Lowell's imagist poetry concentrated on clear, hard, specific imagery as a reaction against the sentimentality that pervaded the previous century's poetry. Others in this group included Ezra Pound, Hilda Doolittle, and Richard Addington. Born in Brookline, Massachusetts, Lowell joined the imagists in England in 1913. She was the sister of Abbott Lawrence Lowell, a progressive president of Harvard University, and Percival Lowell, the discoverer of the planet Pluto. Lowell's volume of poems *What's O'Clock* won the Pulitzer Prize in 1925.

With almost haiku-like simplicity, Amy Lowell juxtaposes the particular against the universal. The poem is a simple statement, well within Lowell's imagist roots, which leaves the reader with a lovely picture of glittering ponds.

*G*reatly shining,
The Autumn moon floats in the thin sky;
And the fish-ponds shake their backs and flash their dragon scales
As she passes over them.

Meaning and Idea

1. Who or what is the "she" in the last line? Why "she" instead of "he"? To whom or to what does the pronoun *their* refer in line 3?

2. What is the weather of this poem? How do you know from the sparse description?

3. Describe the scene and action of this short poem in plain prose, as objectively as possible.

4. How does the title of the poem supplement the description?

Language, Form, Structure

1. What is Lowell's *purpose* in this poem? For what reasons do you think she chose to express that purpose in such a short poem? Do you think she was successful?

2. In line 3, Lowell relies on metaphoric description. Explain the meaning of the line in your own words. How is using metaphor here effective for the poem's impact? Why? Identify any other metaphors in the poem.

3. With what feeling does the poem leave you? To which of the reader's senses does it most appeal? Refer to specific elements of the poem to support your opinion.

4. What is the connection between the word *shining* in line 1 and *flash* in line 3? Is it an effective connection? How does it relate to the descriptive scene?

5. What is the significance of the title?

Ideas for Writing

1. The Japanese poem form of haiku makes use, like Lowell does, of extreme economy of description to create a dominant impression. Choose a limited scene to describe—perhaps a street corner or your favorite "hiding place"—and describe it two times: first, in an objectively detailed paragraph; second, in a three- to five-line impressionistic poem which relies on metaphoric description.

2. Imagine Lowell's scene as clearly as possible. Then, in either a short poem or a paragraph, describe the same scene during a summer day. Try to parallel her descriptive movement.

3. In writing a poem about an autumn night pond scene, Lowell selected just a few elements of the scene to describe. In a few paragraphs, discuss your response to the brevity and extreme selectivity of this poem. What is gained by it? What is lost by it? Does it represent any judgment about the scene on Lowell's part? Does it leave you feeling fulfilled or wanting more? Why?

Ozymandias

Percy Bysshe Shelley

Percy Bysshe Shelley (1792–1822) is considered among the greatest poets of the romantic era. He was a sensitive nonconformist who as a boy at Eton was nicknamed "Mad Shelley." Later, he was dismissed from Oxford for writing *The Necessity of Atheism.* He was, however, a quiet and modest man. In 1816, he married Mary Gordon, who the next year wrote the classic horror story *Frankenstein.* In 1822, Shelley drowned in a boating accident, and in the romantic fashion, his body was burned on the beach by his friends.

"Ozymandias" displays Shelley's attraction to mythological legend as it combines with his self-proclaimed abhorrence of "religious, political, and domestic oppression." In this poem, he demonstrates the irony of tyrannical bravura while leaving us on a typically romantic landscape.

I met a traveller from an antique land
Who said: Two vast and trunkless legs of stone
Stand in the desert . . . Near them, on the sand,
Half sunk, a shattered visage lies, whose frown,
And wrinkled lip, and sneer of cold command,   5
Tell that its sculptor well those passions read
Which yet survive, stamped on these lifeless things,
The hand that mocked them, and the heart that fed:
And on the pedestal these words appear:
"My name is Ozymandias, king of kings: 10
Look on my works, ye Mighty, and despair!"
Nothing beside remains. Round the decay
Of that colossal wreck, boundless and bare
The lone and level sands stretch far away.

Meaning and Idea

1. Ozymandias is the Greek name for the Egyptian pharaoh Ramses II. According to the description in the poem, what physical characteristics do you know about Ozymandias? From what lines do you learn this? What kind of attitude did he project, according to Shelley's description?

2. What is the "antique land" mentioned here? What, exactly, does the traveller describe to the speaker of this poem?

3. Summarize, in your own words, the statement that appears on the pedestal.

Language, Form, Structure

1. *Irony* refers to the disparity between what is said and what is meant (verbal irony) or what should be and what actually is (situational irony). What is the main situational irony of this poem? What sort of verbal irony exists here as well?

2. Why is *lifeless* a particularly good descriptive word in line 7? Aside from its literal meaning for the poem, what ironic or connotative meanings does it carry here? What are the possible meanings for the word *mocked* in line 8?

3. What are the uses of the verb *survive* in line 7? How does it refer to the phrase that precedes it? How does it refer to the verbal constructions that follow it?

4. What are the special meanings in this poem for the following words: vast; visage; sneer; read; mocked; pedestal; despair; boundless.

Ideas for Writing

1. Choose a situation that you expected to turn out one way but that in fact turned out in some other way. Describe in detail your expectations; then, describe the actual outcome.

2. Write a description of some place or some thing you have seen which was either decayed, eroded, or destroyed. Concentrate on visual details.

3. Write a paragraph in which you discuss the effectiveness of Shelley's use of irony in this poem. How do you think it enhanced or detracted from the impact of the poem?

My Mother's Mother

Edna O'Brien

Since the 1960s Edna O'Brien has published over 15 novels and collections of short stories, despite frequent censorship in her native country because of her frank, sensuous portrayals of women and their lives. O'Brien was born in County Clare in 1932 and educated in Dublin. "My Mother's Mother," from her 1984 collection, *A Fanatic Heart,* is a captivating short story filled with sensory detail and evocative settings. In it, a daughter begins to learn firsthand not only the aphorism "Absence makes the heart grow fonder," but also that the lesson itself is a double-edged sword.

I loved my mother, yet I was glad when the time came to go to her   1
mother's house each summer. It was a little house in the mountains and it commanded a fine view of the valley and the great lake below. From the front door, glimpsed through a pair of very old binoculars, one could see the entire Shannon Lake studded with various islands. On a summer's day this was a thrill. I would be put standing on a kitchen chair, while someone held the binoculars, and sometimes I marveled though I could not see at all, as the lenses had not been focused properly. The sunshine made everything better, and though we were not down by the lake, we imagined dipping our feet in it, or seeing people in boats fishing and then stopping to have a picnic. We imagined lake water lapping.

I felt safer in that house. It was different from our house, not so imposing,   2
a cottage really, with no indoor water and no water closet. We went for buckets of water to the well, a different well each summer. These were a source of miracle to me, these deep cold wells, sunk into the ground, in a kitchen garden, or a paddock, or even a long distance away, wells that had been divined since I was last there. There was always a tin scoop nearby so that one could fill the bucket to the very brim. Then of course the full bucket was an occasion of trepidation, because one was supposed not to spill. One often brought the bucket to the very threshold of the kitchen and then out of excitement or clumsiness some water would get splashed onto the concrete floor and there would be admonishments, but it was not like the admonishments in our own house, it was not calamitous.

My grandfather was old and thin and hoary when I first saw him. His skin   3
was the color of a clay pipe. After the market day he would come home in the pony and trap drunk, and then as soon as he stepped out of the trap he would stagger and fall into a drain or whatever. Then he would roar for help, and his grandson, who was in his twenties, would pick him up, or rather, drag him along the ground and through the house and up the stairs to his feather bed, where he moaned and groaned. The bedroom was above the kitchen, and in the night we would be below, around the fire, eating warm soda bread and drinking cocoa. There was nothing like it. The fresh bread would only be an hour out of the pot and cut in thick pieces and dolloped with butter and greengage jam. The green-

gage jam was a present from the postmistress, who gave it in return for the grazing of a bullock. She gave marmalade at a different time of year and a barmbrack at Halloween. He moaned upstairs, but no one was frightened of him, not even his own wife, who chewed and chewed and said, "Bad cess to them that give him the drink." She meant the publicans. She was a minute woman with a minute face and her thin hair was pinned up tightly. Her little face, though old, was like a bud, and when she was young she had been beautiful. There was a photo of her to prove it.

Sitting with them at night I thought that maybe I would not go home at all. 4 Maybe I would never again lie in bed next to my mother, the two of us shivering with expectancy and with terror. Maybe I would forsake my mother.

"Maybe you'll stay here," my aunt said, as if she had guessed my thoughts. 5

"I couldn't do that," I said, not knowing why I declined, because indeed the 6 place had definite advantages. I stayed up as late as they did. I ate soda bread and jam to my heart's content, I rambled around the fields all day, admiring sally trees, elder bushes, and the fluttering flowers, I played "shop" or I played teaching in the little dark plantation, and no one interfered or told me to stop doing it. The plantation was where I played secrets, and always I knew the grownups were within shouting distance, if a stranger or a tinker should surprise me there. It was pitch dark and full of young fir trees. The ground was a carpet of bronzed fallen fir needles. I used to kneel on them for punishment, after the playing.

Then when that ritual was done I went into the flower garden, which being 7 full of begonias and lupins was a mass of bright brilliant colors. Each area had its own color, as my aunt planned it that way. I can see them now, those bright reds, like nail varnish, and those yellows like the gauze of a summer dress and those pale blues like old people's eyes, with the bees and the wasps luxuriating in each petal, or each little bell, or each flute, and feel the warmth of the place, and the drone of the bees, and see again tea towels and gray flannelette drawers that were spread out on the hedge to dry. The sun garden, they called it. My aunt got the seeds and just sprinkled them around, causing marvelous blooms to spring up. They even had tulips, whereas at home we had only a diseased rambling rose on a silvered arch and two clumps of devil's pokers. Our garden was sad and windy, the wind had made holes and indentations in the hedges, and the dogs had made further holes where they slept and burrowed. Our house was larger, and there was better linoleum on the floor, there were brass rods on the stairs, and there was a flush lavatory, but it did not have the same cheeriness and it was imbued with doom.

Still, I knew that I would not stay in my grandmother's forever. I knew it 8 for certain when I got into bed and then desperately missed my mother, and missed the little whispering we did, and the chocolate we ate, and I missed the smell of our kind of bedclothes. Theirs were gray flannel, which tickled the skin, as did the loose feathers, and their pointed ends kept irking one. There was a gaudy red quilt that I thought would come to life and turn into a sinister Santa Claus. Except that they had told me that there was no Santa Claus. My aunt told me that, she insisted.

There was my aunt and her two sons, Donal and Joe, and my grandmother ₉
and grandfather. My aunt and Joe would tease me each night, say that there was
no Santa Claus, until I got up and stamped the floor, and in contradicting them
welled up with tears, and then at last, when I was on the point of breaking down,
they would say that there was. Then one night they went too far. They said that
my mother was not my real mother. My real mother, they said, was in Australia
and I was adopted. I could not be told that word. I began to hit the wall and
screech, and the more they insisted, the more obstreperous I became. My aunt
went into the parlor in search of a box of snaps to find a photo of my real mother
and came out triumphant at having found it. She showed me a woman in knicker-
bockers with a big floppy hat. I could have thrown it in the fire so violent was I.
They watched for each new moment of panic and furious disbelief, and then they
got the wind up when they saw I was getting out of control. I began to shake like
the weather conductor on the chapel chimney and my teeth chattered, and before
long I was just this shaking creature, unable to let out any sound, and seeing the
room's contents swim away from me, I felt their alarm almost as I felt my own.
My aunt took hold of my wrist to feel my pulse, and my grandmother held a
spoonful of tonic to my lips, but I spilled it. It was called Parishes Food and was
the color of cooked beetroot. My eyes were haywire. My aunt put a big towel
around me and sat me on her knee, and as the terror lessened, my tears began to
flow and I cried so much that they thought I would choke because of the tears
going back down the throat. They said I must never tell anyone and I must never
tell my mother.

"She is my mother," I said, and they said, "Yes, darling," but I knew that ₁₀
they were appalled at what had happened.

That night I fell out of bed twice, and my aunt had to put chairs next to it to ₁₁
keep me in. She slept in the same room, and often I used to hear her crying for her
dead husband and begging to be reunited with him in heaven. She used to talk to
him and say, "Is that you, Michael, is that you?" I often heard her arms striking
against the headboard, or heavy movements when she got up to relieve herself. In
the daytime we used the fields, but at night we did not go out for fear of ghosts.
There was a gutter in the back kitchen that served as a channel, and twice a week
she put disinfectant in it. The crux in the daytime was finding a private place and
not being found or spied on by anyone. It entailed much walking and then much
hesitating so as not to be seen.

The morning after the fright, they pampered me, scrambled me an egg, and ₁₂
sprinkled nutmeg over it. Then along with that my aunt announced a surprise. Our
workman had sent word by the mail-car man that he was coming to see me on
Sunday and the postman had delivered the message. Oh, what a glut of happiness.
Our workman was called Carnero and I loved him too. I loved his rotting teeth
and his curly hair and his strong hands and his big stomach, which people referred
to as his "corporation." He was nicknamed Carnero after a boxer. I knew that
when he came he would have bars of chocolate, and maybe a letter or a silk hanky
from my mother, and that he would lift me up in his arms and swing me around
and say "Sugarbush." How many hours were there until Sunday, I asked.

Yet that day, which was Friday, did not pass without event. We had a visitor— 13
a man. I will never know why but my grandfather called him Tim, whereas his real
name was Pat, but my grandfather was not to be told that. Tim, it seems, had died
and my grandfather was not to know, because if any of the locals died, it brought
his own death to his mind and he dreaded death as strenuously as did all the others.
Death was some weird journey that you made alone and unbefriended, once you
had embarked on it. When my aunt's husband had died, in fact had been shot by the
Black and Tans, my aunt had to conceal the death from her own parents, so irrational were they about the subject. She had to stay up at home the evening her husband's remains were brought to the chapel, and when the chapel bell rang out inter-
mittently, as it does for a death, and they asked who it was, again and again, my
poor aunt had to conceal her own grief, be silent about her own tragedy, and pretend that she did not know. Next day she went to the funeral on the excuse that it
was some forester whom her husband knew. Her husband was supposed to be transferred to a barracks a long way off, and meanwhile she was going to live with her
parents and bring her infant sons until her husband found accommodation. She
invented a name for the district where her husband was supposed to be, it was in the
North of Ireland, and she invented letters that she had received from him, and the
news of the Troubles up there. Eventually, I expect, she told them, and I expect they
collapsed and broke down. In fact, the man who brought these imaginary letters
would have been Tim, since he had been the postman, and it was of his death my
grandfather must not be told. So there in the porch, in a worn suit, was a man called
Pat answering to the name of Tim, and the news that a Tim would have, such as how
were his family and what crops had he put in and what cattle fairs had he been to.
I thought that it was peculiar that he could answer for another, but I expect that
everyone's life story was identical.

Sunday after Mass I was down by the little green gate skipping and waiting 14
for Carnero. As often happens, the visitor arrives just when we look away. The
cuckoo called, and though I knew I would not see her, I looked in a tree where
there was a ravaged bird's nest, and at that moment heard Carnero's whistle. I ran
down the road, and at once he hefted me up onto the crossbar of his bicycle.

"Oh, Carnero," I cried. There was both joy and sadness in our reunion. He 15
had brought me a bag of tinned sweets, and the most glamorous present—as we
got off the bicycle near the little gate he put it on me. It was a toy watch—a most
beautiful red, and each bit of the bracelet was the shape and color of a raspberry.
It had hands, and though they did not move, that did not matter. One could pull
the bracelet part by its elastic thread and cause it to snap in or out. The hands were
black and curved like an eyelash. He would not say where he had got it. I had only
one craving, to stay down there by the gate with him and admire the watch and
talk about home. I could not talk to him in front of them because a child was not
supposed to talk or have any wants. He was puffing from having cycled uphill and
began to open his tie, and taking it off, he said, "This bloody thing." I wondered
who he had put it on for. He was in his Sunday suit and had a fishing feather in
his hat.

"Oh, Carnero, turn the bike around and bring me home with you."   16

Such were my unuttered and unutterable hopes. Later my grandfather   17
teased me and said was it in his backside I saw Carnero's looks, and I said no, in
every particle of him.

That night as we were saying the Rosary my grandfather let out a shout,   18
slouched forward, knocking the wooden chair and hitting himself on the rungs of
it, then falling on the cement floor. He died delirious. He died calling on his
Maker. It was ghastly. Joe was out and only my grandmother and aunt were there
to assist. They picked him up. His skin was purple, the exact color of the iron
tonic, and his eyes rolled so that they were seeing every bit of the room, from the
ceiling, to the whitewashed wall, to the cement floor, to the settle bed, to the cans
of milk, seeing and bulging. He writhed like an animal and then let out a most
beseeching howl, and that was it. At that moment my aunt remembered I was
there and told me to go into the parlor and wait. It was worse in there, pitch dark,
and I in a place where I did not know my footing or my way around. I'd only been
in there once, to fetch a teapot and a sugar tongs when Tim came. Had it been in
our own house I would have known what to cling to, the back of a chair, the tas-
sel of a blind, the girth of a plaster statue, but in there I held on to nothing and
thought how the thing he dreaded had come to pass and now he was finding out
those dire things that all his life his mind had shirked from.

"May he rest in peace, may the souls of the faithful departed rest in peace."   19

It was that for two days, along with litanies and mourners smoking clay   20
pipes, plates being passed around and glasses filled. My mother and father were
there, among the mourners. I was praised for growing, as if it were something I
myself had caused to happen. My mother looked older in black, and I wished she
had worn a georgette scarf, something to give her a bit of brightness around the
throat. She did not like when I said that, and sent me off to say the Confiteor and
three Hail Marys. Her eyes were dry. She did not love her own father. Neither
did I. Her sister and she would go down into the far room and discuss whether
to bring out another bottle of whiskey or another porter cake, or whether it was
time to offer the jelly. They were reluctant, the reason being that some provisions
had to be held over for the next day, when the special mourners would come up
after the funeral. Whereas that night half the parish was there. My grandfather
was laid out upstairs in a brown habit. He had stubble on his chin and looked like
a frosted plank lying there, gray-white and inanimate. As soon as they had paid
their respects, the people hurried down to the kitchen and the parlor, for the eats
and the chat. No one wanted to be with the dead man, not even his wife, who had
gone a bit funny and was asking my aunt annoying questions about the food and
the fire, and how many priests were going to serve at the High Mass.

"Leave that to us," my mother would say, and then my grandmother would   21
retell the world what a palace my mother's house was, and how it was the nicest
house in the countryside, and my mother would say "Shhhh," as if she were being
disgraced. My father said, "Well, missy," to me twice, and a strange man gave me
sixpence. It was a very thin, worn sixpence and I thought it would disappear. I

called him Father, out of reverence, because he looked like a priest, but he was in fact a boatman.

The funeral was on an island on the Shannon. Most of the people stayed on the quay, but we, the family, piled into two row-boats and followed the boat that carried the coffin. It was a jolty ride, with big waves coming in over us and our feet getting drenched. The island itself was full of cows. The sudden arrivals made them bawl and race about, and I thought it was quite improper to see that happening while the remains were being lowered and buried. It was totally desolate, and though my aunt sniffled a bit, and my grandmother let out ejaculations, there was no real grief, and that was the saddest thing.

Next day they burned his working clothes and threw his muddy boots on the manure heap. Then my aunt sewed black diamonds of cloth on her clothes, on my grandmother's, and on Joe's. She wrote a long letter to her son in England, and enclosed black diamonds of cloth for him to stitch onto his effects. He worked in Liverpool in a motorcar factory. Whenever they said Liverpool, I thought of a whole mound of bloodied liver, but then I would look down at my watch and be happy again and pretend to tell the time. The house was gloomy. I went off with Joe, who was mowing hay, and sat with him on the mowing machine and fell slightly in love. Indoors was worst, what with my grandmother sighing and recalling old times, such as when her husband tried to kill her with a carving knife, and then she would snivel and miss him and say, "The poor old creature, he wasn't prepared . . ."

Out in the fields Joe fondled my knee and asked was I ticklish. He had a lovely long face and a beautiful whistle. He was probably about twenty-four, but he seemed old, especially because of a slouchy hat and because of a pair of trousers that were several times too big for him. When the mare passed water he nudged me and said, "Want lemonade?" and when she broke wind he made disgraceful plopping sounds with his lips. He and I ate lunch on the headland and lolled for a bit. We had bread and butter, milk from a flask, and some ginger cake that was left over from the funeral. It had gone damp. He sang, "You'll be lonely, little sweetheart, in the spring," and smiled a lot at me, and I felt very privileged. I knew that all he would do was tickle my knees, and the backs of my knees, because at heart he was shy and not like some of the local men who would want to throw you to the ground and press themselves over you so that you would have to ask God for protection. When he lifted me onto the machine, he said that we would bring out a nice little cushion on the morrow so that I would have a soft seat. But on the morrow it rained and he went off to the sawmill to get shelving, and my aunt moaned about the hay getting wet and perhaps getting ruined and possibly there being no fodder for cattle next winter.

That day I got into dire disaster. I was out in the fields playing, talking, and enjoying the rainbows in the puddles, when all of a sudden I decided to run helter-skelter toward the house in case they were cross with me. Coming through a stile that led to the yard, I decided to do a big jump and landed head over heels in the manure heap. I fell so heavily onto it that every bit of clothing got wet and smeared. It was a very massive manure heap, and very squelchy. Each day the cow house was cleaned out and the contents shoveled there, and each week the straw and old nesting from the hen house were dumped there, and so was the pigs' bedding. So it was not like falling into a sack of hay. It was not dry and clean. It was a foul spot I fell into, and as soon as I waded out, I decided it was wise to undress. The pleated skirt was ruined and so was my blouse and my navy cardigan. Damp had gone through to my bodice, and the smell was dreadful. I was trying to wash it off under an outside tap, using a fist of grass as a cloth, when my aunt came out and exclaimed, "Jesus, Mary, and Joseph, glory be to the great God today and tonight, but what have you done to yourself!" I was afraid to tell her that I fell, so I said I was doing washing and she said in the name of God what washing, and then she saw the ruin on the garments. She picked up the skirt and said why on earth had she let me wear it that day, and wasn't it the demon that came with me the day I arrived with my attaché case. I was still trying to wash and not answer this barrage of questions, all beginning with the word "why." As if I knew why! She got a rag and some pumice stone, plus a can of water, and stripped to the skin, I was washed and reprimanded. Then my clothes were put to soak in the can, all except for the skirt, which had to be brought in to dry, and then cleaned with a clothes brush. Mercifully my grandmother was not told.

My aunt forgave me two nights later when she was in the dairy churning 26 and singing. I asked if I could turn the churn handle for a jiff. It was changing from liquid to solid and the handle was becoming stiff. I tried with all my might, but I was not strong enough.

"You will, when you're big," she said, and sang to me. She sang "Far Away 27 in Australia" and then asked what I would like to do when I grew up. I said I would like to marry Carnero, and she laughed and said what a lovely thing it was to be young and carefree. She let me look into the churn to see the mound of yellow butter that had formed. There were drops of water all over its surface, it was like some big bulk that had bathed but had not dried off. She got two sets of wooden pats, and together we began to fashion the butter into dainty shapes. She was quicker at it than I. She made little round balls of butter with prickly surfaces, then she said wouldn't it be lovely if the curate came up for tea. He was a new curate and had rimless spectacles.

The next day she went to the town to sell the butter and I was left to mind 28 the house along with my grandmother. My aunt had promised to bring back a shop cake, and said that, depending on the price, it would be either a sponge cake or an Oxford Lunch, which was a type of fruit cake wrapped in beautiful dun silverish paper. My grandmother donned a big straw hat with a chin strap and looked very distracted. She kept thinking that there was a car or a cart coming into the back yard and had me looking out windows on the alert. Then she got a flush and I had to conduct her into the plantation and sit on the bench next to her, and we were scarcely there when three huge fellows walked in and we knew at once that they were tinkers. The fear is indescribable. I knew that tinkers took one off in their cart, hid one under shawls, and did dire things to one. I knew that they beat their wives and children, got drunk, had fights among themselves, and spent many a night cooling off in the barracks. I jumped up as they came through the gate. My grandmother's mouth fell wide open with shock. One of them carried a shears and the other had a weighing pan in his hand. They asked if we had any sheep's wool and we both said no, no sheep, only cattle. They had evil eyes and gamey looks. There was no knowing what they would do to us. Then they asked if we had any feathers for pillows or mattresses. She was so crazed with fear that she said yes and led the way to the house. As we walked along, I expected a strong hand to be clamped on my shoulder. They were dreadfully silent. Only one had spoken and he had a shocking accent, what my mother would call "a gurrier's." She sent me upstairs to get the two bags of feathers out of the wardrobe, and I knew that she stayed below so that they would not steal a cake or bread or crockery or any other things. She was agreeing on a price when I came down, or rather, requesting a price. The talking member said it was a barter job. We would get a lace cloth in return. She asked how big this cloth was, and he said very big, while his companion put his hand into the bag of feathers to make sure that there was not anything else in there, that we were not trying to fob them off with grass or sawdust or something. She asked where was the cloth. They laughed. They said it was down in the caravan, at the crossroads, ma'am. She knew then she was being cheated, but she tried to stand her ground. She grabbed one end of the bag and said, "You'll not have these."

"D'you think we're mugs?" one of them said, and gestured to the others to 29 pick up the two bags, which they did. Then they looked at us as if they might mutilate us, and I prayed to St. Jude and St. Anthony to keep us from harm. Before going, they insisted on being given new milk. They drank in great slugs.

"Are you afraid of me?" one of the men said to her. 30

He was the tallest of the three and his shirt was open. I could see the hair 31 on his chest, and he had a very funny look in his eyes as if he was not thinking, as if thinking was beyond him. His eyes had a thickness in them. For some reason he reminded me of meat.

"Why should I be afraid of you," she said, and I was so proud of her I would 32 have clapped, but for the tight shave we were in.

She blessed herself several times when they'd gone and decided that what 33 we did had been the practical thing to do, and in fact our only recourse. But when my aunt came back and began an intensive cross-examination, the main contention was how they learned in the first place that there were feathers in the house. My aunt reasoned that they could not have known unless they had been told, they were not fortune-tellers. Each time I was asked, I would seal my lips, as I did not want to betray my grandmother. Each time she was asked, she described them in detail, the holes in their clothes, the safety pins instead of buttons, their villainous looks, and then she mentioned the child, me, and hinted about the things they might have done and was it not the blessing of God that we had got rid of them peaceably! My aunt's son joked about the lace cloth for weeks. He used to affect to admire it, by picking up one end of the black oilcloth on the table and saying, "Is it Brussels lace or is it Carrickmackross?"

Sunday came and my mother was expected to visit. My aunt had washed 34 me the night before in an aluminum pan. I had to sit in it, and was terrified lest my cousin should peep in. He was in the back kitchen shaving and whistling. It was a question of a "Saturday splash for Sunday's dash." My aunt poured a can of water over my head and down my back. It was scalding hot. Then she poured rainwater over me and by contrast it was freezing. She was not a thorough washer like my mother, but all the time she kept saying that I would be like a new pin.

My mother was not expected until the afternoon. We had washed up the din- 35 ner things and given the dogs the potato skins and milk when I started in earnest to look out for her. I went to the gate where I had waited for Carnero, and seeing no sign of her, I sauntered off down the road. I was at the crossroads when I realized how dangerous it was, as I was approaching the spot where the tinkers said their caravan was pitched. So it was back at full speed. The fuchsia was out and so were the elderberries. The fuchsia was like dangling earrings and the riper elderberries were in maroon smudges on the road. I waited in hiding, the better to surprise her. She never came. It was five, and then half past five, and then it was six. I would go back to the kitchen and lift the clock that was face down on the dresser, and then hurry out to my watch post. By seven it was certain that she would not come, although I still held out hope. They hated to see me sniffle, and even hated more when I refused a slice of cake. I could not bear to eat. Might she still come? They said there was no point in my being so spoiled. I was imprisoned at the kitchen table in front of this slice of seed cake. In my mind I lifted the gate hasp a thousand times and saw my mother pass by the kitchen window, as fleeting as a ghost; and by the time we all knelt down to say the Rosary, my imagination had run amuck. I conceived of the worst things, such as she had died, or that my father had killed her, or that she had met a man and eloped. All three were unbearable. In bed I sobbed and chewed on the blanket so as not to be heard, and between tears and with my aunt enjoining me to dry up, I hatched a plan.

On the morrow there was no word or no letter, so I decided to run away. I 36 packed a little satchel with bread, my comb, and, daftly, a spare pair of ankle socks. I told my aunt that I was going on a picnic and affected to be very happy by humming and doing little reels. It was a dry day and the dust rose in whirls under my feet. The dogs followed and I had immense trouble getting them to go back. There were no tinkers' caravans at the crossroads and because of that I was jubilant. I walked and then ran, and then I would have to slow down, and always when I slowed down, I looked back in case someone was following me. While I was running I felt I could elude them, but there was no eluding the loose stones and the bits of rock that were wedged into the dirt road. Twice I tripped. If, coming toward me, I saw two people together, I then felt safe, but if I saw one person it boded ill, as that one person could be mad, or drunk, or likely to accost. On three occasions I had to climb into a field and hide until that one ominous person went by. Fortunately, it was a quiet road, as not many souls lived in that region.

When I came off the dirt road onto the main road, I felt safer, and very soon 37 a man came by in a pony and trap and offered me a lift. He looked a harmless enough person, in a frieze coat and a cloth cap. When I stepped into the trap I was surprised to find two hens clucking and agitating under a seat.

"Would you be one of the Linihans?" he asked, referring to my grand- ₃₈
mother's family.

I said no and gave an assumed name. He plied me with questions. To get ₃₉
the most out of me, he even got the pony to slow down, so as to lengthen the journey. We dawdled. The seat of black leather was held down with black buttons. He
had a tartan rug over him. He spread it out over us both. Quickly I edged out from
under it, complaining about fleas and midges, neither of which there were. It was
a desperately lonely road with only a house here and there, a graveyard, and
sometimes an orchard. The apples looked tempting on the trees. To see each
ripening apple was to see a miracle. He asked if I believed in ghosts and told me
that he had seen the riderless horse on the moors.

"If you're a Minnogue," he said, "you should be getting out here," and he ₄₀
pulled on the reins.

I had called myself a Minnogue because I knew a girl of that name who ₄₁
lived with her mother and was separated from her father. I would like to have
been her.

"I'm not," I said, and tried to be as innocent as possible. I then had to say ₄₂
who I was, and ask if he would drop me in the village.

"I'm passing your gate," he said, and I was terrified that I would have to ask ₄₃
him up, as my mother dreaded strangers, even dreaded visitors, since these diver-
sions usually gave my father the inclination to drink, and once he drank he was
on a drinking bout that would last for weeks, and that was notorious. Therefore I
had to conjure up another lie. It was that my parents were both staying with my
grandmother and that I had been dispatched home to get a change of clothing for
us all. He grumbled at not coming up to our house, but I jumped out of the trap
and said we would ask him to a card party for sure, in December.

There was no one at home. The door was locked and the big key in its cus- ₄₄
tomary place under the pantry window. The kitchen bore signs of my mother having gone out in a hurry, as the dishes were on the table, and on the table, too, were
her powder puff, a near-empty powder box, and a holder of papier-mâché in
which her toiletries were kept. Had she gone to the city? My heart was wild with
envy. Why had she gone without me? I called upstairs, and then hearing no reply,
I went up with a mind that was buzzing with fear, rage, suspicion, and envy. The
beds were made. The rooms seemed vast and awesome compared with the little
crammed rooms of my grandmother's. I heard someone in the kitchen and hurried down with renewed palpitations. It was my mother. She had been to the shop
and got some chocolate. It was rationed because of its being wartime, but she
used to coax the shopkeeper to give her some. He was a bachelor. He liked her.
Maybe that was why she had put powder on.

"Who brought you home, my lady?" she said stiffly. ₄₅

She hadn't come on Sunday. I blurted that out. She said did anyone ever ₄₆
hear such nonsense. She said did I not know that I was to stay there until the end
of August till school began. She was even more irate when she heard that I had
run away. What would they now be thinking but that I was in a bog hole or something. She said had I no consideration and how in heaven's name was she going
to get word to them, an SOS.

"Where's my father?" I asked.   47

"Saving hay," she said.   48

I gathered the cups off the table so as to make myself useful in her eyes.   49
Seeing the state of my canvas shoes and the marks on the ankle socks, she asked
had I come through a river or what. All I wanted to know was why she had not
come on Sunday as promised. The bicycle got punctured, she said, and then asked
did I think that with bunions, corns, and welts she could walk six miles after
doing a day's work. All I thought was that the homecoming was not nearly as tender as I hoped it would be, and there was no embrace and no reunion. She filled
the kettle and I laid clean cups. I tried to be civil, to contain the pique and misery
that was welling up in me. I told her how many trams of hay they had made in her
mother's house, and she said it was a sight more than we had done. She hauled
some scones from a colander in the cupboard and told me I had better eat. She did
not heat them on the top of the oven, and that meant she was still vexed. I knew
that before nightfall she would melt, but where is the use of a thing that comes
too late?

I sat at the far end of the table watching the lines on her brow, watching the   50
puckering, as she wrote a letter to my aunt explaining that I had come home. I
would have to give it to the mail-car man the following morning and ask the postman to deliver it by hand. She said, God only knows what commotion there would
be all that day and into the night looking for me. The ink in her pen gave out, and
I held the near-empty ink bottle sideways while she refilled it.

"Go back to your place," she said, and I went back to the far end of the table   51
like someone glued to her post. I thought of fields around my grandmother's
house and the various smooth stones that I had put on the windowsill. I thought
of the sun garden, of the night my grandfather had died and my vigil in the cold
parlor. I thought of many things. Sitting there, I wanted both to be in our house
and to be back in my grandmother's missing my mother. It was as if I could taste
my pain better away from her, the excruciating pain that told me how much I
loved her. I thought how much I needed to be without her so that I could think of
her, dwell on her, and fashion her into the perfect person that she clearly was not.
I resolved that for certain I would grow up and one day go away. It was a sweet
thought, and it was packed with punishment.

Meaning and Idea

1. Why has O'Brien placed so much vivid imagery and explanation of death
   alongside the same kind of description of life and living things?

2. Is the girl actually adopted? Why do you think so? What other elements in
   the story are or are not the way they seem?

3. Who is the narrator of the story? How old is the narrator of the story now?
   What does being at her grandmother's house make the girl feel about her
   own mother? Do you think the narrator is aware of this?

Language, Form, Structure

1. Compare and contrast the first and last paragraphs of the story. Look particularly at the very last sentences of the final paragraph. How do the narrator's love for her mother and her love for her mother's mother vie for importance? How can the "sweet thought" be "packed with punishment"?

2. Look at the passage, during the grandfather's wake, when the girl is given sixpence and she thinks it is thin and about to disappear. She calls the man "Father out of reverence, because he looked like a priest, but he was in fact a boatman." Discuss what this passage means and what its effect is on the reader.

3. Find three examples of each type of sensory detail: sight, sound, taste, smell, and touch. Also find one long example that incorporates many of these sensory details at the same time.

Ideas for Writing

1. Think of a situation in which you felt homesick or otherwise missed a person or place. Write a descriptive essay about where you were and where you wished to be.

2. Write a descriptive essay about the most "rural," "roughing-it" experience you have ever had. Don't assume that it must be about the country.

3. Reread O'Brien's story. Write an essay about the uses of description in this piece. Think about how and when O'Brien describes things, and when she omits descriptions as well. Which are the most vivid or original passages? Why do you think so?

The Kitchen

Alfred Kazin

Alfred Kazin is a literary and social critic who was born in Brooklyn, New York, in 1915. His studies on American literature include *On Native Grounds* (1942). *Contemporaries* (1962), and *Bright Book of Life* (1973). His various volumes of autobiography have provided a valuable social history, particularly of life among Jewish immigrants to this country at the beginning of the century. The most recent, and perhaps the best-known, of these volumes is *New York Jew,* published in 1978.

In this touching selection from his 1951 autobiographical work *A Walker in the City,* Alfred Kazin uses precise visual images to recapture "the aliveness of the moment" in his child-hood. Through his intimate description of just one room, Kazin evokes all the people and places of the Jewish immigrant section of Bronwsville, Brooklyn, as they appeared years ago.

*I*n Brownsville tenements the kitchen is always the largest room and   1
the center of the household. As a child I felt that we lived in a kitchen to which four other rooms were annexed. My mother, a "home" dressmaker, had her work-shop in the kitchen. She told me once that she had begun dressmaking in Poland at thirteen; as far back as I can remember, she was always making dresses for the local women. She had a innate sense of design, a quick eye for all the subtleties in the latest fashions, even when she despised them, and great boldness. For three or four dollars she would study the fashion magazines with a customer, go with the customer to the remnants store on Belmont Avenue to pick out the material, argue the owner down—all remnants stores, for some reason, were supposed to be shady, as if the owners dealt in stolen goods—and then for days would patiently fit and baste and sew and fit again. Our apartment was always full of women in their housedresses sitting around the kitchen table waiting for a fitting. My little bedroom next to the kitchen was the fitting room. The sewing machine, an old nut-brown Singer with golden scrolls painted along the black arm and engraved along the two tiers of little drawers massed with needles and thread on each side of the treadle, stood next to the window and the great coalblack stove which up to my last year in college was our main source of heat. By December the two outer bedrooms were closed off, and used to chill bottles of milk and cream, cold borscht and jellied calves' feet.

The kitchen held our lives together. My mother worked in it all day long,   2
we ate in it almost all meals except the Passover *seder,* I did my homework and first writing at the kitchen table, and in winter I often had a bed made up for me on three kitchen chairs near the stove. On the wall just over the table hung a long horizontal mirror that sloped to a ship's prow at each end and was lined in cherry wood. It took up the whole wall, and drew every object in the kitchen to itself. The walls were a fiercely stippled white-wash, so often rewhitened by my father

in slack seasons that the paint looked as if it had been squeezed and cracked into the walls. A large electric bulb hung down the center of the kitchen at the end of a chain that had been hooked into the ceiling; the old gas ring and key still jutted out of the wall like antlers. In the corner next to the toilet was the sink at which we washed, and the square tub in which my mother did our clothes. Above it, tacked to the shelf on which were pleasantly ranged square, blue-bordered white sugar and spice jars, hung calendars from the Public National Bank on Pitkin Avenue and the Minsker Progressive Branch of the Workman's Circle; receipts for the payment of insurance premiums, and household bills on a spindle; two little boxes engraved with Hebrew letters. One of these was for the poor, the other to buy back the Land of Israel. Each spring a bearded little man would suddenly appear in our kitchen, salute us with a hurried Hebrew blessing, empty the boxes (sometimes with a sidelong look of disdain if they were not full), hurriedly bless us again for remembering our less fortunate Jewish brothers and sisters, and so take his departure until the next spring, after vainly trying to persuade my mother to take still another box. We did occasionally remember to drop coins in the boxes, but this was usually only on the dreaded morning of "mid-terms" and final examinations, because my mother thought it would bring me luck. She was extremely superstitious, but embarrassed about it, and always laughed at herself whenever, on the morning of an examination, she counseled me to leave the house on my right foot. "I know it's silly," her smile seemed to say, "but what harm can it do? It may calm God down."

     The kitchen gave a special character to our lives; my mother's character. All my memories of that kitchen are dominated by the nearness of my mother sitting all day long at her sewing machine, by the clacking of the treadle against the linoleum floor, by the patient twist of her right shoulder as she automatically pushed at the wheel with one hand or lifted the foot to free the needle where it had got stuck in a thick piece of material. The kitchen was her life. Year by year, as I began to take in her fantastic capacity for labor and her anxious zeal, I realized it was ourselves she kept stitched together. I can never remember a time when she was not working. She worked because the law of her life was work, work and anxiety; she worked because she would have found life meaningless without work. She read almost no English; she could read the Yiddish paper, but never felt she had time to. We were always talking of a time when I would teach her how to read, but somehow there was never time. When I awoke in the morning she was already at her machine, or in the great morning crowd of housewives at the grocery getting fresh rolls for breakfast. When I returned from school she was at her machine, or conferring over *McCall's* with some neighborhood woman who had come in pointing hopefully to an illustration—"Mrs. Kazin! Mrs. Kazin! Make me a dress like it shows here in the picture!" When my father came home from work she had somehow mysteriously interrupted herself to make supper for us, and the dishes cleared and washed, was back at her machine. When I went to bed at night, often she was still there, pounding away at the treadle, hunched over the wheel, her hands steering a piece of gauze under the needle with a finesse that always contrasted sharply with her swollen hands and broken nails. Her left hand had been pierced through when as a girl she had worked in the infamous Triangle Shirtwaist Factory on the East Side. A needle had gone straight through the palm, severing a large vein. They had sewn it up for her so clumsily that a tuft of flesh always lay folded over the palm.

The kitchen was the great machine that set our lives running; it whirred down a little only on Saturdays and holy days. From my mother's kitchen I gained my first picture of life as a white, overheated, starkly lit workshop redolent with Jewish cooking, crowded with women in housedresses, strewn with fashion magazines, patterns, dress material, spools of thread—and at whose center, so lashed to her machine that bolts of energy seemed to dance out of her hands and feet as she worked, my mother stamped the treadle hard against the floor, hard, hard, and silently, grimly at war, beat out the first rhythm of the world for me.

Every sound from the street roared and trembled at our windows—a mother feeding her child on the doorstep, the screech of the trolley cars on Rockaway Avenue, the eternal smash of a handball against the wall of our house, the clatter of *"der Italyéner"*'s cart packed with watermelons, the sing-song of the old-clothes men walking Chester Street, the cries *"Árbes! Árbes! Kinder! Kinder! Heyse gute árbes!"* All day long people streamed into our apartment as a matter of course—"customers," upstairs neighbors, downstairs neighbors, women who would stop in for a half-hour's talk, salesmen, relatives, insurance agents. Usually they came in without ringing the bell—everyone knew my mother was always at home. I would hear the front door opening, the wind whistling through our front hall, and then some familiar face would appear in our kitchen with the same bland, matter-of-fact inquiring look: no need to stand on ceremony: my mother and her kitchen were available to everyone all day long.

At night the kitchen contracted around the blaze of light on the cloth, the patterns, the ironing board where the iron had burned a black border around the tear in the muslin cover; the finished dresses looked so frilly as they jostled on their wire hangers after all the work my mother had put into them. And then I would get that strangely ominous smell of tension from the dress fabrics and the burn in the cover of the ironing board—as if each piece of cloth and paper crushed with light under the naked bulb might suddenly go up in flames. Whenever I pass some small tailoring shop still lit up at night and see the owner hunched over his steam press; whenever in some poorer neighborhood of the city I see through a window some small crowded kitchen naked under the harsh light glittering in the ceiling, I still smell that fiery breath, that warning of imminent fire. I was always holding my breath. What I must have felt most about ourselves, I see now, was that we ourselves were like kindling—that all the hard-pressed pieces of ourselves and all the hard-used objects in that kitchen were like so many slivers of wood that might go up in flames if we came too near the white-blazing filaments in that naked bulb. Our tension itself was fire, we ourselves were forever burning—to live, to get down the foreboding in our souls, to make good.

Twice a year, on the anniversaries of her parents' deaths, my mother placed on top of the ice-box an ordinary kitchen glass packed with wax, the *yortsayt,* and

The Eagle

Alfred, Lord Tennyson

Alfred, Lord Tennyson (1809–1892), along with Robert Browning, is considered a major poet of the early Victorian age. He was the son of a conservative clergyman and was educated at Cambridge, where he early on dedicated himself to poetics. The publication in 1842 of his two-volume *Poems* established his early popularity, and by 1850 he could claim to be England's most popular poet. In that year, he was named Poet Laureate of England. Among his most noted works are his tribute to friendship, *In Memoriam* (1850); his patriotic "The Charge of the Light Brigade" (1854); and his Arthurian verse romance, *The Idylls of the King* (1859–1885).

"The Eagle" is typical of Tennyson's—and the early Victorians'—reliance on smooth, metrical constructions in an attempt to blend romanticism and realism in a way to take them away from pure emotionalism. Notice how, despite the grandeur of the description, the poem is emotionally quite controlled.

*H*e clasps the crag with crooked hands;
Close to the sun in lonely lands,
Ringed with the azure world, he stands.

The wrinkled sea beneath him crawls;
He watches from his mountain walls,   5
And like a thunderbolt he falls.

Meaning and Idea

1. What is the "azure world?" Who is the "he" in the poem?

2. Where is the eagle situated in this poem? What three descriptions in stanza one uphold this placement?

3. What does the eagle do at the end of the poem?

Language, Form, Structure

1. What is the effect of the patterning set up by ending stanza one with "he stands" and stanza two with "he falls"?

2. A *simile* is a figure of speech that compares two things with the use of the word *like* or *as*. A *metaphor* makes a descriptive comparison directly, without *like* or *as*. Where does Tennyson use simile in this poem? Where does he use metaphor?

3. *Personification* is the poetic technique of attributing human feelings or characteristics to inanimate objects or things in nature. Where in his description of the eagle does Tennyson rely on personification? What is its effect? How would the poem be different if he had used *she* or *it* instead of *he* to describe the eagle?

4. Write synonyms for the following words: crag; ringed; azure.

Ideas for Writing

1. Describe a pet you've had or any animal you've observed closely. Make use of personification to enhance your description. Place the animal in its most natural environment.

2. Watch an animal in a park or anywhere outdoors for a few minutes. List objectively five actions the animal performed. Then, write a simile for each action.

3. In this poem, Tennyson's description enables the reader to have a kind of *participation* in the eagle's experience. How is this accomplished? How is this description different from a dictionary definition of an eagle? Write a short analysis of the participatory effect of this poem.

Ode to Autumn

John Keats

John Keats (1795–1821) was the son of a stable hand and an innkeeper's daughter. Unlike his fellow romantic poets, he was little inclined toward cynical or revolutionary statements; instead, he strove only to capture the "people" in nature and in people. Keats originally studied medicine after being orphaned at age 15. Sadly, he contracted tuberculosis—the same disease that had killed his mother and brother—at age 26. It was from that point on that he wrote some of his masterpieces, including "Ode on a Grecian Urn" and "Ode to a Nightingale."

"Ode to Autumn" exemplifies the lyric mastery with which Keats expressed his devotion to beauty and nature. It is a finely crafted poem rich in picturesque and sensory imagery.

Season of mists and mellow fruitfulness,
    Close bosom-friend of the maturing sun;
Conspiring with him how to load and bless
    With fruit the vines that round the thatch-eves run;
To bend with apples the mossed cottage-trees,   5
    And fill all fruit with ripeness to the core;
        To swell the gourd, and plump the hazel shells
With a sweet kernel; to set budding more,
    And still more, larger flowers for the bees,
    Until they think warm days will never cease,   10
        For summer has o'er-brimmed their clammy cells.

Who hath not seen thee oft amid thy store?
    Sometimes whoever seeks abroad may find
Thee sitting careless on a granary floor,
    Thy hair soft-lifted by the winnowing wind;   15
Or on a half-reaped furrow sound asleep,
    Drowsed with the fume of poppies, while thy hook
        Spares the next swath and all its twined flowers:
And sometimes like a gleaner thou dost keep
    Steady thy laden head across a brook;   20
    Or by a cider-press, with patient look,
        Thou watchest the last oozings hours by hours.

Where are the songs of Spring? Ay, where are they?
    Think not of them, thou hast thy music too,—
While barred clouds bloom the soft-dying day,   25
    And touch the stubble-plains with rosy hue;

Then in a wailful choir the small gnats mourn
   Among the river swallows, borne aloft
      Or sinking as the light wind lives or dies;
And full-grown lambs loud bleat from hilly bourn;   30
      Hedge-crickets sing; and now with treble soft
      The red-breast whistles from a garden-croft;
         And gathering swallows twitter in the skies.

Meaning and Idea

1. The speaker is addressing autumn in the poem. Why does he call autumn a friend of the sun? How do autumn and the sun conspire?

2. Explain stanza two in your own words. How is autumn "like a gleaner"?

3. What, according to Keats, is autumn's music?

Language, Form, Structure

1. What is Keats's theme in this poem?

2. What is the focus of imagery in each stanza? How does Keats arrange the imagery within the poem?

3. To which of the five senses does the imagery of this poem appeal? Give an example of an image for each sense you list. Explain each image in your own words.

4. How does Keats use *personification* in the poem? Which stanza makes the most use of personification?

5. Look up the following words in a dictionary: granary; winnowing; furrow; hook; swath; barred; sallow; bleat; bourn; twitter.

Ideas for Writing

1. Write a description, either in prose or verse, of your favorite season. Try to use images that appeal to each of the five senses.

2. Describe and evaluate the syntax and diction of this nineteenth-century poem.

Snow toward Evening

Melville Cane

Melville Cane (1879–1980) was born in Plattsburg, New York, and educated at Columbia University, where he received his law degree. He was primarily a lawyer, yet found enough time to concentrate on his poetry, so that in 1971 he received the Poetry Society of America's gold medal. His collections include *And Pastures New* (1956) and *Snow toward Evening* (1974).

Melville Cane blends direct statement description ("the sky turned gray") with metaphoric description ("From some invisible blossoming tree") to describe a simple, natural event.

Suddenly the sky turned gray,
The day,
Which had been bitter and chill,
Grew soft and still.
Quietly   5
From some invisible blossoming tree
Millions of petals cool and white
Drifted and blew,
Lifted and flew,
Fell with the falling night.   10

Meaning and Idea

1. What is the season described in this poem?

2. During what time of day does this poem occur? Aside from the title, what evidence do you have for your answer? How do you know it's not late at night, for example?

Language, Form, Structure

1. This poem is composed of two sentences, each beginning with an adverb. What are these adverbs? How do they help establish the dominant impression in the poem?

2. How does the use of rhyme contribute to the overall feeling of the poem?

3. How does Cane use *metaphor* as a descriptive technique in this poem? What are the "millions of petals"? What is the "invisible blossoming tree"?

Ideas for Writing

1. Describe an evening snow scene that particularly impressed you.

2. Describe the beginning moments of a simple, natural occurrence. Attempt to use some metaphoric description.

3. Both Cane's poem and Keats's "Autumn" describe seasonal scenes in nature. Which do you find more effective and more evocative? Why?

CROSSOVER

1. Percy Bysshe Shelley, Amy Lowell, Alfred Lord Tennyson, John Keats, and Melville Cane bring the poet's eye to the task of description and turn it into a treasure of original phrasing, intense sensory language, and startling insights. Select any two or three of the poets in this chapter and compare and contrast their strategies for describing the topics of the poems. Which poem has the most unique phrasing? Which images are most indelible in your mind? Draw liberally from the poets' language to support your point.

2. N. Scott Momaday in "The Last of the Kiowas," E. B. White in "Once More to the Lake," Edna O'Brien in "My Mother's Mother," and Alfred Kazin in "The Kitchen" all write about places rooted in memory. How does each author use memory to contribute to meaning? What does the act of remembering add to the intensity of the descriptions?

Chapter Two

■

NARRATION

In most cultures we find an exalted place for the story, the narrative with a clear march of scenes that reports a notable sequence of events in vivid language. Stories reflect the reaches of human experience. People delight in narratives—whether fiction or fact, imagined or historical. Even our modern sensibilities, so obviously in flux as a result of the entertainment technologies and the media explosion, show no diminished love of stories. Afternoon soap operas, prime-time comedy and adventure series, and the popular films of our decade build their appeals upon narrative frameworks. The fictions we read, too, of course—the novels, short stories, and plays of our age—take much of their life from narrative, as do popular songs and poems. Essays also rely upon narrative structures; when Aristotle identified narration as one of the four categories of prose forms (including description, exposition, and argumentation), it was clearly an acknowledgment of the value of the story for its own sake.

READING NARRATIVE

As speakers, listeners, readers, and writers, we are tireless narrators. We're always telling and listening to stories just for the fun of them. The Canadian novelist Alice Munro identifies this impulse in *Lives of Girls and Women:* "Aunt Elspeth and Auntie Grace told stories. It did not seem as if they were telling them to me, to entertain me, but as if they would have told them anyway, for their own pleasure, even if they had been alone." In this spirit, narratives in this chapter are appealing because they give pleasure to readers. This is not to say that the narratives here have no further goal. Certainly "A Wagner Matinée," the lead piece in this chapter, delights us by stating the precise sensory details that arouse Aunt Georgiana's joy at hearing a concert after many years; but the dramatic final sentence of the story brings her sacrifices into sudden and shocking perspective. With the contrast between Aunt Georgiana's life of deprivation and a life in which musical performances are familiar ecstasies, Willa Cather is asserting the centrality of art to human experience. Similarly, Raymond Carver's accretion of details in his narrative essay, "My Father's Life," forces us to think again about fate, life, and reminiscence. The essay is great writing because it provides a stirring commentary on human nature, and the narrative structure makes the point more forcefully than any other. All narratives, whether fiction or fact, prose or poetry, share the common bond of purpose. Readers seek out the point of the story and use it as a mark of the story's success. Today's stories may no longer have a moral, in the narrow sense, but the effective story will still, at the very least, present an understanding or raise a question, even if it offers no easy solution. "Why is this writer telling us this?" is the most important question we can ask about any piece of narration.

What in fact does a story do? A story breaks the ice: "It's great being back here talking to this Kiwanis Club in Charleston. Why, twenty years ago, when I was a small girl growing up in Parkersburg, Virginia, I. . . ." A story gives essential information: "My car was parked on the corner of Clark and Wabash, officer, when I saw a man leap out the door of the 7–11 and. . . ." Stories connect us to other people and provide a frame or a mirror to our own lives. Stories prod our imaginations, our consciousness, our humanity. They win us over. They wear us down. Sometimes they push us to action.

Experienced readers of narrative can identify two general approaches. One is the *narrative summary* where the writer covers large segments of time, skips over some events to highlight others, and aims for broad comprehensive impressions in the minds of readers more than for a highly detailed vision of discrete scenes. Writers of history, memoirs, and biography, as well as news and sports reporters, often will rely upon narrative summaries. Essayists, too, will use this technique and so will novelists, poets, and short story writers. When you read Carver's essay in this chapter, you will see narrative summary in one of its best forms. The other approach is the *narrative moment* where the writer chooses a limited time frame and explores all its details for an intense, comprehensive view of a flash of time. Most selections here follow this format. Relying upon character, dialogue, plot, and concrete sensory language, the narrative moment is like a sequence of frames on a piece of film that presents carefully chosen details for the viewer. The selection from *Native Son,* along with many others in this chapter, underscores how effective this method is in holding a reader's attention. We're not suggesting any single approach here—writers may use both narrative summary and narrative moments in a novel or poem or story or essay—but as alert readers we want to be aware of how we arrive where writers want to take us. Hence, the distinction between narrative summary and narrative moment is useful.

Also when we read, we must be aware of the temporal sequence upon which the flesh of the story hangs. Most narratives consist of an orderly *chronology:* First this happened, then that, then some other thing. In using narrative to make a dramatic point, most essayists and fiction writers use this simple arrangement. But experienced writers can and do take great liberties with sequence. A story can begin *in medias res*—in the midst of things—where readers suddenly find themselves in the heat of an event that does not evolve from an orderly march of hours and minutes and seconds. With such stories we often must fill in details on our own, reconstructing pieces as we go along, or waiting for information that may be revealed later on about earlier events. Or skillful writers may rely upon *flashback,* where they freeze the current narrative, whisking us back in time to explore an earlier event, then returning to the present moment. Yet even in the hands of the most talented writer, the flashback risks confusing readers. Note when you read "A Wagner Matinée" how Cather moves you back and forth in time with great skill, but how you must nonetheless concentrate carefully on these temporal shifts in order to keep the story properly focused. The heart of narrative is time—the writer's vision of reality is inseparable from the way he or she views time and its impact upon characters, events, and ideas—and you want to pay particular attention to sequence as you read.

WRITING NARRATIVE

To encourage practice in writing narrative, this chapter asks you to concentrate on the story pretty much for its own sake. Later on, you will use narrative as a means for advancing ideas in expository frameworks, but here the story itself is the thing. Your objective is to transform events into clear, vivid prose.

PURPOSE AND AUDIENCE

At least once, we have all sat almost transfixed by boredom as we listened to a rambling, pointless story. As soon as someone has to ask about a piece of writing, "What is this all about?" you've exhausted whatever patience your readers may possess. Thus in choosing your narrative you must be very clear yourself on why you are telling about this particular event. Ask yourself this question as you are brainstorming: "What am I trying to demonstrate with this story?" Write down your answer so that your purpose does not escape you and so that you can see if it holds up. Stating your purpose too generally will not help much: "to answer," "to shock," "to stimulate"—these are not particularly useful statements of purpose because they provide little guidance as you develop the narrative framework. Suppose you saw close up a fire blazing through a section of your town and you wanted to write a narrative about it. Notice how each of the purposes below would stimulate a different story line about the same event.

Topic: The October 1984 fire on Walker Street
Purpose:

1. To show the bravery of an understaffed volunteer fire department

2. To follow the actions of a suspicious bystander

3. To show how people clutching their possessions poured from the houses and shops engulfed in flames

4. To trace the events from the first sparks at the corner grocery store to the conflagration that swept through the neighborhood

5. To show the orderly evacuation of 600 children from Birch Lane Elementary School

Not all of these are mutually exclusive. You could combine 1 and 3, for example, or 3 and 4. The point is that your narrative should focus on some purpose that is absolutely clear to you and that you finally make clear to your reader. You might want to state your purpose in a *thesis sentence,* sometimes called a *main idea sentence,* somewhere in your introduction. "Three racing figures in yellow slickers and black boots (this is all there is to the Lewis Valley Volunteer Fire Department) contained the worst fire in our town in twenty years, saving more than a dozen lives before Walker Street lay in a heap of ashes." Or you may choose not to state a thesis or main idea; instead, you may want readers to be able to discover your purpose on their own by concentrating thoughtfully on your story. In either case you must *be able* to state your purpose even if it is just as a check on the integrity of your narrative.

Very much related to the purpose of your narrative is the audience you want to read it. Many of the writing exercises in this chapter suggest an audience, and your instructor may define a readership too. But you should be prepared to identify your own audience. For whom are you writing this narrative? If you wrote about the fire in a report to the mayor of Lewis Valley, in a front page news story for the *Lewis Valley Gazette,* or in a letter to your sister back East, your narrative in each case would differ sharply from the other. Thinking about your audience as you shape your story will help you select appropriate details and eliminate extraneous ones. Also, a good sense of audience will help you develop an appropriate point of view. Would your readers expect you to be as objective as possible? Would they want you to place yourself in the scene as a participant-observer sharing subjective feelings and reactions? Either of these points of view would have a major impact upon the tone and structure of your narrative.

PROCESS

Your first step is to find a story worth telling. But it's not accurate to think only in terms of dazzling incidents in the lives of superstars. In simple, everyday activities the sensitive, observing eye can find terrific stories. Walter Prichard Eaton, as a freshman at Harvard more than thirty years ago, recalls how his instructors encouraged him to develop "the daily theme eye." He writes, "It became needful, then, to watch for and treasure incidents that were sharply dramatic or poignant, moods that were clear and definite, pictures that created a single clean impression. . . . By training the daily theme eye, we watched for and found in the surroundings of our life, as it passed, a heightened picturesqueness, a constant wonder, and added significance."

Like Eaton, we remind you to look around for the best stories and to make today the starting point for a fresh view of the events in your life. Also like Eaton, you might wish to keep a notebook of your impressions, jotting down incidents you see that can open a floodgate of narrative when you sit at your chair ready to develop a draft. Selecting a moment you've only recently experienced almost always assures a high level of intensity in your paper: You'll see the events clearly in your mind's eye because they are fresh and vivid to you, and you'll be able to convey that freshness and vividness to your readers. But memorable past events too can etch themselves on your consciousness, and you'll want to comb the past experiences of your life for narrative worth sharing with your readers.

As you think and write with your audience and purpose in mind, produce a thesis statement, whether or not you ultimately use it in your essay. Your thesis should state your topic for the narrative and should express your opinion or attitude toward it. Also, be aware of the nature and quantity of detail you need to include. Obviously you cannot cover every minute event in the story you are reporting; such thoroughness would simply overwhelm your readers. You have to select details carefully so that they reinforce your objective and so that they keep your readers interested. What you learned about concrete sensory detail in the last chapter will be useful here. Much of your narrative will draw upon images of sound, color, action, smell, and touch.

You must be particularly attentive to time and sequence when you write narrative. Events should follow each other logically, if not chronologically, and readers should never feel adrift in a sea of unconnected events. If you are bold enough to try flashback, be careful not to bounce back and forth from present to past; it will jar your readers. You might wish to make a time line or a simple list of chronological events so that you have at your fingertips the exact order of actions, no matter how you finally present them.

As you link events together, *transitions* will be very useful. Words like *then, later, now, before, after, soon, in a moment*—there are hundreds of others—can help you move from beginning to middle to end. But you must use these connectors judiciously and selectively. A clearly told story makes its own internal connections; events flow naturally from one to the other, and a mechanical use of transitions will obstruct that natural flow.

A last point to consider: dialogue. Almost all stories about people draw upon the natural conversations among characters in the narrative. Listen to the rhythms in everyday speech, and when your characters speak, make their words sound as if real people spoke them. Dialogue, like other details, requires selectivity. Let all spoken language in your story advance the special point you wish to make.

SUMMING UP: NARRATION

Reading Narrative

- Narrative simply means telling a story—whether fiction or fact, imagined or historical.

- Identify the pleasure-giving qualities of the narrative within the context of the writer's purpose—that is, what entertains you about the writer's story, and what is its point?

- Ask yourself about the narrative: "What is this writer telling me?" What sentence (or sentences) helps me state the writer's thesis, that is, the topic of the narrative and the writer's attitude toward that topic?

- Look for the *narrative summary* approach in which the writer covers large time segments and does not aim to include all details.

- Look for the *narrative moment* approach in which the writer aims to explore a limited time frame in all its detail.

- Be attentive to the sequence used by the writer, among them *chronology* (exact time order), *in medias res* (a story started in the midst of things), and *flashback* (movement back in time within a current narrative).

Writing Narrative

- Your narrative should transform events into clear, vivid prose that draws on concrete sensory language.

- Produce a thesis, so that you will be very clear about why you are relating the event; a carefully developed thesis sentence (or *main idea* sentence) will help you state your topic, your attitude toward it, and your purpose for writing.

- Consider your audience for the narrative, and use your sense of audience to help you shape your story, select appropriate details, and eliminate extraneous ones.

- To choose an appropriate narrative, look for stories in the events that surround you. A moment recently experienced often assures a high level of vividness and intensity in your writing; a memorable past event also can stimulate rich, detailed narrative if you concentrate on the event in all its details.

- Use appropriate transitions as needed. Many transitions, such as *now, later,* and *then,* help you move from beginning to middle to end of a narrative.

- Use dialogue—let the characters in your narrative speak—to advance the special point you wish to make in your story.

A Wagner Matinée

Willa Cather

Willa Cather (1876–1947) was amply familiar with the changing social values about which she wrote. Born in Virginia, she was soon on "foreign soil" when her family moved to the Nebraska immigrant town of Red Cloud. Here she gained an abiding respect for the land and the people who made something from it. Her best-known novel is *My Antonia* (1918), the story of the struggles of the prairie girl, Antonia Shimerda.

In "A Wagner Matinée," Willa Cather tells us the story of a life seemingly fulfilled, but inwardly longing. In this story of a woman who appears to have everything, Cather blends flashback with chronological narration to show us what was, what is, and what could have been.

I received one morning a letter, written in pale ink on glossy blue-lined notepaper, and bearing the postmark of a little Nebraska village. This communication, worn and rubbed, looking as if it had been carried for some days in a coat pocket that was none too clean, was from my Uncle Howard, and informed me that his wife had been left a small legacy by a bachelor relative, and that it would be necessary for her to go to Boston to attend the settling of the estate. He requested me to meet her at the station and render her whatever services might be necessary. On examining the date indicated as that of her arrival, I found it to be no later than tomorrow. He had characteristically delayed writing until, had I been away from home for a day, I must have missed my aunt altogether.

The name of my Aunt Georgiana opened before me a gulf of recollection so wide and deep that, as the letter dropped from my hand, I felt suddenly a stranger to all the present conditions of my existence, wholly ill at ease and out of place amid the familiar surroundings of my study. I became, in short, the gangling farm-boy my aunt had known, scourged with chilblains and bashfulness, my hands cracked and sore form the corn husking. I sat again before her parlor organ fumbling the scales with my stiff red fingers, while she, beside me, made canvas mittens for the huskers. The next morning, after preparing my landlady for a visitor, I set out for the station. When the train arrived I had some difficulty in finding my aunt. She was the last of the passengers to alight, and it was not until I got her into the carriage that she seemed really to recognize me. She had come all the way in a day coach; her linen duster had become black with soot and her black bonnet gray with dust during the journey. When we arrived at my boarding house the landlady put her to bed at once and I did not see her again until the next morning.

Whatever shock Mrs. Springer experienced at my aunt's appearance, she considerably concealed. As for myself, I saw my aunt's battered figure with that feeling of awe and respect with which we behold explorers who have left their ears and fingers north of Franz-Joseph Land or their health somewhere along the

Upper Congo. My Aunt Georgiana had been a music teacher at the Boston Conservatory, somewhere back in the later sixties. One summer, while visiting in the
little village among the Green Mountains where her ancestors had dwelt for generations, she had kindled the callow fancy of my uncle, Howard Carpenter, then
an idle, shiftless boy of twenty-one. When she returned to her duties in Boston,
Howard followed her, and the upshot of this infatuation was that she eloped with
him, eluding the reproaches of her family and the criticism of her friends by going
with him to the Nebraska frontier. Carpenter, who, of course, had no money, took
up a homestead in Red Willow County, fifty miles from the railroad. There they
had measured off their land themselves, driving across the prairie in a wagon, to
the wheel of which they had tied a red cotton handkerchief, and counting its revolutions. They built a dug-out in the red hillside, one of those cave dwellings
whose inmates so often reverted to primitive conditions. Their water they got
from the lagoons where the buffalo drank, and their slender stock of provisions
was always at the mercy of roving Indians. For thirty years my aunt had not been
farther than fifty miles from the homestead.

I owed to this woman most of the good that ever came my way in my boy- 4
hood, and had a reverential affection for her. During the years when I was riding
herd for my uncle, my aunt, after cooking the three meals—the first of which was
ready at six o'clock in the morning—and putting the six children to bed, would
often stand until midnight at her ironing-board with me at the kitchen table beside
her, hearing me recite Latin declensions and conjugations, gently shaking me
when my drowsy head sank down over a page of irregular verbs. It was to her, at
her ironing or mending, that I read my first Shakespeare, and her old textbook on
mythology was the first that ever came into my empty hands. She taught me my
scales and exercises on the little parlor organ which her husband had bought her
after fifteen years during which she had not so much as seen a musical instrument. She would sit beside me by the hour, darning and counting, while I struggled with the "Joyous Farmer." She seldom talked to me about music and I understood why. Once when I had been doggedly beating out some easy passages from
an old score of *Euryanthe* I had found among her music books, she came up to
me and, putting her hands over my eyes, gently drew my head back upon her
shoulder, saying tremulously, "Don't love it so well, Clark, or it may be taken
from you."

When my aunt appeared on the morning after her arrival in Boston, she was 5
still in a semi-somnambulant state. She seemed not to realize that she was in the
city where she had spent her youth, the place longed for hungrily half a lifetime.
She had been so wretchedly train-sick throughout the journey that she had no recollection of anything but her discomfort, and, to all intents and purposes, there
were but a few hours of nightmare between the farm in Red Willow County and
my study on Newbury Street. I had planned a little pleasure for her that afternoon,
to repay her for some of the glorious moments she had given me when we used
to milk together in the straw-thatched cowshed and she, because I was more than
usually tired, or because her husband had spoken sharply to me, would tell me of
the splendid performance of the *Huguenots* she had seen in Paris, in her youth.

At two o'clock the Symphony Orchestra was to give a Wagner program, 6
and I intended to take my aunt; though, as I conversed with her, I grew doubtful
about her enjoyment of it. I suggested our visiting the Conservatory and the Common before lunch, but she seemed altogether too timid to wish to venture out. She
questioned me absently about various changes in the city, but she was chiefly concerned that she had forgotten to leave instructions about feeding half-skimmed
milk to a certain weakling calf, "old Maggie's calf, you know, Clark," she
explained, evidently having forgotten how long I had been away. She was further
troubled because she had neglected to tell her daughter about the freshly opened
kit of mackerel in the cellar, which would spoil if it were not used directly.

I asked her whether she had ever heard any of the Wagnerian operas, and 7
found that she had not, though she was perfectly familiar with their respective situations, and had once possessed the piano score of *The Flying Dutchman.* I began
to think it would be best to get her back to Red Willow County without waking
her, and regretted having suggested the concert.

From the time we entered the concert hall, however, she was a trifle less 8
passive and inert, and for the first time seemed to perceive her surroundings. I had
felt some trepidation lest she might become aware of her queer country clothes,
or might experience some painful embarrassment at stepping suddenly into the
world to which she had been dead for a quarter of a century. But again, I found
how superficially I had judged her. She sat looking about her with eyes as impersonal, almost as stony, as those with which the granite Rameses in a museum
watches the froth and fret that ebbs and flows about his pedestal. I have seen this
same aloofness in old miners who drift into the Brown Hotel at Denver, their
pockets full of bullion, their linen soiled, their haggard faces unshaven; standing
in the thronged corridors as solitary as though they were still in a frozen camp on
the Yukon.

The matinée audience was made up chiefly of women. One lost the contour 9
of faces and figures, indeed any effect of line whatever, and there was only the
color of bodies past counting, the shimmer of fabrics soft and fine, silky and
sheer; red, mauve, pink, blue, lilac, purple, ecru, rose, yellow, cream, and white,
all the colors that an impressionist finds in a sunlight landscape, with here and
there the dead shadow of a frock coat. My Aunt Georgiana regarded them as
though they had been so many daubs of tube-paint on a palette.

When the musicians came out and took their places, she gave a little stir of 10
anticipation, and looked with quickening interest down over the rail at that invari-
able grouping, perhaps the first wholly familiar thing that had greeted her eye
since she had left old Maggie and her weakling calf. I could feel how all those
details sank into her soul, for I had not forgotten how they had sunk into mine
when I came fresh from plowing forever and forever between green aisles of corn,
where, as in a treadmill, one might walk from daybreak to dusk without perceiving a shadow of change. The clean profiles of the musicians, the gloss of their
linen, the dull black of their coats, the beloved shapes of the instruments, the
patches of yellow light on the smooth, varnished bellies of the 'cellos and the bass

viols in the rear, the restless, wind-tossed forest of fiddle necks and bows—I recalled how, in the first orchestra I ever heard, those long bow-strokes seemed to draw the heart out of me, as a conjurer's stick reels out yards of paper ribbon from a hat.

The first number was the *Tannhauser* overture. When the horns drew out the first strain of the "Pilgrims' Chorus," Aunt Georgiana clutched my coat sleeve. Then it was I first realized that for her this broke a silence of thirty years. With the battle between the two motives, with the frenzy of the Venusberg theme and its ripping of strings, there came to me an overwhelming sense of the waste and wear we are so powerless to combat; and I saw again the tall, naked house on the prairie, black and grim as a wooden fortress; the black pond where I had learned to swim, its margin pitted with sun-dried cattle tracks; the rain gullied clay banks about the naked house, the four dwarf ash seedlings where the dishcloths were always hung to dry before the kitchen door. The world there was the flat world of the ancients; to the east, a cornfield that stretched to daybreak; to the west, a corral that reached to sunset; between, the conquests of peace, dearer-bought than those of war.

The overture closed, my aunt released my coat sleeve, but she said nothing. She sat staring dully at the orchestra. What, I wondered, did she get from it? She had been a good pianist in her day, I knew, and her musical education had been broader than that of most music teachers of a quarter of a century ago. She had often told me of Mozart's operas and Meyerbeer's, and I could remember her sing, years ago, certain melodies of Verdi. When I had fallen ill with a fever in her house she used to sit by my cot in the evening—when the cool night wind blew in through the faded mosquito netting tacked over the window and I lay watching a certain bright star that burned red above the cornfield—and sing "Home to our mountain, O let us return!" in a way fit to break the heart of a Vermont boy near dead of homesickness already.

I watched her closely through the prelude to *Tristan and Isolde,* trying vainly to conjecture what that seething turmoil of strings and winds might mean to her, but she sat mutely staring at the violin bows that drove obliquely downward, like the pelting streaks of rain in a summer shower. Had this music any message for her? Had she enough left to at all comprehend this power which had kindled the world since she had left it? I was in a fever of curiosity, but Aunt Georgiana sat silent upon her peak in Darien. She preserved this utter immobility throughout the number from *The Flying Dutchman,* though her fingers worked mechanically upon her black dress, as if, of themselves, they were recalling the piano score they had once played. Poor hands! They had been stretched and twisted into mere tentacles to hold and lift and knead with; on one of them a thin worn band that had once been a wedding ring. As I pressed and gently quieted one of these groping hands, I remembered with quivering eyelids their services for me in other days.

Soon after the tenor began the "Prize Song," I heard a quick drawn breath, and turned to my aunt. Her eyes were closed, but the tears were glistening on her cheeks, and I think, in a moment more, they were in my eyes as well. It never really dies, then—the soul which can suffer so excruciatingly and so interminably; it withers to the outward eye only; like that strange moss which can lie on a dusty shelf half a century, and yet, if placed in water, grows green again. She wept so throughout the development and elaboration of the melody.

During the intermission before the second half, I questioned my aunt and found that the "Prize Song" was not new to her. Some years before there had drifted to the farm in Red Willow County a young German, a tramp cow-puncher, who had sung in the chorus at Bayreuth when he was a boy, along with the other peasant boys and girls. On a Sunday morning he used to sit on his gingham-sheeted bed in the hands' bedroom which opened off the kitchen, cleaning the leather of his boots and saddle, singing the "Prize Song," while my aunt went about her work in the kitchen. She had hovered over him until she had prevailed upon him to join the country church, though his sole fitness for this step, in so far as I could gather, lay in his boyish face, and his possession of this divine melody. Shortly afterward, he had gone to town on the Fourth of July, been drunk for several days, lost his money at a faro table, ridden a saddled Texas steer on a bet, and disappeared with a fractured collarbone. All this my aunt told me huskily, wanderingly, as though she were talking in the weak lapses of illness. 15

"Well, we have come to better things than the old *Trovatore,* at any rate, Aunt Georgie?" I queried, with a well-meant effort at jocularity. 16

Her lip quivered and she hastily put her handkerchief up to her mouth. From behind it she murmured, "And you have been hearing this ever since you left me, Clark?" Her question was the gentlest and saddest of reproaches. 17

The second half of the program consisted of four numbers from the *Ring,* and closed with Siegfried's funeral march. My aunt wept quietly but almost continuously, as a shallow vessel overflows in a rain-storm. From time to time her dim eyes looked up at the lights, burning softly under their dull glass globes. 18

The deluge of sound poured on and on; I never knew what she found in the shining current of it; I never knew how far it bore her, or past what happy islands. From the trembling of her face, I could well believe that before the last number she had been carried out where the myriad graves are, into the gray, nameless burying grounds of the sea, or into some world of death vaster yet, where, from the beginning of the world, hope has lain down with hope and dream with dream and, renouncing, slept. 19

The concert was over; the people filed out of the hall chattering and laughing, glad to relax and find the living level again, but my kinswoman made no effort to rise. The harpist slipped the green felt cover over his instrument; the flute-players shook the water from their mouth-pieces; the men of the orchestra went out one by one, leaving the stage to the chairs and music stands, empty as a winter cornfield. 20

I spoke to my aunt. She burst into tears and sobbed pleadingly. "I don't want to go, Clark, I don't want to go!" 21

I understood. For her, just outside the concert hall, lay the black pond with the cattle-tracked bluffs; the tall, unpainted house, with weather-curled boards, 22 naked as a tower; the crook-backed ash seedlings where the dishcloths hung to dry; the gaunt, moulting turkeys picking up refuse about the kitchen door.

Meaning and Idea

1. Where was Aunt Georgiana born? Where did she live at the time of the story? For how long? Why did she move there? What is her attitude toward that place? Does that attitude change at all during the course of the story?

2. Why did Aunt Georgiana seldom talk about music?

3. What kind of relationship do you think Aunt Georgiana had with her husband? How can you tell?

4. Who is Wagner? Which of his musical works are played at the matinée? How do Aunt Georgiana's reactions change with each piece? How does Cather use different pieces to further the narrative?

5. At one point, Clark states, "I began to think it would be best to get her back to Red Willow County without waking her. . . ." What is the meaning of this statement? Why does he think it?

6. Toward the end of the story, the narrator states, "It never really dies, then." What is the "it" in this statement?

Language, Form, Structure

1. To what does Clark compare his aunt's trip? To what does he compare her weeping? How else are comparisons used in this story?

2. What is the conflict in this story? How does Cather develop it? How is it resolved?

3. How is the technique of *flashback* used here? For what purpose? How does Cather maintain narrative unity with the flashbacks?

4. How is color imagery used in the narrative? Give specific examples.

5. Explain each of the following adjectival phrases from the story: reverential affection; gangling farmboy; semi-somnambulant state; wretchedly train-sick; quivering eyelids."

Ideas for Writing

1. Tell about an experience with a member of your family whom you hadn't seen in a number of years, but recently saw. How did you behave in this situation? How had you both changed? How had you stayed the same?

2. Narrate a particularly emotional experience of yours that centered on a musical performance, a play, a film, a poetry reading, or an art or museum exhibit.

3. Write a short commentary on your reaction to Cather's portrayal of the two characters. Do you feel you have sufficient knowledge of either or both of the characters to believe their actions and reactions? Do you have a clear visual impression of the characters? Why?

From *Narrative of the Life of Frederick Douglass, An American Slave*

Frederick Douglass

At the age of 21, Frederick Douglass escaped to the North. Born a slave in Maryland, he had to teach himself to read and write, and yet he went on to become a renowned editor, writer, orator, and statesman of his time. He served as a U.S. Marshall and as Consul General to Haiti, and he had been a counselor to four presidents before he died in 1895.

His autobiography was a firsthand account of slavery; no such narrative had existed before. Leaders of the abolitionist movement quickly saw the appeal of Douglass's involvement in the cause. He was wary at first, concerned that such a bold stance by a runaway slave was dangerous. But he overcame that fear and became one of the most important political voices of his time.

I was born in Tuckahoe, near Hillsborough, and about twelve miles   1
from Easton, in Talbot county, Maryland. I have no accurate knowledge of my age, never having seen any authentic record containing it. By far the larger part of the slaves know as little of their ages as horses know of theirs, and it is the wish of most masters within my knowledge to keep their slaves thus ignorant. I do not remember to have ever met a slave who could tell of his birthday. They seldom come nearer to it than planting-time, harvest-time, cherry-time, spring-time, or fall-time. A want of information concerning my own was a source of unhappiness to me even during childhood. The white children could tell their ages. I could not tell why I ought to be deprived of the same privilege. I was not allowed to make any inquiries of my master concerning it. He deemed all such inquiries on the part of a slave improper and impertinent, and evidence of a restless spirit. The nearest estimate I can give makes me now between twenty-seven and twenty-eight years of age. I come to this, from hearing my master say, some time during 1835, I was about seventeen years old.

My mother was named Harriet Bailey. She was the daughter of Isaac and   2
Betsey Bailey, both colored, and quite dark. My mother was of a darker complexion than either my grandmother or grandfather.

My father was a white man. He was admitted to be such by all I ever heard   3
speak of my parentage. The opinion was also whispered that my master was my father; but of the correctness of this opinion, I know nothing; the means of knowing was withheld from me. My mother and I were separated when I was but an infant—before I knew her as my mother. It is a common custom, in the part of Maryland from which I ran away, to part children from their mothers at a very early age. Frequently, before the child has reached its twelfth month, its mother

is taken from it, and hired out on some farm a considerable distance off, and the child is placed under the care of an old woman, too old for field labor. For what this separation is done, I do not know, unless it be to hinder the development of the child's affection toward its mother, and to blunt and destroy the natural affection of the mother for the child. This is the inevitable result.

I never saw my mother, to know her as such, more than four or five times in my life; and each of these times was very short in duration, and at night. She was hired by a Mr. Stewart, who lived about twelve miles from my home. She made her journeys to see me in the night, travelling the whole distance on foot, after the performance of her day's work. She was a field hand, and a whipping is the penalty of not being in the field at sunrise, unless a slave has special permission from his or her master to the contrary—a permission which they seldom get, and one that gives to him that gives it the proud name of being a kind master. I do not recollect of ever seeing my mother by the light of day. She was with me in the night. She would lie down with me, and get me to sleep, but long before I waked she was gone. Very little communication ever took place between us. Death soon ended what little we could have while she lived, and with it her hardships and suffering. She died when I was about seven years old, on one of my master's farms, near Lee's Mill. I was not allowed to be present during her illness, at her death, or burial. She was gone long before I knew any thing about it. Never having enjoyed, to any considerable extent, her soothing presence, her tender and watchful care, I received the tidings of her death with much the same emotions I should have probably felt at the death of a stranger.

Called thus suddenly away, she left me without the slightest intimation of who my father was. The whisper that my master was my father, may or may not be true; and, true or false, it is of but little consequence to my purpose whilst the fact remains, in all its glaring odiousness, that slaveholders have ordained, and by law established, that the children of slave women shall in all cases follow the condition of their mothers; and this is done too obviously to administer to their own lusts, and make a gratification of their wicked desires profitable as well as pleasurable; for by this cunning arrangement, the slaveholder, in cases not a few, sustains to his slaves the double relation of master and father.

I know of such cases; and it is worthy of remark that such slaves invariably suffer greater hardships, and have more to contend with, than others. They are, in the first place, a constant offense to their mistress. She is ever disposed to find fault with them; they can seldom do any thing to please her; she is never better pleased than when she sees them under the lash, especially when she suspects her husband of showing to his mulatto children favors which he withholds from his black slaves. The master is frequently compelled to sell this class of his slaves, out of deference to the feelings of his white wife; and cruel as the deed may strike any one to be, for a man to sell his own children to human flesh-mongers, it is often the dictate of humanity for him to do so; for, unless he does this, he must not only whip them himself; but must stand by and see one white son tie up his brother, of but few shades darker complexion than himself, and ply the gory lash to his naked back; and if he lisp one word of disapproval, it is set down to his parental partiality, and only makes a bad matter worse, both for himself and the slave whom he would protect and defend.

Every year brings with it multitudes of this class of slaves. It was doubtless in consequence of a knowledge of this fact, that one great statesman of the south predicted the downfall of slavery by the inevitable laws of population. Whether this prophecy is ever fulfilled or not, it is nevertheless plain that a very different-looking class of people are springing up at the south, and are now held in slavery, from those originally brought to this country from Africa; and if their increase will do no other good, it will do away the force of the argument, that God cursed Ham, and therefore American slavery is right. If the lineal descendants of Ham are alone to be scripturally enslaved, it is certain that slavery at the south must soon become unscriptural; for thousands are ushered into the world, annually, who, like myself, owe their existence to white fathers, and those fathers most frequently their own masters.

I have had two masters. My first master's name was Anthony. I do not remember his first name. He was generally called Captain Anthony—a title which, I presume, he acquired by sailing a craft on the Chesapeake Bay. He was not considered a rich slaveholder. He owned two or three farms, and about thirty slaves. His farms and slaves were under the care of an overseer. The overseer's name was Plummer. Mr. Plummer was a miserable drunkard, a profane swearer, and a savage monster. He always went armed with a cowskin and a heavy cudgel. I have known him to cut and slash the women's heads so horribly, that even master would be enraged at his cruelty, and would threaten to whip him if he did not mind himself. Master, however, was not a humane slaveholder. It required extraordinary barbarity on the part of an overseer to affect him. He was a cruel man, hardened by a long life of slaveholding. He would at times seem to take great pleasure in whipping a slave. I have often been awakened at the dawn of day by the most heart-rending shrieks of an own aunt of mine, whom he used to tie up to a joist, and whip upon her naked back till she was literally covered with blood. No words, no tears, no prayers, from his gory victim, seemed to move his iron heart from its bloody purpose. The louder she screamed, the harder he whipped; and where the blood ran fastest, there he whipped longest. He would whip her to make her scream, and whip her to make her hush; and not until overcome by fatigue, would he cease to swing the blood-clotted cowskin. I remember the first time I ever witnessed this horrible exhibition. I was quite a child, but I well remember it. I never shall forget it whilst I remember any thing. It was the first of a long series of such outrages, of which I was doomed to be a witness and a participant. It struck me with awful force. It was the blood-stained gate, the entrance to the hell of slavery, through which I was about to pass. It was a most terrible spectacle. I wish I could commit to paper the feelings with which I beheld it.

This occurrence took place very soon after I went to live with my old master, and under the following circumstances. Aunt Hester went out one night,— where or for what I do not know,—and happened to be absent when my master desired her presence. He had ordered her not to go out evenings, and warned her that she must never let him catch her in company with a young man, who was paying attention to her belonging to Colonel Lloyd. The young man's name was Ned Roberts, generally called Lloyd's Ned. Why master was so careful of her, may be safely left to conjecture. She was a woman of noble form, and of graceful proportions, having very few equals, and fewer superiors, in personal appearance, among the colored or white women of our neighborhood.

Aunt Hester had not only disobeyed his orders in going out, but had been so found in company with Lloyd's Ned; which circumstance, I found, from what he said while whipping her, was the chief offence. Had he been a man of pure morals himself, he might have been thought interested in protecting the innocence of my aunt; but those who knew him will not suspect him of any such virtue. Before he commenced whipping Aunt Hester, he took her into the kitchen, and stripped her from neck to waist, leaving her neck, shoulders, and back, entirely naked. He then told her to cross her hands, calling her at the same time a d——d b——h. After crossing her hands, he tied them with a strong rope, and led her to a stool under a large hook in the joist, put in for the purpose. He made her get upon the stool, and tied her hands to the hook. She now stood fair for his infernal purpose. Her arms were stretched up at their full length, so that she stood upon the ends of her toes. He then said to her, "Now, you d——d b——h, I'll learn you how to disobey my orders!" and after rolling up his sleeves, he commenced to lay on the heavy cowskin, and soon the warm, red blood (amid heart-rending shrieks from her, and horrid oaths from him) came dripping to the floor. I was so terrified and horror-stricken at the sight, that I hid myself in a closet, and dared not venture out till long after the bloody transaction was over. I expected it would be my turn next. It was all new to me. I had never seen any thing like it before. I had always lived with my grandmother on the outskirts of the plantation, where she was put to raise the children of the younger women. I had therefore been, until now, out of the way of the bloody scenes that often occurred on the plantation.

My master's family consisted of two sons, Andrew and Richard; one daughter, Lucretia, and her husband, Captain Thomas Auld. They lived in one house, upon the home plantation of Colonel Edward Lloyd. My master was Colonel Lloyd's clerk and superintendent. He was what might be called the overseer of the overseers. I spent two years of childhood on this plantation in my old master's family. It was here that I witnessed the bloody transaction recorded in the first chapter; and as I received my first impressions of slavery on this plantation, I will give some description of it, and of slavery as it there existed. The plantation is about twelve miles north of Easton, in Talbot county, and is situated on the border of Miles River. The principal products raised upon it were tobacco, corn, and wheat. These were raised in great abundance; so that, with the products of this and the other farms belonging to him, he was able to keep in almost constant employment a large sloop, in carrying them to market at Baltimore. This sloop was named Sally Lloyd, in honor of one of the colonel's daughters. My master's son-in-law, Captain Auld, was master of the vessel; she was otherwise manned by the colonel's own slaves. Their names were Peter, Isaac, Rich, and Jake. These were esteemed very highly by the other slaves, and looked upon as the privileged ones of the plantation; for it was no small affair, in the eyes of the slaves, to be allowed to see Baltimore.

Colonel Lloyd kept from three to four hundred slaves on his home planta- 12 tion, and owned a large number more on the neighboring farms belonging to him. The names of the farms nearest to the home plantation were Wye Town and New Design. "Wye Town" was under the overseership of a man named Noah Willis. New Design was under the overseership of a Mr. Townsend. The overseers of these, and all the rest of the farms, numbering over twenty, received advice and direction from the managers of the home plantation. This was the great business place. It was the seat of government for the whole twenty farms. All disputes among the overseers were settled here. If a slave was convicted of any high misdemeanor, became unmanageable, or evinced a determination to run away, he was brought immediately here, severely whipped, put on board the sloop, carried to Baltimore, and sold to Austin Woolfolk, or some other slave-trader, as a warning to the slaves remaining.

Here, too, the slaves of all the other farms received their monthly allowance 13 of food, and their yearly clothing. The men and women slaves received, as their monthly allowance of food, eight pounds of pork, or its equivalent in fish, and one bushel of corn meal. Their yearly clothing consisted of two coarse linen shirts, one pair of linen trousers, like the shirts, one jacket, one pair of trousers for winter, made of coarse negro cloth, one pair of stockings, and one pair of shoes; the whole of which could not have cost more than seven dollars. The allowance of the slave children was given to their mothers, or the old women having the care of them. The children unable to work in the field had neither shoes, stockings, jackets, nor trousers, given to them; their clothing consisted of two coarse linen shirts per year. When these failed them, they went naked until the next allowance-day. Children from seven to ten years old, of both sexes, almost naked, might be seen at all seasons of the year.

There were no beds given the slaves, unless one coarse blanket be consid- 14 ered such, and none but the men and women had these. This, however, is not considered a very great privation. They find less difficulty from the want of beds, than from the want of time to sleep; for when their day's work in the field is done, the most of them having their washing, mending, and cooking to do, and having few or none of the ordinary facilities for doing either of these, very many of their sleeping hours are consumed in preparing for the field the coming day; and when this is done, old and young, male and female, married and single, drop down side by side, on one common bed,—the cold, damp floor,—each covering himself or herself with their miserable blankets; and here they sleep till they are summoned to the field by the driver's horn. At the sound of this, all must rise, and be off to the field. There must be no halting; every one must be at his or her post; and woe betides them who hear not this morning summons to the field; for if they are not awakened by the sense of hearing, they are by the sense of feeling: no age nor sex finds any favor. Mr. Severe, the overseer, used to stand by the door of the quarter, armed with a large hickory stick and heavy cowskin, ready to whip any one who was so unfortunate as not to hear, or, from any other cause, was prevented from being ready to start for the field at the sound of the horn.

Mr. Severe was rightly named: he was a cruel man. I have seen him whip ₁₅ a woman, causing the blood to run half an hour at the time; and this, too, in the midst of her crying children, pleading for their mother's release. He seemed to take pleasure in manifesting his fiendish barbarity. Added to his cruelty, he was a profane swearer. It was enough to chill the blood and stiffen the hair of an ordinary man to hear him talk. Scarce a sentence escaped him but that was commenced or concluded by some horrid oath. The field was the place to witness his cruelty and profanity. His presence made it both the field of blood and of blasphemy. From the rising till the going down of the sun, he was cursing, raving, cutting, and slashing among the slaves of the field, in the most frightful manner. His career was short. He died very soon after I went to Colonel Lloyd's; and he died as he lived, uttering, with his dying groans, bitter curses and horrid oaths. His death was regarded by the slaves as the result of a merciful providence.

Mr. Severe's place was filled by a Mr. Hopkins. He was a very different ₁₆ man. He was less cruel, less profane, and made less noise, than Mr. Severe. His course was characterized by no extraordinary demonstrations of cruelty. He whipped, but seemed to take no pleasure in it. He was called by the slaves a good overseer.

The home plantation of Colonel Lloyd wore the appearance of a country ₁₇ village. All the mechanical operations for all the farms were performed here. The shoemaking and mending, the blacksmithing, cartwrighting, coopering, weaving, and grain-grinding, were all performed by the slaves on the home plantation. The whole place wore a business-like aspect very unlike the neighboring farms. The number of houses, too, conspired to give it advantage over the neighboring farms. It was called by the slaves the *Great House Farm*. Few privileges were esteemed higher, by the slaves of the out-farms, than that of being selected to do errands at the Great House Farm. It was associated in their minds with greatness. A representative could not be prouder of his election to a seat in the American Congress, than a slave on one of the out-farms would be of his election to do errands at the Great House Farm. They regarded it as evidence of great confidence reposed in them by their overseers; and it was on this account, as well as a constant desire to be out of the field from under the driver's lash, that they esteemed it a high privilege, one worth careful living for. He was called the smartest and most trusty fellow, who had this honor conferred upon him the most frequently. The competitors for this office sought as diligently to please their overseers, as the office-seekers in the political parties seek to please and deceive the people. The same traits of character might be seen in Colonel Lloyd's slaves, as are seen in the slaves of the political parties.

The slaves selected to go to the Great House Farm, for the monthly ₁₈ allowance for themselves and their fellow-slaves, were peculiarly enthusiastic. While on their way, they would make the dense old woods, for miles around, reverberate with their wild songs, revealing at once the highest joy and the deepest sadness. They would compose and sing as they went along, consulting neither time nor tune. The thought that came up, came out—if not in the word, in the sound;— and as frequently in the one as in the other. They would sometimes sing the most pathetic sentiment in the most rapturous tone, and the most rapturous sentiment in the most pathetic tone. Into all of their songs they would manage to weave something of the Great House Farm. Especially would they do this, when leaving home. They would then sing most exultingly the following words:—

I am going away to the Great House Farm!

O, Yea! O, Yea! O!

This they would sing, as a chorus, to words which to many would seem unmeaning jargon, but which, nevertheless, were full of meaning to themselves. I have sometimes thought that the mere hearing of those songs would do more to impress some minds with the horrible character of slavery, than the reading of whole volumes of philosophy on the subject could do.

I did not, when a slave, understand the deep meaning of those rude and 19 apparently incoherent songs. I was myself within the circle; so that I neither saw nor heard as those without might see and hear. They told a tale of woe which was then altogether beyond my feeble comprehension; they were tones loud, long, and deep; they breathed the prayer and complaint of souls boiling over with the bitterest anguish. Every tone was a testimony against slavery, and a prayer to God for deliverance from chains. The hearing of those wild notes always depressed my spirit, and filled me with ineffable sadness. I have frequently found myself in tears while hearing them. The mere recurrence to those songs, even now, afflicts me; and while I am writing these lines, an expression of feeling has already found its way down my cheek. To those songs I trace my first glimmering conception of the dehumanizing character of slavery. I can never get rid of that conception. Those songs still follow me, to deepen my hatred of slavery, and quicken my sympathies for my brethren in bonds. If any one wishes to be impressed with the soul-killing effects of slavery, let him go to Colonel Lloyd's plantation, and, on allowance-day, place himself in the deep pine woods, and there let him, in silence, analyze the sounds that shall pass through the chambers of his soul,—and if he is not thus impressed, it will only be because "there is no flesh in his obdurate heart."

I have often been utterly astonished, since I came to the north, to find per- 20 sons who could speak of the singing, among slaves, as evidence of their contentment and happiness. It is impossible to conceive of a greater mistake. Slaves sing most when they are most unhappy. The songs of the slave represent the sorrows of his heart; and he is relieved by them, only as an aching heart is relieved by its tears. At least, such is my experience. I have often sung to drown my sorrow, but seldom to express my happiness. Crying for joy, and singing for joy, were alike uncommon to me while in the jaws of slavery. The singing of a man cast away upon a desolate island might be as appropriately considered as evidence of contentment and happiness, as the singing of a slave; the songs of the one and of the other are prompted by the same emotion.

Meaning and Idea

1. What is "the inevitable result" of separating a slave mother from her child? What is Douglass referring to when he notes the "glaring odiousness" of how "the children of slave women must follow the condition of their mothers"? Why would these types of measures be a part of slavery?

2. Douglass says his Aunt Hester was consistently whipped by their master and that his own first memory of a whipping was one of these experiences. Why did Master Anthony pick on her? What made the whipping Douglass describes particularly harsh?

3. What was the source for the singing that the slaves often did? Explain the honor and enthusiasm the slaves associated with traveling to Baltimore or the Great House Farm. Why were the singing and enthusiasm especially intense on "allowance" day?

Language, Form, Structure

1. The excerpt from Douglass's autobiography contains detailed descriptions of slave life: clothes, food, bedding, the driver's horn, what the plantation was like. What is the effect of this detail? How do the details help flesh out the narrative?

2. Think about what Douglass knows about his own parentage and what he knows about the status and population of mulatto slaves. At times he seems to speak of these and other matters in an impersonal way, and at times he speaks quite personally. What is the effect of this technique? How does he achieve it?

3. Define the following words and use each in a sentence: impertinent; inevitable; duration; intimation; odiousness; ordained; obdurate.

Ideas for Writing

1. Examine a series of related events that you have experienced. First list the events in the order in which they occurred. Now think about why they happened and what they meant to you when they happened. What do they mean to you now? Write an essay that recounts these experiences and feelings. Be sure to create an appropriate introduction and conclusion.

2. Write a narrative essay about your experience with a highly regimented system you have been a part of. For instance, you could write about the necessities of being a college student (enrolling, registering, attending, studying, living conditions, costs, commuting, getting grades). Be sure your

essay is about the *system* and your experiences while a part of it, not *just* your experiences.

3. The excerpt from Douglass's autobiography shifts back and forth between the detailed recounting of events or circumstances and more stylistic, philosophic examinations of what these things meant. Write an essay that examines why Douglass does this and what the effect is.

There's Been a Death in the Opposite House

Emily Dickinson

"The recluse of Amherst," Emily Dickinson (1830–1886) became one of the world's most renowned poets without ever leaving her home in Amherst, Massachusetts. Critics argue still whether Dickinson, most of whose poems were not published until after her death, wrote from a life fully lived or from one almost fully repressed. She wrote eloquently of love and devotion, yet she did not sustain an intimate romantic relationship nor did she every marry. In all, Dickinson's collected poems leave us a rich expression of universal values and meanings.

Dickinson's "There's Been a Death in the Opposite House" tells readers both of the closeness of death and of the transparency of events in a small, country town. Though a simple narrative, the poem leaves one with a deep feeling and respect for the event.

*T*here's been a death in the opposite house
As lately as today.
I know it by the numb look
Such houses have alway.

The neighbors rustle in and out,   5
The doctor drives away.
A window opens like a pod,
Abrupt, mechanically;
Somebody flings a mattress out,
The children hurry by;   10
They wonder if it died on that,
I used to when a boy.

The minister goes stiffly in
As if the house were his,
And he owned all the mourners now,   15
And little boys besides;

And then the milliner, and the man
Of the appalling trade,
To take the measure of the house.
There'll be that dark parade   20

Of tassels and of coaches soon;
It's easy as a sign,
The intuition of the news
In just a country town.

Meaning and Idea

1. How does the speaker know that a death has occurred? What images support this knowledge? How does the speaker feel about death?

2. What is a *milliner?* Why is the milliner important to the scene? Who is "the man/Of the appalling trade"?

3. According to the poem, why is it so easy to tell that a death has occurred in a country town?

Language, Form, Structure

1. Who is the audience for this poem? How do you know? The narrative structure here is extraordinarily simple. How does Dickinson take the reader from event to event? What transitions help the narrative movement?

2. Which verbs best convey simple crisp actions? Which adjectives best reflect the issue of death?

3. Contrast the meaning of the word *house* in lines 1 and 19.

4. Which lines in the poem come closest to stating Dickinson's main point?

5. Look up the following words in a dictionary: numb; rustle; flings; measure (noun); intuition.

Ideas for Writing

1. Write a page or two in which you narrate an early experience with death. Try to re-create the scene as clearly as possible.

2. Tell a story of an incident that you think is either uniquely rural or uniquely urban. In other words, tell of an incident that probably would not occur in the same way in the opposite environment.

3. The speaker of this poem is a man (refer to line 12), yet the poet is a woman. Do you feel Dickinson adequately portrays a man's point of view? Would there by any difference between a man's and a woman's point of view about this scene? In general, do you think writers can easily write through the eyes of a character of the opposite sex? Draw on examples from your reading.

Native Son

Richard Wright

Richard Wright (1908–1960) was one of America's foremost black writers, alternately praised and scorned for his dramatic, often angry accounts of black life and radical politics. Born on a cotton plantation near Natchez, Mississippi, Wright grew up impoverished and orphaned. His decision to join the American Communist Party in Chicago during the Great Depression significantly influenced his outlook in such books as *Native Son* (1940), which he wrote under the auspices of a Guggenheim fellowship. He also wrote the autobiographical *Black Boy* (1945) and a chronicle of his eventual dissatisfaction with communism contributed to a collection of ex-communist writing, *The God That Failed* (1950).

When *Native Son* first appeared in 1940, it shook the literary world with its brutally realistic account of anger, alienation, and violence within the black community. The novel's dramatic climax, a murder, is foreshadowed in this selection when the narrator writes of the protagonist, Bigger: "He knew that the moment he allowed what his life meant to enter fully into his consciousness, he would either kill himself or someone else."

CHAPTER 1

*B*rrrrriiiiiiiiiiiiiiiiiiiiiiiiiing!   1

An alarm clock clanged in the dark and silent room. A bed spring creaked.   2
A woman's voice sang out impatiently:

"Bigger, shut that thing off!"   3

A surly grunt sounded above the tinny ring of metal. Naked feet swished   4
dryly across the planks in the wooden floor and the clang ceased abruptly.

"Turn on the light, Bigger."   5

"Awright," came a sleepy mumble.   6

Light flooded the room and revealed a black boy standing in a narrow space   7
between two iron beds, rubbing his eyes with the backs of his hands. From a bed
to his right, the woman spoke again:

"Buddy, get up from there! I got a big washing on my hands today, and I   8
want you all out of here."

Another black boy rolled from bed and stood up. The woman also rose and   9
stood in her nightgown.

"Turn your heads so I can dress," she said.   10

The two boys averted their eyes and gazed into a far corner of the room.   11

The woman rushed out of her nightgown and put on a pair of step-ins. She   12
turned to the bed from which she had risen and called:

"Vera! Get up from there!"   13

"What time is it, Ma?" asked a muffled, adolescent voice from beneath a quilt.   14

"Get up from there, I say!"   15

"O.K., Ma." 16

A brown-skinned girl in a cotton gown got up and stretched her arms above 17 her head and yawned. Sleepily, she sat on a chair and fumbled with her stockings. The two boys kept their faces averted while their mother and sister put on enough clothes to keep them from feeling ashamed; and the mother and sister did the same while the boys dressed. Abruptly, they all paused, holding their clothes in their hands, their attention caught by a light tapping in the thinly plastered walls of the room. They forgot their conspiracy against shame and their eyes strayed apprehensively over the floor.

"There he is again, Bigger!" the woman screamed, and the tiny one-room 18 apartment galvanized into violent action. A chair toppled as the woman, half-dressed and in her stocking feet, scrambled breathlessly upon the bed. Her two sons, barefoot, stood tense and motionless, their eyes searching anxiously under the bed and chairs. The girl ran into a corner, half-stooped and gathered the hem of her slip into both of her hands and held it tightly over her knees.

"Oh! Oh!" she wailed. 19

"There he goes!" 20

The woman pointed a shaking finger. Her eyes were round with fascinated 21 horror.

"Where?" 22

"I don't see 'im!" 23

"Bigger, he's behind the trunk!" the girl whimpered. 24

"Vera!" the woman screamed. "Get up here on the bed! Don't let that thing 25 *bite* you!"

Frantically, Vera climbed upon the bed and the woman caught hold of her. 26 With their arms entwined about each other, the black mother and the brown daughter gazed open-mouthed at the trunk in the corner.

Bigger looked round the room wildly, then darted to a curtain and swept it 27 aside and grabbed two heavy iron skillets from a wall above a gas stove. He whirled and called softly to his brother, his eyes glued to the trunk.

"Buddy !" 28

"Yeah?" 29

"Here; take this skillet." 30

"O.K." 31

"Now, get over by the door!" 32

"O.K." 33

Buddy crouched by the door and held the iron skillet by its handle, his arm 34 flexed and poised. Save for the quick, deep breathing of the four people, the room was quiet. Bigger crept on tiptoe toward the trunk with the skillet clutched stiffly in his hand, his eyes dancing and watching every inch of the wooden floor in front of him. He paused and, without moving an eye or muscle, called:

"Buddy !" 35

"Hunh?" 36

"Put that box in front of the hole so he can't get out!" 37

"O.K." 38

Buddy ran to a wooden box and shoved it quickly in front of a gaping hole   39
in the molding and then backed again to the door, holding the skillet ready. Bigger eased to the trunk and peered behind it cautiously. He saw nothing. Carefully,
he stuck out his bare foot and pushed the trunk a few inches.

"There he is!" the mother screamed again.   40

A huge black rat squealed and leaped at Bigger's trouser-leg and snagged it   41
in his teeth, hanging on. "Goddamn!" Bigger whispered fiercely, whirling and
kicking out his leg with all the strength of his body. The force of his movement
shook the rat loose and it sailed through the air and struck a wall. Instantly, it
rolled over and leaped again. Bigger dodged and the rat landed against a table leg.
With clenched teeth, Bigger held the skillet; he was afraid to hurl it, fearing that
he might miss. The rat squeaked and turned and ran in a narrow circle, looking
for a place to hide; it leaped again past Bigger and scurried on dry rasping feet to
one side of the box and then to the other, searching for the hole. Then it turned
and reared upon its hind legs.

"Hit 'im, Bigger!" Buddy shouted.   42

"Kill 'im!" the woman screamed.   43

The rat's belly pulsed with fear. Bigger advanced a step and the rat emitted   44
a long thin song of defiance, its black beady eyes glittering, its tiny forefeet paw-
ing the air restlessly. Bigger swung the skillet; it skidded over the floor, missing
the rat, and clattered to a stop against a wall.

"Goddamn !"   45

The rat leaped. Bigger sprang to one side. The rat stopped under a chair and   46
let out a furious screak. Bigger moved slowly backward toward the door.

"Gimme that skillet, Buddy," he asked quietly, not taking his eyes from   47
the rat.

Buddy extended his hand. Bigger caught the skillet and lifted it high in the   48
air. The rat scuttled across the floor and stopped again at the box and searched
quickly for the hole; then it reared once more and bared long yellow fangs, pip-
ing shrilly, belly quivering.

Bigger aimed and let the skillet fly with a heavy grunt. There was a shat-   49
tering of wood as the box caved in. The woman screamed and hid her face in her
hands. Bigger tiptoed forward and peered.

"I got 'im," he muttered, his clenched teeth bared in a smile. "By God, I   50
got 'im."

He kicked the splintered box out of the way and the flat black body of the   51
rat lay exposed, its two long yellow tusks showing distinctly. Bigger took a shoe
and pounded the rat's head, crushing it, cursing hysterically:

"You sonofabitch!"   52

The woman on the bed sank to her knees and buried her face in the quilts   53
and sobbed:

"Lord, Lord, have mercy. . . ."   54

"Aw, Mama," Vera whimpered, bending to her. "Don't cry. It's dead now."   55

The two brothers stood over the dead rat and spoke in tones of awed   56
admiration.

"Gee, but he's a big bastard."   57

"That sonofabitch could cut your throat."   58

"He's over a foot long."   59

"How in hell do they get so big?"   60

"Eating garbage and anything else they can get."   61

"Look, Bigger, there's a three-inch rip in your pant-leg."   62

"Yeah; he was after me, all right."   63

"Please, Bigger, take 'im out," Vera begged.   64

"Aw, don't be so scary," Buddy said.   65

The woman on the bed continued to sob. Bigger took a piece of newspaper   66
and gingerly lifted the rat by its tail and held it out at arm's length.

"Bigger, take 'im out," Vera begged again.   67

Bigger laughed and approached the bed with the dangling rat, swinging it   68
to and fro like a pendulum, enjoying his sister's fear.

"Bigger!" Vera gasped convulsively; she screamed and swayed and closed   69
her eyes and fell headlong across her mother and rolled limply from the bed to
the floor.

"Bigger, for God's sake!" the mother sobbed, rising and bending over Vera.   70
"Don't do that! Throw that rat out!"

He laid the rat down and started to dress.   71

"Bigger, help me lift Vera to the bed," the mother said.   72

He paused and turned round.   73

"What's the matter?" he asked, feigning ignorance.   74

"Do what I asked you, will you, boy?"   75

He went to the bed and helped his mother lift Vera. Vera's eyes were closed.   76
He turned away and finished dressing. He wrapped the rat in a newspaper and
went out of the door and down the stairs and put it into a garbage can at the corner of an alley. When he returned to the room his mother was still bent over Vera,
placing a wet towel upon her head. She straightened and faced him, her cheeks
and eyes wet with tears and her lips tight with anger.

"Boy, sometimes I wonder what makes you act like you do."   77

"What I do now?" he demanded belligerently.   78

"Sometimes you act the biggest fool I ever saw."   79

"What you talking about?"   80

"You scared your sister with that rat and she *fainted*! Ain't you got no sense   81
at all?"

"Aw, I didn't know she was that scary."   82

"Buddy!" the mother called.   83

"Yessum."   84

"Take a newspaper and spread it over that spot."   85

"Yessum ."   86

Buddy opened out a newspaper and covered the smear of blood on the floor   87
where the rat had been crushed. Bigger went to the window and stood looking out
abstractedly into the street. His mother glared at his back.

"Bigger, sometimes I wonder why I birthed you," she said bitterly.   88

Bigger looked at her and turned away.   89

"Maybe you oughtn't've. Maybe you ought to left me where I was."   90

"You shut your sassy mouth!"   91

"Aw, for chrissakes!" Bigger said, lighting a cigarette.   92

"Buddy, pick up them skillets and put 'em in the sink," the mother said. 93

"Yessum."   94

Bigger walked across the floor and sat on the bed. His mother's eyes fol- 95
lowed him.

"We wouldn't have to live in this garbage dump if you had any manhood in   96
you," she said.

"Aw, don't start that again."   97

"How you feel, Vera?" the mother asked.   98

Vera raised her head and looked about the room as though expecting to see 99
another rat.

"Oh, Mama!"   100

"You poor thing!"   101

"I couldn't help it. Bigger scared me."   102

"Did you hurt yourself?"   103

"I bumped my head."   104

"Here; take it easy. You'll be all right."   105

"How come Bigger acts that way?" Vera asked, crying again.   106

"He's just crazy," the mother said. "Just plain dumb black crazy."   107

"I'll be late for my sewing class at the Y.W.C.A.," Vera said.   108

"Here; stretch out on the bed. You'll feel better in a little while," the mother 109
said.

She left Vera on the bed and turned a pair of cold eyes upon Bigger.   110

"Suppose you wake up some morning and find your sister dead? What   111
would you think then?" she asked. "Suppose those rats cut our veins at night
when we sleep? Naw! Nothing like that ever bothers you! All you care about is
your own pleasure! Even when the relief offers you a job you won't take it till
they threaten to cut off your food and starve you! Bigger, honest, you the most
no-countest man I ever seen in all my life!"

"You done told me that a thousand times," he said, not looking round.   112

"Well, I'm telling you agin! And mark my word, some of these days you   113
going to set down and cry. Some of these days you going to wish you had made
something out of yourself, instead of just a tramp. But it'll be too late then."

"Stop prophesying about me," he said.   114

"I prophesy much as I please! And if you don't like it, you can get out. We 115
can get along without you. We can live in one room just like we living now, even
with you gone," she said.

"Aw, for chrissakes!" he said, his voice filled with nervous irritation. 116

"You'll regret how you living some day," she went on. "If you don't stop 117
running with that gang of yours and do right you'll end up where you never
thought you would. You think I don't know what you boys is doing, but I do. And

the gallows is at the end of the road you traveling, boy. Just remember that." She turned and looked at Buddy. "Throw that box outside, Buddy."

"Yessum."   118

There was silence. Buddy took the box out. The mother went behind the   119
curtain to the gas stove. Vera sat up in bed and swung her feet to the floor.

"Lay back down, Vera," the mother said.   120

"I feel all right now, Ma. I got to go to my sewing class."   121

"Well, if you feel like it, set the table," the mother said, going behind the   122
curtain again. "Lord, I get so tired of this I don't know what to do," her voice floated plaintively from behind the curtain. "All I ever do is try to make a home for you children and you don't care."

"Aw, Ma," Vera protested. "Don't say that."   123

"Vera, sometimes I just want to lay down and quit."   124

"Ma, please don't say that."   125

"I can't last many more years, living like this."   126

"I'll be old enough to work soon, Ma."   127

"I reckon I'll be dead then. I reckon God'll call me home."   128

Vera went behind the curtain, and Bigger heard her trying to comfort his   129
mother. He shut their voices out of his mind. He hated his family because he knew that they were suffering and that he was powerless to help them. He knew that the moment he allowed himself to feel to its fullness how they lived, the shame and misery of their lives, he would be swept out of himself with fear and despair. So he held toward them an attitude of iron reserve; he lived with them, but behind a wall, a curtain. And toward himself he was even more exacting. He knew that the moment he allowed what his life meant to enter fully into his consciousness, he would either kill himself or someone else. So he denied himself and acted tough.

He got up and crushed his cigarette upon the window sill. Vera came into   130
the room and placed knives and forks upon the table.

"Get ready to eat, you-all," the mother called.   131

He sat at the table. The odor of frying bacon and boiling coffee drifted to   132
him from behind the curtain. His mother's voice floated to him in song.

Life is like a mountain railroad
  With an engineer that's brave
We must make the run successful
  From the cradle to the grave. . . .

The song irked him, and he was glad when she stopped and came into the   133
room with a pot of coffee and a plate of crinkled bacon. Vera brought the bread in and they sat down. His mother closed her eyes and lowered her head and mumbled,

"Lord, we thank Thee for the food You done placed before us for the nour-   134
ishment of our bodies. Amen." She lifted her eyes and without changing her tone of voice, said, "You going to have to learn to get up earlier than this, Bigger, to hold a job."

He did not answer or look up.   135

"You want me to pour you some coffee?" Vera asked.   136

"Yeah."   137

"You going to take the job, ain't you, Bigger?" his mother asked.   138

He laid down his fork and stared at her.   139

"I told you last night I was going to take it. How many times you want to   140
ask me?"

"Well, don't bite her head off," Vera said. "She only asked you a question."   141

"Pass the bread and stop being smart."   142

"You know you have to see Mr. Dalton at five-thirty," his mother said.   143

"You done said that ten times."   144

"I don't want you to forget, son."   145

"And you know how you can forget," Vera said.   146

"Aw, lay off Bigger," Buddy said. "He told you he was going to take   147
the job."

"Don't tell 'em nothing," Bigger said.   148

"You shut your mouth, Buddy, or get up from this table," the mother said.   149
"I'm not going to take any stinking sass from you. One fool in the family's enough."

"Lay off, Ma," Buddy said.   150

"Bigger's setting here like he ain't glad to get a job," she said.   151

"What you want me to do? Shout?" Bigger asked.   152

"Oh, Bigger!" his sister said.   153

"I wish you'd keep your big mouth out of this!" he told his sister.   154

"If you get that job," his mother said in a low, kind tone of voice, busy slic-   155
ing a loaf of bread, "I can fix up a nice place for you children. You could be comfortable and not have to live like pigs."

"Bigger ain't decent enough to think of nothing like that," Vera said.   156

"God, I wish you-all would let me eat," Bigger said.   157

His mother talked on as though she had not heard him and he stopped   158
listening.

"Ma's talking to you, Bigger," Vera said.   159

"So what?"   160

"Don't be that way, Bigger!"   161

He laid down his fork and his strong black fingers gripped the edge of the   162
table; there was silence save for the tinkling of his brother's fork against a plate.
He kept staring at his sister till her eyes fell.

"I wish you'd let me eat," he said again.   163

As he ate he felt that they were thinking of the job he was to get that evening   164
and it made him angry; he felt that they had tricked him into a cheap surrender.

"I need some carfare," he said.

"Here's all I got," his mother said, pushing a quarter to the side of his plate.   165

He put the quarter in his pocket and drained his cup of coffee in one long   166
swallow. He got his coat and cap and went to the door.   167

"You know, Bigger," his mother said, "if you don't take that job the relief'll
cut us off. We won't have any food."   168

"I told you I'd take it!" he shouted and slammed the door.   169

Meaning and Idea

1. Why does the family practice a "conspiracy against shame" as they dress each morning? What is their morning routine? What does the scene tell us about their living conditions?

2. What accounts for Bigger's "sassiness"? Why has he "denied himself and acted tough"? From whom do we get that information, the narrator or a character? What is the difference in the information gathered from each? Quote exact lines in your answer.

3. What is the main reason the mother wants Bigger to get a job? Do you think that this is her only reason? Why? What other reasons might she have?

Language, Form, Structure

1. How is *sound imagery* used in the opening of this selection? Why is it an effective beginning? List specific sound words drawn from the first few paragraphs.

2. This selection is a good example of the use of *narrative moment.* Trace Wright's development of this narrative moment. How is it realistic or not? Complete or not? How does Wright use transitions to keep the story line flowing smoothly and swiftly?

3. The rat is not actually named as such until well into the narration of the incident. How do we know that it actually *is* a rat from the very beginning? What are the clues, both obvious and subtle, to its identity?

4. How does the use of *dialogue* affect the pacing and feeling of the story? *Dialect* is a special regional or cultural use of a language. How does Wright use dialect in this selection? Why does he do so?

5. Use each of the following words correctly in a sentence of your own: surly; averted; entwined; poised; rasping; pendulum; irked.

Ideas for Writing

1. Following the pattern of a narrative moment, write about a single dangerous incident that you, or someone you know, recently experienced.

2. Narrate an angry interaction among three people—either people you know or characters you create. Try to write the entire narration using dialogue almost exclusively.

3. In this selection, Wright uses a few distinct voices—those of the four characters as well as that of the narrator. How is the narrator's voice significantly different from those of the characters? Do you think that this difference is appropriate or not? How does it affect your reading of the selection?

Incident

Countee Cullen

Countee Cullen (1903–1946) was born in New York City. He is considered, along with W. E. B. Du Bois, Langston Hughes, Claude McKay, and Jean Toomer, among the leading writers of the Harlem Renaissance of the 1920s. The Renaissance was a literary and arts movement that chronicled black life and celebrated black pride. Cullen's contribution was his poetry, in which he intertwined traditional forms with black themes and syntax. Among his best-known volumes of poetry are *Color* (1925) and *Copper Sun* (1927).

In this rhymed, simple three-stanza poem, Countee Cullen tells of a single event, which was in fact indicative of a cultural attitude that fostered millions of similar "incidents." As you read, think of how the idea of the poem reflects common moments in our everyday life.

*O*nce *riding in old Baltimore*
    Heart-filled, head-filled with glee,
I saw a Baltimorean
    Keep looking straight at me.

Now I was eight and very small,   5
    And he was no whit bigger,
And so I smiled, but he poked out
    His tongue, and called me, "Nigger."

I saw the whole of Baltimore
    From May until December;   10
Of all the things that happened there
    That's all that I remember.

Meaning and Idea

1. The "incident" here is very straightforward. Tell what actually happened in a single sentence.

2. About how old was the person who called the narrator "Nigger"? How do you know?

3. What is the effect of the incident on the narrator? What is the immediate change in his attitude? He says he was in Baltimore "From May until December," but how can you tell that the effects were longer lasting than that?

Language, Form, Structure

1. How does stanza three differ from the first two stanzas? From what does it derive its effectiveness?

2. Comment on the meaning and tone of the phrase "no whit bigger." What does it tell us about the time frame of this incident?

3. What is the relation between the poem's title and its story? What transitions does the poet use to make the narrative structure clear?

Ideas for Writing

1. Tell of a seemingly simple incident or comment that deeply affected you. What were the circumstances? What were the results?

2. Tell about a time when you intentionally or inadvertently insulted someone. Why did you insult the person? How did you feel, and what did you do afterward?

3. Write a brief paper to explain whether or not you are satisfied with the format of a poem for telling this story. Do you think it would have been more effective written as a prose narrative? Why or why not?

The Witch's Husband

Judith Ortiz Cofer

Judith Ortiz Cofer was born in Puerto Rico in 1952, and she and her family emigrated to New York in 1956. She received a B.A. degree from Augusta College in 1974 and went on to earn an M.A. degree from Florida Atlantic in 1977. She has taught English and Spanish in many parts of Florida and Georgia. Cofer has written several books of poetry and two novels.

The following selection is from *Silent Dancing,* a memoir about her family and their lives in both Puerto Rico and the United States. In this selection she tells how her grandmother's narrative skills kept Cofer from accomplishing a goal.

*M*y grandfather has misplaced his words again. He is trying to find   1
my name in the kaleidoscope of images that his mind has become. His face brightens like a child's who has just remembered his lesson. He points to me and says my mother's name. I smile back and kiss him on the cheek. It doesn't matter what names he remembers anymore. Every day he is more confused, his memory slipping back a little further in time. Today he has no grandchildren yet. Tomorrow he will be a young man courting my grandmother again, quoting bits of poetry to her. In months to come, he will begin calling her Mamá.

I have traveled to Puerto Rico at my mother's request to help her deal with   2
the old people. My grandfather is physically healthy but his dementia is severe. My grandmother's heart is making odd sounds again in her chest. Yet she insists on taking care of the old man at home herself. She will not give up her house, though she has been warned that her heart might fail in her sleep without proper monitoring, that is, in a nursing home or a relative's care. Her response is typical of her famous obstinacy: "*Bueno,*" she says, "I will die in my own bed."

I am now at her house, waiting for my opportunity to talk "sense" into her.   3
As a college teacher in the United States I am supposed to represent the voice of logic; I have been called in to convince *la abuela,* the family's proud matriarch, to step down—to allow her children to take care of her before she kills herself with work. I spent years at her house as a child but have lived in the States for most of my adult life. I learned to love and respect this strong woman who with five children of her own had found a way to help many others. She was a legend in the pueblo for having more foster children than anyone else. I have spoken with people my mother's age who told me that they had spent up to a year at Abuela's house during emergencies and hard times. It seems extraordinary that a woman would willingly take on such obligations. And, frankly, I am a bit appalled at what I have begun to think of as "the martyr complex" in Puerto Rican women, that is, the idea that self-sacrifice is a woman's lot and her privilege. A good woman is defined by how much suffering and mothering she can do in one lifetime. Abuela

is the all-time champion in my eyes. Her life has been entirely devoted to others. Not content to bring up two sons and three daughters as the Depression raged on, followed by the war that took one of her sons, she had also taken on other people's burdens. This had been the usual pattern with one exception that I knew of: the year that Abuela spent in New York, apparently undergoing some kind of treatment of her heart while she was still a young woman. My mother was five or six years old, and there were three other children who had been born by that time, too. They were given into the care of Abuela's sister, Delia. The two women traded places for the year. Abuela went to live in her sister's apartment in New York City, while the younger woman took over Abuela's duties at the house in Puerto Rico. Grandfather was a shadowy figure in the background during that period. My mother doesn't say much about what went on during that year, only that her mother was sick and away for months. Grandfather seemed absent, too, since he worked all of the time. Though they missed Abuela, they were well taken care of.

I am sitting on a rocking chair on the porch of her house. She is facing me from a hammock she made when her first baby was born. My mother was rocked 4
on the hammock. I was rocked on that hammock, and when I brought my daughter as a baby to Abuela's house, she was held in Abuela's sun-browned arms, my porcelain pink baby, and rocked to a peaceful sleep, too. Abuela sits there and smiles as the breeze of a tropical November brings the scent of her roses and her herbs to us. She is proud of her garden. In front of the house she grows flowers and lush trailing plants; in the back, where the mango tree gives shade, she has an herb garden. From this patch of weedy-looking plants came all the remedies of my childhood, for anything from a sore throat to menstrual cramps. Abuela had a recipe for every pain a child could dream up, and she brought it to your bed in her own hands smelling of the earth. For a moment I am content to sit in her comforting presence. She is rotund now—a small-boned brown-skinned earth mother—with a big heart and temper to match. My grandfather comes to stand at the screen door. He has forgotten how the latch works. He pulls at the knob and moans softly, rattling it. With some effort Abuela gets down from the hammock. She opens the door, gently guiding the old man to a chair at the end of the porch. There be begins anew his constant search for the words he needs. He tries various combinations, but they don't work as language. Abuela pats his hand and motions for me to follow her into the house. We sit down at opposite ends of her sofa.

She apologizes to me as if for a misbehaving child.   5

"He'll quiet down," she says. "He does not like to be ignored."   6

I take a deep breath in preparation for my big lecture to Grandmother. This   7
is the time to tell her that she has to give up trying to run this house and take care of others at her age. One of her daughters is prepared to take her in. Grandfather is to be sent to a nursing home. Before I can say anything Abuela says, "*Mi amor*, would you like to hear a story?"

I smile, surprised at her offer. These are the same words that stopped me in   8
my tracks as a child, even in the middle of a tantrum. Abuela could always entrance me with one of her tales.

I nodded. Yes, my sermon could wait a little longer, I thought.   9

"Let me tell you an old, old story I heard when I was a little girl.   10

"There was once a man who became worried and suspicious when he noticed   11
that his wife disappeared from their bed every night for long periods of time. Wanting to find out what she was doing before confronting her, the man decided to stay
awake at night and keep guard. For hours he watched her every movement through
half-closed eyelids with his ears perked up like those of a burro.

"Then just about midnight, when the night was as dark as the bottom of a   12
cauldron, he felt his wife slipping out of bed. He saw her go to the wardrobe and
take out a jar and a little paintbrush. She stood naked by the window, and when
the church bells struck twelve, she began to paint her entire body with the paintbrush, dipping it into the jar. As the bells tolled the hour, she whispered these
words: *I don't believe in the Church, or in God, or in the Virgin Mary.* As soon as
this was spoken, she rose from the ground and flew into the night like a bird.

"Astounded, the man decided not to say anything to his wife the next day,   13
but to try to find out where she went. The following night, the man pretended to
sleep and waited until she had again performed her little ceremony and flown
away, then he repeated her actions exactly. He soon found himself flying after her.
Approaching a palace, he saw many other women circling the roof, taking turns
going down the chimney. After the last had descended, he slid down the dark hole
that led to the castle's bodega, where food and wine were stored. He hid himself
behind some cases of wine and watched the women greet each other.

"The witches, for that's what they were, were the wives of his neighbors   14
and friends, but he at first had trouble recognizing them, for, like his wife, they
were all naked. With much merriment, they took the meats and cheeses that hung
from the bodega's rafters and laid a table for a feast. They drank the fine wines
right from the bottles, like men in a cantina, and danced wildly to eerie music
from invisible instruments. They spoke to each other in a language that he did not
understand, words that sounded like a cat whose tail has been stepped on. Still,
horrible as their speech was, the food they prepared smelled delicious. Cautiously
placing himself in the shadows near one of the witches, he extended his hand for
a plate. He was given a steaming dish of stewed tongue. Hungrily, he took a bite;
it was tasteless. The other witches had apparently noticed the same thing because
they sent one of the younger ones to find some salt. But when the young witch
came back into the room with a salt shaker in her hand, the man forgot himself
and exclaimed, 'Thank God the salt is here.'

"On hearing God's name, all the witches took flight immediately, leaving   15
the man completely alone in the darkened cellar. He tried the spell for flight that
had brought him there, but it did not work. It was no longer midnight, and it was
obviously the wrong incantation for going *up* a chimney. He tried all night to get
out of the place, which had been left in shambles by the witches, but it was locked
up as tight as heaven is to a sinner. Finally, he fell asleep from exhaustion and
slept until dawn, when he heard footsteps approaching. When he saw the heavy
door being pushed open, he hid himself behind a cask of wine.

"A man in rich clothes walked in, followed by several servants. They were ₁₆ armed with heavy sticks as if out to kill someone. When the man lit his torch and saw the chaos in the cellar, broken bottles strewn on the floor, meats and cheeses half eaten and tossed everywhere, he cried out in such a rage that the man hiding behind the wine cask closed his eyes and committed his soul to God. The owner of the castle ordered his servants to search the whole bodega, every inch of it, until they discovered how vandals had entered his home. It was a matter of minutes before they discovered the witch's husband, curled up like a stray dog, and—worse—painted the color of a vampire bat, without a stitch of clothing.

"They dragged him to the center of the room and beat him with their sticks ₁₇ until the poor man thought that his bones had been pulverized and he would have to be poured into his grave. When the castle's owner said that he thought the poor wretch had learned his lesson, the servants tossed him naked onto the road. The man was so sore that he slept right there on the public *camino,* oblivious to the stares and insults of all who passed him. When he awakened in the middle of the night and found himself naked, dirty, bloody, and miles from his home, he swore to himself right then and there that he would never, for anything in the world, follow his wife on her nightly journeys again."

"Colorín, colorado." Abuela claps her hands three times, chanting the ₁₈ childhood rhyme for ending a story, *"Este cuento se ha acabado."* She smiles at me, shifting her position on the sofa to be able to watch Grandfather muttering to himself on the porch. I remember those eyes on me when I was a small child. Their movements seemed to be triggered by a child's actions, like those holograms of the Holy Mother that were popular with Catholics a few years ago—you couldn't get away from their mesmerizing gaze.

"Will you tell me about your year in New York, Abuela?" I surprise myself ₁₉ with the question. But suddenly I need to know about Abuela's lost year. It has to be another good story.

She looks intently at me before she answers. Her eyes are my eyes, same ₂₀ dark brown color, almond shape, and the lids that droop a little: called by some "bedroom eyes"; to others they are a sign of a cunning nature. "Why are you looking at me that way?" is a question I am often asked.

"I wanted to leave home," she says calmly, as though she had been expect- ₂₁ ing the question from me all along.

"You mean abandon your family?" I am really taken aback by her words. ₂₂

"Yes, *hija.* That is exactly what I mean. Abandon them. Never to return." ₂₃

"Why?" ₂₄

"I was tired. I was young and pretty, full of energy and dreams." She smiles ₂₅ as Grandfather breaks into song standing by himself on the porch. A woman passing by with a baby in her arms waves at him. Grandfather sings louder, something about a man going to his exile because the woman he loves has rejected him. He finishes the song on a long note and continues to stand in the middle of the tiled porch as if listening for applause. He bows.

Abuela shakes her head, smiling a little, as if amused by his antics, then she 26
finishes her sentence. "Restless, bored. Four children and a husband all demanding more and more from me."

"So you left the children with your sister and went to New York?" I say, try- 27
ing to keep the mixed emotions I was feeling out of my voice. I look at the serene
old woman in front of me and cannot believe that she once left four children and
a loving husband to go live alone in a faraway country.

"I had left him once before, but he found me. I came back home, but on the 28
condition that he never follow me anywhere again. I told him the next time I
would not return." She is silent, apparently falling deep into thought.

"You were never really sick," I say, though I am afraid that she will not 29
resume her story. But I want to know more about this woman whose life I thought
was an open book.

"I *was* sick. Sick at heart. And he knew it," she says, keeping her eyes on 30
Grandfather, who is standing as still as a marble statue on the porch. He seems to
be listening intently for something.

"The year in New York was his idea. He saw how unhappy I was. He knew 31
I needed to taste freedom. He paid my sister Delia to come take care of the children. He also sublet her apartment for me, though he had to take a second job to
do it. He gave me money and told me to go."

"What did you do that year in New York?" I am both stunned and fascinated 32
by Abuela's revelation.

"I worked as a seamstress in a fancy dress shop. And. . . . *y pues, hija"—* 33
she smiles at me as if I should know something without being told—"I lived."

"Why did you come back?" I ask. 34

"Because I love him," she says, "and I missed my children." 35

He is scratching at the door. Like a small child he has traced the sound of 36
Abuela's voice back to her. She lets him in, guiding him gently by the hand. Then
she eases him down on his favorite rocking chair. He begins to nod; soon he will
be sound asleep, comforted by her proximity, secure in his familiar surroundings.
I wonder how long it will take him to revert to infantilism. The doctors say he is
physically healthy and may live for many years, but his memory, verbal skills, and
ability to control his biological functions will deteriorate rapidly. He may end his
days bedridden, perhaps comatose. My eyes fill with tears as I look at the lined
face of this beautiful and gentle old man. I am in awe of the generosity of spirit
that allowed him to give a year of freedom to the woman he loved, not knowing
whether she would ever return to him. Abuela has seen my tears and moves over
on the sofa to sit near me. She slips an arm around my waist and pulls me close.
She kisses my wet cheek. Then she whispers softly into my ear, "And in time, the
husband either began forgetting that he had seen her turn into a witch, or believed
that he had just dreamed it." She takes my face into her hands. "I am going to take
care of your grandfather until one of us dies. I promised him when I came back
that I would never leave home again unless he asked me to: he never did. He never
asked any questions."

I hear my mother's car pull up into the driveway. She will wait there for me. 37
I will have to admit that I failed in my mission. I will argue Abuela's case without
revealing her secret. As far as everyone is concerned she went away to recover from
problems with her heart. That part is true in both versions of the story.

At the door she gives me the traditional blessing, adding with a wink, 38
"Colorín, colorado." My grandfather, hearing her voice, smiles in his sleep.

Meaning and Idea

1. Why has Cofer come to Puerto Rico in the first place? Is she surprised
   when she realizes that, instead of convincing her grandmother of
   something, she herself has become convinced of something instead? How
   do you know?

2. Does the grandmother know the granddaughter's topic before she even
   begins to talk? How do you know? What is the significance of the story of
   the witch? Does the grandmother know that the story about the witch's
   husband will be so timely? Why do you think so?

3. This essay contains several narratives. Summarize them briefly. How do
   they all serve the same purpose or relate to the same theme?

Language, Form, Structure

1. Throughout the beginning of the essay, the writer moves easily between
   memories of the setting, tales and history regarding her grandmother, the
   grandfather's state, and the two women moving about the house and then
   beginning their conversation. How does this flow of subjects affect the
   reader? What linguistic or rhetorical strategies does Cofer use to help the
   reader? For example, comment on her use of transitions, thesis statement,
   and sensory detail.

2. What is the effect of using Spanish words the way Cofer does? Find and
   define as many of them as you can. Suppose Cofer used only the English
   equivalents of these words. How would they affect the theme and the
   atmosphere of the selection?

3. Define the following words: dementia; obstinacy; martyr; tantrum;
   cauldron; incantation; shambles; oblivious; holograms; mesmerizing;
   serene; revelation; proximity.

Ideas for Writing

1. Write an essay in which you narrate a story that someone told to you—a
   family member, a friend, someone you hold dear. Be sure to describe the
   setting fully, and also the situation in which the person related the tale.

Thus, you will be telling two stories, the story that the person told you *and* the story of the person's telling you the story.

2. Write an essay in which you narrate the experience or activities of an elderly person, whom you know or know of, in order to argue for or against that person's continuing his or her current living situation.

3. Reread Cofer's essay and write an essay about what she calls the "martyr complex." Use examples you know of or have personally experienced to explain the existence or nonexistence of the complex among women.

The Chimney Sweeper

William Blake

By trade, William Blake (1757–1827) was a painter and an engraver. Yet he was also an eccentric poet; much of his poetry derives from mystical visions and communications which he trusted as much as—or more than—his conscious reality. The "romantic school" shunned him because of his mysticism and abstruseness, and his poetry was all but ignored in his time. Today, however, we count his two major collections of poetry, *Songs of Innocence* (1789) and *Songs of Experience* (1794), among the most lyrical, profound delvings into human existence.

Collected in Blake's second major volume, *Songs of Experience,* "The Chimney Sweeper" is indicative of the poet's indignation at society's treatment of poor and homeless children. Blake's concerns, in general, are with social evils, and these concerns pervade the whole collection.

*W*hen *my mother died I was very young,*
And my father sold me while yet my tongue
Could scarcely cry " 'weep! 'weep! 'weep! 'weep!"
So your chimneys I sweep, and in soot I sleep.

There's little Tom Dacre, who cried when his head,   5
That curled like a lamb's back, was shaved; so I said,
"Hush, Tom! never mind it, for, when your head's bare,
You know that the soot cannot spoil your white hair."

And so he was quiet, and that very night,
As Tom was sleeping, he had such a sight!   10
That thousands of sweepers, Dick, Joe, Ned, and Jack,
Were all of them locked up in coffins of black.

And by came an Angel who had a bright key,
And he opened the coffins and set them all free;
Then down a green plain leaping, laughing, they run,   15
And wash in a river, and shine in the sun.

Then naked and white, all their bags left behind,
They rise upon clouds and sport in the wind;
And the Angel told Tom, if he'd be a good boy,
He'd have God for his father, and never want joy.   20

And so Tom awoke, and we rose in the dark,
And got with our bags and our brushes to work.
Though the morning was cold, Tom was happy and warm;
So if all do their duty they need not fear harm.

Meaning and Idea

1. What do you know about the boy who narrates this poem? What can you discern about his character and his attitude towards life?

2. What is the "sight" of line 10?

3. Summarize the boy's dream (lines 11–20) in your own words.

Language, Form, Structure

1. *Dramatic irony* is the difference between what a narrator says and what the writer intends or knows. How is this poem an example of dramatic irony? How do you interpret the boy's dream? If a *symbol* is something that is both what it is and something else with a larger, more important meaning, how may the dream be viewed as *symbolic*?

2. What is the effect of the repetition of *weep* in line 3?

3. How does Blake use images of lightness and darkness to heighten the drama of this poem?

Ideas for Writing

1. Write a narrative of how a recent dream led you to some resolution of a difficult situation. Be sure to narrate the dream as well.

2. Write a short story—or write a poem—about an unfortunate person you have met.

3. This poem comes from Blake's *Songs of Experience.* Write a paragraph or two that tell in what ways you might consider this poem a "song." Draw specific examples from "The Chimney Sweeper" to support your point.

Araby

James Joyce

Deservedly considered the writer who forever changed the face of modern fiction, James Joyce (1882–1942) was born into a middle-class family in Dublin, Ireland. Educated at Jesuit boarding schools and later at University College, Dublin, James Joyce soon divorced himself physically (though not emotionally) from Irish nationalism and Irish Catholicism. He spent almost all his postcollege years outside Ireland, living and working in such places as Paris, Zurich, and Trieste. His works, some of which are marked by such radical experiments in form and content as "stream of consciousness" narration, include the eloquent *Dubliners* (1914), the semiautobiographical *A Portrait of the Artist as a Young Man* (1916), the monumental *Ulysses* (1922), and the extraordinary (if a little abstruse) *Finnegan's Wake* (1939). Unfortunately, Joyce's creative genius was not justly recognized until after his death.

"Araby" is one of the fifteen literary gems that compose Joyce's collection of short stories, *Dubliners,* written between 1904 and 1907. Although some readers may be awed by the creative ambiguities of Joyce's other works, *Dubliners,* his early fiction, is easily accessible. In "Araby" he tells the story of a young man overcome by his confusions of love and infatuation, imagination and reality, freedom and commitment.

North Richmond Street, being blind, was a quaint street except at the hour when the Christian Brothers School set the boys free. An uninhabited house of two storeys stood at the blind end, detached from its neighbours in a square ground. The other houses of the street, conscious of decent lives within them, gazed at one another with brown imperturbable faces.

The former tenant of our house, a priest, had died in the back drawing-room. Air, musty from having been long enclosed, hung in all the rooms, and the waste room behind the kitchen was littered with old useless papers. Among these I found a few paper-covered books, the pages of which were curled and damp: *The Abbott,* by Walter Scott, *The Devout Communicant* and *The Memoirs of Vidocq.* I liked the last best because its leaves were yellow. The wild garden behind the house contained a central apple-tree and a few straggling bushes under one of which I found the late tenant's rusty bicycle-pump. He had been a very charitable priest; in his will he had left all his money to institutions and the furniture of his house to his sister.

When the short days of winter came dusk fell before we had well eaten our dinners. When we met in the street the houses had grown sombre. The space of sky above us was the colour of ever-changing violet and towards it the lamps of the street lifted their feeble lanterns. The cold air stung us and we played till our bodies glowed. Our shouts echoed in the silent street. The career of our play brought us through the dark muddy lanes behind the houses where we ran the gauntlet of the rough tribes from the cottages, to the back doors of the dark dripping gardens where odours arose from the ashpits, to the dark odorous stables where a coachman smoothed and combed the horse or shook music from the buckled harness. When we returned to the street light from the kitchen windows had filled the areas. If my uncle was seen turning the corner we hid in the shadow until we had seen him safely housed. Or if Mangan's sister came out on the doorstep to call her brother in to his tea we watched her from our shadow peer up and down the street. We waited to see whether she would remain or go in and, if she remained, we left our shadow and walked up to Mangan's steps resignedly. She was waiting for us, her figure defined by the light from the half-opened door. Her brother always teased her before he obeyed and I stood by the railings looking at her. Her dress swung as she moved her body and the soft rope of her hair tossed from side to side.

Every morning I lay on the floor in the front parlour watching her door. The 4 blind was pulled down to within an inch of the sash so that I could not be seen. When she came out on the doorstep my heart leaped. I ran to the hall, seized my books and followed her. I kept her brown figure always in my eye and, when we came near the point at which our ways diverged, I quickened my pace and passed her. This happened morning after morning. I had never spoken to her, except for a few casual words, and yet her name was like a summons to all my foolish blood.

Her image accompanied me even in places the most hostile to romance. On 5 Saturday evenings when my aunt went marketing I had to go to carry some of the parcels. We walked through the flaring streets, jostled by drunken men and bargaining women, amid the curses of labourers, the shrill litanies of shop-boys who stood on guard by the barrels of pigs' cheeks, the nasal chanting of street-singers, who sang a *come-all-you* about O'Donovan Rossa, or a ballad about the troubles in our native land. These noises converged in a single sensation of life for me: I imagined that I bore my chalice safely through a throng of foes. Her name sprang to my lips at moments in strange prayers and praises which I myself did not understand. My eyes were often full of tears (I could not tell why) and at times a flood from my heart seemed to pour itself out into my bosom. I thought little of the future. I did not know whether I would ever speak to her or not or, if I spoke to her, how I could tell her of my confused adoration. But my body was like a harp and her words and gestures were like fingers running upon the wires.

One evening I went into the back drawing-room in which the priest had 6 died. It was a dark rainy evening and there was no sound in the house. Through one of the broken panes I heard the rain impinge upon the earth, the fine incessant needles of water playing in the sodden beds. Some distant lamp or lighted window gleamed below me. I was thankful that I could see so little. All my senses seemed to desire to veil themselves and, feeling that I was about to slip from them, I pressed the palms of my hands together until they trembled, murmuring: *"O love! O love!"* many times.

At last she spoke to me. When she addressed the first words to me I was so 7 confused that I did not know what to answer. She asked me was I going to *Araby.* I forgot whether I answered yes or no. It would be a splendid bazaar, she said she would love to go.

"And why can't you?" I asked. 8

While she spoke she turned a silver bracelet round and round her wrist. She 9
could not go, she said, because there would be a retreat that week in her convent.
Her brother and two other boys were fighting for their caps and I was alone at the
railings. She held one of the spikes, bowing her head towards me. The light from
the lamp opposite our door caught the white curve of her neck, lit up her hair that
rested there and, falling, lit up the hand upon the railing. It fell over one side of her
dress and caught the white border of a petticoat, just visible as she stood at ease.

"It's well for you," she said. 10

"If I go," I said, "I will bring you something." 11

What innumerable follies laid waste my waking and sleeping thoughts after 12
that evening! I wished to annihilate the tedious intervening days. I chafed against
the work of school. At night in my bedroom and by day in the classroom her
image came between me and the page I strove to read. The syllables of the word
Araby were called to me through the silence in which my soul luxuriated and cast
an Eastern enchantment over me. I asked for leave to go to the bazaar on Saturday night. My aunt was surprised and hoped it was not some Freemason affair. I
answered few questions in class. I watched my master's face pass from amiabil-
ity to sternness; he hoped I was not beginning to idle. I could not call my wandering thoughts together. I had hardly any patience with the serious work of life
which, now that it stood between me and my desire, seemed to me child's play,
ugly monotonous child's play.

On Saturday morning I reminded my uncle that I wished to go to the bazaar 13
in the evening. He was fussing at the hallstand, looking for the hat-brush, and
answered me curtly:

"Yes, boy, I know." 14

As he was in the hall I could not go into the front parlour and lie at the win- 15
dow. I left the house in bad humour and walked slowly towards the school. The
air was pitilessly raw and already my heart misgave me.

When I came home to dinner my uncle had not yet been home. Still it was 16
early. I sat staring at the clock for some time and, when its ticking began to irri-
tate me, I left the room. I mounted the staircase and gained the upper part of the
house. The high cold empty gloomy rooms liberated me and I went from room to
room singing. From the front window I saw my companions playing below in the
street. Their cries reached me weakened and indistinct and, leaning my forehead
against the cool glass, I looked over at the dark house where she lived. I may have
stood there for an hour, seeing nothing but the brown-clad figure cast by my
imagination, touched discreetly by the lamplight at the curved neck, at the hand
upon the railings and at the border below the dress.

When I came downstairs again I found Mrs. Mercer sitting at the fire. She 17
was an old garrulous woman, a pawnbroker's widow, who collected used stamps
for some pious purpose. I had to endure the gossip of the tea-table. The meal was
prolonged beyond an hour and still my uncle did not come. Mrs. Mercer stood up
to go: she was sorry she couldn't wait any longer, but it was after eight o'clock

and she did not like to be out late, as the night air was bad for her. When she had gone I began to walk up and down the room, clenching my fists. My aunt said:

"I'm afraid you may put off your bazaar for this night of Our Lord." 18

At nine o'clock I heard my uncle's latchkey in the halldoor. I heard him 19 talking to himself and heard the hallstand rocking when it had received the weight of his overcoat. I could interpret these signs. When he was midway through his dinner I asked him to give me the money to go to the bazaar. He had forgotten.

"The people are in bed and after their first sleep now," he said. 20

I did not smile. My aunt said to him energetically: 21

"Can't you give him the money and let him go? You've kept him late 22 enough as it is."

My uncle said he was very sorry he had forgotten. He said he believed in 23 the old saying: "All work and no play makes Jack a dull boy." He asked me where I was going and, when I had told him a second time he asked me did I know *The Arab's Farewell to his Steed.* When I left the kitchen he was about to recite the opening lines of the piece to my aunt.

I held a florin tightly in my hand as I strode down Buckingham Street 24 towards the station. The sight of the streets thronged with buyers and glaring with gas recalled to me the purpose of my journey. I took my seat in a third-class carriage of a deserted train. After an intolerable delay the train moved out of the station slowly. It crept onward among ruinous houses and over the twinkling river. At Westland Row Station a crowd of people pressed to the carriage doors; but the porters moved them back, saying that it was a special train for the bazaar. I remained alone in the bare carriage. In a few minutes the train drew up beside an improvised wooden platform. I passed out on the road and saw by the lighted dial of a clock that it was ten minutes to ten. In front of me was a large building which displayed the magical name.

I could not find any sixpenny entrance and, fearing that the bazaar would 25 be closed, I passed in quickly through a turnstile, handing a shilling to a weary-looking man. I found myself in a big hall girdled at half its height by a gallery. Nearly all the stalls were closed and the greater part of the hall was in darkness. I recognised a silence like that which pervades a church after a service. I walked into the centre of the bazaar timidly. A few people were gathered about the stalls which were still open. Before a curtain, over which the words *Café Chantant* were written in coloured lamps, two men were counting money on a salver. I listened to the fall of the coins.

Remembering with difficulty why I had come I went over to one of the 26 stalls and examined porcelain vases and flowered tea-sets. At the door of the stall a young lady was talking and laughing with two young gentlemen. I remarked their English accents and listened vaguely to their conversation.

"O, I never said such a thing!" 27

"O, but you did!" 28

"O, but I didn't!" 29

"Didn't she say that?" 30

"Yes. I heard her." 31

"O, there's a . . . fib!"   32

Observing me the young lady came over and asked me did I wish to buy 33 anything. The tone of her voice was not encouraging; she seemed to have spoken to me out of a sense of duty. I looked humbly at the great jars that stood like eastern guards at either side of the dark entrance to the stall and murmured:

"No, thank you."   34

The young lady changed the position of one of the vases and went back to 35 the two young men. They began to talk of the same subject. Once or twice the young lady glanced at me over her shoulder.

I lingered before her stall, though I knew my stay was useless, to make my 36 interest in her wares seem the more real. Then I turned away slowly and walked down the middle of the bazaar. I allowed the two pennies to fall against the sixpence in my pocket. I heard a voice call from one end of the gallery that the light was out. The upper part of the hall was now completely dark.

Gazing up into the darkness I saw myself as a creature driven and derided 37 by vanity; and my eyes burned with anguish and anger.

Meaning and Idea

1. Describe the environment in which the narrator lives. What does he find special about it? What is the significance of the details which he chooses to emphasize, especially in the opening paragraphs?

2. What are the narrator's feelings toward Mangan's sister? On what are they based? What image of her does his imagination create? How close is it to her reality? Why is she always referred to as "Mangan's sister" rather than be her own name?

3. Is Mangan's sister older or younger than the narrator? How do you know?

4. What promise does the narrator make to Mangan's sister? Does he keep it? Why? Describe what happens. What do you think will be the consequences to the narrator?

5. How old do you think the narrator is when he is telling this story? How can you tell?

Language, Form, Structure

1. How is personification (see page 58) used in the beginning paragraphs of the story? How does it bear on the narrator's character and his choices?

2. Trace the uses of color imagery in the story. What are the predominant colors? How do they help set the tone of the story? What is the special significance of the colors used to describe Mangan's sister?

3. Joyce wrote of his stories as having "moments of epiphany"—that is, sudden, great realizations that change the course of the protagonist's

actions. What is the "moment of epiphany" in this story? How is it foreshadowed? Imagine this story without its special moment. What does the moment of epiphany contribute to the story as a whole?

4. What is the theme of this story? How does the title support the theme?

5. Select 10 words from this story which were unfamiliar to you and use them in sentences of your own.

Ideas for Writing

1. Write a narrative about a time you made a promise to someone, one which you decided not to keep. Why didn't you keep it? What were the consequences?

2. Write a narrative of a moment in which you felt alone, although you may have been in the midst of a crowd. Concentrate on details of the environment.

3. In *Dubliners,* the book of stories in which "Araby" was collected, Joyce wanted to write about the "paralysis"—or emotional immobilization—of life in Dublin as he knew it. Write a short analysis of this story in relation to the theme of paralysis. Who or what is paralyzed here?

Salvation

Langston Hughes

Langston Hughes (1902–1967) was one of America's foremost poets, essayists, dramatists, and fiction writers whose self-proclaimed desire as a writer was "to explain and illuminate the Negro condition in America." After being elected class poet in grammar school
in Lincoln, Illinois, Hughes first gained adult recognition as a poet when he was a busboy
at a hotel in Washington, D.C. He left some poems by the plate of the poet Vachel Lindsay, who fortunately recognized his talent.

"Salvation" is a selection from Hughes's autobiography, *The Big Sea* (1940). In it, he tells
of his "conversion" to Christ in the midst of peer and community pressure. The narrative
informs us of young Hughes's difficult situation, his fanciful reaction to it, and both the
short- and long-term effects of his actions.

I was saved from sin when I was going on thirteen. But not really   1
saved. It happened like this. There was a big revival at my Auntie Reed's church.
Every night for weeks there had been much preaching, singing, praying, and
shouting, and some very hardened sinners had been brought to Christ, and the
membership of the church had grown by leaps and bounds. Then just before the
revival ended, they held a special meeting for children, "to bring the young lambs
to the fold." My aunt spoke of it for days ahead. That night I was escorted to the
front row and placed on the mourners' bench with all the other young sinners,
who had not yet been brought to Jesus.

My aunt told me that when you were saved you saw a light, and something   2
happened to you inside! And Jesus came into your life! And God was with you
from then on! She said you could see and hear and feel Jesus in your soul. I
believed her. I had heard a great many old people say the same thing and it
seemed to me they ought to know. So I sat there calmly in the hot, crowded
church, waiting for Jesus to come to me.

The preacher preached a wonderful rhythmical sermon, all moans and   3
shouts and lonely cries and dire pictures of hell, and then he sang a song about
the ninety and nine safe in the fold, but one little lamb was left out in the cold.
Then he said: "Won't you come? Won't you come to Jesus? Young lambs, won't
you come?" And he held out his arms to all us young sinners there on the mourners' bench. And the little girls cried. And some of them jumped up and went to
Jesus right away. But most of us just sat there.

A great many old people came and knelt around us and prayed, old women   4
with jet-black faces and braided hair, old men with work-gnarled hands. And the
church sang a song about the lower lights are burning, some poor sinners to be
saved. And the whole building rocked with prayer and song.

Still I kept waiting to *see* Jesus.   5

Finally all the young people had gone to the altar and were saved, but one   6
boy and me. He was a rounder's son named Westley. Westley and I were surrounded by sisters and deacons praying. It was very hot in the church, and getting
late now. Finally Westley said to me in a whisper: "God damn! I'm tired o' sitting
here. Let's get up and be saved." So he got up and was saved.

Then I was left all alone on the mourners' bench. My aunt came and knelt   7
at my knees and cried, while prayers and songs swirled all around me in the little church. The whole congregation prayed for me alone, in a mighty wail of
moans and voices. And I kept waiting serenely for Jesus, waiting, waiting—but
he didn't come. I wanted to see him, but nothing happened to me. Nothing! I
wanted something to happen to me, but nothing happened.

I heard the songs and the minister saying: "Why don't you come? My dear   8
child, why don't you come to Jesus? Jesus is waiting for you. He wants you. Why
don't you come? Sister Reed, what is this child's name?"

"Langston," my aunt sobbed.   9

"Langston, why don't you come? Why don't you come and be saved? Oh,   10
Lamb of God! Why don't you come?"

Now it was really getting late. I began to be ashamed of myself, holding   11
everything up so long. I began to wonder what God thought about Westley, who
certainly hadn't seen Jesus either, but who was now sitting proudly on the platform, swinging his knickerbockered legs and grinning down at me, surrounded by
deacons and old women on their knees praying. God had not struck Westley dead
for taking his name in vain or for lying in the temple. So I decided that maybe to
save further trouble, I'd better lie, too, and say that Jesus had come, and get up
and be saved.

So I got up.   12

Suddenly the whole room broke into a sea of shouting, as they saw me rise.   13
Waves of rejoicing swept the place. Women leaped in the air. My aunt threw her
arms around me. The minister took me by the hand and led me to the platform.

When things quieted down, in a hushed silence, punctuated by a few ecsta-   14
tic "Amens," all the new young lambs were blessed in the name of God. Then joyous singing filled the room.

That night, for the last time in my life but one—for I was a big boy twelve   15
years old—I cried. I cried, in bed alone, and couldn't stop. I buried by head under
the quilts, but my aunt heard me. She woke up and told my uncle I was crying
because the Holy Ghost had come into my life, and because I had seen Jesus. But
I was really crying because I couldn't bear to tell her that I had lied, that I had
deceived everybody in the church, that I hadn't seen Jesus, and that now I didn't
believe there was a Jesus anymore, since he didn't come to help me.

Meaning and Idea

1. In your own words, describe the atmosphere of the revival meeting. What
   was its purpose?

2. Who are the "lambs" to be saved?

3. Who is most concerned about Langston's "salvation"? Why? Do you think they are sincere?

4. Why does Westley get "saved"? Why does Langston decide to be saved, too?

5. What are the immediate consequences of Langston's actions? What are the long-range consequences?

Language, Form, Structure

1. How do the first two sentences serve as a thesis for this essay? What conflict do they present which must be resolved within the narrative?

2. About midway through the essay, what *allusion* (see page 56) helps place the time period of this narrative? Approximately what time period is it?

3. What is the value of *dialogue* in this selection? Where is it used most effectively? How would paragraph 6, for example, be different if Hughes had omitted Westley's line of dialogue?

4. How is sound imagery used in this essay? Where is it used most vibrantly?

5. How does Hughes slightly change the time frame of the essay in the last sentence?

6. Check the dictionary meanings for: dire; gnarled; rounder; deacons. Use each word in an original sentence.

Ideas for Writing

1. Tell about a time when you told a lie. Be sure to set the situation, tell about the actual event of the lie, and discuss the consequences.

2. Narrate an incident in which you did something you thought you *had* to do but didn't really *want* to do. Explain why you did it—what pressures affected you most strongly. Tell about your feelings afterward.

3. What do you consider the most effective prose narrative techniques in this essay? You might consider, for example, language, sentence structure, temporal sequencing, characterization, or dialogue. In a paragraph or two, explain your choice by analyzing examples from the text.

The Tell-Tale Heart

Edgar Allan Poe

Edgar Allan Poe (1809–1849) was born in Boston. After his mother died when he was only two years old, he was adopted by John Allan of Richmond, Virginia. Poe eventually returned to Boston, then made homes in New York and Baltimore. Known mostly for his macabre and tormented stories and poems, Poe was also a literary critic of some merit. In fact, in one critical essay, he set down guidelines for the writing of the short story which are still relevant over a hundred years later. In 1835, Poe became editor of the *Southern Literary Messenger* and for much of his life held similar editorial positions. However, his life was beset with difficulties and tragedies: poverty; the illness and death of his 13-year-old bride; bitter personal battles; his own physical and mental dissolution. Poe was found unconscious in a gutter in Baltimore in 1849, where he died soon after.

First published in the January 1843 edition of *The Pioneer,* "The Tell-Tale Heart" is Poe's classic gothic horror tale. Colored by the obviously deranged mind of its narrator, this story is a good example of an interior dramatic monologue, in which one character speaks to himself alone.

*T*rue!—nervous—very, very dreadfully nervous I had been and am; but why *will* you say that I am mad? The disease had sharpened my senses—not destroyed—not dulled them. Above all was the sense of hearing acute. I heard all things in the heaven and in the earth. I heard many things in hell. How, then, am I mad? Hearken! and observe how healthily—how calmly I can tell you the whole story.   1

It is impossible to say how first the idea entered my brain; but once conceived, it haunted me day and night. Object there was none. Passion there was none. I loved the old man. He had never wronged me. He had never given me insult. For his gold I had no desire. I think it was his eye! yes, it was this! One of his eyes resembled that of a vulture—a pale blue eye, with a film over it. Whenever it fell upon me, my blood ran cold; and so by degrees—very gradually—I made up my mind to take the life of the old man, and thus rid myself of the eye for ever.   2

Now this is the point. You fancy me mad. Madmen know nothing. But you should have seen *me*. You should have seen how wisely I proceeded—with what caution—with what foresight—with what dissimulation I went to work! I was never kinder to the old man than during the whole week before I killed him. And every night, about midnight, I turned the latch of his door and opened it—oh, so gently! And then, when I had made an opening sufficient for my head, I put in a dark lantern, all closed, closed, so that no light shone out, and then I thrust in my head. Oh, you would have laughed to see how cunningly I thrust it in! I moved it slowly—very, very slowly, so that I might not disturb the old man's sleep. It took me an hour to place my whole head within the opening so far that I could see him   3 as he lay upon his bed. Ha!—would a madman have been so wise as this? And then, when my head was well in the room, I undid the lantern cautiously—oh, so cautiously—cautiously (for the hinges creaked)—I undid it just so much that a single thin ray fell upon the vulture eye. And this I did for seven long nights— every night just at midnight—but I found the eye always closed; and so it was impossible to do the work; for it was not the old man who vexed me, but his Evil Eye. And every morning, when the day broke, I went boldly into the chamber, and spoke courageously to him, calling him by name in a hearty tone, and inquiring how he had passed the night. So you see he would have been a very profound old man, indeed, to suspect that every night, just at twelve, I looked in upon him while he slept.

Upon the eighth night I was more than usually cautious in opening the door. 4
A watch's minute hand moves more quickly than did mine. Never before that night had I *felt* the extent of my own powers—of my sagacity. I could scarcely contain my feelings of triumph. To think that there I was, opening the door, little by little, and he not even to dream of my secret deeds or thoughts. I fairly chuck- led at the idea; and perhaps he heard me; for he moved on the bed suddenly, as if startled. Now you may think that I drew back—but no. His room was as black as pitch with the thick darkness (for the shutters were close fastened, through fear of robbers), and so I knew that he could not see the opening of the door, and I kept pushing it on steadily, steadily.

I had my head in, and was about to open the lantern, when my thumb 5
slipped upon the tin fastening, and the old man sprang up in the bed, crying out "Who's there?"

I kept quite still and said nothing. For a whole hour I did not move a mus- 6
cle, and in the meantime I did not hear him lie down. He was still sitting up in the bed listening;—just as I have done, night after night, hearkening to the death watches in the wall.

Presently I heard a slight groan, and I knew it was the groan of mortal ter- 7
ror. It was not a groan of pain or of grief—oh, no!—it was the low stifled sound that arises from the bottom of the soul when overcharged with awe. I knew the sound well. Many a night, just at midnight, when all the world slept, it was welled up from my own bosom, deepening, with its dreadful echo, the terrors that dis- tracted me. I say I knew it well. I knew what the old man felt, and pitied him, although I chuckled at heart. I knew that he had been lying awake ever since the first slight noise, when he had turned in the bed. His fears had been ever since growing upon him. He had been trying to fancy them causeless, but could not. He had been saying to himself—"It is nothing but the wind in the chimney—it is only a mouse crossing the floor," or "it is merely a cricket which has made a single chirp." Yes, he has been trying to comfort himself with these suppositions; but he had found all in vain. *All in vain;* because Death, in approaching him, had stalked with his black shadow before him, and enveloped the victim. And it was the mournful influence of the unperceived shadow that caused him to feel—although he neither saw nor heard—to *feel* the presence of my head within the room.

When I had waited a long time, very patiently, without hearing him lie 8
down, I resolved to open a little—a very, very little crevice in the lantern. So I
opened it—you cannot imagine how stealthily, stealthily, until, at length, a single
dim ray, like the thread of a spider, shot from out the crevice and full upon the
vulture eye.

It was open—wide, wide open—and I grew furious as I gazed upon it. I saw 9
it with perfect distinctness—all a dull blue, with a hideous veil over it that chilled
the very marrow in my bones; but I could see nothing else of the old man's face or
person: for I had directed the ray as if by instinct, precisely upon the damned spot.

And now have I not told you that what you mistake for madness is but over- 10
acuteness of the senses? —now, I say, there came to my ears a low, dull, quick
sound, such as a watch makes when enveloped in cotton. I knew *that* sound well
too. It was the beating of the old man's heart. It increased my fury, as the beating
of a drum stimulates the soldier into courage.

But even yet I refrained and kept still. I scarcely breathed. I held the lantern 11
motionless. I tried how steadily I could maintain the ray upon the eye. Meantime
the hellish tattoo of the heart increased. It grew quicker and quicker, and louder
and louder every instant. The old man's terror *must* have been extreme! It grew
louder, I say, louder every moment! —do you mark me well? I have told you that
I am nervous: so I am. And now at the dead hour of the night, amid the dreadful
silence of that old house, so strange a noise as this excited me to uncontrollable
terror. Yet, for some minutes longer I refrained and stood still. But the beating
grew louder, louder! I thought the heart must burst. And now a new anxiety seized
me—the sound would be heard by a neighbor! The old man's hour had come!
With a loud yell, I threw open the lantern and leaped into the room. He shrieked
once—once only. In an instant I dragged him to the floor, and pulled the heavy
bed over him. I then smiled gaily, to find the deed so far done. But, for many minutes, the heart beat on with a muffled sound. This, however, did not vex me; it
would not be heard through the wall. At length it ceased. The old man was dead.
I removed the bed and examined the corpse. Yes, he was stone, stone dead. I
placed my hand upon the heart and held it there many minutes. There was no pul-
sation. He was stone dead. His eye would trouble me no more.

If still you think me mad, you will think so no longer when I describe the 12
wise precautions I took for the concealment of the body. The night waned and I
worked hastily, but in silence. First of all I dismembered the corpse. I cut off the
head and the arms and the legs.

I then took up three planks from the flooring of the chamber, and deposited 13
all between the scantlings. I then replaced the boards so cleverly, so cunningly,
that no human eye—not even *his*—could have detected any thing wrong. There
was nothing to wash out—no stain of any kind—no blood-spot whatever. I had
been too wary for that. A tub had caught all—ha! ha!

When I had made an end of these labors, it was four o'clock—still dark as 14
midnight. As the bell sounded the hour, there came a knocking at the street door.
I went down to open it with a light heart,—for what had I *now* to fear? There
entered three men, who introduced themselves, with perfect suavity, as officers of

the police. A shriek had been heard by a neighbor during the night; suspicion of foul play had been aroused; information had been lodged at the police office, and they (the officers) had been deputed to search the premises.

I smiled,—for *what* had I to fear? I bade the gentlemen welcome. The shriek, I said, was my own in a dream. The old man, I mentioned, was absent in the country. I took my visitors all over the house. I bade them search—search *well*. I led them, at length, to *his* chamber. I showed them his treasures, secure, undisturbed. In the enthusiasm of my confidence, I brought chairs into the room, and desired them *here* to rest from their fatigues, while I myself, in the wild audacity of my perfect triumph, placed my own seat upon the very spot beneath which reposed the corpse of the victim.

The officers were satisfied. My *manner* had convinced them. I was singularly at ease. They sat, and while I answered cheerily, they chatted familiar things. But, ere long, I felt myself getting pale and wished them gone. My head ached, and I fancied a ringing in my ears: but still they sat and still chatted. The ringing became more distinct:—it continued and became more distinct: I talked more freely to get rid of the feeling: but it continued and gained definitiveness—until, at length, I found that the noise was *not* within my ears.

No doubt I now grew *very* pale;—but I talked more fluently, and with a heightened voice. Yet the sound increased—and what could I do? It was *a low, dull, quick sound—much such a sound as a watch makes when enveloped in cotton.* I gasped for breath—and yet the officers heard it not. I talked more quickly—more vehemently; but the noise steadily increased. I arose and argued about trifles, in a high key and with violent gesticulations, but the noise steadily increased. Why *would* they not be gone? I paced the floor to and fro with heavy strides, as if excited to fury by the observation of the men—but the noise steadily increased. Oh God! what *could* I do? I foamed—I raved—I swore! I swung the chair upon which I had been sitting, and grated it upon the boards, but the noise arose over all and continually increased. It grew louder—louder—*louder*! And still the men chatted pleasantly, and smiled. Was it possible they heard not? Almighty God!—no, no! They heard!—they suspected!—they *knew*!—they were making a mockery of my horror!—this I thought, and this I think. But any thing was better than this agony! Any thing was more tolerable than this derision! I could bear those hypocritical smiles no longer! I felt that I must scream or die!—and now—again!—hark! louder! louder! louder! *louder*!—

"Villains!" I shrieked, "dissemble no more! I admit the deed!—tear up the planks!—here, here!—it is the beating of his hideous heart!"

Meaning and Idea

1. If not madness, what does the narrator claim is the effect of his disease? Does he try to convince the reader that he is not mad?

2. Throughout the story, the narrator claims to know well the old man's feelings. How can the narrator actually know those feelings?

3. How does the narrator explain the shriek that brought the police to the house? How does he deal with the police?

4. Given the events as related by the narrator, could he indeed still be haunted by the heart beating? Why? How does this assertion influence one's belief in the rest of the story?

5. In the last paragraph, the narrator describes his actions at trying to drown out the noise of the heart. What does he do? If these actions were true, would the three men still have "chatted pleasantly"? What do you suspect was the truth of the incident? Why?

Language, Form, Structure

1. This story is an example of the *I-narrative* form, or first-person narrative, in which the protagonist tells the events that happen to him and others. Also, this I-narrative is an example of a dramatic monologue. To whom does the narrator address himself? Why?

2. In the first paragraph, the narrator claims, "Above all was the sense of hearing acute." Poe then makes use of numerous auditory images throughout the story. Go through the tale again and list, in order, all the auditory imagery you find. How does this acute sense of hearing eventually cause the narrator's downfall?

3. The narrator's madness causes him to make certain highly ironic statements. Reread the opening three paragraphs, then choose and explain what you consider the most ironic statements.

4. There is a great deal of repetition of words and phrases in this narrative. What is the purpose of these repetitions? What do they indicate about the narrator's emotional state? How do they affect the rhythm of the story?

5. Look up the meanings of the following words: acute; sagacity; stealthily; hideous; vex; waned; suavity; audacity; trifles; gesticulations. Then use each of these words in a sentence of your own.

Ideas for Writing

1. Make up a horror story of your own and narrate it through an unreliable first-person narrator. Try to make it as dramatic as possible.

2. Narrate the most horrible true incident you've ever witnessed. Attempt to create a fearful tone.

3. Write an essay in which you analyze the narrator of "A Tell-Tale Heart." Unlike a third-person narrative where the reader can generally trust the narrator with no reservations, in any I-narrative the reader must apply certain tests to the narrator's reliability. For example, we must ascertain whether or not the narrator is crazy, drunk, in a heightened emotional state,

a habitual liar, and so on. Clearly the I-narrator in this story is *un*reliable. In that case, what information *can* you obtain from this story? Why would Poe choose to write in this motif? Do you believe any of the story? Which part? Why? What do you suppose *is* the true story here?

In what other stories or books have you questioned the narrator's veracity? How did they compare with this story?

My Father's Life

Raymond Carver

Raymond Carver was born in 1939 in Clatskanie, Oregon. He studied at Humboldt State College and the University of Iowa and then worked a variety of jobs—janitor, stockboy, editor, creative writing instructor—to support his family. All the time, he wrote and began to earn the critical acclaim he now receives. Among other awards, he has been the recipient of a National Endowment for the Arts "Discovery" Award, a Guggenheim fellowship, and the prestigious Strauss Living Award. His poems, essays, and stories have been widely published in magazines, and his narrative sparseness has caused some to compare him to Hemingway. His collections of fiction include *Will You Please Be Quiet, Please* (1976), *What We Talk about When We Talk about Love* (1981), and *Cathedral* (1983).

"My Father's Life" first appeared in the "First Person" column of magazine in September 1984. In it, Carver remembers his father, senses the convergences and divergences of their lives, and at last, consigns his father to memory.

[1]

My dad's name was Clevie Raymond Carver. His family called him Raymond and friends called him C.R. I was named Raymond Clevie Carver Jr. I hated the "Junior" part. When I was little my dad called me Frog, which was okay. But later, like everybody else in the family, he began calling me Junior. He went on calling me this until I was thirteen or fourteen and announced that I wouldn't answer to that name any longer. So he began calling me Doc. From then [2] until his death, on June 17, 1967, he called me Doc, or else Son.

When he died, my mother telephoned my wife with the news. I was away from my family at the time, between lives, trying to enroll in the School of Library Science at the University of Iowa. When my wife answered the phone, my mother blurted out, "Raymond's dead!" For a moment, my wife thought my mother was telling her that I was dead. Then my mother made it clear *which* Raymond she was talking about and my wife said, "Thank God. I thought you meant [3] *my* Raymond."

My dad walked, hitched rides, and rode in empty boxcars when he went from Arkansas to Washington State in 1934, looking for work. I don't know whether he was pursuing a dream when he went out to Washington. I doubt it. I don't think he dreamed much. I believe he was simply looking for steady work at decent pay. Steady work was meaningful work. He picked apples for a time and then landed a construction laborer's job on the Grand Coulee Dam. After he'd put aside a little money, he bought a car and drove back to Arkansas to help his folks, my grandparents, pack up for the move west. He said later that they were about to starve down there, and this wasn't meant as a figure of speech. It was during that short while in Arkansas, in a town called Leola, that my mother met my dad on the sidewalk as he came out of a tavern. [4]

"He was drunk," she said. "I don't know why I let him talk to me. His eyes were glittery. I wish I'd had a crystal ball." They'd met once, a year or so before, at a dance. He'd had girlfriends before her, my mother told me. "Your dad always had a girlfriend, even after we married. He was my first and last. I never had 5 another man. But I didn't miss anything."

They were married by a justice of the peace on the day they left for Washington, this big, tall country girl and a farmhand-turned-construction worker. My mother spent her wedding night with my dad and his folks, all of them camped 6 beside the road in Arkansas.

In Omak, Washington, my dad and mother lived in a little place not much bigger than a cabin. My grandparents lived next door. My dad was still working on the dam, and later, with the huge turbines producing electricity and the water backed up for a hundred miles into Canada, he stood in the crowd and heard Franklin D. Roosevelt when he spoke at the construction site. "He never mentioned those guys who died building that dam," my dad said. Some of his friends 7 had died there, men from Arkansas, Oklahoma, and Missouri.

He then took a job in a sawmill in Clatskanie, Oregon, a little town alongside the Columbia River. I was born there, and my mother has a picture of my dad standing in front of the gate to the mill, proudly holding me up to face the camera. My bonnet is on crooked and about to come untied. His hat is pushed back on his forehead, and he's wearing a big grin. Was he going in to work or just finishing his shift? It doesn't matter. In either case, he had a job and a family. These 8 were his salad days.

In 1941 we moved to Yakima, Washington, where my dad went to work as a saw filer, a skilled trade he'd learned in Clatskanie. When war broke out, he was given a deferment because his work was considered necessary to the war effort. Finished lumber was in demand by the armed services, and he kept his saws so 9 sharp they could shave the hair off your arm.

After my dad had moved us to Yakima, he moved his folks into the same neighborhood. By the mid-1940s the rest of my dad's family—his brother, his sister, and her husband, as well as uncles, cousins, nephews, and most of their extended family and friends—had come out from Arkansas. All because my dad came out first. The men went to work at Boise Cascade, where my dad worked, and the women packed apples in the canneries. And in just a little while, it seemed—according to my mother—everybody was better off than my dad. "Your dad couldn't keep money," my mother said. "Money burned a hole in his pocket. 10 He was always doing for others."

The first house I clearly remember living in, at 1515 South Fifteenth Street, in Yakima, had an outdoor toilet. On Halloween night, or just any night, for the hell of it, neighbor kids, kids in their early teens, would carry our toilet away and leave it next to the road. My dad would have to get somebody to help him bring it home. Or these kids would take the toilet and stand it in somebody else's backyard. Once they actually set it on fire. But ours wasn't the only house that had an outdoor toilet. When I was old enough to know what I was doing, I threw rocks at the other toilets when I'd see someone go inside. This was called bombing the toilets. After a while, though, everyone went to indoor plumbing until, suddenly, our toilet was the last outdoor one in the neighborhood. I remember the shame I felt when my third-grade teacher, Mr. Wise, drove me home from school one day.   11 I asked him to stop at the house just before ours, claiming I lived there.

I can recall what happened one night when my dad came home late to find that my mother had locked all the doors on him from the inside. He was drunk, and we could feel the house shudder as he rattled the door. When he'd managed to force open a window, she hit him between the eyes with a colander and knocked him out. We could see him down there on the grass. For years afterward, I used to pick up this colander—it was as heavy as a rolling pin—and imagine   12 what it would feel like to be hit in the head with something like that.

It was during this period that I remember my dad taking me into the bedroom, sitting me down on the bed, and telling me that I might have to go live with my Aunt LaVon for a while. I couldn't understand what I'd done that meant I'd have to go away from home to live. But this, too—whatever prompted it—must have blown over, more or less, anyway, because we stayed together, and I didn't   13 have to go live with her or anyone else.

I remember my mother pouring his whiskey down the sink. Sometimes she'd pour it all out and sometimes, if she was afraid of getting caught, she'd only pour half of it out and then add water to the rest. I tasted some of his whiskey once   14 myself. It was terrible stuff, and I don't see how anybody could drink it.

After a long time without one, we finally got a car, in 1949 or 1950, a 1938 Ford. But it threw a rod the first week we had it, and my dad had to have the motor   15 rebuilt.

"We drove the oldest car in town," my mother said. "We could have had a Cadillac for all he spent on car repairs." One time she found someone else's tube of lipstick on the floorboard, along with a lacy handkerchief. "See this?" she said   16 to me. "Some floozy left this in the car."

Once I saw her take a pan of warm water into the bedroom where my dad was sleeping. She took his hand from under the covers and held it in the water. I stood in the doorway and watched. I wanted to know what was going on. This would make him talk in his sleep, she told me. There were things she needed to   17 know, things she was sure he was keeping from her.

Every year or so, when I was little, we would take the North Coast Limited across the Cascade Range from Yakima to Seattle and stay in the Vance Hotel and eat, I remember, at a place called the Dinner Bell Cafe. Once we went to Ivar's   18 Acres of Clams and drank glasses of warm clam broth.

In 1956, the year I was to graduate from high school, my dad quit his job at the mill in Yakima and took a job in Chester, a little sawmill town in northern California. The reasons given at the time for his taking the job had to do with a higher hourly wage and the vague promise that he might, in a few years' time, succeed to the job of head filer in this new mill. But I think, in the main, that my dad had grown restless and simply wanted to try his luck elsewhere. Things had gotten a little too predictable for him in Yakima. Also, the year before, there had been the deaths, within six months of each other, of both his parents.

But just a few days after graduation, when my mother and I were packed to move to Chester, my dad penciled a letter to say he'd been sick for a while. He didn't want us to worry, he said, but he'd cut himself on a saw. Maybe he'd got a tiny sliver of steel in his blood. Anyway, something had happened and he'd had to miss work, he said. In the same mail was an unsigned postcard from somebody down there telling my mother that my dad was about to die and that he was drinking "raw whiskey."

When we arrived in Chester, my dad was living in a trailer that belonged to the company. I didn't recognize him immediately. I guess for a moment I didn't want to recognize him. He was skinny and pale and looked bewildered. His pants wouldn't stay up. He didn't look like my dad. My mother began to cry. My dad put his arm around her and patted her shoulder vaguely, like he didn't know what this was all about, either. The three of us took up life together in the trailer, and we looked after him as best we could. But my dad was sick, and he couldn't get any better. I worked with him in the mill that summer and part of the fall. We'd get up in the mornings and eat eggs and toast while we listened to the radio, and then go out the door with our lunch pails. We'd pass through the gate together at eight in the morning, and I wouldn't see him again until quitting time. In November I went back to Yakima to be closer to my girlfriend, the girl I'd made up my mind I was going to marry.

He worked at the mill in Chester until the following February, when he collapsed on the job and was taken to the hospital. My mother asked if I would come down there and help. I caught a bus from Yakima to Chester, intending to drive them back to Yakima. But now, in addition to being physically sick, my dad was in the midst of a nervous breakdown, though none of us knew to call it that at the time. During the entire trip back to Yakima, he didn't speak, not even when asked a direct question. ("How do you feel, Raymond?" "You okay, Dad?") He'd communicate, if he communicated at all, by moving his head or by turning his palms up as if to say he didn't know or care. The only time he said anything on the trip, and for nearly a month afterward, was when I was speeding down a gravel road in Oregon and the car muffler came loose. "You were going too fast," he said.

Back in Yakima a doctor saw to it that my dad went to a psychiatrist. My mother and dad had to go on relief, as it was called, and the county paid for the psychiatrist. The psychiatrist asked my dad, "Who is the President?" He'd had a question put to him that he could answer. "Ike," my dad said. Nevertheless, they put him on the fifth floor of Valley Memorial Hospital and began giving him electroshock treatments. I was married by then and about to start my own family. My dad was still locked up when my wife went into this same hospital, just one floor down, to have our first baby. After she had delivered, I went upstairs to give my dad the news. They let me in through a steel door and showed me where I could find him. He was sitting on a couch with a blanket over his lap. *Hey,* I thought. *What in hell is happening to my dad?* I sat down next to him and told him he was a grandfather. He waited a minute and then he said, "I feel like a grandfather." That's all he said. He didn't smile or move. He was in a big room with a lot of other people. Then I hugged him, and he began to cry. [23]

Somehow he got out of there. But now came the years when he couldn't work and just sat around the house trying to figure what next and what he'd done wrong in his life that he'd wound up like this. My mother went from job to crummy job. Much later she referred to that time he was in the hospital, and those years just afterward, as "when Raymond was sick." The word *sick* was never the [24] same for me again.

In 1964, through the help of a friend, he was lucky enough to be hired on at a mill in Klamath, California. He moved down there by himself to see if he could hack it. He lived not far from the mill, in a one-room cabin not much different from the place he and my mother had started out living in when they went west. He scrawled letters to my mother, and if I called she'd read them aloud to me over the phone. In the letters, he said it was touch and go. Every day that he went to work, he felt like it was the most important day of his life. But every day, he told her, made the next day that much easier. He said for her to tell me he said hello. If he couldn't sleep at night, he said, he thought about me and the good times we used to have. Finally, after a couple of months, he regained some of his confidence. He could do the work and didn't think he had to worry that he'd let [25] anybody down ever again. When he was sure, he sent for my mother.

He'd been off from work for six years and had lost everything in that time—home, car, furniture, and appliances, including the big freezer that had been my mother's pride and joy. He'd lost his good name too—Raymond Carver was someone who couldn't pay his bills—and his self-respect was gone. He'd even lost his virility. My mother told my wife, "All during that time Raymond was sick we slept together in the same bed, but we didn't have relations. He wanted to a few times, but nothing happened. I didn't miss it, but I think he wanted to, [26] you know."

During those years I was trying to raise my own family and earn a living. But, one thing and another, we found ourselves having to move a lot. I couldn't keep track of what was going down in my dad's life. But I did have a chance one Christmas to tell him I wanted to be a writer. I might as well have told him I wanted to become a plastic surgeon. "What are you going to write about?" he wanted to know. Then as if to help me out, he said, "Write about stuff you know about. Write about some of those fishing trips we took." I said I would, but I knew I wouldn't. "Send me what you write," he said. I said I'd do that, but then I didn't. I wasn't writing anything about fishing, and I didn't think he'd particularly care about, or even necessarily understand, what I was writing in those days. [27] Besides, he wasn't a reader. Not the sort, anyway, I imagined I was writing for.

Then he died. I was a long way off, in Iowa City, with things still to say to him. I didn't have the chance to tell him goodbye, or that I thought he was doing [28] great at his new job. That I was proud of him for making a comeback.

My mother said he came in from work that night and ate a big supper. Then he sat at the table by himself and finished what was left of a bottle of whiskey, a bottle she found hidden in the bottom of the garbage under some coffee grounds a day or so later. Then he got up and went to bed, where my mother joined him a little later. But in the night she had to get up and make a bed for herself on the couch. "He was snoring so loud I couldn't sleep," she said. The next morning when she looked in on him, he was on his back with his mouth open, his cheeks caved in. *Gray-looking,* she said. She knew he was dead—she didn't need a doctor to tell her that. But she called one anyway, and then she called my wife.

Among the pictures my mother kept of my dad and herself during those early days in Washington was a photograph of him standing in front of a car, holding a beer and a stringer of fish. In the photograph he is wearing his hat back on his forehead and has this awkward grin on his face. I asked her for it and she gave it to me, along with some others. I put it up on my wall, and each time we moved, I took the picture along and put it up on another wall. I looked at it carefully from time to time, trying to figure out some things about my dad, and maybe myself in the process. But I couldn't. My dad just kept moving further and further away from me and back into time. Finally, in the course of another move, I lost the photograph. It was then that I tried to recall it, and at the same time make an attempt to say something about my dad, and how I thought that in some important ways we might be alike. I wrote the poem when I was living in an apartment house in an urban area south of San Francisco, at a time when I found myself, like my dad, having trouble with alcohol. The poem was a way of trying to connect with him.

Photograph of My Father in His Twenty-Second Year

October. Here in this dank, unfamiliar kitchen
I study my father's embarrassed young man's face.
Sheepish grin, he holds in one hand a string
of spiny yellow perch, in the other a bottle of Carlsberg beer.

In jeans and flannel shirt, he leans against the front fender of a 1934 Ford.
He would like to pose brave and hearty for his posterity,
wear his old hat cocked over his ear.
All his life my father wanted to be bold.

But the eyes give him away, and the hands
that limply offer the string of dead perch
and the bottle of beer. Father, I love you,
yet how can I say thank you, I who can't hold my liquor either
and don't even know the places to fish.

The poem is true in its particulars, except that my dad died in June and not October, as the first word of the poem says. I wanted a word with more than one syllable to it to make it linger a little. But more than that, I wanted a month appropriate to what I felt at the time I wrote the poem—month of short days and failing light, smoke in the air, things perishing. June was summer nights and days, graduations, my wedding anniversary, the birthday of one of my children. June wasn't a month your father died in.

After the service at the funeral home, after we had moved outside, a woman I didn't know came over to me and said, "He's happier where he is now." I stared at this woman until she moved away. I still remember the little knob of a hat she was wearing. Then one of my dad's cousins—I didn't know the man's name—reached out and took my hand. "We all miss him," he said, and I knew he wasn't ₃₂ saying it just to be polite.

I began to weep for the first time since receiving the news. I hadn't been able to before. I hadn't had the time, for one thing. Now, suddenly, I couldn't stop. I held my wife and wept while she said and did what she could do to comfort me ₃₃ there in the middle of that summer afternoon.

I listened to people say consoling things to my mother, and I was glad that my dad's family had turned up, had come to where he was. I thought I'd remember everything that was said and done that day and maybe find a way to tell it sometime. But I didn't. I forgot it all, or nearly. What I do remember is that I heard our name used a lot that afternoon, my dad's name and mine. But I knew they were talking about my dad. *Raymond,* these people kept saying in their beautiful voices out of my childhood. *Raymond.*

Meaning and Idea

1. How did Carver's mother and father meet? What was her reaction to him? How did she feel about him in later life?

2. Why was Carver embarrassed about his home in Yakima?

3. Trace the geographic movement of Carver's father.

4. How does Carver's father get sick? What are the results of that sickness?

5. What parallels between his own life and his father's life does Carver write about? What is his opinion of these similarities?

6. What sort of person was Carver's father? What is your reaction to him? What was Carver's?

Language, Form, Structure

1. How does Carver use *narrative summary* (see page 65) throughout this essay? How does it affect the tone of the writing? How does Carver maintain unity throughout the essay? What words or phrases are often repeated?

2. What is the use of *dialogue* in this essay? How does it enhance the narration?

3. Essentially, this essay is a chronological narrative of the life of Carver's father. Yet the paragraph just after the poem seems to break the chronology momentarily. What is the purpose of this break?

4. What is the effect of the terse line: "Then he died"?

5. Why does Carver include the full text of the poem in this essay? How is its tone different from the narrative tone? Could he have summarized the poem's contents just as easily?

6. Throughout the essay, Carver uses various colloquialisms such as *floozy, raw whiskey,* and *crummy.* Explain the meanings of these, and find and explain three other colloquialisms.

Ideas for Writing

1. Narrate the history of one of your closest family members. Attempt to follow Carver's pattern of highlighting through narrative summary.

2. Select one incident from the narration you wrote in response to question one in this section, and expand it to a two- or three-paragraph narration of its own.

3. Write a brief analysis of Carver's style as evidenced in "My Father's Life." Carver, who is primarily a fiction writer, is known for his terse, compact, narrative summary style. Do the same stylistic qualities emerge here? What are the effects of this style upon the reader? Draw specific examples from the selection to make your point.

Jacklight

Louise Erdrich

Louise Erdrich was born in Minnesota in 1954 and grew up in North Dakota as a member of the Turtle Mountain Chippewas. Her father, of German descent, and mother, part Chippewa, both worked at the Bureau of Indian Affairs School there.

Though her writing often focuses on Native Americans, she has written about both parts of her heritage. "Jacklight," the title poem from her first collection of poetry and the selection below, is an example. This theme alone indicates the complexity of the poem's topic. Erdrich has a degree in anthropology from Dartmouth College (1976) and one in creative writing from Johns Hopkins (1979).

> The same Chippewa word is used both for
> flirting and hunting game, while another
> Chippewa word connotes both using force in
> intercourse and also killing a bear with
> one's bare hands.
>
> > > *R.W. Dunning,* Social and Economic
> > > Change among the Northern Ojibwa
> > > (1959)

We have come to the edge of the woods,
out of brown grass where we slept, unseen,
out of knotted twigs, out of leaves creaked shut,
out of hiding.

At first the light wavered, glancing over us.   5
Then it clenched to a fist of light that pointed,
searched out, divided us.
Each took the beams like direct blows the heart answers.
Each of us moved forward alone.

We have come to the edge of the woods,   10
drawn out of ourselves by this night sun,
this battery of polarized acids,
that outshines the moon.

We smell them behind it
but they are faceless, invisible.   15
We smell the raw steel of their gun barrels,
mink oil on leather, their tongues of sour barley.

We smell their mothers buried chin-deep in wet dirt.
We smell their fathers with scoured knuckles,
teeth cracked from hot marrow.　　　　　　　　　　　20
We smell their sisters of crushed dogwood, bruised apples,
of fractured cups and concussions of burnt hooks.

We smell their breath steaming lightly behind the jacklight.
We smell the itch underneath the caked guts on their clothes.
We smell their minds like silver hammers　　　　　　25

cocked back, held in readiness
for the first of us to step into the open.

We have come to the edge of the woods,
out of brown grass where we slept, unseen,
out of leaves creaked shut, out of our hiding.　　　　30
We have come here too long.

It is their turn now,
their turn to follow us. Listen,
they put down their equipment.
It is useless in the tall brush.　　　　　　　　　　35
And now they take the first steps, not knowing
how deep the woods are and lightless.
How deep the woods are.

Meaning and Idea

1. Who are the "we" in the poem? Who are the "them"? What would you say was the theme of the poem?

2. A jacklight is a light used as a lure while hunting or fishing. What is the poem referring to with the use of the word? How does the title "Jacklight" help frame the meaning of the poem?

3. What does it mean that "It is their turn now," that "they" go in to the tall brush, and that "they" do not know how deep and lightless the woods are?

Language, Form, Structure

1. What is the story of this poem, that is, its narrative? Tell the story in your own words, being sure to keep the sequence clear.

2. What is the purpose of the opening quote from Dunning? How does it contribute to your understanding of the poem?

3. Which words or phrases best illustrate that theme? Why do you think the narrator repeats the phrase "How deep the woods are"?

4. Find as many separate descriptions of "we" and "they" and their actions as possible. Examine and categorize these descriptions. How do they characterize "we" and "they"?

5. Define these words from the poem: polarized; scoured; marrow.

Ideas for Writing

1. Write a narrative from the point of view of a hunter seeking game in the woods. What does the hunter see, do, think?

2. Write a narrative essay that continues the story of the speaker in the poem. What happens next?

3. Write an essay in which you analyze the effectiveness of Erdrich's poem. What main point is she trying to make? How well has she succeeded in making that point?

CROSSOVER

1. Frederick Douglass, Richard Wright, Countee Cullen, and Langston Hughes all provide windows on the experience of growing up as African-Americans. Select two or three of these writers, and write an essay that identifies common and differing elements in their portrayed experiences.

2. Judith Ortiz Cofer in "The Witch's Husband" and Edna O'Brien in "My Mother's Mother" both write about the influence of a grandmother on the narrator's sensibilities. What seems most memorable about each grandmother? Write an essay exploring each writer's assertion about her grandmother along with your own insight into your own grandmother's (or grandfather's) life and influence on you or others.

Chapter Three

■

EXEMPLIFICATION

The process of exemplification is such an essential part of the way we think, the way we talk and argue and respond, that it may seem odd to consider it as a writer's option. Simply put, exemplification means providing examples to illustrate an idea with particulars.

As a case in point, if you wanted to illustrate Dickens's skill at characterization, you could present a single well-developed example—the example of Pip, say, the main character in *Great Expectations*. Or, to make a point about the extraordinary defensive playing by the Yankees and the Braves, you might provide a blow-by-blow retelling of the pitching duel in the last inning of some crucial game between them. In each case, you'd probably infuse the one example with details. In the first, you'd draw upon paraphrases and quotations from the novel. In the second, you'd provide concrete sensory images and narrative particulars to bring to life the final breathless moments of play.

A single extended example can make a strong case; yet we are equally impressed with cumulative exemplification. Here, the writer provides a series of illustrations, the accretion of related yet different instances making the original point grow and solidify. Thus, if you wanted to use *Great Expectations* to demonstrate Dickens's talent for character development, you might deal with Miss Haversham, the convict Magwitch, and Estella, as well as with Pip. Similarly, if you were touting the Yankees' defense, you might want to point to instances of skillful fielding by the third baseman, the shortstop, and the right fielder, as well as to the masterful job on the mound. Cumulative exemplification provides the reader with many illustrations of the writer's point.

Examples move readers beyond generalizations. As a means for anchoring general ideas in specifics, examples are essential rhetorical strategies to writers of stories, novels, essays, and poems.

READING EXEMPLIFICATION

As you read instances to support a writer's position, your critical faculties should engage this question: Are these examples solid illustrations of the point? No matter how clever or amusing they may be, the examples must pertain to the writer's purpose in the essay. Sometimes the writer will list examples, expecting through accumulation of supporting information to win you over, as George Orwell does here, in order to convince us to acknowledge his good memories of Crossgates School:

> I have good memories of Crossgates, among a horde of bad ones. Sometimes on summer afternoons there were wonderful expeditions across the Downs, or to Beachy Head, where one bathed dangerously among the chalk boulders and came home covered with cuts. And there were still more wonderful midsummer evenings when, as a special treat, we were not driven off to bed as usual but allowed to wander about the grounds in the long twilight, ending up with a plunge into the swimming bath at about nine o'clock. There was the joy of waking early on summer mornings and getting in an hour's undisturbed reading (Ian Hay, Thackeray, Kipling and H.G. Wells were the favourite authors of my boyhood) in the sunlit, sleeping

dormitory. There was also cricket, which I was no good at but with which I conducted a sort of hopeless love affair up to the age of about eighteen. And there was
the pleasure of keeping caterpillars—the silky green and purple puss-moth, the
ghostly green poplar-hawk, the privet hawk, large as one's third finger, specimens
of which could be illicitly purchased for sixpence at a shop in the town—and, when
one could escape long enough from the master who was "taking the walk," there
was the excitement of dredging the dew-ponds on the Downs for enormous newts
with orange-coloured bellies. This business of being out for a walk, coming across
something of fascinating interest and then being dragged away from it by a yell
from the master, like a dog jerked onwards by the leash, is an important feature of
school life, and helps to build up the conviction, so strong in many children, that the
things you most want to do are always unattainable.

To support the general statement in the first sentence, each subsequent sentence in the paragraph provides a different example. The last sentence develops
yet another generalization from the examples. Drawing upon personal experiences, Orwell advances his examples with concrete sensory details—"bathed
dangerously among the chalk boulders," "in the silent, sleeping dormitory," "the
silky green and purple puss-moth"—but he does not expand any one example to
any particular degree. Notice how deftly he moves us from one instance to the
next. Words and phrases like "And then there were still more," "there was also,"
"And then there was" link the instances by repetition and transitions.

In this selection from *Manchild in the Promised Land,* Claude Brown wants
to convince us of the strange things he saw down South, but he uses only a few
examples, each somewhat more expanded than Orwell's:

Down South seemed like a dream when I was on the train going back to New York.
I saw a lot of things down South that I never saw in my whole life before and most
of them I didn't ever want to see again. I saw a great big old burly black man hit a
pig in the head with the back of an ax. The pig screamed, oink-oinked a few times,
lay down, and started kicking and bleeding . . . and died. When he was real little,
I used to chase him, catch him, pick him up, and play catch with him. He was a
greedy old pig, but I used to like him. One day when it was real cold, I ate a piece
of that pig, and I still liked him. One day I saw Grandma kill a rattlesnake with a
hoe. She chopped the snake's head off in the front yard, and I sat on the porch and
watched the snake's body keep wiggling till it was nighttime. And I saw an old
brown hound dog named Old Joe eat a rat one day, right out in the front yard. He
caught the rat in the woodpile and started tearing him open. Old Joe was eating
everything in the rat. He ate something that looked like the yellow part in an egg,
and I didn't eat eggs for a long time after that. I saw a lady rat have a lot of little
baby rats on a pile of tobacco leaves. She had to be a lady, because my first-grade
teacher told a girl that ladies don't cry about little things, and the rat had eleven little hairless pink rats, and she didn't even squeak about it.

I made a gun down South out of a piece of wood, some tape, a piece of tire-
tube rubber, a nail, some wire, a piece of pipe, and a piece of door hinge. And I saw
nothing but blood where my right thumbnail used to be after I shot it for the first

time. That nail grew back, little by little. I saw a lot of people who had roots worked on them, but I never saw anybody getting roots worked on them.

Down South sure was a crazy place, and it was good to be going back to New York.

Here, too, images of color, sound, and action make the instances come alive. Note how Brown develops the example of the pig by jerking us back and forth in time. In wrenching the chronology, he sustains the shock of the pig's death. The example takes on special significance because of the temporally disconnected memories the writer associates with the murdered animal. Brown uses *and* as a transitional device at the start of several sentences. The repeated phrase "down South" also helps to connect the examples smoothly.

Both Orwell and Brown write from personal experience and support their examples with concrete sensory details. However, many writers do not call exclusively upon events in their lives; and they use other kinds of details to support a point through exemplification. You should be aware of some of these techniques as you read. Writers will draw upon facts, the language of numbers, statistics, and cases. They will draw upon quotations or paraphrases chosen from experts in the field. They will summarize. They will cite historical or scientific evidence to advance their ideas. Whatever the nature of the details, good writing always provides them, and you should pay careful attention to the kind of concrete support that a writer will use to make the instances come alive. Note the details in this paragraph from Theodore Ziolkowski's "The Existential Anxieties of Engineering":

> Novels portraying the moral anxiety of engineering did not cease to be written after World War I, of course. Literary genres do not disappear so quickly. Some thirty years later Frederick Philip Grove's *Master of the Mill* (1944) recapitulates all the characteristics of the genre. In this powerful Canadian classic, the engineer Samuel Clark learns that his family's milling empire, which supplies 90 percent of the nation's flour, was founded by a criminal act of his father. Clark is unsuccessful in his efforts to assume the responsibility, to compensate for the crime by social welfare, and to protect his own son from the inherited guilt. His plans for social reform fail; the workers are displaced by technology; and his son is shot during a strike of the enraged millers. By the time Clark dies, he realizes that the great pyramidal mill of seventeen stories had always ruled his destiny and determined his every action. "The history of the mill had been his history"—as much so as the submarines, tunnels, and bridges of the earlier novels. Having destroyed its creator and disenfranchised its former workers, it survives as a symbol of the engineer's moral anxiety.

In the first two sentences Ziolkowski asserts that post–World War I novels about "the moral anxiety of engineering" did not vanish. As an example, he presents Grove's 1944 *Master of the Mill;* and then, to support the example, Ziolkowski provides specific details from that novel, including a quotation in the next to the last sentence. It is interesting to see here how only one example, richly expanded with detail, serves very nicely to make the point.

Which writer—Orwell, Brown, or Ziolkowski—has used the right number of examples and the appropriate degree of detail? Of course, there is no answer to that question. As a critical reader, you need to decide for yourself whether the examples and supporting details clarify the point. If you're left just short of being convinced or are overwhelmed with more than you need, the writer may have seriously misjudged his audience.

In addition to the quantity and quality of the examples, you should look also for their manner of arrangement. Does the writer present the instances chronologically—in the order in which they occurred? Does he or she present them according to importance, building from the least to the most significant example? Do you detect any logic in the scheme of arrangement that the writer has used? Why are the examples presented in the order that you see them? As you read the selections in this chapter, in particular Walt Whitman's "There Was a Child Went Forth," Maxine Kingston's "Family Ghosts," and James Thurber's "Courtship through the Ages," you should consider the relation between the examples and their method of arrangement.

WRITING EXEMPLIFICATION

Many topics lend themselves to development through examples, and as you think about your topic, you should be able to list a number of instances to use as possible means of support in your essay. Suppose you wanted to write about the personality of your old family car, an '82 Chevy, with which you associate many happy memories. You could develop an essay through description alone, showing your reader with careful, loving details all the memorable features of this automobile. Or you could narrate one particular trip you took in which your beat-up sedan served as vehicle, living room, dining room, and bedroom on a slow trip to Maine from your home in Dallas. Or, if you wanted to point to a number of pleasant associations, you would reach for exemplification, using two or three instances to show readers the range of memories this car provides for you. The point here is that the topic and your view of how to develop it will suggest an appropriate rhetorical scheme. You start with a sense of your topic and an idea of your purpose in writing about it, and then you consider the strategy that will help you best achieve your goal.

As with all the rhetorical models you're exploring in this book, try not to think of exemplification as an isolated form. Often you see it working hand in hand with description, narration, comparison and contrast, or definition. In writing an exemplification paper about your memories of your old auto, no doubt you'd weave in concrete sensory details. You might tell two or three brief stories about the car, and you might compare and contrast the instances with each other. Again, the rhetorical form you choose should always serve your purpose and suit your intended audience.

PURPOSE AND AUDIENCE

The nature of the instances you choose for your exemplification paper will depend upon what your aim is in your essay and upon who your intended reader is. As we pointed out earlier, it's hard to find a topic that cannot be approached through exemplification, so you probably won't have much trouble in identifying an appropriate subject or in generating examples to support your ideas. Sources for examples are many. The most familiar, of course, is personal experience. Thus, as a start, you might want to search your memory, your own personal past history, to identify instances you could expand with details. Or you could use a topic idea to stimulate new experiences that you could record accurately and share with your readers. To provide examples of the crush of holiday shoppers at a local mall, you could try to recall those harried buyers who'd impressed you during your last shopping spree; but you might tap a fresher source of details if you returned to the mall, pencil in hand, to observe the hustle and bustle around you carefully. Many writers will draw upon their imaginations for details, spinning hypotheses, metaphors, or analogies to support an issue with a pointed example. Comparing one shopper, as she trails down the aisle in a clothing store, to a long-necked crane poking and pecking and staring at racks of blouses and dresses might make your point creatively and delight your readers.

In addition to personal experience, all you read in books, newspapers, and magazines, all you hear on the radio, in class, out on the street, and all you see in the movies and on television are remarkable sources for examples to use in your writing. When you have identified a topic, have thought of what you wish to say about it, and have considered what your audience might expect in your essay, don't hesitate to talk your idea over with friends; to watch some local programs on your Public Broadcasting System or on network television; or to check your topic in the card catalogue, the *Readers' Guide for Periodical Literature,* or the *Social Science and Humanities Index* in your library. Your audience might expect solid details drawn from nonexperiential sources, and your own purpose in writing might be served by examples taken from careful investigation. If you wanted to write about those holiday shoppers for the Chamber of Commerce, a group you wanted to convince of the need for a better safety plan during peak shopping hours, you'd want to draw upon statistics of accidents and crimes in former years, upon testimony by store owners, managers, and customers at the mall, and upon public records of supplemental budgets for part-time police protection in the mall parking lot and in open areas during December. Intent on persuading your readers to take some course of action, and knowing them to respond to hard data, you might be making a mistake to draw only upon your own personal experiences to make your point.

PROCESS

Jot down some ideas in a list or a scratch outline to help you decide on a topic and a purpose for writing. With some record of your thoughts on paper, you might find an informal outline or some other grouping system useful before you try a draft. Cluster together any ideas that are related to the same example. As in most writing tasks, a thesis sentence will be very helpful, and you should spend considerable time writing a clear one even though you may decide ultimately not to use it in your final draft. In most cases your thesis will be a generalization that your examples will expand.

Keeping audience and purpose in mind, decide on how many examples you need to hold your readers' attention. Will you offer one single instance expanded with precise and appropriate details? Will you offer three or four examples each with some supporting information? Will you offer a simple listing in which you provide numerous examples, none of which is backed up to any large degree with details? Take into account too the nature of the kinds of examples and the details your essay will require. Will you use images of concrete sensory details to anchor your examples? Will you use statistics, cases, or other data? Will you quote from a book, a television program, or an actual interview? Will you summarize a song or a short story or a lab report? Will you *invent* an example? When you give a draft of your paper to a friend, ask him or her to tell you whether your examples are believable, whether they suit your point, and whether you've developed them with adequate detail.

As we suggested before, you'll have to make a decision about how to arrange the examples for the strongest presentation. If they involve narration, a simple chronological arrangement might serve you best. In order to build slowly to the most dramatic instance, many writers will choose an arrangement by importance, saving the most crucial example for last. Whatever your method of arrangement, aim for coherence by linking your examples so that readers move smoothly from instance to instance. To achieve a coherent essay, you'll find that transitions, used moderately, will be useful, as will other connecting devices, such as pronouns, repetition, and coordinate structures.

Keep in mind that the particulars in your essay will hold your readers' attention. No matter how thoughtful or original or surprising your generalizations may be, specific instances make those generalizations more immediate, interesting, and, finally, understandable.

SUMMING UP: EXEMPLIFICATION

Reading Exemplification

- *Exemplification* means the provision of examples to illustrate an idea with particulars.

- Determine whether the writer has provided examples that solidly illustrate the point.

- Determine the writer's thesis and how it lends itself to examples as supporting details.

- Weigh the writer's use of transitional expressions and repetition to connect the examples smoothly.

- Examine the details used to support the point made through exemplification. Writers may use concrete sensory detail, statistics, or cases; they may use quotations or paraphrases from reliable sources; they may summarize or cite historical or scientific evidence.

- Identify how the writer has arranged the details.

Writing Exemplification

- As you define your topic, list a number of instances to use as possible means of support for your essay.

- Consider your aim and your audience, and produce an appropriate thesis that allows the use of exemplification.

- Choose from a variety of sources for your examples, depending upon your aim. These sources may include personal experience; quotations and paraphrases drawn from books, periodicals, and other media; and statistics and cases.

- Share thoughts and ideas with reliable friends and classmates as you develop your topic.

- Make a scratch outline; group together any ideas related to the same example.

- Determine the number of examples you need to hold your readers' attention.

- Determine the most appropriate method of arranging your examples for the strongest presentation.

- Show an early draft to someone you trust, and weigh carefully any advice or recommendations about how to improve your paper.

- To achieve coherence, link your examples so that readers move smoothly from instance to instance; use transitions moderately to connect ideas.

Family Ghosts

Maxine Hong Kingston

Maxine Hong Kingston was born in Stockton, California, in 1940, the daughter of a scholar who has also been a laundry worker and of a midwife who has done field work. Kingston's writing, which focuses on the Chinese and Chinese-American experience, has been aptly described by Susan Cinner as a blend of "myth, legend, history and autobiography into a genre of her own invention." Her honors include the National Book Critics' Circle Award in 1976 for *The Woman Warrior,* which was also named by *Time* magazine as among the top ten nonfiction works of the decade 1970–1980.

In "Family Ghosts," Maxine Hong Kingston uses description, narration, and flashback to set the stage for a ghost story. She derives her tale from ancient Chinese legends, of *Sit Dom Kuei*—semimagical words for which she can better give examples than translations or definitions.

When the thermometer in our laundry reached one hundred and   1
eleven degrees on summer afternoons, either my mother or my father would say that it was time to tell another ghost story so that we could get some good chills up our backs. My parents, my brothers, sisters, great-uncle, and "Third Aunt," who wasn't really our aunt but a fellow villager, someone else's third aunt, kept the presses crashing and hissing and shouted out the stories. Those were our successful days, when so much laundry came in, my mother did not have to pick tomatoes. For breaks we changed from pressing to sorting.

"One twilight," my mother began, and already the chills traveled my back and   2
crossed my shoulders; the hair rose at the nape and the back of the legs, "I was walking home after doctoring a sick family. To get home I had to cross a footbridge. In China the bridges are nothing like the ones in Brooklyn and San Francisco. This one was made from rope, laced and knotted as if by magpies. Actually it had been built by men who had returned after harvesting sea swallow nests in Malaya. They had had to swing over the faces of the Malayan cliffs in baskets they had woven themselves. Though this bridge pitched and swayed in the updraft, no one had ever fallen into the river, which looked like a bright scratch at the bottom of the canyon, as if the Queen of Heaven had swept her great silver hairpin across the earth as well as the sky."

One twilight, just as my mother stepped on the bridge, two smoky columns   3
spiraled up taller than she. Their swaying tops hovered over her head like white cobras, one at either handrail. From stillness came a wind rushing between the smoke spindles. A high sound entered her temple bones. Through the twin whirlwinds she could see the sun and the river, the river twisting in circles, the trees upside down. The bridge moved like a ship, sickening. The earth dipped. She collapsed to the wooden slats, a ladder up the sky, her fingers so weak she could not grip the rungs. The wind dragged her hair behind her, then whipped it forward

across her face. Suddenly the smoke spindles disappeared. The world righted itself, and she crossed to the other side. She looked back, but there was nothing there. She used the bridge often, but she did not encounter those ghosts again.

"They were Sit Dom Kuei," said Great-Uncle. "Sit Dom Kuei."   4

"Yes, of course," said my mother. "Sit Dom Kuei."   5

I keep looking in dictionaries under those syllables. "Kuei" means "ghost,"   6
but I don't find any other words that make sense. I only hear my great-uncle's river-pirate voice, the voice of a big man who had killed someone in New York or Cuba, make the sounds—"Sit Dom Kuei." How do they translate?

When the Communists issued their papers on techniques for combating   7
ghosts, I looked for "Sit Dom Kuei." I have not found them described anywhere, although now I see that my mother won in ghost battle because she can eat anything—quick, pluck out the carp's eyes, one for Mother and one for Father. All heroes are bold toward food. In the research against ghost fear published by the Chinese Academy of Science is the story of a magistrate's servant, Kao Chung, a capable eater who in 1683 ate five cooked chickens and drank ten bottles of wine that belonged to the sea monster with branching teeth. The monster had arranged its food around a fire on the beach and started to feed when Kao Chung attacked. The swan-feather sword he wrested from this monster can be seen in the Wentung County Armory in Shantung today.

Another big eater was Chou Yi-han of Changchow, who fried a ghost. It was   8
a meaty stick when he cut it up and cooked it. But before that it had been a woman out at night.

Chen Luan-feng, during the Yuan Ho era of the T'ang dynasty (A.D. 806–820),   9
ate yellow croaker and pork together, which the thunder god had forbidden. But Chen wanted to incur thunderbolts during drought. The first time he ate, the thunder god jumped out of the sky, its legs like old trees. Chen chopped off the left one. The thunder god fell to the earth, and the villagers could see that it was a blue pig or bear with horns and fleshy wings. Chen leapt on it, prepared to chop its neck and bite its throat, but the villagers stopped him. After that, Chen lived apart as a rainmaker, neither relatives nor the monks willing to bring lightning upon themselves. He lived in a cave, and for years whenever there was drought the villagers asked him to eat yellow croaker and pork together, and he did.

The most fantastic eater of them all was Wei Pang, a scholar-hunter of the   10
Ta Li era of the T'ang dynasty (A.D. 766–779). He shot and cooked rabbits and birds, but he could also eat scorpions, snakes, cockroaches, worms, slugs, beetles, and crickets. Once he spent the night in a house that had been abandoned because its inhabitants feared contamination from the dead man next door. A shining, twinkling sphere came flying through the darkness at Wei. He felled it with three true arrows—the first making the thing crackle and flame; the second dimming it; and the third putting out its lights, sputter. When his servant came running in with a lamp, Wei saw his arrows sticking in a ball of flesh entirely covered with eyes, some rolled back to show the dulling whites. He and the servant pulled out the arrows and cut up the ball into little pieces. The servant cooked the morsels in sesame oil, and the wonderful aroma made Wei laugh. They ate half, saving half to show the household, which would return now.

Big eaters win. When other passers-by stepped around the bundle wrapped ₁₁ in white silk, the anonymous scholar of Hanchow took it home. Inside were three silver ingots and a froglike evil, which sat on the ingots. The scholar laughed at it and chased it off. That night two frogs the size of year-old babies appeared in his room. He clubbed them to death, cooked them, and ate them with white wine. The next night a dozen frogs, together the size of a pair of year-old babies, jumped from the ceiling. He ate all twelve for dinner. The third night thirty small frogs were sitting on his mat and staring at him with their frog eyes. He ate them too. Every night for a month smaller but more numerous frogs came so that he always had the same amount to eat. Soon his floor was like the healthy banks of a pond in spring when the tadpoles, having just turned, sprang in the wet grass. "Get a hedgehog to help eat," cried his family. "I'm as good as a hedgehog," the scholar said, laughing. And at the end of the month the frogs stopped coming, leaving the scholar with the white silk and silver ingots.

Meaning and Idea

1. What was the occasion for Kingston's mother telling a ghost story? What was the desired effect? Summarize the ghost story in your own words.

2. Why did her mother "win" the ghost battle? What generalization does Kingston make about those who conquer ghosts? How many examples of "ghost conquerors" does she offer?

3. Not only does Kingston provide examples of "ghost conquerors," but also within each example she gives instances of different ghost manifestations. List them in the order that they appear. Where does she provide examples of what the "ghosts" really may have been?

Language, Form, Structure

1. How does Kingston arrange her examples of "heroes" against ghosts? Name the examples she provides.

2. Midway through her mother's story, the narrator shifts. From whom to whom does the narration shift? What is the effect of this change? There is also a significant shift in the time sequence in this essay. Where does it occur? What grammatical change signals the shift? Why does it occur?

3. What transitions appear between each example? How does the first sentence of the last paragraph act as a transition?

4. List and define five unusual animal names used in this essay.

Ideas for Writing

1. Have you ever had a supernatural experience, or do you know someone who has? Tell about it and provide examples of what was seen, heard, or felt as supernatural.

2. What was your favorite kind of story when you were a child? Write an essay in which you exemplify this type of story and the purposes it served for you besides pure enjoyment.

3. Kingston's writing often demonstrates a clash of cultures, an old-world Chinese culture and a new-world American culture. Using examples drawn from "Family Ghosts," show whether or not you agree with this point.

The Black Death

Barbara Tuchman

Barbara Tuchman (1912–1989) made history and historical biography an entertaining topic for readers for decades. She attended Radcliffe, where she studied literature and history. Her love of history and of books was what helped her become one of the most prolific and popular historians of the twentieth century.

She received Pulitzer Prizes for *The Guns of August* (1962), about World War I, and for *Stilwell and the American Experience in China* (1971). The following selection comes from *A Distant Mirror: The Calamitous Fourteenth Century* (1978). The detailed and specific way in which she illustrates the Black Plague is a commanding instance of exemplification.

*I*n October 1347, two months after the fall of Calais, Genoese trading ships put into the harbor of Messina in Sicily with dead and dying men at the oars. The ships had come from the Black Sea port of Caffa (now Feodosiya) in the Crimea, where the Genoese maintained a trading post. The diseased sailors showed strange black swellings about the size of an egg or an apple in the armpits and groin. The swellings oozed blood and pus and were followed by spreading boils and black blotches on the skin from internal bleeding. The sick suffered severe pain and died quickly within five days of the first symptoms. As the disease spread, other symptoms of continuous fever and spitting of blood appeared instead of the swellings or buboes. These victims coughed and sweated heavily and died even more quickly, within three days or less, sometimes in 24 hours. In both types everything that issued from the body—breath, sweat, blood from the buboes and lungs, bloody urine, and blood-blackened excrement—smelled foul. Depression and despair accompanied the physical symptoms, and before the end, "death is seen seated on the face."[1]

The disease was bubonic plague, present in two forms: one that infected the bloodstream, causing the buboes and internal bleeding, and was spread by contact; and a second, more virulent pneumonic type that infected the lungs and was spread by respiratory infection. The presence of both at once caused the high mortality and speed of contagion. So lethal was the disease that cases were known of persons going to bed well and dying before they woke, of doctors catching the illness at a bedside and dying before the patient. So rapidly did it spread from one to another that to a French physician, Simon de Covino, it seemed as if one sick person "could infect the whole world."[2] The malignity of the pestilence appeared more terrible because its victims knew no prevention and no remedy.

[1]Anna M. Campbell, *The Black Death and Men of Learning* (New York: Columbia University Press, 1931), 80.
[2]Francis Aidan Gasquet, Abbot, *The Black Death of 1348 and 1349,* 2nd ed. (London, 1908), 41.

    The physical suffering of the disease and its aspects of evil mystery were ₃
expressed in a strange Welsh lament which saw "death coming into our midst like
black smoke, a plague which cuts off the young, a rootless phantom which has no
mercy for fair countenance. Woe is me of the shilling in the armpit! It is seething,
terrible . . . a head that gives pain and causes a loud cry . . . a painful angry
knob. . . . Great is its seething like a burning cinder . . . a grievous thing of
ashy color." Its eruption is ugly like the "seeds of black peas, broken fragments
of brittle sea-coal . . . the early ornaments of black death, cinders of the peelings
of the cockle weed, a mixed multitude, a black plague like half-pence, like
berries. . . ."³

    Rumors of a terrible plague supposedly arising in China and spreading ₄
through Tartary (Central Asia) to India and Persia, Mesopotamia, Syria, Egypt,
and all of Asia Minor had reached Europe in 1346. They told of a death toll so
devastating that all of India was said to be depopulated, whole territories covered
by dead bodies, other areas with no one left alive. As added up by Pope Clement
VI at Avignon, the total of reported dead reached 23,840,000. In the absence of a
concept of contagion, no serious alarm was felt in Europe until the trading ships
brought their black burden of pestilence into Messina while other infected ships
from the Levant carried it to Genoa and Venice.

    By January 1348 it penetrated France via Marseille, and North Africa via ₅
Tunis. Shipborne along coasts and navigable rivers, it spread westward from Marseille through the ports of Languedoc to Spain and northward up the Rhone to Avignon, where it arrived in March. It reached Narbonne, Montpellier, Carcassonne,
and Toulouse between February and May, and at the same time in Italy spread to
Rome and Florence and their hinterlands. Between June and August it reached Bordeaux, Lyon, and Paris, spread to Burgundy and Normandy, and crossed the Channel from Normandy into southern England. From Italy during the same summer it
crossed the Alps into Switzerland and reached eastward to Hungary.

    In a given area the plague accomplished its kill within four to six months ₆
and then faded, except in the larger cities, where, rooting into the close-quartered
population, it abated during the winter, only to reappear in spring and rage for
another six months.

    In 1349 it resumed in Paris, spread to Picardy, Flanders, and the Low Coun- ₇
tries, and from England to Scotland and Ireland as well as to Norway, where a
ghost ship with a cargo of wool and a dead crew drifted offshore until it ran
aground near Bergen. From there the plague passed into Sweden, Denmark, Prus-
sia, Iceland, and as far as Greenland. Leaving a strange pocket of immunity in
Bohemia, and Russia unattacked until 1351, it had passed from most of Europe
by mid-1350. Although the mortality rate was erratic, ranging from one fifth in
some places to nine tenths or almost total elimination in others, the overall estimate of modern demographers has settled—for the area extending from India to
Iceland—around the same figure expressed in Froissart's casual words: "a third

³Philip Ziegler, *The Black Death* (New York, 1969), 190.

of the world died." His estimate, the common one at the time, was not an inspired guess but a borrowing of St. John's figure for mortality from plague in Revelation, the favorite guide to human affairs of the Middle Ages.

A third of Europe would have meant about 20 million deaths. No one knows in truth how many died. Contemporary reports were an awed impression, not an accurate count. In crowded Avignon, it was said, 400 died daily; 7,000 houses emptied by death were shut up; a single graveyard received 11,000 corpses in six weeks; half the city's inhabitants reportedly died, including 9 cardinals or one third of the total, and 70 lesser prelates. Watching the endlessly passing death carts, chroniclers let normal exaggeration take wings and put the Avignon death toll at 62,000 and even at 120,000, although the city's total population was probably less than 50,000.

When graveyards filled up, bodies at Avignon were thrown into the Rhone until mass burial pits were dug for dumping the corpses. In London in such pits corpses piled up in layers until they overflowed. Everywhere reports speak of the sick dying too fast for the living to bury. Corpses were dragged out of homes and left in front of doorways. Morning light revealed new piles of bodies. In Florence the dead were gathered up by the Compagnia della Misericordia—founded in 1244 to care for the sick—whose members wore red robes and hoods masking the face except for the eyes. When their efforts failed, the dead lay putrid in the streets for days at a time. When no coffins were to be had, the bodies were laid on boards, two or three at once, to be carried to graveyards or common pits. Families dumped their own relatives into the pits, or buried them so hastily and thinly "that dogs dragged them forth and devoured their bodies."[4]

Amid accumulating death and fear of contagion, people died without last rites and were buried without prayers, a prospect that terrified the last hours of the stricken. A bishop in England gave permission to laymen to make confession to each other as was done by the Apostles, "or if no man is present then even to a woman," and if no priest could be found to administer extreme unction, "then faith must suffice."[5] Clement VI found it necessary to grant remissions of sin to all who died of the plague because so many were unattended by priests. "And no bells tolled," wrote a chronicler of Siena, "and nobody wept no matter what his loss because almost everyone expected death. . . . And people said and believed, "This is the end of the world.""[6]

In Paris, where the plague lasted through 1349, the reported death rate was 800 a day, in Pisa 500, in Vienna 500 to 600. The total dead in Paris numbered 50,000 or half the population. Florence, weakened by the famine of 1347, lost three to four fifths of its citizens, Venice two thirds, Hamburg and Bremen, though smaller in size, about the same proportion. Cities, as centers of transportation, were more likely to be affected than villages, although once a village

[4]Ziegler, *The Black Death,* 58.
[5]Ziegler, *The Black Death,* 125.
[6]Ferdinand Schevill, *Siena: The History of a Medieval Commune* (New York, 1909), 211.

was infected, its death rate was equally high. At Givry, a prosperous village in Burgundy of 1,200 to 1,500 people, the parish register records 615 deaths in the space of fourteen weeks, compared to an average of thirty deaths a year in the previous decade.[7] In three villages of Cambridgeshire, manorial records show a death rate of 47 percent, 57 percent, and in one case 70 percent.[8] When the last survivors, too few to carry on, moved away, a deserted village sank back into the wilderness and disappeared from the map altogether, leaving only a grass-covered ghostly outline to show where mortals once had lived.

In enclosed places such as monasteries and prisons, the infection of one person usually meant that of all, as happened in the Franciscan convents of Carcassonne and Marseille, where every inmate without exception died. Of the 140 Dominicans at Montpellier only seven survived. Petrarch's brother Gherardo, member of a Carthusian monastery, buried the prior and 34 fellow monks one by one, sometimes three a day, until he was left alone with his dog and fled to look for a place that would take him in.[9] Watching every comrade die, men in such places could not but wonder whether the strange peril that filled the air had not been sent to exterminate the human race. In Kilkenny, Ireland, Brother John Clyn of the Friars Minor, another monk left alone among dead men, kept a record of what had happened lest "things which should be remembered perish with time and vanish from the memory of those who come after us." Sensing "the whole world, as it were, placed within the grasp of the Evil One," and waiting for death to visit him too, he wrote, "I leave parchment to continue this work, if perchance any man survive and any of the race of Adam escape this pestilence and carry on the work which I have begun."[10] Brother John, as noted by another hand, died of the pestilence, but he foiled oblivion.

The largest cities of Europe, with populations of about 100,000, were Paris and Florence, Venice and Genoa. At the next level, with more than 50,000, were Ghent and Bruges in Flanders, Milan, Bologna, Rome, Naples, and Palermo, and Cologne. London hovered below 50,000, the only city in England except York with more than 10,000. At the level of 20,000 to 50,000 were Bordeaux, Toulouse, Montpellier, Marseille, and Lyon in France, Barcelona, Seville, and Toledo in Spain, Siena, Pisa, and other secondary cities in Italy, and the Hanseatic trading cities of the Empire. The plague raged through them all, killing anywhere from one third to two thirds of their inhabitants. Italy, with a total population of 10 to 11 million, probably suffered the heaviest toll. Following the Florentine bankruptcies, the crop failures and workers' riots of 1346–47, the revolt of Cola di Rienzi that plunged Rome into anarchy, the plague came as the peak of successive calamities. As if the world were indeed in the grasp of the Evil One, its

---

[7]Yves Renouard, *"La Peste noirs de 1348–50," Rev. de Paris* (March, 1959), 111.
[8]John Saltmarsh, "Plague and Economic Decline in England in the Later Middle Ages," *Cambridge Historical Journal,* vol. VII, no. 1, 1941
[9]Morris Bishop, *Petrarch and His World* (Bloomington: Indiana University Press, 1963), 273.
[10]Ziegler, *The Black Death,* 195.

first appearance on the European mainland in January 1348 coincided with a fearsome earthquake that carved a path of wreckage from Naples up to Venice. Houses collapsed, church towers toppled, villages were crushed, and the destruction reached as far as Germany and Greece. Emotional response, dulled by horrors, underwent a kind of atrophy epitomized by the chronicler who wrote, "And in these days was burying without sorrowe and wedding without friendschippe."[11]

In Siena, where more than half the inhabitants died of the plague, work was abandoned on the great cathedral, planned to be the largest in the world, and never resumed, owing to loss of workers and master masons and "the melancholy and grief" of the survivors. The cathedral's truncated transept still stands in permanent witness to the sweep of death's scythe. Agnolo di Tura, a chronicler of Siena, recorded the fear of contagion that froze every other instinct. "Father abandoned child, wife husband, one brother another," he wrote, "for this plague seemed to strike through the breath and sight. And so they died. And no one could be found to bury the dead for money or friendship. . . . And I, Angolo di Tura, called the Fat, buried my five children with my own hands, and so did many others likewise."[12]

There were many to echo his account of inhumanity and few to balance it, for the plague was not the kind of calamity that inspired mutual help. Its loathsomeness and deadliness did not herd people together in mutual distress, but only prompted their desire to escape each other. "Magistrates and notaries refused to come and make the wills of the dying" reported a Franciscan friar of Piazza in Sicily; what was worse, "even the priests did not come to hear their confessions."[13] A clerk of the Archbishop of Canterbury reported the same of English priests who "turned away from the care of their benefices from fear of death."[14] Cases of parents deserting children and children their parents were reported across Europe from Scotland to Russia.[15] The calamity chilled the hearts of men, wrote Boccaccio in his famous account of the plague in Florence that serves as introduction to the *Decameron*. "One man shunned another . . . kinsfolk held aloof, brother was forsaken by brother, oftentimes husband by wife; nay, what is more, and scarcely to be believed, fathers and mothers were found to abandon their own children to their fate, untended, unvisited as if they had been strangers." Exaggeration and literary pessimism were common in the 14th century, but the Pope's physician, Guy de Chauliac, was a sober, careful observer who reported the same phenomenon: "A father did not visit his son, nor the son his father. Charity was dead."[16]

Yet not entirely. In Paris, according to the chronicler Jean de Venette, the nuns of the Hotel Dieu or municipal hospital, "having no fear of death, tended the sick with all sweetness and humility." New nuns repeatedly took the places of

[11]George Deaux, *The Black Death, 1347* (London, 1969), 143.
[12]Ziegler, *The Black Death,* 58.
[13]Deaux, *The Black Death,* 49.
[14]Ziegler, *The Black Death,* 261.
[15]J. F. C. Hecker, *The Epidemics of the Middle Ages* (London, 1844), 30.
[16]Gasquet, *The Black Death of 1348 and 1349,* 50–51.

those who died, until the majority "many times renewed by death now rest in peace with Christ as we may piously believe."[17]

When the plague entered northern France in July 1348, it settled first in Normandy and, checked by winter, gave Picardy a deceptive interim until the next summer. Either in mourning or warning, black flags were flown from church towers of the worst-stricken villages of Normandy. "And in that time," wrote a monk of the abbey of Fourcarment, "the mortality was so great among the people of Normandy that those of Picardy mocked them." The same unneighborly reaction was reported of the Scots, separated by a winter's immunity from the English. Delighted to hear of the disease that was scourging the "southrons," they gathered forces for an invasion, "laughing at their enemies." Before they could move, the savage mortality fell upon them too, scattering some in death and the rest in panic to spread the infection as they fled.[18]

In Picardy in the summer of 1349 the pestilence penetrated the castle of Coucy to kill Enguerrand's mother, Catherine, and her new husband. Whether her nine-year-old son escaped by chance or was perhaps living elsewhere with one of his guardians is unrecorded.[19] In nearby Amiens, tannery workers, responding quickly to losses in the labor force, combined to bargain for higher wages.[20] In another place villagers were seen dancing to drums and trumpets, and on being asked the reason, answered that, seeing their neighbors die day by day while their village remained immune, they believed that they could keep the plague from entering "by the jollity that is in us. That is why we dance."[21] Further north in Tournai on the border of Flanders, Gilles li Muisis, Abbot of St. Martin's, kept one of the epidemic's most vivid accounts. The passing bells rang all day and all night, he recorded, because sextons were anxious to obtain their fees while they could. Filled with the sound of mourning, the city became oppressed by fear, so that the authorities forbade the tolling of bells and the wearing of black and restricted funeral services to two mourners. The silencing of funeral bells and of criers' announcements of deaths was ordained by most cities. Siena imposed a fine on the wearing of mourning clothes by all except widows.

Flight was the chief recourse of those who could afford it or arrange it. The rich fled to their country places like Boccaccio's young patricians of Florence, who settled in a pastoral palace "removed on every side from the roads" with "wells of cool water and vaults of rare wines." The urban poor died in their burrows, "and only the stench of their bodies informed neighbors of their deaths." That the poor were more heavily afflicted than the rich was clearly remarked at the time, in the north as in the south. A Scottish chronicler, John of Fordun, stated

[17]Jean Birdsall, trans., and Richard A. Newhall, ed., *Chronicle of Jean de Venette* (New York: Columbia University Press, 1853), 49.

[18]Gasquet, *The Black Death of 1348 and 1349,* 53, and Ziegler, *The Black Death,* 198.

[19]*L'Art de vérifier les dates des faits historiques,* par un Religieux de la Congregation de St.-Maur. vol. XII (Paris, 1818), 237.

[20]Gasquet, *The Black Death of 1348 and 1349,* 57.

[21]Paulin Paris, ed., *Grandes Croniques de France,* vol. VI (Paris, 1838), 486–87.

flatly that the pest "attacked especially the meaner sort and common people— seldom the magnates."[22] Simon de Covino of Montpellier made the same observation. He ascribed it to the misery and want and hard lives that made the poor more susceptible, which was half the truth.[23] Close contact and lack of sanitation was the unrecognized other half. It was noticed too that the young died in greater proportion than the old; Simon de Covino compared the disappearance of youth to the withering of flowers in the fields.[24]

In the countryside peasants dropped dead on the roads, in the fields, in their houses. Survivors in growing helplessness fell into apathy, leaving ripe wheat uncut and livestock untended. Oxen and asses, sheep and goats, pigs and chickens ran wild and they too, according to local reports, succumbed to the pest. English sheep, bearers of the precious wool, died throughout the country. The chronicler Henry Knighton, canon of Leicester Abbey, reported 5,000 dead in one field alone, "their bodies so corrupted by the plague that neither beast nor bird would touch them," and spreading an appalling stench.[25] In the Austrian Alps wolves came down to prey upon sheep and then, "as if alarmed by some invisible warning, turned and fled back into the wilderness." In remote Dalmatia bolder wolves descended upon a plague-stricken city and attacked human survivors.[26] For want of herdsmen, cattle strayed from place to place and died in hedgerows and ditches. Dogs and cats fell like the rest.[27]

The dearth of labor held a fearful prospect because the 14th century lived close to the annual harvest both for food and for next year's seed. "So few servants and laborers were left," wrote Knighton, "that no one knew where to turn for help." The sense of a vanishing future created a kind of dementia of despair. A Bavarian chronicler of Neuberg on the Danube recorded that "Men and women . . . wandered around as if mad" and let their cattle stray "because no one had any inclination to concern themselves about the future."[28] Fields went uncultivated, spring seed unsown. Second growth with nature's awful energy crept back over cleared land, dikes crumbled, salt water reinvaded and soured the lowlands. With so few hands remaining to restore the work of centuries, people felt, in Walsingham's words, that "the world could never again regain its former prosperity."[29]

Though the death rate was higher among the anonymous poor, the known and the great died too. King Alfonso XI of Castile was the only reigning monarch killed by the pest, but his neighbor King Pedro of Aragon lost his wife, Queen

[22]Ziegler, *The Black Death,* 199.
[23]Gasquet, *The Black Death of 1348 and 1349,* 42.
[24]Raymond Cazelles, *"La Peste de 1348–49 en Langue d'oil: épidémic proletarienne et enfantine,"* *Bull philologique et historique* (1962), 293–305.
[25]Ziegler, *The Black Death,* 175.
[26]Ziegler, *The Black Death,* 84, 111.
[27]Gasquet, *The Black Death of 1348 and 1349,* 44, 61.
[28]Ziegler, *The Black Death,* 84.
[29]Henri Denifle, *La Dësolation des églises, monastëres et hopitaux en France pendant la guerre de cent ans,* vol. I (Paris, 1899), 273.

Leonora, his daughter Marie, and a niece in the space of six months. John Cantacuzene, Emperor of Byzantium, lost his son. In France the lame Queen Jeanne and her daughter-in-law Bonne de Luxemburg, wife of the Dauphin, both died in 1349 in the same phase that took the life of Enguerrand's mother. Jeanne, Queen of Navarre, daughter of Louis X, was another victim. Edward III's second daughter, Joanna, who was on her way to marry Pedro, the heir of Castile, died in Bordeaux. Women appear to have been more vulnerable than men, perhaps because being more housebound, they were more exposed to fleas. Boccaccio's mistress Fiammetta, illegitimate daughter of the King of Naples, died, as did Laura, the beloved—whether real or fictional—of Petrarch. Reaching out to us in the future, Petrarch cried, "Oh happy posterity who will not experience such abysmal woe and will look upon our testimony as a fable."[30]

In Florence Giovanni Villani, the great historian of his time, died at 68 in the midst of an unfinished sentence: ". . . *e dure questo pistolenza fino a . . .* (in the midst of this pestilence there came to an end . . .).[31] Siena's master painters, the brothers Ambrogio and Pietro Lorenzetti, whose names never appear after 1348, presumably perished in the plague, as did Andrea Pisano, architect and sculptor of Florence. William of Ockham and the English mystic Richard Rolle of Hampole both disappear from mention after 1349. Francisco Datini, merchant of Prato, lost both his parents and two siblings. Curious sweeps of mortality afflicted certain bodies of merchants in London. All eight wardens of the Company of Cutters, all six wardens of the Hatters, and four wardens of the Goldsmiths died before July 1350. Sir John Pulteney, master draper and four times Mayor of London, was a victim, likewise Sir John Montgomery, Governor of Calais.

Among the clergy and doctors the mortality was naturally high because of the nature of their professions. Out of 24 physicians in Venice, 20 were said to have lost their lives in the plague, although, according to another account, some were believed to have fled or to have shut themselves up in their houses. At Montpellier, site of the leading medieval medical school, the physician Simon de Covino reported that, despite the great number of doctors, "hardly one of them escaped."[32] In Avignon, Guy de Chauliac confessed that he performed his medical visits only because he dared not stay away for fear of infamy, but "I was in continual fear."[33] He claimed to have contracted the disease but to have cured himself by his own treatment; if so, he was one of the few who recovered.

Clerical mortality varied with rank. Although the one-third toll of cardinals reflects the same proportion as the whole, this was probably due to their concentration in Avignon. In England, in strange and almost sinister procession, the

---

[30]Ziegler, *The Black Death,* 45.

[31]Frederick Snell, *The Fourteenth Century* (Edinburgh, 1899), 334.

[32]Campbell, *The Black Death and Men of Learning,* 98, 31.

[33]James Westfall Thompson, *Economic and Social History of Europe in the Later Middle Ages* (New York, 1931), 379.

Archbishop of Canterbury, John Stratford, died in August 1348, his appointed successor died in May 1349, and the next appointee three months later, all three within a year. Despite such weird vagaries, prelates in general managed to sustain a higher survival rate than the lesser clergy. Among bishops the deaths have been estimated at about one in twenty. The loss of priests, even if many avoided their fearful duty of attending the dying, was about the same as among the population as a whole.

Government officials, whose loss contributed to the general chaos, found, on the whole, no special shelter. In Siena four of the nine members of the governing oligarchy died, in France one third of the royal notaries, in Bristol 15 out of the 52 members of the Town Council or almost one third. Tax-collecting obviously suffered, with the result that Philip VI was unable to collect more than a fraction of the subsidy granted him by the Estates in the winter of 1347–48.

Lawlessness and debauchery accompanied the plague as they had during the great plague of Athens of 430 B.C., when according to Thucydides, men grew bold in the indulgence of pleasure: "For seeing how the rich died in a moment and those who had nothing immediately inherited their property, they reflected that life and riches were alike transitory and they resolved to enjoy themselves while they could."[34] Human behavior is timeless. When St. John had his vision of plague in Revelation, he knew from some experience or race memory that those who survived "repented not of the work of their hands. . . . Neither repented they of their murders, nor of their sorceries, nor of their fornication, nor of their thefts."

Meaning and Idea

1. What were the various symptoms of the bubonic plague? Why was the "malignity of the disease" so terrible? How did the survivors dispose of the dead bodies?

2. Give examples of why Tuchman notes that "the plague was not the kind of calamity that inspired mutual help." In what cases *did* people show humanity amid the horrors of the disease? How did the authorities counteract the terrible fear in Tournai? in Siena?

3. What does Tuchman mean by the sentence, "The sense of a vanishing future created a kind of dementia of despair"? What examples does she give to support her observation?

4. Who were some of "the known and the great" who died in the plague? Why was the mortality rate particularly high among doctors and the clergy?

5. Why does Tuchman say in the last paragraph that "Human behavior is timeless"?

[34]Raymond Crawfurd, *Plague and Pestilence in Literature and Art* (Oxford, 1914), 30–31.

Language, Form, Structure

1. How do the first two paragraphs serve as a strong introduction to the selection? Which sentence or sentences best express the thesis of the piece? Why do you think that the writer begins with a narrative of the sailors from the Black Sea port of Caffa?

2. Tuchman uses examples throughout the essay to illustrate different aspects of her topic. Which examples are most vivid? How does the piling up of examples serve to convince you of the accuracy of her observations? How does the writer use quotations from other sources to help make her point? Are these quotations tedious and overwhelming, or are they valuable and dramatic? Support your opinion with references to the text.

3. How does the writer use time, particularly dates, as transitions? What other transitional elements does she use? Does the selection, to your mind, achieve the right level of unity and coherence? In what ways other than the use of transitions does Tuchman aim for these important features of writing?

4. How does the last paragraph serve as a fitting conclusion to the selection?

5. Write definitions for the following words: virulent; contagion; malignity; atrophy; truncated; apathy; dearth; dementia.

Ideas for Writing

1. Imagine yourself as an eyewitness to the bubonic plague in the fourteenth century. Write an essay to describe and analyze the events that surround you and your feelings as a surviving observer. Provide examples from Tuchman as well as from your own imagination, trying to achieve as much historical accuracy as you can.

2. Select a cataclysm—that is, a violent natural occurrence—in recent or current history. Do research, if necessary, and write an essay about it, using the principles of exemplification. You might wish to write about AIDS, the eruption of Mount St. Helens, or the San Francisco earthquake, for example.

3. Write a critical essay about how Tuchman's use of examples in this essay advances her thesis. Point out the strongest use of examples and the weakest.

Courtship through the Ages

James Thurber

James Thurber (1894–1961) was perhaps best known and loved by the American public for his stories, essays, and line drawings in *The New Yorker* magazine, where he was employed for many years after being hired by E. B. White in 1925. Thurber always cast a humorously ironic eye on the human condition. His best-known collections include *Is Sex Necessary?* (with E. B. White, 1929), *The Seal in the Bedroom and Other Predicaments* (1932), *The Thurber Carnival* (1945), and *Thurber Country* (1953).

"Courtship through the Ages," Thurber's accumulation of examples of "love displays" by the male species toward the opposite sex, first appeared in *The New Yorker* in 1939; that same year it was also collected in Thurber's book *My World—and Welcome to It.*

Surely nothing in the astonishing scheme of life can have nonplussed [1] Nature so much as the fact that none of the females of any of the species she created really cared very much for the male, as such. For the past ten million years Nature has been busily inventing ways to make the male attractive to the female, but the whole business of courtship, from the marine annelids up to man, still lumbers heavily along, like a complicated musical comedy. I have been reading the sad and absorbing story in Volume 6 (Cole to Dama) of the *Encyclopaedia Britannica.* In this volume you can learn all about cricket, cotton, costume designing, crocodiles, crown jewels, and Coleridge, but none of these subjects is so interesting as the Courtship of Animals, which recounts the sorrowful lengths to which all males must go to arouse the interest of a lady.

We all know, I think, that Nature gave man whiskers and a mustache with [2] the quaint idea in mind that these would prove attractive to the female. We all know that, far from attracting her, whiskers and mustaches only made her nervous and gloomy, so that man had to go in for somersaults, tilting with lances, and performing feats of parlor magic to win her attention; he also had to bring her candy, flowers, and the furs of animals. It is common knowledge that in spite of all these "love displays" the male is constantly being turned down, insulted, or thrown out of the house. It is rather comforting, then, to discover that the peacock, for all his gorgeous plumage, does not have a particularly easy time in courtship; none of the males in the world do. The first peahen, it turned out, was only faintly stirred by her suitor's beautiful train. She would often go quietly to sleep while he was whisking it around. The *Britannica* tells us that the peacock actually had to learn a certain little trick to wake her up and revive her interest: he had to learn to vibrate his quills so as to make a rustling sound. In ancient times man himself, observing the ways of the peacock, probably tried vibrating his whiskers to make a rustling sound; if so, it didn't get him anywhere. He had to go in for something else; so, among other things, he went in for gifts. It is not unlikely that he got this idea from certain flies and birds who were making no headway at all with rustling sounds.

One of the flies of the family Empidae, who had tried everything, finally hit ³ on something pretty special. He contrived to make a glistening transparent balloon which was even larger than himself. Into this he would put sweetmeats and tidbits and he would carry the whole elaborate envelope through the air to the lady of his choice. This amused her for a time, but she finally got bored with it. She demanded silly little colorful presents, something that you couldn't eat but that would look nice around the house. So the male Empis had to go around gathering flower petals and pieces of bright paper to put into his balloon. On a courtship flight a male Empis cuts quite a figure now, but he can hardly be said to be happy. He never knows how soon the female will demand heavier presents, such as Roman coins and gold collar buttons. It seems probable that one day the courtship of the Empidae will fall down, as man's occasionally does, of its own weight.

The bowerbird is another creature that spends so much time courting the ⁴ female that he never gets any work done. If all the male bowerbirds became nervous wrecks within the next ten or fifteen years, it would not surprise me. The female bowerbird insists that a playground be built for her with a specially constructed bower at the entrance. This bower is much more elaborate than an ordinary nest and is harder to build; it costs a lot more, too. The female will not come to the playground until the male has filled it up with a great many gifts: silvery leaves, red leaves, rose petals, shells, beads, berries, bones, dice, buttons, cigar bands, Christmas seals, and the Lord knows what else. When the female finally condescends to visit the playground, she is in a coy and silly mood and has to be chased in and out of the bower and up and down the playground before she will quit giggling and stand still long enough even to shake hands. The male bird is, of course, pretty well done in before the chase starts, because he has worn himself out hunting for eyeglass lenses and begonia blossoms. I imagine that many a bowerbird, after chasing a female for two or three hours, says the hell with it and goes home to bed. Next day, of course, he telephones someone else and the same trying ritual is gone through again. A male bowerbird is as exhausted as a nightclub habitué before he is out of his twenties.

The male fiddler crab has a somewhat easier time, but it can hardly be said ⁵ that he is sitting pretty. He has one enormously large and powerful claw, usually brilliantly colored, and you might suppose that all he had to do was reach out and grab some passing cutie. The very earliest fiddler crabs may have tried this, but, if so, they got slapped for their pains. A female crab will not tolerate any caveman stuff; she never has and she doesn't intend to start now. To attract a female, a fiddler crab has to stand on tiptoe and brandish his claw in the air. If any female in the neighborhood is interested—and you'd be surprised how many are not— she comes over and engages him in light badinage, for which he is not in the mood. As many as a hundred females may pass the time of day with him and go on about their business. By nightfall of an average courting day, a fiddler crab who has been standing on tiptoe for eight or ten hours waving a heavy claw in the air is in pretty sad shape. As in the case of the males of all species, however, he gets out of bed next morning, dashes some water on his face, and tries again.

The next time you encounter a male web-spinning spider, stop and reflect   6
that he is too busy worrying about his love life to have any desire to bite you.
Male web-spinning spiders have a tougher life than any other males in the animal
kingdom. This is because the female web-spinning spiders have very poor eye-
sight. If a male lands on a female's web, she kills him before he has time to lay
down his cane and gloves, mistaking him for a fly or a bumblebee who has tumbled into her trap. Before the species figured out what to do about this, millions
of males were murdered by ladies they called on. It is the nature of spiders to perform a little dance in front of the female, but before a male spinner could get near
enough for the female to see who he was and what he was up to, she would lash
out at him with a flat-iron or a pair of garden shears. One night, nobody knows
when, a very bright male spinner lay awake worrying about calling on a lady who
had been killing suitors right and left. It came to him that this business of dancing as a love display wasn't getting anybody anywhere except the grave. He
decided to go in for web-twitching, or strand-vibrating. The next day he tried it
on one of the nearsighted girls. Instead of dropping in on her suddenly, he stayed
outside the web and began monkeying with one of its strands. He twitched it up
and down and in and out with such a lilting rhythm that the female was charmed.
The serenade worked beautifully; the female let him live. The *Britannica*'s
spider-watchers, however, report that this system is not always successful. Once
in a while, even now, a female will fire three bullets into a suitor or run him
through with kitchen knife. She keeps threatening him from the moment he
strikes the first low notes on the outside strings, but usually by the time he has got
up to the high notes played around the center of the web, he is going to town and
she spares his life.

Even the butterfly, as handsome a fellow as he is, can't always win a mate   7
merely by fluttering around and showing off. Many butterflies have to have scent
scales on their wings. Hepialus carries a powder puff in a perfumed pouch. He
throws perfume at the ladies when they pass. The male tree cricket, Oecanthus,
goes Hepialus one better by carrying a tiny bottle of wine with him and giving
drinks to such doxies as he has designs on. One of the male snails throws darts to
entertain the girls. So it goes, through the long list of animals, from the bristle
worm and his rudimentary dance steps to man and his gift of diamonds and sap-
phires. The golden-eye drake raises a jet of water with his feet as he flies over a
lake; Hepialus has his powder puff, Oecanthus his wine bottle, man his etchings.
It is a bright and melancholy story, the age-old desire of the male for the female,
the age-old desire of the female to be amused and entertained. Of all the creatures
on earth, the only males who could be figured as putting any irony into their
courtship are the grebes and certain other diving birds. Every now and then a
courting grebe slips quietly down to the bottom of a lake and then, with a mighty
"Whoosh!," pops out suddenly a few feet from his girl friend, splashing water all
over her. She seems to be persuaded that this is a purely loving display, but I like
to think that the grebe always has a faint hope of drowning her or scaring her to
death.

I will close this investigation into the mournful burdens of the male with the   8
Britannica's story about a certain Argus pheasant. It appears that the Argus displays himself in front of a female who stands perfectly still without moving a feather. . . . The male Argus the *Britannica* tells about was confined in a cage with a female of another species, a female who kept moving around, emptying ashtrays and fussing with lampshades all the time the male was showing off his talents. Finally, in disgust, he stalked away and began displaying in front of his water trough. He reminds me of a certain male (*Homo sapiens*) of my acquaintance who one night after dinner asked his wife to put down her detective magazine so that he could read her a poem of which he was very fond. She sat quietly enough until he was well into the middle of the thing, intoning with great ardor and intensity. Then suddenly there came a sharp, disconcerting *slap!* It turned out that all during the male's display, the female had been intent on a circling mosquito and had finally trapped it between the palms of her hands. The male in this case did not stalk away and display in front of a water trough; he went over to Tim's and had a flock of drinks and recited the poem to the fellas. I am sure they all told bitter stories of their own about how their displays had been interrupted by females. I am also sure that they all ended up singing "Honey, Honey, Bless Your Heart."

Meaning and Idea

1. On what other piece of writing does Thurber hinge his essay? Why?

2. In paragraph 2, Thurber gives examples of the things men had to do to attract females because their whiskers and mustaches weren't enough. What are those other things? What is the ultimate substitute—the "something else"—mentioned in that paragraph? What examples of it does Thurber include in subsequent paragraphs?

3. Who does Thurber think ultimately has the upper hand in male-female relations? How do you know? How does the last sentence of the essay fit in with his evaluation?

Language, Form, Structure

1. What is the initial generalization that Thurber sets out to support through exemplification? Do you agree with this generalization? Why is exemplification a suitable technique for this essay?

2. Thurber tends to use *hyperbole* (the deliberate exaggeration of an idea or description) quite freely throughout the essay. Give three examples of the most hyperbolic statements. To what purpose does he use hyperbole?

3. An *analogy* is a comparison of two subjects drawn from divergent areas. If you showed point by point the similarities between an ant hill and a crowded train station, you'd be writing an analogy. What is the implicit

analogy throughout this essay? Where in each paragraph is that analogy made most explicitly? What purpose does that explicit analogy serve?

4. How does Thurber arrange his examples in paragraphs 3 through 6? In paragraph 7? Why does he change his arrangement in paragraph 7? Briefly outline Thurber's use of transitions between paragraphs 2 through 7.

5. What is Thurber's attitude toward his topic in this essay? How can you tell? Does he maintain the same attitude throughout the essay?

6. Make certain that you know the meanings of the following words: nonplussed; feats; habitué; badinage; doxies; intoning; ardor.

Ideas for Writing

1. Write a paragraph using examples in which you explain your favorite means of attracting the opposite sex. Which are most effective? Which are least effective?

2. Go to a place where men and women gather socially—a cafeteria, a pub, a lecture hall, for example—and observe their behavior toward each other, especially their means of attracting each other. Write a single generalization about your observation of the scene and support it in an essay of exemplification.

3. Clearly, Thurber uses *irony* here almost to the limits of *sarcasm*. Write a short essay in which you analyze the positive and negative sides of the use of irony in this essay. Support your ideas with specific examples drawn from the text.

There Was a Child Went Forth

Walt Whitman

Whitman affected American poetry profoundly not only because of his wide-ranging subject matter but also because of his experimental verse. Born on New York's Long Island in
1819, he wrote poems infused with such divergent forces as democratic idealism, opera,
Shakespeare, Quaker religious philosophy, sexual openness, and the rhythms of city life.
His magnum opus, *Leaves of Grass* (1855), proclaimed the great freedom of the human
mind, body, and spirit. Whitman died in 1892.

In this poem Whitman provides a series of indelible images in an effort to define the personality of a child. Critics point to many autobiographical lines in "There Was a Child Went
Forth." But the poem goes beyond the concrete experiential world of the poet, a world so
vividly recreated here, to a statement on the relation between human character and experience and the unity of all in nature.

*T*here was a child went forth every day,
And the first object he look'd upon, that object he became,
And that object became part of him for the day or a certain part of the day,
Or for many years or stretching cycles of years.

The early lilacs became part of this child.   5
And grass and white and red morning-glories, and white and red clover, and the
    song of the phoebe-bird,
And the Third-month lambs and the sow's pink-faint litter, and the mare's foal
    and the cow's calf,
And the noisy brood of the barnyard or by the mire of the pond-side,
And the fish suspending themselves so curiously below there, and the beautiful
    curious liquid,
And the water-plants with their graceful flat heads, all became part of him.   10
The field-sprouts of Fourth-month and Fifth-month became part of him,
Winter-grain sprouts and those of the light-yellow corn, and the esculent
    roots of the garden,
And the apple-trees cover'd with blossoms and the fruit afterward, and wood-
    berries, and the commonest weeds by the road,
And the old drunkard staggering home from the outhouse of the tavern whence
    he had lately risen,
And the schoolmistress that pass'd on her way to the school,   15
And the friendly boys that pass'd, and the quarrelsome boys,
And the tidy and fresh-cheek'd girls, and the barefoot negro boy and girl,
And all the changes of city and country wherever he went.

His own parents, he that had father'd him and she that had conceiv'd him
    in her womb and birth'd him,
They gave this child more of themselves than that,   20
They gave him afterward every day, they became part of him.

The mother at home quietly placing the dishes on the suppertable,
The mother with mild words, clean her cap and gown, a wholesome odor
    falling off her person and clothes as she walks by,
The father, strong, self-sufficient, manly, mean, anger'd, unjust,
The blow, the quick loud word, the tight bargain, the crafty lure,   25
The family usages, the language, the company, the furniture, the yearning and
    swelling heart,
Affection that will not be gainsay'd, the sense of what is real, the thought if
    after all it should prove unreal,
The doubts of day-time and the doubts of night-time, the curious whether and
    how,
Whether that which appears so is so, or is it all flashes and specks?
Men and women crowding fast in the streets, if they are not flashes and specks 30
    what are they?
The streets themselves and the facades of houses, and goods in the windows,
Vehicles, teams, the heavy-plank'd wharves, the huge crossing at the ferries,
The village on the highland seen from afar at sunset, the river between,
Shadows, aureola and mist, the light falling on roofs and gables of white or
    brown two miles off,
The schooner near by sleepily dropping down the tide, the little boat slack-   35
    tow'd astern,
The hurrying tumbling waves, quick-broken crests, slapping,
The strata of color'd clouds, the long bar of maroon-tint away solitary by
    itself, the spread of purity it lies motionless in,
The horizon's edge, the flying sea-crow, the fragrance of salt marsh and shore mud,
These became part of that child who went forth every day, and who now goes,
    and will always go forth every day.

Meaning and Idea

1. State in your own words the point Whitman is trying to make with this
   poem. Where does he come closest to stating his purpose? What is the
   value to the poem of the last line in the first stanza (line 4)?

2. What experiences with nature, family, and city are most vivid to you? What
   is the character of the child that Whitman is attempting to draw for us here?

3. What are the doubts and questions aroused by the child's experiences?
   Would you call them typical of a child growing up? Why?

4. Describe the child's father and mother.

Language, Form, Structure

1. Which images are richest in concrete sensory detail? Whitman has a special knack of sketching characters with a series of single words or short phrases. Why are the modifiers describing the father particularly well chosen? What is the effect of placing all the modifiers after the noun *father*?

2. How is this poem an instance of exemplification? Why does Whitman provide a listing of so many details? Why didn't he just choose five or six examples instead of all that you see here? How does the use of all of these examples reinforce the purpose and meaning of the poem?

3. Why does Whitman repeat the phrase "part of him" (or variations of that phrase) in other lines of the poem? What other words or phrases does he repeat? What is your reaction to the last line of the poem? (Compare its meaning to the meaning of the first stanza.)

4. How has Whitman used sentence structure as a unifying element? What is the advantage of beginning so many sentences with the word *and?* with the word *the?*

5. Explain the meanings of the following words: mire; gainsay'd; facades; aureola; strata. Why has Whitman used the terms "Third-month," "Fourth-month," and "Fifth-month"?

Ideas for Writing

1. Write a paragraph entitled "What Am I?" in which you provide a series of concrete sensory images that show the various experiences that helped to shape your personality.

2. Check library resources to investigate the life of some person who interests you. Try to find an identifiable element of character or personality. Then, in an essay, use exemplification to show how experiences in the person's life demonstrate that element of character.

3. A critic of nineteenth-century American literature, F. O. Matthiessen, writes about Whitman: "He understood that language was not 'an abstract construction' made by the learned, but that it had arisen out of the work and needs, the joys and struggles and desires of long generations of humanity, and that it had 'its bases broad and low, close to the ground.' Words are not arbitrary inventions, but the product of human events and customs, the progeny of folkways." Consider the validity of this statement in regard to "There Was a Child Went Forth." Use specific examples from the poem to support your point.

Nobody Loses All the Time

e. e. cummings

The poet Edward Estlin Cummings, who was born in 1894 in Cambridge, Massachusetts, used the signature "e. e. cummings." cummings's strange use of typography, combined with his lyrical language, is viewed by many as one of the most important keys to the "free style" of contemporary poetry. *Is 5* (1926) and *95 Poems* (1958) are foremost among his verse collections, and his *The Enormous Room* (1922) is a forceful prose account of World War I. cummings died in 1962.

cummings's wry exemplification in this poem affords us insight into the general nature of failure and success rather than causing us great anguish about Uncle Sol's failed life.

i had an uncle named
Sol who was a born failure and
nearly everybody said he should have gone
into vaudeville perhaps because my Uncle Sol could
sing McCann He Was A Diver on Xmas Eve like Hell Itself   5
     which
may or may not account for the fact that my Uncle

Sol indulged in that possibly most inexcusable
of all to use a highfalootin phrase
luxuries that is or to
wit farming and be   10
it needlessly
added

my Uncle Sol's farm
failed because the chickens
ate the vegetables so   15
my Uncle Sol had a
chicken farm till the
skunks ate the chickens when

my Uncle Sol
had a skunk farm but   20
the skunks caught cold and
died and so
my Uncle Sol imitated the
skunks in a subtle manner

or by drowning himself in the watertank   25
but somebody who'd given my Uncle Sol a Victor
Victrola and records while he lived presented to
him upon the auspicious occasion of his decease a
scrumptious not to mention splendiferous funeral with
tall boys in black gloves and flowers and everything and   30

i remember we all cried like the Missouri
when my Uncle Sol's coffin lurched because
somebody pressed a button
(and down went
my Uncle   35
Sol

and started a worm farm)

Meaning and Idea

1. What examples in the poem support the assertion that Uncle Sol was "a born failure"?

2. What is the speaker's attitude toward Uncle Sol? Can you really categorize it as sorrow even at the funereal ending?

3. What is the relation between Sol's vaudevillian talents and his failures? Might cummings be trying to impart a message to us? If so, what is it?

Language, Form, Structure

1. What is the relation between the title of the poem and the examples it sets forth? If "nobody loses all the time," is there any example of Uncle Sol's "success" in life?

2. What is the tone of this poem? How does the way it is set up on the page contribute to that tone? Do any words or expressions especially affect the tone?

3. How does cummings connect the various illustrations here? Are the transitions smooth? Which ones do you think serve the poem best?

4. Write definitions for the following words: subtle; auspicious; decease (as a noun); scrumptious; lurched.

Ideas for Writing

1. Choose a person you know (not a celebrity) whom you consider to be a success. Write a short character sketch that focuses on the person's success using the cumulative technique of exemplification.

2. Choose any aspect of human nature and write a paragraph to define that aspect through extended exemplification.

3. The introduction to this chapter of *Great Writing* states that "The process of exemplification is . . . an essential part of the way . . . we talk and argue and respond." What elements of cummings's poem make his use of exemplification seem very commonplace, very *un*literary?

I Discover Moses and the Bulrushers

Mark Twain

Mark Twain was the pen name used by Samuel Langhorne Clemens (1835–1910). Twain was a teller of tales of and for the people. Additionally, he was a perceptive journalist, a biting satirist, and a world traveler (by his mid-thirties, he'd already been throughout the United States, Hawaii, Europe, and Palestine). Born in Hannibal, Missouri, he was the first major American writer born and raised west of the Mississippi River, which became the lifeblood of so much of his writing. His works exhibit the full range of his talents, as well as the breadth of his experiences and emotions. His major books include *Roughing It* (1872), *The Adventures of Tom Sawyer* (1876), *Life on the Mississippi* (1883), *Adventures of Huckleberry Finn* (1885), *The Prince and the Pauper* (1882), *A Connecticut Yankee in King Arthur's Court* (1889), and *The Mysterious Stranger* (1916).

"I Discover Moses and the Bulrushers" is the opening chapter of Twain's *Adventures of Huckleberry Finn. Huck Finn* was the third in a series of books about the Mississippi, which also included *Tom Sawyer* and *Life on the Mississippi. Huckleberry Finn* is generally considered the most complex and mature of the three—a kind of folk epic written by one of America's major humorists who did not ignore the dark side of our civilization. Twain's style in *Huck Finn* is rarely polemical; he opts instead for the rich descriptive details and examples evidenced in this first chapter.

You don't know about me without you have read a book by the name   1
of *The Adventures of Tom Sawyer;* but that ain't no matter. That book was made by Mr. Mark Twain, and he told the truth, mainly. There was things which he stretched, but mainly he told the truth. That is nothing. I never seen anybody but lied one time or another, without it was Aunt Polly, or the widow, or maybe Mary. Aunt Polly—Tom's Aunt Polly, she is—and Mary, and the Widow Douglas is all told about in that book, which is mostly a true book, with some stretchers, as I said before.

Now the way that the book winds up is this: Tom and me found the money   2
that the robbers hid in the cave, and it made us rich. We got six thousand dollars apiece—all gold. It was an awful sight of money when it was piled up. Well, Judge Thatcher he took it and put it out at interest, and it fetched us a dollar a day apiece all the year round—more than a body could tell what to do with. The Widow Douglas she took me for her son, and allowed she would sivilize me; but it was rough living in the house all the time, considering how dismal regular and decent the widow was in all her ways; and so when I couldn't stand it no longer I lit out. I got into my old rags and my sugar-hogshead again, and was free and satisfied. But Tom Sawyer he hunted me up and said he was going to start a band of robbers, and I might join if I would go back to the widow and be respectable. So I went back.

The widow she cried over me, and called me a poor lost lamb, and she ₃
called me a lot of other names, too, but she never meant no harm by it. She put
me in them new clothes again, and I couldn't do nothing but sweat and sweat, and
felt all cramped up. Well, then, the old thing commenced again. The widow rung
a bell for supper, and you had to come to time. When you got to the table you
couldn't go right to eating, but you had to wait for the widow to tuck down her
head and grumble a little over the victuals, though there warn't really anything
the matter with them—that is, nothing only everything was cooked by itself. In a
barrel of odds and ends it is different; things get mixed up, and the juice kind of
swaps around, and the things go better.

After supper she got out her book and learned me about Moses and the Bul- ₄
rushers, and I was in a sweat to find out all about him; but by and by she let it out
that Moses had been dead a considerable long time; so then I didn't care no more
about him, because I don't take no stock in dead people.

Pretty soon I wanted to smoke, and asked the widow to let me. But she ₅
wouldn't. She said it was a mean practice and wasn't clean, and I must try to not
do it any more. That is just the way with some people. They get down on a thing
when they don't know nothing about it. Here she was abothering about Moses,
which was no kin to her, and no use to anybody, being gone, you see, yet finding
a power of fault with me for doing a thing that had some good in it. And she took
snuff, too; of course that was all right, because she done it herself.

Her sister, Miss Watson, a tolerable slim old maid, with goggles on, had just ₆
come to live with her, and took a set at me now with a spelling book. She worked
me middling hard for about an hour, and then the widow made her ease up. I
couldn't stood it much longer. Then for an hour it was deadly dull, and I was fid-
gety. Miss Watson would say, "Don't put your feet up there, Huckleberry"; and
"Don't scrunch up like that, Huckleberry—set up straight"; and pretty soon she
would say, "Don't gap and stretch like that, Huckleberry—why don't you try to
behave?" Then she told me all about the bad place, and I said I wished I was there.
She got mad then, but I didn't mean no harm. All I wanted was to go somewheres;
all I wanted was a change, I warn't particular. She said it was wicked to say what
I said; said she wouldn't say it for the whole world; *she* was going to live so as to
go to the good place. Well, I couldn't see no advantage in going where she was
going, so I made up my mind I wouldn't try for it. But I never said so, because it
would only make trouble, and wouldn't do no good.

Now she had got a start, and she went on and told me all about the good ₇
place. She said all a body would have to do there was to go around all day long
with a harp and sing, forever and ever. So I didn't think much of it. But I never
said so. I asked her if she reckoned Tom Sawyer would go there, and she said not
by considerable sight. I was glad about that, because I wanted him and me to be
together.

Miss Watson she kept pecking at me, and it got tiresome and lonesome. By ₈
and by they fetched the niggers in and had prayers, and then everybody was off
to bed. I went up to my room with a piece of candle, and put it on the table. Then
I set down in a chair by the window and tried to think of something cheerful, but

it warn't no use. I felt so lonesome I most wished I was dead. The stars were shining, and the leaves rustled in the woods ever so mournful; and I heard an owl, away off, who-whooing about somebody that was dead, and a whippowill and a dog crying about somebody that was going to die; and the wind was trying to whisper something to me, and I couldn't make out what it was, and so it made the cold shivers run over me. Then away out in the woods I heard that kind of a sound that a ghost makes when it wants to tell about something that's on its mind and can't make itself understood, and so can't rest easy in its grave, and has to go about that way every night grieving. I got so downhearted and scared I did wish I had some company. Pretty soon a spider went crawling up my shoulder, and I flipped it off and it lit in the candle; and before I could budge it was all shriveled up. I didn't need anybody to tell me that that was an awful bad sign and would fetch me some bad luck, so I was scared and most shook the clothes off of me. I got up and turned around in my tracks three times and crossed my breast every time; and then I tied up a little lock of my hair with a thread to keep witches away. But I hadn't no confidence. You do that when you've lost a horseshoe that you've found, instead of nailing it up over the door, but I hadn't ever heard anybody say it was any way to keep off bad luck when you'd killed a spider.

I set down again, a-shaking all over, and got out my pipe for a smoke; for the house was all as still as death now, and so the widow wouldn't know. Well, after a long time I heard the clock away off in the town go boom—boom—boom—twelve licks; and all still again—stiller than ever. Pretty soon I heard a twig snap down in the dark amongst the trees—something was a-stirring. I set still and listened. Directly I could just barely hear a *"me-yow! me-yow!"* down there. That was good! Says I, *"me-yow! me-yow!"* as soft as I could, and then I put out the light and scrambled out of the window on to the shed. Then I slipped down to the ground and crawled in among the trees, and, sure enough, there was Tom Sawyer waiting for me.

Meaning and Idea

1. What is the biblical story of Moses and the bulrushes (note the difference in spelling)? What is the significance of that story to Huck's narration?

2. Throughout this chapter, how does Huck exemplify "how dismal regular and decent" the Widow Douglas was? List the examples and paraphrase each. What is the worst example of her righteousness? What are Huck's reactions to her decency?

3. What is meant by "the bad place"? Why does Huck tell Miss Watson that he wishes he were there? What is "the good place"? Why doesn't Huck want to be there?

4. What causes Huck's lonesomeness? How does he deal with it?

5. What examples of superstitious behavior and belief does Huck provide? What do his superstitions tell you about his character?

Language, Form, Structure

1. What sort of narration is this? How is the point of view appropriate to the story?

2. How does Twain use exemplification in this chapter from *Huckleberry Finn?* How does he use narrative summary? What is the advantage of using narrative summary here?

3. How does the narrator arrange the examples in this selection? How does time sequence influence the arrangement?

4. How is dialect important in this story? List five examples of dialectical usage. For each, write a standard English equivalent.

Ideas for Writing

1. Select an authority figure whose sense of propriety or decorum you question. Summarize the person's attitudes, then proceed to explain them through exemplification.

2. Do you believe in any particular superstition? If so, write a paragraph in which you explain your belief through cumulative exemplification.

3. If you define *tone* as the author's attitude toward his subject, write a reaction to the tone of this selection, especially as it is affected by Huck's use of dialect. How does the dialect affect your understanding or enjoyment of the piece? How does Twain feel about Huck? About the Widow Douglas? Miss Watson? Huck's milieu in general?

We Real Cool

Gwendolyn Brooks

Gwendolyn Brooks was born in 1917 and moved to Chicago at a very early age. Her deceptively simple, powerful poetry is a lyrical voice for the black and inner-city cultures of Chicago's south side. Brooks's mother, a former teacher, encouraged her daughter's literary interests. The poet's father provided a central image for her work: a capable and dignified but quite ordinary black man.

In 1950, Brooks became the first African-American woman to win the Pulitzer Prize. She was named poet laureate of Illinois in 1969, a post she still holds today. The easy flow of her words and the way she is inspired by rhythm are well suited to her subjects and themes; but sometimes this poetic skill hides a beguiling, ironic aspect. "We Real Cool" is just such an example.

The Pool Players
Seven at the Golden Shovel

We real cool. We
Left School. We

Lurk late. We   5
Strike straight. We

Sing sin. We
Thin gin. We

Jazz June. We
Die soon.   10

Meaning and Idea

1. What is the theme of the poem? Who are "We"? How many of them are there? Does the poet think they are truly "cool"? How can you tell?

2. What examples in the poem indicate the lifestyles the speakers lead? What do "Jazz June," "Thin gin," and those other expressions mean?

3. Is the last sentence of the poem, "We / Die soon," coming from the same point of view as the previous line? Whose or what kind of awareness does the poet express in these last words? It may be useful to count the number of *We*'s and the number of "players."

Language, Form, Structure

1. Think about the rhythm of the poem. Speak the poem aloud if you have not already actually *listened* to it. What special elements do you note about the rhythm? How does the poet achieve this rhythm? Why has she chosen this rhythm?

2. Can you tell what the poet's attitude toward the pool players is? Which of the following best describes that attitude: *admiration, contempt, pity, sarcasm?* What does the reader *know* about the speakers based on what they say and/or their attitudes?

3. Be sure you know all the possible meanings for "lurk," "thin," and "jazz."

Ideas for Writing

1. Think of a person who you feel is or was misdirected or misguided. Write an essay that presents examples to explain what caused this misdirection. Don't forget to include what you feel results from this person's lifestyle.

2. Think of a person who you feel is "trouble." Why do you feel this way? What are the examples that brought you to your point of view? Now, using the examples to support your point, create an essay on the topic.

3. Think about the elements of the poem that you find the strongest. In an essay, explain what the theme of the poem is, why the poem's elements work so well, and how they reveal and support that theme.

My Last Duchess

Robert Browning

Along with Tennyson, Robert Browning (1812–1889) is considered a shining poet of the late Victorian period. He was raised in an artistic and cultured family of nonconformists— a sort of "pre-Bohemian" English intellectual group. Browning's own education was excellent and well-rounded, and in his early teens he began to write poetry, heavily influenced by Shelley. Browning is considered the master of the dramatic monologue and his three most popular poems in this vein are *My Last Duchess, Fra Lippo Lippi,* and *Andrea Del Sarto.* His other well-known works include *Rabbi Ben Ezra* (1864) and the popular children's classic *The Pied Piper of Hamelin* (1842). He was happily married to the poet Elizabeth Barrett Browning.

Browning's "My Last Duchess" is considered one of the best-crafted and most consistent revelations of character in all of English poetry. Browning has the Duke of Ferrara (a man probably as powerful as a monarch in sixteenth-century Italy) choose just the right descriptive details and examples to reveal to us the full extent of his massive egotism.

FERRARA

*T*hat's my last duchess painted on the wall,
Looking as if she were alive. I call
That piece a wonder, now; Fra Pandolf's hands
Worked busily a day, and there she stands.
Will't please you sit and look at her? I said   5
"Fra Pandolf" by design, for never read
Strangers like you that pictured countenance,
The depth and passion of its earnest glance,
But to myself they turned (since none puts by
The curtain I have drawn for you, but I)   10
And seemed as they would ask me, if they durst,
How such a glance came there; so, not the first
Are you to turn and ask thus. Sir, 'twas not
Her husband's presence only, called that spot
Of joy into the Duchess' cheek; perhaps   15
Fra Pandolf chanced to say, "Her mantle laps
Over my lady's wrist too much," or, "Paint
Must never hope to reproduce the faint
Half-blush that dies along her throat." Such stuff
Was courtesy, she thought, and cause enough   20
For calling up that spot of joy. She had
A heart—how shall I say?—too soon made glad,

Too easily impressed; she liked whate'er
She looked on, and her looks went everywhere.
Sir, 'twas all one! My favor at her breast,   25
The dropping of the daylight in the West,
The bough of cherries some officious fool
Broke in the orchard for her, the white mule
She rode with round the terrace—all and each
Would draw from her alike the approving speech,   30
Or blush, at least. She thanked men—good! but thanked
Somehow—I know not how—as if she ranked
My gift of a nine-hundred-years-old name
With anybody's gift. Who'd stoop to blame
This sort of trifling? Even had you skill   35
In speech—which I have not—to make your will
Quite clear to such an one, and say, "Just this
Or that in you disgusts me; here you miss,
Or there exceed the mark"—and if she let
Herself be lessoned so, nor plainly set   40
Her wits to yours, forsooth, and made excuse—
E'en then would be some stooping; and I choose
Never to stoop. Oh, sir, she smiled, no doubt,
Whene'er I passed her; but who passed without
Much the same smile? This grew; I gave commands;   45
Then all smiles stopped together. There she stands
As if alive. Will't please you rise? We'll meet
The company below, then. I repeat,
The Count your master's known munificence
Is ample warrant that no just pretense   50
Of mine for dowry will be disallowed;
Though his fair daughter's self, as I avowed
At starting, is my object. Nay, we'll go
Together down, sir. Notice Neptune, though,
Taming a sea-horse, thought a rarity,   55
Which Claus of Innsbruck cast in bronze for me.

Meaning and Idea

1. "My Last Duchess" is considered one of the foremost examples of dramatic
   monologue in English. A *dramatic monologue* is a form of lyric poetry in
   which a character reveals—to another person, but without dialogue—his
   inner self at a particular moment and situation. What is the situation in this
   monologue? To whom is the Duke of Ferrara speaking? What does the
   duke reveal about himself to the speaker?

2. What does the duke think was *right* about his duchess? What does he think
   was *wrong* with her?

3. What is the meaning of lines 21–23: "She had / A heart—how shall I say?— too soon made glad, / Too easily impressed"? How does the duke support his allegation?

4. Within the poem's dramatic context, what do you suppose were the "commands" of line 45? Why did all smiles stop after their fulfillment?

5. What, according to the duke, was his ultimate gift to the duchess? How did she receive it?

Language, Form, Structure

1. Within the dramatic context of the monologue, what is the duke's purpose in relating this story? Do you think he has any ulterior motives? What are they? What is the significance of the word *last* in the first line of the poem?

2. How does *exemplification* operate in this poem? How are the examples important in revealing the meaning?

3. What is the use of *dramatic irony* in this poem? (*Dramatic irony* refers to a condition where the reader knows the truth of a situation to be other than what is presented.)

4. Write dictionary definitions for the following words: countenance; durst; mantle; bough; officious; lessoned; munificence; pretense; dowry.

Ideas for Writing

1. Choose a nonabstract painting that you enjoy, and make a narrative generalization about it. Then describe the painting in a paragraph supporting your generalization with examples drawn from the painting.

2. Write a paragraph in which you attempt to convince someone of the rightness or wrongness of an action by using exemplification as your support technique.

Good Times

Lucille Clifton

Lucille Clifton was born in 1936 in upstate New York and graduated from Howard University. She is the recipient of a National Endowment for the Arts grant, among other awards, and has taught at the Columbia University School of the Arts. She says of herself, "I am a black woman poet, and I sound like one." Her poetry is characterized by understatement and succinctness, and although her poems often deal with the nitty-gritty difficulties of life, they are essentially affirmative and optimistic. Clifton's collections of poetry include *Good Times* (1969), *Good News about the Earth* (1972), and *An Ordinary Woman* (1974).

Lucille Clifton's "Good Times" is ultimately a social commentary in which the examples are often ironically double-edged.

*M*y Daddy has paid the rent
and the insurance man is gone
and the lights is back on
and my uncle Brud has hit
for one dollar straight   5
and they is good times
good times
good times

My Mama has made bread
and Grampaw has come   10
and everybody is drunk
and dancing in the kitchen
and singing in the kitchen
oh these is good times
good times   15
good times

oh children think about the
good times

Meaning and Idea

1. In a single sentence, state the main point of this poem. Is Clifton writing about good times or their opposite?

2. What is the meaning of the lines "and my uncle Brud has hit / for one dollar straight"?

3. What examples of "good times" does the speaker give? How do the examples convey the social status of the speaker?

4. At the end of the poem, why does the speaker tell the children to "think about the / good times"?

Language, Form, Structure

1. What is the general tone of this poem? Does that tone seem at all to contradict the title? How?

2. What is the significance of the stanza divisions of this poem? How does it allow Clifton to arrange her examples?

3. Is there irony in this poem? If so, what kind of irony is it? How does the poet achieve it? What is its purpose?

4. What is the role of repetition in this poem? What does it contribute to the poem's meaning? Notice how the only transition is the word *and.* Why does Clifton use this word eight times? What is the purpose of repeating the words *good times* seven times?

Ideas for Writing

1. Write an exemplification essay called "Good Times" or "Bad Times." Draw upon your own experiences to illustrate your point.

2. Write a paragraph in which you give examples to explain "success." Attempt to be ironic, and end your paragraph with a caution to your readers.

3. This poem is written in very colloquial language. Some "purist" readers of poetry still object to such "unexalted" language being used for poetry. In general, how do you react to poetry of this sort? What else have you read with similar language use (either poetry or prose)? In your answer, make specific references to this and other works.

Clutter

William Zinsser

William Zinsser was born in New York in 1922 and received an A. B. degree from Prince-ton in 1944. He served in North Africa in World War II, and worked as a journalist and an editor for many years before he began to teach. He has said, "The only way to learn to write is to force yourself to produce a certain number of words on a regular basis," and that is just what he has done. He has produced some 20 books and countless articles over the years.

On Writing Well, the source for the next selection, is an important and commonly used work on the art of expository writing. By instruction and example, Zinsser show us exactly what uncluttered writing is.

*F*ighting clutter is like fighting weeds—the writer is always slightly   1
behind. New varieties sprout overnight, and by noon they are part of American speech. Consider what President Nixon's aide John Dean accomplished in just one day of testimony on TV during the Watergate hearings. The next day every-one in American was saying "at this point in time" instead of "now."

Consider all the prepositions that are draped onto verbs that don't need   2
any help. We no longer head committees. We head them up. We don't face prob-lems anymore. We face up to them when we can free up a few minutes. A small detail, you may say—not worth bothering about. It *is* worth bothering about. Writing improves in direct ratio to the number of things we can keep out of it that shouldn't be there. "Up" in "free up" shouldn't be there. To write clean English you must examine every word you put on paper. You'll find a surpris-ing number that don't serve any purpose.

Take the adjective "personal," as in "a personal friend of mine," "his per-   3
sonal feeling" or "her personal physician." It's typical of hundreds of words that can be eliminated. The personal friend has come into the language to distinguish him or her from the business friend, thereby debasing both language and friend-ship. Someone's feeling *is* that person's personal feeling—that's what "his" and "her" mean. As for the personal physician, that's the man or woman summoned to the dressing room of a stricken actress so she won't have to be treated by the impersonal physician assigned to the theater. Someday I'd like to see that person identified as "her doctor." Physicians are physicians, friends are friends. The rest is clutter.

Clutter is the laborious phrase that has pushed out the short word that means   4
the same thing. Even before John Dean, people had stopped saying "now." They were saying "currently," or "at the present time," or "presently" (which means "soon"). Yet the idea can always be expressed by "now" to mean the immediate moment ("Now I can see him"), or by "today" to mean the historical present

("Today prices are high"), or simply by a form of the verb "to be" ("It is raining"). There's no need to say, "At the present time we are experiencing precipitation."

Speaking of which, we are experiencing considerable difficulty getting *that* word out of the language. Even your dentist will ask if you are experiencing any pain. If he had his own kid in the chair he would say, "Does it hurt?" He would, in short, be himself. By using a more pompous phrase in his professional role, he not only sounds more important; he blunts the painful edge of truth. It's the language of the flight attendant demonstrating the oxygen mask that will drop down if the plane should run out of air. "In the unlikely possibility that the aircraft should experience such an eventuality," she begins—a phrase so oxygen-depriving in itself that we are prepared for any disaster. As for her request to "kindly extinguish all smoking materials," I often wonder what materials are smoking. It's a terrifying sentence.

Clutter is the ponderous euphemism that turns a slum into a depressed socioeconomic area, a salesman into a marketing representative, garbage collectors into waste-disposal personnel and the town dump into the volume reduction unit. I think of Bill Mauldin's cartoon of two hoboes riding a freight car. One of them says, "I started as a simple bum, but now I'm hard-core unemployed." Clutter is political correctness gone amok. I saw an ad for a boys' camp designed to provide "individual attention for the minimally exceptional."

Clutter is the official language used by corporations to hide their mistakes. When the Digital Equipment Corporation recently eliminated 3,000 jobs, its statement didn't mention layoffs; those were "involuntary methodologies." When an Air Force missile crashed, it "impacted with the ground prematurely." When General Motors had a plant shutdown, that was a "volume-related production-schedule adjustment." Today a company that goes belly-up has "a negative cash-flow position."

Clutter is the language of the Pentagon throwing dust in the eyes of the populace by calling an invasion a "reinforced protective reaction strike" and by justifying its vast budgets on the need for "counterforce deterrence." How can we grasp such vaporous double-talk? As George Orwell pointed out in "Politics and the English Language," an essay written in 1946 but cited frequently during the Vietnam and Cambodia years of Presidents Johnson and Nixon, "Political speech and writing are largely the defense of the indefensible. . . .Thus political language has to consist largely of euphemism, question-begging and sheer cloudy vagueness." Orwell's warning that clutter is not just a nuisance but a deadly tool has come true in the recent decades of American military adventurism in Southeast Asia, Central America and other parts of the world.

Verbal camouflage reached new heights during General Alexander Haig's tenure as secretary of state during the Reagan administration. Before Haig, nobody had thought of saying "at this juncture of maturization" to mean "now." He told the American people that he saw "improved pluralization" in El Salvador, that terrorism could be fought with "meaningful sanctionary teeth" and that intermediate nuclear missiles were "at the vortex of cruciality." As for any worries the public might harbor, his message—reduced to one-syllable words—was "leave it to Al." What he actually said was, "We must push this to a lower decibel of public fixation. I don't think there's much of a learning curve to be achieved in this area of content."

I could go on quoting examples from various fields—every profession has its growing arsenal of jargon to fire at the layman and hurl him back from its walls. But the list would be tedious. The point of raising it now is to serve notice that clutter is the enemy, whatever form it takes. It slows the reader and makes the writer seem pretentious.

Beware, then, of the long word that's no better than the short word: "assistance" (help), "numerous" (many), "facilitate" (ease), "individual" (man or woman), "remainder" (rest), "initial" (first), "implement" (do), "sufficient" (enough), "attempt" (try), "referred to as" (called), and hundreds more. Beware of all the slippery new fad words for which the language already has equivalents: overview and quantify, paradigm and parameter, optimize and maximize, prioritize and potentialize. They are all weeds that will smother what you write. Don't dialogue with someone you can talk to. Don't interface with anybody.

Just as insidious are the little word clusters with which we explain how we propose to go about our explaining, or which inflate a simple preposition or conjunction into a whole windy phrase. "I might add," "It should be pointed out," "It is interesting to note"—how many sentences begin with these dreary clauses announcing what the writer is going to do next? If you might add, add it. If it should be pointed out, point it out. If it is interesting to note, *make* it interesting. Being told that something is interesting is the surest way of tempting the reader to find it dull; are we not all stupefied by what follows when someone says, "This will interest you"? As for the windy inflations, they are the countless phrases like "with the possible exception of" (except), "due to the fact that" (because), "he totally lacked the ability to" (he couldn't), "until such time as" (until), "for the purpose of" (for).

Is there any way to recognize clutter at a glance? Here's a device my students at Yale found helpful. I would put brackets around any component in a piece of writing that wasn't doing useful work. Often just one word got bracketed: the unnecessary preposition appended to a verb ("order up"), or the adverb that carries the same meaning as the verb ("smile happily"), or the adjective that states a known fact ("tall skyscraper"). Often my brackets surrounded the little qualifiers that weaken any sentence they inhabit ("a bit," "sort of"), or announcements like "I'm tempted to say," or phrases like "in a sense," which don't mean anything. Sometimes my brackets surrounded an entire sentence—the one that essentially repeats what the previous sentence said, or that says something readers don't need to know or can figure out for themselves. Most first drafts can be cut by 50 percent. They are swollen with words and phrases that do no new work.

My reason for bracketing superfluous words instead of crossing them out was to avoid violating the students' sacred prose. I wanted to leave the sentence intact for them to analyze. I was saying, "I may be wrong, but I think this can be deleted and the meaning won't be affected. But *you* decide: read the sentence without the bracketed material and see if it works." In the early weeks of the term I handed back papers that were festooned with brackets. Entire paragraphs were bracketed. But soon the students learned to put mental brackets around their own clutter, and by the end of the term their papers were almost clean. Today many of those students are professional writers, and they tell me, "I still see your brackets—they're following me through life."

You can develop the same eye. Look for the clutter in your writing and prune it ruthlessly. Be grateful for everything you can throw away. Reexamine each sentence you put on paper. Is every word doing new work? Can any thought be expressed with more economy? Is anything pompous or pretentious or faddish? Are you hanging on to something useless just because you think it's beautiful? 15

Simplify, simplify. 16

Meaning and Idea

1. Zinsser's thesis is quite obvious. When a room or a house is filled with "clutter," what does it look like? What is Zinsser saying about language that suffers from clutter?

2. What examples does the writer provide to help you see what he means by clutter? What is the *ponderous euphemism*?

3. How do corporations and the government contribute to clutter?

4. Answer the question Zinsser raises: "Is there any way to recognize clutter at a glance?"

5. Considering the title of Zinsser's book, *On Writing Well*, what do you think of the tactic he espouses?

Language, Form, Structure

1. What is the effect of the simile in the opening sentence? What other figures of speech lend clarity and focus to Zinsser's piece?

2. How does the use of the many examples he provides strengthen Zinsser's argument? How does Zinsser himself avoid clutter?

3. What does Zinsser gain by talking about small amounts of clutter (unnecessary prepositions, and then self-evident adjectives) before he begins to discuss more "substantial" examples?

4. Comment on the last line—two words, really, that serve as the closing of the selection. In what ways is this the perfect conclusion to the topic Zinsser has selected?

5. Define the following words and use each in a sentence: debasing; laborious; pompous; ponderous; euphemism; amok; vaporous; fixation; jargon; tedious; pretentious; insidious; stupefied; superfluous.

Ideas for Writing

1. Find an example, in a newspaper or a magazine, of the kind of "clutter" Zinsser criticizes, and rewrite it to state more clearly what the writer intended.

2. Write an essay called "Simplify, Simplify" in which you use examples to propose ways of streamlining some element of your life—your eating or study habits, getting to school or work, or your own writing, for example.

3. Paying special attention to paragraphs 7 and 8, write an essay in which you discuss the uses and abuses of the kind of language Zinsser discusses.

CROSSOVER

1. Barbara Tuchman in "The Black Death" (this chapter) and Susan Sontag in "Two Diseases" (Chapter Five) explore the physical and social repercussions of epidemic disease. Which examples of different aspects of disease seem most powerful to you? Why? What techniques seem most effective?

2. Maxine Hong Kingston in "Family Ghosts" (this chapter) and Langston Hughes in "Salvation" (Chapter Two) consider powerful childhood experiences in potent communities. How does each author characterize his or her community? What specific details contribute to the overall characterization?

Chapter Four

■

PROCESS

In early recorded literature we can identify the impulse to explain and to understand how to perform some task. "Make thee an ark of gopher wood," proclaims the voice of the Lord of the Old Testament to Noah; "rooms shalt thou make in the ark, and shalt pitch it within and without with pitch."

> And this is how thou shalt make it: the length of the ark three hundred cubits, the breadth of it fifty cubits, and the height of it thirty cubits. A light shalt thou make to the ark, and to a cubit shalt thou finish it upward; and the door of the ark shalt thou set in the side thereof; with lower, second, and third stories shalt thou make it. And I, behold, I do bring the flood of waters upon the earth, to destroy all flesh, wherein is the breath of life, from under heaven; every thing that is in the earth shall perish. But I will establish My covenant with thee; and thou shalt come into the ark, thou, and thy sons, and thy wife, and thy sons' wives, with thee. And of every living thing of all flesh, two of every sort shalt thou bring into the ark, to keep them alive with thee; they shall be male and female. Of the fowl after their kind, and of the cattle after their kind, of every creeping thing of the ground after its kind, two of every sort shall come unto thee, to keep them alive. And take thou unto thee of all food that is eaten and gather it to thee; and it shall be for food for thee, and for them. Thus did Noah; according to all that God commanded him, so did he.

Certainly, the simplicity of language and the precise sequence of events belie the complexity of the tasks here—it would be no easy task to make an ark simply by following these instructions—but in this explanation from the Book of Genesis you have a striking example of *process analysis* as a key element in early creative literature.

Simply put, the general concept of analysis is the attempt to break something down into parts in an effort to make the whole clear and understandable. When you analyze a novel or a poem, for example, you look carefully at the words and sentences, the chapters or stanzas to give you insights into the total work. Sometimes *causal analysis* motivates your exploration; when you examine a historical event—the Boxer Rebellion, say, or the invasion of Cambodia—you may be looking for the chain of causes and effects that make the situation comprehensible. (See Chapter Seven.) *Process analysis* states and explains the steps required to do or to make something or to show how something is (or was) done or is (or was) made.

READING PROCESS ANALYSIS

The distinction above between learning how to do or make something and learning how it is done or made is not simply semantic. Rather, the distinction lies at the heart of process analysis as a reflection of thought and as a means of broadening knowledge for readers.

The modern reading public has an ongoing love affair with "how-to" books; these books line shelf after shelf in trade book stores everywhere. The cover of an issue of *Publisher's Weekly,* the journal of the book industry, showed for one publisher more than twenty "do-it-yourself" volumes issued in a single year: how to design and build deck patios, basic remodeling techniques, how to build and use greenhouses, and how to design and install outdoor lighting, just to name a few. As a further indication of our seemingly endless attraction to books on process, the *New York Times* Book Review now includes the category "Advice, How-to, and Miscellaneous" in the list of weekly best sellers, a list that for years and years reported on only the two familiar groups, "Fiction" and "Nonfiction." We all want instructions on how to perform some process so that we ourselves can perform it in our backyards, under the hoods of our automobiles, in the solitude of our homes. When Hemingway writes to his 1920 *Toronto Star* readers (see pages 199 to 201), he tells them exactly what steps to take in order to camp out successfully. Even today we can follow the process and duplicate it. Hemingway wrote this piece so that anyone interested in a short stay in the great outdoors could get the most out of it.

Yet as readers we are equally interested in learning about processes that we have no intention of duplicating. We simply want to see a thing from the inside out, so to speak. We read with rapt attention about how homemade bombs are built or about how flappers made bathtub gin, never thinking for a moment to try schemes like these ourselves. When we read about how music boxes work, how the FBI captured one of its most wanted criminals, or how a woman born in the slums of Chicago became a multimillionaire as a banker, we are seeking information for its own sake, our joy here simply in learning the steps that produced some situation that fascinates us. Thoreau's goal in the selection from *Walden* reprinted here is to tell you how, not how to. Similarly, Ovid explains step-by-step procedures without the slightest interest in getting his readers to try to copy them. Sometimes writers explain a process so clearly that it could be copied, even if the author had not so intended it. Anthony Trollope wants you to understand how *he* goes about writing, but he lays out the process so clearly that *you* might easily use his techniques to become a prolific, if obsessive, writer.

Despite the array of topics that face a reader interested in processes, good "how-to" writing shares a common ground, and alert readers have certain expectations. Perhaps the first here (as for all writing) is clarity. Do you understand the point of the process essay? In other words, can you determine the thesis? And does the writer make the steps comprehensible? An omitted step, an undefined term, an inappropriate assumption of the reader's prior knowledge can turn a process into mayhem. What frustration is greater than trying to put together a utility cabinet, a gas grill, or a motorized toy from accompanying instructions and finding some abstruse technical term at a critical stage in the assembly? Or wondering with consternation how anyone other than a genius in engineering could advance from one step to the next simply by following the available instructions?

Readers of process analysis, like readers of narrative, usually expect to find a clear chronological sequence, although there are other possibilities. If we expect to carry out the steps ourselves, the relation of the steps to each other is especially important. When we read about process for pleasure and for information—as opposed to reading simply as the fastest and most efficient way to do something (the way we read recipes, for example, or instructions for assembling a stereo)— we also expect the writing to be interesting. Often a writer will depart from chronology to give an example, to provide some relevant background details, to define terms, or to give a lively example. But no matter how much the narrative sequence may recede, its framework is usually there as a necessary guide to the steps being explained.

WRITING PROCESS ANALYSIS

In writing process analysis, perhaps more than in any other kind of writing, you, the writer, become a teacher, and you have to be as well informed about your subject as the best teacher always is. When you explain how something is done or made, you are showing the complexities of an operation to someone who may have little knowledge about your subject. Thus, if you're revealing a process that you know how to perform quite well, have performed often, and hope to stimulate someone else to duplicate, your experience should shine in your prose. Readers should recognize with ease how much you are a master of this process. If you're analyzing a process you've investigated but have not ever attempted, readers should have no questions about your authority to write. Your explanations must be securely grounded in relevant, up-to-date, comprehensive information. In advance of selecting a topic to explore through process analysis, then, you should address these questions:

1. What process can I perform well enough to explain to people who might want to try it themselves or who just might want to know how the process is carried out?

2. What process interests me enough to make me want to research it adequately and to present it clearly in an explanation readers can follow easily?

PURPOSE AND AUDIENCE

You have options in regard to your purpose for writing as you consider a topic for development through process analysis. You should decide whether you want primarily to give instructions or to give information. Certainly these two purposes overlap, but it's important to acknowledge some differences. Giving instructions implies a desire on behalf of reader and writer alike to take action. If you're explaining how to plant a garden of perennials, for example, you'd want the reader to be able to follow your directions on a piece of land in his or her own backyard, and the reader would have the same expectations. If you're writing essentially to give information, on the other hand, you'll be explaining a process you probably would not expect anyone to act upon. Nevertheless, your reader should see easily how this process is achieved and should understand fully how an orderly procedure leads to a realistic end. A consideration of your purpose in writing a process paper is incomplete without considerable thought about your audience. It's comfortable, and sometimes accurate, to assume that anyone who chooses to read *instructions* has a need or a desire for them, and so the writer can count on the readers' loyal interest in the subject right from the start. It's true that most people who choose to read a book called *How to Build a Deck Patio* would have ambitions in the future for expanding their outdoor living space. Such people want to build a deck, and, already motivated and charged with self-interest, they turn to a book for help in realizing their goal.

But it's not always true that instructions are read by captive audiences only. Assume for a moment that you're leafing through a popular magazine and you come across a piece called "How to Tune Up Your Car: Ten Simple Steps for People with Ten Thumbs and Two Left Hands." Being unmechanical, you might be one of those who ordinarily shiver and turn the page when you see anything that requires taking things apart and putting them together. But this essay, from its title at least, may be talking your language. You're fed up with the high costs of car maintenance at a service station, and you'll take a chance on reading this essay to see if in fact even a clod like you can follow the process and master it. Here, then, the writer would have been wrong to assume only a captive readership. A good part of this essay would have to go toward capturing and engaging the reader. It's certain that a writer who chose a title like the one we've mentioned above knows how little his audience understands about tuning cars and how important it is to woo that audience from the start.

Furthermore, assuming that you have only an eager, dedicated audience for your instructions can make for sloppy writing. In some cases the easiest way to present a set of instructions is just to number and list them briefly with accompanying illustrations and be done with it. But if you've ever struggled with supposedly simple lists and pictures on the cartons of do-it-yourself products, you know what it means to long for fuller explanations—complete sentences, detailed paragraphs!—when there is no slot into which an equally nonexistent Flap A must fit, or when four nuts and three bolts remain to complete a unit that demands three nuts and four bolts. Even interested readers deserve clear, careful prose. Besides, for the kind of process paper that you will write to give instructions at school or on the job, the real audience—your instructor, your fellow classmates, or your coworkers—will almost certainly not have a passion for or an interest in your essay topic. You might be able to tick off 15 quick steps for curing ich in tropical fish; and if you were writing for an amateur collector who had lost a tank of mollies and swordtails to the disease, she might be reading your essay with rapt attention. But if your teacher or the fellow in the next row has no interest in home aquariums, your essay will have to win these people over as much as it will have to teach them how to carry out those basic steps for bacteria-free fish. Although *your* purpose might be to give directions, readers who have no special interest in advance of following them may, despite your goals, be reading only information. Your paper should acknowledge both readerships by avoiding complaisance at all costs.

When you analyze a process essentially to convey information, as opposed to writing essentially to give directions, you should always work to draw your reader in, and that rule of thumb should guide a process essay of any kind. You should be weighing your audience's stake in reading your paper. What chord can you strike that will hold your reader's interest? How can you convince your readers that what you say will amuse or inform or surprise them to a high enough degree to warrant their taking the time to read?

Consideration of (and for) your audience raises another question that you must face as you plan and develop your paper. How much can you assume that your audience knows about your topic? This is an important question because the response will guide your level of vocabulary and the scope and depth of detail you must include. Suppose you wanted to explain a quick method you'd developed for adding cuffs to trouser legs or coat sleeves. If your intended audience were a group of young, single males or females who had never held a needle in their hands, you'd have to consider as technical vocabulary some of the basic language required to explain the process, words like *hem, hemline, basting, thimble, finish, blind stitch,* just to name a few. If you didn't provide definitions at least for some of these, you couldn't be sure that your readers would understand what you were talking about. And for such an audience you couldn't assume much advance knowledge of any steps in the process. You'd have to spell out everything from how to hold the garment to how to knot the thread at the end of the needle. However, for an audience of experienced homemakers who had sewn lots of hems and seams before, you could assume a thorough working knowledge of sewing vocabulary and could skip the most elementary steps, fairly confident that your readers knew the basics of needlework.

You can see even from this brief section how complex an issue audience is for the writer of process analysis. It's never easy to know exactly what your audience is like, even when you might know pretty well who they are—your teacher, say, or the group of cowriters with whom you've been working in class. Professional writers have similar problems: For example, a writer doing a piece for *Mademoiselle,* a magazine ostensibly for fashion-conscious, upper-middle-class young women, has no guarantee that every reader is equal in knowledge, language, and background to understand an article on the use of weight machines to firm up flabby muscles, or on the process of buying good wines, or on planting a window garden. Some writers of process, then, will define their own audience and refer overtly to it in the paper, weaving their assumptions about the readership into the essay itself. Hemingway makes clear in the first couple of paragraphs of "Camping Out" that he is writing not to experienced campers and fishing enthusiasts but to bona fide amateurs. The writer whose title is "How to Tune Up Your Car: Ten Simple Steps for People with Ten Thumbs and Two Left Hands" has defined his audience directly in the title. The strategy of naming your audience for all to see can help you draw in otherwise reluctant readers. Your audience may not in fact be the audience you've defined; but once they know exactly for whom you're aiming, they might be willing to suspend disbelief, so to speak, and to join temporarily the group you're trying to reach. Aware of the readers that Hemingway is addressing, even long-time fishermen could enjoy the good-humored recommendations the writer offers to novices.

PROCESS

Spend some time identifying a process you want to write about by considering the two questions raised on page 186. If you choose to give directions for a process you know how to do well, you'll have to reflect a while on the various steps required to carry it out. The more experienced you are, the more automatic your actions become; you may have to bring to a level of conscious thought some of the steps you haven't dwelled on for years. If you choose to give information about a process that interests you, you may have to spend some time in the library looking at books and magazines that will fill in any gaps of knowledge.

Once you have a topic and have duly considered audience and purpose, perhaps the best way to begin is to make a rough list of all the steps required in the process. Once you have your list, look it over carefully. Be sure that you have not left anything out. Are there preparatory steps to take, for example? Is there equipment that must be gathered together before beginning? Should objects be measured or counted beforehand? Should you provide an overview or some background information, including, perhaps, a history of the process, the reasons for your interest in it, the ultimate goals of the process, or your intention to examine in great detail only certain phases of the analysis?

You'll also need to examine as objectively as you can the terminology that appears on your list. Identify specialized terms, and plan to define them for your readers.

Look too with special attention at the sequence of steps you've listed. Do they follow each other chronologically? Most process analyses proceed through an orderly sequence of time: Readers have to know what to do first, what to do next, and what to do after that. But you do have other options, and you might want to rearrange the steps on your list. In explaining how you clean a six-room apartment efficiently, you might reject the apparent chronological sequence—"First I clean the bedrooms. . . .Then I wash the bathroom floor. . . . Last I do the kitchen." Instead you might arrange information by importance or by level of difficulty. "The easiest part of the job is vacuuming the carpet on all the floors. . . .The most difficult task is dusting the top corners in the rooms with high ceilings." (This order may be chronological as well, that is, if you do the simple work first and the tough work last, but it does not have to be.)

Another option is to arrange the information in order of physical location. Here you'd move the reader from place to place in the house, your organizing principle based on the spatial relation of the rooms. Or you could decide on some other logical sequence, sorting information according to an interesting scheme you've worked out. "I have learned that cleaning a six-room house should proceed only in one of these ways: the 'once-over-lightly' approach, the 'I'm starting to get serious about this mess' approach, and the 'pull out the stops because the folks are coming tonight' approach." Whatever order you choose should be meaningful, however, and should help the reader understand the process. A revised version of your list should guide you as you develop your drafts.

The sample sentence in the paragraph directly above helps to illustrate once again the all-important thesis, the one sentence that states the main point of your essay. Notice how the writer draws you into his unusual approach to house cleaning through an amusing set of options. Whether or not you are interested in house cleaning (high on almost everyone's most-tedious-things-to-do list), you'd probably want to read an essay that stated its thesis in such an off-beat way. Further to the point, whether the writer ultimately uses this draft thesis sentence in the essay or uses instead some other version of it edited for brevity, or whether the writer decides not to use a thesis sentence at all, counting instead on the readers' ability to determine the thesis on their own, is irrelevant. The fact that the writer can *produce* a thesis, however, is a sure step toward a successful paper. Keeping the thesis in mind helps the writer stay on task and unify the various ideas in the essay around the main point.

Remember that you're trying to engage your reader's interest, so you should resist writing your process paper as a mere list of steps. You might relate a personal incident that sheds light on why you chose to analyze this particular process or that taught you the quickest and the simplest way to do the job. You might investigate the effects or consequences of the process. You might draw upon concrete sensory language to give an immediacy and drama to the steps you're explaining. You might insist upon the importance of knowing how to master this process or of understanding how it is achieved. You might develop an appropriate comparison or analogy. You might provide diagrams, drawings, photographs, maps, charts, or graphs to illustrate the text of your essay.

And don't ignore your style. Prune from early drafts any details that risk making your paper wordy or unnecessarily complicated. Check your vocabulary for jargon, excessively technical terms, or key words that you failed to define. Pay particular attention to transitions. It's easy to overdo time or step markers— *"first"* do this, *then* do that, *next* do something else"—but you will need some of them to help your readers know when one step ends and another begins.

SUMMING UP: PROCESS

Reading Process Analysis

- Process analysis states and explains the steps required to do or make something or to show how something is (or was) done or is (or was) made.

- Examine the writer's thesis for its relation to a rhetorical approach based on process analysis.

- Consider all the steps included in the process analysis: Are they clear, complete, and comprehensible?

- Pay attention to new terms.

- Examine the sequence: Has the writer provided a clear chronology of steps (when appropriate) and linked the steps logically?

- Identify the elements that hold your interest: What aspects of language and presentation does the writer use to engage your attention?

- If the writer expects you to duplicate the process, identify the elements that will allow you to achieve that goal.

Writing Process Analysis

- Understand your role as a teacher when your write process analysis; your writing must show mastery or authority over the process you are explaining.

- Ground your explanations of the process in relevant, up-to-date, comprehensive information.

- To identify a topic for process analysis, look for an activity that you can perform well enough to explain how someone can duplicate it or simply how someone might want to know how to carry out the process; or look for an interesting process that you might want to research and present clearly for readers to follow easily.

- Decide on whether you want to give instructions or information.

- Thoroughly consider the audience you are writing for; win them over to your topic even though they might not have any intrinsic interest in it.

- Produce a thesis that carefully defines the parameters of your intentions in writing your process paper.

- Determine how much your audience needs to know about the topic and direct your writing to fulfilling those needs by defining key terms, spelling out essential steps in the process, and drawing on clear language and sentence style.

On Keeping a Notebook

Joan Didion

Born in Sacramento, California, in 1934, Joan Didion is a novelist, a screenwriter, and a film critic, but she has also won great acclaim as an essayist. Her dry style prompted the novelist James Dickey to call her "the finest woman prose stylist writing in English today." She is not a baby boomer, but her cool detachment often links her to that generation. She won the Vogue Prix de Paris award in 1956 with an essay she wrote during her last year at Berkeley and has been writing professionally ever since.

The following essay, from *Slouching towards Bethlehem* (1968), is a fine example of the shrewd, incisive writing she produces and of the process she goes through as she creates it.

" '*T*hat woman Estelle,'" the note reads, "'is partly the reason why   1
George Sharp and I are separated today.' *Dirty crepe-de-Chine wrapper, hotel bar, Wilmington RR, 9:45 A.M. August Monday morning.*"

Since the note is in my notebook, it presumably has some meaning to me. I   2
study it for a long while. At first I have only the most general notion of what I was doing on an August Monday morning in the bar of the hotel across from the Pennsylvania Railroad station in Wilmington, Delaware (waiting for a train? missing one? 1960? 1961? why Wilmington?), but I do remember being there. The woman in the dirty crepe-de-Chine wrapper had come down from her room for a beer, and the bartender had heard before the reason why George Sharp and she were separated today. "Sure," he said, and went on mopping the floor. "You told me." At the other end of the bar is a girl. She is talking, pointedly, not to the man beside her but to a cat lying in the triangle of sunlight cast through the open door. She is wearing a plaid silk dress from Peck & Peck, and the hem is coming down.

Here is what it is: the girl has been on the Eastern Shore, and now she is   3
going back to the city, leaving the man beside her, and all she can see ahead are the viscous summer sidewalks and the 3A.M. long-distance calls that will make her lie awake and then sleep drugged through all the steaming mornings left in August (1960? 1961?). Because she must go directly from the train to lunch in New York, she wishes that she had a safety pin for the hem of the plaid silk dress, and she also wishes that she could forget about the hem and the lunch and stay in the cool bar that smells of disinfectant and malt and make friends with the woman in the crepe-de-Chine wrapper. She is afflicted by a little self-pity, and she wants to compare Estelles. That is what that was all about.

Why did I write it down? In order to remember, of course, but exactly what   4
was it I wanted to remember? How much of it actually happened? Did any of it? Why do I keep a notebook at all? It is easy to deceive oneself on all those scores. The impulse to write things down is a peculiarly compulsive one, inexplicable to

those who do not share it, useful only accidentally, only secondarily, in the way that any compulsion tries to justify itself. I suppose that it begins or does not begin in the cradle. Although I have felt compelled to write things down since I was five years old, I doubt that my daughter ever will, for she is a singularly blessed and accepting child, delighted with life exactly as life presents itself to her, unafraid to go to sleep and unafraid to wake up. Keepers of private notebooks are a different breed altogether, lonely and resistant rearrangers of things, anxious malcontents, children afflicted apparently at birth with some presentiment of loss.

My first notebook was a Big Five tablet, given to me by my mother with the sensible suggestion that I stop whining and learn to amuse myself by writing down my thoughts. She returned the tablet to me a few years ago; the first entry is an account of a woman who believed herself to be freezing to death in the Arctic night, only to find, when day broke, that she had stumbled onto the Sahara Desert, where she would die of the heat before lunch. I have no idea what turn of a five-year-old's mind could have prompted so insistently, "ironic" and exotic a story, but it does reveal a certain predilection for the extreme which has dogged me into adult life; perhaps if I were analytically inclined I would find it a truer story than any I might have told about Donald Johnson's birthday party or the day my cousin Brenda put Kitty Litter in the aquarium.

So the point of my keeping a notebook has never been, nor is it now, to have an accurate factual record of what I have been doing or thinking. That would be a different impulse entirely, an instinct for reality which I sometimes envy but do not possess. At no point have I ever been able successfully to keep a diary; my approach to daily life ranges from the grossly negligent to the merely absent, and on those few occasions when I have tried dutifully to record a day's events, boredom has so overcome me that the results are mysterious at best. What is this business about "shopping, typing piece, dinner with E, depressed"? Shopping for what? Typing what piece? Who is E? Was this "E" depressed, or was I depressed? Who cares?

In fact I have abandoned altogether that kind of pointless entry; instead I tell what some would call lies. "That's simply not true," the members of my family frequently tell me when they come up against my memory of a shared event. "The party was *not* for you, the spider was *not* a black widow, *it wasn't that way at all*." Very likely they are right, for not only have I always had trouble distinguishing between what happened and what merely might have happened, but I remain unconvinced that the distinction, for my purposes, matters. The cracked crab that I recall having for lunch the day my father came home from Detroit in 1945 must certainly be embroidery, worked into the day's pattern to lend verisimilitude; I was ten years old and would not now remember the cracked crab. The day's events did not turn on cracked crab. And yet it is precisely that fictitious crab that makes me see the afternoon all over again, a home movie run all too often, the father bearing gifts, the child weeping, an exercise in family love and guilt. Or that is what it was to me. Similarly, perhaps it never did snow that August in Vermont; perhaps there never were flurries in the night wind, and maybe no one else felt the ground hardening and summer already dead even as we pretended to bask in it, but that was how it felt to me, and it might as well have snowed, could have snowed, did snow.

How it felt to me: that is getting closer to the truth about a notebook. I some- 8 times delude myself about why I keep a notebook, imagine that some thrifty virtue derives from preserving everything observed. See enough and write it down, I tell myself, and then some morning when the world seems drained of wonder, some day when I am only going through the motions of doing what I am supposed to do, which is write—on that bankrupt morning I will simply open my notebook and there it will all be, a forgotten account with accumulated interest, paid passage back to the world out there: dialogue overheard in hotels and elevators and at the hat-check counter in Pavillon (one middle-aged man shows his hat-check to another and says, "That's my old football number"); impressions of Bettina Aptheker[1] and Benjamin Sonnenberg[2] and Teddy ("Mr. Acapulco") Stauffer[3]; careful *aperçus* about tennis bums and failed fashion models and Greek shipping heiresses, one of whom taught me a significant lesson (a lesson I could have learned from F. Scott Fitzgerald, but perhaps we all must meet the very rich for ourselves) by asking, when I arrived to interview her in her orchid-filled sitting room on the second day of a paralyzing New York blizzard, whether it was snowing outside.

I imagine, in other words, that the notebook is about other people. But of 9 course it is not. I have no real business with what one stranger said to another at the hat-check counter in Pavillon; in fact I suspect that the line "That's my old football number" touched not my own imagination at all, but merely some memory of something once read, probably "The Eighty-Yard Run." Nor is my concern with a woman in a dirty crepe-de-Chine wrapper in a Wilmington bar. My stake is always, of course, in the unmentioned girl in the plaid silk dress. *Remember what it was to be me:* that is always the point.

It is a difficult point to admit. We are brought up in the ethic that others, any 10 others, all others, are by definition more interesting than ourselves; taught to be diffident, just this side of self-effacing ("You're the least important person in the room and don't forget it," Jessica Mitford's[4] governess would hiss in her ear on the advent of any social occasion; I copied that into my notebook because it is only recently that I have been able to enter a room without hearing some such phrase in my inner ear.) Only the very young and the very old may recount their dreams at breakfast, dwell upon self, interrupt with memories of beach picnics and favorite Liberty lawn dresses and the rainbow trout in a creek near Colorado Springs. The rest of us are expected, rightly, to affect absorption in other people's favorite dresses, other people's trout.

And so we do. But our notebooks give us away, for however dutifully we 11 record what we see around us, the common denominator of all we see is always,

---

[1]A leader of the free speech movement at Berkeley in the 1960s.
[2]Public relations expert.
[3]Band leader who opened his own nightclub as a retiree in Acapulco.
[4]British writer who investigates unethical practices in government and business.

transparently, shamelessly, the implacable "I." We are not talking here about the kind of notebook that is patently for public consumption, a structural conceit for binding together a series of graceful *pensées,* we are talking about something private, about bits of the mind's string too short to use, an indiscriminate and erratic assemblage with meaning only for its maker.

And sometimes even the maker has difficulty with the meaning. There does 12 not seem to be, for example, any point in my knowing for the rest of my life that, during 1964, 720 tons of soot fell on every square mile of New York City, yet there it is in my notebook, labeled "FACT." Nor do I really need to remember that Ambrose Bierce liked to spell Leland Stanford's name "£eland $tanford" or that "smart women almost always wear black in Cuba," a fashion hint without much potential for practical application. And does not the relevance of these notes seem marginal at best?:

> In the basement museum of the Inyo County Courthouse in Independence, California, sign pinned to a mandarin coat: "This MANDARIN COAT was often worn by Mrs. Minnie S. Brooks when giving lectures on her TEAPOT COLLECTION."

> Redhead getting out of car in front of Beverly Wilshire Hotel, chinchilla stole, Vuitton bags with tags reading:
>
> > MRS LOU FOX
> > HOTEL SAHARA
> > VEGAS

Well, perhaps not entirely marginal. As a matter of fact, Mrs. Minnie S. 13 Brooks and her MANDARIN COAT pull me back into my own childhood, for although I never knew Mrs. Brooks and did not visit Inyo County until I was thirty, I grew up in just such a world, in houses cluttered with Indian relics and bits of gold ore and ambergris and the souvenirs my Aunt Mercy Farnsworth brought back from the Orient. It is a long way from that world to Mrs. Lou Fox's world, where we all live now, and is it not just as well to remember that? Might not Mrs. Minnie S. Brooks help me to remember what I am? Might not Mrs. Lou Fox help me to remember what I am not?

But sometimes the point is harder to discern. What exactly did I have in 14 mind when I noted down that it cost the father of someone I know $650 a month to light the place on the Hudson in which he lived before the Crash? What use was I planning to make of this line by Jimmy Hoffa[5]: "I may have my faults, but being wrong ain't one of them"? And although I think it interesting to know where the girls who travel with the Syndicate have their hair done when they find themselves on the West Coast, will I ever make suitable use of it? Might I not be better off just passing it on to John O'Hara?[6] What is a recipe for sauerkraut doing in my notebook? What kind of magpie keeps this notebook? *"He was born the*

[5]United States labor leader who disappeared mysteriously in 1971.
[6]American novelist who died in 1970.

night the Titanic went down." That seems a nice enough line, and I even recall
who said it, but is it not really a better line in life than it could ever be in fiction?

But of course that is exactly it: not that I should ever use the line, but that I   15
should remember the woman who said it and the afternoon I heard it. We were on
her terrace by the sea, and we were finishing the wine left from lunch, trying to
get what sun there was, a California winter sun. The woman whose husband was
born the night the *Titanic* went down wanted to rent her house, wanted to go back
to her children in Paris. I remember wishing that I could afford the house, which
cost $1,000 a month. "Someday you will," she said lazily. "Someday it all
comes." There in the sun on her terrace it seemed easy to believe in someday, but
later I had a low-grade afternoon hangover and ran over a black snake on the way
to the supermarket and was flooded with inexplicable fear when I heard the
checkout clerk explaining to the man ahead of me why she was finally divorcing
her husband. "He left me no choice," she said over and over as she punched the
register. "He has a little seven-month-old baby by her, he left me no choice." I
would like to believe that my dread then was for the human condition, but of
course it was for me, because I wanted a baby and did not then have one and
because I wanted to own the house that cost $1,000 a month to rent and because
I had a hangover.

It all comes back. Perhaps it is difficult to see the value in having one's self   16
back in that kind of mood, but I do see it; I think we are well advised to keep on
nodding terms with the people we used to be, whether we find them attractive
company or not. Otherwise they turn up unannounced and surprise us, come hammering on the mind's door at 4 A.M. of a bad night and demand to know who
deserted them, who betrayed them, who is going to make amends. We forget all
too soon the things we thought we could never forget. We forget the loves and the
betrayals alike, forget what we whispered and what we screamed, forget who we
were. I have already lost touch with a couple of people I used to be; one of them,
a seventeen-year-old, presents little threat, although it would be of some interest
to me to know again what it feels like to sit on a river levee drinking vodka-and-
orange-juice and listening to Les Paul and Mary Ford and their echoes sing "How
High the Moon" on the car radio. (You see I still have the scenes: but I no longer
perceive myself among those present, no longer could even improvise the dialogue.) The other one, a twenty-three-year-old, bothers me more. She was always
a good deal of trouble, and I suspect she will reappear when I least want to see
her, skirts too long, shy to the point of aggravation, always the injured party, full
of recriminations and little hurts and stories I do not want to hear again, at once
saddening me and angering me with her vulnerability and ignorance, an appari-
tion all the more insistent for being so long banished.

It is a good idea, then, to keep in touch, and I suppose that keeping in   17
touch is what notebooks are all about. And we are all on our own when it comes
to keeping those lines open to ourselves: your notebook will never help me, nor
mine you. *"So what's new in the whiskey business?"* What could that possibly
mean to you? To me it means a blonde in a Pucci bathing suit sitting with a couple of fat men by the pool at the Beverly Hills Hotel. Another man approaches,

and they all regard one another in silence for a while. "So what's new in the whiskey business?" one of the fat men finally says by way of welcome, and the blonde stands up, arches one foot and dips it in the pool, looking all the while at the cabaña where Baby Pignatari is talking on the telephone. That is all there is to that, except that several years later I saw the blonde coming out of Saks Fifth Avenue in New York with her California complexion and a voluminous mink coat. In the harsh wind that day she looked old and irrevocably tired to me, and even the skins in the mink coat were not worked the way they were doing them that year, not the way she would have wanted them done, and there is the point of the story. For a while after that I did not like to look in the mirror, and my eyes would skim the newspapers and pick out only the deaths, the cancer victims, the premature coronaries, the suicides, and I stopped riding the Lexington Avenue IRT because I noticed for the first time that all the strangers I had seen for years—the man with the seeing-eye dog, the spinster who read the classified pages every day, the fat girl who always got off with me at Grand Central—looked older than they once had.

It all comes back. Even that recipe for sauerkraut: even that brings it back. 18 I was on Fire Island when I first made that sauerkraut, and it was raining, and we drank a lot of bourbon and ate the sauerkraut and went to bed at ten, and I listened to the rain and the Atlantic and felt safe. I made the sauerkraut again last night and it did not make me feel any safer, but that is, as they say, another story.

Meaning and Idea

1. Why does Didion keep a notebook? Is it to capture something? Truth? Reality? Something else?

2. What did her very first notebook entry, done as a child, indicate about the kind of notebook she was likely to keep?

3. Didion says her "approach to daily life ranges from the grossly negligent to the merely absent." What is your sense of this insight? Does Didion's habit of keeping a notebook imply negligence or absence? Why do you think so?

4. "I suppose that keeping in touch is what notebooks are all about," writes Didion. What does she mean by this comment?

Language, Form, Structure

1. What is the thesis of this piece? How did you determine it?

2. If you wanted to follow Didion's example of keeping a notebook, what specific steps explained here could you take? Or is this essay an example of explaining "how" rather than "how to"? Explain your answer.

3. Didion calls her entries "bits of the mind's string too short to use." What does she mean? Reexamine the essay and find the transition points between the "bits" and what she expands them to.

4. In the first sentence of the last paragraph, "It all comes back," what is "It"? The sentence seems quite ambiguous and yet, somehow, it is not. Why? What is your reaction, in general, to the concluding paragraph?

5. Define the following words and use each in a sentence: crepe-de-Chine; viscous; predilection; implacable; *pensées;* ambergris; recriminations; diffident; assemblage; malcontents; presentiment; verisimilitude; *aperçus.*

Ideas for Writing

1. Think of a process that has long and regularly been a part of your life but also has evolved over time. Write an essay about this process and its evolution. For instance, you might choose something like doing homework, playing a musical instrument, or cooking for large holiday parties.

2. Think about the process you follow in writing an essay for your English or composition class. Do you make false starts? Do you have good ideas which somehow never appear in a final draft? Write an essay about your process of writing an essay, complete with descriptions of what makes writing difficult and with sample experiences.

3. Is Didion's essay only for other keepers of notebooks, other writers? Write an essay to analyze what you think Didion's purposes are in recounting her habits to a public audience.

Camping Out

Ernest Hemingway

Ernest Hemingway (1898–1961) is perhaps America's best-known and most widely read modern writer. He was born in Oak Park, Illinois, and started his career as a journalist for the *Kansas City Star.* Wounded while serving as a volunteer ambulance driver in France, Hemingway became part of the "lost generation" of American expatriate writers in Paris in the 1920s. Nick Adams, his alter-ego fictional hero, first appeared in Hemingway's collection of stories, *In Our Time,* in 1924. That book was followed by, among others, *The Sun Also Rises* (1926), *A Farewell to Arms* (1929), *For Whom the Bell Tolls* (1940), and *The Old Man and the Sea* (1952)—all characterized by Hemingway's renowned crisp simplicity. After leaving Paris, Hemingway lived, wrote, hunted, and caroused in Key West, Cuba, Montana, and Africa. He received the Nobel Prize for Literature in 1954. A despondent Hemingway shot himself in 1961.

This piece originally appeared in the *Toronto Star,* for which Hemingway was the Paris correspondent, in the 1920s *before* he established himself as a major writer. In this process analysis, we can observe the roots of the author's well-known fascination with outdoor life and his simplicity in writing.

*T*housands of people will go into the bush this summer to cut the   1
high cost of living. A man who gets his two weeks' salary while he is on vacation should be able to put those two weeks in fishing and camping and be able to save one week's salary clear. He ought to be able to sleep comfortably every night, to eat well every day and to return to the city rested and in good condition.

But if he goes into the woods with a frying pan, an ignorance of black flies   2
and mosquitoes, and a great and abiding lack of knowledge about cookery the chances are that his return will be very different. He will come back with enough mosquito bites to make the back of his neck look like a relief map of the Caucasus. His digestion will be wrecked after a valiant battle to assimilate half-cooked or charred grub. And he won't have had a decent night's sleep while he has been gone.

He will solemnly raise his right hand and inform you that he has joined the   3
grand army of never-agains. The call of the wild may be all right, but it's a dog's life. He's heard the call of the tame with both ears. Waiter, bring him an order of milk toast.

In the first place he overlooked the insects. Black flies, no-see-ums, deer   4
flies, gnats and mosquitoes were instituted by the devil to force people to live in cities where he could get at them better. If it weren't for them everybody would live in the bush and he would be out of work. It was a rather successful invention.

But here are lots of dopes that will counteract the pests. The simplest per-   5
haps is oil of citronella. Two bits' worth of this purchased at any pharmacist's will be enough to last for two weeks in the worst fly and mosquito-ridden country.

Rub a little on the back of your neck, your forehead and your wrists before 6 you start fishing, and the blacks and skeeters will shun you. The odor of citronella is not offensive to people. It smells like gun oil. But the bugs do hate it.

Oil of pennyroyal and eucalyptol are also much hated by mosquitoes, and 7 with citronella they form the basis for many proprietary preparations. But it is cheaper and better to buy the straight citronella. Put a little on the mosquito netting that covers the front of your pup tent or canoe tent at night, and you won't be bothered.

To be really rested and get any benefit out of a vacation a man must get a 8 good night's sleep every night. The first requisite for this is to have plenty of cover. It is twice as cold as you expect it will be in the bush four nights out of five, and a good plan is to take just double the bedding that you think you will need. An old quilt that you can wrap up in is as warm as two blankets.

Nearly all outdoor writers rhapsodize over the browse bed. It is all right for 9 the man who knows how to make one and has plenty of time. But in a succession of one-night camps on a canoe trip all you need is level ground for your tent floor and you will sleep all right if you have plenty of covers under you. Take twice as much cover as you think that you will need, and then put two-thirds of it under you. You will sleep warm and get your rest.

When it is clear weather you don't need to pitch your tent if you are only 10 stopping for the night. Drive four stakes at the head of your made-up bed and drape your mosquito bar over that, then you can sleep like a log and laugh at the mosquitoes.

Outside of insects and bum sleeping the rock that wrecks most camping 11 trips is cooking. The average tyro's idea of cooking is to fry everything and fry it good and plenty. Now, a frying pan is a most necessary thing to any trip, but you also need the old stew kettle and the folding reflector baker.

A pan of fried trout can't be bettered and they don't cost any more than 12 ever. But there is a good and bad way of frying them.

The beginner puts his trout and his bacon in and over a brightly burning 13 fire, the bacon curls up and dries into a dry tasteless cinder and the trout is burned outside while it is still raw inside. He eats them and it is all right if he is only out for the day and going home to a good meal at night. But if he is going to face more trout and bacon the next morning and other equally well-cooked dishes for the remainder of two weeks he is on the pathway to nervous dyspepsia.

The proper way is to cook over coals. Have several cans of Crisco or Coto- 14 suet or one of the vegetable shortenings along that are as good as lard and excellent for all kinds of shortening. Put the bacon in and when it is about half cooked lay the trout in the hot grease, dipping them in corn meal first. Then put the bacon on top of the trout and it will baste them as it slowly cooks.

The coffee can be boiling at the same time and in a smaller skillet pancakes 15 being made that are satisfying the other campers while they are waiting for the trout.

With the prepared pancake flours you take a cupful of pancake flour and 16 add a cup of water. Mix the water and flour and as soon as the lumps are out it is ready for cooking. Have the skillet hot and keep it well greased. Drop the batter in and as soon as it is done on one side loosen it in the skillet and flip it over. Apple butter, syrup or cinnamon and sugar go well with the cakes.

While the crowd have taken the edge from their appetites with flapjacks the 17 trout have been cooked and they and the bacon are ready to serve. The trout are crisp outside and firm and pink inside and the bacon is well done—but not too done. If there is anything better than that combination the writer has yet to taste it in a lifetime devoted largely and studiously to eating.

The stew kettle will cook you dried apricots when they have resumed their 18 predried plumpness after a night of soaking, it will serve to concoct a mulligan in, and it will cook macaroni. When you are not using it, it should be boiling water for the dishes.

In the baker, mere man comes into his own, for he can make a pie that to 19 his bush appetite will have it all over the product that mother used to make, like a tent. Men have always believed that there was something mysterious and diffi-cult about making a pie. Here is a great secret. There is nothing to it. We've been kidded for years. Any man of average office intelligence can make at least as good a pie as his wife.

All there is to a pie is a cup and a half of flour, one-half teaspoonful of salt, 20 one-half cup of lard and cold water. That will make pie crust that will bring tears of joy into your camping partners' eyes.

Mix the salt with the flour, work the lard into the flour, make it up into a 21 good workmanlike dough with cold water. Spread some flour on the back of a box or something flat, and pat the dough around a while. Then roll it out with what-ever kind of round bottle you prefer. Put a little more lard on the surface of the sheet of dough and then slosh a little flour on and roll it up and then roll it out again with the bottle.

Cut out a piece of the rolled out dough big enough to line a pie tin. I like 22 the kind with holes in the bottom. Then put in your dried apples that have soaked all night and been sweetened, or your apricots, or your blueberries, and then take another sheet of the dough and drape it gracefully over the top, soldering it down at the edges with your fingers. Cut a couple of slits in the top dough sheet and prick it a few times with a fork in an artistic manner.

Put it in the baker with a good slow fire for forty-five minutes and then take 23 it out and if your pals are Frenchmen they will kiss you. The penalty for knowing how to cook is that the others will make you do all the cooking.

It is all right to talk about roughing it in the woods. But the real woodsman 24 is the man who can be really comfortable in the bush.

Meaning and Idea

1. Explain in your own words the overall process that Hemingway analyzes in this essay. What subprocesses does he explain as parts of the overall process? Choose one of those subprocesses and explain it fully.

2. According to the essay, what are some of the advantages of spending your vacation camping out?

3. What are the best ways "to counteract the pests"?

4. What are the bad and good ways to cook trout? What other cooking preparations does Hemingway explain?

5. Is Hemingway in favor of "roughing it"? How do you know? Analyze the first and last paragraphs in light of your answer.

Language, Form, Structure

1. Which sentences best state Hemingway's purpose in this essay? Where does he define his audience?

2. How do the first two paragraphs establish the organization of this process analysis? Where does the process analysis actually begin? What is the purpose of the writing up to that point?

3. How does Hemingway use exemplification in this essay? How does he use description?

4. Write sentences showing that you know the meaning of the following words: assimilate; valiant; requisite; rhapsodize; tyro; dyspepsia; mulligan; concoct; soldering.

Ideas for Writing

1. What is your favorite vacation activity? Write a process analysis telling others how to enjoy a similar vacation experience.

2. Choose some common activity—commuting to work, studying, working out, making a pie crust—and write an essay that tells how to do it correctly as opposed to how to do it incorrectly.

3. The intended audience for "Camping Out" was originally urban newspaper readers in the 1920s. Write an essay in which you analyze Hemingway's use of language. Is the word choice appropriate to his audience? How appropriate is the style of the essay to a 1990s newspaper readership? Would you suggest any modifications if the essay were to be published in a newspaper today?

250 Words Every Quarter of an Hour

Anthony Trollope

Anthony Trollope (1815–1882) is known for his realistic novels about the lives of ordinary middle- and upper-middle-class people of Victorian England. Though his later novels became more politically and sociologically oriented, his most famous works are the series of Barsetshire novels about daily life in that fictional county, which include *The Warden* (1855), *The Small House at Allington* (1864), and *The Last Chronicle of Barset* (1867).

In this section from Trollope's *Autobiography*, he gives us an intimate view of the processes and results of his own writing habits. In this way, he suggests a daily process which "will produce as much as a man ought to write."

*A*ll those who have lived as literary men,—working daily as literary [1] labourers,—will agree with me that three hours a day will produce as much as a man ought to write. But then, he should so have trained himself that he shall be able to work continuously during those three hours,—so have tutored his mind that it shall not be necessary for him to sit nibbling his pen, and gazing at the wall before him, till he shall have found the words with which he wants to express his ideas. It had at this time become my custom,—and it still is my custom, though of late I have become a little lenient with myself,—to write with my watch before me, and to require from myself 250 words every quarter of an hour. I have found that the 250 words have been forthcoming as regularly as my watch went. But my three hours were not devoted entirely to writing. I always began my task by reading the work of the day before, an operation which would take me half an hour, and which consisted chiefly in weighing with my ear the sound of the words and phrases. I would strongly recommend this practice to all tyros in writing. That their work should be read after it has been written is a matter of course,—that it should be read twice at least before it goes to the printers, I take to be a matter of course. But by reading what he has last written, just before he recommences his task, the writer will catch the tone and spirit of what he is then saying, and will avoid the fault of seeming to be unlike himself. This division of time allowed me to produce over ten pages of an ordinary novel volume a day, and if kept up through ten months, would have given as its results three novels of three volumes each in the year. . . .

I have never written three novels in a year, but by following the plan above [2] described I have written more than as much as three volumes; and by adhering to it over a course of years, I have been enabled to have always on hand,—for some time back now,—one or two or even three unpublished novels in my desk beside me. Were I to die now there are three such,—besides *The Prime Minister,* half of which only has as yet been issued. One of these has been six years finished, and has never seen the light since it was first tied up in the wrapper which now contains it. I look forward with some grim pleasantry to its publication after another period of six years, and to the declaration of the critics that it has been the work of a period of life at which the power of writing novels has passed from me.

Meaning and Idea

1. Outline, in your own words, Trollope's daily writing process.

2. According to the author, how many hours each day should a writer write? What special procedure should begin that time period? How long does this procedure take Trollope?

3. Explain what Trollope considers the minimal revision process. What is its main purpose? Explain the meaning of "avoid the fault of seeming to sound unlike himself."

4. What for Trollope were the results of adhering to the process he describes?

Language, Form, Structure

1. About whom is Trollope writing? For whom is he writing? What word in the essay helps to identify his intended audience?

2. How does Trollope organize the steps of his process?

3. What is the tone of this selection? Do you detect any tonal change in the last sentence? What is it?

4. Where does the writer use metaphors? Identify them.

5. Write the dictionary meanings of the following words: lenient; tyros; recommences; grim; pleasantry.

Ideas for Writing

1. Choose an activity which you do daily for a limited period of time. Write a short process analysis which would be beneficial to others desiring to do the same activity.

2. Write a process analysis of some intellectual pursuit, other than writing, which you practice. You might choose reading, thinking, or solving a mathematical problem, for example. Gear your analysis to novices to the pursuit.

3. Write a paper in which you evaluate Trollope's advice on writing. How realistic or effective do you find his advice? You might wish to compare his suggestions to the processes of other writers which you have read or heard about. What further advice would you add?

The Creation

Ovid

Ovid, the name by which we know Publius Ovidius Naso, was born to a wealthy family in the hill country outside Rome in 43 B.C. He began writing verse at age 12 and a few years later moved to Rome. In the year A.D. 8, Emperor Augustus exiled Ovid to a small town on the Black Sea for various scandalous indiscretions. He died in that town in A.D. 18, survived by his third wife and his writings, among them *The Art of Love, Heroines, On Make-Up,* and the *Metamorphoses.*

This selection, translated by Rolfe Humphries, is the opening poem of Book I of Ovid's *Metamorphoses,* or *Stories of Changing Forms,* which is a novel-length series of poems described by John Crowe Ransom as "a key to the literary and religious culture of the ancients." This selection describes the most fundamental process of all, a version of which appears in every mythology and culture.

*B*efore the ocean was, or earth, or heaven,
Nature was all alike, a shapelessness,
Chaos, so-called, all rude and lumpy matter,
Nothing but bulk, inert, in whose confusion
Discordant atoms warred: there was no sun   5
To light the universe; there was no moon
With slender silver crescents filling slowly;
No earth hung balanced in surrounding air;
No sea reached far along the fringe of shore.
Land, to be sure, there was, and air, and ocean,   10
But land on which no man could stand, and water
No man could swim in, air no man could breathe,
Air without light, substance forever changing,
Forever at war: within a single body
Heat fought with cold, wet fought with dry, the hard   15
Fought with the soft, things having weight contended
With weightless things.
          Till God, or kindlier Nature,
Settled all argument, and separated
Heaven from earth, water from land, our air   20
From the high stratosphere, a liberation
So things evolved, and out of blind confusion
Found each its place, bound in eternal order.
The force of fire, that weightless element,
Leaped up and claimed the highest place in heaven;   25
Below it, air; and under them the earth

Sank with its grosser portions; and the water,
Lowest of all, held up, held in, the land.

Whatever god it was, who out of chaos
Brought order to the universe, and gave it   30
Division, subdivision, he molded earth,
In the beginning, into a great globe,
Even on every side, and bade the waters
To spread and rise, under the rushing winds,
Surrounding earth; he added ponds and marshes,   35
He banked the river-channels, and the waters
Feed earth or run to sea, and that great flood
Washes on shores, not banks. He made the plains
Spread wide, the valleys settle, and the forest
Be dressed in leaves; he made the rocky mountains   40
Rise to full height, and as the vault of Heaven
Has two zones, left and right, and one between them
Hotter than these, the Lord of all Creation
Marked on the earth the same design and pattern.
The torrid zone too hot for men to live in,   45
The north and south too cold, but in the middle
Varying climate, temperature and season.
Above all things the air, lighter than earth,
Lighter than water, heavier than fire,
Towers and spreads; there mist and cloud assemble,   50
And fearful thunder and lightning and cold winds,
But these, by the Creator's order, held
No general dominion; even as it is,
These brothers brawl and quarrel; though each one
Has his own quarter, still, they come near tearing   55
The universe apart. Eurus is monarch
Of the lands of dawn, the realms of Araby,
The Persian ridges under the rays of morning.
Zephyrus holds the west that glows at sunset,
Boreas, who makes men shiver, holds the north,   60
Warm Auster governs in the misty southland,
And over them all presides the weightless ether,
Pure without taint of earth.
        These boundaries given,
Behold, the stars, long hidden under darkness,   65
Broke through and shone, all over the spangled heaven,
Their home forever, and the gods lived there,
And shining fish were given the waves for dwelling
And beasts the earth, and birds the moving air.

But something else was needed, a finer being,   70
More capable of mind, a sage, a ruler,
So Man was born, it may be, in God's image,
Or Earth, perhaps, so newly separated
From the old fire of Heaven, still retained
Some seed of the celestial force which fashioned   75
Gods out of living clay and running water.
All other animals look downward; Man,
Alone, erect, can raise his face toward Heaven.

Meaning and Idea

1. Paraphrase Ovid's description of the universe before creation.

2. Describe the process of chaos becoming order as it is presented in this poem.

3. What was the relationship among universal opposing forces before the creation? What examples does Ovid provide to support this theory? How does that condition change after the creation? What brought about the change?

4. Identify the following Roman gods whom Ovid alludes to: Eurus; Zephyrus; Boreas; Auster.

5. What, according to the poem, was the purpose for humankind in the creation? At what point in the creation does humanity appear?

Language, Form, Structure

1. In a four-line preface to the *Metamorphoses,* Ovid wrote:

   > My intention is to tell of bodies changed
   > To different forms; the gods, who made the changes,
   > Will help me—or I hope so—with a poem
   > That runs from the world's beginning to our own days.

   How does this short poem serve as an appropriate beginning to the process described in "The Creation"?

2. What is the use of description and narration in this poem? How do they enhance the process analysis?

3. Look up the following words in a dictionary: rude; inert; fringe; stratosphere; bade; torrid; dominion; ether; taint; celestial.

Ideas for Writing

1. Write an essay that analyzes a creative process with which you are familiar. Attempt to use imagery as much as possible.

2. Select some natural process (leaves turning color, for example), and write an analysis explaining it to readers.

3. Write a prose version of Ovid's "The Creation" for a modern audience, paying particular attention to the "how-this-was-done" elements.

On Economy

Henry David Thoreau

Henry David Thoreau (1817–1862) along with Ralph Waldo Emerson helped move the mid-nineteenth-century American literary center from New York to Boston. Thoreau was a man of deeds, a nonconformist, a social critic. He graduated from Harvard, though he eschewed the professional opportunities that education provided him, choosing instead a quiet life in Concord, Massachusetts, where he was born. His most famous writings are *Walden* (1854), his account of natural living at Walden Pond, and the essay "Civil Disobedience," which significantly influenced the philosophy and tactics of Mahatma Ghandi.

In *Walden* Thoreau describes his experiment in living a solitary, self-sufficient, somewhat ascetic life at Walden Pond. In this selection from that book, he addresses the processes by which he learned to live a life of fiscal and emotional economy. He readily admits personal pride in his accomplishments, but also hopes that what he learned will benefit his readers.

*N*ear the end of March, 1845, I borrowed an axe and went down to the woods by Walden Pond, nearest to where I intended to build my house, and began to cut down some tall, arrowy white pines, still in their youth, for timber. It is difficult to begin without borrowing, but perhaps it is the most generous course thus to permit your fellow-men to have an interest in your enterprise. The owner of the axe, as he released his hold on it, said that it was the apple of his eye; but I returned it sharper than I received it. It was a pleasant hillside where I worked, covered with pine woods, through which I looked out on the pond, and a small open field in the woods where pines and hickories were springing up. The ice in the pond was not yet dissolved, though there were some open spaces, and it was all dark-colored and saturated with water. There were some slight flurries of snow during the days that I worked there; but for the most part when I came out on to the railroad, on my way home, its yellow sand-heap stretched away gleaming in the hazy atmosphere, and the rails shone in the spring sun, and I heard the lark and pewee and other birds already come to commence another year with us. They were pleasant spring days, in which the winter of man's discontent was thawing as well as the earth, and the life that had lain torpid began to stretch itself. One day, when my axe had come off and I had cut a green hickory for a wedge, driving it with a stone, and had placed the whole to soak in a pond-hole in order to swell the wood, I saw a striped snake run into the water, and he lay on the bottom, apparently without inconvenience, as long as I stayed there, or more than a quarter of an hour; perhaps because he had not yet fairly come out of the torpid state. It appeared to me that for a like reason men remain in their present low and primitive condition; but if they should feel the influence of the spring of springs arousing them, they would of necessity rise to a higher and more ethereal life. I had previously seen the snakes in frosty mornings in my path with portions of their bodies still numb and inflexible, waiting for the sun to thaw them. On the

1st of April it rained and melted the ice, and in the early part of the day, which was very foggy, I heard a stray goose groping about over the pond and cackling as if lost, or like the spirit of the fog.

So I went on for some days cutting and hewing timber, and also studs and rafters, all with my narrow axe, not having many communicable or scholar-like thoughts, singing to myself,— 2

> Men say they know many things;
> But lo! they have taken wings,—
> The arts and sciences,
> And a thousand appliances:
> The wind that blows
> Is all that anybody knows.

I hewed the main timbers six inches square, most of the studs on two sides only, and the rafters and floor timbers on one side, leaving the rest of the bark on, so that they were just as straight and much stronger than sawed ones. Each stick was carefully mortised or tenoned by its stump, for I had borrowed other tools by this time. My days in the woods were not very long ones; yet I usually carried my dinner of bread and butter, and read the newspaper in which it was wrapped, at noon, sitting amid the green pine boughs which I had cut off, and to my bread was imparted some of their fragrance, for my hands were covered with a thick coat of pitch. Before I had done I was more the friend than the foe of the pine tree, though I had cut down some of them, having become better acquainted with it. Sometimes a rambler in the wood was attracted by the sound of my axe, and we chatted pleasantly over the chips which I had made.

By the middle of April, for I made no haste in my work, but rather made the most of it, my house was framed and ready for the raising. I had already bought the shanty of James Collins, an Irishman who worked on the Fitchburg Railroad, for boards. James Collins' shanty was considered an uncommonly fine one. When I called to see it he was not at home. I walked about the outside, at first unobserved from within, the window was so deep and high. It was of small dimensions, with a peaked cottage roof, and not much else to be seen, the dirt being raised five feet all around as if it were a compost heap. The roof was the soundest part, though a good deal warped and made brittle by the sun. Doorsill there was none, but a perennial passage for the hens under the door-board. Mrs. C came to the door and asked me to view it from the inside. The hens were driven in by my approach. It was dark, and had a dirt floor for the most part, dank, clammy, and aguish, only here a board and there a board which would not bear removal. She lighted a lamp to show me the inside of the roof and the walls, and also that the board floor extended under the bed, warning me not to step into the cellar, a sort of dust hole two feet deep. In her own words, they were "good boards overhead, good boards all around, and a good window,"—of two whole squares originally, only the cat had passed out that way lately. There was a stove, a bed, and a place to sit, an infant in the house where it was born, a silk parasol, gilt-framed 3 looking-glass, and a patent new coffee-mill nailed to an oak sapling, all told. The bargain was soon concluded, for James had in the meanwhile returned. I to pay four dollars and twenty-five cents to-night, he to vacate at five to-morrow morning, selling to nobody else meanwhile: I to take possession at six. It were well, he said, to be there early, and anticipate certain indistinct but wholly unjust claims on the score of ground rent and fuel. This he assured me was the only encumbrance. At six I passed him and his family on the road. One large bundle held their all,—bed, coffee-mill, looking-glass, hens,—all but the cat; she took to the woods and became a wild cat, and as I learned afterward, trod in a trap set for woodchucks, and so became a dead cat at last.

I took down this dwelling the same morning, drawing the nails, and removed it to the pond-side by small cartloads, spreading the boards on the grass there to bleach and warp back again in the sun. One early thrush gave me a note or two as I drove along the woodland path. I was informed treacherously by a young Patrick that neighbor Seeley, an Irishman, in the intervals of the carting, transferred the still tolerable, straight, and drivable nails, staples, and spikes to his pocket, and then stood when I came back to pass the time of day, and look freshly up, unconcerned, with spring thoughts, at the devastation; there being a dearth of work, as he said. He was there to represent spectatordom, and help make this seemingly insignificant event one with the removal of the gods of Troy.

I dug my cellar in the side of a hill sloping to the south, where a woodchuck had formerly dug his burrow, down through sumach and blackberry roots, and the lowest stain of vegetation, six feet square by seven deep, to a fine sand where potatoes would not freeze in any winter. The sides were left shelving, and not stoned; but the sun having never shone on them, the sand still keeps its place. It was but two hours' work. I took particular pleasure in this breaking of ground, for in almost all latitudes men dig into the earth for an equable temperature. Under the most splendid house in the city is still to be found the cellar where they store their roots as of old, and long after the superstructure has disappeared posterity remark its dent in the earth. The house is still but a sort of porch at the entrance of a burrow.

At length, in the beginning of May, with the help of some of my acquaintances, rather to improve so good an occasion for neighborliness than from any necessity, I set up the frame of my house. No man was ever more honored in the character of his raisers than I. They are destined, I trust, to assist at the raising of loftier structures one day. I began to occupy my house on the 4th of July, as soon as it was boarded and roofed, for the boards were carefully feather-edged and lapped, so that it was perfectly impervious to rain, but before boarding I laid the foundation of a chimney at one end, bringing two cartloads of stones up the hill from the pond in my arms. I built the chimney after my hoeing in the fall, before a fire became necessary for warmth, doing my cooking in the meanwhile out of doors on the ground, early in the morning: which mode I still think is in some respects more convenient and agreeable than the usual one. When it stormed before my bread was baked, I fixed a few boards over the fire, and sat under them to watch my loaf, and passed some pleasant hours in that way. In those days, when my hands were much employed, I read but little, but the least scraps of paper which lay on the ground, my holder, or tablecloth, afforded me as much entertainment, in fact answered the same purpose as the Iliad.

It would be worth the while to build still more deliberately than I did, con- 7
sidering, for instance, what foundation a door, a window, a cellar, a garret, have in the nature of man, and perchance never raising any superstructure until we found a better reason for it than our temporal necessities even. There is some of the same fitness in a man's building his own house that there is in a bird's build- ing its own nest. Who knows but if men constructed their dwellings with their own hands, and provided food for themselves and families simply and honestly enough, the poetic faculty would be universally developed, as birds universally sing when they are so engaged? But alas! we do like cowbirds and cuckoos, which lay their eggs in nests which other birds have built, and cheer no traveler with their chattering and unmusical notes. Shall we forever resign the pleasure of construction to the carpenter? What does architecture amount to in the experience of the mass of men? I never in all my walks came across a man engaged in so sim- ple and natural an occupation as building his house. We belong to the community. It is not the tailor alone who is the ninth part of a man; it is as much the preacher, and the merchant, and the farmer. Where is this division of labor to end? and what object does it finally serve? No doubt another *may* also think for me; but it is not therefore desirable that he should do so to the exclusion of my thinking for myself.

True, there are architects so called in this country, and I have heard of one 8
at least possessed with the idea of making architectural ornaments have a core of truth, a necessity, and hence a beauty, as if it were a revelation to him. All very well perhaps from his point of view, but only a little better than the common dilettantism. A sentimental reformer in architecture, he began at the cornice, not at the foundation. It was only how to put a core of truth within the ornaments, that every sugarplum, in fact, might have an almond or caraway seed in it,— though I hold that almonds are most wholesome without the sugar,—and not how the inhabitant, the indweller, might build truly within and without, and let the ornaments take care of themselves. What reasonable man ever supposed that ornaments were something outward and in the skin merely,—that the tortoise got his spotted shell, or the shell-fish its mother-o'-pearl tints, by such a contract as the inhabitants of Broadway their Trinity Church? But a man has no more to do with the style of architecture of his house than a tortoise with that of its shell: nor need the soldier be so idle as to try to paint the precise *color* of his virtue on his standard. The enemy will find it out. He may turn pale when the trial comes. This man seemed to me to lean over the cornice, and timidly whisper his half truth to the rude occupants who really knew it better than he. What of architec- tural beauty I now see, I know has gradually grown from within outward, out of the necessities and character of the indweller, who is the only builder,—out of some unconscious truthfulness, and nobleness, without ever a thought for the appearance; and whatever additional beauty of this kind is destined to be pro-

duced will be preceded by a like unconscious beauty of life. The most interesting dwellings in this country, as the painter knows, are the most unpretending, humble log huts and cottages of the poor commonly; it is the life of the inhabitants whose shells they are, and not any peculiarity in their surfaces merely, which makes them *picturesque;* and equally interesting will be the citizen's suburban box, when his life shall be as simple and as agreeable to the imagination, and there is as little straining after effect in the style of his dwelling. A great proportion of architectural ornaments are literally hollow, and a September gale would strip them off, like borrowed plumes, without injury to the substantials. They can do without *architecture* who have no olives nor wines in the cellar. What if an equal ado were made about the ornaments of style in literature, and the architects of our Bibles spent as much time about their cornices as the architects of our churches do? So are made the *belles-lettres* and the *beaux-arts* and their professors. Much it concerns a man, forsooth, how a few sticks are slanted over him or under him, and what colors are daubed upon his box. It would signify somewhat, if, in any earnest sense, *he* slanted them and daubed it; but the spirit having departed out of the tenant, it is of a piece with constructing his own coffin,—the architecture of the grave,—and "carpenter" is but another name for "coffin-maker." One man says, in his despair or indifference to life, take up a handful of the earth at your feet, and paint your house that color. Is he thinking of his last and narrow house? Toss up a copper for it as well. What an abundance of leisure he must have! Why do you take up a handful of dirt? Better paint your house your own complexion; let it turn pale or blush for you. An enterprise to improve the style of cottage architecture! When you have got my ornaments ready, I will wear them.

Before winter I built a chimney, and shingled the sides of my house, which were already impervious to rain, with imperfect and sappy shingles made of the first slice of the log, whose edges I was obliged to straighten with a plane. 9

I have thus a tight shingled and plastered house, ten feet wide by fifteen long, and eight-feet posts, with a garret and a closet, a large window on each side, two trap-doors, one door at the end, and a brick fireplace opposite. The exact cost of my house, paying the usual price for such materials as I used, but not counting the work, all of which was done by myself, was as follows; and I give the details because very few are able to tell exactly what their houses cost, and fewer still, if any, the separate cost of the various materials which compose them:— 10

Boards	$8 03½,	mostly shanty boards
Refuse shingles for roof and sides	4 00	
Laths	1 25	
Two second-hand windows with glass	2 43	
One thousand old brick	4 00	
Two casks of lime	2 40	That was high.

Hair	0 31	More than I needed.
Mantle-tree iron	0 15	
Nails	3 90	
Hinges and screws.	0 14	
Latch	0 10	
Chalk.	0 01	
Transportation	1 40	{ I carried a good part on my back
	———	
In all	$28 12½	

These are all the materials, excepting the timber, stones, and sand, which I 11 claimed by squatter's right. I have also a small woodshed adjoining, made chiefly of the stuff which was left after building the house.

I intend to build me a house which will surpass any on the main street in 12 Concord in grandeur and luxury, as soon as it pleases me as much and will cost me no more than my present one.

I thus found that the student who wishes for a shelter can obtain one for a 13 lifetime at an expense not greater than the rent which he now pays annually. If I seem to boast more than is becoming, my excuse is that I brag for humanity rather than for myself; and my shortcomings and inconsistencies do not affect the truth of my statement. Notwithstanding much cant and hypocrisy,—chaff which I find it difficult to separate from my wheat, but for which I am as sorry as any man,—I will breathe freely and stretch myself in this respect, it is such a relief to both the moral and physical system; and I am resolved that I will not through humility become the devil's attorney. I will endeavor to speak a good word for the truth. At Cambridge College the mere rent of a student's room, which is only a little larger than my own, is thirty dollars each year, though the corporation had the advantage of building thirty-two side by side and under one roof, and the occupant suffers the inconvenience of many and noisy neighbors, and perhaps a residence in the fourth story. I cannot but think that if we had more true wisdom in these respects, not only less education would be needed, because, forsooth, more would already have been acquired, but the pecuniary expense of getting an education would in a great measure vanish. Those conveniences which the student requires at Cambridge or elsewhere cost him or somebody else ten times as great a sacrifice of life as they would with proper management on both sides. Those things for which the most money is demanded are never the things which the student most wants. Tuition, for instance, is an important item in the term bill, while for the far more valuable education which he gets by asso-ciating with the most cultivated of his contemporaries no charge is made. The mode of founding a college is, commonly, to get up a subscription of dollars and cents, and then, following blindly the principles of a division of labor to its extreme,—a principle which should never be followed but with circumspec-tion,—to call in a contractor who makes this a subject of speculation, and he employs Irishmen or other operatives actually to lay the foundations, while the students that are to be are said to be fitting themselves for it; and for these oversights successive generations have to pay. I think that it would be *better than this,* for the students, or those who desire to be benefited by it, even to lay the foundation themselves. The student who secures his coveted leisure and retirement by systematically shirking any labor necessary to man obtains but an ignoble and unprofitable leisure, defrauding himself of the experience which alone can make leisure fruitful. "But," says one, "you do not mean that the students should go to work with their hands instead of their heads?" I do not mean that exactly, but I mean something which he might think a good deal like that; I mean that they should not *play* life, or *study* it merely, while the community supports them at this expensive game, (but earnestly *live* it from beginning to end.) How could youths better learn to live than by at once trying the experiment of living? Methinks this would exercise their minds as much as mathematics. If I wished a boy to know something about the arts and sciences, for instance, I would not pursue the common course, which is merely to send him into the neighborhood of some professor, where anything is professed and practiced but the art of life;— to survey the world through a telescope or a microscope, and never with his natural eye; to study chemistry, and not learn how his bread is made, or mechanics, and not learn how it is earned; to discover new satellites to Neptune, and not detect the motes in his eyes, or to what vagabond he is a satellite himself; or to be devoured by the monsters that swarm all around him, while contemplating the monsters in a drop of vinegar. Which would have advanced the most at the end of a month,—the boy who had made his own jackknife from the ore which he had dug and smelted, reading as much as would be necessary for this—or the boy who had attended the lectures on metallurgy at the Institute in the meanwhile, and had received a Rodgers penknife from his father? Which would be most likely to cut his fingers? . . .To my astonishment I was informed on leaving college that I had studied navigation!—why, if I had taken one turn down the harbor I should have known more about it. Even the *poor* student studies and is taught only *political* economy, while that economy of living which is synonymous with philosophy is not even sincerely professed in our colleges. The consequence is, that while he is reading Adam Smith, Ricardo, and Say, he runs his father in debt irretrievably.

As with our colleges, so with a hundred "modern improvements;" there is an illusion about them; there is not always a positive advance. The devil goes on exacting compound interest to the last for his early share and numerous succeeding investments in them. Our inventions are wont to be pretty toys, which distract our attention from serious things. They are but improved means to an unimproved end, an end which it was already but too easy to arrive at; as railroads lead to Boston or New York. We are in great haste to construct a magnetic telegraph from Maine to Texas; but Maine and Texas, it may be, have nothing important to communicate. Either is in such a predicament as the man who was earnest to be introduced to a distinguished deaf woman, but when he was presented, and one end of

14

her ear trumpet was put into his hand, had nothing to say. As if the main object were to talk fast and not to talk sensibly. We are eager to tunnel under the Atlantic and bring the Old World some weeks nearer to the New; but perchance the first news that will leak through into the broad, flapping American ear will be that the Princess Adelaide has the whooping cough. After all, the man whose horse trots a mile a minute does not carry the most important messages; he is not an evangelist, nor does he come round eating locusts and wild honey. I doubt if Flying Childers ever carried a peck of corn to mill.

One says to me, "I wonder that you do not lay up money; you love to travel; you might take the cars and go to Fitchburg today and see the country." But I am wiser than that. I have learned that the swiftest traveller is he that goes afoot. I say to my friend, Suppose we try who will get there first. The distance is thirty miles; the fare ninety cents. That is almost a day's wages. I remember when wages were sixty cents a day for laborers on this very road. Well, I start now on foot, and get there before night; I have travelled at that rate by the week together. You will in the meanwhile have earned your fare, and arrive there sometime to-morrow, or possibly this evening, if you are lucky enough to get a job in season. Instead of going to Fitchburg, you will be working here the greater part of the day. And so, if the railroad reached round the world, I think that I should keep ahead of you; and as for seeing the country and getting experience of that kind, I should have to cut your acquaintance altogether.

Such is the universal law, which no man can ever outwit, and with regard to the railroad even we may say it is as broad as it is long. To make a railroad round the world available to all mankind is equivalent to grading the whole surface of the planet. Men have an indistinct notion that if they keep up this activity of joint stocks and spades long enough all will at length ride somewhere, in next to no time, and for nothing; but though a crowd rushes to the depot, and the conductor shouts "All aboard!" when the smoke is blown away and the vapor condensed, it will be perceived that a few are riding, but the rest are run over,—and it will be called, and will be, "A melancholy accident." No doubt they can ride at last who shall have earned their fare, that is, if they survive so long, but they will probably have lost their elasticity and desire to travel by that time. This spending of the best part of one's life earning money in order to enjoy a questionable liberty during the least valuable part of it reminds me of the Englishman who went to India to make a fortune first, in order that he might return to England and live the life of a poet. He should have gone up garret at once. "What!" exclaim a million Irishmen starting up from all the shanties in the land, "is not this railroad which we have built a good thing?" Yes, I answer, *comparatively* good, that is, you might have done worse; but I wish, as you are brothers of mine, that you could have spent your time better than digging in this dirt.

Before I finished my house, wishing to earn ten or twelve dollars by some honest and agreeable method, in order to meet my unusual expenses, I planted about two acres and a half of light and sandy soil near it chiefly with beans, but also a small part with potatoes, corn, peas, and turnips. The whole lot contains eleven acres, mostly growing up to pines and hickories, and was sold the preceding season for eight dollars and eight cents an acre. One farmer said that it was "good for nothing but to raise cheeping squirrels on." I put no manure whatever on this land, not being the owner, but merely a squatter, and not expecting to cultivate so much again, and I did not quite hoe it all once. I got out several cords of stumps in plowing, which supplied me with fuel for a long time, and left small circles of virgin mould, easily distinguishable through the summer by the greater luxuriance of the beans there. The dead and for the most part unmerchantable wood behind my house, and the drift wood from the pond, have supplied the remainder of my fuel. I was obliged to hire a team and a man for the plowing, though I held the plow myself. My farm outgoes for the first season were, for implements, seed, work, etc., $14.72½. The seed corn was given me. This never costs anything to speak of unless you plant more than enough. I got twelve bushels of beans, and eighteen bushels of potatoes, beside some peas and sweet corn. The yellow corn and turnips were too late to come to anything. My whole income from the farm was

Deducting the outgoes $23 44	
	14 72½
There are left $8 71½,	

beside produce consumed and on hand at the time this estimate was made of the value of $4.50,—the amount on hand much more than balancing a little grass which I did not raise. All things considered, that is, considering the importance of a man's soul and of to-day, notwithstanding the short time occupied by my experiment, nay, partly even because of its transient character, I believe that that was doing better than any farmer in Concord did that year.

The next year I did better still, for I spaded up all the land which I required, about a third of an acre, and I learned from the experience of both years, not being in the least awed by many celebrated works on husbandry, Arthur Young among the rest, that if one would live simply and eat only the crop which he raised, and raise no more than he ate, and not exchange it for an insufficient quantity of more luxurious and expensive things, he would need to cultivate only a few rods of ground, and that it would be cheaper to spade up that than to use oxen to plow it, and to select a fresh spot from time to time than to manure the old, and he could do all his necessary farm work as it were with his left hand at odd hours in the summer; and thus he would not be tied to an ox, or horse, or cow, or pig, as at present. I desire to speak impartially on this point, and as one not interested in the success or failure of the present economical and social arrangements. I was more independent than any farmer in Concord, for I was not anchored to a house or farm, but could follow the bent of my genius, which is a very crooked one, every moment. Beside being better off than they already, if my house had been burned or my crops had failed, I should have been nearly as well off as before.

I am wont to think that men are not so much the keepers of herds as herds are the keepers of men, the former are so much the freer. Men and oxen exchange work; but if we consider necessary work only, the oxen will be seen to have greatly the advantage, their farm is so much the larger. Man does some of his part of the exchange work in his six weeks of haying, and it is no boy's play. Certainly no nation that lived simply in all respects, that is, no nation of philosophers, would commit so great a blunder as to use the labor of animals. True, there never was and is not likely soon to be a nation of philosophers, nor am I certain it is desirable that there should be. However, *I* should never have broken a horse or bull and taken him to board for any work he might do for me, for fear I should become a horse-man or a herds-man merely; and if society seems to be the gainer by so doing, are we certain that what is one man's gain is not another's loss, and that the stable-boy has equal cause with his master to be satisfied? Granted that some public works would not have been constructed without this aid, and let man share the glory of such with the ox and horse; does it follow that he could not have accomplished works yet more worthy of himself in that case? When men begin to do, not merely unnecessary or artistic, but luxurious and idle work, with their assistance, it is inevitable that a few do all the exchange work with the oxen, or, in other words, become the slaves of the strongest. Man thus not only works for the animal within him, but, for a symbol of this, he works for the animal without him. Though we have many substantial houses of brick or stone, the prosperity of the farmer is still measured by the degree to which the barn overshadows the house. This town is said to have the largest houses for oxen, cows, and horses hereabouts, and it is not behindhand in its public buildings; but there are very few halls for free worship or free speech in this county. It should not be by their architecture, but why not even by their power of abstract thought, that nations should seek to commemorate themselves? How much more admirable the Bhagvat-Geeta than all the ruins of the East! Towers and temples are the luxury of princes. A simple and independent mind does not toil at the bidding of any prince. Genius is not a retainer to any emperor, nor is its material silver, or gold, or marble, except to a trifling extent. To what end, pray, is so much stone hammered? In Arcadia, when I was there, I did not see any hammering stone. Nations are possessed with an insane ambition to perpetuate the memory of themselves by the amount of hammered stone they leave. What if equal pains were taken to smooth and polish their manners? One piece of good sense would be more memorable than a monument as high as the moon. I love better to see stones in place. The grandeur of Thebes was a vulgar grandeur. More sensible is a rod of stone wall that bounds an honest man's field than a hundred-gated Thebes that has wandered farther from the true end of life. The religion and civilization which are barbaric and heathenish build splendid temples; but what you might call Christianity does not. Most of the stone a nation hammers goes toward its tomb only.

It buries itself alive. As for the Pyramids, there is nothing to wonder at in them so much as the fact that so many men could be found degraded enough to spend their lives constructing a tomb for some ambitious booby, whom it would have been wiser and manlier to have drowned in the Nile, and then given his body to the dogs. I might possibly invent some excuse for them and him, but I have no time for it. As for the religion and love of art of the builders, it is much the same all the world over, whether the building be an Egyptian temple or the United States Bank. It costs more than it comes to. The mainspring is vanity, assisted by the love of garlic and bread and butter. Mr. Balcom, a promising young architect, designs it on the back of his Vitruvius, with hard pencil and ruler, and the job is let out to Dobson & Sons, stonecutters. When the thirty centuries begin to look down on it, mankind begin to look up at it. As for your high towers and monuments, there was a crazy fellow once in this town who undertook to dig through to China, and he got so far that, as he said, he heard the Chinese pots and kettles rattle; but I think that I shall not go out of my way to admire the hole which he made. Many are concerned about the monuments of the West and the East,—to know who built them. For my part, I should like to know who in those days did not build them,—who were above such trifling. But to proceed with my statistics.

By surveying, carpentry, and day-labor of various other kinds in the village 20 in the meanwhile, for I have as many trades as fingers, I had earned $13.34. The expense of food for eight months, namely, from July 4th to March 1st, the time when these estimates were made, though I lived there more than two years,—not counting potatoes, a little green corn, and some peas, which I had raised, nor considering the value of what was on hand at the last date,—was

Rice $1 73½		
Molasses 1 73	Cheapest form of the saccharine.	
Rye meal 1 04¾		
Indian meal. 0 99¾	Cheaper than rye.	
Pork 0 22		
Flour. 0 88	{ Costs more than Indian meal, both money and trouble.	
Sugar 0 80		
Lard 0 65		
Apples 0 25		
Dried apple. 0 22		
Sweet potatoes. . . . 0 10		
One pumpkin 0 6		
One watermelon . . . 0 2		
Salt. 0 3		

Yes, I did eat $8.74, all told; but I should not thus unblushingly publish my guilt, if I did not know that most of my readers were equally guilty with myself, and that their deeds would look no better in print. The next year I sometimes caught a mess of fish for my dinner, and once I went so far as to slaughter a woodchuck which ravaged my bean-field,—effect his transmigration, as a Tartar would say,— and devour him, partly for experiment's sake; but though it afforded me a momentary enjoyment, notwithstanding a musky flavor, I saw that the longest use would not make that a good practice, however it might seem to have your woodchucks ready dressed by the village butcher.

Clothing and some incidental expenses within the same dates, though little ²¹ can be inferred from this item, amounted to

$8 40¾
Oil and some household utensils 2 00

So that all the pecuniary outgoes, excepting for washing and mending, which for the most part were done out of the house, and their bills have not yet been received,—and these are all and more than all the ways by which money necessarily goes out in this part of the world,—were

House $28 12½
Farm one year 14 72½
Food eight months 8 74
Clothing, etc., eight months 8 40¾
Oil, etc., eight months. 2 00
$61 99¾

I address myself now to those of my readers who have a living to get. And to meet this I have for farm produce sold

Earned by day-labor $23 44
13 44
In all. $36 78,

which subtracted from the sum of the outgoes leaves a balance of $25.21¾ on the one side,—this being very nearly the means with which I started, and the measure of expenses to be incurred,—and on the other, beside the leisure and independence and health thus secured, a comfortable house for me as long as I choose to occupy it.

These statistics, however accidental and therefore uninstructive they may 22 appear, as they have a certain completeness, have a certain value also. Nothing was given me of which I have not rendered some account. It appears from the above estimate, that my food alone cost me in money about twenty-seven cents a week. It was, for nearly two years after this, rye and Indian meal without yeast, potatoes, rice, a very little salt pork, molasses, and salt; and my drink, water. It was fit that I should live on rice, mainly, who loved so well the philosophy of India. To meet the objections of some inveterate cavillers, I may as well state, that if I dined out occasionally, as I always had done, and I trust shall have opportunities to do again, it was frequently to the detriment of my domestic arrangements. But the dining out, being, as I have stated, a constant element, does not in the least affect a comparative statement like this.

I learned from my two years' experience that it would cost incredibly little 23 trouble to obtain one's necessary food, even in this latitude; that a man may use as simple a diet as the animals, and yet retain health and strength. I have made a satisfactory dinner, satisfactory on several accounts, simply off a dish of purslane (*Portulaca oleracea*) which I gathered in my cornfield, boiled and salted. I give the Latin on account of the savoriness of the trivial name. And pray what more can a reasonable man desire, in peaceful times, in ordinary noons, than a sufficient number of ears of green sweet corn boiled, with the addition of salt? Even the little variety which I used was a yielding to the demands of appetite, and not of health. Yet men have come to such a pass that they frequently starve, not for want of necessaries, but for want of luxuries; and I know a good woman who thinks that her son lost his life because he took to drinking water only.

The reader will perceive that I am treating the subject rather from an eco- 24 nomic than a dietetic point of view, and he will not venture to put my abstemiousness to the test unless he has a well-stocked larder.

Bread I at first made of pure Indian meal and salt, genuine hoe-cakes, which 25 I baked before my fire out of doors on a shingle or the end of a stick of timber sawed off in building my house; but it was wont to get smoked and to have a piny flavor. I tried flour also; but have at last found a mixture of rye and Indian meal most convenient and agreeable. In cold weather it was no little amusement to bake several small loaves of this in succession, tending and turning them as carefully as an Egyptian his hatching eggs. They were a real cereal fruit which I ripened, and they had to my senses a fragrance like that of other noble fruits, which I kept in as long as possible by wrapping them in cloths. I made a study of the ancient and indispensable art of bread-making, consulting such authorities as offered, going back to the primitive days and first invention of the unleavened kind, when from the wildness of nuts and meats men first reached the mildness and refinement of this diet, and travelling gradually down in my studies through that accidental souring of the dough which, it is supposed, taught the leavening process, and through the various fermentations thereafter, till I came to "good, sweet, wholesome bread," the staff of life. Leaven, which some deem the soul of bread, the *spiritus* which fills its cellular tissue, which is religiously preserved like the vestal fire,—some precious bottleful, I suppose, first brought over in the

Mayflower, did the business for America, and its influence is still rising, swelling, spreading, in cerealian billows over the land,—this seed I regularly and faithfully procured from the village, till at length one morning I forgot the rules, and scalded my yeast; by which accident I discovered that even this was not indispensable,—for my discoveries were not by the synthetic but analytic process,—and I have gladly omitted it since, though most housewives earnestly assured me that safe and wholesome bread without yeast might not be, and elderly people prophesied a speedy decay of the vital forces. Yet I find it not to be an essential ingredient, and after going without it for a year am still in the land of the living; and I am glad to escape the trivialness of carrying a bottleful in my pocket, which would sometimes pop and discharge its contents to my discomfiture. It is simpler and more respectable to omit it. Man is an animal who more than any other can adapt himself to all climates and circumstances. Neither did I put any sal-soda, or other acid or alkali, into my bread. It would seem that I made it according to the recipe which Marcus Porcius Cato gave about two centuries before Christ. "Panem depsticium sic facito. Manus mortariumque bene lavato. Farinam in mortarium indito, aquae paulatim addito, subigitoque pulchre. Ubi bene subegeris, defingito, coquitoque sub testu." Which I take to mean, "Make kneaded bread thus. Wash your hands and trough well. Put the meal into the trough, add water gradually, and knead it thoroughly. When you have kneaded it well, mould it, and bake it under a cover," that is, in a baking-kettle. Not a word about leaven. But I did not always use this staff of life. At one time, owing to the emptiness of my purse, I saw none of it for more than a month.

Every New Englander might easily raise all his own breadstuffs in this land 26 of rye and Indian corn, and not depend on distant and fluctuating markets for them. Yet so far are we from simplicity and independence that, in Concord, fresh and sweet meal is rarely sold in the shops, and hominy and corn in a still coarser form are hardly used by any. For the most part the farmer gives to his cattle and hogs the grain of his own producing, and buys flour, which is at least no more wholesome, at a greater cost, at the store. I saw that I could easily raise my bushel or two of rye and Indian corn, for the former will grow on the poorest land, and the latter does not require the best, and grind them in a hand-mill, and so do without rice and pork; and if I must have some concentrated sweet, I found by experiment that I could make a very good molasses either of pumpkins or beets, and I knew that I needed only to set out a few maples to obtain it more easily still, and while these were growing I could use various substitutes beside those which I have named. "For," as the Forefathers sang,—

> we can make liquor to sweeten our lips
> Of pumpkins and parsnips and walnut-tree chips.

Finally, as for salt, that grossest of groceries, to obtain this might be a fit occasion for a visit to the seashore, or, if I did without it altogether, I should probably drink the less water. I do not learn that the Indians ever troubled themselves to go after it.

Thus I could avoid all trade and barter, so far as my food was concerned, 27 and having a shelter already, it would only remain to get clothing and fuel. The

pantaloons which I now wear were woven in a farmer's family,—thank Heaven there is so much virtue still in man; for I think the fall from the farmer to the operative as great and memorable as that from the man to the farmer;—and in a new country, fuel is an encumbrance. As for a habitat, if I were not permitted still to squat, I might purchase one acre at the same price for which the land I cultivated was sold—namely, eight dollars and eight cents. But as it was, I considered that I enhanced the value of the land by squatting on it.

There is a certain class of unbelievers who sometimes ask me such questions as, if I think that I can live on vegetable food alone; and to strike at the root of the matter at once,—for the root is faith,—I am accustomed to answer such, that I can live on board nails. If they cannot understand that, they cannot understand much that I have to say. For my part, I am glad to hear of experiments of this kind being tried; as that a young man tried for a fortnight to live on hard, raw corn on the ear, using his teeth for all mortar. The squirrel tribe tried the same and succeeded. The human race is interested in these experiments, though a few old women who are incapacitated for them, or who own their thirds in mills, may be alarmed.

Meaning and Idea

1. What does Thoreau mean by *economy?* (You may want to check a dictionary definition of the word and compare Thoreau's use of it.) Briefly summarize what Thoreau considers the importance of economy.

2. What is the "experiment" Thoreau mentions? What does Thoreau identify as the nonmonetary personal gains of his experiment?

3. Toward the end of the essay, Thoreau claims, "Thus I could avoid all trade and barter, so far as my food was concerned." Describe the process by which he achieved this condition. What are Thoreau's general suggestions to his audience about economizing on food?

4. What is the author's attitude toward modernization? How does he exemplify his attitude?

5. Thoreau writes in this essay, "my discoveries were not by the synthetic but analytic process." Interpret the meaning of this statement in light of your reading of the essay.

Language, Form, Structure

1. What is the main process which Thoreau explains in this essay? Outline the steps he describes. How does he accomplish the transitions between these steps? How does he arrange them? What is the time span covered by the essay? What stages of the overall process occur at different points in this time span?

2. What is the overall purpose of this selection? In other words, what is Thoreau trying to teach his audience about the process of their lives? Into

what categories of daily life and necessities does he divide his overall process analysis?

3. How does Thoreau use description in this essay? Which descriptive details do you find freshest? Which sensory appeals are particularly vivid? Where does Thoreau use data to support his point? Why do you think he uses data?

4. Throughout the essay, Thoreau makes numerous comparisons of the steps of his process to the processes of nature. Identify some of these comparisons. What do they add to the tone and style of the essay?

   He also makes several comparisons to Greek mythology. Identify them and explain their purpose.

5. How does Thoreau analyze the process of human beings becoming subservient to their work animals? How might this section be read metaphorically?

6. Identify the meanings of ten of the following words from the essay. Then add five more definitions of words unfamiliar to you in the reading that do not appear on this list: ethereal; perennial; dank; dearth; posterity; revelation; dilettantism; ado; *belles-lettres;* cant; pecuniary; coveted; perpetuate; heathenish; transmigration.

Ideas for Writing

1. Write about a long-term project you attempted either recently or in the past. Analyze the process by which you approached and carried out this project.

2. In the form of a letter, write to a friend who has trouble managing money and propose a process by which he or she could be more financially responsible.

3. In an essay respond to the following question: Would you classify "economy" as a *how* or a *how-to* process analysis? Support your answer with specific references to Thoreau's essay.

The Rocking-Horse Winner

D. H. Lawrence

D. H. Lawrence was born in 1885 in the English Midlands coal-mining town of Eastwood, the son of a coal miner. Lawrence was ambivalent about his background—he found it overly materialistic and repressive, yet he used it as the basis for nearly all his fiction. In 1912, he ran off with his wife-to-be, Frieda, and they lived outside of England for most of their lives—in Australia, Italy, Germany, Mexico, and the United States. Lawrence's fiction—including *Sons and Lovers* (1913), *The Rainbow* (1915), *Women in Love* (1920), and *Lady Chatterley's Lover* (1928)—created great uproars for its literary daring and so-called immorality. Lawrence, who was also a prolific critical and travel writer, died of tuberculosis in southern France in 1930; his ashes rest in Taos, New Mexico.

"The Rocking-Horse Winner" shows us how need—real or imagined—can sometimes overcome life itself. Notice how Lawrence uses processes of both building up and deterioration to develop the narrative line.

*T*here was a woman who was beautiful, who started with all the 1 advantages, yet she had no luck. She married for love, and the love turned to dust. She had bonny children, yet she felt they had been thrust upon her, and she could not love them. They looked at her coldly, as if they were finding fault with her. And hurriedly she felt she must cover up some fault in herself. Yet what it was that she must cover up she never knew. Nevertheless, when her children were present, she always felt the centre of her heart go hard. This troubled her, and in her manner she was all the more gentle and anxious for her children, as if she loved them very much. Only she herself knew that at the centre of her heart was a hard little place that could not feel love, no, not for anybody. Everybody else said of her: "She is such a good mother. She adores her children." Only she herself, and her children themselves, knew it was not so. They read it in each other's eyes.

There were a boy and two little girls. They lived in a pleasant house, with 2 a garden, and they had discreet servants, and felt themselves superior to anyone in the neighbourhood.

Although they lived in style, they felt always an anxiety in the house. There 3 was never enough money. The mother had a small income, and the father had a small income, but not nearly enough for the social position which they had to keep up. The father went into town to some office. But though he had good prospects, these prospects never materialised. There was always the grinding sense of the shortage of money, though the style was always kept up.

At last the mother said: "I will see if *I* can't make something." But she did 4 not know where to begin. She racked her brains, and tried this thing and the other, but could not find anything successful. The failure made deep lines come into her face. Her children were growing up, they would have to go to school. There must be more money, there must be more money. The father, who was always very handsome and expensive in his tastes, seemed as if he never *would* be able to do anything worth doing. And the mother, who had a great belief in herself, did not succeed any better, and her tastes were just as expensive.

And so the house came to be haunted by the unspoken phrase: *There must* 5 *be more money! There must be more money!* The children could hear it all the time, though nobody said it aloud. They heard it at Christmas, when the expensive and splendid toys filled the nursery. Behind the shining modern rocking-horse, behind the smart doll's house, a voice would start whispering: "There *must* be more money! There *must* be more money!" And the children would stop playing, to listen for a moment. They would look into each other's eyes, to see if they had all heard. And each one saw in the eyes of the other two that they too had heard. "There *must* be more money! There *must* be more money!"

It came whispering from the springs of the still-swaying rocking-horse, and 6 even the horse, bending his wooden, champing head, heard it. The big doll, sitting so pink and smirking in her new pram, could hear it quite plainly, and seemed to be smirking all the more self-consciously because of it. The foolish puppy, too, that took the place of the teddy-bear, he was looking so extraordinarily foolish for no other reason but that he heard the secret whisper all over the house: "There *must* be more money!

Yet nobody ever said it aloud. The whisper was everywhere, and therefore 7 no one spoke it. Just as no one ever says: "We are breathing!" in spite of the fact that breath is coming and going all the time.

"Mother," said the boy Paul one day, "Why do we always use uncle's, or 8 else a taxi?"

"Because we're the poor members of the family," said the mother. 9

"But why *are* we, mother?" 10

"Well—I suppose," she said slowly and bitterly, "it's because your father 11 has no luck."

The boy was silent for some time. 12

"Is luck money, mother?" he asked, rather timidly. 13

"No, Paul. Not quite. It's what causes you to have money." 14

"Oh!" said Paul vaguely. "I thought when Uncle Oscar said *filthy lucker,* it 15 meant money."

"*Filthy lucre* does mean money," said the mother. "But it's lucre, not luck." 16

"Oh!" said the boy. "Then what *is* luck, mother?" 17

"It's what causes you to have money. If you're lucky you have money. 18 That's why it's better to be born lucky than rich. If you're rich, you may lose your money. But if you're lucky, you will always get more money."

"Oh! Will you? And is father not lucky?" 19

"Very unlucky, I should say," she said bitterly. 20

The boy watched her with unsure eyes. 21

"Why?" he asked. 22

"I don't know. Nobody ever knows why one person is lucky and another 23 unlucky."

"Don't they? Nobody at all? Does *nobody* know?"   24

"Perhaps God. But He never tells."   25

"He ought to, then. And aren't you lucky either, mother?"   26

"I can't be, if I married an unlucky husband."   27

"But by yourself, aren't you?"   28

"I used to think I was, before I married. Now I think I am very unlucky   29
indeed."

"Why?"   30

"Well—never mind! Perhaps I'm not really," she said.   31

The child looked at her to see if she meant it. But he saw, by the lines of her   32
mouth, that she was only trying to hide something from him.

"Well, anyhow," he said stoutly, "I'm a lucky person."   33

"Why?" said his mother, with a sudden laugh.   34

He stared at her. He didn't even know why he had said it.   35

"God told me," he asserted, brazening it out.   36

"I hope He did, dear!" she said, again with a laugh, but rather bitter.   37

"He did, mother!"   38

"Excellent!" said the mother, using one of her husband's exclamations.   39

The boy saw she did not believe him; or rather, that she paid no attention to   40
his assertion. This angered him somewhat, and made him want to compel her
attention.

He went off by himself, vaguely, in a childish way, seeking for the clue to   41
"luck." Absorbed, taking no heed of other people, he went about with a sort of
stealth, seeking inwardly for luck. He wanted luck, he wanted it, he wanted it.
When the two girls were playing dolls in the nursery, he would sit on his big
rocking-horse, charging madly into space, with a frenzy that made the little girls
peer at him uneasily. Wildly the horse careened, the waving dark hair of the boy
tossed, his eyes had a strange glare in them. The little girls dared not speak to him.

When he had ridden to the end of his mad little journey, he climbed down   42
and stood in front of his rocking-horse, staring fixedly into its lowered face. Its
red mouth was slightly open, its big eye was wide and glassy-bright.

"Now!" he would silently command the snorting steed. "Now, take me to   43
where there is luck! Now take me!"

And he would slash the horse on the neck with the little whip he had asked   44
Uncle Oscar for. He *knew* the horse could take him to where there was luck, if
only he forced it. So he would mount again and start on his furious ride, hoping
at last to get there. He knew he could get there.

"You'll break your horse, Paul!" said the nurse.   45

"He's always riding like that! I wish he'd leave off!" said his elder sister   46
Joan.

But he only glared down on them in silence. Nurse gave him up. She could   47
make nothing of him. Anyhow, he was growing beyond her.

One day his mother and his Uncle Oscar came in when he was on one of   48
his furious rides. He did not speak to them.

"Hallo, you young jockey! Riding a winner?" said his uncle.   49

"Aren't you growing too big for a rocking-horse? You're not a very little   50
boy any longer, you know," said his mother.

But Paul only gave a blue glare from his big, rather close-set eyes. He   51
would speak to nobody when he was in full tilt. His mother watched him with an
anxious expression on her face.

At last he suddenly stopped forcing his horse into the mechanical gallop   52
and slid down.

"Well, I got there!" he announced fiercely, his blue eyes still flaring, and his   53
sturdy long legs straddling apart.

"Where did you get to?" asked his mother.   54

"Where I wanted to go," he flared back at her.   55

"That's right, son!" said Uncle Oscar. "Don't you stop till you get there.   56
What's the horse's name?"

"He doesn't have a name," said the boy.   57

"Gets on without all right?" asked the uncle.   58

"Well, he has different names. He was called Sansovino last week."   59

"Sansovino, eh? Won the Ascot. How did you know this name?"   60

"He always talks about horse-races with Bassett," said Joan.   61

The uncle was delighted to find that his small nephew was posted with all   62
the racing news. Bassett, the young gardener, who had been wounded in the left
foot in the war and had got his present job through Oscar Cresswell, whose bat-
man he had been, was a perfect blade of the "turf." He lived in the racing events,
and the small boy lived with him.

Oscar Cresswell got it all from Bassett.   63

"Master Paul comes and asks me, so I can't do more than tell him, sir," said   64
Bassett, his face terribly serious, as if he were speaking of religious matters.

"And does he ever put anything on a horse he fancies?"   65

"Well—I don't want to give him away—he's a young sport, a fine sport, sir.   66
Would you mind asking him himself? He sort of takes a pleasure in it, and perhaps he'd feel I was giving him away, sir, if you don't mind."

Bassett was serious as a church.   67

The uncle went back to his nephew and took him off for a ride in the car.   68

"Say, Paul, old man, do you ever put anything on a horse?" the uncle asked.   69

The boy watched the handsome man closely.   70

"Why, do you think I oughtn't to?" he parried.   71

"Not a bit of it! I thought perhaps you might give me a tip for the Lincoln."   72

The car sped on into the country, going down to Uncle Oscar's place in   73
Hampshire.

"Honour bright?" said the nephew.   74

"Honour bright, son!" said the uncle.   75

"Well, then, Daffodil."   76

"Daffodil! I doubt it, sonny. What about Mirza?"   77

"I only know the winner," said the boy. "That's Daffodil."   78

"Daffodil, eh?"   79

There was a pause. Daffodil was an obscure horse comparatively.   80

"Uncle!"   81

"Yes, son?"   82

"You won't let it go any further, will you? I promised Bassett."   83

"Bassett be damned, old man! What's he got to do with it?"   84

"We're partners. We've been partners from the first. Uncle, he lent me my   85
first five shillings, which I lost. I promised him, honour bright, it was only
between me and him; only you gave me that ten-schilling note I started winning
with, so I thought you were lucky. You won't let it go any further, will you?"

The boy gazed at his uncle from those big, hot, blue eyes, set rather close   86
together. The uncle stirred and laughed uneasily.

"Right you are, son! I'll keep your tip private. Daffodil, eh? How much are   87
you putting on him?"

"All except twenty pounds," said the boy. "I keep that in reserve."   88

The uncle thought it a good joke.   89

"You keep twenty pounds in reserve, do you, you young romancer? What   90
are you betting, then?"

"I'm betting three hundred," said the boy gravely. "But it's between you and   91
me, Uncle Oscar! Honour bright?"

The uncle burst into a roar of laughter.   92

"It's between you and me all right, you young Nat Gould," he said, laugh-   93
ing. "But where's your three hundred?"

"Bassett keeps it for me. We're partners."   94

"You are, are you! And what is Bassett putting on Daffodil?"   95

"He won't go quite as high as I do, I expect. Perhaps he'll go a hundred and   96
fifty."

"What, pennies?" laughed the uncle.   97

"Pounds," said the child, with a surprised look at his uncle. "Bassett keeps   98
a bigger reserve than I do."

Between wonder and amusement Uncle Oscar was silent. He pursued the   99
matter no further, but he determined to take his nephew with him to the Lincoln
races.

"Now, son," he said, "I'm putting twenty on Mirza, and I'll put five on for   100
you on any horse you fancy. What's your pick?"

"Daffodil, uncle."   101

"No, not the fiver on Daffodil!"   102

"I should if it was my own fiver," said the child.   103

"Good! Good! Right you are! A fiver for me and a fiver for you on Daffodil."   104

The child had never been to a race-meeting before, and his eyes were blue   105
fire. He pursed his mouth tight and watched. A Frenchman just in front had put
his money on Lancelot. Wild with excitement, he flayed his arms up and down,
yelling *"Lancelot! Lancelot!"* in his French accent.

Daffodil came in first, Lancelot second, Mirza third. The child, flushed and   106
with eyes blazing, was curiously serene. His uncle brought him four five-pound
notes, four to one.

"What am I to do with these?" he cried, waving them before the boy's eyes. 107

"I suppose we'll talk to Bassett," said the boy. "I expect I have fifteen hun- 108
dred now; and twenty in reserve; and this twenty."

His uncle studied him for some moments. 109

"Look here, son!" he said. "You're not serious about Bassett and that fifteen 110
hundred, are you?"

"Yes, I am. But it's between you and me, uncle. Honour bright?" 111

"Honour bright all right, son! But I must talk to Bassett." 112

"If you'd like to be a partner, uncle, with Bassett and me, we could all be 113
partners. Only, you'd have to promise, honour bright, uncle, not to let it go
beyond us three. Bassett and I are lucky, and you must be lucky, because it was
your ten shillings I started winning with. . . ."

Uncle Oscar took both Bassett and Paul into Richmond Park for an after- 114
noon, and there they talked.

"It's like this, you see, sir," Bassett said. "Master Paul would get me talk- 115
ing about racing events, spinning yarns, you know, sir. And he was always keen
on knowing if I'd made or if I'd lost. It's about a year since, now, that I put five
shillings on Blush of Dawn for him: and we lost. Then the luck turned, with that
ten shillings he had from you: that we put on Singhalese. And since that time, it's
been pretty steady, all things considering. What do you say, Master Paul?"

"We're all right when we're sure," said Paul. "It's when we're not quite sure 116
that we go down."

"Oh, but we're careful then," said Bassett. 117

"But when are you *sure?*" smiled Uncle Oscar. 118

"It's Master Paul, sir," said Bassett in a secret, religious voice. "It's as if he 119
had it from heaven. Like Daffodil, now, for the Lincoln. That was as sure as eggs."

"Did you put anything on Daffodil?" asked Oscar Cresswell.

"Yes, sir. I made my bit." 120

"And my nephew?" 121

Bassett was obstinately silent, looking at Paul. 122

"I made twelve hundred, didn't I, Bassett? I told uncle I was putting three 123
hundred on Daffodil." 124

"That's right," said Bassett, nodding.

"But where's the money?" asked the uncle. 125

"I keep it safe locked up, sir. Master Paul he can have it any minute he likes 126
to ask for it." 127

"What, fifteen hundred pounds?"

"And twenty! And *forty,* that is, with the twenty he made on the course." 128

"It's amazing!" said the uncle. 129

"If Master Paul offers you to be partners, sir, I would, if I were you: if you'll 130
excuse me," said Bassett. 131

Oscar Cresswell thought about it.

"I'll see the money," he said. 132

133

They drove home again, and, sure enough, Bassett came round to the 134 garden-house with fifteen hundred pounds in notes. The twenty pounds reserve was left with Joe Glee, in the Turf Commission deposit.

"You see, it's all right, uncle, when I'm *sure!* Then we go strong, for all 135 we're worth. Don't we, Bassett?"

"We do that, Master Paul." 136

"And when are you sure?" said the uncle, laughing. 137

"Oh, well, sometimes I'm *absolutely* sure, like about Daffodil," said the 138 boy; "and sometimes I have an idea; and sometimes I haven't even an idea, have I, Bassett? Then we're careful, because we mostly go down."

"You do, do you! And when you're sure, like about Daffodil, what makes 139 you sure, sonny?"

"Oh, well, I don't know," said the boy uneasily. "I'm sure, you know, uncle; 140 that's all."

"It's as if he had it from heaven, sir," Bassett reiterated. 141

"I should say so!" said the uncle. 142

But he became a partner. And when the Leger was coming on Paul was 143 "sure" about Lively Spark, which was a quite inconsiderable horse. The boy insisted on putting a thousand on the horse, Bassett was for five hundred, and Oscar Cresswell two hundred. Lively Spark came in first, and the betting had been ten to one against him. Paul had made ten thousand.

"You see," he said, "I was absolutely sure of him." 144

Even Oscar Cresswell had cleared two thousand. 145

"Look here, son," he said, "this sort of thing makes me nervous." 146

"It needn't, uncle! Perhaps I shan't be sure again for a long time." 147

"But what are you going to do with your money?" asked the uncle. 148

"Of course," said the boy, "I started it for mother. She said she had no luck, 149 because father is unlucky, so I thought if *I* was lucky, it might stop whispering."

"What might stop whispering?" 150

"Our house. I *hate* our house for whispering." 151

"What does it whisper?" 152

"Why—why"—the boy fidgeted—"why, I don't know. But it's always 153 short of money, you know, uncle."

"I know it, son, I know it." 154

"You know people send mother writs, don't you, uncle?" 155

"I'm afraid I do," said the uncle. 156

"And then the house whispers, like people laughing at you behind your 157 back. It's awful, that is! I thought if I was lucky—"

"You might stop it," added the uncle. 158

The boy watched him with big blue eyes, that had an uncanny cold fire in 159 them, and he said never a word.

"Well, then!" said the uncle. "What are we doing?" 160

"I shouldn't like mother to know I was lucky," said the boy. 161

"Why not, son?"   162

"She'd stop me."   163

"I don't think she would."   164

"Oh!"—and the boy writhed in an odd way—"I *don't* want her to know,   165
uncle."

"All right, son! We'll manage it without her knowing."   166

They managed it very easily. Paul, at the other's suggestion, handed over   167
five thousand pounds to his uncle, who deposited it with the family lawyer, who
was then to inform Paul's mother that a relative had put five thousand pounds into
his hands, which sum was to be paid out a thousand pounds at a time, on the
mother's birthday, for the next five years.

"So she'll have a birthday present of a thousand pounds for five successive   168
years," said Uncle Oscar. "I hope it won't make it all the harder for her later."

Paul's mother had her birthday in November. The house had been "whis-   169
pering" worse than ever lately, and, even in spite of his luck, Paul could not bear
up against it. He was very anxious to see the effect of the birthday letter, telling
his mother about the thousand pounds.

When there were no visitors, Paul now took his meals with his parents, as   170
he was beyond the nursery control. His mother went into town nearly every day.
She had discovered that she had an odd knack of sketching furs and dress materials, so she worked secretly in the studio of a friend who was the chief "artist"
for the leading drapers. She drew the figures of ladies in furs and ladies in silk
and sequins for the newspaper advertisements. This young woman artist earned
several thousand pounds a year, but Paul's mother only made several hundreds,
and she was again dissatisfied. She so wanted to be first in something, and she did
not succeed, even in making sketches for drapery advertisements.

She was down to breakfast on the morning of her birthday. Paul watched   171
her face as she read her letters. He knew the lawyer's letter. As his mother read it,
her face hardened and became more expressionless. Then a cold, determined look
came on her mouth. She hid the letter under the pile of others, and said not a word
about it.

"Didn't you have anything nice in the post for your birthday, mother?" said   172
Paul.

"Quite moderately nice," she said, her voice cold and absent.   173

She went away to town without saying more.   174

But in the afternoon Uncle Oscar appeared. He said Paul's mother had had   175
a long interview with the lawyer, asking if the whole five thousand could not be
advanced at once, as she was in debt.

"What do you think, uncle?" said the boy.   176

"I leave it to you, son."   177

"Oh, let her have it, then! We can get some more with the other," said the boy.   178

"A bird in the hand is worth two in the bush, laddie!" said Uncle Oscar.   179

"But I'm sure to *know* for the Grand National; or the Lincolnshire; or else   180
the Derby. I'm sure to know for *one* of them," said Paul.

So Uncle Oscar signed the agreement, and Paul's mother touched the whole 181 five thousand. Then something very curious happened. The voices in the house suddenly went mad, like a chorus of frogs on a spring evening. There were certain new furnishings, and Paul had a tutor. He was *really* going to Eton, his father's school, in the following autumn. There were flowers in the winter, and a blossoming of the luxury Paul's mother had been used to. And yet the voices in the house, behind the sprays of mimosa and almondblossom, and from under the piles of iridescent cushions, simply trilled and screamed in a sort of ecstasy: "There *must* be more money! Oh-h-h; there *must* be more money. Oh, now now-w! Now-w-w—there *must* be more money!—more than ever! More than ever!"

It frightened Paul terribly. He studied away at his Latin and Greek with his 182 tutor. But his intense hours were spent with Bassett. The Grand National had gone by: he had not "known," and had lost a hundred pounds. Summer was at hand. He was in agony for the Lincoln. But even for the Lincoln he didn't "know," and he lost fifty pounds. He became wild-eyed and strange, as if something were going to explode in him.

"Let it alone, son! Don't you bother about it!" urged Uncle Oscar. But it 183 was as if the boy couldn't really hear what his uncle was saying.

"I've got to know for the Derby! I've got to know for the Derby!" the child 184 reiterated, his big blue eyes blazing with a sort of madness.

His mother noticed how overwrought he was. 185

"You'd better go to the seaside. Wouldn't you like to go now to the seaside, 186 instead of waiting? I think you'd better," she said, looking down at him anxiously, her heart curiously heavy because of him.

But the child lifted his uncanny blue eyes. 187

"I couldn't possibly go before the Derby, mother!" he said. "I couldn't 188 possibly!"

"Why not?" she said, her voice becoming heavy when she was opposed. 189 "Why not? You can still go from the seaside to see the Derby with your Uncle Oscar, if that's what you wish. No need for you to wait here. Besides, I think you care too much about these races. It's a bad sign. My family has been a gambling family, and you won't know till you grow up how much damage it has done. But it has done damage. I shall have to send Bassett away, and ask Uncle Oscar not to talk racing to you, unless you promise to be reasonable about it: go away to the seaside and forget it. You're all nerves!"

"I'll do what you like, mother, so long as you don't send me away till after 190 the Derby," the boy said.

"Send you away from where? Just from this house?" 191

"Yes," he said, gazing at her. 192

"Why, you curious child, what makes you care about this house so much, 193 suddenly? I never knew you loved it."

He gazed at her without speaking. He had a secret within a secret, some- 194 thing he had not divulged, even to Bassett or to his Uncle Oscar.

But his mother, after standing undecided and a little bit sullen for some 195 moments, said:

"Very well, then! Don't go to the seaside till after the Derby, if you don't 196 wish it. But promise me you won't let your nerves go to pieces. Promise you won't think so much about horse-racing and *events,* as you call them!"

"Oh no," said the boy casually. "I won't think much about them, mother. 197 You needn't worry. I wouldn't worry, mother, if I were you."

"If you were me and I were you," said his mother, "I wonder what we 198 *should* do!"

"But you know you needn't worry, mother, don't you?" the boy repeated. 199

"I should be awfully glad to know it," she said wearily. 200

"Oh, well, you *can,* you know. I mean, you *ought* to know you needn't 201 worry," he insisted.

"Ought I? Then I'll see about it," she said. 202

Paul's secret of secrets was his wooden horse, that which had no name. 203 Since he was emancipated from a nurse and a nursery-governess, he had had his rocking-horse removed to his own bedroom at the top of the house.

"Surely you're too big for a rocking-horse!" his mother had remonstrated. 204

"Well, you see, mother, till I can have a *real* horse, I like to have *some* sort 205 of animal about," had been his quaint answer.

"Do you feel he keeps you company?" she laughed. 206

"Oh yes! He's very good, he always keeps me company, when I'm there," 207 said Paul.

So the horse, rather shabby, stood in an arrested prance in the boy's bedroom. 208

The Derby was drawing near, and the boy grew more and more tense. He 209 hardly heard what was spoken to him, he was very frail, and his eyes were really uncanny. His mother had sudden strange seizures of uneasiness about him. Sometimes, for half an hour, she would feel a sudden anxiety about him that was almost anguish. She wanted to rush to him at once, and know he was safe.

Two nights before the Derby, she was at a big party in town, when one of 210 her rushes of anxiety about her boy, her first-born, gripped her heart till she could hardly speak. She fought with the feeling, might and main, for she believed in common sense. But it was too strong. She had to leave the dance and go downstairs to telephone to the country. The children's nursery-governess was terribly surprised and startled at being rung up in the night.

"Are the children all right, Miss Wilmot?" 211

"Oh yes, they are quite all right." 212

"Master Paul? Is he all right?" 213

"He went to bed as right as a trivet. Shall I run up and look at him?" 214

"No," said Paul's mother reluctantly. "No! Don't trouble. It's all right. 215 Don't sit up. We shall be home fairly soon." She did not want her son's privacy intruded upon.

"Very good," said the governess. 216

It was about one o'clock when Paul's mother and father drove up to their 217 house. All was still. Paul's mother went to her room and slipped off her white fur cloak. She had told her maid not to wait up for her. She heard her husband down-stairs, mixing a whisky and soda.

And then, because of the strange anxiety at her heart, she stole upstairs to [218] her son's room. Noiselessly she went along the upper corridor. Was there a faint noise? What was it?

She stood, with arrested muscles, outside his door, listening. There was a [219] strange, heavy, and yet not loud noise. Her heart stood still. It was a soundless noise, yet rushing and powerful. Something huge, in violent, hushed motion. What was it? What in God's name was it? She ought to know. She felt that she knew the noise. She knew what it was.

Yet she could not place it. She couldn't say what it was. And on and on it [220] went, like a madness.

Softly, frozen with anxiety and fear, she turned the doorhandle. [221]

The room was dark. Yet in the space near the window, she heard and saw [222] something plunging to and fro. She gazed in fear and amazement.

Then suddenly she switched on the light, and saw her son, in his green pyja- [223] mas, madly surging on the rocking-horse. The blaze of light suddenly lit him up, as he urged the wooden horse, and lit her up, as she stood, blonde, in her dress of pale green and crystal, in the doorway.

"Paul!" she cried. "Whatever are you doing?" [224]

"It's Malabar!" he screamed in a powerful, strange voice. "It's Malabar!" [225]

His eyes blazed at her for one strange and senseless second, as he ceased [226] urging his wooden horse. Then he fell with a crash to the ground, and she, all her tormented motherhood flooding upon her, rushed to gather him up.

But he was unconscious, and unconscious he remained, with some brain- [227] fever. He talked and tossed, and his mother sat stonily by his side.

"Malabar! It's Malabar! Bassett, Bassett, I *know!* It's Malabar!" [228]

So the child cried, trying to get up and urge the rocking-horse that gave him [229] his inspiration.

"What does he mean by Malabar?" asked the heart-frozen mother. [230]

"I don't know," said the father stonily. [231]

"What does he mean by Malabar?" she asked her brother Oscar. [232]

"It's one of the horses running for the Derby," was the answer. [233]

And, in spite of himself, Oscar Cresswell spoke to Bassett, and himself put [234] a thousand on Malabar: at fourteen to one.

The third day of the illness was critical: they were waiting for a change. The [235] boy, with his rather long, curly hair, was tossing ceaselessly on the pillow. He nei-ther slept nor regained consciousness, and his eyes were like blue stones. His mother sat, feeling her heart had gone, turned actually into a stone.

In the evening, Oscar Cresswell did not come, but Bassett sent a message, [236] saying could he come up for one moment, just one moment? Paul's mother was very angry at the intrusion, but on second thoughts she agreed. The boy was the same. Perhaps Bassett might bring him to consciousness.

The gardener, a shortish fellow with a little brown moustache and sharp lit- [237] tle brown eyes, tiptoed into the room, touched his imaginary cap to Paul's mother, and stole to the bedside, staring with glittering, smallish eyes at the tossing, dying child.

"Master Paul!" he whispered. "Master Paul! Malabar came in first all right, a clean win. I did as you told me. You've made over seventy thousand pounds, you have; you've got over eighty thousand. Malabar came in all right, Master Paul."

"Malabar! Malabar! Did I say Malabar, mother? Did I say Malabar? Do you think I'm lucky, mother? I knew Malabar, didn't I? Over eighty thousand pounds! I call that lucky, don't you, mother? Over eighty thousand pounds! I knew, didn't I know I knew? Malabar came in all right. If I ride my horse till I'm sure, then I tell you, Bassett, you can go as high as you like. Did you go for all you were worth, Bassett?"

"I went a thousand on it, Master Paul."

"I never told you, mother, that if I can ride my horse, and *get there,* then I'm absolutely sure—oh absolutely! Mother, did I ever tell you? I *am* lucky!"

"No, you never did," said his mother.

But the boy died in the night.

And even as he lay dead, his mother heard her brother's voice saying to her: "My God, Hester, you're eighty-odd thousand to the good, and a poor devil of a son to the bad. But, poor devil, poor devil, he's best gone out of a life where he rides his rocking-horse to find a winner."

Meaning and Idea

1. Describe Paul's character. How does his home environment affect him? What does he hope to accomplish in this story? Does he manage it? How and why does he die?

2. Who are the other main characters in this story? How does each of them contribute to the overall process of the story?

3. According to Paul's mother, what is the relation between luck and money? What process derives from that relation?

4. What do the voices in the house say? Why? How do they change after the first windfall of money? Why?

Language, Form, Structure

1. What is the overall process described in this story? Who is most responsible for enacting that process? What are his or her motivations to follow through on that process?

2. What is the theme of this story? What is its tone? Describe the relation between theme and tone here. Why is process analysis used as one of the organizing techniques?

3. The overall process here is divided into smaller processes, among them Paul's ritual on the rocking horse and the process of placing bets. Describe these two processes. What other smaller processes help form the overall process? Describe at least two of them.

4. How does repetition function in this story?

5. Write meanings for each of the following figurative expressions from this story: racked her brains; *filthy lucre*; unsure eyes; compel her attention; brazening it out; in full tilt; spinning yarns; an arrested prance. Then use each phrase in a sentence of your own.

Ideas for Writing

1. Explain a process that you used to get something you wanted very much. Be sure to indicate your motivations for beginning the process and tell whether you actually got what you wanted.

2. Describe a process by which you solved a major problem for yourself or someone else. Use narration and dialogue to enhance your analysis.

3. In interpreting this story, critics have often read the overall process involved as a metaphor either for Paul's "coming of age" (that is, his adolescence) or for what Lawrence viewed as the corruptness of the society in which it takes place. What is your response to these interpretations? Do you think either, or both, is valid? If so, in what ways? If not, why? Do you think there are any other metaphoric values attached to the processes of the story?

The Baby Myna

Ved Mehta

Ved Mehta was born in Lahore, India (now Pakistan), in 1934, and became an American citizen in 1975. Educated at Oxford and Harvard, Mehta began his schooling at schools for the blind in Bombay, India, and Little Rock, Arkansas, where his father had sent him to escape the life of degradation and poverty so often the fate of Asian blind children. The main part of Mehta's essay and story writing was accomplished while he was a contributing editor to *The New Yorker* magazine. His explanations of Indian lifestyles are collected in such works as *Walking the Indian Streets* (1960), the biographical *Daddyji* (1972) and *Mamaji* (1979), *The Photographs of Chachji* (1980), and the autobiographical *Vedi* (1982). Among Mehta's honors are a Guggenheim fellowship and a Ford Foundation grant.

In this vignette from his autobiographical *Vedi*, Ved Mehta skillfully blends description and narration to explain the various processes involved in his getting, training, and ultimately losing his pet myna bird, Sweetie.

*O*ne day, Sher Singh returned from leave in his village in the Kangara District, in the hills, with a baby myna for me. "I have brought you a friend," he said. "It's a baby myna. It's one of the only birds in the world that can talk. It's just the right age to learn to talk." 1

I was excited. I went with Sher Singh to the Mozang Chowk and bought a wire cage with a door, a metal floor, and a little swing. The cage had a hook at the top, and I hung it in my room. (We were temporarily living in our own house, at 11 Temple Road.) I got a couple of brass bowls—one for water, the other for grain—and filled them up and put them in the cage. I got a brush for cleaning out the cage. I named the myna Sweetie. The name came to me just out of the sky. 2

"How do you catch a baby myna?" I asked Sher Singh. 3

"It's difficult, Vedi Sahib. There are very few of them around, and you have to know where a baby myna is resting with her mother. You have to slip up on them in the middle of the night, when they are sleeping in their nest, and throw a cover over them and hope that you catch the baby, because only baby myna can learn to talk. Sometimes the mother myna will nip at your finger, and there are people in my village who are constantly getting their fingers nipped at because they have been trying to catch a baby myna." 4

At first, Sweetie was so small that she could scarcely fly even a few inches. I would sit her on my shoulder and walk around the room. She would dig her nervous, trembling claws through my shirt and into my shoulder as she tried to keep her balance, fluttering around my ear and sending off little ripples of air. But Sweetie grew fast, and soon she was flying around my room. Before I opened her cage to fill up the bowls or clean the floor, I would have to shut the door. She would often nip at my finger and escape from the cage. She would go and perch on the mantelpiece. When I ran to the mantelpiece to catch her, she 5 would fly up to the curtain rod. When I climbed up onto the windowsill and shook the curtain, she would fly back to the mantelpiece. Sometimes she would be so silent that I would wonder if she was still in the room. Other times, I would hear her flying all around the room—now she would be by the window, now by the overhead light, her wings beating against the pane and the lampshade. I would make kissing sounds, as I had heard Sher Singh make them. I would call to her—"Sweetie! Sweetie!" I would whistle affectionately. I would run frenetically from one end of the room to the other. I would scream with rage. But she wouldn't come to me. I would somehow have to summon Sher Singh through the closed door, and then give him a cue to come in when I thought she wasn't near the door, and he would have to prance around the room and somehow catch her with his duster.

"She's a real hill girl, all right, flying around like that," he would say.   6

When we had finally got her back in the cage, I would scold her roundly,   7
but it didn't seem to do much good.

"Vedi Sahib, you'll lose her, like your eyes, if you don't keep her always in   8
the cage," Sher Singh said.

"But then how can I feed her? How can I clean out her cage?"   9

"I will do all that, Vedi Sahib. And, because I can see, I can watch her."   10

"But I like looking after her," I said.   11

"You'll lose her, Vedi Sahib," he said. "And mind your finger. She's getting   12
big."

I devised a way of filling her bowls and cleaning some of the cage's floor   13
by surreptitiously sticking my fingers between the wires. But now and again I would want to feel her on her swing or take her out and hold her, and then she would nip at my finger and sometimes draw blood. She would escape and give me a real run around the room.

Every time I passed Sweetie's cage, I would say "Hello, Sweetie," and wait   14
for her to talk. But she would only flutter in the cage or, at most, make her swing squeak.

"Are you sure Sweetie can talk?" I asked Sher Singh.   15

"All baby mynas from Kangara can learn to talk," he said.   16

"Are you sure she is from Kangara?"   17

"Only mynas from Kangara have a black patch on the throat. You can feel   18
it, and you can ask anyone—it's as black as coal."

I took Sweetie out of her cage. I held her tight in one hand and tried to feel   19
the patch on her throat with the other. She screamed and tried to bite my finger, but I finally found the patch. It was a little soft, downy raised circle that throbbed with her pulse.

"What do mynas sound like when they talk?" I later asked Sher Singh.   20

"They have the voice of the Kangara, of a Kangara hill girl."   21

"What is that?"   22

"The Punjab hills, the leaves in the wind, the waterfall on a mountainside—   23
you know, Vedi Sahib, it's the sound of a peacock spreading its wings in Kangara at dawn."

One day, I passed her cage and said, "Hello, Sweetie." 24

"Hello, Sweetie," she answered. 25

I jumped. I don't know how I had expected her voice to sound, but it was thin, 26 sharp, and defiant—at once whiny and abrasive—like three treble notes on the harmonium played very fast. Her words assaulted my ears—"Sweetie" was something that film stars called each other on the screen, and sounded very naughty.

I had scarcely taken in the fact that Sweetie could really speak when she 27 repeated "Hello, Sweetie." She kept on repeating it, hour after hour. "Hello, Sweetie" would suddenly explode into the air like a firecracker.

Try as I would, I couldn't teach her to say anything else. All the same, there 28 was something thrilling and comforting in having my own film star in the cage, and I got so used to her enticing outbursts that I missed them when she kept quiet or was dozing.

Every evening, at the time when my big sisters and my big brother went to 29 play hockey or some other game with their school friends, it was Sher Singh's duty to take me for a walk to Lawrence Gardens. There I would ride the merry-go-round—a big, creaky thing with wooden seats and a metal railing—while Sher Singh ran alongside. It would revolve and lurch, tipping this way and that way, filling me with terror and excitement. On the ground, I would throw off my shoes and run up and down the hillocks. They were covered with damp, soft grass and occasional patches of dead grass. The grass would caress, tickle, and prick my feet. All around, there were the light, cheerful sounds of sighted children running and playing and of birds flying and perching and calling. In the distance, there was the solitary, mournful song of a nightingale.

I felt sorry that Sweetie, shut up in the house, couldn't enjoy the company 30 of other birds, and one evening I insisted that we take her along in her cage and let her enjoy the fresh air and the life of Lawrence Gardens, even if it was only through the wires of her cage.

"But don't let her out of the cage," Sher Singh said. "She is a spirit from the 31 hills. She will fly back to Kangara."

"Fly all the way to Kangara! She would die without food or water. Besides, 32 she is my friend. She wouldn't leave me."

"Vedi Sahib, you know how loyal Kangara servants are?" 33

"No one could be more loyal than you, Sher Singh." 34

"Well, Kangara mynas are as disloyal as Kangara servants are loyal. You 35 can love a beloved myna all you want to, give her all the grain to eat you want to, give her all the water to drink you want to, and at the first opportunity she will nip at your finger and fly away. But you can kick a servant from Kangara and he will still give you first-class service."

"Why is that?" 36

"Because servants from Kangara, like mynas, have breathed the Himalayan 37 air and are free spirits. A Kangara servant is a servant by choice—but no myna is in a cage by choice."

I couldn't follow exactly what Sher Singh was saying, but I laughed. Anyway, I insisted that we take Sweetie with us. 38

At Lawrence Gardens, I had no intention of taking Sweetie out of her cage, but when she heard the other birds she set up such a racket that children and servants who usually took little notice of me wandered toward us to find out what I was doing to the poor myna. They said all kinds of things: 39

"She is lonely." 40

"He's keeping her a prisoner." 41

"Tch, tch! He can't play with other children, so he won't let his myna play with other birds." 42

"She'll fly away to Kangara!" I cried. 43

People laughed, hooted, and jeered. "She's so small she probably can't even fly up to that tree." 44

"Why are you pointing? He doesn't know how high that tree is." 45

I suddenly got an idea. I had with me a ball of strong, fortified string that Brother Om used for flying kites. I took Sweetie out of the cage and, while I held her screaming and biting in my hands, I had Sher Singh tie up her legs with the string. Then I caught hold of the ball and let her go, and the people about us clapped and cheered. I started giving her string, and she flew high up and pulled and tugged. I gave her more string and let her lead me where she would around the grass. I thought it was a wonderful game. Before I knew what had happened, her weight at the end of the string was gone, and the limp string had fluttered down on me. 46

"She's bitten through the string! Look, she's bitten through the string!" everyone shouted, running away. 47

"Sher Singh, catch her! Catch her!" I cried. "Bring Sweetie back!" 48

"I think I see her!" he called, running off. 49

A few minutes later, Sher Singh came back. "She's nowhere to be found, Vedi Sahib. She's gone, Sahib—gone straight back to Kangara. You will now have to get along without Sweetie." 50

Sher Singh and I looked for her all over Lawrence Gardens, calling "Sweetie! Sweetie!" until it was dark and everyone had left. Then Sher Singh and I walked home with the empty cage. 51

Meaning and Idea

1. What is a myna? Why would it be a particularly attractive pet for a child?

2. What problems does the blind child Vedi have with the infant bird? What advice does Sher Singh give him? Why is Vedi reluctant to accept it?

3. How does Sher Singh's description of what the bird's voice would sound like compare with what Vedi actually hears once Sweetie learns to talk?

4. What plan does Vedi put into action for releasing Sweetie at Lawrence Gardens? How does it fail?

Language, Form, Structure

1. How does Ved Mehta use narration as the organizing technique for this selection? How does narration enhance the analysis of the various processes?

2. What is the main point of the selection? As part of a chapter from a long book, "The Baby Myna" understandably lacks a thesis sentence. What might a thesis sentence for this selection include? Write one that you think would be appropriate.

3. What does the tone of this essay tell you about Mehta's feelings about his childhood? How?

4. Write meanings for the following words: frenetically; prance; roundly; surreptitiously; defiant; abrasive; harmonium; enticing; lurch; fortified.

Ideas for Writing

1. If you have ever had a pet, explain the process by which you trained it to do something. Be sure to include any failures you experienced in this process before you were successful.

2. Using narration as your organizing principle, write a process analysis of how you learned to do something during your childhood.

3. Ved Mehta, as you may have picked up from context clues, has been blind since his childhood. How does this knowledge affect your reading of this selection? Does it make you reevaluate the descriptive passages or the overall tone and development of the process analysis? What other famous writers can you think of who were blind? How do you think their blindness affected their writing?

The Gold Worker

Camara Laye

Camara Laye (1928–1980) was born the son of a goldsmith in Kouroussa, French Guinea. His writings focus on the sharp contrast between traditional rural culture and modern urban lifestyles, a relationship that mirrors his own experience of leaving a tribal system to study and work in Paris. Among his best-known works are *The Dark Child* (1953) and *A Dream of Africa* (1971). Laye was also a contributor to numerous African, European, and American journals.

In *The Dark Child*, drawn from his childhood memory, Camara Laye explains the "magical" process of his father's work as a goldsmith. Technical process, though easily identifiable in this selection, is artfully crafted into a vivid narration.

Of all the different kinds of work my father engaged in, none fasci-   1
nated me so much as his skill with gold. No other occupation was so noble, no other needed such a delicate touch. And then, every time he worked in gold it was like a festival—indeed it *was* a festival—that broke the monotony of ordinary working days.

So, if a woman, accompanied by a go-between, crossed the threshold of the   2
workshop, I followed her in at once. I knew what she wanted: she had brought some gold, and had come to ask my father to transform it into a trinket. She had collected it in the placers of Siguiri where, crouching over the river for months on end, she had patiently extracted grains of gold from the mud.

These women never came alone. They knew my father had other things to   3
do than make trinkets. And even when he had the time, they knew they were not the first to ask a favor of him, and that, consequently, they would not be served before others.

Generally, they required the trinket for a certain date, for the festival of   4
Ramadan or the Tabaski or some other family ceremony or dance.

Therefore, to enhance their chances of being served quickly and to more   5
easily persuade my father to interrupt the work before him, they used to request the services of an official praise-singer, a go-between, arranging in advance the fee they were to pay him for his good offices.

The go-between installed himself in the workshop, tuned up his *cora*,   6
which is our harp, and began to sing my father's praises. This was always a great event for me. I heard recalled the lofty deeds of my father's ancestors and their names from the earliest times. As the couplets were reeled off it was like watching the growth of a great genealogical tree that spread its branches far and wide and flourished its boughs and twigs before my mind's eye. The harp played an accompaniment to this vast utterance of names, expanding it with notes that were now soft, now shrill.

I could sense my father's vanity being inflamed, and I already knew that after having sipped this milk-and-honey he would lend a favorable ear to the woman's request. But I was not alone in my knowledge. The woman also had seen my father's eyes gleaming with contented pride. She held out her grains of gold as if the whole matter were settled. My father took up his scales and weighed the gold.   7

"What sort of trinket do you want?" he would ask.   8

"I want. . . ."   9

And then the woman would not know any longer exactly what she wanted because desire kept making her change her mind, and because she would have liked all the trinkets at once. But it would have taken a pile of gold much larger than she had brought to satisfy her whim, and from then on her chief purpose in life was to get hold of it as soon as she could.   10

"When do you want it?"   11

Always the answer was that the trinket was needed for an occasion in the near future.   12

"So! You are in that much of a hurry? Where do you think I shall find the time?"   13

"I am in a great hurry, I assure you."   14

"I have never seen a woman eager to deck herself out who wasn't in a great hurry! Good! I shall arrange my time to suit you. Are you satisfied?"   15

He would take the clay pot that was kept specially for smelting gold, and would pour the grains into it. He would then cover the gold with powdered charcoal, a charcoal he prepared by using plant juices of exceptional purity. Finally, he would place a large lump of the same kind of charcoal over the pot.   16

As soon as she saw that the work had been duly undertaken, the woman, now quite satisfied, would return to her household tasks, leaving her go-between to carry on with the praise-singing which had already proved so advantageous.   17

At a sign from my father the apprentices began working two sheepskin bellows. The skins were on the floor, on opposite sides of the forge, connected to it by earthen pipes. While the work was in progress the apprentices sat in front of the bellows with crossed legs. That is, the younger of the two sat, for the elder was sometimes allowed to assist. But the younger—this time it was Sidafa—was only permitted to work the bellows and watch while waiting his turn for promotion to less rudimentary tasks. First one and then the other worked hard at the bellows: the flame in the forge rose higher and became a living thing, a genie implacable and full of life.   18

Then my father lifted the clay pot with his long tongs and placed it on the flame.   19

Immediately all activity in the workshop almost came to a halt. During the whole time that the gold was being smelted, neither copper nor aluminum could be worked nearby, lest some particle of these base metals fall into the container which held the gold. Only steel could be worked on such occasions, but the men, whose task that was, hurried to finish what they were doing, or left it abruptly to join the apprentices gathered around the forge. There were so many, and they   20 crowded so around my father, that I, the smallest person present, had to come near the forge in order not to lose track of what was going on.

21 If he felt he had inadequate working space, my father had the apprentices stand well away from him. He merely raised his hand in a simple gesture: at that particular moment he never uttered a word, and no one else would: no one was allowed to utter a word. Even the go-between's voice was no longer raised in song. The silence was broken only by the panting of the bellows and the faint hissing of the gold. But if my father never actually spoke, I know that he was forming words in his mind. I could tell from his lips, which kept moving, while, bending over the pot, he stirred the gold and charcoal with a bit of wood that kept bursting into flame and had constantly to be replaced by a fresh one.

22 What words did my father utter? I do not know. At least I am not certain what they were. No one ever told me. But could they have been anything but incantations? On these occasions was he not invoking the genies of fire and gold, of fire and wind, of wind blown by the blast-pipes of the forge, of fire born of wind, of gold married to fire? Was it not their assistance, their friendship, their espousal that he besought? Yes. Almost certainly he was invoking these genies, all of whom are equally indispensable for smelting gold.

23 The operation going on before my eyes was certainly the smelting of gold, yet something more than that: a magical operation that the guiding spirits could regard with favor or disfavor. That is why, all around my father, there was absolute silence and anxious expectancy. Though only a child, I knew there could be no craft greater than the goldsmith's. I expected a ceremony; I had come to be present at a ceremony; and it actually was one, though very protracted. I was still too young to understand why, but I had an inkling as I watched the almost religious concentration of those who followed the mixing process in the clay pot.

24 When finally the gold began to melt I could have shouted aloud—and perhaps we all would have if we had not been forbidden to make a sound. I trembled, and so did everyone else watching my father stir the mixture—it was still a heavy paste—in which the charcoal was gradually consumed. The next stage followed swiftly. The gold now had the fluidity of water. The genies had smiled on the operation!

25 "Bring me the brick!" my father would order, thus lifting the ban that until then had silenced us.

26 The brick, which an apprentice would place beside the fire, was hollowed out, generously greased with Galam butter. My father would take the pot off the fire and tilt it carefully while I would watch the gold flow into the brick, flow like liquid fire. True, it was only a very sparse trickle of fire, but how vivid, how brilliant! As the gold flowed into the brick the grease sputtered and flamed and emitted a thick smoke that caught in the throat and stung the eyes, leaving us all weeping and coughing.

27 But there were times when it seemed to me that my father ought to turn this task over to one of his assistants. They were experienced, had assisted him hundreds of times, and could certainly have performed the work well. But my father's lips moved and those inaudible, secret words, those incantations he addressed to one we

could not see or hear, was the essential part. Calling on the genies of fire, of wind, of gold and exorcising the evil spirits—this was a knowledge he alone possessed.

By now the gold had been cooled in the hollow of the brick, and my father 28 began to hammer and stretch it. This was the moment when his work as a gold-smith really began. I noticed that before embarking on it he never failed to stroke the little snake stealthily as it lay coiled up under the sheepskin. I can only assume that this was his way of gathering strength for what remained to be done, the most trying part of his task.

But was it not extraordinary and miraculous that on these occasions the lit- 29 tle black snake was always coiled under the sheepskin? He was not always there. He did not visit my father every day. But he was always present whenever there was gold to be worked. His presence was no surprise to *me*. After that evening when my father had spoken of the guiding spirit of his race I was no longer aston-ished. The snake was there intentionally. He knew what the future held. Did he tell my father? I think that he most certainly did. Did he tell him everything? I have another reason for believing firmly that he did.

The craftsman who works in gold must first of all purify himself. That is, 30 he must wash himself all over and, of course, abstain from all sexual commerce during the whole time. Great respecter of ceremony as he was, it would have been impossible for my father to ignore these rules. Now, I never saw him make these preparations. I saw him address himself to his work without any apparent pre-liminaries. From that moment it was obvious that, forewarned in a dream by his black guiding spirit of the task which awaited him in the morning, my father must have prepared for it as soon as he arose, entering his workshop in a state of purity, his body smeared with the secret potions hidden in his numerous pots of magical substances; or perhaps he always came into his workshop in a state of ritual purity. I am not trying to make him out a better man than he was—he was a man and had his share of human frailties—but he was always uncompromising in his respect for ritual observance.

The woman for whom the trinket was being made, and who had come often 31 to see how the work was progressing, would arrive for the final time, not wanting to miss a moment of this spectacle—as marvelous to her as to us—when the gold wire, which my father had succeeded in drawing out from the mass of molten gold and charcoal, was transformed into a trinket.

There she would be. Her eyes would devour the fragile gold wire, follow- 32 ing it in its tranquil and regular spiral around the little slab of metal which sup-ported it. My father would catch a glimpse of her and I would see him slowly beginning to smile. Her avid attention delighted him.

"Are you trembling?" he would ask.   33
"Am I trembling?"   34
And we would all burst out laughing at her. For she would be trembling! 35 She would be trembling with covetousness for the spiral pyramid in which my father would be inserting, among the convolutions, tiny grains of gold. When he had finally finished by crowning the pyramid with a heavier grain, she would dance in delight.

No one—no one at all—would be more enchanted than she as my father slowly turned the trinket back and forth between his fingers to display its perfection. Not even the praise-singer whose business it was to register excitement would be more excited than she. Throughout this metamorphosis he did not stop speaking faster and ever faster, increasing his tempo, accelerating his praises and flatteries as the trinket took shape, shouting to the skies my father's skill.

For the praise-singer took a curious part—I should say rather that it was direct and effective—in the work. He was drunk with the joy of creation. He shouted aloud in joy. He plucked his *cora* like a man inspired. He sweated as if he were the trinket-maker, as if he were my father, as if the trinket were his creation. He was no longer a hired censer-bearer, a man whose services anyone could rent. He was a man who created his song out of some deep inner necessity. And when my father, after having soldered the large grain of gold that crowned the summit, held out his work to be admired, the praise-singer would no longer be able to contain himself. He would begin to intone the *douga,* the great chant which is sung only for celebrated men and which is danced for them alone.

But the *douga* is a formidable chant, a provocative chant, a chant which the praise-singer dared not sing, and which the man for whom it is sung dared not dance before certain precautions had been taken. My father had taken them as soon as he woke, since he had been warned in a dream. The praise-singer had taken them when he concluded his arrangements with the woman. Like my father he had smeared his body with magic substances and had made himself invulnerable to the evil genies whom the *douga* inevitably set free; these potions made him invulnerable also to rival praise-singers, perhaps jealous of him, who awaited only this song and the exaltation and loss of control which attended it, in order to begin casting their spells.

At the first notes of the *douga* my father would arise and emit a cry in which happiness and triumph were equally mingled; and brandishing in his right hand the hammer that was the symbol of his profession and in his left a ram's horn filled with magic substances, he would dance the glorious dance.

No sooner had he finished, than workmen and apprentices, friends and customers in their turn, not forgetting the woman for whom the trinket had been created, would flock around him, congratulating him, showering praises on him and complimenting the praise-singer at the same time. The latter found himself laden with gifts—almost his only means of support, for the praise-singer leads a wandering life after the fashion of the troubadours of old. Aglow with dancing and the praises he had received, my father would offer everyone cola nuts, that small change of Guinean courtesy.

Now all that remained to be done was to redden the trinket in a little water to which chlorine and sea salt had been added. I was at liberty to leave. The festival was over! But often as I came out of the workshop my mother would be in the court, pounding millet or rice, and she would call to me:

"Where have you been?" although she knew perfectly well where I had been.

"In the workshop."

"Of course. Your father was smelting gold. Gold! Always gold!"   43
And she would beat the millet or rice furiously with her pestle.   44
"Your father is ruining his health!"   45
"He danced the *douga*."   46
"The *douga!* The *douga* won't keep him from ruining his eyes. As for you,   47
you would be better off playing in the courtyard instead of breathing dust and
smoke in the workshop."

My mother did not like my father to work in gold. She knew how danger-   48
ous it was: a trinket-maker empties his lungs blowing on the blowpipe and his
eyes suffer from the fire. Perhaps they suffer even more from the microscopic precision which the work requires. And even if there had been no such objections
involved, my mother would scarcely have relished this work. She was suspicious
of it, for gold can not be smelted without the use of other metals, and my mother
thought it was not entirely honest to put aside for one's own use the gold which
the alloy had displaced. However, this was a custom generally known, and one
which she herself had accepted when she took cotton to be woven and received
back only a piece of cotton cloth half the weight of the original bundle.

Meaning and Idea

1. What function does the official praise-singer serve in negotiations between
   the woman and the narrator's father? How does the praise-singer continue
   to participate in the creation of the trinket?

2. Why is there "absolute silence and anxious expectancy" in the workshop?

3. When does the work of the skillful goldsmith really begin? How does the
   snake figure in the work?

4. What elements of ceremony and superstition do you note here? Why does
   the narrator say that his father "was always uncompromising in his respect
   for ritual observance"? How, in fact, is the day for working the gold "like a
   festival"?

5. What is the *douga?* How does the father prepare himself for it?

Language, Form, Structure

1. How does the writer make this highly technical process lively and
   enjoyable for his readers?

2. How does the first paragraph serve as an appropriate introduction to the
   selection? Which sentence in the introduction might be considered as a
   thesis sentence?

3. How do description and narration serve as transitional devices here? What
   transitional words and phrases help link the elements of the selection
   together?

4. Explain the following simile from the essay: "As the couplets were reeled off it was like watching the growth of a great genealogical tree." Explain the following metaphor: "after having sipped this milk-and-honey, he would lend a favorable ear to the woman's request." Find and explain at least two other metaphors and two other similes in the selection.

5. Choose ten of the following words and write definitions for them: trinket; shrill; vanity; smelting; apprentices; bellows; rudimentary; incantations; invoke; espousal; inaudible; covetousness; metamorphosis; intone.

Ideas for Writing

1. Describe the process by which you learned to do something in your childhood. Try to include how your perception of the process now is different from what it was then.

2. Explain any technical process with which you are familiar. Use narration and description to make the process analysis lively.

3. This selection is a childhood memory explained from the perspective of an adult. In an essay, evaluate Laye's ability to connect those two perspectives.

How to Become a Better Writer

Lorrie Moore

Born in Glen Falls, New York, and educated at Sarah Lawrence and Cornell, Lorrie Moore teaches English at the University of Wisconsin at Madison and has published three books and several articles.

She writes the following selection, which comes from her novel *Self Help,* mockingly in the second person. Moore set out to appropriate the "how-to" form for fiction. "I was interested in whatever tensions resulted when a writer foisted the fictional experience of the 'I' of the first person." We can easily read her short story as a process essay describing "how not to."

*F*irst, try to be something, anything, else. A movie star/astronaut. A movie star/missionary. A movie star/kindergarten teacher. President of the World. Fail miserably. It is best if you fail at an early age—say, fourteen. Early, critical disillusionment is necessary so that at fifteen you can write long haiku sequences about thwarted desire. It is a pond, a cherry blossom, a wind brushing against sparrow wing leaving for mountain. Count the syllables. Show it to your mom. She is tough and practical. She has a son in Vietnam and a husband who may be having an affair. She believes in wearing brown because it hides spots. She'll look briefly at your writing, then back up at you with a face blank as a donut. She'll say: "How about emptying the dishwasher?" Look away. Shove the forks in the fork drawer. Accidentally break one of the freebie gas station glasses. This is the required pain and suffering. This is only for starters.

In your high school English class look at Mr. Killian's face. Decide faces are important. Write a villanelle about pores. Struggle. Write a sonnet. Count the syllables: nine, ten, eleven, thirteen. Decide to experiment with fiction. Here you don't have to count syllables. Write a short story about an elderly man and woman who accidentally shoot each other in the head, the result of an inexplicable malfunction of a shotgun which appears mysteriously in their living room one night. Give it to Mr. Killian as your final project. When you get it back, he has written on it: "Some of your images are quite nice, but you have no sense of plot." When you are home, in the privacy of your own room, faintly scrawl in pencil beneath his black-inked comments: "Plots are for dead people, pore-face."

Take all the babysitting jobs you can get. You are great with kids. They love you. You tell them stories about old people who die idiot deaths. You sing them songs like "Blue Bells of Scotland," which is their favorite. And when they are in their pajamas and have finally stopped pinching each other, when they are fast asleep, you read every sex manual in the house, and wonder how on earth anyone could ever do those things with someone they truly loved. Fall asleep in a chair reading Mr. McMurphy's *Playboy*. When the McMurphys come home, they will tap you on the shoulder, look at the magazine in your lap, and grin. You will want to die. They will ask you if Tracey took her medicine all right. Explain, yes, she did, that you promised her a story if she would take it like a big girl and that seemed to work out just fine. "Oh, marvelous," they will exclaim.

Try to smile proudly. 4

Apply to college as a child psychology major. 5

As a child psychology major, you have some electives. You've always liked 6 birds. Sign up for something called "The Ornithological Field Trip." It meets Tuesdays and Thursdays at two. When you arrive at Room 134 on the first day of class, everyone is sitting around a seminar table talking about metaphors. You've heard of these. After a short, excruciating while, raise your hand and say diffidently, "Excuse me, isn't this Birdwatching One-oh-one?" The class stops and turns to look at you. They seem to all have one face—giant and blank as a vandalized clock. Someone with a beard booms out, "No, this is Creative Writing." Say: "Oh—right," as if perhaps you knew all along. Look down at your schedule. Wonder how the hell you ended up here. The computer, apparently, has made an error. You start to get up to leave and then don't. The lines at the registrar this week are huge. Perhaps you should stick with this mistake. Perhaps your creative writing isn't all that bad. Perhaps it is fate. Perhaps this is what your dad meant when he said, "It's the age of computers, Francie, it's the age of computers."

Decide that you like college life. In your dorm you meet many nice people. 7 Some are smarter than you. And some, you notice, are dumber than you. You will continue, unfortunately, to view the world in exactly these terms for the rest of your life.

The assignment this week in creative writing is to narrate a violent hap- 8 pening. Turn in a story about driving with your Uncle Gordon and another one about two old people who are accidentally electrocuted when they go to turn on a badly wired desk lamp. The teacher will hand them back to you with comments: "Much of your writing is smooth and energetic. You have, however, a ludicrous notion of plot." Write another story about a man and a woman who, in the very first paragraph, have their lower torsos accidentally blitzed away by dynamite. In the second paragraph, with the insurance money, they buy a frozen yogurt stand together. There are six more paragraphs. You read the whole thing out loud in class. No one likes it. They say your sense of plot is outrageous and incompetent. After class someone asks you if you are crazy.

Decide that perhaps you should stick to comedies. Start dating someone who 9 is funny, someone who has what in high school you called a "really great sense of humor" and what now your creative writing class calls "self-contempt giving rise to comic form." Write down all of his jokes, but don't tell him you are doing this. Make up anagrams of his old girlfriend's name and name all of your socially handicapped characters with them. Tell him his old girlfriend is in all of your stories and then watch how funny he can be, see what a really great sense of humor he can have.

Your child psychology advisor tells you you are neglecting courses in your 10 major. What you spend the most time on should be what you're majoring in. Say yes, you understand.

In creative writing seminars over the next two years, everyone continues to 11 smoke cigarettes and ask the same things: "But does it work?" "Why should we care about this character?" "Have you earned this cliché?" These seem like important questions.

On days when it is your turn, you look at the class hopefully as they scour 12 your mimeographs for a plot. They look back up at you, drag deeply, and then smile in a sweet sort of way.

You spend too much time slouched and demoralized. Your boyfriend sug- 13 gests bicycling. Your roommate suggests a new boyfriend. You are said to be self-mutilating and losing weight, but you continue writing. The only happiness you have is writing something new, in the middle of the night, armpits damp, heart pounding, something no one has yet seen. You have only those brief, fragile, untested moments of exhilaration when you know: you are a genius. Understand what you must do. Switch majors. The kids in your nursery project will be disappointed, but you have a calling, an urge, a delusion, an unfortunate habit. You have, as your mother would say, fallen in with a bad crowd.

Why write? Where does writing come from? These are questions to ask 14 yourself? They are like: Where does dust come from? Or: Why is there war? Or: If there's a God, then why is my brother now a cripple?

These are questions that you keep in your wallet, like calling cards. These 15 are questions, your creative writing teacher says, that are good to address in your journals but rarely in your fiction.

The writing professor this fall is stressing the Power of the Imagination. 16 Which means he doesn't want long descriptive stories about your camping trip last July. He wants you to start in a realistic context but then to alter it. Like recombinant DNA. He wants you to let your imagination sail, to let it grow big-bellied in the wind. This is a quote from Shakespeare.

Tell your roommate your great idea, your great exercise of imaginative 17 power: a transformation of Melville to contemporary life. It will be about mono-mania and the fish-eat-fish world of life insurance in Rochester, New York. The first line will be "Call me Fishmeal," and it will feature a menopausal suburban husband named Richard, who because he is so depressed all the time is called "Mopey Dick" by his witty wife Elaine. Say to your roommate: "Mopey Dick, get it?" Your roommate looks at you, her face blank as a large Kleenex. She comes up to you, like a buddy, and puts an arm around your burdened shoulders. "Listen, Francie," she says, slow as speech therapy. "Let's go out and get a big beer."

The seminar doesn't like this one either. You suspect they are beginning to feel sorry for you. They say: "You have to think about what is happening. Where is the story here?"

18

The next semester the writing professor is obsessed with writing from personal experience. You must write from what you know, from what has happened to you. He wants deaths, he wants camping trips. Think about what has happened to you. In three years there have been three things: you lost your virginity; your parents got divorced; and your brother came home from a forest ten miles from the Cambodian border with only half a thigh, a permanent smirk nestled into one corner of his mouth.

19

About the first you write: "It created a new space, which hurt and cried in a voice that wasn't mine, 'I'm not the same anymore, but I'll be okay.'"

20

About the second you write an elaborate story of an old married couple who stumble upon an unknown land mine in their kitchen and accidentally blow themselves up. You call it: "For Better or for Liverwurst."

21

About the last you write nothing. There are no words for this. Your typewriter hums. You can find no words.

22

At undergraduate cocktail parties, people say, "Oh, you write? What do you write about?" Your roommate, who has consumed too much wine, too little cheese, and no crackers at all, blurts: "Oh, my god, she always writes about her dumb boyfriend."

23

Later on in life you will learn that writers are merely open, helpless texts with no real understanding of what they have written and therefore must half-believe anything and everything that is said of them. You, however, have not yet reached this stage of literary criticism. You stiffen and say, "I do not," the same way you said it when someone in the fourth grade accused you of really liking oboe lessons and your parents really weren't just making you take them.

24

Insist you are not very interested in any one subject at all, that you are interested in the music of language, that you are interested in—in—syllables, because they are the atoms of poetry, the cells of the mind, the breath of the soul. Begin to feel woozy. Stare into your plastic wine cup.

25

"Syllables?" you will hear someone ask, voice trailing off, as they glide slowly toward the reassuring white of the dip.

26

Begin to wonder what you do write about. Or if you have anything to say. Or if there even is such a thing as a thing to say. Limit these thoughts to no more than ten minutes a day; like sit-ups, they can make you thin.

27

You will read somewhere that all writing has to do with one's genitals. Don't dwell on this. It will make you nervous.

28

Your mother will come visit you. She will look at the circles under your ₂₉ eyes and hand you a brown book with a brown briefcase on the cover. It is entitled: *How to Become a Business Executive.* She has also brought the *Names for Baby* encyclopedia you asked for; one of your characters, the aging clown-school teacher, needs a new name. Your mother will shake her head and say: "Francie, Francie, remember when you were going to be a child psychology major?"

Say: "Mom, I like to write." ₃₀

She'll say: "Sure you like to write. Of course. Sure you like to write." ₃₁

Write a story about a confused music student and title it: "Schubert Was the ₃₂ One with the Glasses, Right?" It's not a big hit, although your roommate likes the part where the two violinists accidentally blow themselves up in a recital room. "I went out with a violinist once," she says, snapping her gum.

Thank god you are taking other courses. You can find sanctuary in ₃₃ nineteenth-century ontological snags and invertebrate courting rituals. Certain globular mollusks have what is called "Sex by the Arm." The male octopus, for instance, loses the end of one arm when placing it inside the female body during intercourse. Marine biologists call it "Seven Heaven." Be glad you know these things. Be glad you are not just a writer. Apply to law school.

From here on in, many things can happen. But the main one will be this: ₃₄ you decide not to go to law school after all, and, instead, you spend a good, big chunk of your adult life telling people how you decided not to go to law school after all. Somehow you end up writing again. Perhaps you go to graduate school. Perhaps you work odd jobs and take writing courses at night. Perhaps you are working on a novel and writing down all the clever remarks and intimate personal confessions you hear during the day. Perhaps you are losing your pals, your acquaintances, your balance.

You have broken up with your boyfriend. You now go out with men who, ₃₅ instead of whispering "I love you," shout: "Do it to me, baby." This is good for your writing.

Sooner or later you have a finished manuscript more or less. People look at ₃₆ it in a vaguely troubled sort of way and say, "I'll bet becoming a writer was always a fantasy of yours, wasn't it?" Your lips dry to salt. Say that of all the fantasies possible in the world, you can't imagine being a writer even making the top twenty. Tell them you were going to be a child psychology major. "I bet," they always sigh, "you'd be great with kids." Scowl fiercely. Tell them you're a walking blade.

Quit classes. Quit jobs. Cash in old savings bonds. Now you have time like ₃₇ warts on your hands. Slowly copy all of your friends' addresses into a new address book.

Vacuum. Chew cough drops. Keep a folder full of fragments.   38

An eyelid darkening sideways.

World as conspiracy.

Possible plot? A woman gets on a bus.

Suppose you threw a love affair and nobody came.

At home drink a lot of coffee. At Howard Johnson's order the cole slaw.   39
Consider how it looks like the soggy confetti of a map: where you've been, where
you're going—"You Are Here," says the red star on the back of the menu.

Occasionally a date with a face blank as a sheet of paper asks you whether   40
writers often become discouraged. Say that sometimes they do and sometimes
they do. Say it's a lot like having polio.

"Interesting," smiles your date, and then he looks down at his arm hairs and   41
starts to smooth them, all, always, in the same direction.

Meaning and Idea

1. Moore's story is about the process of becoming a writer, or the process of
    not becoming one, depending on how you look at the piece. What are the
    basic elements in the process she describes? If you wanted to be a writer,
    which of her recommendations would you attempt to practice? Why?

2. How do the adverse experiences of the narrator affect her? In what way do
    they skew her vision of the writer's craft? What is the most humorous detail
    here in the catalogue of steps to take to become a better writer?

3. Are we supposed to take Moore's advice seriously? How can you tell? Why
    has she chosen a humorous form of presentation as opposed to a more
    serious one?

Language, Form, Structure

1. Why does Moore choose to write this fictional piece in the second
    person—as advice to "you"?

2. How does the writer achieve the humorous effects here? How does she use
    irony, exaggeration, one-liners, non sequiturs, and other devices to make
    readers laugh?

3. What is your reaction to the first line of the selection? How does it relate to
    the title? How do the first line and the rest of the first paragraph establish
    the humorous dimensions of the piece?

4. Moore writes a number of brief or one-sentence paragraphs. Why does she
    do so, do you think? What do they contribute to her overall intent? How do
    they affect the process being described?

5. How do the last two paragraphs provide an appropriate conclusion for this fictional piece? Why does the date smooth his arm hairs? What does this gesture tell you about Moore's view of what the world thinks of the writer's struggles?

6. Define the following words and use each in a sentence: thwarted; diffidently; ludicrous; demoralized; recombinant; monomania; woozy; sanctuary; ontological.

Ideas for Writing

1. Using the second person, explain a frustrating process as an essay of advice to someone. You may choose, in fact, to make this a how-*not*-to essay.

2. Write an essay that attempts to answer one or both of these two questions from Moore's essay: "Why write? Where does writing come from?" Draw upon the strategies of process analysis to develop your paper.

3. Write a critical essay in which you analyze the comic effects in this selection. Draw liberally from the piece to illustrate how Moore made you laugh.

CROSSOVER ▬▬▬▬▬▬▬▬▬▬▬▬▬▬▬▬

1. Ernest Hemingway in "Camping Out" (this chapter), E. B. White in "Once More to the Lake" (Chapter One), and Jack London in "To Build a Fire" (Chapter Seven) offer reflections on nature. How do their views of the natural world differ? Which essay engages you most with the powers of living things? What techniques does the writer use to affect you? Write an essay to explore these questions.

2. In this chapter, Anthony Trollope in "250 Words Every Quarter of an Hour," Joan Didion in "On Keeping a Notebook," and Lorrie Moore in "How to Become a Better Writer" tell about how they approach aspects of writing. Which selection makes writing most attractive? Which selection makes writing least attractive? What elements of writing does each piece stress to make its point? Write an essay to explore these questions.

Chapter Five

■

COMPARISON

Where would we be without the ability to see things in relation to other things? Making comparisons, seeing similarities or differences (or both) is essential for making the judgments we live by. Is he large or small, beautiful or ugly, kind or cruel? Is she attentive or blasé, energetic or lethargic, coy or ostentatious? To answer such questions intelligently we often ask another question: "*Compared* to whom?" Making comparisons allows us to think more deeply. Indeed, thought without comparisons is not really thought as we know it. A mind overtaken by an obsession, for example, is a mind stuck in a single vision, unable to look about with an eye open to relationships and comparisons.

Comparative thinking is a particularly human gift that enables us to organize experience and to make the serious and fanciful connections that help us evaluate the conditions of our daily lives.

READING COMPARISON

Careful readers know that for the best writers, the comparative faculty is a steady apparatus. The writer of fiction or drama develops one character with another in mind and depends on readers or viewers seeing these created people in relation to one another. We appreciate the nobility of an Othello, for example, more clearly in relation to the vile actions of an Iago, or the vulnerable youth of Romeo and Juliet in relation to their ruling elders.

The worlds of comedy and tragedy alike are populated with characters meant for the reader to compare—Mutt and Jeff, Felix and Oscar, Lenny and George, and the list goes on—clear opposites meant to illuminate each other. Many writers, then, make generous use of explicit and implicit comparisons. This is as true for the writer of essays as for the writer of imaginative literature. Patterns emerge and generalizations come forth as the essayist in "Once More to the Lake" (see Chapter Two) considers subjects relatively. E. B. White's trip to the lake with his son gains meaning for both the writer and the reader as White *compares* the stay to those of his childhood. Without the pressure of these other memories, White's descriptions might have evoked a sense of place but could never have conveyed the rich sense of time and of life passing by. Similarly, readers confronted with Susan Sontag's comparison in this chapter between the public's perceptions about cancer and tuberculosis learn much about our entrenched habits in thinking about and dealing with disease. The primitive dread, shame, and disgust that for centuries marked attitudes toward TB have attached themselves in the modern age to our attitude toward cancer and cancer patients. Sontag's comparison urges us to review our thinking, to cast off old prejudices and phobias, and to assume the enlightened consciousness and behavior permitted by the advancing science of our century. Her historical perspective allows us to view cancer with increased hope as well. Like TB, so long the dreaded "killer," cancer too can be understood and conquered, both mentally and physically. The essay deepens from the apt comparison.

In reading poetry, we are confronted again and again with comparisons. Poets can structure their poems with comparisons, exploring two subjects at once. Such basic comparisons appear in poems like "The Naked and the Nude" (Chapter

Eight) and "Richard Cory" (Chapter Nine). These comparisons help readers see subjects dynamically—Nakedness versus Nudity town patrician versus town folk. But poets work in fanciful comparisons as well, comparing a lover to a summer's day, home life to a hag-ridden dream, an unfulfilled dream to a raisin in the sun.

Figurative devices help us compare things in an imaginative fashion. Through metaphor, for example, we can make statements that tell special truths. In Tennyson's "The Eagle" (Chapter One) we read about the eagle's "hands" and accept this, though, in actuality, the eagle doesn't have hands but talons. By writing "hands," however, the poet is able to convey to us the bird's extraordinarily strong, firm grasp and to suggest to the reader that his subject is human, or is as important as a human. Had Tennyson written *claws,* we might have found ourselves thinking in a more mundane context—chicken feet and so on. Poems, like our daily lives, are filled with metaphors (a thing is said to be something it really is not—but really *is* if you think about it) and similes (a thing is said to be *like* something it really is not—but really *is* if you think about it). In poetry, as in life, these comparisons can be fresh. Or they can be overused—big as a house, long as the day, eats like a bird, he's a monster, he's an animal, and so on. The similes and metaphors that we use daily may be trite, but they reflect nonetheless our very human desire to see elements in our lives comparatively. In the comparisons offered by figurative language (metaphor, simile, and others) the writer sets something from one class of things (or people or ideas) against something from another class of things. Such comparisons are the opposites of those comparisons we spoke of earlier in which two or more things of the *same* class are compared—two trips, two diseases, two people, two newspapers. Hence, with figurative language a person is compared to an animal—a horse, let's say, because of the quality shared with horses—largeness, endurance, strength, appetite, range of emotions. Or a person is compared to something superhuman in order to emphasize some extraordinary features—she sings like an angel, he's built like a god, and so on. There is pleasure in breaking down barriers between classifications in order to see our world more vividly: combs have teeth, shoes have tongues, corn grows in ears, trees have arms. The metaphors and similes we use again and again in our daily lives might show wear from overuse, but they reflect our desire to see comparisons, to make connections, to play with seeing and saying.

Reading good poetry gives us the chance to enjoy unique comparisons—the poet's similes and metaphors. Langston Hughes's "Dream Deferred," a poem you will read in Chapter Seven, is a prime example of the use of figurative device to shock us into awareness about both language and the human condition. Who would ever think, for example, of a deferred dream as being like an infected wound? And yet by making this comparison and others equally startling in their originality, Hughes makes us see its validity and makes us see as well the ability of language to transport us to new areas of feeling and thought.

The comparisons presented in this chapter are both sensible—comparing within classes—and fanciful—comparing things from different classes. Each in its way will help you to see subjects freshly with the understanding that comes from comparative thinking.

WRITING COMPARISON

In writing comparisons, more perhaps than in any other writing, you must plan with care. The comparison paper presents you with a double challenge: to discuss two things at once. Therefore as you approach your discussion of these two things—two ideas, two people, two places—you must reflect at length upon matters such as purpose, audience, and organization.

PURPOSE AND AUDIENCE

Often as you write in college, the assignment itself will clarify your purpose. Indeed, some instructors use the term *compare* to mean "to state likenesses," and *contrast* to mean "to state differences." For our purpose, however, we are using the term *compare* to mean both or either (similarities and differences) depending on your subject and your thinking.

When the two items in your comparison are very different on the surface— separated by time, nationality, or what-have-you—stressing likenesses would seem more appropriate because the differences are already so apparent. A paper comparing horses and humans would require little attention to the contrasting features of the animals. Everyone knows the two differ dramatically; what readers want to know is what the writer sees as similarities.

But when the two items you wish to compare are on the surface very similar, stressing differences makes for a more enlightening discussion. In comparing manual and electric typewriters, you would spend most of your time detailing the differences between the old and the new technologies. But there are no absolutes. If your employer asked you to compare IBM and Apple computers, you would probably pay careful attention to likenesses as well as differences.

Often, however, subjects are both alike and not alike. Rock groups like the Beatles and the Rolling Stones, for example, share much—the time they began, their popularity, the death of group members, and so on. However, the groups are very different in tone, image, and style. To give your writing a purpose, you must decide which way to go. If you stress differences, it does not mean you will not deal with likenesses at all, only that you won't dwell on them. Perhaps an introductory paragraph can state the obvious similarities and the rest of the paper can explore distinctions. Or, if you find similarities most interesting, then you may wish to consider obvious differences first in a paragraph or two and then move on to your main concern and purpose: that the two groups, for example, had more in common than they knew they had; that they each in their own way, however unwittingly, fell prey to the violence of the times.

An effective, persuasive comparison paper must have a purpose—to show likenesses or differences *primarily*. Without this purpose, you risk providing a mere catalogue of features and qualities to no good end. And you want to consider the value of expressing the purpose of your comparison paper in an original statement of thesis. For example, the comparison paper built on thesis statements, such as "There are many similarities between X and Y but also many differences," may be a clear enough paper but one bound to bore the reader. The paper that rests on a daring thesis like Sontag's, for example—that our *similar* responses to two very *different* diseases reflect a continuing negative impulse in our psyche and culture—grabs the reader's attention and holds it. The purpose of comparison, then, is to stress similarities *or* differences *in order to make a point.* It's the additional point that distinguishes the humdrum sorting of qualities from the engaging essay.

As for audience—again, as in other kinds of essays, the reader makes a big difference for the writer. How much does the reader know about the subject? How much background must you give? What are the readers' social, political, or aesthetic inclinations? What are their cultural backgrounds? How old are they? For example, your analysis of the Beatles and the Rolling Stones for an American or a British audience would be very different from your analysis of them for an Asian audience. Your analysis will differ, too, depending on whether the reader was listening to pop music when these groups were in their heydey or whether the reader was "tuned in to" other music at the time or was possibly not yet alive!

PROCESS

First determine what two subjects you wish to compare in your paper. As you consider your subjects, make sure that you have a sound basis for comparison. Ask yourself, are they of the same class of things—two music groups, two plays, two heroes, two books, two treaties? If you find that the subjects you're thinking of comparing are *not* of the same class, then ask yourself if the "stretch" pays off. Does the fanciful comparison allow you to present something in a new light, or is it simply the result of a quick or an idiosyncratic idea?

Once you have two items for your comparison and have assured yourself that you have a sound basis for comparison, you are ready to identify the features to consider in the comparison. Some writers find a grid a useful tool for this stage of prewriting. Use a grid like the accompanying one or some other note-taking system that allows you to generate the points in your comparison and the details and examples that develop or illustrate these points.

Topics for Comparison

	A._____	B._____
Points		
of		
Comparison		

Next, look over the notes on your grid to see what you can say about your two topics. Where you have the most detail should give you a clue about where you have the most to say.

Formulate a thesis sentence that joins the two subjects in an interesting formulation: "Despite obvious differences . . . X and Y's similarities show them both to be expressions of popular urges," or some such sentence.

With your thesis and your points of comparison developed, you are ready to organize your essay. Organization is critical for any essay, but in the comparison essay it is doubly important. Without careful planning, your essay can end up being an analysis of one of your subjects on a few points and then an analysis of the other on some other points—two separate analyses with no comparisons drawn. Or your essay, without proper planning, can easily become a lopsided affair, with ample discussion of one subject and a race through the next.

The effective comparison paper is balanced and consistent. If you discuss the history of one subject, you should discuss the history of the other; if you discuss the appearance of one subject, you should discuss the appearance of the other.

As you plan, you must decide on an appropriate scheme. Do you wish to discuss one subject covering all the points of comparison and then go on to the next subject covering the same points? Then your paper might look like this:

A.

> 1.
>
> 2.
>
> 3.

B.

> 1.
>
> 2.
>
> 3.

Or do you wish to allow the points of comparison to structure your discussion? Then your paper might look like this:

> 1. History   A.
>
>   B.
>
> 2. Appearance   A.
>
>   B.
>
> 3. Sound   A.
>
>   B.

The first way allows for a fuller presentation of each of the topics on its own terms and for a more inductive approach. The second permits a more dynamic discussion with the relationship being stated throughout. If you choose the first arrangement, you will need to plan to make some more explicit statements of comparison at the end of the essay once you have laid out the different points for each of the two subjects.

Finally, as you write your comparison paper, you will want to make use of the transitional phrases that ease movement from one topic to the other— *similarly, likewise, in contrast, on the other hand, however,* and so on. These phrases will help you and the reader to navigate the complicated process of comparative analysis.

SUMMING UP: COMPARISON

Reading Comparison

- Comparison and contrast means to show similarities and differences between objects and ideas.

- Be attentive to the terms of the writer's comparison—that is, be clear about what is being compared to what.

- Identify the writer's thesis: What is her reason for making the comparison? What is her opinion about or attitude toward the topic she has chosen to explore through comparison and contrast strategies?

- Look for the writer's use of figurative expressions, which often help him compare things in an imaginative fashion. Simile, metaphor, personification—these and other figurative devices, by expressing ideas in comparative terms, help readers see issues freshly and vividly.

Writing Comparison

- Decide on the two objects or ideas you wish to present together, and weigh your audience and your purpose carefully, as well as your method of organization.

- Generally, comparison papers deal with both similarities and differences, yet with one taking the primary spotlight.

- If the two items you want to compare in your paper are very different on the surface, stress their likenesses; the differences will already be quite apparent. If you wish to compare items that are very similar on the surface, stress the differences.

- Develop a thesis statement that tells readers the purpose of your paper to stress similarities or differences. Join the two topics in an interesting formulation as you state your topic clearly; and as you indicate the primary focus of your topic, make sure the reader knows that you are using the comparison strategy *to make a point.*

- Determine your intended audience and, considering what your reader knows about the topic, provide appropriate detail.

- In your prewriting on the topic, generate a list of the points you wish to make in the comparison and of the details and examples that develop or illustrate these points.

- Balance your presentation by considering points in relation to *both* topics, not just one.

- Decide on an appropriate scheme for organization:

  Treat each subject separately, presenting all the points of comparison for one of the items of your topic, then covering the same points for the second item

  OR

  Treat each point of the comparison, presenting the two items in relation to each point

- Use transitional phrases carefully to help you move from one aspect of the topic to another. Words and phrases like *similarly, in contrast,* and *on the other hand* help you connect ideas smoothly.

Shakespeare's Gifted Sister

Virginia Woolf

Virginia Woolf (1882–1941) is today considered one of the most important writers in the development of modernist fiction. She lived with her husband, editor and publisher Leonard Woolf, her sister Vanessa (a painter), and Vanessa's husband Clive Bell (an art critic) as a part of the famous Bloomsbury group in England. This group was to include people such as novelist E. M. Forster, poet T. S. Eliot, art historian Roger Fry, and economist John Maynard Keynes, all of whom became renowned, in one way or another, for their progressive thought and lifestyles. Virginia and Leonard founded the Hogarth Press, which published her work, Eliot's, and Freud's (the first editions in English), among other great writers. Her widely admired fiction includes *Mrs. Dalloway* (1925), *To the Lighthouse* (1927), *Orlando* (1928), and *The Waves* (1931). She also left us a rich repository of essays. After years of battling mental illness, she committed suicide in 1941.

This selection, from her 1929 book *A Room of One's Own*, sets an imaginative, fictional context allowing Woolf to explore the inequities between men and women. Notice how she manages to balance description and exemplification of the real with the abstract as she looks at Elizabethan literature.

*F*or it is a perennial puzzle why no woman wrote a word of that 1 extraordinary literature when every other man, it seemed, was capable of song or sonnet. What were the conditions in which women lived, I asked myself; for fiction, imaginative work that is, is not dropped like a pebble upon the ground, as science may be; fiction is like a spider's web, attached ever so lightly perhaps, but still attached to life at all four corners. Often the attachment is scarcely perceptible; Shakespeare's plays, for instance, seem to hang there complete by themselves. But when the web is pulled askew, hooked up at the edge, torn in the middle, one remembers that these webs are not spun in mid-air by incorporeal creatures, but are the work of suffering human beings, and are attached to grossly material things, like health and money and the houses we live in. . . .

But what I find deplorable . . . is that nothing is known about women 2 before the eighteenth century. I have no model in my mind to turn about this way and that. Here am I asking why women did not write poetry in the Elizabethan age, and I am not sure how they were educated; whether they were taught to write; whether they had sitting-rooms to themselves; how many women had children before they were twenty-one; what, in short, they did from eight in the morning till eight at night. They had no money, evidently; according to Professor Trevelyan they were married whether they liked it or not before they were out of the nursery, at fifteen or sixteen very likely. It would have been extremely odd, even upon this showing, had one of them suddenly written the plays of Shakespeare. I concluded, and I thought of that old gentleman, who is dead now, but was a bishop, I think, who declared that it was impossible for any woman, past, present, or to come, to have the genius of Shakespeare. He wrote to the papers about it. He also told a lady who applied to him for information that cats do not as a matter of fact go to heaven, though they have, he added, souls of a sort. How much thinking those old gentlemen used to save one! How the borders of ignorance shrank back at their approach! Cats do not go to heaven. Women cannot write the plays of Shakespeare.

Be that as it may, I could not help thinking, as I looked at the works of ₃ Shakespeare on the shelf, that the bishop was right at least in this; it would have been impossible, completely and entirely, for any woman to have written the plays of Shakespeare in the age of Shakespeare. Let me imagine, since facts are so hard to come by, what would have happened had Shakespeare had a wonderfully gifted sister, called Judith, let us say. Shakespeare himself went, very probably—his mother was an heiress—to the grammar school, where he may have learnt Latin—Ovid, Virgil and Horace—and the elements of grammar and logic. He was, it is well known, a wild boy who poached rabbits, perhaps shot a deer, and had, rather sooner than he should have done, to marry a woman in the neighbourhood, who bore him a child rather quicker than was right. That escapade sent him to seek his fortune in London. He had, it seemed, a taste for the theatre; he began by holding horses at the stage door. Very soon he got work in the theatre, became a successful actor, and lived at the hub of the universe, meeting everybody, knowing everybody, practising his art on the boards, exercising his wits in the streets, and even getting access to the palace of the queen. Meanwhile his extraordinarily gifted sister, let us suppose, remained at home. She was as adventurous, as imaginative, as agog to see the world as he was. But she was not sent to school. She had no chance of learning grammar and logic, let alone of reading Horace and Virgil. She picked up a book now and then, one of her brother's perhaps, and read a few pages. But then her parents came in and told her to mend the stockings or mind the stew and not moon about with books and papers. They would have spoken sharply but kindly, for they were substantial people who knew the conditions of life for a woman and loved their daughter—indeed, more likely than not she was the apple of her father's eye. Perhaps she scribbled some pages up in an apple loft on the sly, but was careful to hide them or set fire to them. Soon, however, before she was out of her teens, she was to be betrothed to the son of a neighbouring wool-stapler. She cried out that marriage was hateful to her, and for that she was severely beaten by her father. Then he ceased to scold her. He begged her instead not to hurt him, not to shame him in this matter of her marriage. He would give her a chain of beads or a fine petticoat, he said; and there were tears in his eyes. How could she disobey him? How could she break his heart? The force of her own gift alone drove her to it. She made up a small parcel of her belongings, let herself down by a rope one summer's night and took the road to London. She was not seventeen. The birds that sang in the hedge were not more musical than she was. She had the quickest fancy, a gift like her brother's, for the tune of words. Like him, she had a taste for the theatre. She stood at the stage door; she wanted to act, she said. Men laughed in her face. The manager—a fat, loose-lipped man—guffawed. He bellowed something about poodles dancing and women acting—no woman, he said, could possibly be an actress. He hinted—you can imagine what. She could get no training in her craft. Could she even seek her dinner in a tavern or roam the streets at midnight? Yet her genius was for fiction and lusted to feed abundantly upon the lives of men and women and the study of their ways. At last—for she was very young, oddly like Shakespeare the poet in her face, with the same grey eyes and rounded brows—at last Nick Greene the actor-manager took pity on her; she found herself with child by that gentleman and so—who shall measure the heat and violence of the poet's heart when caught and tangled in a woman's body?—killed herself one winter's night and lies buried at some crossroads where the omnibuses now stop outside the Elephant and Castle.

That, more or less, is how the story would run, I think, if a woman in Shakespeare's day had had Shakespeare's genius. But for my part, I agree with the deceased bishop, if such he was—it is unthinkable that any woman in Shakespeare's day should have had Shakespeare's genius. For genius like Shakespeare's is not born among labouring, uneducated, servile people. It was not born in England among the Saxons and the Britons. It is not born today among the working classes. How, then, could it have been born among women whose work began, according to Professor Trevelyan, almost before they were out of the nursery, who were forced to it by their parents and held to it by all the power of law and custom? Yet genius of a sort must have existed among women as it must have existed among the working classes.

Meaning and Idea

1. What is Woolf's specific thesis about Shakespeare and his imaginary sister? How is that specific thesis indicative of her overall thesis comparing the lives and creative endeavors of men and women? Summarize briefly what that overall thesis says.

2. What is Woolf's opinion of the contrast between scientific and creative works?

3. How do Woolf's references to the "deceased bishop" exemplify her views concerning how men generally think about women? What other specific examples of such thinking does she offer?

4. What is the Elephant and Castle? What does the last line of the third paragraph indicate about Shakespeare's sister's relative importance?

5. Why does Woolf agree that it would have been "unthinkable" for a woman in Elizabethan times to have achieved Shakespeare's genius? How is she using the term *genius*? Is this a conclusion with which she is happy?

Language, Form, Structure

1. Which developmental pattern for a comparison essay does Woolf follow here? How does she balance the two sides of her comparison? Prepare a

point-by-point outline of Woolf's comparison between William and "Judith" Shakespeare. What does she say about their comparative schooling? Writing? Marriages? Results of creative impulses?

2. What generally is Woolf's tone in this essay—sorrowful, angry, comic, sarcastic, ironic? Find three examples from the essay which contribute to that tone.

3. Interpret the following lines as a generalization of Woolf's attitude about the relationship between men and women throughout the ages: "at last Nick Greene the actor-manager took pity on her; she found herself with child by that gentleman and so—"

4. Identify the paragraphs which constitute the introduction, body, and conclusion to this essay.

5. Look up definitions for the following words: perennial; perceptible; askew; incorporeal; poached; escapade; hub; guffawed; betrothed; lusted; servile. Now choose any five and use them in original sentences.

Ideas for Writing

1. Write an essay in which you compare the life and achievements of a famous man with the life and achievements of his imaginary sister. Use the block method of organization, taking care to balance both sections.

2. Write a short essay in which you compare how you and your best friend approach a similar task.

3. Virginia Woolf wrote this piece in the 1920s, whereas Shakespeare wrote in the late 1500s to mid-1600s. How does Woolf make her ideas apply to twentieth-century life? Do you feel that her analysis is relevant to the relations between women and men today? Explain.

Two Kinds

Amy Tan

Born in Oakland, California, in 1952 soon after her parents arrived in the United States, Amy Tan has a sensibility that is resonant with that of many first-generation, immigrant Americans, neither Chinese nor American but identifying strongly with both. Tan's first novel, *The Joy Luck Club* (1989), wrestled with these very themes.

The novel, composed of sixteen interconnected stories narrated by four Chinese-born mothers and their four American-born daughters, is deeply concerned with issues of love, loss, identity, and growth. Jing-mei (June) Woo is one of the daughters in the book. In the following selection, she and her mother embark upon a classic family struggle.

*M*y mother believed you could be anything you wanted to be in America. You could open a restaurant. You could work for the government and get good retirement. You could buy a house with almost no money down. You could become rich. You could become instantly famous.

"Of course you can be prodigy, too," my mother told me when I was nine. "You can be best anything. What does Auntie Lindo know? Her daughter, she is only best tricky."

America was where all my mother's hopes lay. She had come here in 1949 after losing everything in China: her mother and father, her family home, her first husband, and two daughters, twin baby girls. But she never looked back with regret. There were so many ways for things to get better.

We didn't immediately pick the right kind of prodigy. At first my mother thought I could be a Chinese Shirley Temple. We'd watch Shirley's old movies on TV as though they were training films. My mother would poke my arm and say, "*Ni Kan*"—You watch. And I would see Shirley tapping her feet, or singing a sailor song, or pursing her lips into a very round O while saying, "Oh my goodness."

"*Ni kan*," said my mother as Shirley's eyes flooded with tears. "You already know how. Don't need talent for crying!"

Soon after my mother got this idea about Shirley Temple, she took me to a beauty training school in the Mission district and put me in the hands of a student who could barely hold the scissors without shaking. Instead of getting big fat curls, I emerged with an uneven mass of crinkly black fuzz. My mother dragged me off to the bathroom and tried to wet down my hair.

"You look like Negro Chinese," she lamented, as if I had done this on purpose.

The instructor of the beauty training school had to lop off these soggy clumps to make my hair even again. "Peter Pan is very popular these days," the instructor assured my mother. I now had hair the length of a boy's, with straight-across bangs that hung at a slant two inches above my eyebrows. I liked the hair-cut and it made me actually look forward to my future fame.

In fact, in the beginning, I was just as excited as my mother, maybe even more 9
so. I pictured this prodigy part of me as many different images, trying each one on
for size. I was a dainty ballerina girl standing by the curtains, waiting to hear the
right music that would send me floating on my tiptoes. I was like the Christ child
lifted out of the straw manger, crying with holy indignity. I was Cinderella stepping
from her pumpkin carriage with sparkly cartoon music filling the air.

In all of my imagingings, I was filled with a sense that I would soon 10
become *perfect.* My mother and father would adore me. I would be beyond
reproach. I would never feel the need to sulk for anything.

But sometimes the prodigy in me became impatient. "If you don't hurry up 11
and get me out of here, I'm disappearing for good," it warned. "And then you'll
always be nothing."

Every night after dinner, my mother and I would sit at the Formica kitchen 12
table. She would present new tests, taking her examples from stories of amazing
children she had read in *Ripley's Believe It or Not,* or *Good Housekeeping,*
Reader's Digest, and a dozen other magazines she kept in a pile in our bathroom.
My mother got these magazines from people whose houses she cleaned. And
since she cleaned many houses each week, we had a great assortment. She would
look through them all, searching for stories about remarkable children.

The first night she brought out a story about a three-year-old boy who knew 13
the capitals of all the states and even most of the European countries. A teacher
was quoted as saying the little boy could also pronounce the names of the foreign
cities correctly.

"What's the capital of Finland?" my mother asked me, looking at the mag- 14
azine story.

All I knew was the capital of California, because Sacramento was the name 15
of the street we lived on in Chinatown. "Nairobi!" I guessed, saying the most foreign word I could think of. She checked to see if that was possibly one way to
pronounce "Helsinki" before showing me the answer.

The tests got harder—multiplying numbers in my head, finding the queen 16
of hearts in a deck of cards, trying to stand on my head without using my hands,
predicting the daily temperatures in Los Angeles, New York, and London.

One night I had to look at a page from the Bible for three minutes and then 17
report everything I could remember. "Now Jehoshaphat had riches and honor in
abundance and . . . that's all I remember, Ma," I said.

And after seeing my mother's disappointed face once again, something 18
inside of me began to die. I hated the tests, the raised hopes and failed expectations. Before going to bed that night, I looked in the mirror above the bathroom
sink and when I saw only my face staring back—and that it would always be this
ordinary face—I began to cry. Such a sad, ugly girl! I made high-pitched noises
like a crazed animal, trying to scratch out the face in the mirror.

And then I saw what seemed to be the prodigy side of me—because I had 19
never seen that face before. I looked at my reflection blinking so I could see more
clearly. The girl staring back at me was angry, powerful. This girl and I were the

same. I had new thoughts, willful thoughts, or rather thoughts filled with lots of won'ts. I won't let her change me, I promised myself. I won't be what I'm not.

So now on nights when my mother presented her tests, I performed list-²⁰ lessly, my head propped on one arm. I pretended to be bored. And I was. I got so bored I started counting the bellows of the foghorns out on the bay while my mother drilled me in other areas. The sound was comforting and reminded me of the cow jumping over the moon. And the next day, I played a game with myself, seeing if my mother would give up on me before eight bellows. After a while I usually counted only one, maybe two bellows at most. At last she was beginning to give up hope.

Two or three months had gone by without any mention of my being a prodigy ²¹ again. And then one day my mother was watching "The Ed Sullivan Show" on TV. The TV was old and the sound kept shorting out. Every time my mother got halfway up from the sofa to adjust the set, the sound would go back on and Ed would be talking. As soon as she sat down, Ed would go silent again. She got up, the TV broke into loud piano music. She sat down. Silence. Up and down, back and forth, quiet and loud. It was like a stiff embraceless dance between her and the TV set. Finally she stood by the set with her hand on the sound dial.

She seemed entranced by the music, a little frenzied piano piece with this ²² mesmerizing quality, sort of quick passages and then teasing lilting ones before it returned to the quick playful parts.

"*Ni kan*," my mother said, calling me over with hurried hand gestures. ²³ "Look here."

I could see why my mother was fascinated by the music. It was being ²⁴ pounded out by a little Chinese girl, about nine years old, with a Peter Pan haircut. The girl had the sauciness of a Shirley Temple. She was proudly modest like a proper Chinese child. And she also did this fancy sweep of a curtsy, so that the fluffy skirt of her white dress cascaded slowly to the floor like the petals of a large carnation.

In spite of these warning signs, I wasn't worried. Our family had no piano ²⁵ and we couldn't afford to buy one, let alone reams of sheet music and piano lessons. So I could be generous in my comments when my mother bad-mouthed the little girl on TV.

"Play note right, but doesn't sound good! No singing sound," complained ²⁶ my mother.

"What are you picking on her for?" I said carelessly. "She's pretty good. ²⁷ Maybe she's not the best, but she's trying hard." I knew almost immediately I would be sorry I said that.

"Just like you," she said. "Not the best. Because you not trying." She gave ²⁸ a little huff as she let go of the sound dial and sat down on the sofa.

The little Chinese girl sat down also to play an encore of "Anitra's Dance" ²⁹ by Grieg. I remember the song, because later on I had to learn how to play it.

Three days after watching "The Ed Sullivan Show," my mother told me ³⁰ what my schedule would be for piano lessons and piano practice. She had talked to Mr. Chong, who lived on the first floor of our apartment building. Mr. Chong was a retired piano teacher and my mother had traded housecleaning services for weekly lessons and a piano for me to practice on every day, two hours a day, from four until six.

When my mother told me this, I felt as though I had been sent to hell. I 31 whined and then kicked my foot a little when I couldn't stand it anymore.

"Why don't you like me the way I am? I'm *not* a genius! I can't play the 32 piano. And even if I could, I wouldn't go on TV if you paid me a million dollars!" I cried.

My mother slapped me. "Who ask you be genius?" she shouted. "Only ask 33 you be your best. For your sake. You think I want you be genius? Hnnh! What for! Who ask you!"

"So ungrateful," I heard her mutter in Chinese. "If she had as much talent 34 as she has temper, she would be famous now."

Mr. Chong, whom I secretly nicknamed Old Chong, was very strange, 35 always tapping his fingers to the silent music of an invisible orchestra. He looked ancient in my eyes. He had lost most of the hair on top of his head and he wore thick glasses and had eyes that always looked tired and sleepy. But he must have been younger than I thought, since he lived with his mother and was not yet married.

I met Old Lady Chong once and that was enough. She had this peculiar 36 smell like a baby that had done something in its pants. And her fingers felt like a dead person's, like an old peach I once found in the back of the refrigerator; the skin just slid off the meat when I picked it up.

I soon found out why Old Chong had retired from teaching piano. He was 37 deaf. "Like Beethoven!" he shouted to me. "We're both listening only in our head!" And he would start to conduct his frantic silent sonatas.

Our lessons went like this. He would open the book and point to different 38 things, explaining their purpose: "Key! Treble! Bass! No sharps or flats! So this is C major! Listen now and play after me!"

And then he would play the C scale a few times, a simple chord, and then, 39 as if inspired by an old, unreachable itch, he gradually added more notes and running trills and a pounding bass until the music was really something quite grand.

I would play after him, the simple scale, the simple chord and then I just 40 played some nonsense that sounded like a cat running up and down on top of garbage cans. Old Chong smiled and applauded and then said, "Very good! But now you must learn to keep time!"

So that's how I discovered that Old Chong's eyes were too slow to keep up 41 with the wrong notes I was playing. He went through the motions in half-time. To help me keep rhythm, he stood behind me, pushing down on my right shoulder for every beat. He balanced pennies on top of my wrists so I would keep them still as I slowly played scales and arpeggios. He had me curve my hand around an apple and keep that shape when playing chords. He marched stiffly to show me how to make each finger dance up and down, staccato like an obedient little solider.

He taught me all these things, and that was how I also learned I could be ₄₂ lazy and get away with mistakes, lots of mistakes. If I hit the wrong notes because I hadn't practiced enough, I never corrected myself. I just kept playing in rhythm. And Old Chong kept conducting his own private reverie.

So maybe I never really gave myself a fair chance. I did pick up the basics ₄₃ pretty quickly, and I might have become a good pianist at that young age. But I was so determined not to try, not to be anybody different that I learned to play only the most ear-splitting preludes, the most discordant hymns.

Over the next year, I practiced like this, dutifully in my own way. And then ₄₄ one day I heard my mother and her friend Lindo Jong both talking in a loud bragging tone of voice so others could hear. It was after church, and I was leaning against the brick wall wearing a dress with stiff white petticoats. Auntie Lindo's daughter, Waverly, who was about my age, was standing farther down the wall about five feet away. We had grown up together and shared all the closeness of two sisters squabbling over crayons and dolls. In other words, for the most part, we hated each other. I thought she was snotty. Waverly Jong had gained a certain amount of fame as "Chinatown's Littlest Chinese Chess Champion."

"She bring home too many trophy," lamented Auntie Lindo that Sunday. ₄₅ "All day she play chess. All day I have no time do nothing but dust off her winnings." She threw a scolding look at Waverly, who pretended not to see her.

"You lucky you don't have this problem," said Auntie Lindo with a sigh to ₄₆ my mother.

And my mother squared her shoulders and bragged: "Our problem worser ₄₇ than yours. If we ask Jing-mei wash dish, she hear nothing but music. It's like you can't stop this natural talent."

And right then, I was determined to put a stop to her foolish pride. ₄₈

A few weeks later, Old Chong and my mother conspired to have me play in ₄₉ a talent show which would be held in the church hall. By then, my parents had saved up enough to buy me a secondhand piano, a black Wurlitzer spinet with a scarred bench. It was the showpiece of our living room.

For the talent show, I was to play a piece called "Pleading Child" from the ₅₀ Schumann's *Scenes from Childhood*. It was a simple, moody piece that sounded more difficult than it was. I was supposed to memorize the whole thing, playing the repeat parts twice to make the piece sound longer. But I dawdled over it, playing a few bars and then cheating, looking up to see what notes followed, I never really listened to what I was playing. I daydreamed about being somewhere else, about being someone else.

The part I liked to practice best was the fancy curtsy: right foot out, touch ₅₁ the rose on the carpet with a pointed foot, sweep to the side, left leg bends, look up and smile.

My parents invited all the couples from the Joy Luck Club to witness my ₅₂ debut. Auntie Lindo and Uncle Tin were there. Waverly and her two older brothers had also come. The first two rows were filled with children both younger and older that I was. The littlest ones got to go first. They recited simple nursery rhythms, squawked out tunes on miniature violins, twirled Hula Hoops, pranced in pink ballet tutus, and when they bowed or curtsied, the audience would sigh in unison, "Awww," and then clap enthusiastically.

When my turn came, I was very confident. I remember my childish excite- 53 ment. It was as if I know, without a doubt, that the prodigy side of me really did exist. I had no fear whatsoever, no nervousness. I remember thinking to myself, This is it! This is it! I looked out over the audience, at my mother's blank face, my father's yawn, Auntie Lindo's stiff-lipped smile, Waverly's sulky expression. I had on a white dres layered with sheets of lace, and a pink bow in my Peter Pan haircut. As I sat down I envisioned people jumping to their feet and Ed Sullivan rushing up to introduce me to everyone on TV.

And I started to play. It was so beautiful. I was so caught up in how lovely 54 I looked that at first I didn't worry how I would sound: So it was a surprise to me when I hit the first wrong note and I realized something didn't sound quite right. And then I hit another and another followed that. A chill started at the top of my head and began to trickle down. Yet I couldn't stop playing, as though my hands were bewitched. I kept thinking my fingers would adjust themselves back, like a train switching to the right track. I played this strange jumble through two repeats, the sour notes staying with me all the way to the end.

When I stood up, I discovered my legs were shaking. Maybe I had just been 55 nervous and the audience, like Old Chong, had seen me go through the right motions and had not heard anything wrong at all. I swept my right foot out, went down on my knee, looked up and smiled. The room was quiet, except for Old Chong, who was beaming and shouting, "Bravo! Bravo! Well done!" But then I saw my mother's face, her stricken face. The audience clapped weakly, and as I walked back to my chair, with my whole face quivering as I tried not to cry, I heard a little boy whisper loudly to his mother, "That was awful," and the mother whispered back, "Well, she certainly tried."

And now I realized how many people were in the audience, the whole world 56 it seemed. I was aware of eyes burning into my back. I felt the shame of my mother and father as they sat stiffly throughout the rest of the show.

We could have escaped during intermission. Pride and some strange sense of 57 honor must have anchored my parents to their chairs. And so we watched it all: the eighteen-year-old boy with a fake mustache who did a magic show and juggled flaming hoops while riding a unicycle. The breasted girl with white makeup who sang from *Madama Butterfly* and got honorable mention. And the eleven-year-old boy who won first prize playing a tricky violin song that sounded like a busy bee.

After the show, the Hsus, the Jongs, and the St. Clairs from the Joy Luck 58 Club came up to my mother and father.

"Lots of talented kids," Auntie Lindo said vaguely, smiling broadly.   59

"That was somethin' else," said my father, and I wondered if he was refer- 60 ring to me in a humorous way, or whether he even remembered what I had done.

Waverly looked at me and shrugged her shoulders. "You aren't a genius like 61 me," she said matter-of-factly. And if I hadn't felt so bad, I would have pulled her braids and punched her stomach.

But my mother's expression was what devastated me: a quiet, blank look 62 that said she had lost everything. I felt the same way, and it seemed as if everybody were now coming up, like gawkers at the scene of an accident, to see what parts were actually missing. When we got on the bus to go home, my father was humming the busy-bee tune and my mother was silent. I kept thinking she wanted to wait until we got home before shouting at me. But when my father unlocked the door to our apartment, my mother walked in then went to the back, into the bedroom. No accusations. No blame. And in a way, I felt disappointed. I had been waiting for her to start shouting, so I could shout back and cry and blame her for all my misery.

I assumed my talent-show fiasco meant I never had to play the piano again. 63 But two days later, after school, my mother came out of the kitchen and saw me watching TV.

"Four clock," she reminded me as if it were any other day. I was stunned, 64 as though she were asking me to go through the talent-show torture again. I wedged myself more tightly in front of the TV.

"Turn off TV," she called from the kitchen five minutes later. 65

I didn't budge. And then I decided. I didn't have to do what my mother said 66 anymore. I wasn't her slave. This wasn't China. I had listened to her before and look what happened. She was the stupid one.

She came out from the kitchen and stood in the arched entryway of the liv- 67 ing room. "Four clock," she said once again, louder.

"I'm not going to play anymore," I said nonchalantly. "Why should I? I'm 68 not a genius."

She walked over and stood in front of the TV. I saw her chest was heaving 69 up and down in an angry way.

"No!" I said, and I now felt stronger, as if my true self had finally emerged. 70 So this was what had been inside me all along.

"No! I won't!" I screamed. 71

She yanked me by the arm, pulled me off the floor, snapped off the TV. She 72 was frighteningly strong, half pulling, half carrying me toward the piano as I kicked the throw rugs under my feet. She lifted me up and onto the hard bench. I was sobbing by now, looking at her bitterly. Her chest was heaving even more and her mouth was open, smiling crazily as if she were pleased I was crying.

"You want me to be someone that I'm not!" I sobbed. "I'll never be the kind 73 of daughter you want me to be!"

"Only two kinds of daughters," she shouted in Chinese. "Those who are 74 obedient and those who follow their own mind! Only one kind of daughter can live in this house. Obedient daughter!"

"Then I wish I wasn't your daughter. I wish you weren't my mother," I 75 shouted. As I said these things I got scared. I felt like worms and toads and slimy things were crawling out of my chest, but it also felt good, as if this awful side of me had surfaced, at last.

"Too late change this," said my mother shrilly.   76

And I could sense her anger rising to its breaking point. I wanted to see it   77
spill over. And that's when I remembered the babies she had lost in China, the
ones we never talked about. "Then I wish I'd never been born!" I shouted. "I wish
I were dead! Like them."

It was as if I had said the magic words. Alakazam!—and her face went   78
blank, her mouth closed, her arms went slack, and she backed out of the room,
stunned, as if she were blowing away like a small brown leaf, thin, brittle, lifeless.

It was not the only disappointment my mother felt in me. In the years that   79
followed, I failed her so many times, each time asserting my own will, my right
to fall short of expectations. I didn't get straight A's. I didn't become class president. I didn't get into Stanford. I dropped out of college.

For unlike my mother, I did not believe I could be anything I wanted to be.   80
I could only be me.

Meaning and Idea

1. What is this selection about? What is the basic comparison that Tan draws?
    What other comparisons are in the piece?

2. What is a prodigy? Why does the narrator's mother want her to be a
    prodigy? How does the Chinese girl on "The Ed Sullivan Show" contribute
    to the levels of comparison here?

3. The mother explains what she sees as the two kinds of daughters. What is
    the child's response to her mother? Who is right, do you think?

4. Explain the meaning of the sentences, "For unlike my mother, I did not
    believe I could be anything I wanted to be. I could only be me." How are
    these two lines together both hopeful and hopeless? Do you agree with the
    sentiment expressed here? Or do you agree with the mother? Why?

Language, Form, Structure

1. How does the title of the selection help establish the rhetorical pattern of
    the piece? What do you think "two kinds" refers to—the daughter and
    some imagined perfect child, the daughter and the musical prodigy on "The
    Ed Sullivan Show," the daughter and the mother, all of these? Defend your
    answers.

2. Identify the various transition points in the selection where the time seems
    to shift. How does Tan achieve the necessary coherence? Where does she
    use narrative elements in this piece?

3. Tan uses a number of figures of speech here. Identify several that you find
    vivid. How do they help you visualize the scene? What other imagery does
    Tan use?

4. Define the following words and use each in a sentence: prodigy; indignity; listlessly; bellows; embraceless; sauciness; cascaded; sonatas; arpeggios; reverie; petticoats; squabbling; spinet; moody; dawdled; stricken.

Ideas for Writing

1. Write an essay in which you discuss having to learn or do one or many things because a parent or other relative insisted that you should. Compare and contrast what you wanted to what your relative wanted. In the ensuing conflicts, show who, if anyone, was victor.

2. Recount an event from your childhood or youth which you held in one perspective at the time but hold in a different perspective now. Write a comparison of the two attitudes and explain the changes.

3. Reread the Tan selection, and look for and list as many elements of similarity and difference between the mother and daughter as possible. Now think about all the different pairs of people who are compared throughout the essay. How many "twos" are there? Write an essay in which you discuss the many possible meanings of Tan's title.

The Secret Sharer

Joseph Conrad

Joseph Conrad (1857–1924), who was born in Poland as Jozef Teodor Konrad Nalecz Korzeniowski, did not speak a word of English until he was 21. At the age of 14, he went to sea for the first time as a gunrunner, and by 1884 he was a master mariner in the British Merchant Service (having become a naturalized British citizen in 1886). In all, he spent 20 years at sea all over the globe, surviving shipwrecks and observing the rich details of life which we find in his fiction. Conrad is considered one of the most important crossover writers from the Victorian to the modern era, and his importance in shaping both the technical and the thematic course of modern literature can never be underestimated. Quite popular in his own lifetime, he left a legacy of such works as *The Nigger of the "Narcissus"* (1897), *Heart of Darkness* (1899), *Lord Jim* (1900), *Nostromo* (1904), *The Secret Agent* (1907), *Victory* (1915), and a number of short story collections.

Some critics claim that Conrad's subtle and haunting "The Secret Sharer," published in 1907, is among the most important shapers of the course of modern fiction. The basis of the overriding comparison—a man versus his "other self"—set the stage for the twentieth-century fascination with split personalities (pathological or not), the struggle to find one's "true self," and the need to resolve opposing forces in order to attain freedom. As you read, pay special attention to the intricate, multilevel weaving of the fabric of contrasts and comparisons.

I

*O*n my right hand there were lines of fishing-stakes resembling a mysterious system of half-submerged bamboo fences, incomprehensible in its division of the domain of tropical fishes, and crazy of aspect as if abandoned for ever by some nomad tribe of fishermen now gone to the other end of the ocean; for there was no sign of human habitation as far as the eye could reach. To the left a group of barren islets, suggesting ruins of stone walls, towers, and blockhouses, had its foundations set in a blue sea that itself looked solid, so still and stable did it lie below my feet; even the track of light from the westering sun shone smoothly, without that animated glitter which tells of an imperceptible ripple. And when I turned my head to take a parting glance at the tug which had just left us anchored outside the bar, I saw the straight line of the flat shore joined to the stable sea, edge to edge, with a perfect and unmarked closeness, in one levelled floor half brown, half blue under the enormous dome of the sky. Corresponding in their insignificance to the islets of the sea, two small clumps of trees, one on each side of the only fault in the impeccable joint, marked the mouth of the river Meinam we had just left on the first preparatory stage of our homeward journey; and, far back on the inland level, a larger and loftier mass, the grove surrounding the great Paknam pagoda, was the only thing on which the eye could rest from the vain task of exploring the monotonous sweep of the horizon. Here and there gleams as of a few scattered pieces of silver marked the windings of the great river; and on the nearest of them, just within the bar, the tug steaming right into the land became lost to my sight, hull and funnel and masts, as though the impassive earth had swallowed her up without an effort, without a tremor. My eye followed the light cloud of her smoke, now here, now there, above the plain, according to the devious curves of the stream, but always fainter and farther away, till I lost it at last behind the mitre-shaped hill of the great pagoda. And then I was left alone with my ship, anchored at the head of the Gulf of Siam.

She floated at the starting-point of a long journey, very still in an immense stillness, the shadows of her spars flung far to the eastward by the setting sun. At that moment I was alone on her decks. There was not a sound in her—and around us nothing moved, nothing lived, not a canoe on the water, not a bird in the air, not a cloud in the sky. In this breathless pause at the threshold of a long passage we seemed to be measuring our fitness for a long and arduous enterprise, the appointed task of both our existences to be carried out, far from all human eyes, with only sky and sea for spectators and for judges. 2

There must have been some glare in the air to interfere with one's sight, because it was only just before the sun left us that my roaming eyes made out beyond the highest ridge of the principal islet of the group something which did away with the solemnity of perfect solitude. The tide of darkness flowed on swiftly; and with tropical suddenness a swarm of stars came out above the shadowy earth, while I lingered yet, my hand resting lightly on my ship's rail as if on the shoulder of a trusted friend. But, with all that multitude of celestial bodies staring down at one, the comfort of quiet communion with her was gone for good. And there were also disturbing sounds by this time—voices, footsteps forward; the steward flitted along the maindeck, a busily ministering spirit; a hand-bell tinkled urgently under the poop-deck. . . . 3

I found my two officers waiting for me near the supper table, in the lighted cuddy. We sat down at once, and as I helped the chief mate, I said: 4

"Are you aware that there is a ship anchored inside the islands? I saw her mastheads above the ridge as the sun went down." 5

He raised sharply his simple face, overcharged by a terrible growth of whisker, and emitted his usual ejaculations: "Bless my soul, sir! You don't say so!" 6

My second mate was a round-cheeked, silent young man, grave beyond his years, I thought; but as our eyes happened to meet I detected a slight quiver on his lips. I looked down at once. It was not my part to encourage sneering on board my ship. It must be said, too, that I knew very little of my officers. In consequence of certain events of no particular significance, except to myself, I had been appointed to the command only a fortnight before. Neither did I know much of the hands forward. All these people had been together for eighteen months or so, and my position was that of the only stranger on board. I mention this because it has some bearing on what is to follow. But what I felt most was my being a stranger to the ship; and if all the truth must be told, I was somewhat of a stranger 7 to myself. The youngest man on board (barring the second mate), and untried as yet by a position of the fullest responsibility, I was willing to take the adequacy of the others for granted. They had simply to be equal to their tasks; but I wondered how far I should turn out faithful to that ideal conception of one's own personality every man sets up for himself secretly.

Meantime the chief mate, with an almost visible effect of collaboration on the part of his round eyes and frightful whiskers, was trying to evolve a theory of the anchored ship. His dominant trait was to take all things into earnest consideration. He was of a painstaking turn of mind. As he used to say, he "liked to account to himself" for practically everything that came in his way, down to a miserable scorpion he had found in his cabin a week before. The why and the wherefore of that scorpion—how it got on board and came to select his room rather than the pantry (which was a dark place and more what a scorpion would be partial to), and how on earth it managed to drown itself in the inkwell of his writing-desk—had exercised him infinitely. The ship within the islands was much more easily accounted for; and just as we were about to rise from table he made his pronouncement. She was, he doubted not, a ship from home lately arrived. Probably she drew too much water to cross the bar except at the top of spring tides. Therefore she went into that natural harbour to wait for a few days in preference to remaining in an open roadstead. 8

"That's so," confirmed the second mate, suddenly, in his slightly hoarse voice. "She draws over twenty feet. She's the Liverpool ship *Sephora* with a cargo of coal. Hundred and twenty-three days from Cardiff." 9

We looked at him in surprise. 10

"The tugboat skipper told me when he came on board for your letters, sir," explained the young man. "He expects to take her up the river the day after tomorrow." 11

After thus overwhelming us with the extent of his information he slipped out of the cabin. The mate observed regretfully that he "could not account for that young fellow's whims." What prevented him telling us all about it at once, he wanted to know. 12

I detained him as he was making a move. For the last two days the crew had had plenty of hard work, and the night before they had very little sleep. I felt painfully that I—a stranger—was doing something unusual when I directed him to let all hands turn in without setting an anchor-watch. I proposed to keep on deck myself till one o'clock or thereabouts. I would get the second mate to relieve me at that hour. 13

"He will turn out the cook and the steward at four," I concluded, "and then give you a call. Of course at the slightest sign of any sort of wind we'll have the hands up and make a start at once." 14

He concealed his astonishment. "Very well, sir." Outside the cuddy he put his head in the second mate's door to inform him of my unheard-of caprice to take a five hours' anchor-watch on myself. I heard the other raise his voice incredulously—"What? The Captain himself?" Then a few more murmurs, a door closed, then another. A few moments later I went on deck. 15

My strangeness, which had made me sleepless, had prompted that unconven- 16
tional arrangement, as if I had expected in those solitary hours of the night to get on
terms with the ship of which I knew nothing, manned by men of whom I knew very
little more. Fast alongside a wharf, littered like any ship in port with a tangle of
unrelated things, invaded by unrelated shore people, I had hardly seen her yet properly. Now, as she lay cleared for sea, the stretch of her main-deck seemed to me very
fine under the stars. Very fine, very roomy for her size, and very inviting. I
descended the poop and paced the waist, my mind picturing to myself the coming
passage through the Malay Archipelago, down the Indian Ocean, and up the
Atlantic. All its phases were familiar enough to me, every characteristic, all the
alternatives which were likely to face me on the high seas—everything! . . .
except the novel responsibility of command. But I took heart from the reasonable
thought that the ship was like other ships, the men like other men, and that the sea
was not likely to keep any special surprises expressly for my discomfiture.

Arrived at that comforting conclusion, I bethought myself of a cigar and 17
went below to get it. All was still down there. Everybody at the after end of the
ship was sleeping profoundly. I came out again on the quarter-deck, agreeably at
ease in my sleeping-suit on that warm breathless night, barefooted, a glowing
cigar in my teeth, and, going forward, I was met by the profound silence of the
fore end of the ship. Only as I passed the door of the forecastle I heard a deep,
quiet, trustful sigh of some sleeper inside. And suddenly I rejoiced in the great
security of the sea as compared with the unrest of the land, in my choice of that
untempted life presenting no disquieting problems, invested with an elementary
moral beauty by the absolute straightforwardness of its appeal and by the single-
ness of its purpose.

The riding-light in the fore-rigging burned with a clear, untroubled, as if 18
symbolic, flame, confident and bright in the mysterious shades of the night. Passing on my way aft along the other side of the ship, I observed that the rope side-
ladder, put over, no doubt, for the master of the tug when he came to fetch away
our letters, had not been hauled in as it should have been. I became annoyed at
this, for exactitude in small matters is the very soul of discipline. Then I reflected
that I had myself peremptorily dismissed my officers from duty, and by my own
act had prevented the anchor-watch being formally set and things properly
attended to. I asked myself whether it was wise ever to interfere with the established routine of duties even from the kindest of motives. My action might have
made me appear eccentric. Goodness only knew how that absurdly whiskered
mate would "account" for my conduct, and what the whole ship thought of that
informality of their new captain. I was vexed with myself.

Not from compunction certainly, but, as it were mechanically, I proceeded 19
to get the ladder in myself. Now a side-ladder of that sort is a light affair and
comes in easily, yet my vigorous tug, which should have brought it flying on
board, merely recoiled upon my body in a totally unexpected jerk. What the
devil! . . . I was so astounded by the immovableness of that ladder that I
remained stock-still, trying to account for it to myself like that imbecile mate of
mine. In the end, of course, I put my head over the rail.

The side of the ship made an opaque belt of shadow on the darkling glassy ₂₀ shimmer of the sea. But I saw at once something elongated and pale floating very close to the ladder. Before I could form a guess a faint flash of phosphorescent light, which seemed to issue suddenly from the naked body of a man, flickered in the sleeping water with the elusive, silent play of summer lightning in a night sky. With a gasp I saw revealed to my stare a pair of feet, the long legs, a broad livid back immersed right up to the neck in a greenish cadaverous glow. One hand, awash, clutched the bottom rung of the ladder. He was complete but for the head. A headless corpse! The cigar dropped out of my gaping mouth with a tiny plop and a short hiss quite audible in the absolute stillness of all things under heaven. At that I suppose he raised up his face, a dimly pale oval in the shadow of the ship's side. But even then I could only barely make out down there the shape of his black-haired head. However, it was enough for the horrid, frost-bound sensation which had gripped me about the chest to pass off. The moment of vain exclamations was past, too. I only climbed on the spare spar and leaned over the rail as far as I could, to bring my eyes nearer to that mystery floating alongside.

As he hung by the ladder, like a resting swimmer, the sea-lightning played ₂₁ about his limbs at every stir; and he appeared in it ghastly, silvery, fish-like. He remained as mute as a fish, too. He made no motion to get out of the water, either. It was inconceivable that he should not attempt to come on board, and strangely troubling to suspect that perhaps he did not want to. And my first words were prompted by just that troubled incertitude.

"What's the matter?" I asked in my ordinary tone, speaking down to the ₂₂ face upturned exactly under mine.

"Cramp," it answered, no louder. Then slightly anxious, "I say, no need to ₂₃ call any one."

"I was not going to," I said. ₂₄

"Are you alone on deck?" ₂₅

"Yes." ₂₆

I had somehow the impression that he was on the point of letting go the lad- ₂₇ der to swim away beyond my ken—mysterious as he came. But, for the moment, this being appearing as if he had risen from the bottom of the sea (it was certainly the nearest land to the ship) wanted only to know the time. I told him. And he, down there, tentatively:

"I suppose your captain's turned in?" ₂₈

"I am sure he isn't," I said. ₂₉

He seemed to struggle with himself, for I heard something like the low, bit- ₃₀ ter murmur of doubt. "What's the good?" His next words came out with a hesi- tating effort.

"Look here, my man. Could you call him out quietly?" ₃₁

I thought the time had come to declare myself. ₃₂

"*I* am the captain." ₃₃

I heard a "By Jove!" whispered at the level of the water. The phosphores- ₃₄ cence flashed in the swirl of the water all about his limbs, his other hand seized the ladder.

"My name's Leggatt."   35

The voice was calm and resolute. A good voice. The self-possession of that   36
man had somehow induced a corresponding state in myself. It was very quietly
that I remarked:

"You must be a good swimmer."   37

"Yes. I've been in the water practically since nine o'clock. The question for   38
me now is whether I am to let go this ladder and go on swimming till I sink from
exhaustion, or—to come on board here."

I felt this was no mere formula of desperate speech, but a real alternative in   39
the view of a strong soul. I should have gathered from this that he was young;
indeed, it is only the young who are ever confronted by such clear issues. But at
the time it was pure intuition on my part. A mysterious communication was established already between us two—in the face of that silent, darkened tropical sea. I
was young, too; young enough to make no comment. The man in the water began
suddenly to climb up the ladder, and I hastened away from the rail to fetch some
clothes.

Before entering the cabin I stood still, listening in the lobby at the foot of   40
the stairs. A faint snore came through the closed door of the chief mate's room.
The second mate's door was on the hook, but the darkness in there was absolutely
soundless. He, too, was young and could sleep like a stone. Remained the steward, but he was not likely to wake up before he was called. I got a sleeping-suit
out of my room and, coming back on deck, saw the naked man from the sea sitting on the main-hatch, glimmering white in the darkness, his elbows on his knees
and his head in his hands. In a moment he had concealed his damp body in a
sleeping-suit of the same grey-stripe pattern as the one I was wearing and followed me like my double on the poop. Together we moved right aft, barefooted,
silent.

"What is it?" I asked in a deadened voice, taking the lighted lamp out of the   41
binnacle, and raising it to his face.

"An ugly business."   42

He had rather regular features; a good mouth; light eyes under somewhat   43
heavy, dark eyebrows; a smooth, square forehead; no growth on his cheeks; a
small, brown moustache, and a well-shaped, round chin. His expression was concentrated, meditative, under the inspecting light of the lamp I held up to his face;
such as a man thinking hard in solitude might wear. My sleeping-suit was just
right for his size. A well-knit young fellow of twenty-five at most. He caught his
lower lip with the edge of white, even teeth.

"Yes," I said, replacing the lamp in the binnacle. The warm, heavy tropical   44
night closed upon his head again.

"There's a ship over there," he murmured.   45

"Yes, I know. The *Sephora*. Did you know of us?"   46

"Hadn't the slightest idea. I am the mate of her———" He paused and cor-   47
rected himself. "I should say I *was*."

"Aha! Something wrong?"   48

"Yes. Very wrong indeed. I've killed a man."   49

"What do you mean? Just now?"   50

"No, on the passage. Weeks ago.Thirty-nine south. When I say a man—"   51

"Fit of temper," I suggested, confidently.   52

The shadowy, dark head, like mine, seemed to nod imperceptibly above the   53
ghostly grey of my sleeping-suit. It was, in the night, as though I had been faced
by my own reflection in the depths of a sombre and immense mirror.

"A pretty thing to have to own up to for a Conway boy," murmured my dou-   54
ble, distinctly.

"You're a Conway boy?"   55

"I am," he said, as if startled. Then, slowly . . . "Perhaps you too—"   56

It was so; but being a couple of years older I had left before he joined. After   57
a quick interchange of dates a silence fell; and I thought suddenly of my absurd
mate with his terrific whiskers and the "Bless my soul—you don't say so" type
of intellect. My double gave me an inkling of his thoughts by saying: "My father's
a parson in Norfolk. Do you see me before a judge and jury on that charge? For
myself I can't see the necessity. There are fellows that an angel from heaven——
And I am not that. He was one of those creatures that are just simmering all the
time with a silly sort of wickedness. Miserable devils that have no business to live
at all. He wouldn't do his duty and wouldn't let anybody else do theirs. But what's
the good of talking! You know well enough the sort of ill-conditioned snarling
cur——"

He appealed to me as if our experiences had been as identical as our   58
clothes. And I knew well enough the pestiferous danger of such a character where
there are no means of legal repression. And I knew well enough also that my double there was no homicidal ruffian. I did not think of asking him for details, and
he told me the story roughly in brusque, disconnected sentences. I needed no
more. I saw it all going on as though I were myself inside that other sleeping-suit.

"It happened while we were setting a reefed foresail, at dusk. Reefed fore-   59
sail! You understand the sort of weather. The only sail we had left to keep the ship
running; so you may guess what it had been like for days. Anxious sort of job,
that. He gave me some of his cursed insolence at the sheet. I tell you I was over-
done with this terrific weather that seemed to have no end to it. Terrific, I tell
you—and a deep ship. I believe the fellow himself was half crazed with funk. It
was no time for gentlemanly reproof, so I turned round and felled him like an ox.
He up and at me. We closed just as an awful sea made for the ship. All hands saw
it coming and took to the rigging, but I had him by the throat, and went on shaking him like a rat, the men above us yelling, 'Look out! look out!' Then a crash
as if the sky had fallen on my head. They say that for over ten minutes hardly anything was to be seen of the ship—just the three masts and a bit of the forecastle
head and of the poop all awash driving along in a smother of foam. It was a miracle that they found us, jammed together behind the forebits. It's clear that I
meant business, because I was holding him by the throat still when they picked
us up. He was black in the face. It was too much for them. It seems they rushed
us aft together, gripped as we were, screaming 'Murder!' like a lot of lunatics, and

broke into the cuddy. And the ship running for her life, touch and go all the time, any minute her last in a sea fit to turn your hair grey only a-looking at it. I understand that the skipper, too, started raving like the rest of them. The man had been deprived of sleep for more than a week, and to have this sprung on him at the height of a furious gale nearly drove him out of his mind. I wonder they didn't fling me overboard after getting the carcass of their previous ship-mate out of my fingers. They had rather a job to separate us, I've been told. A sufficiently fierce story to make an old judge and a respectable jury sit up a bit. The first thing I heard when I came to myself was the maddening howling of that endless gale, and on that the voice of the old man. He was hanging on to my bunk, staring into my face out of his sou'wester.

"'Mr. Leggatt, you have killed a man. You can act no longer as chief mate 60
of this ship.'"

His care to subdue his voice made it sound monotonous. He rested a hand 61
on the end of the skylight to steady himself with, and all that time did not stir a limb, so far as I could see. "Nice little tale for a quiet tea-party," he concluded in the same tone.

One of my hands, too, rested on the end of the skylight; neither did I stir a 62
limb, so far as I knew. We stood less than a foot from each other. It occurred to me that if old "Bless my soul—you don't say so" were to put his head up the companion and catch sight of us, he would think he was seeing double, or imagine himself come upon a scene of weird witchcraft; the strange captain having a quiet confabulation by the wheel with his own grey ghost. I became very much concerned to prevent anything of the sort. I heard the other's soothing undertone.

"My father's a parson in Norfolk," it said. Evidently he had forgotten he had 63
told me this important fact before. Truly a nice little tale.

"You had better slip down into my stateroom now," I said, moving off 64
stealthily. My double followed my movements; our bare feet made no sound; I let him in, closed the door with care, and, after giving a call to the second mate, returned on deck for my relief.

"Not much sign of any wind yet," I remarked when he approached. 65

"No, sir. Not much," he assented, sleepily, in his hoarse voice, with just 66
enough deference, no more, and barely suppressing a yawn.

"Well, that's all you have to look out for. You have got your orders." 67

"Yes, sir." 68

I paced a turn or two on the poop and saw him take up his position face for- 69
ward with his elbow in the ratlines of the mizzenrigging before I went below. The mate's faint snoring was still going on peacefully. The cuddy lamp was burning over the table on which stood a vase with flowers, a polite attention from the ship's provision merchant—the last flowers we should see for the next three months at the very least. Two bunches of bananas hung from the beam symmetrically, one on each side of the rudder-casing. Everything was as before in the ship—except that two of her captain's sleeping-suits were simultaneously in use, one motionless in the cuddy, the other keeping very still in the captain's stateroom.

It must be explained here that my cabin had the form of the capital letter L 70 the door being within the angle and opening into the short part of the letter. A couch was to the left, the bed-place to the right; my writing-desk and the chronometers' table faced the door. But any one opening it, unless he stepped right inside, had no view of what I call the long (or vertical) part of the letter. It contained some lockers surmounted by a bookcase; and a few clothes, a thick jacket or two, caps, oilskin coat, and such like, hung on hooks. There was at the bottom of that part a door opening into my bathroom, which could be entered also directly from the saloon. But that way was never used.

The mysterious arrival had discovered the advantage of this particular 71 shape. Entering my room, lighted strongly by a big bulkhead lamp swung on gimbals above my writing-desk, I did not see him anywhere till he stepped out quietly from behind the coats hung in the recessed part.

"I heard somebody moving about, and went in there at once," he whispered. 72

I, too, spoke under my breath. 73

"Nobody is likely to come in here without knocking and getting permission." 74

He nodded. His face was thin and the sunburn faded, as though he had been 75 ill. And no wonder. He had been, I heard presently, kept under arrest in his cabin for nearly seven weeks. But there was nothing sickly in his eyes or in his expression. He was not a bit like me, really; yet, as we stood leaning over my bed-place, whispering side by side, with our dark heads together and our backs to the door, anybody bold enough to open it stealthily would have been treated to the uncanny sight of a double captain busy talking in whispers with his other self.

"But all this doesn't tell me how you came to hang on to our side-ladder," 76 I inquired, in the hardly audible murmurs we used, after he had told me something more of the proceedings on board the *Sephora* once the bad weather was over.

"When we sighted Java Head I had had time to think all those matters out 77 several times over. I had six weeks of doing nothing else, and with only an hour or so every evening for a tramp on the quarter-deck."

He whispered, his arms folded on the side of my bed-place, staring through 78 the open port. And I could imagine perfectly the manner of this thinking out—a stubborn if not a steadfast operation; something of which I should have been perfectly incapable.

"I reckoned it would be dark before we closed with the land," he continued, 79 so low that I had to strain my hearing, near as we were to each other, shoulder touching shoulder almost. "So I asked to speak to the old man. He always seemed very sick when he came to see me—as if he could not look me in the face. You know, that foresail saved the ship. She was too deep to have run long under bare poles. And it was I that managed to set it for him. Anyway, he came. When I had him in my cabin—he stood by the door looking at me as if I had the halter round my neck already—I asked him right away to leave my cabin door unlocked at night while the ship was going through Sunda Straits. There would be the Java coast within two or three miles, off Angier Point. I wanted nothing more. I've had a prize for swimming my second year in the Conway."

"I can believe it," I breathed out. 80

"God only knows why they locked me in every night. To see some of their 81 faces you'd have thought they were afraid I'd go about at night strangling people. Am I a murdering brute? Do I look it? By Jove! if I had been he wouldn't have trusted himself like that into my room. You'll say I might have chucked him aside and bolted out, there and then—it was dark already. Well, no. And for the same reason I wouldn't think of trying to smash the door. There would have been a rush to stop me at the noise, and I did not mean to get into a confounded scrimmage. Somebody else might have got killed—for I would not have broken out only to get chucked back, and I did not want any more of that work. He refused, looking more sick than ever. He was afraid of the men, and also of that old second mate of his who had been sailing with him for years—a grey-headed old humbug; and his steward, too, had been with him devil knows how long—seventeen years or more—a dogmatic sort of loafer who hated me like poison, just because I was the chief mate. No chief mate ever made more than one voyage in the *Sephora,* you know. Those two old chaps ran the ship. Devil only knows what the skipper wasn't afraid of (all his nerve went to pieces altogether in that hellish spell of bad weather we had)—of what the law would do to him—of his wife, perhaps. Oh, yes! she's on board. Though I don't think she would have meddled. She would have been only too glad to have me out of the ship in any way. The 'brand of Cain' business, don't you see. That's all right. I was ready enough to go off wandering on the face of the earth—and that was price enough to pay for an Abel of that sort. Anyhow, he wouldn't listen to me. 'This thing must take its course. I represent the law here.' He was shaking like a leaf. 'So you won't?' 'No!' 'Then I hope you will be able to sleep on that,' I said, and turned my back on him. 'I wonder that *you* can,' cries he, and locks the door.

"Well, after that, I couldn't. Not very well. That was three weeks ago. We 82 have had a slow passage through the Java Sea; drifted about Carimata for ten days. When we anchored here they thought, I suppose, it was all right. The nearest land (and that's five miles) is the ship's destination; the consul would soon set about catching me; and there would have been no object in bolting to these islets there. I don't suppose there's a drop of water on them. I don't know how it was, but to-night that steward, after bringing me my supper, went out to let me eat it, and left the door unlocked. And I ate it—all there was, too. After I had finished I strolled out on the quarter-deck. I don't know that I meant to do anything. A breath of fresh air was all I wanted, I believe. Then a sudden temptation came over me. I kicked off my slippers and was in the water before I had made up my mind fairly. Somebody heard the splash and they raised an awful hullabaloo. 'He's gone! Lower the boats! He's committed suicide! No, he's swimming.' Certainly I was swimming. It's not so easy for a swimmer like me to commit suicide by drowning. I landed on the nearest islet before the boat left the ship's side. I heard them pulling about in the dark, hailing, and so on, but after a bit they gave up. Everything quieted down and the anchorage became as still as death. I sat down on a stone and began to think. I felt certain they would start searching for me at daylight. There was no place to hide on those stony things—and if there had been, what would have been the good? But now I was clear of that ship, I was not going back. So after a while I took off all my clothes, tied them up in a bundle with a stone inside, and dropped them in the deep water on the outer side of that islet. That was suicide enough for me. Let them think what they liked, but I didn't mean to drown myself. I meant to swim till I sank—but that's not the same thing. I struck out for another of these little islands, and it was from that one that I first saw your riding-light. Something to swim for. I went on easily, and on the way I came upon a flat rock a foot or two above water. In the daytime, I dare say, you might make it out with a glass from your poop. I scrambled up on it and rested myself for a bit. Then I made another start. That last spell must have been over a mile."

His whisper was getting fainter and fainter, and all the time he stared straight out through the port-hole, in which there was not even a star to be seen. I had not interrupted him. There was something that made comment impossible in his narrative, or perhaps in himself; a sort of feeling, a quality, which I can't find a name for. And when he ceased, all I found was a futile whisper: "So you swam for our light?" [83]

"Yes—straight for it. It was something to swim for. I couldn't see any stars low down because the coast was in the way, and I couldn't see the land, either. The water was like glass. One might have been swimming in a confounded thousand-feet deep cistern with no place for scrambling out anywhere; but what I didn't like was the notion of swimming round and round like a crazed bullock before I gave out; and as I didn't mean to go back . . . No. Do you see me being hauled back, stark naked, off one of these little islands by the scruff of the neck and fighting like a wild beast? Somebody would have got killed for certain, and I did not want any of that. So I went on. Then your ladder——" [84]

"Why didn't you hail the ship?" I asked, a little louder. [85]

He touched my shoulder lightly. Lazy footsteps came right over out heads and stopped. The second mate had crossed from the other side of the poop and might have been hanging over the rail, for all we knew. [86]

"He couldn't hear us talking—could he?" My double breathed into my very ear, anxiously. [87]

His anxiety was an answer, a sufficient answer, to the question I had put to him. An answer containing all the difficulty of that situation. I closed the porthole quietly, to make sure. A louder word might have been overheard. [88]

"Who's that?" he whispered then. [89]

"My second mate. But I don't know much more of the fellow than you do." [90]

And I told him a little about myself. I had been appointed to take charge while I least expected anything of the sort, not quite a fortnight ago. I didn't know either the ship or the people. Hadn't had the time in port to look about me or size anybody up. And as to the crew, all they knew was that I was appointed to take the ship home. For the rest, I was almost as much of a stranger on board as himself, I said. And at the moment I felt it most acutely. I felt that it would take very little to make me a suspect person in the eyes of the ship's company. [91]

He had turned about meantime; and we, the two strangers in the ship, faced 92 each other in identical attitudes.

"Your ladder——" he murmured, after a silence. "Who'd have thought of 93 finding a ladder hanging over at night in a ship anchored out here! I felt just then a very unpleasant faintness. After the life I've been leading for nine weeks, any-body would have got out of condition. I wasn't capable of swimming round as far as your rudderchains. And, lo and behold! there was a ladder to get hold of. After I gripped it I said to myself, 'What's the good?' When I saw a man's head look-ing over I thought I would swim away presently and leave him shouting—in whatever language it was. I didn't mind being looked at. I—I liked it. And then you speaking to me so quietly—as if you had expected me—made me hold on a little longer. It had been a confounded lonely time—I don't mean while swim-ming. I was glad to talk a little to somebody that didn't belong to the *Sephora*. As to asking for the captain, that was a mere impulse. It could have been no use, with all the ship knowing about me and the other people pretty certain to be round here in the morning. I don't know—I wanted to be seen, to talk with somebody, before I went on. I don't know what I would have said. . . . 'Fine night, isn't it?' or something of the sort."

"Do you think they will be round here presently?" I asked with some 94 incredulity.

"Quite likely," he said, faintly. 95

He looked extremely haggard all of a sudden. His head rolled on his 96 shoulders.

"H'm. We shall see then. Meantime get into that bed," I whispered. "Want 97 help? There."

It was a rather high bed-place with a set of drawers underneath. This amaz- 98 ing swimmer really needed the lift I gave him by seizing his leg. He tumbled in, rolled over on his back, and flung one arm across his eyes. And then, with his face nearly hidden, he must have looked exactly as I used to look in that bed. I gazed upon my other self for a while before drawing across carefully the two green serge curtains which ran on a brass rod. I thought for a moment of pinning them together for greater safety, but I sat down on the couch, and once there I felt unwilling to rise and hunt for a pin. I would do it in a moment. I was extremely tired, in a peculiarly intimate way, by the strain of stealthiness, by the effort of whispering and the general secrecy of this excitement. It was three o'clock by now and I had been on my feet since nine, but I was not sleepy; I could not have gone to sleep. I sat there, fagged out, looking at the curtains, trying to clear my mind of the confused sensation of being in two places at once, and greatly both-ered by an exasperating knocking in my head. It was a relief to discover suddenly that it was not in my head at all, but on the outside of the door. Before I could col-lect myself the words "Come in" were out of my mouth, and the steward entered with a tray, bringing in my morning coffee. I had slept, after all, and I was so frightened that I shouted, "This way! I am here, steward," as though he had been miles away. He put down the tray on the table next the couch and only then said, very quietly, "I can see you are here, sir." I felt him give me a keen look, but I dared not meet his eyes just then. He must have wondered why I had drawn the curtains of my bed before going to sleep on the couch. He went out, hooking the door open as usual.

I heard the crew washing decks above me. I knew I would have been told 99 at once if there had been any wind. Calm, I thought, and I was doubly vexed. Indeed, I felt dual more than ever. The steward reappeared suddenly in the doorway. I jumped up from the couch so quickly that he gave a start.

"What do you want here?"   100

"Close your port, sir—they are washing decks."   101

"It is closed," I said, reddening.   102

"Very well, sir." But he did not move from the doorway and returned my 103 stare in an extraordinary, equivocal manner for a time. Then his eyes wavered, all his expression changed, and in a voice unusually gentle, almost coaxingly:

"May I come in to take the empty cup away, sir?"   104

"Of course!" I turned my back on him while he popped in and out. Then I 105 unhooked and closed the door and even pushed the bolt. This sort of thing could not go on very long. The cabin was as hot as an oven, too. I took a peep at my double, and discovered that he had not moved, his arm was still over his eyes; but his chest heaved; his hair was wet; his chin glistened with perspiration. I reached over him and opened the port.

"I must show myself on deck," I reflected.   106

Of course, theoretically, I could do what I liked, with no one to say nay to 107 me within the whole circle of the horizon; but to lock my cabin door and take the key away I did not dare. Directly I put my head out of the companion I saw the group of my two officers, the second mate barefooted, the chief mate in long india-rubber boots, near the break of the poop, and the steward half-way down the poopladder talking to them eagerly. He happened to catch sight of me and dived, the second ran down on the main-deck shouting some order or other, and the chief mate came to meet me, touching his cap.

There was a sort of curiosity in his eye that I did not like. I don't know 108 whether the steward had told them that I was "queer" only, or downright drunk, but I know the man meant to have a good look at me. I watched him coming with a smile which, as he got into point-blank range, took effect and froze his very whiskers. I did not give him time to open his lips.

"Square the yards by lifts and braces before the hands go to breakfast." 109

It was the first particular order I had given on board that ship; and I stayed 110 on deck to see it executed, too. I had felt the need of asserting myself without loss of time. That sneering young cub got taken down a peg or two on that occasion, and I also seized the opportunity of having a good look at the face of every foremast man as they filed past me to go to the after braces. At breakfast time, eating nothing myself, I presided with such frigid dignity that the two mates were only too glad to escape from the cabin as soon as decency permitted; and all the time the dual working of my mind distracted me almost to the point of insanity. I was constantly watching myself, my secret self, as dependent on my actions as my own personality, sleeping in that bed, behind that door which faced me as I sat at the head of the table. It was very much like being mad, only it was worse because one was aware of it.

I had to shake him for a solid minute, but when at last he opened his eyes 111 it was in the full possession of his senses, with an inquiring look.

"All's well so far," I whispered. "Now you must vanish into the bathroom." 112

He did so, as noiseless as a ghost, and then I rang for the steward, and fac- 113 ing him boldly, directed him to tidy up my stateroom while I was having my bath—"and be quick about it." As my tone admitted of no excuses, he said, "Yes, sir," and ran off to fetch his dust-pan and brushes. I took a bath and did most of my dressing, splashing, and whistling softly for the steward's edification, while the secret sharer of my life stood drawn up bolt upright in that little space, his face looking very sunken in daylight, his eyelids lowered under the stern, dark line of his eyebrows drawn together by a slight frown.

When I left him there to go back to my room the steward was finishing dust- 114 ing. I sent for the mate and engaged him in some insignificant conversation. It was, as it were, trifling with the terrific character of his whiskers; but my object was to give him an opportunity for a good look at my cabin. And then I could at last shut, with a clear conscience, the door of my stateroom and get my double back into the recessed part. There was nothing else for it. He had to sit still on a small folding stool, half smothered by the heavy coats hanging there. We listened to the steward going into the bathroom out of the saloon, filling the water-bottles there, scrubbing the bath, setting things to rights, whisk, bang, clatter—out again into the saloon— turn the key—click. Such was my scheme for keeping my second self invisible. Nothing better could be contrived under the circumstances. And there we sat; I at my writing-desk ready to appear busy with some papers, he behind me out of sight of the door. It would not have been prudent to talk in daytime; and I could not have stood the excitement of that queer sense of whispering to myself. Now and then, glancing over my shoulder, I saw him far back there, sitting rigidly on the low stool, his bare feet close together, his arms folded, his head hanging on his breast—and perfectly still. Anybody would have taken him for me.

I was fascinated by it myself. Every moment I had to glance over my shoul- 115 der. I was looking at him when a voice outside the door said:

"Beg pardon, sir."   116

"Well!" . . . I kept my eyes on him, and so when the voice outside the door 117 announced, "There's ship's boat coming our way, sir," I saw him give a start—the first movement he had made for hours. But he did not raise his bowed head.

"All right. Get the ladder over."   118

I hesitated. Should I whisper something to him? But what? His immobility 119 seemed to have been never disturbed. What could I tell him he did not know already? . . . Finally I went on deck.

II

The skipper of the *Sephora* had a thin red whisker all round his face, and 120 the sort of complexion that goes with hair of that colour; also the particular, rather smeary shade of blue in the eyes. He was not exactly a showy figure; his shoulders were high, his stature but middling—one leg slightly more bandy than the other. He shook hands, looking vaguely around. A spiritless tenacity was his main characteristic, I judged. I behaved with a politeness which seemed to disconcert him. Perhaps he was shy. He mumbled to me as if he were ashamed of what he was saying; gave his name (it was something like Archbold—but at this distance of years I hardly am sure), his ship's name, and a few other particulars of that sort, in the manner of a criminal making a reluctant and doleful confession. He had had terrible weather on the passage out—terrible—terrible—wife aboard, too.

By this time we were seated in the cabin and the steward brought in a tray 121 with a bottle and glasses. "Thanks! No." Never took liquor. Would have some water, though. He drank two tumblerfuls. Terrible thirsty work. Ever since daylight had been exploring the islands round his ship.

"What was that for—fun?" I asked, with an appearance of polite interest.   122

"No!" He signed. "Painful duty."   123

As he persisted in his mumbling and I wanted my double to hear every 124 word, I hit upon the notion of informing him that I regretted to say I was hard of hearing.

"Such a young man, too!" he nodded, keeping his smeary blue, unintelli- 125 gent eyes fastened upon me. "What was the cause of it—some disease?" he inquired, without the least sympathy and as if he thought that, if so, I'd got no more than I deserved.

"Yes; disease," I admitted in a cheerful tone which seemed to shock him. 126 But my point was gained, because he had to raise his voice to give me his tale. It is not worth while to record that version. It was just over two months since all this had happened, and he had thought so much about it that he seemed completely muddled as to its bearings, but still immensely impressed.

"What would you think of such a thing happening on board your own ship? 127 I've had the *Sephora* for these fifteen years. I am a well-known shipmaster."

He was densely distressed—and perhaps I should have sympathised with 128 him if I had been able to detach my mental vision from the unsuspected sharer of my cabin as though he were my second self. There he was on the other side of the bulkhead, four or five feet from us, no more, as we sat in the saloon. I looked politely at Captain Archbold (if that was his name), but it was the other I saw, in a grey sleeping-suit, seated on a low stool, his bare feet close together, his arms folded, and every word said between us falling into the ears of his dark head bowed on his chest.

"I have been at sea now, man and boy, for seven-and-thirty years, and I've 129 never heard of such a thing happening in an English ship. And that it should be my ship. Wife on board, too."

I was hardly listening to him. 130

"Don't you think," I said, "that the heavy sea which, you told me, came 131 aboard just then might have killed the man? I have seen the sheer weight of a sea kill a man very neatly, by simply breaking his neck."

"Good God!" he uttered, impressively, fixing his smeary blue eyes on me. 132 "The sea! No man killed by the sea ever looked like that." He seemed positively scandalised at my suggestion. And as I gazed at him, certainly not prepared for anything original on his part, he advanced his head close to mine and thrust his tongue out at me so suddenly that I couldn't help starting back.

After scoring over my calmness in this graphic way he nodded wisely. If I 133 had seen the sight, he assured me, I would never forget it as long as I lived. The weather was too bad to give the corpse a proper sea burial. So next day at dawn they took it up on the poop, covering its face with a bit of bunting; he read a short prayer, and then, just as it was, in its oilskins and long boots, they launched it amongst those mountainous seas that seemed ready every moment to swallow up the ship herself and the terrified lives on board of her.

"That reefed foresail saved you," I threw in. 134

"Under God—it did," he exclaimed fervently. "It was by a special mercy, I 135 firmly believed, that it stood some of those hurricane squalls."

"It was the setting of that sail which——" I began. 136

"God's own hand in it," he interrupted me. "Nothing less could have done 137 it. I don't mind telling you that I hardly dared give the order. It seemed impossible that we could touch anything without losing it, and then our last hope would have been gone."

The terror of that gale was on him yet. I let him go on for a bit, then said, 138 casually—as if returning to a minor subject:

"You were very anxious to give up your mate to the shore people, I believe?" 139

He was. To the law. His obscure tenacity on that point had in it something 140 incomprehensible and a little awful; something, as it were, mystical, quite apart from his anxiety that he should not be suspected of "countenancing any doings of that sort." Seven-and-thirty virtuous years at sea, of which over twenty of immaculate command, and the last fifteen in the *Sephora,* seemed to have laid him under some pitiless obligation.

"And you know," he went on, groping shamefacedly amongst his feelings, 141 "I did not engage that young fellow. His people had some interest with my owners. I was in a way forced to take him on. He looked very smart, very gentlemanly, and all that. But do you know—I never liked him, somehow. I am a plain man. You see, he wasn't exactly the sort for the chief mate of a ship like the *Sephora.*"

I had become so connected in thoughts and impressions with the secret 142 sharer of my cabin that I felt as if I, personally, were being given to understand that I, too, was not the sort that would have done for the chief mate of a ship like the *Sephora.* I had no doubt of it in my mind.

"Not at all the style of man. You understand," he insisted, superfluously, 143 looking hard at me.

I smiled urbanely. He seemed at a loss for a while.   144

"I suppose I must report a suicide."   145

"Beg pardon?"   146

"Sui-cide! That's what I'll have to write to my owners directly I get in."   147

"Unless you manage to recover him before to-morrow," I assented, dispas-   148
sionately. . . . "I mean, alive."

He mumbled something which I really did not catch, and I turned my ear to   149
him in a puzzled manner. He fairly bawled:

"The land—I say, the mainland is at least seven miles off my anchorage."   150

"About that."   151

My lack of excitement, of curiosity, of surprise, of any sort of pronounced   152
interest, began to arouse his distrust. But except for the felicitous pretence of
deafness I had not tried to pretend anything. I had felt utterly incapable of playing the part of ignorance properly, and therefore was afraid to try. It is also certain that he had brought some ready-made suspicions with him, and that he
viewed my politeness as a strange and unnatural phenomenon. And yet how else
could I have received him? Not heartily! That was impossible for psychological
reasons, which I need not state here. My only object was to keep off his inquiries.
Surlily? Yes, but surliness might have provoked a point-blank question. From its
novelty to him and from its nature, punctilious courtesy was the manner best calculated to restrain the man. But there was the danger of his breaking through my
defence bluntly. I could not, I think, have met him by a direct lie, also for psychological (not moral) reasons. If he had only known how afraid I was of his
putting my feeling of identity with the other to the test! But, strangely enough—
(I thought of it only afterwards)—I believe that he was not a little disconcerted by
the reverse side of that weird situation, by something in me that reminded him of
the man he was seeking—suggested a mysterious similitude to the young fellow
he had distrusted and disliked from the first.

However that might have been, the silence was not very prolonged. He took   153
another oblique step.

"I reckon I had no more than a two-mile pull to your ship. Not a bit more."   154

"And quite enough, too, in this awful heat," I said.   155

Another pause full of mistrust followed. Necessity, they say, is mother of   156
invention, but fear, too, is not barren of ingenious suggestions. And I was afraid
he would ask me point-blank for news of my other self.

"Nice little saloon, isn't it?" I remarked, as if noticing for the first time the   157
way his eyes roamed from one closed door to the other. "And very well fitted out,
too. Here, for instance," I continued, reaching over the back of my seat negli-
gently and flinging the door open, "is my bathroom."

He made an eager movement, but hardly gave it a glance. I got up, shut the   158
door of the bath-room, and invited him to have a look around, as if I were very
proud of my accommodation. He had to rise and be shown around, but he went
through the business without any raptures whatever.

"And now we'll have a look at my stateroom," I declared, in a voice as loud   159
as I dared to make it, crossing the cabin to the starboard side with purposely
heavy steps.

He followed me in and gazed around. My intelligent double had vanished. 160 I played my part.

"Very convenient—isn't it?"   161

"Very nice. Very comf . . ." He didn't finish and went out brusquely as if 162 to escape from some unrighteous wiles of mine. But it was not to be. I had been too frightened not to feel vengeful; I felt I had him on the run, and I meant to keep him on the run. My polite insistence must have had something menacing in it, because he gave in suddenly. And I did not let him off a single item; mate's room, pantry, storerooms, the very sail-locker which was also under the poop—he had to look into them all. When at last I showed him out on the quarter-deck he drew a long, spiritless sigh, and mumbled dismally that he must really be going back to his ship now. I desired my mate, who had joined us, to see to the captain's boat.

The man of whiskers gave a blast on the whistle which he used to wear 163 hanging round his neck, and yelled, "*Sephora*'s away!" My double down there in my cabin must have heard, and certainly could not feel more relieved than I. Four fellows came running out from somewhere forward and went over the side, while my own men, appearing on deck too, lined the rail. I escorted my visitor to the gangway ceremoniously, and nearly overdid it. He was a tenacious beast. On the very ladder he lingered, and in that unique, guiltily conscientious manner of sticking to the point:

"I say . . . you . . . you don't think that——"   164

I covered his voice loudly: 165

"Certainly not. . . . I am delighted. Goodbye."   166

I had an idea of what he meant to say, and just saved myself by the privi- 167 lege of defective hearing. He was too shaken generally to insist, but my mate, close witness of that parting, looked mystified and his face took on a thoughtful cast. As I did not want to appear as if I wished to avoid all communication with my officers, he had the opportunity to address me.

"Seems a very nice man. His boat's crew told our chaps a very extraordi- 168 nary story, if what I am told by the steward is true. I suppose you had it from the captain, sir?"

"Yes. I had a story from the captain."   169

"A very horrible affair—isn't it, sir?"   170

"It is."   171

"Beats all these tales we hear about murders in Yankee ships."   172

"I don't think it beats them. I don't think it resembles them in the least."   173

"Bless my soul—you don't say so! But of course I've no acquaintance 174 whatever with American ships, not I, so I couldn't go against your knowledge. It's horrible enough for me . . . But the queerest part is that those fellows seemed to have some idea the man was hidden aboard here. They had really. Did you ever hear of such a thing?"

"Preposterous—isn't it?"   175

We were walking to and fro athwart the quarter-deck. No one of the crew 176 forward could be seen (the day was Sunday), and the mate pursued:

"There was some little dispute about it. Our chaps took offence. 'As if we 177 would harbour a thing like that,' they said. 'Wouldn't you like to look for him in our coal-hole?' Quite a tiff. But they made it up in the end. I suppose he did drown himself. Don't you, sir?"

"I don't suppose anything."   178

"You have no doubt in the matter, sir?"   179

"None whatever."   180

I left him suddenly. I felt I was producing a bad impression, but with my 181 double down there it was most trying to be on deck. And it was almost as trying to be below. Altogether a nerve-trying situation. But on the whole I felt less torn in two when I was with him. There was no one in the whole ship whom I dared take into my confidence. Since the hands had got to know his story, it would have been impossible to pass him off for any one else, and an accidental discovery was to be dreaded now more than ever. . . .

The steward being engaged in laying the table for dinner, we could talk only 182 with our eyes when I first went down. Later in the afternoon we had a cautious try at whispering. The Sunday quietness of the ship was against us; the stillness of air and water around her was against us; the elements, the men were against us—everything was against us in our secret partnership; time itself—for this could not go on forever. The very trust in Providence was, I suppose, denied to his guilt. Shall I confess that this thought cast me down very much? And as to the chapter of accidents which counts for so much in the book of success, I could only hope that it was closed. For what favourable accident could be expected?

"Did you hear everything?" were my first words as soon as we took up our 183 position side by side, leaning over my bed-place.

He had. And the proof of it was his earnest whisper, "The man told you he 184 hardly dared to give the order."

I understood the reference to be to that saving foresail.   185

"Yes. He was afraid of it being lost in the setting."   186

"I assure you he never gave the order. He may think he did, but he never 187 gave it. He stood there with me on the break of the poop after the maintopsail blew away, and whimpered about our last hope—positively whimpered about it and nothing else—and the night coming on! To hear one's skipper go on like that in such weather was enough to drive any fellow out of his mind. It worked me up into a sort of desperation. I just took it into my own hands and went away from him, boiling, and——But what's the use telling you? *You* know! . . . Do you think that if I had not been pretty fierce with them I should have got the men to do anything? Not it! The bo's'n perhaps? Perhaps! It wasn't a heavy sea—it was a sea gone mad! I suppose the end of the world will be something like that; and a man may have the heart to see it coming once and be done with it—but to have to face it day after day——I don't blame anybody. I was precious little better than the rest. Only—I was an officer of that old coal-wagon, anyhow——"

"I quite understand," I conveyed that sincere assurance into his ear. He was 188 out of breath with whispering; I could hear him pant slightly. It was all very simple. The same strung-up force which had given twenty-four men a chance, at least, for their lives, had, in a sort of recoil, crushed an unworthy mutinous existence.

But I had no leisure to weigh the merits of the matter—footsteps in the ₁₈₉
saloon, a heavy knock. "There's enough wind to get under way with, sir." Here
was the call of a new claim upon my thoughts and even upon my feelings.

"Turn the hands up," I cried through the door. "I'll be on deck directly."   ₁₉₀

I was going out to make the acquaintance of my ship. Before I left the cabin ₁₉₁
our eyes met—the eyes of the only two strangers on board. I pointed to the
recessed part where the little camp-stool awaited him and laid my finger on my
lips. He made a gesture—somewhat vague—a little mysterious, accompanied by
a faint smile, as if of regret.

This is not the place to enlarge upon the sensations of a man who feels for ₁₉₂
the first time a ship move under his feet to his own independent word. In my case
they were not unalloyed. I was not wholly alone with my command; for there was
that stranger in my cabin. Or rather, I was not completely and wholly with her.
Part of me was absent. That mental feeling of being in two places at once affected
me physically as if the mood of secrecy had penetrated my very soul. Before an
hour had elapsed since the ship had begun to move, having occasion to ask the
mate (he stood by my side) to take a compass bearing of the Pagoda, I caught
myself reaching up to his ear in whispers. I say I caught myself, but enough had
escaped to startle the man. I can't describe it otherwise than by saying that he
shied. A grave, preoccupied manner, as though he were in possession of some
perplexing intelligence, did not leave him henceforth. A little later I moved away
from the rail to look at the compass with such a stealthy gait that the helmsman
noticed it—and I could not help noticing the unusual roundness of his eyes. These
are trifling instances, though it's to no commander's advantage to be suspected of
ludicrous eccentricities. But I was also more seriously affected. There are to a
seaman certain words, gestures, that should in given conditions come as naturally,
as instinctively as the winking of a menaced eye. A certain order should spring on
to his lips without thinking; a certain sign should get itself made, so to speak,
without reflection. But all unconscious alertness had abandoned me. I had to
make an effort of will to recall myself back (from the cabin) to the conditions of
the moment. I felt that I was appearing an irresolute commander to those people
who were watching me more or less critically.

And, besides, there were the scares. On the second day out, for instance, ₁₉₃
coming off the deck in the afternoon (I had straw slippers on my bare feet) I
stopped at the open pantry door and spoke to the steward. He was doing something there with his back to me. At the sound of my voice he nearly jumped out
of his skin, as the saying is, and incidentally broke a cup.

"What on earth's the matter with you?" I asked, astonished.   ₁₉₄

He was extremely confused. "Beg your pardon, sir. I made sure you were ₁₉₅
in your cabin."

"You see I wasn't."   ₁₉₆

"No, sir. I could have sworn I had heard you moving in there not a moment ₁₉₇
ago. It's most extraordinary . . . very sorry, sir."

I passed on with an inward shudder. I was so identified with my secret dou- ₁₉₈
ble that I did not even mention the fact in those scanty, fearful whispers we

exchanged. I suppose he had made some slight noise of some kind or other. It would have been miraculous if he hadn't at one time or another. And yet, haggard as he appeared, he looked always perfectly self-controlled, more than calm— almost invulnerable. On my suggestion he remained almost entirely in the bathroom, which, upon the whole, was the safest place. There could be really no shadow of an excuse for any one ever wanting to go in there, once the steward had done with it. It was a very tiny place. Sometimes he reclined on the floor, his legs bent, his head sustained on one elbow. At others I would find him on the camp-stool, sitting in his grey sleeping-suit and with his cropped dark hair like a patient, unmoved convict. At night I would smuggle him into my bed-place, and we would whisper together, with the regular footfalls of the officer of the watch passing and repassing over our heads. It was an infinitely miserable time. It was lucky that some tins of fine preserves were stowed in a locker in my stateroom; hard bread I could always get hold of; and so he lived on stewed chicken, paté de foie gras, asparagus, cooked oysters, sardines—on all sorts of abominable sham delicacies out of tins. My early morning coffee he always drank; and it was all I dared do for him in that respect.

Every day there was the horrible manoeuvring to go through so that my 199 room and then the bath-room should be done in the usual way. I came to hate the sight of the steward, to abhor the voice of that harmless man. I felt that it was he who would bring on the disaster of discovery. It hung like a sword over our heads.

The fourth day out, I think (we were then working down the east side of the 200 Gulf of Siam, tack for tack, in light winds and smooth water)—the fourth day, I say, of this miserable juggling with the unavoidable, as we sat at our evening meal, that man, whose slightest movement I dreaded, after putting down the dishes ran up on deck busily. This could not be dangerous. Presently he came down again; and then it appeared that he had remembered a coat of mine which I had thrown over a rail to dry after having been wetted in a shower which had passed over the ship in the afternoon. Sitting stolidly at the head of the table I became terrified at the sight of the garment on his arm. Of course he made for my door. There was no time to lose.

"Steward," I thundered. My nerves were so shaken that I could not govern 201 my voice and conceal my agitation. This was the sort of thing that made my terrifically whiskered mate tap his forehead with his forefinger. I had detected him using that gesture while talking on deck with a confidential air to the carpenter. It was too far to hear a word, but I had no doubt that this pantomime could only refer to the strange new captain.

"Yes, sir," the pale-faced steward turned resignedly to me. It was this mad- 202 dening course of being shouted at, checked without rhyme or reason, arbitrarily chased out of my cabin, suddenly called into it, sent flying out of his pantry on incomprehensible errands, that accounted for the growing wretchedness of his expression.

"Where are you going with that coat?"   203
"To your room, sir."   204
"Is there another shower coming?"   205

"I'm sure I don't know, sir. Shall I go up again and see, sir?"   206

"No! never mind."   207

My object was attained, as of course my other self in there would have 208 heard everything that passed. During this interlude my two officers never raised their eyes off their respective plates; but the lip of that confounded cub, the second mate, quivered visibly.

I expected the steward to hook my coat on and come out at once. He was 209 very slow about it; but I dominated my nervousness sufficiently not to shout after him. Suddenly I became aware (it could be heard plainly enough) that the fellow for some reason or other was opening the door of the bath-room. It was the end. The place was literally not big enough to swing a cat in. My voice died in my throat and I went stony all over. I expected to hear a yell of surprise and terror, and made a movement, but had not the strength to get on my legs. Everything remained still. Had my second self taken the poor wretch by the throat? I don't know what I could have done next moment if I had not seen the steward come out of my room, close the door, and then stand quietly by the sideboard.

"Saved," I thought. "But, no! Lost! Gone! He was gone!"   210

I laid my knife and fork down and leaned back in my chair. My head swam. 211 After a while, when sufficiently recovered to speak in a steady voice, I instructed my mate to put the ship round at eight o'clock himself.

"I won't come on deck," I went on. "I think I'll turn in, and unless the wind 212 shifts I don't want to be disturbed before midnight. I feel a bit seedy."

"You did look middling bad a little while ago," the chief mate remarked 213 without showing any great concern.

They both went out, and I stared at the steward clearing the table. There was 214 nothing to be read on that wretched man's face. But why did he avoid my eyes, I asked myself. Then I thought I should like to hear the sound of his voice.

"Steward!"   215

"Sir!" Startled as usual.   216

"Where did you hang up that coat?"   217

"In the bath-room, sir." The usual anxious tone. "It's not quite dry yet, sir." 218

For some time longer I sat in the cuddy. Had my double vanished as he had 219 come? But of his coming there was an explanation, whereas his disappearance would be inexplicable . . . I went slowly into my dark room, shut the door, lighted the lamp, and for a time dared not turn round. When at last I did I saw him standing bolt-upright in the narrow recessed part. It would not be true to say I had a shock, but an irresistible doubt of his bodily existence flitted through my mind. Can it be, I asked myself, that he is not visible to other eyes than mine? It was like being haunted. Motionless, with a grave face, he raised his hands slightly at me in a gesture which meant clearly, "Heavens! what a narrow escape!" Narrow indeed. I think I had come creeping quietly as near insanity as any man who has not actually gone over the border. That gesture restrained me, so to speak.

The mate with the terrific whiskers was now putting the ship on the other 220 tack. In the moment of profound silence which follows upon the hands going to their stations I heard on the poop his raised voice: "Hard alee!" and the distant shout of the order repeated on the maindeck. The sails, in that light breeze, made but a faint fluttering noise. It ceased. The ship was coming round slowly; I held my breath in the renewed stillness of expectation; one wouldn't have thought that there was a single living soul on her decks. A sudden brisk shout, "Mainsail haul!" broke the spell, and in the noisy cries and rush overhead of the men running away with the main-brace we two, down in my cabin, came together in our usual position by the bed-place.

He did not wait for my question. "I heard him fumbling here and just man- [221] aged to squat myself down in the path," he whispered to me. "The fellow only opened the door and put his arm in to hang the coat up. All the same——"

"I never thought of that," I whispered back, even more appalled than before [222] at the closeness of the shave, and marvelling at that something unyielding in his character which was carrying him through so finely. There was no agitation in his whisper. Whoever was being driven distracted, it was not he. He was sane. And the proof of his sanity was continued when he took up the whispering again.

"It would never do for me to come to life again." [223]

It was something that a ghost might have said. But what he was alluding to [224] was his old captain's reluctant admission of the theory of suicide. It would obviously serve his turn—if I had understood at all the view which seemed to govern the unalterable purpose of his action.

"You must maroon me as soon as ever you can get amongst these islands [225] off the Cambodge shore," he went on.

"Maroon you! We are not living in a boy's adventure tale," I protested. His [226] scornful whispering took me up.

"We aren't indeed! There's nothing of a boy's tale in this. But there's nothing [227] else for it. I want no more. You don't suppose I am afraid of what can be done to me? Prison or gallows or whatever they may please. But you don't see me coming back to explain such things to an old fellow in a wig and twelve respectable tradesmen, do you? What can they know whether I am guilty or not—or of *what* I am guilty, either? That's my affair. What does the Bible say? 'Driven off the face of the earth.' Very well. I am off the face of the earth now. As I came at night so I shall go."

"Impossible!" I murmured. "You can't. [228]

"Can't? . . . Not naked like a soul on the Day of Judgment. I shall freeze [229] on to this sleeping-suit. The Last Day is not yet—and . . . you have understood thoroughly. Didn't you?"

I felt suddenly ashamed of myself. I may say truly that I understood—and [230] my hesitation in letting that man swim away from my ship's side had been a mere sham sentiment, a sort of cowardice.

"It can't be done now till next night," I breathed out. "The ship is on the off- [231] shore tack and the wind may fail us."

"As long as I know that you understand," he whispered. "But of course you [232] do. It's a great satisfaction to have got somebody to understand. You seem to have been there on purpose." And in the same whisper, as if we two whenever we talked had to say things to each other which were not fit for the world to hear, he added, "It's very wonderful."

We remained side by side talking in our secret way—but sometimes silent ₂₃₃ or just exchanging a whispered word or two at long intervals. And as usual he stared through the port. A breath of wind came now and again into our faces. The ship might have been moored in dock, so gently and on an even keel she slipped through the water, that did not murmur even at our passage, shadowy and silent like a phantom sea.

At midnight I went on deck, and to my mate's great surprise put the ship ₂₃₄ round on the other tack. His terrible whiskers flitted round me in silent criticism. I certainly should not have done it if it had been only a question of getting out of that sleepy gulf as quickly as possible. I believe he told the second mate, who relieved him, that it was a great want of judgment. The other only yawned. That intolerable cub shuffled about so sleepily and lolled against the rails in such a slack, improper fashion that I came down on him sharply.

"Aren't you properly awake yet?"   ₂₃₅

"Yes, sir! I am awake."   ₂₃₆

"Well, then, be good enough to hold yourself as if you were. And keep a ₂₃₇ look-out. If there's any current we'll be closing with some islands before daylight."

The east side of the gulf is fringed with islands, some solitary, others in ₂₃₈ groups. On the blue background of the high coast they seem to float on silvery patches of calm water, arid and grey, or dark green and rounded like clumps of evergreen bushes, with the larger ones, a mile or two long, showing the outlines of ridges, ribs of grey rock under the dank mantle of matted leafage. Unknown to trade, to travel, almost to geography, the manner of life they harbour is an unsolved secret. There must be villages—settlements of fishermen at least—on the largest of them, and some communication with the world is probably kept up by native craft. But all that forenoon, as we headed for them, fanned along by the faintest of breezes, I saw no sign of man or canoe in the field of the telescope I kept on pointing at the scattered group.

At noon I gave no orders for a change of course, and the mate's whiskers ₂₃₉ became much concerned and seemed to be offering themselves unduly to my notice. At last I said:

"I am going to stand right in. Quite in—as far as I can take her."   ₂₄₀

The stare of extreme surprise imparted an air of ferocity also to his eyes, ₂₄₁ and he looked truly terrific for a moment.

"We're not doing well in the middle of the gulf," I continued, casually. "I ₂₄₂ am going to look for the land breezes to-night."

"Bless my soul! Do you mean, sir, in the dark amongst the lot of all them ₂₄₃ islands and reefs and shoals?"

"Well—if there are any regular land breezes at all on this coast one must ₂₄₄ get close inshore to find them, mustn't one?"

"Bless my soul!" he exclaimed again under his breath. All that afternoon he ₂₄₅ wore a dreamy, contemplative appearance which in him was a mark of perplexity. After dinner I went into my stateroom as if I meant to take some rest. There we two bent our dark heads over a half-unrolled chart lying on my bed.

"There," I said. "It's got to be Koh-ring. I've been looking at it ever since 246 sunrise. It has got two hills and a low point. It must be inhabited. And on the coast opposite there is what looks like the mouth of a biggish river—with some town, no doubt, not far up. It's the best chance for you that I can see."

"Anything. Koh-ring let it be."   247

He looked thoughtfully at the chart as if surveying chances and distances 248 from a lofty height—and following with his eyes his own figure wandering on the blank land of Cochin-China, and then passing off that piece of paper clean out of sight into uncharted regions. And it was as if the ship had two captains to plan her course for her. I had been so worried and restless running up and down that I had not had the patience to dress that day. I had remained in my sleeping-suit, with straw slippers and a soft floppy hat. The closeness of the heat in the gulf had been most oppressive, and the crew were used to see me wandering in that airy attire.

"She will clear the south point as she heads now," I whispered into his ear. 249 "Goodness only knows when, though, but certainly after dark. I'll edge her in to half a mile, as far as I may be able to judge in the dark——"

"Be careful," he murmured, warningly—and I realised suddenly that all my 250 future, the only future for which I was fit, would perhaps go irretrievably to pieces in any mishap to my first command.

I could not stop a moment longer in the room. I motioned him to get out of 251 sight and made my way on the poop. That unplayful cub had the watch. I walked up and down for a while thinking things out, then beckoned him over.

"Send a couple of hands to open the two quarter-deck ports," I said, mildly. 252

He actually had the impudence, or else so forgot himself in his wonder at 253 such an incomprehensible order, as to repeat:

"Open the quarter-deck ports! What for, sir?"   254

"The only reason you need concern yourself about is because I tell you to 255 do so. Have them opened wide and fastened properly."

He reddened and went off, but I believe made some jeering remark to the 256 carpenter as to the sensible practice of ventilating a ship's quarter-deck. I know he popped into the mate's cabin to impart the fact to him because the whiskers came on deck, as it were by chance, and stole glances at me from below—for signs of lunacy or drunkenness, I suppose.

A little before supper, feeling more restless than ever, I rejoined, for a 257 moment, my second self. And to find him sitting so quietly was surprising, like something against nature, inhuman.

I developed my plan in a hurried whisper.   258

"I shall stand in as close as I dare and then put her round. I will presently 259 find means to smuggle you out of here into the sail-locker, which communicates with the lobby. But there is an opening, a sort of square for hauling the sails out, which gives straight on the quarter-deck and which is never closed in fine weather, so as to give air to the sails. When the ship's way is deadened in stays and all the hands are aft at the main-braces you will have a clear road to slip out and get overboard through the open quarter-deck port. I've had them both fastened up. Use a rope's end to lower yourself into the water so as to avoid a splash—you know. It could be heard and cause some beastly complication."

He kept silent for a while, then whispered, "I understand." 260

"I won't be there to see you go," I began with an effort. "The rest . . . I only 261 hope I have understood, too."

"You have. From first to last"—and for the first time there seemed to be a fal- 262 tering, something strained in his whisper. He caught hold of my arm, but the ring- ing of the supper bell made me start. He didn't, though; he only released his grip.

After supper I didn't come below again till well past eight o'clock. The 263 faint, steady breeze was loaded with dew; and the wet, darkened sails held all there was of propelling power in it. The night, clear and starry, sparkled darkly, and the opaque, lightless patches shifting slowly against the low stars were the drifting islets. On the port bow there was a big one more distant and shadowily imposing by the great space of sky it eclipsed.

On opening the door I had a back view of my very own self looking at a 264 chart. He had come out of the recess and was standing near the table.

"Quite dark enough," I whispered. 265

He stepped back and learned against my bed with a level, quiet glance. I sat 266 on the couch. We had nothing to say to each other. Over our heads the officer of the watch moved here and there. Then I heard him move quickly. I knew what that meant. He was making for the companion; and presently his voice was outside my door.

"We are drawing in pretty fast, sir. Land looks rather close." 267

"Very well," I answered. "I am coming on deck directly." 268

I waited till he was gone out of the cuddy, then rose. My double moved too. 269 The time had come to exchange our last whispers, for neither of us was ever to hear each other's natural voice.

"Look here!" I opened a drawer and took out three sovereigns. "Take this 270 anyhow. I've got six and I'd give you the lot, only I must keep a little money to buy some fruit and vegetables for the crew from native boats as we go through Sunda Straights."

He shook his head. 271

"Take it," I urged him, whispering desperately. "No one can tell what——" 272

He smiled and slapped meaningly the only pocket of the sleeping-jacket. It 273 was not safe, certainly. But I produced a large old silk handkerchief of mine, and tying the three pieces of gold in a corner, pressed it on him. He was touched, I suppose, because he took it at last and tied it quickly round his waist under the jacket, on his bare skin.

Our eyes met; several seconds elapsed, till, our glances still mingled, I 274 extended my hand and turned the lamp out. Then I passed through the cuddy, leaving the door of my room wide open. . . . "Steward!"

He was still lingering in the pantry in the greatness of his zeal, giving a rub- 275 up to a plated cruet stand the last thing before going to bed. Being careful not to wake up the mate, whose room was opposite, I spoke in an undertone.

He looked round anxiously. "Sir!" 276

"Can you get me a little hot water from the galley?" 277

"I am afraid, sir, the galley fire's been out for some time now." 278

"Go and see." 279

He flew up the stairs.   280

"Now," I whispered, loudly, into the saloon—too loudly, perhaps, but I was 281
afraid I couldn't make a sound. He was by my side in an instant—the double captain slipped past the stairs—through a tiny dark passage . . . a sliding door. We
were in the sail-locker, scrambling on our knees over the sails. A sudden thought
struck me. I saw myself wandering barefooted, bareheaded, the sun beating on
my dark poll. I snatched off my floppy hat and tried hurriedly in the dark to ram
it on my other self. He dodged and fended off silently. I wonder what he thought
had come to me before he understood and suddenly desisted. Our hands met grop-
ingly, lingered united in a steady, motionless clasp for a second. . . . No word
was breathed by either of us when they separated.

I was standing quietly by the pantry door when the steward returned.   282

"Sorry, sir. Kettle barely warm. Shall I light the spirit-lamp?"   283

"Never mind."   284

I came out on deck slowly. It was now a matter of conscience to shave the 285
land as close as possible—for now he must go overboard whenever the ship was
put in stays. Must! There could be no going back for him. After a moment I
walked over to leeward and my heart flew into my mouth at the nearness of the
land on the bow. Under any other circumstances I would not have held on a
minute longer. The second mate had followed me anxiously.

I looked on till I felt I could command my voice.   286

"She will weather," I said then in a quiet tone.   287

"Are you going to try that, sir?" he stammered out incredulously.   288

I took no notice of him and raised my tone just enough to be heard by the 289
helmsman.

"Keep her good full."   290

"Good full, sir."   291

The wind fanned my cheek, the sails slept, the world was silent. The strain 292
of watching the dark loom of the land grow bigger and denser was too much for
me. I had shut my eyes—because the ship must go closer. She must! The stillness
was intolerable. Were we standing still?

When I opened my eyes the second view started my heart with a thump. 293
The black southern hill of Koh-ring seemed to hang right over the ship like a towering fragment of the everlasting night. On that enormous mass of blackness there
was not a gleam to be seen, not a sound to be heard. It was gliding irresistibly
towards us and yet seemed already within reach of the hand. I saw the vague figures of the watch grouped in the waist, gazing in awed silence.

"Are you going on, sir?" inquired an unsteady voice at my elbow.   294

I ignored it. I had to go on.   295

"Keep her full. Don't check her way. That won't do now," I said, warningly. 296

"I can't see the sails very well," the helmsman answered me, in strange, 297
quavering tones.

Was she close enough? Already she was, I won't say in the shadow of the 298
land, but in the very blackness of it, already swallowed up as it were, gone too
close to be recalled, gone from me altogether.

"Give the mate a call," I said to the young man who stood at my elbow as ₂₉₉ still as death. "And turn all hands up."

My tone had a borrowed loudness reverberated from the height of the land. ₃₀₀ Several voices cried out together: "We are all on deck, sir."

Then stillness again, with the great shadow gliding closer, towering higher, ₃₀₁ without a light, without a sound. Such a hush had fallen on the ship that she might have been a bark of the dead floating in slowly under the very gate of Erebus.

"My God! Where are we?" ₃₀₂

It was the mate moaning at my elbow. He was thunderstruck, and as it were ₃₀₃ deprived of the moral support of his whiskers. He clapped his hands and absolutely cried out, "Lost!"

"Be quiet," I said, sternly. ₃₀₄

He lowered his tone, but I saw the shadowy gesture of his despair. "What ₃₀₅ are we doing here?"

"Looking for the land wind." ₃₀₆

He made as if to tear his hair, and addressed me recklessly. ₃₀₇

"She will never get out. You have done it, sir. I knew it'd end in something ₃₀₈ like this. She will never weather, and you are too close now to stay. She'll drift ashore before she's round. O my God!"

I caught his arm as he was raising it to batter his poor devoted head, and ₃₀₉ shook it violently.

"She's ashore already," he wailed, trying to tear himself away. ₃₁₀

"Is she? . . . Keep good full there!" ₃₁₁

"Good full, sir," cried the helmsman in a frightened, thin, childlike voice. ₃₁₂

I hadn't let go the mate's arm and went on shaking it. "Ready about, do you ₃₁₃ hear? You go forward"—shake—"and stop there"—shake—"and hold your noise"—shake—"and see these headsheets properly overhauled"—shake, shake—shake.

And all the time I dared not look towards the land lest my heart should fail ₃₁₄ me. I released my grip at last and he ran forward as if fleeing for dear life.

I wondered what my double there in the sail-locker thought of this com- ₃₁₅ motion. He was able to hear everything—and perhaps he was able to understand why, on my conscience, it had to be thus close—no less. My first order "Hard alee!" re-echoed ominously under the towering shadow of Koh-ring as if I had shouted in a mountain gorge. And then I watched the land intently. In that smooth water and light wind it was impossible to feel the ship coming-to. No! I could not feel her. And my second self was making now ready to slip out and lower himself overboard. Perhaps he was gone already. . . ?

The great black mass brooding over our very mastheads began to pivot ₃₁₆ away from the ship's side silently. And now I forgot the secret stranger ready to depart, and remembered only that I was a total stranger to the ship. I did not know her. Would she do it? How was she to be handled?

I swung the mainyard and waited helplessly. She was perhaps stopped, and ₃₁₇ her very fate hung in the balance, with the black mass of Koh-ring like the gate of the everlasting night towering over her taffrail. What would she do now? Had she way on her yet? I stepped to the side swiftly, and on the shadowy water I could see nothing except a faint phosphorescent flash revealing the glassy smoothness of the sleeping surface. It was impossible to tell—and I had not learned yet the feel of my ship. Was she moving? What I needed was something easily seen, a piece of paper, which I could throw overboard and watch. I had nothing on me. To run down for it I didn't dare. There was no time. All at once my strained, yearning stare distinguished a white object floating within a yard of the ship's side. White on the black water. A phosphorescent flash passed under it. What was that thing? . . . I recognised my own floppy hat. It must have fallen off his head . . . and he didn't bother. Now I had what I wanted—the saving mark for my eyes. But I hardly thought of my other self, now gone from the ship, to be hidden for ever from all friendly faces, to be a fugitive and a vagabond on the earth, with no brand of the curse on his sane forehead to stay a slaying hand . . . too proud to explain.

And I watched the hat—the expression of my sudden pity for his mere 318 flesh. It had been meant to save his homeless head from the dangers of the sun. And now—behold—it was saving the ship, by serving me for a mark to help out the ignorance of my strangeness. Ha! It was drifting forward, warning me just in time that the ship had gathered sternway.

"Shift the helm," I said in a low voice to the seaman standing still like a 319 statue.

The man's eyes glistened wildly in the binnacle light as he jumped round 320 to the other side and spun round the wheel.

I walked to the break of the poop. On the overshadowed deck all hands 321 stood by the forebraces waiting for my order. The stars ahead seemed to be gliding from right to left. And all was so still in the world that I heard the quiet remark, "She's round," passed in a tone of intense relief between two seamen.

"Let go and haul."   322

The foreyards ran round with a great noise, amidst cheery cries. And now 323 the frightful whiskers made themselves heard giving various orders. Already the ship was drawing ahead. And I was alone with her. Nothing! no one in the world should stand now between us, throwing a shadow on the way of silent knowledge and mute affection, the perfect communion of a seaman with his first command.

Walking to the taffrail, I was in time to make out, on the very edge of a 324 darkness thrown by a towering black mass like the very gateway of Erebus—yes, I was in time to catch an evanescent glimpse of my white hat left behind to mark the spot where the secret sharer of my cabin and of my thoughts, as though he were my second self, had lowered himself into the water to take his punishment: a free man, a proud swimmer striking out for a new destiny.

Meaning and Idea

1. Who is the narrator of the story? What is his post on the boat? How does he feel about his responsibilities?

2. Where is the ship at the start of the story? At sea? In port? In what part of the world? Where is it headed?

3. What is the *Sephora?* What is Leggatt's relation to the *Sephora?* What crime has Leggatt committed? How? Why? What is his background?

4. Describe the narrator's room. What shape is it? Of what importance are these details to the story?

5. What does the narrator do at the end of the story? What does Leggatt do? Why does the narrator go along with this?

Language, Form, Structure

1. What is the main point of this story? What comparisons and contrasts does Conrad use to advance his theme? Pay particular attention to the characters and to the setting as you answer this question.

2. Conrad relies on repetitive devices in this story. For example, he repeats the word *stranger* throughout the first few pages. Also, throughout the story, the captain continuously refers to Leggatt as "my double"—or some variation of that description. What is the effect of the repetitions?

3. Find specific references that indicate the sensory reality of Leggatt for the captain. Find specific references to Leggatt's possible "ghostliness." How do the two interpretations of Leggatt compare? Why is it important that throughout the story Leggatt is dressed in the captain's sleeping suit?

4. How does the description in the first paragraph foreshadow the more important comparisons and contrasts to come? What does it tell us about the captain's situation?

5. Interpret the possible meaning of the title "The Secret Sharer." About midway through the story, the captain actually names Leggatt "the secret sharer," yet toward the end he calls Leggatt "the secret stranger." Compare these two descriptions.

6. Select fifteen words from this story with which you were unfamiliar and write dictionary definitions for them. Select your words on this basis: five descriptive words; five nouns; five verbs.

Ideas for Writing

1. Compare two crucial choices that you have made concerning love. Show how the nature, enactment or process, and results of these choices compare.

2. Write a comparison of two very different feelings you have had about yourself at different times in your life. You may want to consider feelings about your personality, your goals, your looks, etc. Which perspective now seems more important to you? Why?

3. The great critical controversy about "The Secret Sharer" is, quite simply, whether or not Leggatt is real. Write an analysis, drawing on specific references to the text, in which you explain your point of view on this matter. You may want to consider whether it is indeed possible to read the story on two levels simultaneously.

The Ruined Maid

Thomas Hardy

Thomas Hardy (1840–1928) was born in Dorset, Wessex, England, and there received a liberal education with a special concentration in Latin and Greek. His father having been a master mason, Hardy chose architecture as his intended profession and moved to London in 1862 to apprentice. He practiced as an architect until 1874, when his first critically acclaimed novel, *Far from the Madding Crowd,* appeared. His four best, and most widely read, novels followed closely: *The Return of the Native* (1878), *The Mayor of Casterbridge* (1886), *Tess of the D'Urbervilles* (1891), and *Jude the Obscure* (1896). Unfortunately, the strongly passionate *Jude* shocked Victorian critical circles, and Hardy's response was to abandon writing novels in favor of composing poetry. He is buried in "Poets' Corner" in Westminster Abbey in London.

In "The Ruined Maid" Hardy uses dialogue to express two views of what, because of moral considerations, is an ambiguous condition. As you finish this poem, consider whether the two speakers' opinions are ultimately more the same or more different.

"*O*'Melia, my dear, this does everything crown!
Who could have supposed I should meet you in Town?
And whence such fair garments, such prosperi-ty"—
"Oh didn't you know I'd been ruined?" said she.

—"You left us in tatters, without shoes or socks,   5
Tired of digging potatoes, and spudding up docks;
And now you've gay bracelets and bright feathers three!"—
"Yes: that's how we dress when we're ruined," said she.

—"At home in the barton you said 'thee' and 'thou,'
And 'thik oon,' and 'theäs oon,' and 't'other'; but now   10
Your talking quite fits 'ee for high compa-ny!"—
"Some polish is gained with one's ruin," said she.

—"Your hands were like paws then, your face blue and bleak
But now I'm bewitched by your delicate cheek,
And your little gloves fit as on any la-dy!"—   15
"We never do work when we're ruined," said she.

—"You used to call home-life a hag-ridden dream,
And you'd sigh, and you'd sock; but at present you seem
To know not of megrims or melancho-ly!"—
"True. One's pretty lively when ruined," said she.   20

—"I wish I had feathers, a fine sweeping gown,
And a delicate face, and could strut about Town!"—
"My dear—a raw country girl, such as you be,
Cannot quite expect that. You ain't ruined," said she.

Meaning and Idea

1. What is the setting for this conversation? Who are the two speakers? What is their relationship?

2. What is the first speaker's attitude toward 'Melia! What is 'Melia's attitude toward the speaker? Where and how do we learn of these attitudes?

3. Why does 'Melia call herself "ruined"? Is she using that term ironically? How do her old and new lives compare? What is Hardy's attitude about her "ruination"? What is his attitude toward the first speaker?

Language, Form, Structure

1. How is comparison an appropriate format for the theme of this poem? Why is dialogue an effective means to support the comparison? What main point does the poem make?

2. What words suggest 'Melia's newfound sophistication? What words suggest that this sophistication is only a veneer?

3. See if you can find meanings for the following words. Use a collegiate-sized dictionary, since several have archaic, specialized, or dialectical meanings: crown; spudding up docks; barton; sock; megrims.

Ideas for Writing

1. Write an imaginary dialogue in which a person "sizes up" an old acquaintance after not seeing him or her for a long time. Be sure to keep a consistent point of view throughout.

2. Write a short essay in which you discuss the friend you've known longest in terms of how he or she has changed since five (more or less) years ago. You should include two specific bases of comparison.

3. In this poem, Hardy expresses a comparison in dialogue. Do you feel that dialogue adequately supports the theme here? Making allowances for the fact that the poem was written over 80 years ago, how realistic do you find the dialogue?

Digging

Seamus Heaney

Seamus Heaney was born in 1939 in County Derry and attended Queen's University in Belfast. He has taught extensively in Ireland and the United States, and currently works at Harvard, where he spends half his time. The rest of the year he is in Belfast. He is both critically acclaimed and well known by the public at large, quite a feat considering his subject matter and his political interests.

His fluid yet muscled style smoothly elaborates the topic at hand without covering it in sticky, overwrought language. Critic Richard Ellman has said Heaney "does not overwhelm his subjects; rather he allows them a certain freedom from him, and his sharp conjunctions with them leave their authority and his undiminished."

*B*etween my finger and my thumb
The squat pen rests; snug as a gun.

Under my window, a clean rasping sound
When the spade sinks into gravelly ground.
My father, digging. I look down   5

Till his straining rump among the flowerbeds
Bends low, comes up twenty years away
Stooping in rhythm through potato drills
Where he was digging.

The coarse boot nestled on the lug, the shaft   10
Against the inside knee was levered firmly.
He rooted out tall tops, buried the bright edge deep
To scatter new potatoes that we picked
Loving their cool hardness in our hands.

By God, the old man could handle a spade.   15
Just like his old man.

My grandfather cut more turf in a day
Than any other man on Toner's bog.
Once I carried him milk in a bottle
Corked sloppily with paper. He straightened up   20
To drink it, then fell to right away

Nicking and slicing neatly, heaving sods

Over his shoulder, going down and down
For the good turf. Digging.

The cold smell of potato mould, the squelch and slap   25
Of soggy peat, the curt cuts of an edge
Through living roots awaken in my head.
But I've no spade to follow men like them.

Between my finger and my thumb
The squat pen rests.   30
I'll dig with it.

Meaning and Idea

1. How many generations does the poem present? Why does the speaker bring in both his grandfather and his father? What does the poet achieve here?

2. What is actually being compared in the poem, other than the three men and what they do? How does the comparison both delight and instruct the reader? In what ways can a pen and a shovel be thought of as related tools? Avoiding the obvious, how are they both similar and different? How is a writer like a digger?

3. Why does the speaker admire his father and his grandfather so? Why does he not follow in their footsteps? What is the meaning of the line "But I've no spade to follow men like them"?

Language, Form, Structure

1. The poet jumps back and forth in time in this short poem. How does he move the reader smoothly from one time frame to another? How do transitions help him achieve the movement? What does narrative structure contribute to the poem?

2. Heaney uses a staccato style of short, direct sentences throughout. How does this stylistic approach help convey the poem's meaning? In what ways does the style duplicate the actual act of digging in the ground?

3. Why does Heaney avoid describing in detail the work of a poet? Although writing poetry may not seem a physical, strenuous act, how does the poet manage to convey its physicality and its validity? Remember that, in fact, the only way we get to see the generations of men here is through the poem itself!

4. What does the simile in the second line, "snug as a gun," contribute to the poem? Why has the poet used such an image—he never again takes up the comparison and what it implies. How is a pen like a gun? And why does the poet twice use the word *squat* to describe the pen?

5. What would you say is the main point of the poem? Write a single sentence to state it.

6. Define the following words and use each in a sentence: squat; lug; bog; sods; squelch; peat; curt.

Ideas for Writing

1. Write a paper in which you compare and contrast the work of a member of your family with your own kind of work.

2. Write an essay in which you compare writing to another physical act. Search for similarities and differences beyond the apparent.

3. Write an essay that evaluates Heaney's use of comparisons and his use of sensory language. Which images do you find most original? most shocking?

Two Diseases

Susan Sontag

Susan Sontag, born in New York City in 1933, is known for her astute writings about contemporary culture. She has continually surprised readers and critics alike with her range of subject and interpretation, which defy any one "label." Her work has taken the form of fiction, essays, and films. Sontag's fiction includes the novels *The Benefactor, Death Kit,* and, most recently, *Volcano Lover,* as well as the short-story collection *I, etcetera.* Her essay collections include *Against Interpretation* (1966), *About Photography* (1977), *Illness as Metaphor* (1978), and *Under the Sign of Saturn* (1980).

In "Two Diseases" (taken from Chapters 1 and 2 of *Illness as Metaphor*) Sontag uses comparison and contrast techniques to challenge the "trappings of metaphor" which have surrounded two of the worst killers of this and the past centuries—cancer and tuberculosis. Pay close attention to the ways in which Sontag uses historical development, allusions, and exemplification.

*T*wo diseases have been spectacularly, and similarly, encumbered by   1
the trappings of metaphor: tuberculosis and cancer.

The fantasies inspired by TB in the last century, by cancer now, are responses   2
to a disease thought to be intractable and capricious—that is, a disease not understood—in an era in which medicine's central premise is that all diseases can be cured. Such a disease is, by definition, mysterious. For as long as its cause was not understood and the ministrations of doctors remained so ineffective, TB was thought to be an insidious, implacable theft of a life. Now it is cancer's turn to be the disease that doesn't knock before it enters, cancer that fills the role of an illness experienced as a ruthless, secret invasion—a role it will keep until, one day, its etiology becomes as clear and its treatment as effective as those of TB have become.

Although the way in which disease mystifies is set against a backdrop of   3
new expectations, the disease itself (once TB, cancer today) arouses thoroughly old-fashioned kinds of dread. Any disease that is treated as a mystery and acutely enough feared will be felt to be morally, if not literally, contagious. Thus, a surprisingly large number of people with cancer find themselves being shunned by relatives and friends and are the object of practices of decontamination by members of their household, as if cancer, like TB, were an infectious disease. Contact with someone afflicted with a disease regarded as a mysterious malevolency inevitably feels like a trespass; worse, like the violation of a taboo. The very names of such diseases are felt to have a magic power. In Stendhal's *Armance* (1827), the hero's mother refuses to say "tuberculosis," for fear that pronouncing the word will hasten the course of her son's malady. And Karl Menninger has observed (in *The Vital Balance*) that "the very word 'cancer' is said to kill some patients who would not have succumbed (so quickly) to the malignancy from which they suffer." This observation is offered in support of anti-intellectual

pieties and a facile compassion all too triumphant in contemporary medicine and psychiatry. "Patients who consult us because of their suffering and their distress and their disability," he continues, "have every right to resent being plastered with a damning index tab." Dr. Menninger recommends that physicians generally abandon "names" and "labels" ("our function is to help these people, not to further afflict them")—which would mean, in effect, increasing secretiveness and medical paternalism. It is not naming as such that is pejorative or damning, but the name "cancer." As long as a particular disease is treated as an evil, invincible predator, not just a disease, most people with cancer will indeed be demoralized by learning what disease they have. The solution is hardly to stop telling cancer patients the truth, but to rectify the conception of the disease, to demythicize it.

When, not so many decades ago, learning that one had TB was tantamount ⁴ to hearing a sentence of death—as today, in the popular imagination, cancer equals death—it was common to conceal the identity of their disease from tuberculars and, after they died, from their children. Even with patients informed about their disease, doctors and family were reluctant to talk freely. "Verbally I don't learn anything definite," Kafka wrote to a friend in April 1924 from the sanatorium where he died two months later, "since in discussing tuberculosis . . . everybody drops into a shy, evasive, glassy-eyed manner of speech." Conventions of concealment with cancer are even more strenuous. In France and Italy it is still the rule for doctors to communicate a cancer diagnosis to the patient's family but not to the patient; doctors consider that the truth will be intolerable to all but exceptionally mature and intelligent patients. (A leading French oncologist has told me that fewer than a tenth of his patients know they have cancer.) In America—in part because of the doctors' fear of malpractice suits—there is now much more candor with patients, but the country's largest cancer hospital mails routine communications and bills to outpatients in envelopes that do not reveal the sender, on the assumption that the illness may be a secret from their families. Since getting cancer can be a scandal that jeopardizes one's love life, one's chance of promotion, even one's job, patients who know what they have tend to be extremely prudish, if not outright secretive, about their disease. And a federal law, the 1966 Freedom of Information Act, cites "treatment for cancer" in a clause exempting from disclosure matters whose disclosure "would be an unwarranted invasion of personal privacy." It is the only disease mentioned.

All this lying to and by cancer patients is a measure of how much harder it ⁵ has become in advanced industrial societies to come to terms with death. As death is now an offensively meaningless event, so that disease widely considered a synonym for death is experienced as something to hide. The policy of equivocating about the nature of their disease with cancer patients reflects the conviction that dying people are best spared the news that they are dying, and that the good death is the sudden one, best of all if it happens while we're unconscious or asleep. Yet the modern denial of death does not explain the extent of the lying and the wish to be lied to; it does not touch the deepest dread. Someone who has had a coronary is at least as likely to die of another one within a few years as someone with cancer is likely to die soon from cancer. But no one thinks of concealing the truth from a cardiac patient: there is nothing shameful about a heart attack. Cancer patients are lied to, not just because the disease is (or is thought to be) a death sentence, but because it is felt to be obscene—in the original meaning of that word: ill-omened, abominable, repugnant to the senses. Cardiac disease implies a weakness, trouble, failure that is mechanical; there is no disgrace, nothing of the taboo that once surrounded people afflicted with TB and still surrounds those who have cancer. The metaphors attached to TB and to cancer imply living processes of a particularly resonant and horrid kind.

Throughout most of their history, the metaphoric uses of TB and cancer crisscross and overlap. The *Oxford English Dictionary* records "consumption" in use as a synonym for pulmonary tuberculosis as early as 1398. (John of Trevisa: "Whan the blode is made thynne, soo folowyth consumpcyon and wastyng.") But the pre-modern understanding of cancer also invokes the notion of consumption. The OED gives as the early figurative definition of cancer: "Anything that frets, corrodes, corrupts, or consumes slowly and secretly." (Thomas Paynell in 1528: "A canker is a melancolye impostume eatynge partes of the bodye.") The earliest literal definition of cancer is a growth, lump, or protuberance, and the disease's name—from the Greek *karkinos* and the Latin *cancer*, both meaning crab—was inspired, according to Galen, by the resemblance of an external tumor's swollen veins to a crab's legs, not, as many people think, because a metastatic disease crawls or creeps like a crab. But etymology indicates that tuberculosis was also once considered a type of abnormal extrusion: the word tuberculosis—from the Latin *tuberculum,* the diminutive of *tuber,* bump, swelling—means a morbid swelling, protuberance, projection, or growth. Rudolf Virchow, who founded the science of cellular pathology in the 1850s, thought of the tubercle as a tumor.

Thus, from late antiquity until quite recently, tuberculosis was— typologically—cancer. And cancer was described, like TB, as a process in which the body was consumed. The modern conceptions of the two diseases could not be set until the advent of cellular pathology. Only with the microscope was it possible to grasp the distinctiveness of cancer, as a type of cellular activity, and to understand that the disease did not always take the form of an external or even palpable tumor. (Before the mid-nineteenth century, nobody could have identified leukemia as a form of cancer.) And it was not possible definitively to separate cancer from TB until after 1882, when tuberculosis was discovered to be a bacterial infection. Such advances in medical thinking enabled the leading metaphors of the two diseases to become truly distinct and, for the most part, contrasting. The modern fantasy about the cancer could then begin to take shape—a fantasy which from the 1920s on would inherit most of the problems dramatized by the fantasies about TB, but with the two diseases and their symptoms conceived in quite different, almost opposing, ways.

TB is understood as a disease of one organ, the lungs, while cancer is understood as a disease that can turn up in any organ and whose outreach is the whole body.

TB is understood as a disease of extreme contrasts: white pallor and red 9
flush, hyperactivity alternating with languidness. The spasmodic course of the
disease is illustrated by what is thought of as the prototypical TB symptom,
coughing. The sufferer is wracked by coughs, then sinks back, recovers breath,
breathes normally; then coughs again. Cancer is a disease of growth (sometimes
visible; more characteristically, inside), of abnormal, ultimately lethal growth that
is measured, incessant, steady. Although there may be periods in which tumor
growth is arrested (remissions), cancer produces no contrasts like the oxymorons
of behavior—febrile activity, passionate resignation—thought to be typical of
TB. The tubercular is pallid some of the time; the pallor of the cancer patient is
unchanging.

TB makes the body transparent. The X-rays, which are the standard diag- 10
nostic tool, permit one, often for the first time, to see one's insides—to become
transparent to oneself. While TB is understood to be, from early on, rich in visible symptoms (progressive emaciation, coughing, languidness, fever), and can be
suddenly and dramatically revealed (the blood on the handkerchief), in cancer the
main symptoms are thought to be, characteristically, invisible—until the last
stage, when it is too late. The disease, often discovered by chance or through a
routine medical checkup, can be far advanced without exhibiting any appreciable
symptoms. One has an opaque body that must be taken to a specialist to find out
if it contains cancer. What the patient cannot perceive, the specialist will determine by analyzing tissues taken from the body. TB patients may see their X-rays
or even possess them: the patients at the sanatorium in *The Magic Mountain* carry
theirs around in their breast pockets. Cancer patients don't look at their biopsies.

TB was—still is—thought to produce spells of euphoria, increased 11
appetite, exacerbated sexual desire. Part of the regimen for patients in *The Magic
Mountain* is a second breakfast, eaten with gusto. Cancer is thought to cripple
vitality, make eating an ordeal, deaden desire. Having TB was imagined to be an
aphrodisiac, and to confer extraordinary powers of seduction. Cancer is considered to be de-sexualizing. But it is characteristic of TB that many of its symptoms
are deceptive—liveliness that comes from enervation, rosy cheeks that look like
a sign of health but come from fever—and an upsurge of vitality may
be a sign of approaching death. (Such gushes of energy will generally be self-
destructive, and may be destructive of others; recall the Old West legend of Doc
Holliday, the tubercular gunfighter released from moral restraints by the ravages
of his disease.) Cancer has only true symptoms.

TB is disintegration, febrilization, dematerialization; it is a disease of 12
liquids—the body turning to phlegm and mucus and sputum and, finally, blood—
and of air, of the need for better air. Cancer is degeneration, the body tissues turning to something hard. Alice James, writing in her journal a year before she died
from cancer in 1892, speaks of "this unholy granite substance in my breast." But
this lump is alive, a fetus with its own will. Novalis, in an entry written around
1798 for his encyclopedia project, defines cancers, along with gangrene, as "full-
fledged *parasites*—they grow, are engendered, engender, have their structure,

secrete, eat." Cancer is a demonic pregnancy. St. Jerome must have been thinking of a cancer when he wrote: "The one there with his swollen belly is pregnant with his own death" (*"Alius tumenti aqualiculo mortem parturit"*). Though the course of both diseases is emaciating, losing weight from TB is understood very differently from losing weight from cancer. In TB the person is "consumed," burned up. In cancer, the patient is "invaded" by alien cells, which multiply, causing an atrophy or blockage of bodily functions. The cancer patient "shrivels" (Alice James's word) or "shrinks" (Wilhelm Reich's word).

TB is a disease of time; it speeds up life, highlights it, spiritualizes it. In both English and French, consumption "gallops." Cancer has stages rather than gaits; it is (eventually) "terminal." Cancer works slowly, insidiously: the standard euphemism in obituaries is that someone has "died after a long illness." Every characterization of cancer describes it as slow, and so it was first used metaphorically. "The word of hem crepith as a kankir," Wyclif wrote in 1382 (translating a phrase in II Timothy 2:17); and among the earliest figurative uses of cancer are as a metaphor for "idleness" and "sloth." Metaphorically, cancer is not so much a disease of time as a disease or pathology of space. Its principal metaphors refer to topography (cancer "spreads" or "proliferates" or is "diffused"; tumors are surgically "excised"), and its most dreaded consequence, short of death, is the mutilation or amputation of part of the body.

TB is often imagined as a disease of poverty and deprivation—of thin garments, thin bodies, unheated rooms, poor hygiene, inadequate food. The poverty may not be as literal as Mimi's garret in *La Bohème*; the tubercular Marguerite Gautier in *La Dame aux camélias* lives in luxury, but inside she is a waif. In contrast, cancer is a disease of middle-class life, a disease associated with affluence, with excess. Rich countries have the highest cancer rates, and the rising incidence of the disease is seen as resulting, in part, from a diet rich in fat and proteins and from the toxic effluvia of the industrial economy that creates affluence. The treatment of TB is identified with the stimulation of appetite, cancer treatment with nausea and the loss of appetite. The undernourished nourishing themselves—alas, to no avail. The overnourished, unable to eat.

The TB patient was thought to be helped, even cured, by a change in environment. There was a notion that TB was a wet disease, a disease of humid and dank cities. The inside of the body became damp ("moisture in the lungs" was a favored locution) and had to be dried out. Doctors advised travel to high, dry places—the mountains, the desert. But no change of surroundings is thought to help the cancer patient. The fight is all inside one's own body. It may be, is increasingly thought to be, something in the environment that has caused the cancer. But once cancer is present, it cannot be reversed or diminished by a move to a better (that is, less carcinogenic) environment.

TB is thought to be relatively painless. Cancer is thought to be, invariably, excruciatingly painful. TB is thought to provide an easy death, while cancer is the spectacularly wretched one. For over a hundred years TB remained the preferred way of giving death a meaning—an edifying, refined disease. Nineteenth-century literature is stocked with descriptions of almost symptomless, unfrightened, beatific deaths from TB, particularly of young people, such as Little Eva in *Uncle Tom's Cabin* and Dombey's son Paul in *Dombey and Son* and Smike in *Nicholas Nickleby,* where Dickens described TB as the "dread disease" which "refines" death.

> if its grosser aspect . . . in which the struggle between soul and body is so gradual, quiet, and solemn, and the result so sure, that day by day, and grain by grain, the mortal part wastes and withers away, so that the spirit grows light and sanguine with its lightening load. . . .

Contrast these ennobling, placid TB deaths with the ignoble, agonizing cancer deaths of Eugene Gant's father in Thomas Wolfe's *Of Time and the River* and of the sister in Bergman's film *Cries and Whispers.* The dying tubercular is pictured as made more beautiful and more soulful; the person dying of cancer is portrayed as robbed of all capacities of self-transcendence, humiliated by fear and agony.

Meaning and Idea

1. What two diseases does the essay explore? How does Sontag characterize each of them?

2. What is Sontag's main point about the relation between the two diseases?

3. How, according to Sontag, have we formed our ideas about the diseases? What do you think she hopes to accomplish with this essay?

4. What does Sontag say about the realities of the relation between social standing or economic condition and the two diseases she is exploring? What does she say about the images we have of these relations? What is the common connection among cancer, death, and dying in our society?

5. What, if anything, can you generalize from this essay to another terrible disease—AIDS, multiple sclerosis, or muscular dystrophy, for example?

Language, Form, Structure

1. As you know, this essay comes from Sontag's book *Illness as Metaphor.* Explain how the title of the book applies to this selection.

2. How does Sontag move back and forth between her two subjects? She uses few transitional expressions, and yet the essay holds together. How do you explain this coherence?

3. Throughout the essay, Sontag uses numerous historical references and literary allusions. Identify a few of them. How are they selected? What is their nature? For what purpose does Sontag include them? Which do you consider more effective, the literary or the statistical allusions?

4. Sontag calls attention to the metaphoric uses of the terms *tuberculosis* and *cancer.* Why?

5. What is the meaning of Sontag's final sentences (after the Dickens quote)? How do they serve as a fitting conclusion?

6. Make a list of any unfamiliar words you find in this essay, and write definitions for them.

Ideas for Writing

1. Write a comparison of the two things that you fear most. Describe how they affect you, and attempt to blend both similarities and differences without losing your focus.

2. Select a social condition (for example, poverty, gentrification, child abuse) about which you have firsthand knowledge or have acquired firsthand experience over the past five to ten years. Compare the manifestations and processes of that condition as it existed five to ten years ago with its present existence. In your essay, make the process of change (or lack of change) clear to your reader.

3. Sontag's essay is very complete, almost encyclopedic. What might that completeness say about her attitude toward the subject? Bear in mind that Sontag herself had recently fought cancer when she wrote this essay. Does that fact color your opinion of this essay? How?

The Allegory of the Cave

Plato

The Greek philosopher Plato (427?–347 B.C.) is considered to be among the greatest of world philosophers and the ancestor of much of modern philosophy. He was a student of Socrates, and his dialogues—including *Phaedo, Symposium,* and *Phaedrus*—are thought to be records of his conversations with Socrates and other students.

"The Allegory of the Cave" comes from the *Republic,* Plato's work about an ideal world. This allegory relies on the traditional Socratic method of a dialectic—that is, a questioning dialogue—aimed at arriving at a general truth, or a Platonic Form (an Ideal Truth). Notice how, through comparison, Plato attempts to make that Ideal a part of the world of "human affairs" as well as of "the upper world."

And now, I said, let me show in a figure how far our nature is 1 enlightened or unenlightened: Behold! human beings living in an underground den, which has a mouth open towards the light and reaching all along the end; here they have been from their childhood, and have their legs and necks chained so that they cannot move, and can only see before them, being prevented by the chains from turning round their heads. Above and behind them a fire is blazing at a distance, and between the fire and the prisoners there is a raised way; and you will see, if you look, a low wall built along the way, like the screen which marionette players have in front of them, over which they show the puppets.

I see. 2

And do you see, I said, men passing along the wall carrying all sorts of ves- 3 sels, and statues and figures of animals made of wood and stone and various materials, which appear over the wall? Some of them are talking, others silent.

You have shown me a strange image, and they are strange prisoners. 4

Like ourselves, I replied; and they see only their own shadows, or the shad- 5 ows of one another, which the fire throws on the opposite wall of the cave?

True, he said; how could they see anything but the shadows if they were 6 never allowed to move their heads?

And of the objects which are being carried in like manner they would only 7 see the shadows?

Yes, he said. 8

And if they were able to converse with one another, would they not suppose 9 that they were naming what was actually before them?

Very true. 10

And suppose further that the prison had an echo which came from the other 11 side, would they not be sure to fancy when one of the passers-by spoke that the voice which they heard came from the passing shadow?

No question, he replied. 12

To them, I said, the truth would be literally nothing but the shadows of the 13 images.

That is certain. 14

And now look again, and see what will naturally follow if the prisoners are 15 released, and disabused of their error. At first, when any of them is liberated and compelled suddenly to stand up and turn his neck round and walk and look towards the light, he will suffer sharp pains; the glare will distress him and he will be unable to see the realities of which in his former state he had seen the shadows; and then conceive some one saying to him, that what he saw before was an illusion, but that now, when he is approaching nearer to being and his eye is turned towards more real existence, he has a clearer vision—what will be his reply? And you may further imagine that his instructor is pointing to the objects as they pass and requiring him to name them—will he not be perplexed? Will he not fancy that the shadows which he formerly saw are truer than the objects which are now shown to him?

Far truer. 16

And if he is compelled to look straight at the light, will he not have a pain 17 in his eyes which will make him turn away to take refuge in the objects of vision which he can see, and which he will conceive to be in reality clearer than the things which are now being shown to him?

True, he said. 18

And suppose once more, that he is reluctantly dragged up a steep and 19 rugged ascent, and held fast until he is forced into the presence of the sun himself, is he not likely to be pained and irritated? When he approaches the light his eyes will be dazzled and he will not be able to see anything at all of what are now called realities.

Not all in a moment, he said. 20

He will require to grow accustomed to the sight of the upper world. And 21 first he will see the shadows best, next the reflections of men and other objects in the water, and then the objects themselves; then he will gaze upon the light of the moon and the stars and the spangled heaven; and he will see the sky and the stars by night better than the sun or the light of the sun by day?

Certainly. 22

Last of all he will be able to see the sun, and not mere reflections of him in 23 the water, but he will see him in his own proper place, and not in another; and he will contemplate him as he is.

Certainly. 24

He will then proceed to argue that this is he who gives the season and the 25 years, and is the guardian of all that is in the visible world, and in a certain way the cause of all things which he and his fellows have been accustomed to behold?

Clearly, he said, he would first see the sun and then reason about him. 26

And when he remembered his old habitation, and the wisdom of the den 27 and his fellow-prisoners, do you not suppose that he would felicitate himself on the change, and pity them?

Certainly, he would. 28

And if they were in the habit of conferring honors among themselves on 29 those who were quickest to observe the passing shadows and to remark which of them went before, and which followed after, and which were together; and who were therefore best able to draw conclusions as to the future, do you think that he would care for such honors and glories, or envy the possessors of them? Would he not say with Homer,

Better to be the poor servant of a poor master,

and to endure anything, rather than their manner?

Yes, he said, I think that he would rather suffer anything than entertain these 30 false notions and live in this miserable manner.

Imagine once more, I said, such an one coming suddenly out of the sun to 31 be replaced in his old situation; would he not be certain to have his eyes full of darkness?

To be sure, he said. 32

And if there were a contest, and he had to compete in measuring the shad- 33 ows with the prisoners who had never moved out of the den, while his sight was still weak, and before his eyes had become steady (and the time which would be needed to acquire this new habit of sight might be very considerable) would he not be ridiculous? Men would say to him that up he went and down he came with- out his eyes; and that it was better not even to think of ascending; and if any one tried to loose another and lead him up to the light, let them only catch the offender, and they would put him to death.

No question, he said. 34

This entire allegory, I said, you may now append, dear Glaucon, to the pre- 35 vious argument; the prison-house is the world of sight, the light of fire is the sun, and you will not misapprehend me if you interpret the journey upwards to be the ascent of the soul into the intellectual world according to my poor belief, which, at your desire, I have expressed—whether rightly or wrongly God knows. But, whether true or false, my opinion is that in the world of knowledge the idea of good appears last of all, and is seen only with an effort; and, when seen, is also inferred to be the universal author of all things beautiful and right, parent of light and of the lord of light in this visible world, and the immediate source of reason and truth in the intellectual; and that this is the power upon which he who would act rationally either in public or private life must have his eye fixed.

I agree, he said, as far as I am able to understand you. 36

Moreover, I said, you must not wonder that those who attain to this beatific 37 vision are unwilling to descend to human affairs; for their souls are ever hasten- ing into the upper world where they desire to dwell; which desire of theirs is very natural, if our allegory may be trusted.

Yes, very natural. 38

And is there anything surprising in one who passes from divine contempla- 39 tions to the evil state of man, misbehaving himself in a ridiculous manner; if, while his eyes are blinking and before he has become accustomed to the sur- rounding darkness, he is compelled to fight in courts of law, or in other places, about the images or the shadows of images of justice, and is endeavouring to meet the conceptions of those who have never yet seen absolute justice?

Anything but surprising, he replied.   40

Any one who has common sense will remember that the bewilderments of   41
the eyes are of two kinds, and arise from two causes, either from coming out of the light or from going into the light, which is true of the mind's eye, quite as much as of the bodily eye; and he who remembers this when he sees any one whose vision is perplexed and weak, will not be too ready to laugh; he will first ask whether that soul of man has come out of the brighter life, and is unable to see because unaccustomed to the dark, or having turned from darkness to the day is dazzled by excess of light. And he will count the one happy in his condition and state of being, and he will pity the other; or, if he have a mind to laugh at the soul which comes from below into the light, there will be more reason in this than in the laugh which greets him who returns from above out of the light into the den.

That, he said, is a very just distinction.   42

Meaning and Idea

1. Who is speaking to whom in this selection? What are they talking about? Do the two speakers maintain similar or dissimilar opinions?

2. Describe the conditions and activities of the prisoners in the cave. What is the contrast in perceptions of things between remaining prisoners and newly released ones? Between prisoners and those who have been outside the cave for a while? Compare the attitude of a prisoner toward his fellow prisoners before and after leaving the cave.

3. How, according to Plato, does someone learn truth?

4. Toward the end of this allegory, with what are the two realms compared or contrasted? How does Plato compare the process of coming out of the light to going into the light? Which does he feel is preferable? Why?

Language, Form, Structure

1. Plato makes use of *allegory* in this selection. What is an allegory? How is this dialogue allegorical?

2. In what ways does Plato use process analysis here? Briefly outline the processes described. Which is, overall, the most important process?

3. Look up the meanings of the following words: enlightened; glare; perplexed; ascent; dazzled; felicitate; append; misapprehend; rationally; endeavoring.

Ideas for Writing

1. Write a dialogue in which two speakers argue opposing sides of an issue. Write only in dialogue, with no authorial commentary or analysis.

2. Choose an abstract concept and write a comparison essay in which you explore two points of view concerning that abstraction.

3. How effective is the allegory in helping Plato make his point? Write an analysis in which you draw on specific references to the text.

My Mistress' Eyes Are Nothing Like the Sun

William Shakespeare

The world's most acknowledged literary figure is William Shakespeare (1564–1616). Born in Stratford-on-Avon, England, on April 26, 1564, he never attended university and was, by his own admission, a poor and unmotivated student. After moving to London with his wife Ann Hathaway, Shakespeare became involved as a dramatist and actor with the Globe Theatre there and was extremely popular in his day. He was somewhat careless with the manuscripts of his now invaluable plays and sonnets. In fact, if not for the efforts of his friends, we might not today have many of his masterpieces, which include, of course, *Hamlet, Macbeth, King Lear, Othello, The Comedy of Errors, The Merchant of Venice, Romeo and Juliet,* and *The Tempest*—the list goes on and on! Shakespeare returned to Stratford-on-Avon at the age of 50 and died there two years later.

In this love sonnet, Shakespeare uses comparison in such a way that we might at first think of it as a "hate sonnet." Notice how he begins to change course in lines 11–12, then makes his purpose clear in lines 13–14.

*M*y mistress' eyes are nothing like the sun;
Coral is far more red than her lips' red:
If snow be white, why then her breasts are dun;
If hairs be wires, black wires grow on her head.
I have seen roses damasked, red and white,   5

But no such roses see I in her cheeks;
And in some perfumes is there more delight
Than in the breath that from my mistress reeks.
I love to hear her speak, yet well I know
That music hath a far more pleasing sound: 10
I grant I never saw a goddess go,—
My mistress, when she walks, treads on the ground.
   And yet, by heaven, I think my love as rare
   As any she belied with false compare.

Meaning and Idea

1. Who is the speaker of the poem? To whom is he speaking?

2. About whom does the speaker speak? What qualities does he stress about that person?

Language, Form, Structure

1. In this sonnet does Shakespeare rely primarily on similarities or on differences? How does the speaker arrange his descriptive comparisons of his mistress? What is the nature of most of the comparisons?

2. What do the last two lines of the sonnet say about Shakespeare's reasoning in the poem? For what purpose did he use the comparisons which preceded the last two lines?

3. How does Shakespeare use negatives to make what is ultimately a highly positive statement?

4. To learn the meanings of some of the following words, it may be necessary to consult a dictionary such as the *Oxford English Dictionary,* since many of the meanings are archaic: dun; damasked; reeks; grant; belied.

Ideas for Writing

1. Write a description of some person you like very much, but develop your description using negative comparisons of that person's features to other objects. Be sure that at the end of the description, your real purpose is clear.

2. In a paragraph, describe the ugliest person you know (either physically or emotionally ugly). Then, in another paragraph, describe that same person through the eyes of someone who loves him or her.

3. Some commentators on this poem have suggested that Shakespeare wrote the sonnet not to his mistress, but with a more metaphoric idea in mind. Write a piece in which you explore another meaning or value of the poem. Support your response with specific analyses of references in the poem.

Fire and Ice

Robert Frost

Although Robert Frost is well known as a New England poet, he was in fact born in San Francisco in 1874. After a brief stay in England (1912–1914), where he first gained fame as a poet, Frost settled in New Hampshire, where he lived most of his days, until his death in 1963. Frost the poet is sometimes deceptively simple; underlying his dramatic accounts of the New England people and landscape, there is often deep symbolism and lyricism. His collected poems were published posthumously in 1967; he received four Pulitzer Prizes for poetry, in 1924, 1931, 1937, and 1943.

In this short, almost deceptively singsong poem, Robert Frost compares two notions of the way the world will end.

Some say the world will end in fire,
Some say in ice.
From what I've tasted of desire
I hold with those who favor fire.
But if it had to perish twice,   5
I think I know enough of hate
To say that for destruction ice
Is also great
And would suffice.

Meaning and Idea

1. Who, literally, are those who "say the world will end in fire"? Who are those who say "in ice"? Which group does Frost favor? Why?

2. What impossible occurrence does the poet describe? Why?

3. State, in a single sentence, Frost's meaning in this poem.

Language, Form, Structure

1. Refer back to your answer to question 1 in the Meaning and Idea section above. Then, state how Frost uses the two groups to symbolize other things. Explain this symbolic meaning.

2. This poem is quite sparse, yet Frost implicitly creates very graphic images. Describe them and explain how he creates them.

3. What special meanings does Frost employ when he writes "tasted" and "hold with"?

Ideas for Writing

1. What do you consider the most negative social trend among your peers? Write an essay in which you compare two ways in which this trend manifests itself.

2. Write a paragraph in which you compare two methods of doing something creative—either a natural process (such as growing sprouts) or an abstract process (such as writing a poem).

3. The Bauhaus school of design is famous for its edict: "Less is more." Write a short essay in which you respond to Frost's poem within the context of the Bauhaus statement.

A Comparison

Sylvia Plath

Sylvia Plath (1932–1963) was born in Boston to well-educated immigrant parents. She graduated from Smith College and took a master's degree at Cambridge University on a Fulbright scholarship. She was a melancholy person, as reflected in her poetry collections, such as *The Collossus* (1960), *Ariel* (1965), and *Winter Trees* (1972). She was married to the British poet Ted Hughes, with whom she lived in England and the United States. Her autobiographical novel *The Bell-Jar* (1963) records her emotional ups and down, which culminated finally in her suicide at the age of 30.

This essay, written just a year before Plath's suicide, playfully compares the life and art of novelists and poets. Notice how she fully details the difficulties of each, and comes out clearly on the side of her first love.

*H*ow I envy the novelist! I imagine him—better say her, for it is the 1
women I look to for . . . a parallel—I imagine her, then, pruning a rosebush with
a large pair of shears, adjusting her spectacles, shuffling about among the teacups,
humming, arranging ashtrays or babies, absorbing a slant of light, a fresh edge to
the weather, and piercing, with a kind of modest, beautiful X-ray vision, the psychic interiors of her neighbors—her neighbors on trains, in the dentist's waiting
room, in the corner teashop. To her, this fortunate one, what is there that *isn't* relevant! Old shoes can be used, doorknobs, air letters, flannel nightgowns, cathe-
drals, nail varnish, jet planes, rose arbors and budgerigars; little mannerisms—the
sucking at a tooth, the tugging at a hemline—any weird or warty or fine or despicable thing. Not to mention emotions, motivations—those rumbling, thunderous
shapes. Her business is time, the way it shoots forward, shunts back, blooms,
decays and double-exposes itself. Her business is people in Time. And she, it
seems to me, has all the time in the world. She can take a century if she likes, a
generation, a whole summer.

I can take about a minute. 2

I'm not talking about epic poems. We all know how long *they* can take. I'm 3
talking about the smallish, unofficial garden-variety poem. How shall I describe
it?—a door opens, a door shuts. In between you have had a glimpse: a garden, a
person, a rainstorm, a dragonfly, a heart, a city. I think of those round glass Victorian paperweights which I remember, yet can never find—a far cry from the
plastic mass-productions which stud the toy counters in Woolworth's. This sort of
paperweight is a clear globe, self-complete, very pure, with a forest or village or
family group within it. You turn it upside down, then back. It snows. Everything
is changed in a minute. It will never be the same in there—not the fir trees, nor
the gables, nor the faces.

So a poem takes place. 4

And there is really so little room! So little time! The poet becomes an expert 5
packer of suitcases:

> The apparition of these faces in the crowd;
> Petals on a wet black bough.

There it is: the beginning and the end in one breath. How would the novel- 6
ist manage that? In a paragraph? In a page? Mixing it, perhaps, like paint, with a
little water, thinning it, spreading it out.

Now I am being smug, I am finding advantages. 7

If a poem is concentrated, a closed fist, then a novel is relaxed and expan- 8
sive, an open hand: it has roads, detours, destinations; a heart line, a head line;
morals and money come into it. Where the first excludes and stuns, the open hand
can touch and encompass a great deal in its travels.

I have never put a toothbrush in a poem. 9

I do not like to think of all the things, familiar, useful and worthy things, I 10
have never put into a poem. I did, once, put a yew tree in. And that yew tree
began, with astounding egotism, to manage and order the whole affair. It was not
a yew tree by a church on a road past a house in a town where a certain woman
lived . . . and so on, as it might have been in a novel. Oh, no. It stood squarely
in the middle of my poem, manipulating its dark shades, the voices in the church-
yard, the clouds, the birds, the tender melancholy with which I contemplated it—
everything! I couldn't subdue it. And, in the end, my poem was a poem about a
yew tree. That yew tree was just too proud to be a passing black mark in a novel.

Perhaps I shall anger some poets by implying that the *poem* is proud. The 11
poem, too, can include everything, they will tell me. And with far more precision
and power than those baggy, disheveled and undiscriminate creatures we call novels. Well, I concede these poets their steamshovels and old trousers. I really *don't*
think poems should be all that chaste. I would, I think, even concede a toothbrush,
if the poem was a real one. But these apparitions, these poetical toothbrushes, are
rare. And when they do arrive, they are inclined, like my obstreperous yew tree,
to think themselves singled out and rather special.

Not so in novels. 12

There the toothbrush returns to its rack with beautiful promptitude and is 13
forgot. Time flows, eddies, meanders, and people have leisure to grow and alter
before our eyes. The rich junk of life bobs all about us: bureaus, thimbles, cats,
the whole much-loved, well-thumbed catalog of the miscellaneous which the
novelist wishes us to share. I do not mean that there is no pattern, no discernment,
no rigorous ordering here.

I am only suggesting that perhaps the pattern does not insist so much. 14

The door of the novel, like the door of the poem, also shuts. 15

But not so fast, nor with such manic, unanswerable finality. 16

Meaning and Idea

1. Why does Plath choose to make her imaginary novelist a woman? How does that make her comparison more relevant and genuine?

2. What does Plath mean by "the smallish, unofficial garden-variety poem"? To what does she compare it? Why does she call it "unofficial"?

3. Summarize briefly how Plath contrasts the process of poetry writing with the process of novel writing. Are they more alike or more different?

4. What is the significance of the "toothbrush" mentioned frequently throughout Plath's essay? Explain the line, in terms of the comparison, "I have not put a toothbrush in a poem."

5. Whom do you think Plath intended as an audience for this essay?

Language, Form, Structure

1. What organizational techniques does Plath use to compare her likes and dislikes for poems versus novels? What transitions help move the essay along smoothly?

2. Explain how Plath uses a single-sentence paragraph ("I can take about a minute.") to balance a richly detailed paragraph such as the one which precedes it.

3. The two lines quoted in paragraph 5 constitute a complete, famous imagist poem by Ezra Pound called "In a Station of the Metro." How does Plath use it to support her poem-novel comparison?

4. How does Plath use the poetic technique of *personification* in this essay? How does personification support process analysis in the essay? What other techniques of poetry does she use?

5. Identify the following words from the essay: budgerigars; mannerisms; despicable; egotism; chaste; concede; obstreperous; promptitude; meanders; discernment; manic.

Ideas for Writing

1. Select a poem and a work of fiction that deal with similar themes or subjects. Write a brief essay to compare them. In your conclusion, indicate which you like better and why.

2. Select an activity you enjoy and compare it to another activity in the same category; for example, playing soccer versus playing football (sports); growing flowers versus growing vegetables (gardening); fixing cars versus fixing televisions (mechanical repair).

3. Plath was almost exclusively a poet, although she is perhaps most widely known for her autobiographical novel *The Bell-Jar*. Identify what you see as poetic elements in "A Comparison." What evidences do you find of a poet behind the prose in this essay?

A Slow Walk of Trees

Toni Morrison

Toni Morrison, an editor at Random House and a much admired novelist, was born near Cleveland in 1931. In 1953 she received her B.A. from Howard University, and in 1955 she earned her M.A. at Cornell. Her novels focus on the black experience, historical and modern, using a unique blend of historical fact and personal mythos. She has also written or edited several works of nonfiction. In 1993 she won the Nobel Prize for literature.

In this essay, Morrison shows that Grandmother Ardelia Willis had one set of beliefs, grandfather John Solomon Willis another. This contrast between Morrison's forebears helped formulate her views on the historical and modern-day fortunes and misfortunes of black people in America. Notice how the author keeps offering yet "another slant" on this issue.

*H*is name was John Solomon Willis, and when at age 5 he heard   1
from the old folks that "the Emancipation Proclamation was coming," he crawled under the bed. It was his earliest recollection of what was to be his habitual response to the promises of white people: horror and an instinctive yearning for safety. He was my grandfather, a musician who managed to hold on to his violin but not his land. He lost all 88 acres of his Indian mother's inheritance to legal predators who built their fortunes on the likes of him. He was an unreconstructed black pessimist who, in spite of or because of emancipation, was convinced for 85 years that there was no hope whatever for black people in this country. His rancor was legitimate, for he, John Solomon, was not only an artist but a first-rate carpenter and farmer, reduced to sending home to his family money he made playing the violin because he was not able to find work. And this during the years when almost half the black male population were skilled craftsmen who lost their jobs to white ex-convicts and immigrant farmers.

His wife, however, was of a quite different frame of mind and believed that   2
all things could be improved by faith in Jesus and an effort of the will. So it was she, Ardelia Willis, who sneaked her seven children out of the back window into the darkness, rather than permit the patron of their sharecropper's existence to become their executioner as well, and headed north in 1912, when 99.2 percent of all black people in the U.S. were native-born and only 60 percent of white Americans were. And it was Ardelia who told her husband that they could not stay in the Kentucky town they ended up in because the teacher didn't know long division.

They have been dead now for 30 years and more and I still don't know   3
which of them came closer to the truth about the possibilities of life for black people in this country. One of their grandchildren is a tenured professor at Princeton. Another, who suffered from what the Peruvian poet called "anger that breaks a man into children," was picked up just as he entered his teens and emotionally

lobotomized by the reformatories and mental institutions specifically designed to serve him. Neither John Solomon nor Ardelia lived long enough to despair over one or swell with pride over the other. But if they were alive today each would have selected and collected enough evidence to support the accuracy of the other's original point of view. And it would be difficult to convince either one that the other was right.

Some of the monstrous events that took place in John Solomon's America   4 have been duplicated in alarming detail in my own America. There was the public murder of a President in a theater in 1865 and the public murder of another President on television in 1963. The Civil War of 1861 had its encore as the civil-rights movement of 1960. The torture and mutilation of a black West Point Cadet (Cadet Johnson Whittaker) in 1880 had its rerun with the 1970's murders of students at Jackson State College, Texas Southern and Southern University in Baton Rouge. And in 1976 we watch for what must be the thousandth time a pitched battle between the children of slaves and the children of immigrants—only this time, it is not the New York draft riots of 1863, but the busing turmoil in Paul Revere's home town, Boston.

Hopeless, he's said. Hopeless. For he was certain that white people of every   5 political, religious, geographical and economic background would band together against black people everywhere when they felt the threat of our progress. And a hundred years after he sought safety from the white man's "promise," somebody put a bullet in Martin Luther King's brain. And not long before that some excellent samples of the master race demonstrated their courage and virility by dynamiting some little black girls to death. If he were here now, my grandfather, he would shake his head, close his eyes and pull out his violin—too polite to say, "I told you so." And his wife would pay attention to the music but not to the sadness in her husband's eyes, for she would see what she expected to see—not the occasional historical repetition, but, *like the slow walk of certain species of trees from the flatlands up into the mountains,* she would see the signs of irrevocable and permanent change. She, who pulled her girls out of an inadequate school in the Cumberland Mountains, knew all along that the gentlemen from Alabama who had killed the little girls would be rounded up. And it wouldn't surprise her in the least to know that the number of black college graduates jumped 12 percent in the last three years; 47 percent in 20 years. That there are 140 black mayors in this country; 14 black judges in the District Circuit, 4 in the Courts of Appeals and one on the Supreme Court. That there are 17 blacks in Congress, one in the Senate; 276 in state legislatures—223 in state houses, 53 in state senates. That there are 112 elected black police chiefs and sheriffs, 1 Pulitzer Prize winner; 1 winner of the Prix de Rome; a dozen or so winners of the Guggenheim; 4 deans of predominently white colleges. . . . Oh, her list would go on and on. But so would John Solomon's sweet sad music.

While my grandparents held opposite views on whether the fortunes of black   6 people were improving, my own parents struck similarly opposed postures, but from another slant. They differed about whether the moral fiber of white people would ever improve. Quite a different argument. The old folks argued about how and if black people could improve themselves, who could be counted on to help us, who would hinder us and so on. My parents took issue over the question of whether it was possible for white people to improve. They assumed that black people were the humans of the globe, but had serious doubts about the quality and existence of white humanity. Thus my father, distrusting every word and every gesture of every white man on earth, assumed that the white man who crept up the stairs one afternoon had come to molest his daughters and threw him down the stairs and then our tricycle after him. (I think my father was wrong, but considering what I have seen since, it may have been very healthy for me to have witnessed that as my first black-white encounter.) My mother, however, *believed* in them— their possibilities. So when the meal we got on relief was bug-ridden, she wrote a long letter to Franklin Delano Roosevelt. And when white bill collectors came to our door, it was she who received them civilly and explained in a sweet voice that we were people of honor and that the debt would be taken care of. Her message to Roosevelt got through—our meal improved. Her message to the bill collectors did not always get through and there was occasional violence when my father (self-exiled to the bedroom for fear he could not hold his temper) would hear that her reasonableness had failed. My mother was always wounded by these scenes, for she thought the bill collector knew that she loved good credit more than life and that being in arrears on a payment horrified her probably more than it did him. So she thought he was rude because he was white. For years she walked to utility companies and department stores to pay bills in person and even now she does not seem convinced that checks are legal tender. My father loved excellence, worked hard (he held three jobs at once for 17 years) and was so outraged by the suggestion of personal slackness that he could explain it to himself only in terms of racism. He was a fastidious worker who was frightened of one thing: unemployment. I can remember now the doomsday-cum-graveyard sound of "laid off" and how the minute school was out he asked us, "Where you workin'?" Both my parents believed that all succor and aid came from themselves and their neighborhood, since "they"—white people in charge and those not in charge but in obstructionist positions—were in some way fundamentally, genetically corrupt.

So I grew up in a basically racist household with more than a child's share [7] of contempt for white people. And for each white friend I acquired who made a small crack in that contempt, there was another who repaired it. For each one who related to me as a person, there was one who in my presence at least, became actively "white." And like most black people of my generation, I suffer from racial vertigo that can be cured only by taking what one needs from one's ancestors. John Solomon's cynicism and his deployment of his art as both weapon and solace, Ardelia's faith in the magic that can be wrought by sheer effort of the will; my mother's openmindedness in each new encounter and her habit of trying reasonableness first; my father's temper, his impatience and his efforts to keep "them" (throw them) out of his life. And it is out of these learned and selected attitudes that I look at the quality of life for my people in this country now. These widely disparate and sometimes conflicting views, I suspect, were held not only by me, but by most black people. Some I know are clearer in their positions, have not sullied their anger with optimism or dirtied their hope with despair. But most of us are plagued by a sense of being worn shell-thin by constant repression and hostility as well as the impression of being buoyed by visible testimony of tremendous strides. There *is* repetition of the grotesque in our history. And there *is* the miraculous walk of trees. The question is whether our walk is progress or merely movement. O.J. Simpson leaning on a Hertz car *is* better than the Gold Dust Twins on the back of a soap box. But is "Good Times" better than Stepin Fetchit? Has the first order of business been taken care of? Does the law of the land work for us?

Are white people who murder black people punished with at least the same 8 dispatch that sends black teen-age truants to Coxsackie? Can we relax now and discuss "The Jeffersons" instead of genocide? Or is the difference between the two only the difference between a greedy pointless white life-style and a messy pointless black death? Now that Mr. Poitier and Mr. Belafonte have shot up all the racists in "Buck and the Preacher," have they all gone away? Can we really move into better neighborhoods and not be set on fire? Is there anybody who will lay me a $5 bet on it?

The past decade is a fairly good index of the odds at which you lay your 9 money down.

Ten years ago in Queens, as black people like me moved into a neighbor- 10 hood 20 minutes away from the Triborough Bridge, "for sale" signs shot up in front of white folks' houses like dandelions after a hot spring rain. And the black people smiled. "Goody, goody," said my neighbor. "Maybe we can push them on out to the sea. You think?"

Now I live in another neighborhood, 20 minutes away from the George 11 Washington Bridge, and again the "for sale" signs are pushing up out of the ground. Fewer, perhaps, and for different reasons, perhaps. Still the Haitian lady and I smile at each other. "My, my," she says "they goin' on up to the hills? Seem like they just come from there." "The woods," I say. "They like to live in the woods." She nods with infinite understanding, then shrugs. The Haitians have already arranged for one mass in the church to be said in French, already have their own newspaper, stores, community center. That's not movement. That's progress.

But the decade has other revelations. Ten years ago, young, bright, ener- 12 getic blacks were sought out, pursued and hired into major corporations, major networks, and onto the staffs of newspapers and national magazines. *Many survived that courtship, some even with their souls intact.* Newscasters, corporate lawyers, marketing specialists, journalists, production managers, plant foremen, college deans. But many more spend a lot of time on the telephone these days, or at the typewriter preparing résumés, which they send out (mostly to friends now) with little notes attached: "Is there anything you know of?" Or they think there is a good book in the story of what happened to them, the great hoax that was played on them. They are right, of course, about the hoax, for many of them were given elegant executive jobs with the work drained out. Work minus power. Work minus decision-making. Work minus dominion. Affirmative Action Make Believe that a lot of black people *did* believe because they also believed that the white people in those nice offices were not like the ones in the general store or in the plumbers' union—that they were fundamentally kind, or fair, or something. Anything but the desperate prisoners of economics they turned out to be, holding on to their dominion with a tenacity and sang-froid that can only be described as Nixonian. So the bright and the black (architects, reporters, vice-presidents in charge of public relations) walk the streets right along with that astounding 38 percent of the black teen-aged female work force that does not have and never has had a job. So the black female college graduate earns two-thirds of what a white male high-school dropout earns. So the black people who put everything into community-action programs supported by Government funds have found themselves bereft of action bereft of funds and all but bereft of community.

This decade has been rife with disappointment in practically every place 13 where we thought we saw permanent change: Hostos, CUNY, and the black-studies departments that erupted like minivolcanoes on campuses all over the nation; easy integrations of public-school systems; acceleration of promotion in factories and businesses. But now when we describe what has happened we cannot do it without using the verbs of upheaval and destruction: Open admission *closes;* minority-student quotas *fall* or *discontinue;* salary gaps between blacks and whites *widen;* black-studies departments *merge.* And the only growth black people can count on is in the prison population and the unemployment line. Even busing, which used to be a plain, if emotional, term at best, has now taken on an adjective normally reserved for rape and burglary—it is now called "forced" busing.

All of that counts, but I'm not sure that in the long haul it matters. Maybe 14 Ardelia Willis had the best idea. One sees signs of her vision and the fruits of her prophecy in spite of the dread-lock statistics. The trees *are* walking, albeit slowly and quietly and without the fanfare of a cross-country run. It seems that at last black people have abandoned our foolish dependency on the Government to do the work that we once thought all of its citizenry would be delighted to do. Our love affair with the Federal Government is over. We misjudged the ardor of its attention. We thought its majority constituency would *prefer* having their children grow up among happy, progressive, industrious, contented black children rather than among angry, disenchanted and dangerous ones. That the profit motive of industry alone would keep us employed and therefore spending, and that our poverty was bad for business. We thought landlords wanted us to have a share in our neighborhoods and therefore love and care for them. That city governments wanted us to control our schools and therefore preserve them.

We were wrong. And now, having been eliminated from the lists of urgent 15 national priorities, from TV documentaries and the platitudes of editorials, black people have chosen, or been forced to seek safety from the white man's promise, but happily not under a bed. More and more there is the return to Ardelia's ways: the exercise of the will, the recognition of obstacles as only that—obstacles, not fixed stars. Black judges are fixing appropriate rather than punitive bail for black "offenders" and letting the rest of the community of jurisprudence scream. Young black women are leaving plush Northern jobs to sit in their living rooms and teach black children, work among factory women and spend months finding money to finance the college education of young blacks. Groups of blacks are buying huge tracts of land in the South and cutting off entirely the dependency of whole communities on grocery chains. For the first time, significant numbers of black people are returning or migrating to the South to focus on the acquisition of land, the transferral of crafts and skills, and the sharing of resources, the rebuilding of neighborhoods.

In the shambles of closing admissions, falling quotas, widening salary gaps and merging black-studies departments, builders and healers are working quietly among us. They are not like the heroes of old, the leaders we followed blindly and upon whom we depended for everything, or the blacks who had accumulated wealth for its own sake, fame, medals or some public acknowledgment of success. These are the people whose work is real and pointed and clear in its application to the race. Some are old and have been at work for a long time in and out of the public eye. Some are new and just finding out what their work is. But they are unmistakably the natural aristocrats of the race. The ones who refuse to imitate, to compromise, and who are indifferent to public accolade. Whose work is free or priceless. They take huge risks economically and personally. They are not always popular, even among black people, but they are the ones whose work black people respect. They are the healers. Some are nowhere near the public eye: Ben Chavis, preacher and political activist languishing now in North Carolina prisons; Robert Moses, a pioneering activist; Sterling Brown, poet and teacher; Father Al McKnight, land reformer; Rudy Lombard, urban sociologist; Lerone Bennett, historian; C.L.R. James, scholar; Alyce Gullattee, psychologist and organizer. Others are public legends: Judge Crockett, Judge Bruce Wright, Stevie Wonder, Ishmael Reed, Miles Davis, Richard Pryor, Muhammad Ali, Fannie Lou Hamer, Eubie Blake, Angela Davis, Bill Russell. . . .

But a complete roll-call is neither fitting nor necessary. They know who they are and so do we. They clarify our past, make livable our present and are certain to shape our future. And since the future is where our immortality as a race lies, no overview of the state of black people at this time can ignore some speculation on the only ones certain to live it—the children.

They are both exhilarating and frightening, those black children, and a source of wonderment to me. Although statistics about black teen-age crime and the "failure" of the courts to gut them are regularly printed and regularly received with outrage and fear, the children I know and see, those born after 1960, do not make such great copy. They are those who have grown up with nothing to prove to white people, whose perceptions of themselves are so new, so different, so focused they appear to me to be either magnificent hybrids or throwbacks to the time when our ancestors were called "royal." They are the baby sisters of the sit-in generation, the sons of the neighborhood blockbusters, the nephews of jailed revolutionaries, and a huge number who have had college graduates in their families for three and four generations. I though we had left them nothing to love and nothing to want to know. I thought that those who exhibited some excitement about their future had long ago looked into the eyes of their teachers and were either saddened or outraged by the death of possibility they found there. I thought that those who were interested in the past had looked into the faces of their parents and seen betrayal. I thought the state had deprived them of a land and the landlords and banks had deprived them of a turf. So how is it that, with nothing to love, nothing they need to know, landless, turfless, minus a future and a past, these black children look us dead in the eye? They seem not to know how to apologize. And even when they are wrong they do not ask for forgiveness. It is as though they are waiting for us to apologize to them, to beg their pardon, to seek their approval. What species of black is this that not only does not choose to grovel, but doesn't know how? How will they keep jobs? How will they live? Won't they be killed before they reproduce? But they are unafraid. Is it because they refuse to see the world as we did? Is it because they have rejected both land and turf to seek instead a world? Maybe they finally got the message that we had been shouting into their faces; that they *live* here, *belong* here on this planet earth and that it is *theirs*. So they watch us with the eyes of poets and carpenters and musicians and scholars and other people who know who they are because they have invented themselves and know where they are going because they have envisioned it. All of which would please Ardelia—and John Solomon, too, I think. After all, he did hold on to his violin.

Meaning and Idea

1. Summarize the grandfather's thinking about the progress of black people. Summarize the grandmother's thinking. How do they compare? Whose thinking does the writer favor?

2. Briefly describe each of the grandparents' backgrounds.

3. How does Morrison compare the status and conditions of blacks from 10 years ago with those today? What is her point in that comparison? Why does she call the "prisoners of economics" *Nixonian?* How does this section fit in with her overall historical comparison?

4. On the first list of "the ones whose work black people respect," how many names do you recognize? Do you think Morrison meant those names to be recognizable? What is her point?

Language, Form, Structure

1. What is Morrison's thesis in this essay? Does she ever state it exactly? If so, where? If not, how can you tell what her main point is?

2. What is the initial comparison the writer develops? How does Morrison use it as the seed to develop a comparison in a larger context? What is that comparison?

3. How does Morrison use data in this essay? Give three examples and analyze each for its significance and use in the essay. What generalization do the data support?

4. How does Morrison use references to popular culture? Why are they effective? How do they influence the organization and coherence of the essay?

5. In the conclusion to this essay, the author makes use of a series of questions. What is their purpose? Does she mean for them to be answered? Why or why not? What tone do they create? How do they serve as a fitting conclusion to the essay?

6. Define the following words from the essay: predators; rancor; fastidious; succor; vertigo; solace; disparate; sang-froid; rife; albeit; accolade; grovel. Choose five of these terms, and use them in sentences of your own.

Ideas for Writing

1. Write a comparison between your parents' and your own outlook on a key political, social, or historical issue. Attempt to blend objective data with vivid, sometimes metaphoric descriptions.

2. Do you remember any time in your childhood when your grandparents, parents, or a close older relative told you how something *would be* when you grew up? Compare what you were told with what you know to be true.

3. What is the relation between Morrison's intended audience and her style, outlook, choice of information, and use of language? She wrote this piece originally for the *New York Times* magazine. How do you think her audience influenced her? How do you think they received the article? What significance is added in that the article first appeared on the day of the U.S. Bicentennial? In your analysis make specific references to the text.

Everyday Use

Alice Walker

Born into a family of sharecroppers in Eatonton, Georgia, in 1944, Alice Walker later attended college at Spelman and Sarah Lawrence and was active in the civil rights move- ment. Now she regularly teaches at various universities and contributes to *Ms.* magazine. Of her several novels, *The Color Purple* won the Pulitzer Prize in 1983 and went on to become a popular film. The following selection comes from *In Love and Trouble: Stories of Black Women.*

Walker has said of herself and her work, "I am committed to exploring the oppressions, the insanities, the loyalties, and the triumphs of black women." "Everyday Use" is a gentle, revealing story of love, understanding, and heritage.

I will wait for her in the yard that Maggie and I made so clean and   1
wavy yesterday afternoon. A yard like this is more comfortable than most people
know. It is not just a yard. It is like an extended living room. When the hard clay
is swept clean as a floor and the fine sand around the edges lined with tiny, irregular grooves anyone can come and sit and look up into the elm tree and wait for
the breezes that never come inside the house.

Maggie will be nervous until after her sister goes: she will stand hopelessly   2
in corners homely and ashamed of the burn scars down her arms and legs, eyeing
her sister with a mixture of envy and awe. She thinks her sister has held life
always in the palm of one hand, that "no" is a word the world never learned to say
to her.

You've no doubt seen those TV shows where the child who has "made it"   3
is confronted, as a surprise, by her own mother and father, tottering in weakly
from backstage. (A pleasant surprise, of course: What would they do if parent and
child came on the show only to curse out and insult each other?) On TV mother
and child embrace and smile into each other's faces. Sometimes the mother and
father weep, the child wraps them in her arms and leans across the table to tell
how she would not have made it without their help. I have seen these programs.

Sometimes I dream a dream in which Dee and I are suddenly brought   4
together on a TV program of this sort. Out of a dark and soft-seated limousine I
am ushered into a bright room filled with many people. There I meet a smiling,
gray, sporty man like Johnny Carson who shakes my hand and tells me what a
fine girl I have. Then we are on the stage and Dee is embracing me with tears in
her eyes. She pins on my dress a large orchid, even though she has told me once
that she thinks orchids are tacky flowers.

In real life I am a large, big-boned woman with rough, man-working hands.   5
In the winter I wear flannel nightgowns to bed and overalls during the day. I can
kill and clean a hog as mercilessly as a man. My fat keeps me hot in zero weather.

I can work all day, breaking ice to get water for washing. I can eat pork liver cooked over the open fire minutes after it comes steaming from the hog. One winter I knocked a bull calf straight in the brain between the eyes with a sledge hammer and had the meat hung up to chill before nightfall. But of course all this does not show on television. I am the way my daughter would want me to be: a hundred pounds lighter, my skin like a uncooked barley pancake. My hair glistens in the hot bright lights. Johnny Carson has much to do to keep up with my quick and witty tongue.

But that is a mistake. I know even before I wake up. Who ever knew a John- 6
son with a quick tongue? Who can even imagine me looking a strange white man in the eye? It seems to me I have talked to them always with one foot raised in flight, with my head turned in whichever way is farthest from them. Dee, though. She would always look anyone in the eye. Hesitation was no part of her nature.

"How do I look, Mama?" Maggie says, showing just enough of her thin 7
body enveloped in pink skirt and red blouse for me to know she's there, almost hidden by the door.

"Come out into the yard," I say. 8

Have you ever seen a lame animal, perhaps a dog run over by some care- 9
less person rich enough to own a car, sidle up to someone who is ignorant enough to be kind to him? That is the way my Maggie walks. She has been like this, chin on chest, eyes on ground, feet in shuffle, ever since the fire that burned the other house to the ground.

Dee is lighter than Maggie, with nicer hair and a fuller figure. She's a 10
woman now, though sometimes I forget. How long ago was it that the other house burned? Ten, twelve years? Sometimes I can still hear the flames and feel Maggie's arm sticking to me, her hair smoking and her dress falling off her in little black papery flakes. Her eyes seemed stretched open, blazed open by the flames reflected in them. And Dee, I see her standing off under the sweet gum tree she used to dig gum out of; a look of concentration on her face as she watched the last dingy gray board of the house fall in toward the red-hot brick chimney. Why don't you do a dance around the ashes? I'd wanted to ask her. She had hated the house that much.

I used to think she hated Maggie, too. But that was before we raised the 11
money, the church and me, to send her to Augusta to school. She used to read to us without pity; forcing words, lies, other folks' habits, whole lives upon us two, sitting trapped and ignorant underneath her voice. She washed us in a river of make-believe, burned us with a lot of knowledge we didn't necessarily need to know. Pressed us to her with the serious way she read, to shove us away at just the moment, like dimwits, we seemed about to understand.

Dee wanted nice things. A yellow organdy dress to wear to her graduation 12
from high school; black pumps to match a green suit she'd made from an old suit somebody gave me. She was determined to stare down any disaster in her efforts. Her eyelids would not flicker for minutes at a time. Often I fought off the temptation to shake her. At sixteen she had a style of her own: and knew what style was.

I never had an education myself. After second grade the school was closed ₁₃ down. Don't ask me why: in 1927 colored asked fewer questions than they do now. Sometimes Maggie reads to me. She stumbles along good-naturedly but can't see well. She knows she is not bright. Like good looks and money, quickness passed her by. She will marry John Thomas (who has mossy teeth in an earnest face) and then I'll be free to sit here and I guess just sing church songs to myself. Although I never was a good singer. Never could carry a tune. I was always better at a man's job. I used to love to milk till I was hoofed in the side in '49. Cows are soothing and slow and don't bother you, unless you try to milk them the wrong way.

I have deliberately turned my back on the house. It is three rooms, just like ₁₄ the one that burned, except the roof is tin; they don't make shingle roofs any more. There are no real windows, just some holes cut in the sides, like the portholes in a ship, but not round and not square, with rawhide holding the shutters up on the outside. The house is in a pasture, too, like the other one. No doubt when Dee sees it she will want to tear it down. She wrote me once that no matter where we "choose" to live, she will manage to come see us. But she will never bring her friends. Maggie and I thought about this and Maggie asked me, "Mama, when did Dee ever *have* any friends?"

She had a few. Furtive boys in pink shirts hanging about on washday after ₁₅ school. Nervous girls who never laughed. Impressed with her they worshiped the well-turned phrase, the cute shape, the scalding humor that erupted like bubbles in lye. She read to them.

When she was courting Jimmy T. she didn't have much time to pay to us, ₁₆ but turned all her faultfinding power on him. He *flew* to marry a cheap gal from a family of ignorant flashy people. She hardly had time to recompose herself.

When she comes I will meet—but there they are! ₁₇

Maggie attempts to make a dash for the house, in her shuffling way, but I ₁₈ stay her with my hand. "Come back here," I say. And she stops and tries to dig a well in the sand with her toe.

It is hard to see them clearly through the strong sun. But even the first ₁₉ glimpse of leg out of the car tells me it is Dee. Her feet were always neat-looking, as if God himself had shaped them with a certain style. From the other side of the car comes a short, stocky man. Hair is all over his head a foot long and hanging from his chin like a kinky mule tail. I hear Maggie suck in her breath. "Uhnnnh," is what it sounds like. Like when you see the wriggling end of a snake just in front of your foot on the road. "Uhnnnh."

Dee next. A dress down to the ground, in this hot weather. A dress so loud ₂₀ it hurts my eyes. There are yellows and oranges enough to throw back the light of the sun. I feel my whole face warming from the heat waves it throws out. Earrings, too, gold and hanging down to her shoulders. Bracelets dangling and making noises when she moves her arm up to shake the folds of the dress out of her armpits. The dress is loose and flows, and as she walks closer, I like it. I hear Maggie go "Uhnnnh" again. It is her sister's hair. It stands straight up like the wool on a sheep. It is black as night and around the edges are two long pigtails that rope about like small lizards disappearing behind her ears.

"Wa-su-zo-Tean-o!" she says, coming on in that gliding way the dress 21 makes her move. The short stocky fellow with the hair to his navel is all grinning and he follows up with "Asalamalakim, my mother and sister!" He moves to hug Maggie but she falls back, right up against the back of my chair. I feel her trembling there and when I look up I see the perspiration falling off her chin.

"Don't get up," says Dee. Since I am stout it takes something of a push. You 22 can see me trying to move a second or two before I make it. She turns, showing white heels through her sandals, and goes back to the car. Out she peeks next with a Polaroid. She stoops down quickly and lines up picture after picture of me sitting there in front of the house with Maggie cowering behind me. She never takes a shot without making sure the house is included. When a cow comes nibbling around the edge of the yard she snaps it and me and Maggie *and* the house. Then she puts the Polaroid in the back seat of the car, and comes up and kisses me on the forehead.

Meanwhile Asalamalakim is going through the motions with Maggie's 23 hand. Maggie's hand is as limp as a fish, and probably as cold, despite the sweat, and she keeps trying to pull it back. It looks like Asalamalakim wants to shake hands but wants to do it fancy. Or maybe he don't know how people shake hands. Anyhow, he soon gives up on Maggie.

"Well," I say. "Dee." 24

"No, Mama," she says. "Not 'Dee.' Wangero Leewanika Kemanjo!" 25

"What happened to 'Dee'?" I wanted to know. 26

"She's dead." Wangero said. "I couldn't bear it any longer being named 27 after the people who oppress me."

"You know as well as me you was named after your aunt Dicie." I said. 28 Dicie is my sister. She named Dee. We called her "Big Dee" after Dee was born.

"But who was *she* named after?" asked Wangero. 29

"I guess after Grandma Dee," I said. 30

"And who was she named after?" asked Wangero. 31

"Her mother," I said, and saw Wangero was getting tired. "That's about as 32 far back as I can trace it," I said. Though, in fact, I probably could have carried it back beyond the Civil War through the branches.

"Well," said Asalamalakim, "there you are." 33

"Uhnnnh," I heard Maggie say. 34

"There I was not," I said, "before 'Dicie' cropped up in our family, so why 35 should I try to trace it that far back?"

He just stood there grinning, looking down on me like somebody inspect- 36 ing a Model A car. Every once in a while he and Wangero sent eye signals over my head.

"How do you pronounce this name?" I asked. 37

"You don't have to call me by it if you don't want to," said Wangero. 38

"Why shouldn't I?" I asked. "If that's what you want us to call you, we'll 39
call you."

"I know it might sound awkward at first," said Wangero. 40

"I'll get used to it," I said. "Ream it out again." 41

Well, soon we got the name out of the way. Asalamalakim had a name twice 42
as long and three times as hard. After I tripped over it two or three times he told
me to just call him Hakim-a-barber. I wanted to ask him was he a barber, but I
didn't really think he was, so I didn't ask.

"You must belong to those beef-cattle peoples down the road," I said. They 43
said "Asalamalakim" when they met you, too, but they didn't shake hands.
Always too busy: feeding the cattle, fixing the fences, putting up salt-lick shel-
ters, throwing down hay. When the white folks poisoned some of the heard the
men stayed up all night with rifles in their hands. I walked a mile and a half just
to see the sight.

Hakim-a-barber said, "I accept some of their doctrines, but farming and 44
raising cattle is not my style." (They didn't tell me, and I didn't ask, whether
Wangero [Dee] had really gone and married him.)

We sat down to eat and right away he said he didn't eat collards and pork 45
was unclean. Wangero, though, went on through the chitlins and corn bread, the
greens and everything else. She talked a blue streak over the sweet potatoes.
Everything delighted her. Even the fact that we still used the benches her daddy
made for the table when we couldn't afford to buy chairs.

"Oh, Mama!" she cried. Then turned to Hakim-a-barber. "I never knew how 46
lovely these benches are. You can feel the rump prints," she said, running her
hands underneath her and along the bench. Then she gave a sigh and her hand
closed over Grandma Dee's butter dish. "That's it!" she said. "I knew there was
something I wanted to ask you if I could have." She jumped up from the table and
went over in the corner where the churn stood, the milk in its clabber by now. She
looked at the churn and looked at it.

"This churn top is what I need," she said. "Didn't Uncle Buddy whittle it 47
out of a tree you all used to have?"

"Yes," I said. 48

"Uh huh," she said happily. "And I want the dasher, too." 49

"Uncle Buddy whittle that, too?" asked the barber. 50

Dee (Wangero) looked up at me. 51

"Aunt Dee's first husband whittled the dash," said Maggie so low you 52
almost couldn't hear her. "His name was Henry, but they called him Stash."

"Maggie's brain is like an elephant's," Wangero said, laughing. "I can use 53
the churn top as a centerpiece for the alcove table," she said, sliding a plate over
the churn, "and I'll think of something artistic to do with the dasher."

When she finished wrapping the dasher the handle stuck out. I took it for a 54
moment in my hands. You didn't even have to look close to see where hands pushing the dasher up and down to make butter had left a kind of sink in the wood. In
fact, there were a lot of small sinks; you could see where thumbs and fingers had

sunk into the wood. It was beautiful light yellow wood, from a tree that grew in the yard where Big Dee and Stash had lived.

After dinner Dee (Wangero) went to the trunk at the foot of my bed and 55 started rifling through it. Maggie hung back in the kitchen over the dishpan. Out came Wangero with two quilts. They had been pieced by Grandma Dee and then Big Dee and me had hung them on the quilt frames on the front porch and quilted them. One was in the Lone Star pattern. The other was Walk Around the Mountain. In both of them were scraps of dresses Grandma Dee had worn fifty and more years ago. Bits and pieces of Grandpa Jarrell's Paisley shirts. And one teeny faded blue piece, about the size of a penny matchbox, that was from Great Grandpa Ezra's uniform that he wore in the Civil War.

"Mama," Wangero said sweet as a bird. "Can I have these old quilts?"   56

I heard something fall in the kitchen, and a minute later the kitchen door 57 slammed.

"Why don't you take one or two of the others?" I asked "These old things 58 was just done by me and Big Dee from some tops your grandma pieced before she died."

"No," said Wangero. "I don't want those. They are stitched around the bor- 59 ders by machine."

"That's to make them last better," I said.   60

"That's not the point," said Wangero. "These are all pieces of dresses 61 Grandma used to wear. She did all this stitching by hand. Imagine!" She held the quilts securely in her arms, stroking them.

"Some of the pieces, like those lavender ones, come from old clothes her 62 mother handed down to her," I said, moving up to touch the quilts. Dee (Wangero) moved back just enough so that I couldn't reach the quilts. They already belonged to her.

"Imagine!" she breathed again, clutching them closely to her bosom.   63

"The truth is," I said, "I promised to give them quilts to Maggie, for when 64 she marries John Thomas."

She gasped like a bee had stung her.   65

"Maggie can't appreciate these quilts!" she said. "She'd probably be back- 66 ward enough to put them to everyday use."

"I reckon she would," I said. "God knows I been saving 'em for long 67 enough with nobody using 'em. I hope she will!" I didn't want to bring up how I had offered Dee (Wangero) a quilt when she went away to college. Then she had told me they were old-fashioned, out of style.

"But they're *priceless*!" she was saying now, furiously, for she has a tem- 68 per. "Maggie would put them on the bed and in five years they'd be in rags. Less than that!"

"She can always make some more," I said. "Maggie knows how to quilt." 69

Dee (Wangero) looked at me with hatred. "You just will not understand. 70 The point is these quilts, *these* quilts!"

"Well," I said, stumped. "What would *you* do with them?"   71

"Hang them," she said. As if that was the only thing you *could* do with quilts.   72

Maggie by now was standing in the door. I could almost hear the sound her feet made as they scraped over each other.   73

"She can have them, Mama," she said, like somebody used to never winning anything, or having anything reserved for her. "I can 'member Grandma Dee without the quilts."   74

I looked at her hard. She had filled her bottom lip with checkerberry snuff and it gave her face a kind of dopey, hangdog look. It was Grandma Dee and Big Dee who taught her how to quilt herself. She stood there with her scarred hands hidden in the folds of her skirt. She looked at her sister with something like fear but she wasn't mad at her. This was Maggie's portion. This was the way she knew God to work.   75

When I looked at her like that something hit me in the top of my head and ran down to the soles of my feet. Just like when I'm in church and the spirit of God touches me and I get happy and shout. I did something I never had done before: hugged Maggie to me, then dragged her on into the room, snatched the quilts out of Miss Wangero's hands and dumped them into Maggie's lap. Maggie just sat there on my bed with her mouth open.   76

"Take one or two of the others," I said to Dee.   77

But she turned without a word and went out to Hakim-a-barber.   78

"You just don't understand," she said, as Maggie and I came out to the car.   79

"What don't I understand?" I wanted to know.   80

"Your heritage," she said. And then she turned to Maggie, kissed her, and said, "You ought to try to make something of yourself, too, Maggie. It's really a new day for us. But from the way you and Mama still live you'd never know it."   81

She put on some sunglasses that hid everything above the tip of her nose and her chin.   82

Maggie smiled; maybe at the sunglasses. But a real smile, not scared. After we watched the car dust settle I asked Maggie to bring me a dip of snuff. And then the two of us sat there just enjoying, until it was time to go in the house and go to bed.   83

Meaning and Idea

1. What are the essential features of the women's personalities—"I" (Momma), Maggie, and Dee (Wangero)? What features do they have in common? How are they different?

2. What is Maggie's reaction to the man who accompanies Dee? Why does she react as she does?

3. Why did Dee change her name? How do Momma and Maggie feel about this change? Why do they react as they do?

4. Wangero seems to reject much of her earlier life, yet she eagerly seeks to take with her objects from Momma's house. How do you account for her interest in the churn top, the dasher, and the handmade quilts?

5. Why does Momma refuse to give Wangero the quilts when she first asks? Why does Maggie agree to let them go, however? What does she mean by the line "I can 'member Grandma Dee without the quilts"?

6. Why does Momma hug Maggie? Momma makes this action seem as if it grew out of a religious epiphany. What made Momma feel as if the spirit of God had touched her? How does she finally resolve the issue of who gets the quilts? Why does she make the decision she makes?

Language, Form, Structure

1. This piece has many levels of comparison and contrast—between the two sisters, between Momma and each of her daughters, between the "new day" and the old ways for African Americans. Discuss the various elements of comparison here. How do the contrastive behaviors help you understand the characters?

2. How does Walker's use of language make us see how cruel Dee is as she leaves? How is the last paragraph, in its homey simplicity, a vindication of the life that Momma and Maggie live as opposed to the life Dee lives?

3. The word *Asalamalakim* is really a greeting. Is it also Wangero's friend's name? Why do you think that Momma uses the word as the man's name?

4. Discuss these phrases for their sensory diction and meaning: eyeing her sister with a mixture of envy and awe; man-working hands; mossy teeth in an earnest face; furtive boys in pink shirts; scalding humor that erupted like bubbles in lye.

Ideas for Writing

1. Think of two people you know who have different ways of dealing with their heritage and write a comparison-and-contrast essay about them.

2. Mothers and daughters, fathers and sons can often represent classical conflicts in their attitudes and behaviors toward each other. Write an essay about a mother and daughter or a father and son whom you know; show how they compare and contrast.

3. Write an essay in which you consider the characters in this fictional piece. How do they compare and contrast with each other? How has Walker succeeded through comparison-and-contrast strategies in making the characters alive and memorable for the reader?

CROSSOVER

1. Virginia Woolf in "Shakespeare's Gifted Sister," Amy Tan in "Two Kinds," and Alice Walker in "Everyday Use" all write about women, family, and the traditions that shape their lives. Write an essay that identifies the common elements of women's lives explored in at least two of these selections. Identify differences, too, in the authors' perspectives on women, family, and tradition.

2. Thomas Hardy in "The Ruined Maid" and William Shakespeare in "My Mistress' Eyes Are Nothing Like the Sun" both use comic elements to explore their female subjects. How effective is each of these as a comic statement? What elements make each funny? What goals beyond the comic does each poem seem to reach for?

■

Chapter Six

CLASSIFICATION

As thinking animals we are forever dividing things up in our minds and putting them back together in a new way. Basic to much of this analytic thinking is the effort to classify myriad experiences and phenomena into meaningful categories. Related objects look clearer and more sensible when sorted into like groups.

Classification usually works hand in hand with division (or analysis). In *division,* you break something down into discrete elements. In *classification,* you place like members of a group into categories. Generally, the intent of division is to take one large object, concept, or idea and to split it so that its parts are clear. To understand the structure of a newspaper, you might divide it into departments—news, sports, advertising, human interest, and so on. The intent of classification is to identify groups by putting together items with common properties. You come closer to understanding newspaper advertisements if you look at specific examples of personal ads, want ads, department store ads, supermarket ads, and so on. Division breaks a large unit down into its pieces; classification builds groups up by collecting common examples.

Think of almost any subject and imagine where we would be without our well-honed habits of division and classification for mental sorting. Take the simple but necessary task of housekeeping, for example. Faced with items piled high during a busy week, we must turn to division and classification as an aid. We divide the items in our pile—clothing, books, papers, sports equipment, CDs, games. Then we put similar items together into a large category, building to a group identity so to speak. Thus, a deflated soccer ball, a worn pair of Nikes, a catcher's mitt, two stained sweatbands, a surfboard—these specific objects help us create the category of "sports equipment." Classifying our housekeeping objects even further, we can see other possibilities for groupings. Clothing falls into categories—dirty and clean, sports and dressy, daytime and evening, and so on. These categories can be even further split: You might classify the clean clothing, for example, into underwear, slacks, shirts; the dirty into nonwashable and washable; the washable into cold, warm, and hot, or bleach and no bleach.

Classification, in short, helps us order our lives, and this ordering can be either humble, as you saw above, or more lofty, as, for example, when we group countries by their economic or political systems, people by their learning styles or creative talents, colleges by their courses of study. Through classification, we can make sensible groupings not only of our daily lives but also of the complex issues that emerge in every area of human activity and study. Indeed, without classification, advanced and systematic thinking could not exist. Chemists first divide the world into organic and inorganic objects and then proceed to subdivide each of these categories further. Biologists classify living things into large groups that are further subdivided to link common creatures. Literary critics classify writing—fiction, poetry, drama, essays—and then make smaller groups within the larger ones.

For the writer, in any area or discipline, classification is essential. Rich details, observations, and examples may be the writer's stock-in-trade, but through appropriate groupings, the writer can link ideas that otherwise might lose force.

READING CLASSIFICATION

As we read classification, we are reminded of the human invention involved in the undertaking. All the selections in this chapter eschew common categories and instead offer the reader fresh mental containers for classifying the various subjects at hand.

Malcolm Cowley's essay "The National Heartbeat: 'We-ness' and 'Me-ness'" allows us to see our age under a modern political microscope. Through his classification of this century's politics as "me"-oriented or "we"-oriented, conservative and then progressive, a back-and-forth pendulum swing between two poles, Cowley helps us to see our century as patterned and to predict the tone of our next era. The two groups and the characteristics of their members enrich our understanding of contemporary politics. Similarly, George Orwell's now classic essay "Politics and the English Language" uses classification to help us view politics from a fresh perspective. Orwell categorizes the "tricks" that many modern prose writers, especially political writers, use to cover over truth, and his classification helps us both to read with greater awareness of demagoguery in print and to write purer and truer prose ourselves.

Classification is a particularly powerful tool for helping us see the patterns and habits of political and social life. But through classification we also can come to an understanding of life's subtle meanings. Dylan Thomas's poem "Do Not Go Gentle into That Good Night" classifies dying men into types. Thomas shows the ways of men as they face death—wise men, good men, wild men, and grave men. By means of his classification, he brings us to a unique view—for his dying father and for us, the readers—of how to face the end of life. Phillip Lopate in "Modern Friendships" reviews classical opinions of friendship in order to establish a new taxonomy of the word for modern times, elucidating both relations and conditions of late-twentieth-century life.

The selections included in this chapter suggest the wide range of subjects that the strategy of classification can help to illuminate, the fresh and novel categories we can use to help us see patterns in personal, public, and artistic life. And the selections demonstrate how writers use their fresh classifications to advance original theses, bringing complex categories to their persuasive purposes.

WRITING CLASSIFICATION

Much of what you are called upon to write requires some classification—breaking down your subject into classes or groups of similar members. You want to write about a poem; well, then chances are you will want to explore the *kind* of poem it is. Is it a sonnet, a ballad, a haiku? How can you classify it according to stanzaic form? Or you might try classifying the poem according to literary genre—epic, lyric, dramatic monologue—or according to subject—love poem, war poem, historical poem. You may do much more besides classifying the poem in your paper, certainly, but writing on almost any topic, in almost any discipline, you will see that classification plays an important role. And it is not just in determining where your subject stands—what class of thing it is—that you call upon classification as a writer. Further analysis of your subject may compel you to make steady use of classification by grouping and categorizing your ideas and observations. In writing about a poem, let's say, you may prepare for the task by jotting down your many thoughts as you read. But then you use some rudimentary classification system to help you sort your many thoughts into different groups: thoughts on imagery, thoughts on word choice, thoughts on characters in the poem perhaps. And then within each of these groups you may find yourself using classification again. In discussing word choice you may classify into denotative meanings (dictionary meanings) and connotative meanings (the meanings that have clustered about the word through usage), or Latinate and Anglo-Saxon words, or abstract and concrete words, and so on—classifying within each of your categories.

Because categorization is a much-used tool in thinking and writing, it is worthwhile to practice writing classification. Again, as with writing of any kind, in preparing the classification paper you will draw on many of the writer's strategies—description, exemplification, and so on. In this writing exercise, however, you will use classification as the controlling strategy. But, as with any strategy, your purpose should be to advance a point or position, to use rhetorical technique to develop a coherent thesis.

PURPOSE AND AUDIENCE

Classification by definition reflects an act of individual judgment. People, chemicals, flora, and fauna do not come into the world neatly fitting into categories; *people* put them into categories in order to make better sense of them and to make the world more orderly through these understandings.

You must make many decisions as you think about exploring a topic through classification. Do you want to be funny or serious? Do you want to criticize or to persuade? Classification is an able tool and lends itself to many purposes. You want to write about your family, let's say. Well, classifying family members into ranters, ravers, whimperers, and pouters—categorizing their behavior when hurt or angry—will help you to develop your thoughts along a comic vein, to think about your family in humorous terms, and to make your reader laugh. But perhaps it's a very serious matter to you when your family are angry or hurt. Well, then you will classify them very differently: You'll discuss those in your family who hold their anger in and those in your family who let their anger go. How you classify depends on how you see your subject.

Readers naturally take to classification because readers, being human, like to see the world made comprehensible and like to see the sorts of arrangements others can make. But without sufficient planning and invention on the part of the writer, classification, like comparison, can grow tedious. Beware, then, of papers whose ideas are merely informational, with little point of view expressed. An essay with the following thesis risks boring the reader terribly: "My teachers fall into three categories: those with degrees in science, those with degrees in the humanities, and those with degrees in the social sciences." True, some lively description of teachers and their habits might make such a thesis come to life. But if the writer settles simply for cataloguing information in this clinical way, readers, unless they are especially interested in the subject, will soon lose interest. How much more engaging, then, to build your own special perception into your classification. "My teachers fall into three categories: friend, mother-surrogate, confessor." Or if you're using a common classification scheme to group them—science, humanities, social science, say—then chances are that you can heighten your reader's attention if you build a point of view into your thesis. "Here at Dovery College my teachers in major academic areas—science, humanities, social science—operate from the same educational assumption: that writing is learning and learning is writing." As we said, the reader with a special interest in or knowledge of a subject may be tolerant or even enthusiastic about a classification essay that is purely informational. But your own lively perspective will add a unique tone to the essay and will engage your audience. Be sure, then, to think about your audience and its relation to your subject, as well as your own relation to the subject, as you prepare your classification essay.

PROCESS

Your first step in designing an essay in classification is to select the principle by which you will classify. Many subjects you might choose to write about lend themselves to varied classification systems. You want to write a classification essay on microcomputers, let's say. You should decide whether you want to classify by price, make, power, availability of software, compatibility, or what have you. Produce a thesis statement that expresses both your topic and your attitude toward it. Once you've decided on the principle that goes best with your interests, as well as your audience's knowledge and interest, stick with this principle as you develop your paper. Keep your categories discrete and do not overlap them. Classifying microcomputers as low-priced, mainframe, medium-priced, microcomputers, IBMs, and high-priced would reflect confused thinking and would lead to a confusing paper.

You must also be careful to be as complete as possible when you develop your various categories. A classification of urban transportation into automobiles and buses is clearly an incomplete classification. A complete classification would have to include trains, subways, and taxis as well. Although Cowley's two large groups are complex and original, you should be aware of the pitfalls in simplistic divisions into two groups only, these and everything else. Classifying films into the successful and the unsuccessful or foods into the nutritious and the nonnutritious creates categories too large and diffuse to be meaningful. A good rule of thumb to help you achieve a relatively complete classification system is to present at least three groups. Depending on your purpose, you might have to approach your topic exhaustively, omitting no categories whatsoever. And you should pay some attention to exceptions: Do examples exist that defy the orderly system you have created? To ignore them is to stack the deck, and an intelligent reader will mistrust you for it. If as you plan your classification paper you find you have too many categories to manage, then modify your subject so that you and your reader don't feel either overwhelmed by too much material or cheated by a big purpose not successfully developed.

When your categories are set, decide on how you will arrange them in your paper. If you're classifying literary genres, will you move chronologically, referring as you name the groups to their origins in time? Will you present them by considering the simpler forms first and then the more complex? Or will you follow public sensibilities by organizing your categories from the least to the most popular forms?

Classifications require the writer to attend to a good deal at once. The effective classification is one whose sections get more or less equal attention. If you devote lots of space to one or two of your categories and skimp on another, your essay will be unsatisfactory in shape and consistency.

Writing classification demands rigorous thinking and careful planning. The rewards of this effort, however, are many, as you and your readers see a subject illuminated by this important reflective act.

SUMMING UP: CLASSIFICATION

Reading Classification

- Working along with *division*, which means breaking something down into discrete elements, *classification* means placing like members of a group into categories.

- Identify the categories that the writer has established and try to determine why he has chosen those categories.

- Determine how the stated (or implied) thesis identifies the classification strategy.

- As you examine the classification piece, ask how the categories enlighten your understanding of the topic. Do the groupings help you understand complex issues?

Writing Classification

- Breaking your subject into classes or groups of similar members.

- Be aware that each group may lend itself to further classification.

- Decide on your purpose for classifying the topic you have chosen and convey that purpose either explicitly in a thesis sentence or by indirection as you explore the features of the topic.

- Be sure to express a point of view toward the topic and the classification strategy in order to avoid a merely informational paper with no embedded attitude or opinion about the essay's subject.

- Consider the audience's needs and interests: what elements of your writing will engage their interest in the topic you wish to develop through classification.

- Weighing your own interests and your audience's knowledge and interests, determine the principle by which you will develop your classification paper and stick with that principle as you develop it.

- Keep your established categories discrete and do not overlap them.

- Be sure that your categories present a complete classification scheme for the topic: Do not omit any categories that are essential for the paper's proper development.

- Beware of simplistic categories that produce groupings too large or diffuse; aim for at least three groups for a relatively complete classification system.

- Pay attention to the possibilities of exceptions to your classification scheme and treat the exceptions honestly for your readers.

- Avoid a classification scheme that produces too many categories; modify your subject if you find that you have too many groups.

- As you develop your draft, determine an appropriate method of grouping the categories you have established.

- Treat the various categories with more or less equal attention; avoid skimping on details in one category as you provide a great deal of information in another.

Politics and the English Language

George Orwell

George Orwell was the name adopted by the English writer Eric Arthur Blair (1903–1950). Although he is a socialist, Orwell is perhaps best known for his fable-novel *Animal Farm* (1946), which is highly critical of communism, and for his *1984* (1949), which presented a frightening view of a totalitarian world society. His autobiographical *Down and Out in Paris and London* (1933) and his literary criticism are considered among the best European writing of the first half of the century.

Orwell published "Politics and the English Language" in 1945; it is now considered among the finest contemporary treatises on the use of language. In this essay Orwell makes connections among thought and language processes, social corruption, and politics, employing classification as an organizational technique for his many examples and astute analyses.

*M*ost people who bother with the matter at all would admit that the   1
English language is in a bad way, but it is generally assumed that we cannot by conscious action do anything about it. Our civilisation is decadent, and our language—so the argument runs—must inevitably share in the general collapse. It follows that any struggle against the abuse of language is a sentimental archaism, like preferring candles to electric light or hansom cabs to aeroplanes. Underneath this lies the half-conscious belief that language is a natural growth and not an instrument which we shape for our own purposes.

Now, it is clear that the decline of a language must ultimately have politi-   2
cal and economic causes: it is not due simply to the bad influence of this or that individual writer. But an effect can become a cause, reinforcing the original cause and producing the same effect in an intensified form, and so on indefinitely. A man may take to drink because he feels himself to be a failure, and then fail all the more completely because he drinks. It is rather the same thing that is happening to the English language. It becomes ugly and inaccurate because our thoughts are foolish, but the slovenliness of our language makes it easier for us to have foolish thoughts. The point is that the process is reversible. Modern English, especially written English, is full of bad habits which spread by imitation and which can be avoided if one is willing to take the necessary trouble. If one gets rid of these habits one can think more clearly, and to think clearly is a necessary first step towards political regeneration: so that the fight against bad English is not frivolous and is not the exclusive concern of professional writers. I will come back to this presently, and I hope that by that time the meaning of what I have said here will have become clearer. Meanwhile, here are five specimens of the English language as it is now habitually written.

These five passages have not been picked out because they are especially ₃ bad—I could have quoted far worse if I had chosen—but because they illustrate various of the mental vices from which we now suffer. They are a little below the average, but are fairly representative samples. I number them so that I can refer back to them when necessary:

1. I am not, indeed, sure whether it is not true to say that the Milton who once seemed not unlike a seventeenth-century Shelley had not become, out of an experience ever more bitter in each year, more alien [*sic*] to the founder of that Jesuit sect which nothing could induce him to tolerate.

Professor Harold Laski (Essay in *Freedom of Expression*).

2. Above all, we cannot play ducks and drakes with a native battery of idioms which prescribes such egregious collocations of vocables as the Basic *put up with* for *tolerate* or *put at a loss* for *bewilder.*

Professor Lancelot Hogben *(Interglossa).*

3. On the one side we have the free personality: by definition it is not neurotic, for it has neither conflict nor dream. Its desires, such as they are, are transparent, for they are just what institutional approval keeps in the forefront of consciousness; another institutional pattern would alter their number and intensity; there is little in them that is natural, irreducible, or culturally dangerous. But *on the other side,* the social bond itself is nothing but the mutual reflection of these self-secure integrities. Recall the definition of love. Is not this the very picture of a small academic? Where is there a place in this hall of mirrors for either personality or fraternity?

Essay on psychology in *Politics* (New York).

4. All the "best people" from the gentlemen's clubs, and all the frantic Fascist captains, united in common hatred of Socialism and bestial horror of the rising tide of the mass revolutionary movement, have turned to acts of provocation, to foul incendiarism, to medieval legends of poisoned wells, to legalise their own destruction to proletarian organisations, and rouse the agitated petty-bourgeoisie to chauvinistic fervour on behalf of the fight against the revolutionary way out of the crisis.

Communist pamphlet.

5. If a new spirit *is* to be infused into this old country, there is one thorny and contentious reform which must be tackled, and that is the humanisation and galvanisation of the BBC. Timidity here will bespeak canker and atrophy of the soul. The heart of Britain may be sound and of strong beat, for instance, but the British lion's roar at present is like that of Bottom in Shakespeare's *Midsummer Night's Dream*— as gentle as any sucking dove. A virile new Britain cannot continue indefinitely to be traduced in the eyes, or rather ears, of the world by the effete languors of Langham Place, brazenly masquerading as "standard English". When the Voice of Britain is heard at nine o'clock, better far and infinitely less ludicrous to hear aitches honestly dropped than the present priggish, inflated, inhibited, school-ma'amish arch braying of blameless bashful mewing maidens!

Letter in *Tribune*.

Each of these passages has faults of its own, but, quite apart from avoidable   4
ugliness, two qualities are common to all of them. The first is staleness of
imagery: the other is lack of precision. The writer either has a meaning and cannot express it, or he inadvertently says something else, or he is almost indifferent
as to whether his words mean anything or not. This mixture of vagueness and
sheer incompetence is the most marked characteristic of modern English prose,
and especially of any kind of political writing. As soon as certain topics are
raised, the concrete melts into the abstract and no one seems able to think of turns
of speech that are not hackneyed: prose consists less and less of *words* chosen for
the sake of their meaning, and more of *phrases* tacked together like the sections
of a prefabricated hen-house. I list below, with notes and examples, various of the
tricks by means of which the work of prose construction is habitually dodged:

Dying metaphors.   A newly invented metaphor assists thought by evoking a   5
visual image, while on the other hand a metaphor which is technically "dead"
(e.g. *iron resolution*) has in effect reverted to being an ordinary word and can generally be used without loss of vividness. But in between these two classes there
is a huge dump of worn-out metaphors which have lost all evocative power and
are merely used because they save people the trouble of inventing phrases for
themselves. Examples are: *Ring the changes on, take up the cudgels for, toe the
line, ride roughshod over, stand shoulder to shoulder with, play into the hands of,
no axe to grind, grist to the mill, fishing in troubled waters, rift within the lute, on
the order of the day, Achilles' heel, swan song, hotbed.* Many of these are used
without knowledge of their meaning (what is a "rift", for instance?), and incom-
patible metaphors are frequently mixed, a sure sign that the writer is not interested in what he is saying. Some metaphors now current have been twisted out of
their original meaning without those who use them even being aware of the fact.
For example, *toe the line* is sometimes written *tow the line.* Another example is
the hammer and the anvil, now always used with the implication that the anvil
gets the worst of it. In real life it is always the anvil that breaks the hammer, never
the other way about: a writer who stopped to think what he was saying would be
aware of this, and would avoid perverting the original phrase.

Operators, or verbal false limbs.   These save the trouble of picking out appropri-   6
ate verbs and nouns, and at the same time pad each sentence with extra syllables
which give it an appearance of symmetry. Characteristic phrases are: *render inop-
erative, militate against, prove unacceptable, make contact with, be subjected to,
give rise to, give grounds for, have the effect of, play a leading part (rôle) in, make
itself felt, take effect, exhibit a tendency to, serve the purpose of,* etc. etc. The
keynote is the elimination of simple verbs. Instead of being a single word, such
as *break, stop, spoil, mend, kill,* a verb becomes a *phrase,* made up of a noun or
adjective tacked on to some general-purposes verb such as *prove, serve, form,
play, render.* In addition, the passive voice is wherever possible used in preference
to the active, and noun constructions are used instead of gerunds (*by examination
of* instead of *by examining*). The range of verbs is further cut down by means of

the *-ise* and *de-* formations, and banal statements are given an appearance of profundity by means of the *not un-* formation. Simple conjunctions and prepositions are replaced by such phrases as *with respect to, having regard to, the fact that, by dint of, in view of, in the interests of, on the hypothesis that*; and the ends of sentences are saved from anticlimax by such resounding commonplaces as *greatly to be desired, cannot be left out of account, a development to be expected in the near future, deserving of serious consideration, brought to a satisfactory conclusion,* and so on and so forth.

Pretentious diction. Words like *phenomenon, element, individual* (as noun) [7] *objective, categorical, effective, virtual, basic, primary, promote, constitute, exhibit, exploit, utilise, eliminate, liquidate,* are used to dress up simple statements and give an air of scientific impartiality to biased judgements. Adjectives like *epoch-making, epic, historic, unforgettable, triumphant, age-old, inevitable, inexorable, veritable,* are used to dignify the sordid processes of international politics, while writing that aims at glorifying war usually takes on an archaic colour, its characteristic words being: *realm, throne, chariot, mailed fist, trident, sword, shield, buckler, banner, jackboot, clarion.* Foreign words and expressions such as *cul de sac, ancien régime, deus ex machina, mutatis mutandis, status quo, Gleichschaltung, Weltanschauung,* are used to give an air of culture and elegance. Except for the useful abbreviations *i.e., e.g.,* and *etc.,* there is no real need for any of the hundreds of foreign phrases now current in English. Bad writers, and especially scientific, political and sociological writers, are nearly always haunted by the notion that Latin or Greek words are grander than Saxon ones, and unnecessary words like *expedite, ameliorate, predict, extraneous, deracinated, clandestine, sub-aqueous* and hundreds of others constantly gain ground from their Anglo-Saxon opposite numbers.[1] The jargon peculiar to Marxist writing (*hyena, hangman, cannibal, petty bourgeois, these gentry, lacquey, flunkey, mad dog, White Guard,* etc.) consists largely of words and phrases translated from Russian, German or French; but the normal way of coining a new word is to use a Latin or Greek root with the appropriate affix and, where necessary, the *-ise* formation. It is often easier to make up words of this kind (*deregionalise, impermissible, extra-marital, non-fragmentatory* and so forth) than to think up the English words that will cover one's meaning. The result, in general, is an increase in slovenliness and vagueness.

Meaningless words. In certain kinds of writing, particularly in art criticism and [8] literary criticism, it is normal to come across long passages which are almost

---

[1] An interesting illustration of this is the way in which the English flower names which were in use till very recently are being ousted by Greek ones; *snapdragon* becoming *antirrhinum, forget-me-not* becoming *myosotis,* etc. It is hard to see any practical reason for this change of fashion: it is probably due to an instinctive turning-away from the more homely word and a vague feeling that the Greek word is scientific.

completely lacking in meaning.[2] Words like *romantic, plastic, values, human, dead, sentimental, natural, vitality,* as used in art criticism, are strictly meaningless, in the sense that they not only do not point to any discoverable object, but are hardly even expected to do so by the reader. When one critic writes, "The outstanding features of Mr X's work is its living quality," while another writes, "The immediately striking thing about Mr X's work is its peculiar deadness," the reader accepts this as a simple difference of opinion. If words like *black* and *white* were involved, instead of the jargon words *dead* and *living,* he would see at once that language was being used in an improper way. Many political words are similarly abused. The word *Fascism* has now no meaning except in so far as it signifies "something not desirable." The words *democracy, socialism, freedom, patriotic, realistic, justice,* have each of them several different meanings which cannot be reconciled with one another. In the case of a word like *democracy,* not only is there no agreed definition, but the attempt to make one is resisted from all sides. It is almost universally felt that when we call a country democratic we are praising it: consequently the defenders of every kind of régime claim that it is a democracy, and fear that they might have to stop using the word if it were tied down to any one meaning. Words of this kind are often used in a consciously dishonest way. That is, the person who uses them has his own private definition, but allows his hearer to think he means something quite different. Statements like *Marshal Pétain was a true patriot, The Soviet press is the freest in the world, The Catholic Church is opposed to persecution,* are almost always made with intent to deceive. Other words used in variable meanings, in most cases more or less dishonestly, are: *class, totalitarian, science, progressive, reactionary, bourgeois, equality.*

Now that I have made this catalogue of swindles and perversions, let me   9 give another example of this kind of writing that they lead to. This time it must of its nature be an imaginary one. I am going to translate a passage of good English into modern English of the worst sort. Here is a well-known verse from *Ecclesiastes*:

> I returned, and saw under the sun, that the race is not to the swift, nor the battle to the strong, neither yet bread to the wise, nor yet riches to men of understanding, nor yet favour to men of skill; but time and chance happeneth to them all.

Here it is in modern English:

> Objective consideration of contemporary phenomena compels the conclusion that success or failure in competitive activities exhibits no tendency to be commensurate with innate capacity, but that a considerable element of the unpredictable must invariably be taken into account.

---

[2]Example: "Comfort's catholicity of perception and image, strangely Whitmanesque in range, almost the exact opposite in aesthetic compulsion, continues to evoke that trembling atmospheric accumulative hinting at a cruel, an inexorably serene timelessness. . . . Wrey Gardiner scores by aiming at simple bullseyes with precision. Only they are not so simple, and through this contented sadness runs more than the surface bitter-sweet of resignation." (*Poetry Quarterly.*)

This is a parody, but not a very gross one. Exhibit 3, above, for instance, contains several patches of the same kind of English. It will be seen that I have not made a full translation. The beginning and ending of the sentence follow the original meaning fairly closely, but in the middle the concrete illustrations—race, battle, bread—dissolve into the vague phrase "success or failure in competitive activities." This had to be so, because no modern writer of the kind I am discussing—no one capable of using phrases like "objective consideration of contemporary phenomena"—would ever tabulate his thoughts in that precise and detailed way. The whole tendency of modern prose is away from concreteness. Now analyse these two sentences a little more closely. The first contains 49 words but only 60 syllables, and all its words are those of everyday life. The second contains 38 words of 90 syllables: 18 of its words are from Latin roots, and one from Greek. The first sentence contains six vivid images, and only one phrase ("time and chance") that could be called vague. The second contains not a single fresh, arresting phrase, and in spite of its 90 syllables it gives only a shortened version of the meaning contained in the first. Yet without a doubt it is the second kind of sentence that is gaining ground in modern English. I do not want to exaggerate. This kind of writing is not yet universal, and outcrops of simplicity will occur here and there in the worst-written page. Still, if you or I were told to write a few lines on the uncertainty of human fortunes, we should probably come much nearer to my imaginary sentence than to the one from *Ecclesiastes*.

As I have tried to show, modern writing at its worst does not consist in picking out words for the sake of their meaning and inventing images in order to make the meaning clearer. It consists in gumming together long strips of words which have already been set in order by someone else, and making the results presentable by sheer humbug. The attraction of this way of writing is that it is easy. It is easier—even quicker, once you have the habit—to say *In my opinion it is a not unjustifiable assumption that* than to say *I think*. If you use ready-made phrases, you not only don't have to hunt about for words; you also don't have to bother with the rhythms of your sentences, since these phrases are generally so arranged as to be more or less euphonious. When you are composing in a hurry—when you are dictating to a stenographer, for instance, or making a public speech—it is natural to fall into a pretentious, latinised style. Tags like *a consideration which we shall do well to bear in mind* or *a conclusion to which all of us would readily assent* will save many a sentence from coming down with a bump. By using stale metaphors, similes and idioms, you save much mental effort, at the cost of leaving your meaning vague, not only for your reader but for yourself. This is the significance of mixed metaphors. The sole aim of a metaphor is to call up a visual image. When these images clash—as in *The Fascist octopus has sung its swan song, the jackboot is thrown into the melting-pot*—it can be taken as certain that the writer is not seeing a mental image of the objects he is naming; in other words he is not really thinking. Look again at the examples I gave at the beginning of this essay. Professor Laski (1) uses five negatives in 53 words. One of these is superfluous, making nonsense of the whole passage, and in addition there is the slip *alien* for akin, making further nonsense, and several avoidable pieces of clumsiness which increase the general vagueness. Professor Hogben (2) plays ducks and drakes with a battery which is able to write prescriptions, and, while disapproving of the everyday phrase *put up with,* is unwilling to look *egregious* up in the dictionary and see what it means; (3), if one takes an uncharitable attitude towards it, is simply meaningless: probably one could work out its intended meaning by reading the whole of the article in which it occurs. In (4) the writer knows more or less what he wants to say, but an accumulation of stale phrases chokes him like tea-leaves blocking a sink. In (5) words and meaning have almost parted company. People who write in this manner usually have a general emotional meaning—they dislike one thing and want to express solidarity with another—but they are not interested in the detail of what they are saying. A scrupulous writer, in every sentence that he writes, will ask himself at least four questions, thus: What am I trying to say? What words will express it? What image or idiom will make it clearer? Is this image fresh enough to have an effect? And he will probably ask himself two more: Could I put it more shortly? Have I said anything that is avoidably ugly? But you are not obliged to go to all this trouble. You can shirk it by simply throwing your mind open and letting the ready-made phrases come crowding in. They will construct your sentences for you—even think your thoughts for you, to a certain extent—and at need they will perform the important service of partially concealing your meaning even from yourself. It is at this point that the special connection between politics and the debasement of language becomes clear.

In our time it is broadly true that political writing is bad writing. Where it is ₁₂ not true, it will generally be found that the writer is some kind of rebel, expressing his private opinions, and not a "party line." Orthodoxy, of whatever colour, seems to demand a lifeless, imitative style. The political dialects to be found in pamphlets, leading articles, manifestos, White Papers and the speeches of Under-Secretaries do, of course, vary from party to party, but they are all alike in that one almost never finds in them a fresh, vivid, home-made turn of speech. When one watches some tired hack on the platform mechanically repeating the familiar phrases—*bestial atrocities, iron heel, blood-stained tyranny, free peoples of the world, stand shoulder to shoulder*—one often has a curious feeling that one is not watching a live human being but some kind of dummy: a feeling which suddenly becomes stronger at moments when the light catches the speaker's spectacles and turns them into blank discs which seem to have no eyes behind them. And this is not altogether fanciful. A speaker who uses that kind of phraseology has gone some distance towards turning himself into a machine. The appropriate noises are coming out of his larynx, but his brain is not involved as it would be if he were choosing his words for himself. If the speech he is making is one that he is accustomed to make over and over again, he may be almost unconscious of what he is saying, as one is when one utters the responses in church. And this reduced state of consciousness, if not indispensable, is at any rate favourable to political conformity.

In our time, political speech and writing are largely the defence of the inde- ₁₃ fensible. Things like the continuance of British rule in India, the Russian purges and deportations, the dropping of the atom bombs on Japan, can indeed be defended, but only by arguments which are too brutal for most people to face, and which do not square with the professed aims of political parties. Thus political language has to consist largely of euphemism, question-begging and sheer cloudy vagueness. Defenceless villages are bombarded from the air, the inhabitants driven out into the countryside, the cattle machine-gunned, the huts set on fire with incendiary bullets: this is called *pacification*. Millions of peasants are robbed of their farms and sent trudging along the roads with no more than they can carry: this is called *transfer of population* or *rectification of frontiers*. People are imprisoned for years without trial, or shot in the back of the neck or sent to die of scurvy in Arctic lumber camps: this is called *elimination of unreliable elements*. Such phraseology is needed if one wants to name things without calling up mental pictures of them. Consider for instance some comfortable English professor defending Russian totalitarianism. He cannot say outright, "I believe in killing off your opponents when you can get good results by doing so." Probably, therefore, he will say something like this:

> While freely conceding that the Soviet régime exhibits certain features which the humanitarian may be inclined to deplore, we must, I think, agree that a certain curtailment of the right to political opposition is an unavoidable concomitant of transitional periods, and that the rigours which the Russian people have been called upon to undergo have been amply justified in the sphere of concrete achievement.

The inflated style is itself a kind of euphemism. A mass of Latin words falls 14 upon the facts like soft snow, blurring the outlines and covering up all the details. The great enemy of clear language is insincerity. When there is a gap between one's real and one's declared aims, one turns as it were instinctively to long words and exhausted idioms, like a cuttlefish squirting out ink. In our age there is no such thing as "keeping out of politics." All issues are political issues, and politics itself is a mass of lies, evasions, folly, hatred and schizophrenia. When the general atmosphere is bad, language must suffer. I should expect to find—this is a guess which I have not sufficient knowledge to verify—that the German, Russian and Italian languages have all deteriorated in the last ten or fifteen years, as a result of dictatorship.

But if thought corrupts language, language can also corrupt thought. A bad 15 usage can spread by tradition and imitation, even among people who should and do know better. The debased language that I have been discussing is in some ways very convenient. Phrases like *a not unjustifiable assumption, leaves much to be desired, would serve no good purpose, a consideration which we should do well to bear in mind,* are a continuous temptation, a packet of aspirins always at one's elbow. Look back through this essay, and for certain you will find that I have again and again committed the very faults I am protesting against. By this morning's post I have received a pamphlet dealing with conditions in Germany. The author tells me that he "felt impelled" to write it. I open it at random, and here is almost the first sentence that I see: "(The Allies) have an opportunity not only of achieving a radical transformation of Germany's social and political structure in such a way as to avoid a nationalistic reaction in Germany itself, but at the same time of laying the foundations of a cooperative and unified Europe." You see, he "feels impelled" to write—feels, presumably, that he has something new to say— and yet his words, like cavalry horses answering the bugle, group themselves automatically into the familiar dreary pattern. This invasion of one's mind by ready-made phrases (*lay the foundations, achieve a radical transformation*) can only be prevented if one is constantly on guard against them, and every such phrase anaesthetises a portion of one's brain.

I said earlier that the decadence of our language is probably curable. Those who deny this would argue, if they produced an argument at all, that language merely reflects existing social conditions, and that we cannot influence its development by any direct tinkering with words and constructions. So far as the general tone or spirit of a language goes, this may be true, but it is not true in detail. Silly words and expressions have often disappeared, not through any evolutionary process but owing to the conscious action of a minority. Two recent examples were *explore every avenue* and *leave no stone unturned,* which were killed by the jeers of a few journalists. There is a long list of fly-blown metaphors which could similarly be got rid of if enough people would interest themselves in the job; and it should also be possible to laugh the *not un-* formation out of existence,[3] to reduce the amount of Latin and Greek in the average sentence, to drive out foreign phrases and strayed scientific words, and, in general, to make pretentiousness unfashionable. But all these are minor points. The defence of the English language implies more than this, and perhaps it is best to start by saying what it does *not* imply.

To begin with, it has nothing to do with archaism, with the salvaging of obsolete words and turns of speech, or with the setting-up of a "standard English" which must never be departed from. On the contrary, it is especially concerned with the scrapping of every word or idiom which has outworn its usefulness. It has nothing to do with correct grammar and syntax, which are of no importance so long as one makes one's meaning clear, or with the avoidance of Americanisms, or with having what is called a "good prose style." On the other hand it is not concerned with fake simplicity and the attempt to make written English colloquial. Nor does it even imply in every case preferring the Saxon word to the Latin one, though it does imply using the fewest and shortest words that will cover one's meaning. What is above all needed is to let the meaning choose the word, and not the other way about. In prose, the worst thing one can do with words is to surrender to them. When you think of a concrete object, you think wordlessly, and then, if you want to describe the thing you have been visualising, you probably hunt about till you find the exact words that seem to fit it. When you think of something abstract you are more inclined to use words from the start, and unless you make a conscious effort to prevent it, the existing dialect will come rushing in and do the job for you, at the expense of blurring or even changing

---

[3]One can cure oneself of the *not un-* formation by memorising this sentence: *A not unblack dog was chasing a not unsmall rabbit across a not ungreen field.*

your meaning. Probably it is better to put off using words as long as possible and get one's meaning as clear as one can through pictures or sensations. Afterwards one can choose—not simply *accept*—the phrases that will best cover the meaning, and then switch round and decide what impression one's words are likely to make on another person. This last effort of the mind cuts out all stale or mixed images, all prefabricated phrases, needless repetitions, and humbug and vagueness generally. But one can often be in doubt about the effect of a word or a phrase, and one needs rules that one can rely on when instinct fails. I think the following rules will cover most cases:

i. Never use a metaphor, simile or other figure of speech which you are used to seeing in print.

ii. Never use a long word where a short one will do.

iii. If it is possible to cut a word out, always cut it out.

iv. Never use the passive where you can use the active.

v. Never use a foreign phrase, a scientific word or a jargon word if you can think of an everyday English equivalent.

vi. Break any of these rules sooner than say anything outright barbarous.

These rules sound elementary, and so they are, but they demand a deep change of attitude in anyone who has grown used to writing in the style now fashionable. One could keep all of them and still write bad English, but one could not write the kind of stuff that I quoted in those five specimens at the beginning of this article.

I have not here been considering the literary use of language, but merely 18 language as an instrument for expressing and not for concealing or preventing thought. Stuart Chase and others have come near to claiming that all abstract words are meaningless, and have used this as a pretext for advocating a kind of political quietism. Since you don't know what Fascism is, how can you struggle against Fascism? One need not swallow such absurdities as this, but one ought to recognise that the present political chaos is connected with the decay of language, and that one can probably bring about some improvement by starting at the verbal end. If you simplify your English, you are freed from the worst follies of orthodoxy. You cannot speak any of the necessary dialects, and when you make a stupid remark its stupidity will be obvious, even to yourself. Political language—and with variations this is true of all political parties, from Conservatives to Anarchists—is designed to make lies sound truthful and murder respectable, and to give an appearance of solidity to pure wind. One cannot change this all in a moment, but one can at least change one's own habits, and from time to time one can even, if one jeers loudly enough, send some worn-out and useless phrase—some *jackboot, Achilles' heel, hotbed, melting pot, acid test, veritable inferno* or other lump of verbal refuse—into the dustbin where it belongs.

Meaning and Idea

1. What generally assumed premise about the English language does Orwell describe in the opening paragraph? What is his opinion of that premise? What theory about the condition of the English language does he propose in its place?

2. What is Orwell's analysis of the relation between thought and sloppy language usage?

3. What does Orwell have to say about "staleness of imagery" and "lack of precision" in writing? Name the categories of causes that he enumerates for these two conditions.

4. What is Orwell's basic opinion about the connection between politics and language? What does he say is the primary purpose of overtly political use of language? Does he ever express any of his own political leanings in this essay? If so, where? Support your response with specific references from the text.

5. What is Orwell's attitude toward the need for perfect grammar and syntax? What specific rules does he offer to improve language usage?

Language, Form, Structure

1. The title of this essay promises a connection between politics and language, yet a good deal of the first half of the essay makes no overt mention of politics at all. Where in the first paragraphs does Orwell allude to politics? At what point does he make the connection explicit? Why do you think Orwell follows this structural division of the essay?

2. What is Orwell's purpose in this essay? What is his intended audience? Discuss the relation between purpose and audience in this essay. How do the introduction and the conclusion contribute to the unity of the essay?

3. Analyze Orwell's use of classification here. Are the categories discrete? Do the examples fit the categories appropriately? Orwell relies heavily on process analysis to support his classification of ideas. Outline the process analysis of one particular category that you consider important. What process does he say a "good writer" will undergo for each sentence?

4. Orwell uses quite a few similes throughout this essay. Identify three, and comment on their success in terms of the author's thoughts about concrete versus abstract writing.

5. Use a dictionary to define the following words: decadent; hackneyed; profundity; sordid; jargon; superfluous; scrupulous; shirk; orthodoxy; euphemism. Then use each word in a sentence of your own. Explain the following phrases (use a dictionary if necessary): sentimental archaism; mental vices; arresting phrase; sheer humbug.

Ideas for Writing

1. Classify the worst elements of today's commercial advertising. In your classification, include an analysis of the causes behind the conditions you cite.

2. Write an essay in which you classify pornography in our culture. You may want to organize your writing according to the effects or according to the types of media.

3. How closely does *your* evaluation of the connection between politics and language coincide with Orwell's? What do you consider the worst types of politicalization of language? Select three examples from contemporary nonfiction writing or media commentary, and explain how they represent different types of politicalization.

The Geometer of Race

Stephen Jay Gould

Stephen Jay Gould (1941–   ) is one of the most widely read scientists of our times. An evolutionary biologist trained in geology and paleontology at Antioch and Columbia, Gould has taught at Harvard since 1967. His most recent writings about science and its history are *Eight Little Piggies* (1993), and a collection of essays entitled *Finders, Keepers: Treasures and Oddities of Natural History Collectors* (1994). He has a regular column entitled "This View of Life" in *Natural History* magazine.

Gould's wry, insightful, and always readable style shines in the following essay. As he discusses the father of racial classification and the problematic nature of the system that humanity devised, Gould reveals his own attitudes about the dangers of less than rigorous scientific research.

*I*nteresting stories often lie encoded in names that seem either capri-   1
cious or misconstrued. Why, for example, are political radicals called "left" and their conservative counterparts "right"? In many European legislatures, the most distinguished members sat at the chairman's right, following a custom of courtesy as old as our prejudices for favoring the dominant hand of most people. (These biases run deep, extending well beyond can openers and scissors to language itself, where *dexterous* stems from the Latin for "right," and *sinister* from the word for "left.") Since these distinguished nobles and moguls tended to espouse conservative views, the right and left wings of the legislature came to define a geometry of political views.

Among such apparently capricious names in my own field of biology and   2
evolution, none seems more curious, and none elicits more questions after lectures, than the official designation of light-skinned people in Europe, western Asia, and North Africa as Caucasian. Why should the most common racial group of the Western world be named for a mountain range that straddles Russia and Georgia? Johann Friedrich Blumenbach (1752–1840), the German anatomist and naturalist who established the most influential of all racial classifications, invented this name in 1795, in the third edition of his seminal work, *De Generis Humani Varietate Nativa* (On the Natural Variety of Mankind). Blumenbach's definition cites two reasons for his choice—the maximal beauty of people from this small region, and the probability that humans were first created in this area.

> Caucasian variety. I have taken the name of this variety from Mount Caucasus, both because its neighborhood, and especially its southern slope, produces the most beautiful race of men, I mean the Georgian; and because . . . in that region, if anywhere, it seems we ought with the greatest probability to place the autochthones [original forms] of mankind.

Blumenbach, one of the greatest and most honored scientists of the Enlight-   3
enment, spent his entire career as a professor at the University of Göttingen in
Germany. He first presented *De Generis Humani Varietate Nativa* as a doctoral
dissertation to the medical faculty of Göttingen in 1775, as the Minutemen of
Lexington and Concord began the American Revolution. He then republished the
text for general distribution in 1776, as a fateful meeting in Philadelphia proclaimed our independence. The coincidence of three great documents in 1776—
Jefferson's Declaration of Independence (on the politics of liberty), Adam
Smith's *Wealth of Nations* (on the economics of individualism), and Blumenbach's treatise on racial classification (on the science of human diversity)—
records the social ferment of these decades and sets the wider context that makes
Blumenbach's taxonomy, and his subsequent decision to call the European race
Caucasian, so important for our history and current concerns.

The solution to big puzzles often hinges upon tiny curiosities, easy to miss   4
or to pass over. I suggest that the key to understanding Blumenbach's classification, the foundation of much that continues to influence and disturb us today, lies
in the peculiar criterion he used to name the European race Caucasian—the supposed superior beauty of people from this region. Why, first of all, should a scientist attach such importance to an evidently subjective assessment; and why, secondly, should an aesthetic criterion become the basis of a scientific judgment
about place of origin? To answer these questions, we must compare Blumenbach's original 1775 text with the later edition of 1795, when Caucasians received
their name.

Blumenbach's final taxonomy of 1795 divided all humans into five groups,   5
defined both by geography and appearance—in his order, the Caucasian variety,
for the light-skinned people of Europe and adjacent parts of Asia and Africa; the
Mongolian variety, for most other inhabitants of Asia, including China and Japan;
the Ethiopian variety, for the dark-skinned people of Africa; the American variety, for most native populations of the New World; and the Malay variety, for the
Polynesians and Melanesians of the Pacific and for the aborigines of Australia.
But Blumenbach's original classification of 1775 recognized only the first four of
these five, and united members of the Malay variety with the other people of Asia
whom Blumenbach came to name Mongolian.

We now encounter the paradox of Blumenbach's reputation as the inventor   6
of modern racial classification. The original four-race system, as I shall illustrate
in a moment, did not arise from Blumenbach's observations but only represents,
as Blumenbach readily admits, the classification promoted by his guru Carolus
Linnaeus in the founding document of taxonomy, the *Systema Naturae* of 1758.
Therefore, Blumenbach's only original contribution to racial classification lies in
the later addition of a Malay variety for some Pacific peoples first included in a
broader Asian group.

This change seems so minor. Why, then, do we credit Blumenbach, rather   7
than Linnaeus, as the founder of racial classification? (One might prefer to say
"discredit," as the enterprise does not, for good reason, enjoy high repute these
days.) But Blumenbach's apparently small change actually records a theoretical

shift that could not have been broader, or more portentous, in scope. This change has been missed or misconstrued because later scientists have not grasped the vital historical and philosophical principle that theories are models subject to visual representation, usually in clearly definable geometric terms.

By moving from the Linnaean four-race system to his own five-race scheme, Blumenbach radically changed the geometry of human order from a geographically based model without explicit ranking to a hierarchy of worth, oddly based upon perceived beauty, and fanning out in two directions from a Caucasian ideal. The addition of a Malay category was crucial to this geometric reformulation—and therefore becomes the key to the conceptual transformation rather than a simple refinement of factual information within an old scheme. (For the insight that scientific revolutions embody such geometric shifts, I am grateful to my friend Rhonda Roland Shearer, who portrays these themes in her book *The Flatland Hypothesis*.)

Blumenbach idolized his teacher Linnaeus and acknowledged him as the source of his original fourfold racial classification: "I have followed Linnaeus in the number, but have defined my varieties by other boundaries" (1775 edition). Later, in adding his Malay variety, Blumenbach identified his change as a departure from his old mentor in the most respectful terms: "It became very clear that the Linnaean division of mankind could no longer be adhered to; for which reason I, in this little work, ceased like others to follow that illustrious man."

Linnaeus divided the species *Homo sapiens* into four basic varieties, defined primarily by geography and, interestingly, not in the ranked order favored by most Europeans in the racist tradition—*Americanus, Europaeus, Asiaticus*, and *Afer*, or African. (He also alluded to two other fanciful categories: *ferus* for "wild boys," occasionally discovered in the woods and possibly raised by animals—most turned out to be retarded or mentally ill youngsters abandoned by their parents—and *monstrosus* for hairy men with tails, and other travelers' confabulations.) In so doing, Linnaeus presented nothing original; he merely mapped humans onto the four geographic regions of conventional cartography.

Linnaeus then characterized each of these groups by noting color, humor, and posture, in that order. Again, none of these categories explicitly implies ranking by worth. Once again, Linnaeus was simply bowing to classical taxonomic theories in making these decisions. For example, his use of the four humors reflects the ancient and medieval theory that a person's temperament arises from a balance of four fluids (*humor* is Latin for "moisture")—blood, phlegm, choler (yellow bile), and melancholy (black bile). Depending on which of the four substances dominated, a person would be sanguine (the cheerful realm of blood), phlegmatic (sluggish), choleric (prone to anger), or melancholic (sad). Four geographic regions, four humors, four races.

For the American variety, Linnaeus wrote "*rufus, cholericus, rectus*" (red, choleric, upright); for the European, "*albus, sanguineus, torosus*" (white, sanguine, muscular); for the Asian, "*luridus, melancholicus, rigidus*" (pale yellow, melancholy, stiff); and for the African, "*niger, phlegmaticus, laxus*" (black, phlegmatic, relaxed).

I don't mean to deny that Linnaeus held conventional beliefs about the 13 superiority of his own European variety over others. Being a sanguine, muscular European surely sounds better than being a melancholy, stiff Asian. Indeed, Linnaeus ended each group's description with a more overtly racist label, an attempt to epitomize behavior in just two words. Thus the American was *regitur consuetudine* (ruled by habit); the European, *regitur ritibus* (ruled by custom); the Asian, *regitur opinionibus* (ruled by belief); and the African, *regitur arbitrio* (ruled by caprice). Surely regulation by established and considered custom beats the unthinking rule of habit or belief, and all of these are superior to caprice—thus leading to the implied and conventional racist ranking of Europeans first, Asians and Americans in the middle, and Africans at the bottom.

Nonetheless, and despite these implications, the overt geometry of Linnaeus's model is not linear or hierarchical. When we visualize his scheme as an essential picture in our mind, we see a map of the world divided into four regions, with the people in each region characterized by a list of different traits. In short, Linnaeus's primary ordering principle is cartographic; if he had wished to push hierarchy as the essential picture of human variety, he would surely have listed Europeans first and Africans last, but he started with native Americans instead.

The shift from a geographic to a hierarchical ordering of human diversity 15 must stand as one of the most fateful transitions in the history of Western science—for what, short of railroads and nuclear bombs, has had more practical impact, in this case almost entirely negative, upon our collective lives? Ironically, Blumenbach is the focus of this shift, for his five-race scheme became canonical and changed the geometry of human order from Linnaean cartography to linear ranking—in short, to a system based on putative worth.

I say ironic because Blumenbach was the least racist and most genial of all 16 Enlightenment thinkers. How peculiar that the man most committed to human unity, and to inconsequential moral and intellectual differences among groups, should have changed the mental geometry of human order to a scheme that has served racism ever since. Yet on second thought, this situation is really not so odd— for most scientists have been quite unaware of the mental machinery, and particularly of the visual or geometric implications, lying behind all their theorizing.

An old tradition in science proclaims that changes in theory must be driven 17 by observation. Since most scientists believe this simplistic formula, they assume that their own shifts in interpretation record only their better understanding of newly discovered facts. Scientists therefore tend to be unaware of their own mental impositions upon the world's messy and ambiguous factuality. Such mental impositions arise from a variety of sources, including psychological predisposition and social context. Blumenbach lived in an age when ideas of progress, and the cultural superiority of European ways, dominated political and social life. Implicit, loosely formulated, or even unconscious notions of racial ranking fit well with such a worldview—indeed, almost any other organizational scheme would have seemed anomalous. I doubt that Blumenbach was actively encouraging racism by redrawing the mental diagram of human groups. He was only, and largely passively, recording the social view of his time. But ideas have consequences, whatever the motives or intentions of their promoters.

Blumenbach certainly thought that his switch from the Linnaean four-race 18 system to his own five-race scheme arose only from his improved understanding of nature's factuality. He said as much when he announced his change in the second (1781) edition of his treatise: "Formerly in the first edition of this work, I divided all mankind into four varieties; but after I had more actively investigated the different nations of Eastern Asia and America, and, so to speak, looked at them more closely, I was compelled to give up that division, and to place in its stead the following five varieties, as more consonant to nature." And in the preface to the third edition, of 1795, Blumenbach states that he gave up the Linnaean scheme in order to arrange "the varieties of man according to the truth of nature." When scientists adopt the myth that theories arise solely from observation, and do not grasp the personal and social influences acting on their thinking, they not only miss the causes of their changed opinions; they may even fail to comprehend the deep mental shift encoded by the new theory.

Blumenbach strongly upheld the unity of the human species against an 19 alternative view, then growing in popularity (and surely more conducive to conventional forms of racism), that each major race had been separately created. He ended his third edition by writing: "No doubt can any longer remain but that we are with great probability right in referring all . . . varieties of man . . . to one and the same species."

As his major argument for unity, Blumenbach noted that all supposed racial 20 characteristics grade continuously from one people to another and cannot define any separate and bounded group. "For although there seems to be so great a difference between widely separate nations, that you might easily take the inhabitants of the Cape of Good Hope, the Greenlanders, and the Circassians for so many different species of man, yet when the matter is thoroughly considered, you see that all do so run into one another, and that one variety of mankind does so sensibly pass into the other, that you cannot mark out the limits between them." He particularly refuted the common racist claim that black Africans bore unique features of their inferiority: "There is no single character so peculiar and so universal among the Ethiopians, but what it may be observed on the one hand everywhere in other varieties of men."

Blumenbach, writing eighty years before Darwin, believed that *Homo sapi-* 21 *ens* had been created in a single region and had then spread over the globe. Our racial diversity, he then argued, arose as a result of this spread to other climates and topographies, and to our adoption of different modes of life in these various regions. Following the terminology of his time, Blumenbach referred to these changes as "degenerations"—not intending the modern sense of deterioration, but the literal meaning of departure from an initial form of humanity at the creation (*de* means "from," and *genus* refers to our original stock).

Most of these degenerations, Blumenbach argued, arose directly from dif- 22 ferences in climate and habitat—ranging from such broad patterns as the correlation of dark skin with tropical environments, to more particular (and fanciful) attributions, including a speculation that the narrow eye slits of some Australian aborigines may have arisen in response to "constant clouds of gnats . . .

contracting the natural face of the inhabitants." Other changes, he maintained, arose as a consequence of customs adopted in different regions. For example, nations that compressed the heads of babies by swaddling boards or papoose carriers ended up with relatively long skulls. Blumenbach held that "almost all the diversity of the form of the head in different nations is to be attributed to the mode of life and to art."

Blumenbach believed that such changes, promoted over many generations, [23] could eventually become hereditary. "With the progress of time," Blumenbach wrote, "art may degenerate into a second nature." But he also argued that most racial variations, as superficial impositions of climate and custom, could be easily altered or reversed by moving to a new region or by adopting new behavior. White Europeans living for generations in the tropics could become dark-skinned, while Africans transported as slaves to high latitudes could eventually become white: "Color, whatever be its cause, be it bile, or the influence of the sun, the air, or the climate, is at all events, an adventitious and easily changeable thing, and can never constitute a diversity of species," he wrote.

Convinced of the superficiality of racial variation. Blumenbach defended [24] the mental and moral unity of all peoples. He held particularly strong opinions on the equal status of black Africans and white Europeans. He may have been patronizing in praising "the good disposition and faculties of these our black brethren," but better paternalism than malign contempt. He campaigned for the abolition of slavery and asserted the moral superiority of slaves to their captors, speaking of a "natural tenderness of heart, which has never been benumbed or extirpated on board the transport vessels or on the West India sugar plantations by the brutality of their white executioners."

Blumenbach established a special library in his house devoted exclusively [25] to black authors, singling out for special praise the poetry of Phillis Wheatley, a Boston slave whose writings have only recently been rediscovered: "I possess English, Dutch, and Latin poems by several [black authors], amongst which however above all, those of Phillis Wheatley of Boston, who is justly famous for them, deserves mention here." Finally, Blumenbach noted that many Caucasian nations could not boast so fine a set of authors and scholars as black Africa has produced under the most depressing circumstances of prejudice and slavery: "It would not be difficult to mention entire well-known provinces of Europe, from out of which you would not easily expect to obtain off-hand such good authors, poets, philosophers, and correspondents of the Paris Academy."

Nonetheless, when Blumenbach presented his mental picture of human [26] diversity in his fateful shift away from Linnaean geography, he singled out a particular group as closest to the created ideal and then characterized all other groups by relative degrees of departure from this archetypal standard. He ended up with a system that placed a single race at the pinnacle, and then envisioned two symmetrical lines of departure away from this ideal toward greater and greater degeneration.

We may now return to the riddle of the name Caucasian, and to the signif- [27] icance of Blumenbach's addition of a fifth race, the Malay variety. Blumenbach chose to regard his own European variety as closest to the created ideal and then searched for the subset of Europeans with greatest perfection—the highest of the high, so to speak. As we have seen, he identified the people around Mount Caucasus as the closet embodiments of the original ideal and proceeded to name the entire European race for its finest representatives.

But Blumenbach now faced a dilemma. He had already affirmed the mental [28] and moral equality of all peoples. He therefore could not use these conventional criteria of racist ranking to establish degrees of relative departure from the Caucasian ideal. Instead, and however subjective (and even risible) we view the criterion today, Blumenbach chose physical beauty as his guide to ranking. He simply affirmed that Europeans were most beautiful, with Caucasians as the most comely of all. This explains why Blumenbach, in the first quote cited in this article, linked the maximal beauty of the Caucasians to the place of human origin. Blumenbach viewed all subsequent variations as departures from the originally created ideal— therefore, the most beautiful people must live closest to our primal home.

Blumenbach's descriptions are pervaded by his subjective sense of relative [29] beauty, presented as though he were discussing an objective and quantifiable property, not subject to doubt or disagreement. He describes a Georgian female skull (found close to Mount Caucasus) as "really the most beautiful form of skull which . . . always of itself attracts every eye, however little observant." He then defends his European standard on aesthetic grounds: "In the first place, that stock displays . . . the most beautiful form of the skull, from which, as from a mean and primeval type, the others diverge by most easy gradations . . . Besides, it is white in color, which we may fairly assume to have been the primitive color of mankind, since . . . it is very easy for that to degenerate into brown, but very much more difficult for dark to become white."

Blumenbach then presented all human variety on two lines of successive [30] departure from this Caucasian ideal, ending in the two most degenerate (least attractive, not least morally unworthy or mentally obtuse) forms a humanity— Asian on one side, and Africans on the other. But Blumenbach also wanted to designate intermediary forms between ideal and most degenerate, especially since even gradation formed his primary argument for human unity. In his original four-race system, he could identify native Americans as intermediary between Europeans and Asians, but who would serve as the transitional form between Europeans and Africans?

The four-race system contained no appropriate group. But inventing a fifth [31] racial category as an intermediary between Europeans and Africans would complete the new symmetrical geometry. Blumenbach therefore added the Malay race, not as a minor, factual refinement but as a device for reformulating an entire theory of human diversity. With this one stroke, he produced the geometric transformation from Linnaeus's unranked geographic model to the conventional hierarchy of implied worth that has fostered so much social grief ever since.

> I have allotted the first place to the Caucasian . . . which makes me esteem it the
> primeval one. This diverges in both directions into two, most remote and very

different from each other; on the one side, namely, into the Ethiopian, and on the other into the Mongolian. The remaining two occupy the intermediate positions between the primeval one and these two extreme varieties; that is, the American between the Caucasian and Mongolian; the Malay between the same Caucasian and Ethiopian. [From Blumenbach's third edition.]

Scholars often think that academic ideas must remain at worst, harmless, 32 and at best, mildly amusing or even instructive. But ideas do not reside in the ivory tower of our usual metaphor about academic irrelevance. We are, as Pascal said, a thinking reed, and ideas motivate human history. Where would Hitler have been without racism, Jefferson without liberty? Blumenbach lived as a cloistered professor all his life, but his ideas have reverberated in ways that he never could have anticipated, through our wars, our social upheavals, our sufferings, and our hopes.

I therefore end by returning once more to the extraordinary coincidences of 33 1776—as Jefferson wrote the Declaration of Independence while Blumenbach was publishing the first edition of his treatise in Latin. We should remember the words of the nineteenth-century British historian and moralist Lord Acton, on the power of ideas to propel history:

> It was from America that . . . ideas long locked in the breast of solitary thinkers, and hidden among Latin folios, burst forth like a conqueror upon the world they were destined to transform, under the title of the Rights of Man.

Meaning and Idea

1. According to Gould, what are the racial groups in Blumenbach's final system?

2. How does this 1795 taxonomy differ from Blumenbach's earlier classification and from that of Linnaeus?

3. Why do you think Gould offers extensive explanations of the classifications of race? What functions do the explanations serve? What, if anything, is Gould defending in the essay?

Language, Form, Structure

1. What is Gould's thesis in this essay? How does the first paragraph set the frame for the thesis?

2. What is the effect of Gould's citing other famous texts from 1776? How does this offer corroborating evidence? To what end?

3. Although Gould does not attempt to defend Blumenbach completely, he does list and discuss several beliefs Blumenbach held which are "defensible." Does doing this weaken Gould's argument? Why or why not?

4. Identify places in the selection in which Gould seems most scientific. How does his rigor seem to contribute to his overall point?

5. Why does Gould end the essay with a quote from Lord Acton? Who was Lord Acton? How does the quotation resonate with the thesis? How does the conclusion set a new frame of reference for the thesis?

6. Define the following words and use each in a sentence: capricious; ferment; portentous; confabulations; cartography; canonical; anomalous; adventitious; paternalism; extirpated; risible.

Ideas for Writing

1. Write an essay in which you use and elaborate upon racial classifications to argue either for or against their continued use in society today.

2. Write an essay about racial equality. Draw on current views of the term and classify the various elements that contribute to your view.

3. Write an essay in which you weigh the elements of classification in Gould's piece.

The Girls in Their Summer Dresses

Irwin Shaw

Irwin Shaw (1913–1984) was a novelist, short story writer, playwright, and screenplay writer who was born in Brooklyn, New York, and was educated at Brooklyn College. James Gindin observed that his works "combine sharp commentary and sensitive observation" about the changing social scene, politics, and violence. Shaw was alternately considered a pop writer and a serious writer, and his talents and ironic sense ran the gamut in such works as *Rich Man, Poor Man* (1970), *Nightwork* (1975), and *Beggarman, Thief* (1977).

Irwin Shaw's simple yet lasting "The Girls in Their Summer Dresses," is set in the New York City of the 1930s but could easily pertain to a modern couple. Notice how Shaw develops various levels of affection and response.

*F*ifth Avenue was shining in the sun when they left the Brevoort. 1
The sun was warm, even though it was February, and everything looked like Sunday morning—the buses and the well-dressed people walking slowly in couples and the quiet buildings with the windows closed.

Michael held Frances' arm tightly as they walked toward Washington 2 Square in the sunlight. They walked lightly, almost smiling, because they had slept late and had a good breakfast and it was Sunday. Michael unbuttoned his coat and left it flap around him in the mild wind.

"Look out," Frances said as they crossed Eighth Street. "You'll break your 3 neck."

Michael laughed and Frances laughed with him. 4

"She's not so pretty," Frances said. "Anyway, not pretty enough to take a 5 chance of breaking your neck."

Michael laughed again. "How did you know I was looking at her?" 6

Frances cocked her head to one side and smiled at her husband under the 7 brim of her hat. "Mike, darling," she said.

"O.K.," he said. "Excuse me." 8

Frances patted his arm lightly and pulled him along a little faster toward 9 Washington Square. "Let's not see anybody all day," she said. "Let's just hang around with each other. You and me. We're always up to our neck in people, drinking their Scotch or drinking our Scotch; we only see each other in bed. I want to go out with my husband all day long. I want him to talk only to me and listen only to me."

"What's to stop us?" Michael asked. 10

"The Stevensons. They want us to drop by around one o'clock and they'll 11 drive us into the country."

"The cunning Stevensons," Mike said. "Transparent. They can whistle. 12
They can go driving in the country by themselves."

"Is it a date?" 13

"It's a date." 14

Frances leaned over and kissed him on the tip of the ear. 15

"Darling," Michael said, "this is Fifth Avenue." 16

"Let me arrange a program," Frances said. "A planned Sunday in New York 17
for a young couple with money to throw away."

"Go easy." 18

"First let's go to the Metropolitan Museum of Art," Frances suggested, 19
because Michael had said during the week he wanted to go. "I haven't been there
in three years and there're at least ten pictures I want to see again. Then we can
take the bus down to Radio City and watch them skate. And later we'll go down
to Cavanagh's and get a steak as big as a blacksmith's apron, with a bottle of
wine, and after that there's a French picture at the Filmarte that everybody says—
say, are you listening to me?"

"Sure," he said. He took his eyes off the hatless girl with dark hair, cut 20
dancer-style like a helmet, who was walking past him.

"That's the program for the day," Frances said flatly. "Or maybe you'd just 21
rather walk up and down Fifth Avenue."

"No," Michael said. "Not at all." 22

"You always look at other women," Frances said "Everywhere. Every damn 23
place we go."

"Now, darling," Michael said, "I look at everything. God gave me eyes and 24
I look at women and men and subway excavations and moving pictures and the
little flowers in the field. I casually inspect the universe."

"You ought to see the look in your eyes," Frances said, "as you casually 25
inspect the universe on Fifth Avenue."

"I'm a happily married man." Michael pressed her elbow tenderly. "Exam- 26
ple for the whole twentieth century—Mr. and Mrs. Mike Loomis. Hey, let's have
a drink," he said, stopping.

"We just had breakfast." 27

"Now listen, darling," Mike said, choosing his words with care, "it's a nice 28
day and we both felt good and there's no reason why we have to break it up. Let's
have a nice Sunday."

"All right. I don't know why I started this. Let's drop it. Let's have a good 29
time."

They joined hands consciously and walked without talking among the baby 30
carriages and the old Italian men in their Sunday clothes and the young women
with Scotties in Washington Square Park.

"At least once a year everyone should go to the Metropolitan Museum of 31
Art," Frances said after a while, her tone a good imitation of the tone she used at
breakfast and at the beginning of their walk. "And it's nice on Sunday. There're a
lot of people looking at the pictures and you get the feeling maybe Art isn't on
the decline in New York City, after all—"

"I want to tell you something," Michael said very seriously. "I have not ₃₂ touched another woman. Not once. In all five years."

"All right," Frances said. ₃₃

"You believe that, don't you?" ₃₄

"All right." ₃₅

They walked between the crowded benches, under the scrubby city-park ₃₆ trees.

"I try not to notice it," Frances said, "but I feel rotten inside, in my stom- ₃₇ ach, when we pass a woman and you look at her and I see that look in your eye and that's the way you looked at me the first time. In Alice Maxwell's house. Standing there in the living room, next to the radio, with a green hat on and all those people."

"I remember the hat," Michael said. ₃₈

"The same look," Frances said. "And it makes me feel bad. It makes me feel ₃₉ terrible."

"Sh-h-h, please, darling, sh-h-h." ₄₀

"I think I would like a drink now," Frances said. ₄₁

They walked over to a bar on Eighth Street, not saying anything, Michael ₄₂ automatically helping her over curbstones and guiding her past automobiles. They sat near a window in the bar and the sun streamed in and there was a small, cheerful fire in the fireplace. A little Japanese waiter came over and put down some pretzels and smiled happily at them.

"What do you order after breakfast?" Michael asked. ₄₃

"Brandy, I suppose," Frances said. ₄₄

"Courvoisier," Michael told the waiter. "Two Courvoisiers." ₄₅

The waiter came with the glasses and they sat drinking the brandy in the ₄₆ sunlight. Michael finished half his and drank a little water.

"I look at women," he said. "Correct. I don't say it's wrong or right. I look ₄₇ at them. If I pass them on the street and I don't look at them, I'm fooling you, I'm fooling myself."

"You look at them as though you want them," Frances said, playing with ₄₈ her brandy glass. "Every one of them."

"In a way," Michael said, speaking softly and not to his wife, "in a way ₄₉ that's true. I don't do anything about it, but it's true."

"I know it. That's why I feel bad." ₅₀

"Another brandy," Michael called. "Waiter, two more brandies." ₅₁

He sighed and closed his eyes and rubbed them gently with his fingertips. ₅₂ "I love the way women look. One of the things I like best about New York is the battalions of women. When I first came to New York from Ohio that was the first thing I noticed, the million wonderful women, all over the city. I walked around with my heart in my throat."

"A kid," Frances said. "That's a kid's feeling." ₅₃

"Guess again," Michael said. "Guess again. I'm older now, I'm a man get- ₅₄ ting near middle age, putting on a little fat and I still love to walk along Fifth Avenue at three o'clock on the east side of the street between Fiftieth and Fifty-seventh Streets. They're all out then, shopping, in their furs and their crazy hats, everything all concentrated from all over the world into seven blocks—the best furs, the best clothes, the handsomest women, out to spend money and feeling good about it."

The Japanese waiter put two drinks down, smiling with great happiness.   55

"Everything is all right?" he asked.   56

"Everything is wonderful," Michael said.   57

"If it's just a couple of fur coats," Frances said, "and forty-five dollar hats—"   58

"It's not the fur coats. Or the hats. That's just the scenery for that particular kind of woman. Understand," he said, "you don't have to listen to this."

"I want to listen."   59

"I like the girls in the offices. Neat, with their eyeglasses, smart, chipper,   60 knowing what everything is about. I like the girls on Forty-fourth Street at lunchtime, the actresses, all dressed up on nothing a week. I like the salesgirls in the stores, paying attention to you first because you're a man, leaving lady customers waiting. I got all this stuff accumulated in me because I've been thinking about it for ten years and now you've asked for it and here it is."

"Go ahead," Frances said.   61

"When I think of New York City, I think of all the girls on parade in the   62 city. I don't know whether it's something special with me or whether every man in the city walks around with the same feeling inside him, but I feel as though I'm at a picnic in this city. I like to sit near the women in the theatres, the famous beauties who've taken six hours to get ready and look it. And the young girls at the football games, with the red cheeks, and when the warm weather comes, the girls in their summer dresses." He finished his drink. "That's the story."

Frances finished her drink and swallowed two or three times extra. "You   63 say you love me?"

"I love you."   64

"I'm pretty, too," Frances said. "As pretty as any of them."   65

"You're beautiful," Michael said.   66

"I'm good for you," Frances said, pleading. "I've made a good wife, a good   67 housekeeper, a good friend. I'd do any damn thing for you."

"I know," Michael said. He put his hand out and grasped hers.   68

"You'd like to be free to—" Frances said.   69

"Sh-h-h."   70

"Tell the truth." She took her hand away from under his.   71

Michael flicked the edge of his glass with his finger. "O.K.," he said   72 gently. "Sometimes I feel I would like to be free."

"Well," Frances said, "any time you say."   73

"Don't be foolish." Michael swung his chair around to her side of the table   74 and patted her thigh.

She began to cry silently into her handkerchief, bent over just enough so   75 that nobody else in the bar would notice. "Someday," she said, crying, "you're going to make a move."

Michael didn't say anything. He sat watching the bartender slowly peel a 76
lemon.

"Aren't you?" Frances asked harshly. "Come on, tell me. Talk. Aren't you?" 77

"Maybe," Michael said. He moved his chair back again. "How the hell do I 78
know?"

"You know," Frances persisted. "Don't you know?" 79

"Yes," Michael said after a while, "I know." 80

Frances stopped crying then. Two or three snuffles into the handkerchief 81
and she put it away and her face didn't tell anything to anybody. "At least do me
one favor," she said.

"Sure." 82

"Stop talking about how pretty this woman is or that one. Nice eyes, nice 83
breasts, a pretty figure, good voice." She mimicked his voice. "Keep it to yourself. I'm not interested."

Michael waved to the waiter. "I'll keep it to myself," he said. 84

Frances flicked the corners of her eyes. "Another brandy," she told the 85
waiter.

"Two," Michael said. 86

"Yes, Ma'am, yes, sir," said the waiter, backing away. 87

Frances regarded Michael coolly across the table. "Do you want me to call 88
the Stevensons?" she asked. "It'll be nice in the country."

"Sure," Michael said. "Call them." 89

She got up from the table and walked across the room toward the telephone. 90
Michael watched her walk, thinking what a pretty girl, what nice legs.

Meaning and Idea

1. Into what categories does Michael classify women? Does his energetic
    classification of women make Michael a male chauvinist, or is it just an
    indication of his general appreciation for the opposite sex and for life in
    general, as he claims?

2. To what social class do these characters belong? How do you know?

3. In what ways does Frances classify her relation with Michael?

4. What sort of relationship exists between Frances and Michael?

Language, Form, Structure

1. By what method does Michael classify women? Does he follow any
    system?

2. What is the significance of the title of this story? Could it have been named
    just as easily "The Girls in the Offices," or "The Salesgirls in the Stores,"
    or "The Girls on Forty-fourth Street at Lunchtime?" Why or why not?

3. At one point, the Japanese waiter is described as "smiling with great happiness." What types or levels of happiness does Shaw deal with in the story?

4. In what ways can you read this narrative fiction as classification?

5. Look up and write definitions for: excavations; scrubby; battalions; accumulated; mimicked.

Ideas for Writing

1. Write a few paragraphs in which you classify the members of the opposite sex in your school.

2. Select a single emotion and write a classification of the levels of your reactions to it. You might choose jealousy, fear, love, hate, anxiety, or some other emotion important to you.

3. With whom, Frances or Michael, do you think Shaw's sympathies lie most? Why? What elements of the writing give you this opinion?

Do Not Go Gentle into That Good Night

Dylan Thomas

Dylan Thomas (1914–1953), one of the most flamboyant of modern poets, was born in Swansea, Wales, the son of a schoolteacher. However, Thomas himself was not particularly enamored of school, and he chose instead the life of a writer, publishing his first volume of poems at the age of 20. In 1936, he began a turbulent and dramatic marriage with Caitlin MacNamara, from whom he was often separated in order to give reading and lecture tours in the United States. Thomas is also known for his drama and prose, among which are the voice-play *Under Milkwood* and the delightful *A Child's Christmas in Wales*. Thomas was an excessive drinker, and his alcoholism finally caused his death. Outside the Chelsea Hotel, where he often stayed in New York City, there is a plaque posted to his memory.

"Do Not Go Gentle into That Good Night" was written in 1952 on the occasion of Thomas's father's final illness and just one year before Thomas's own death. In the poet's categorization of the ways in which different types of men face death, we discern a poignant plea to his father.

*D*o not go gentle into that good night,
Old age should burn and rave at close of day;
Rage, rage against the dying of the light.

Though wise men at their end know dark is right,
Because their words had forked no lightning they   5
Do not go gentle into that good night.

Good men, the last wave by, crying how bright
Their frail deeds might have danced in a green bay,
Rage, rage against the dying of the light.

Wild men who caught and sang the sun in flight,   10
And learn, too late, they grieved it on its way
Do not go gentle into that good night.

Grave men, near death, who see with blinding sight
Blind eyes could blaze like meteors and be gay,
Rage, rage against the dying of the light.   15

And you, my father, there on the sad height,
Curse, bless, me now with your fierce tears, I pray.
Do not go gentle into that good night.
Rage, rage against the dying of the light.

Meaning and Idea

1. Whom is the speaker addressing in this poem? How is the address different in stanzas one and six? Why?

2. Into what categories does Thomas classify men who are near death? How are they different from one another? How well do these classifications present a full spectrum of types of people? By what principle do you think Thomas made his selection of categories? Why?

3. What does Thomas ask from his dying father? Is there more than one way to interpret his request? Why does he ask for what he does?

Language, Form, Structure

1. This poem is written according to an intricate French structural form called *villanelle.* Without actually diagramming that form, explain, in your own words, how Thomas uses structure as an organizing technique in this poem. What effect does it produce?

2. What is the irony in the use of the word *grave* in line 13? How is that irony achieved? Why do you think Thomas uses irony here?

3. What is the overall purpose of this poem? How well does Thomas fulfill that purpose? How does classification assist that purpose?

4. Select any words that are not familiar to you from this poem, and write definitions for them.

Ideas for Writing

1. Write a short classification in which you group different types of reactions to an important natural event of your choosing, such as birth, maturation, or death. Address your writing to a specific person for a specific reason.

2. Write a classification essay about different types of people in love. Be sure to include reasons you think they fit into certain categories.

3. In the Author's Prologue to the *Collected Poems of Dylan Thomas* (1957), Thomas writes, "I read somewhere of a shepherd who, when asked why he made from within Fairy rings, ritual observances to the moon to protect his flocks, replied: 'I'd be a damn' fool if I didn't!' These poems, with all their crudities, doubts, and confusions, are written for the love of man and in praise of God, and I'd be a damn' fool if they weren't." Analyze "Do Not Go Gentle into That Good Night" in light of Thomas's stated purpose. Do you see "crudities, doubts, and confusions"? In what way is the poem for the love of man and in praise of God?

Naming of Parts

Henry Reed

Although Henry Reed wrote only two volumes of poetry, his earlier one, *A Map of Verona* (1946), is characterized by a fine combination of feeling and form. The volume is divided into four sections. The first, "Naming of Parts," deals with World War II. Reed's observation is sharp and ironic, and his theme is the futility of war. Born in 1914 in Birmingham, England, Henry Reed was a freelance journalist and teacher. He is best known for his ironic and amusing dramas and radio plays produced by the BBC. His more recent volume of poetry is *Lessons of the War* (1970). He died in 1986.

As you read Henry Reed's "Naming of Parts," play close attention to how the poet intertwines two classifications of simultaneous activities. This poem is a poignant example of Reed's own opinions about war and its activities.

*T*oday we have naming of parts. Yesterday,
We had daily cleaning. And tomorrow morning,
We shall have what to do after firing. But today,
Today we have naming of parts. Japonica
Glistens like coral in all of the neighboring gardens,   5
     And today we have naming of parts.

This is the lower sling swivel. And this
Is the upper sling swivel, whose use you will see,
When you are given your slings. And this is the piling swivel,
Which in your case you have not got. The branches   10
Hold in the gardens their silent, eloquent gestures,
     Which in our case we have not got.

This is the safety-catch, which is always released
With an easy flick of the thumb. And please do not let me
See anyone using his finger. You can do it quite easy   15
If you have any strength in your thumb. The blossoms
Are fragile and motionless, never letting anyone see
     Any of them using their finger.

And this you can see is the bolt. The purpose of this
Is to open the breech, as you see. We can slide it   20
Rapidly backwards and forwards: we call this
Easing the spring. And rapidly backwards and forwards
The early bees are assaulting and fumbling the flowers:
     They call it easing the Spring.

They call it easing the Spring: it is perfectly easy   25
If you have any strength in your thumb: like the bolt,
And the breech, and the cocking-piece, and the point of balance,
Which in our case we have not got; and the almond-blossom
Silent in all of the gardens and the bees going backwards and forwards,
     For today we have naming of parts.   30

Meaning and Idea

1. How does Reed categorize experience in this poem into the "gun world" and the "living world"? Briefly describe the basis of each. What is the relation between the two?

2. What three divisions of activity appear in the first stanza? How does the poet follow through on each division?

3. What is Reed's attitude toward the activities of the training camp? Support your answer with specific references from the poem.

4. To what does the word *parts* in the title refer?

Language, Form, Structure

1. How many speakers are there in this poem? Who are they? How are they different? Where does one voice end and the other begin? Would you call this poem a dialogue? Why or why not?

2. How is time used as a classifying principle in this poem? What are the time periods dealt with?

3. What is the theme of this poem? What is its tone? How do the two affect each other?

4. How is the last stanza structurally different from the others? For what purpose?

5. Define these terms: Japonica; swivel; slings; fragile; assaulting; breech.

Ideas for Writing

1. Classify the various kinds of activities involved in some familiar task. Try to include—in a subtle way—your feelings about the task.

2. Classify the activities or stages that constitute a particular season other than spring.

3. *Double entendre,* a French term meaning "double meaning," identifies a word or expression that simultaneously carries two equally valid meanings and may be used to create irony. How is *double entendre* used in this poem? How does it affect your response to the theme of the poem?

Ecclesiastes

Ecclesiastes is the twenty-first book of the Old Testament. It was originally thought to be composed by Solomon, but scholars now place its writing ca. 300–160 B.C.

Ecclesiastes can be read as a philosophical essay whose theme is that all life needs to be lived happily to the fullest because "all is vanity." The certainty of death, the necessities of wisdom and mercy, and ultimate respect for God's judgments form its philosophical core.

Chapter 3 emphasizes acceptance of the "natural rhythm" of the universe along with enjoyment of one's labors as God's ultimate gift.

CHAPTER 3

*T*o every thing there is a season, and a time to every purpose under the heaven:
2   A time to be born, and a time to die; a time to plant, and a time to pluck up that which is planted;
3   A time to kill, and a time to heal; a time to break down, and a time to build up;
4   A time to weep, and a time to laugh; a time to mourn, and a time to dance;
5   A time to cast away stones, and a time to gather stones together; a time to embrace, and a time to refrain from embracing;
6   A time to get, and a time to lose; a time to keep, and a time to cast away;
7   A time to rend, and a time to sew; a time to keep silence, and a time to speak;
8   A time to love, and a time to hate; a time of war, and a time of peace.
9   What profit hath he that worketh in that wherein he laboureth?
10   I have seen the travail, which God hath given to the sons of men to be exercised in it.
11   He hath made every thing beautiful in his time: also he hath set the world in their heart, so that no man can find out the work that God maketh from the beginning to the end.
12   I know that there is no good in them, but for *a man* to rejoice, and to do good in his life.
13   And also that every man should eat and drink, and enjoy the good of all his labour, it *is* the gift of God.
14   I know that, whatsoever God doeth, it shall be for ever: nothing can be put to it, nor any thing taken from it: and God doeth *it,* that *men* should fear before him.
15   That which hath been is now; and that which is to be hath already been; and God requireth that which is past.
16   And moreover I saw under the sun the place of judgment, *that* wickedness *was* there; and the place of righteousness, that iniquity *was* there.

17   I said in mine heart, God shall judge the righteous and the wicked: for *there is* a time there for every purpose and for every work.

18   I said in mine heart concerning the estate of the sons of men, that God might manifest them, and that they might see that they themselves are beasts.

19   For that which befalleth the sons of men befalleth beasts; even one thing befalleth them: as the one dieth, so dieth the other; yea, they have all one breath; so that a man hath no preeminence above a beast: for all *is* vanity.

20   All go unto one place; all are of the dust, and all turn to dust again.

21   Who knoweth the spirit of man that goeth upward, and the spirit of the beast that goeth downward to the earth?

22   Wherefore I perceive that *there is* nothing better, than that a man should rejoice in his own works; for that *is* his portion: for who shall bring him to see what shall be after him?

Meaning and Idea

1. How, according to this chapter, did God order man's relation to time? What attitude about daily life should derive from that relation?

2. According to the text, are negative emotions and actions permissable? If so, when and why?

Language, Form, Structure

1. This chapter divides into two structural units. Where does the division take place? What is the change? Why does it occur?

2. Verses 1–8 give examples of the "natural flow" of life. Do these examples follow any special patterning or classification? Try to group them into general categories.

3. Define these terms: refrain; rend; travail.

Ideas for Writing

1. Write a classification of your various emotional ups and downs of the past few years.

2. Classify a typical weekday's activities for you from morning to night. How clearly do you usually uphold this classification of activities?

3. This text derives from the traditional King James translation of the Bible. Yet, within the past 20 years or so, many modernized versions of the Bible have appeared—versions that update syntax, try to eliminate the male-oriented language, deal with cultural sensitivities, and so on. How do you feel about the old language versus the new? How do you feel about updated versions of the Bible in general? Why? If possible, find a modified text of this chapter and use specific comparisons to support your opinion.

The National Heartbeat: "We-ness" and "Me-ness"

Malcolm Cowley

Malcolm Cowley (1898–1989) was a literary critic, poet, editor, and social historian. He is well known for his studies of the Lost Generation of American expatriate writers in the 1920s, *Exiles' Return* (1934) and *A Second Flowering* (1973). As editor of the liberal *New Republic,* he organized the 1932 Bonus Expeditionary Force to march to President Hoover's doorstep during the Great Depression to demand their army pensions.

"The National Heartbeat: 'We-ness' and 'Me-ness'" carries into the 1980s Cowley's fine, 60-plus-year history of alert social criticism. As you read, pay attention to his social and cultural classifications and how they differ from what he describes as the mainstream opinions.

So it has been more or less agreed that America is turning right. One pictures a disciplined army of 200 million persons, not counting toddlers, all, as at a word of command, executing a right face and marching off into John Wayne country.

I should question whether there has been any such unanimity, but undoubtedly there has been a change in mood and direction. Liberals now admit to being qualmish about big government. Conservatives are shouting hallelujah! as they band into national lobbies. The watchword in education is "back to basics." College students, those barometers of the future—if one learns to read the dials—have stopped being rebels; instead they plug for marks, worry about finding jobs after graduation, and one reads that their favorite course is Accounting.

But after the turbulent age group of the 1960's, isn't that what might have been expected? Another age group has appeared with its own standards of the good life, and these were pretty certain to be in conflict with the standards of the group that preceded it.

Age groups and the part they have played in American culture—or indeed in any culture—are a subject that has seldom been thoroughly discussed. It first attracted my attention when I was working on the literary records of the so-called Lost Generation. Soon I noted that this was only one of several "generations" in 20th-century American literature. Then I observed that the same phenomenon of conflicting age groups appeared in other fields—art, music, science, public affairs—and was finally mirrored in the general mood of the country. Each new group had its own likes, dislikes, and aspirations, its own "consciousness" or sense of life, and this it tried to impose on older groups and on the future.

But was "generation" the right word for those successive groups? They seemed to come forward at much shorter intervals than the 30-year span of a biological generation. American commentators have preferred to speak in terms of decades, thereby adopting a numerical scheme that lends itself to simple adjectives: the Roaring 20's, the Depression 30's (which were not depressed), the silent or shameful 50's, the rebellious 60's. I noted, however, that this counting by tens doesn't often correspond to the true date either for an age group or for changes in the dominant mood.

I decided to make a chronological table, based on what I remembered or had learned about our century. The result was something like this:

1904–1918: The Age of Reform. Muckrakers, labor novelists, Bull Moose, and finally a crusade to make the world safe for democracy.

1919–1930: The Jazz Age. Wall Street follies, the fast buck, bathtub gin, "The Great Gatsby," expatriation, the crash of '29.

1931–1945: The Depression. Bread lines, the New Deal, Spain, "The Grapes of Wrath," The Hitler-Stalin Pact, and finally the great war that was not a crusade.

1946–1960: The Silent Generation. Security, "making it," the baby boom, the cold war, Joe McCarthy, the New Critics.

1961–1973: The Youth Rebellion. Freedom marches, pot, rock music, "Make love, not war," Vietnam, "The March on the Pentagon," Watergate.

Others might choose different dates for the beginning and end of each period (except when the change in mood was abrupt and unmistakable, as at the end of the two world wars). More often there was a gradual transition, as when the Silent Generation of the 1950's made way for the Youth Rebellion. Did the 60's really begin with John F. Kennedy's Inaugural Address ("Ask what you can do for your country") or only with the bitter news of his assassination? And what about movements like Women's Liberation that have already spanned two eras?

One could argue at length about such questions, but I think that two or three facts might become apparent from my little chart. The first is that there have been five distinct periods—or six, counting the present era—since the turn of the century.

They have lasted for an average of a little less than 15 years, or half the span of a human generation. Finally, one notes that the dominant mood of the country has gone from one extreme to another, and back again, so that periods 30 years apart bear some resemblance to each other. The Old Left of the 1930's fathered the New Left of the 1960's. Now, in the late 1970's, we have the New Right, just as in the late 1940's.

Right . . . left . . . right. Hearing those words so often, we picture the country as following the swing of a giant pendulum. The real process, however, is rather an expansion and contraction of interests on the part of influential minorities. "We-ness" and "me-ness" are the two key words. During an expansive period, the general attention is turned outward to broad issues affecting "us," the nation or the world. The leftists are loud and confident. During a contractive period, attention is focused on "my" success in a stable society. The voices we hear are those of conservatives.

One period has followed another in an immensely slow heartbeat rhythm of diastole followed by systole. The Age of Reform, the Depression, the Youth

Rebellion of the 1960's—all those were expansive periods. In each case they were succeeded by a contractive period: the Jazz Age, the Silent Generation, and now the "me" years after Watergate.

Of course those alternations were shaped by external events, including wars, a depression, and the baby boom. I believe, however, that they also reveal an inner logic and sequence. Perhaps the guiding concept here is disillusionment. The spokesmen for an expansive period are disillusioned when their dream of the future is shattered by such events as the Treaty of Versailles (1919) or the Hitler-Stalin Pact of 1939. A contractive period, with its hunger for personal achievement, or simply for money, leads to another type of disillusionment, this time connected with stress, alienation, corruption, and nervous breakdown. That was what happened toward the end of the Jazz Age, and it may soon happen again, if we can trust college reports.

And then what is to be expected? Putting on my tall, conical wizard's hat and acting the part of an aged seer, I prophesy that some time in the middle 1980's there will be another reaction from me-ness into we-ness, another cresting and falling wave of popular idealism. I don't know what form it will take, since that will depend on events in the world and the nation, but I am sure it is coming.

Meaning and Idea

1. What is Cowley's basic premise in this essay? What is the focus of his evaluation of the changes which have taken place over the years?

2. What is Cowley's opinion of the American political climate of the 1980s? What examples does he offer to support his opinion? What does he say about how college students of that era fit into this political climate?

3. What does the author mean by the phrase "marching off into John Wayne country"? Explain in your own words the meaning of the complete metaphor in the second sentence.

4. What did Cowley mean by *we-ness* and *me-ness*? Why does he identify them as "the two key words"?

5. What did Cowley predict would take place in the mid-1980s? Since we have already passed that time, do you see any evidence of his predictions coming true? How would you characterize Cowley's overall political stance? Do you classify him as a pessimist or an optimist? Why?

Language, Form, Structure

1. According to Cowley, by what classification scheme have most American commentators on culture identified America's consciousness of the twentieth century? What is Cowley's scheme of classification? How is his scheme different? On what basis does he decide to make his categories?

2. Name the special *connotations* that the author applies to the following words or expressions: right; barometers; consciousness; generation; New Left; New Right.

3. How does this essay combine classification with process analysis? Identify and briefly summarize two process analyses used in this essay.

4. Cowley makes use of numerous allusions to political, social, and cultural events. From each of the eras listed on his chart covering the period 1904–1973, choose and explain one fully.

5. Look up the following words in a dictionary, and then use each in a sentence: unanimity; qualmish; turbulent; aspirations; expatriation; contractive; diastole; systole; seer; prophesy.

Ideas for Writing

1. Write a classification of the various cliques or social groups in your school. In your prewriting, be sure to decide on basic principles of classification by which to describe the groups.

2. Write a short classification of either "givers" *or* "takers" among people you have known. Include at least three categories.

3. Do you agree with Cowley's basic division of the ages by means of the "we-ness" and "me-ness" factors? Write a further classification of these two groups based on your own observations. Into which group would you place yourself? Into which group would you place the majority of students in your school? Why?

Modern Friendships

Phillip Lopate

Born in 1943 in Jamaica Heights, New York, Phillip Lopate has written two books of poetry and one novel, and has taught in the Teachers and Writers Collaborative in New York public schools for several years. *Being with Children* is about his time spent in the classroom. This selection is from *Joie de Vivre*, a book of essays published in 1990.

His examination and classification of friendships is of, by, and for his own time. The parameters for and kinds of friendships he discusses are contemporary, and he points out the ways friendship has changed over the years through his many allusions and direct references.

*I*s there anything left to say about friendship after so many great 1 essayists have picked over the bones of the subject? Probably not. Aristotle and Cicero, Seneca and Montaigne, Bacon and Samuel Johnson, Hazlitt, Emerson, and Lamb have all taken their cracks at it; since the ancients, friendship has been a sort of examination subject for the personal essayist. It is partly the very existence of such wonderful prior models that lures the newcomer to follow in the others' footsteps, and partly a self-referential aspect of the genre, since the personal essay is itself an attempt to establish a friendship on the page between writer and reader.

Friendship has been called "love without wings," implying a want of lyri- 2 cal afflatus. On the other hand, the Stoic definition of love ("Love is the attempt to form a friendship inspired by beauty") seems to suggest that friendship came first. Certainly a case can be made that the buildup of affection and the yearning for more intimacy, without the release of sexual activity, keeps friends in a state of sweet-sorrowful itchiness that has as much romantic quality as a love affair. We know that a falling-out between two old friends can leave a deeper and more perplexing hurt than the ending of a love affair, perhaps because we are more pessimistic about the latter's endurance from the start.

Our first attempted friendships are within the family. It is here we practice 3 the techniques of listening sympathetically and proving that we can be trusted, and learn the sort of kindness we can expect in return. I have a sister, one year younger than I, who often took care of me when I was growing up. Once, when I was about fifteen, unable to sleep and shivering uncontrollably with the start of a fever, I decided in the middle of the night to go into her room and wake her. She held me, performing the basic service of a friend—presence—and the chills went away.

There is something tainted about these family friendships, however. This same sister, in her insecure adolescent phase, told me: "You love me because I'm related to you, but if you were to meet me for the first time at a party, you'd think I was a jerk and not worth being your friend." She had me in a bind: I had no way of testing her hypothesis. I should have argued that even if our bond was not freely chosen, our decision to work on it had been. Still, we are quick to dismiss the partiality of our family members when they tell us we are talented, cute, or lovable; we must go out into the world and seduce others.

It is just a few short years from the promiscuity of the sandbox to the tor- 4 mented, possessive feelings of a fifth grader who has just learned that his best and only friend is playing at another classmate's house after school. There may be worse betrayals in store, but probably none is more influential than the sudden fickleness of an elementary school friend who has dropped us for someone more popular after all our careful, patient wooing. Often we lose no time inflicting the same betrayal on someone else, just to ensure that we have got the victimization dynamic right.

What makes friendships in childhood and adolescence so poignant is that 5 we need the chosen comrade to be everything in order to rescue us from the gothic inwardness of family life. Even if we are lucky enough to have several companions, there must be a Best Friend, knightly dubbed as though victor of an Arthurian tournament.

I clung to the romance of the Best Friend all through high school, college, 6 and beyond, until my university circle began to disperse. At that point, in my midtwenties, I also "acted out" the dark competitive side of friendship that can exist between two young men fighting for a place in life and love, by doing the one unforgivable thing: sleeping with my best friend's girl. I was baffled at first that there was no way to repair the damage. I lost this friendship forever, and came away from that debacle much more aware of the amount of injury that friendship can and cannot sustain. Perhaps I needed to prove to myself that friendship was not an all-permissive, resilient bond, like a mother's love, but something quite fragile. Precisely because Best Friendship promotes such a merging of identities, such seeming boundarylessness, the first major transgression of trust can cause the injured party to feel he is fighting for his violated soul against his darkest enemy. There is not much room to maneuver in a best friendship between unlimited intimacy and unlimited mistrust.

Still, it was not until the age of thirty that I reluctantly abandoned the Best 7 Friend expectation and took up a more pluralistic model. At present, I cherish a dozen friends for their unique personalities, without asking that any one be my soul-twin. Whether this alteration constitutes a movement toward maturity or toward cowardly pragmatism is not for me to say. It may be that, in refusing to depend so much on any one friend, I am opting for self-protection over intimacy. Or it may be that, as we advance into middle age, the life problem becomes less that of establishing a tight dyadic bond and more one of making our way in a broader world, "society." Indeed, since Americans have so indistinct a notion of society, we often try to put friendship networks in its place. If a certain intensity is lost in the pluralistic model of friendship, there is also the gain of being able to experience all of one's potential, half-buried selves, through witnessing the spectacle of the multiple fates of our friends. Since we cannot be polygamists in our conjugal life, at least we can do so with friendship. As it happens, the harem of friends, so tantalizing a notion, often translates into feeling pulled in a dozen different directions, with the guilty sense of having disappointed everyone a little. It is also a risky, contrived enterprise to try to make one's friends behave in a friendly manner toward each other: if the effort fails one feels obliged to mediate; if it succeeds two well, one is jealous.

Whether friendship is intrinsically singular and exclusive, or plural and democratic, is a question that has vexed many commentators. Aristotle distinguished three types of friendship in *The Nicomachean Ethics:* "friendship based on utility," such as businessmen cultivating each other for benefit; "friendship based on pleasure," like young people interested in partying; and "perfect friendship." The first two categories Aristotle calls "qualified and superficial friendships," because they are founded on circumstances that could easily change; the last, which is based on admiration for another's good character, is more permanent, but also rarer, because good men "are few." Cicero, who wrote perhaps the best treatise on friendship, also insisted that what brings true friends together is "a mutual belief in each other's goodness." This insistence on virtue as a precondition for true friendship may strike us as impossibly demanding: who, after all, feels himself good nowadays? And yet, if I am honest, I must admit that the friendships of mine which have lasted longest have been with those whose integrity, or humanity, or strength to bear their troubles I continue to admire. Conversely, when I lost respect for someone, however winning he otherwise remained, the friendship petered away almost immediately. "Remove respect from friendship," said Cicero, "and you have taken away the most splendid ornament it possesses."

Montaigne distinguished between friendship, which he saw as a once-in-a-lifetime experience, and the calculating worldly alliances around him, which he thought unworthy of the name. In paying tribute to his late friend Etienne de la Boetie, Montaigne wrote: "Having so little time to last, and having begun so late, for we were both grown men, and he a few years older than I, it could not lose time and conform to the pattern of mild and regular friendships, which need so many precautions in the form of long preliminary association. Our friendship has no other model than itself, and can be compared only with itself. It is not one special consideration, nor two, nor three, nor four, nor a thousand: it is I know not what quintessence of all this mixture, which, having seized my whole will, led it to plunge and lose itself in his; which, having seized his whole will, led it to plunge and lose itself in mine, with equal hunger, equal rivalry. . . . So many coincidences are needed to build up such a friendship that it is a lot if fortune can do it once in three centuries." This seems a bit high hat: since the sixteenth century, our expectations of friendship may have grown more plebeian. Even Emerson, in his grand romantic essay on the subject, allowed as how he was not up to the Castor-and-Pollux standard: "I am not quite so strict in my terms, perhaps because I have never known so high a fellowship as others." Emerson contents himself with a circle of intelligent men and women, but warns us not to throw them together: "You shall have very useful and cheering discourse at several times with two several men, but let all three of you come together, and you shall not have one new and hearty word. Two may talk and one may hear, but three cannot take part in a conversation of the most sincere and searching sort."

Friendship is a long conversation. I suppose I could imagine a nonverbal 10 friendship revolving around shared physical work or sport, but for me, good talk is the point of the thing. Indeed, the ability to generate conversation by the hour is the most promising indication, during its uncertain early stages, that a possible friendship will take hold. In the first few conversations there may be an exaggeration of agreement, as both parties angle for adhesive surfaces. But later on, trust builds through the courage to assert disagreement, through the tactful acceptance that differences of opinion will have to remain.

Some view like-mindedness as both the precondition and product of friend- 11 ship. Myself, I distrust it. I have one friend who keeps assuming that we see the world eye-to-eye. She is intent on enrolling us in a flattering aristocracy of taste, on the short "we" list against the ignorant "they"; sometimes I do not have the strength to fight her need for consensus with my own stubborn disbelief in the existence of any such inner circle of privileged, cultivated sensibility. Perhaps I have too much invested in a view of myself as idiosyncratic to be eager to join any coterie, even a coterie of two. What attracts me to friends' conversation is the give-and-take, not necessarily that we come out at the same point.

"Our tastes and aims and views were identical—and that is where the 12 essence of a friendship must always lie," wrote Cicero. To some extent, perhaps, but then the convergence must be natural, not, as Emerson put it, "a mush of concession. Better be a nettle in the side of your friend than his echo." And Francis Bacon observed that "the best preservative to keep the mind in health is the faithful admonition of a friend."

Friendship is a school for character, allowing us the chance to study in great 13 detail and over time temperaments very different from our own. These charming quirks, these contradictions, these nobilities, these blind spots of our friends we track not out of disinterested curiosity: we must have this information before knowing how far we may relax our guard, how much we may rely on them in crises. The learning curve of friendship involves, to no small extent, filling out this picture of the other's limitations and making peace with the results. (With one's own limitations there may never be peace.) Each time I hit up against a friend's inflexibility I am relieved as well as disappointed: I can begin to predict, and arm myself in advance against repeated bruises. I have one friend who is always late, so I bring a book along when I am to meet her. If I give her a manuscript to read and she promises to look at it over the weekend, I start preparing myself for a month-long wait.

Not that one ever gives up trying to educate the friend to one's needs. I 14 approach such matters experimentally: sometimes I will pride myself in tactfully circumventing the friend's predicted limitation, even if it means relinquishing all hope of getting the response I want; at other times I will confront a problem with intentional tactlessness, just to see if any change is still possible.

I have a dear old friend, Richard, who shies away from personal confi- 15 dences. Years go by without my learning anything about his love life, and he does not encourage the baring of my soul either, much as I like that sort of thing. But we share so many other interests and values that that limitation seems easily borne, most of the time. Once, however, I found myself in a state of emotional despair; I told him I had exhausted my hopes of finding love or success, that I felt suicidal, and he changed the topic, patently embarrassed. I was annoyed both at his emotional rigidity and at my own stupidity—after all, I'd enough friends who ate up this kind of confessional talk, why foist on Richard what I might have predicted he couldn't, or wouldn't, handle? For a while I sulked, annoyed at him for having failed me, but I also began to see my despair through his eyes as melodramatic, childish petulance, and I began to let it go. As it happened, he found other ways during our visit to be so considerate that I ended up feeling better, even without our having had a heart-to-heart talk. I suppose the moral is that a friend can serve as a corrective to our insular miseries simply by offering up his essential otherness.

Though it is often said that with a true friend there is no need to hold anything back ("A friend is a person with whom I may be sincere. Before him I may think aloud," wrote Emerson), I have never found this to be entirely the case. Certain words may be too cruel if spoken at the wrong moment—or may fall on deaf ears, for any number of reasons. I also find with each friend, as they must with me, that some initial resistance, restlessness, psychic weather must be overcome before that tender ideal attentiveness may be called forth. 16

I have a good friend, Charlie, who is often very distracted whenever we first get together. If we are sitting in a cafe he will look around constantly for the waiter, or be distracted by a pretty woman or the restaurant's cat. It would be foolish for me to broach an important subject at such moments, so I resign myself to waiting the half hour or however long it takes until his jumpiness subsides. Or else I draw this pattern grumpily to his attention. Once he has settled down, however, I can tell Charlie virtually anything, and he me. But the candor cannot be rushed. It must be built up to with the verbal equivalent of limbering exercises. 17

The Friendship Scene—a flow of shared confidences, recognitions, humor, advice, speculation, even wisdom—is one of the key elements of modern friendships. Compared to the rest of life, this ability to lavish one's best energies on an activity utterly divorced from the profit motive and free from the routines of domination and inequality that affect most relations (including, perhaps, the selfsame friendship at other times) seems idyllic. The Friendship Scene is by its nature not an everyday occurrence. It represents the pinnacle, the fruit of the friendship, potentially ever-present but not always arrived at. Both friends' dim yet self-conscious awareness that they are wandering conversationally toward a goal that they have previously accomplished but which may elude them this time around creates a tension, an obligation to communicate as sincerely as possible, like actors in an improvisation exercise struggling to shape their baggy material into some climactic form. This very pressure to achieve "quality" communication may induce a sort of inauthentic epiphany, not unlike what happens sometimes in the last ten minutes of a psychotherapy session. But a truly achieved Friendship Scene can be among the best experiences life has to offer. 18

I remember one such afternoon when Michael, a close writer-friend, and I met at a cafeteria on a balmy Saturday in early spring and talked for three and a 19 half hours. There were no outside time pressures that particular afternoon, a rare occurrence for either of us. At first we caught up with our latest business, the sort of items that might have gone into a biweekly bulletin sent to any number of acquaintances. Then gradually we settled into an area of perplexing unresolved impressions. I would tell Michael about A's chance, seemingly hostile remark toward me at a gathering, and he would report that the normally ebullient B looked secretly depressed. These were the memory equivalents of food grains stuck in our teeth, which we were now trying to free with our tongues: anecdotal fragments I was not even sure had any point, until I started fashioning them aloud for Michael's interest. Together we diagnosed our mutual acquaintances, each other's character, and, from there, the way of the world. In the course of our free associations we eventually descended into what was really bothering us. I learned he was preoccupied with the fate of an old college friend who was dying of AIDS, he, that my father was in poor health and needed two operations. We had touched bottom—mortality—and it was reassuring to settle there awhile. Gradually we rose again, drawn back to the questions of ego and career, craft and romance. It was, as I've said, a pretty day, and we ended up walking through a new mall in Houston, gawking at the window displays of that bland emporium with a reawakened curiosity about the consumer treats of America, our attentions turned happily outward now that we had dwelt long enough in the shared privacies of our psyches.

Contemporary urban life, with its tight schedules and crowded appointment ²⁰ books, has helped to shape modern friendship into something requiring a good deal of intentionality and pursuit. You phone a friend and make a date a week or more in advance; then you set aside an evening, like a tryst, during which to squeeze in all your news and advice, confession and opinion. Such intimate compression may add a romantic note to modern friendships, but it also places a strain on the meeting to yield a high quality of meaning and satisfaction, closer to art than life, thereby increasing the chance for disappointment. If I see certain busy or out-of-town friends only once every six months, we must not only catch up on our lives but convince ourselves within the allotted two hours together that we still share a special affinity, an inner track to each other's psyches, or the next meeting may be put off for years. Surely there must be another, saner rhythm to friendship in rural areas—or maybe not? I think about "the good old days" when friends would go on walking tours through England together, when Edith Wharton would bundle poor Henry James into her motorcar and they'd drive to the South of France for a month. I'm not sure my friendships could sustain the strain of travel for weeks at a time, and the truth of the matter is that I've gotten used to this urban arrangement of serial friendship "dates," where the pleasure of the rendezvous is enhanced by the knowledge that it will only last, at most, six hours. If the two of us don't happen to mesh that day (always a possibility)—well, it's only a few hours; and if it should go beautifully, one needs an escape hatch from exaltation as well as disenchantment. I am capable of only so much intense, exciting communication before I start to fade; I come to these encounters equipped with a six-hour oxygen tank. Is this an evolutionary pattern of modern friendship, or only a personal limitation?

Perhaps because I conceive of the modern Friendship Scene as a somewhat 21 theatrical enterprise, a one-act play, I tend to be very affected by the "set," so to speak. A restaurant, a museum, a walk in the park through the zoo, even accompanying a friend on shopping errands—I prefer public turf where the stimulation of the city can play a backdrop to our dialogue, feeding it with details when inspiration flags. True, some of the most cherished friendship scenes have occurred around a friend's kitchen table. The problem with restricting the date to one another's houses is that the entertaining friend may be unable to stop playing the host, or may sink too passively into his or her surroundings. Subtle struggles may also develop over which domicile should serve as the venue.

I have a number of *chez moi* friends, friends who always invite me to come 22 to their homes while evading offers to visit mine. What they view as hospitality I see as a need to control the *mise-en-scène* of friendship. I am expected to fit in where they are most comfortable, while they play lord of the manor, distracted by the props of decor, the pool, the unexpected phone call, the swirl of children, animals, and neighbors. Indeed, *chez moi* friends often tend to keep a sort of open house, so that in going over to see them—for a *tête-à-tête,* I had assumed—I will suddenly find their other friends and neighbors, whom they have also invited, dropping in all afternoon. There are only so many Sundays I care to spend hanging out with a friend's entourage before becoming impatient for a private audience.

Married friends who own their own homes are much more apt to try to draw 23 me into their domestic fold, whereas single people are often more sensitive about establishing a discreet space for the friendship to occur. Perhaps the married assume that a bachelor like myself is desperate for home cooking and a little family life. I have noticed that it is not an easy matter to pry a married friend away from mate and milieu. For married people, especially those with children, the home often becomes the wellspring of all their nurturing feelings, and the single friend is invited to partake in the general flow. Maybe there is also a certain tendency on their parts to kill two birds with one stone: they don't see enough of their spouse and kids, and figure they can visit with you all at the same time. And maybe they need one-on-one friendship less, hampered as they are by responsibilities that no amount of camaraderie or discussion can change. Often friendship in these circumstances is not even a pairing, but a mixing together of two sets of parents and children willy-nilly. What would the ancients say about this? In Rome, according to Bacon, "the whole senate dedicated an altar to Friendship, as to a goddess. . . ." From my standpoint, friendship is a jealous goddess. Whenever a friend of mine marries, I have to fight to overcome the feeling that I am being "replaced" by the spouse. I don't mind sharing a friend with his family milieu—in fact I like it, up to a point—but eventually I must get the friend alone, or else, as a bachelor at a distinct power disadvantage, I risk becoming a mere spectator of familial rituals instead of a key player in the drama of friendship.

A person living alone usually has more control over his or her schedule, 24 hence more energy to give to friendship. If anything, the danger is of investing too much emotional energy in one's friends. When a single person is going through a romantic dry spell he or she often tries to extract the missing passion from a circle of friends. This works only up to a point: the frayed nerves of protracted celibacy can lead to hypersensitive imaginings of slights and rejections, during which times one's platonic friends seem to come particularly into the line of fire.

Today, with the partial decline of the nuclear family and the search for alter- 25
natives to it, we also see attempts to substitute the friendship web for intergenerational family life. Since psychoanalysis has alerted us to regard the family as a minefield of unrequited love, manipulation, and ambivalence, it is only natural that people may look to friendship as a more supportive ground for relation. But in our longing for an unequivocally positive bond, we should beware of sentimentalizing friendship, as saccharine "buddy" movies or certain feminist novels do, of neutering its problematic, destructive aspects. Besides, friendship can never substitute for the true meaning of family: if nothing else, it will never be able to duplicate the family's wild capacity for concentrating neurosis.

In short, friends can't be your family, they can't be your lovers, they can't 26
be your psychiatrists. But they can be your friends, which is plenty. For, as Cicero tells us, "friendship is the noblest and most delightful of all the gifts the gods have given to mankind." And Bacon adds: "it is a mere and miserable solitude to want true friends, without which the world is but a wilderness. . . ."

When I think about the qualities that characterize the best friendships I've 27
known, I can identify five: rapport, affection, need, habit, and forgiveness. Rapport and affection can only take you so far; they may leave you at the formal, outer gate of goodwill, which is still not friendship. A persistent need for the other's company, for their interest, approval, opinion, will get you inside the gates, especially when it is reciprocated. In the end, however, there are no substitutes for habit and forgiveness. A friendship may travel for years on cozy habit. But it is a melancholy fact that unless you are a saint you are bound to offend every friend deeply at least once in the course of time. The friends I have kept the longest are those who forgave me for wronging them, unintentionally, intentionally, or by the plain catastrophe of my personality, time and again. There can be no friendship without forgiveness.

Meaning and Idea

1. Why is Lopate's essay called "Modern Friendships"? What distinction is he drawing?

2. What are Lopate's categories for friendship?

3. What are Lopate's categories for the qualities most important to friendship?

4. Lopate feels that we learn how to create and keep friendships. He also notes that it is sometimes necessary to behave differently with different kinds of friends. What has he learned, in fact, do you think? Where did he get his first lessons? Did he then always know how? Which classical

authors does Lopate attend to most? What does he think about their observations and classifications of friendship?

Language, Form, Structure

1. Especially throughout the first part of his essay, Lopate acknowledges and cites famous writers who have dealt with the topic of friendship or have been "great friends." Does he always completely agree with these others? How is he *using* them?

2. What does the writer achieve by opening his essay with a question?

3. What is the thesis in this essay?

4. The first section of the essay categorizes previous opinions on the topic relative to the writer's own. The second discusses kinds of friendships he has known or had. The third section specifically examines kinds of modern friendships. How is this developing structure useful for Lopate's overall theme?

5. Define the following words, and use each in a sentence: afflatus; stoic; poignant; gothic; debacle; permissive; pluralistic; pragmatism; dyadic; polygamists; conjugal; intrinsically; quintessence; plebeian; coterie; nettle; admonition; borne; foist; petulance; broach; candor; idyllic; epiphany; ebullient.

Ideas for Writing

1. Using classification as the main organizing principle, write an essay called "Modern _____." Fill in the blank with a term of your choice, such as *love, jobs, students, automobiles, films,* or the like.

2. Write your own essay called "Modern Friendships," using a classification scheme to develop your ideas.

3. Identify the three parts of Lopate's essay, and discuss each section's success or quality in relation to his thesis.

CROSSOVER ▬▬▬▬▬▬▬▬▬▬▬▬▬▬▬▬▬▬▬▬▬▬▬

1. Henry Reed's "Naming of Parts" and Wilfred Owen's "Dulce Et Decorum Est" (Chapter Nine) rivet the reader's attention on the destructiveness of war. Write an essay that considers the elements in each poem that most effectively convey the antiwar message.

2. Stephen Jay Gould in "The Geometer of Race" and George Orwell in "Politics and the English Language" write of the relation between language and the way people think. In an essay, explore that connection. What points do the two authors establish in common? In what ways are the authors' positions about language and its repercussions different?

Chapter Seven

■

CAUSATION

Thinking about causes—what produces something—and about effects—what something produces—is an activity both natural and necessary to human life. Questions like, "Why did I do that?", "What happened because I did that?", and "What might happen if I do that?" reflect both our instinctive curiosity and our desire to learn from experience—to explain or control life from our judgments of the past or from our anticipation of the future. Indeed, it is hard to think of an hour passing when our minds are not engaged in causal thinking. The whistling we hear: Is that the kettle, the wind, the radio? That pulsing headache: Is it an emerging cold, tension over an exam, eyestrain, or the day's humidity? And what will result from the headache? Will we miss work, fail a test, finally replace lost eyeglasses, shop for a dehumidifier?

Not surprisingly, great writing throughout history reflects the basic human habit of seeking explanations for why things happen and what occurs after they happen. In almost every culture, early myths explore why the world began and why its inhabitants, human and nonhuman alike, got to be the way they are. Philosophers from Aristotle on have dealt copiously with causal thinking—what it is, how to do it best, how to avoid its traps. For Aristotle, and then for the medieval philosophers who built on his thinking, there existed a taxonomy of causes—*efficient* cause, *material* cause, *formal* cause, *final* cause, to name but a few. For ages, most thinkers saw a *necessary* connection between causes and effects, a connection finally controlled by power from a divine source. In the eighteenth century, however, the philosopher David Hume painted a universe as a place of accidents and coincidences, not of absolute connections between causes and effects. Hume helped to change markedly a long-accepted view of causation. By the twentieth century, the philosopher Bertrand Russell declared the idea of cause a "relic of bygone days."

The stance of men like Russell may be extreme and inaccurate; but it is valuable, for it cautions us away from fast and smug interpretations of why things happen. Essential as it is, the whole undertaking of causal thinking can be treacherous. Rushing to judgment, we can assign the wrong cause to an event or point to an effect that is no more than a coincidence. Chances are that the notion of causality will be with us for as long as humans think critically about events, but going slowly and carefully as we think about why things happen and what follows when something happens seems the only right way to reach sound and useful judgments. The imaginative writer delves steadily and deeply into causes and effects. The great writer eschews snap judgments, tracing the possibilities for why things occur or for the effects of occurrences, and inviting readers to use their own faculties to validate proposed causes and results.

READING CAUSAL ANALYSIS

Read a tale to a child, and the child asks, "Why? Then what?" These questions remain steady ones as we read throughout our lives. In great writing we find minds searching for why things happen—why wars start, why marriages last or fail, why people give up or endure, why kingdoms and civilizations crumble or advance. And great writing takes up the questions beyond these: What happens as a result of certain conditions—*after* wars begin, *after* marriages end, *after* men or women survive, *after* kingdoms fall. What happens then?

The selections in this chapter allow you to see both impulses at work—the search back into causes and the search forward from events into effects.

Reading causation in the masters, we are encouraged to see the subtlety of explanations that guide us away from pat interpretations. Indeed, in the hands of great writers, causal analysis is often more an *asking* or a *suggesting* than a certain *stating* of causes and (or) effects. Edwin Arlington Robinson's poem "Richard Cory" never tells the reader "This is why Richard Cory killed himself"; rather the poet lays out details and patterns that invite the reader to speculate *why*.

Reading causal analyses can teach us much as we approach our own thinking and writing. Great writers remind us to approach the whole undertaking of causation with care, to avoid the quick and facile explanations that lead to error, and to find the explanations that can open our eyes about past events and future possibilities. Yet these writers also help us thrill to the speculation about causes and effects, how these unite in a chain of interactions, what might have occurred had one small event not led to another and another and another. Tobias Wolff's story, aptly called "The Chain," though it is a simple narrative, will intensify your view of how, even when unintended, incidents may link to produce tragic results.

WRITING CAUSAL ANALYSIS

Causal thinking is central to much writing. Again and again, students receive assignments whose major task is the identification and explanation of the cause of a particular phenomenon, the effects of the phenomenon, or both. History courses might ask you to examine in writing the causes or results of a war. Literature courses might ask you to write on causes or effects of character, events, or places. Science courses might ask you to reflect again and again on events leading to or resulting from some occurrence—how a compound forms from two elements in a test tube, say, or the consequences of unchecked atmospheric pollution.

Causal analysis is the dominant undertaking of a good portion of academic assignments and an important contributor to still more. Most writers undertaking a comprehensive analysis of a subject will pay attention to causality, even if their major concerns lie elsewhere. Explaining how to establish a new lawn, for example, a writer might lay out the consequences of too little watering or too much fertilizer, and would therefore be drawing cause and effect into a paper whose main intent was process analysis. In a comparison between two unequally successful socialist economic systems, you certainly would explore for your reader the causes for the failures of one and the gains of the other. Causal analysis, then, is something you must master as a writer in order to investigate many topics in many fields, and must learn to approach with slow and deliberate thinking beforehand.

PURPOSE AND AUDIENCE

While many causal assignments will require you to discuss causes *and* effects, many will require that you decide for yourself on one or the other. Often, then, the first step in clarifying purpose for your causal writing is to determine which you will be considering—causes or effects. Do you want to consider what led up to an event or phenomenon, or do you want to consider what came after it? Furthermore, what you decide to focus on in causal analysis will depend to a great extent on your interests and your point of view. The causes assigned to the same event—World War II, for example—will differ depending on the orientation of the person doing the analysis. A psychologist or a psychologically oriented person may stress the *Übermensch* mentality of the Third Reich. The economist or economically oriented person might stress the striving for control of world capital. The political scientist or someone interested in the study of government might stress the clash of nations or the political orientations of their leaders. All of these approaches may be valid. Usually, important events, like wars, stem from many conditions and occurrences.

Aside from orientation, you must take into account the scope of discussion within that orientation. Generally the causes leading to something are many and connected, as are the results. You must decide whether you wish to consider far-off causes, or immediate causes, underlying causes, or precipitating events. And for results, too, do you wish to write of immediate or far-reaching results, the most important or the least expected? Will you show that causes or effects usually ascribed to an occurrence are simply wrong or inaccurate? If you decide which kinds of causes and effects you wish to include, you will be able to write with much greater purpose and direction.

In part, your audience may determine both the point of view and the scope you adopt. Does your audience have some special interest or intellectual approach? Does it know a good deal about the subject? If so, do you wish to deepen or rather to challenge their knowledge? Explaining the results of a new gene-splicing technique in a journal for geneticists requires one strategy; explaining it to the educated but not nearly so specialized readership of *Omni* or *Scientific American* requires quite another. Although a writer could assume avid interest from both audiences, the range of materials included in essays to each group would differ drastically. And imagine how those two essays would differ from a piece on the causal analysis of gene splicing in the Sunday magazine section of your local newspaper.

PROCESS

To help you think about your purpose in causal analysis, use prewriting strategies to produce a sequence of the events or phenomena involved in the topic you're interested in. If you are uncertain about whether you wish to write about causes, effects, or both, try to draft your time line so that your sequence stretches *back* through events and *forward* through results. Then look over your time line or sequential list and decide what interests you most—what *caused* an event or phenomenon, or what resulted from an event or phenomenon, or both. As you look over your page, ask yourself if you have jotted down many causes, for example, that are psychological in nature. If so, that may tell you something about what you wish to stress in your analysis. Use your sequential list as a rough outline and cross out those items that seem uninteresting or illogical and add other items that might make for a fuller discussion. Suppose you've decided to write about the reasons you and your boyfriend broke up last month. You see as you look at your prewriting that the major problem was a raw competitiveness that underlay the relationship despite its passion and mutual respect. You see, too, that you've listed anxiety over pressure to marry as another cause for the end of the relationship. Well, then, the items you've included about your different tastes in clothing, foods, and good times and your different intellectual interests (you're a business major, he's a poet) may not be relevant in this paper. But you might add another item—the psychological stress caused by your frequent separations.

Once you've decided on your focus—causes, effects, or both—and have roughly outlined and revised possible causes and/or effects, you are ready to look even more critically at your analysis. Causality is an extremely valuable tool for a writer, but without sufficient care, we all too often can fall into illogical thinking, assigning cause or effect when there is neither. Therefore you want to review your list of possible causes and effects for problems in logic. Have you called something an effect just because it happened after something else? Have you called something a cause because something else just happens to follow it? Because it snowed the day you got an A on your calculus final, it does not logically follow that the A *resulted* from the snow or that the snow *caused* the A grade. The two events have nothing logically to do with each other. Logicians call this error in logic *post hoc, ergo propter hoc* (after this, therefore because of this), and you must be on the lookout for this fallacy as you prepare to write. Also, make sure that you have provided a reasonable number of causes and/or effects in your analysis. At times, a single cause or effect is all the writer wishes to convey, but more often than not, several causes and/or several results make for a more enlightened discussion. In truth, causation is no simple affair, and a whole chain of events and conditions precedes and follows almost any event.

When you're ready to write, if you wish to focus on effects, you will most likely start with a brief statement of *cause* and then move on to the main concern of your paper—effects of that cause. If, on the other hand, you're primarily interested in discussing effect, then you will do well to start your paper by briefly identifying and explaining the causes leading to this effect. If you're doing both—an ambitious undertaking in a short essay—then identify your phenomenon at the start of your paper and discuss causes and effects in separate sections so as not to confuse the two. A well-wrought thesis statement that identifies your topic and your intended approach to it will guide your course as you produce your drafts.

The care and attention you give to planning a paper of causal analysis is worth the effort. Causal thinking is vital, helping us to explain past events and to learn for the future. The well-reasoned causal analysis can teach much to both the writer and the reader.

SUMMING UP: CAUSATION

Reading Causal Analysis

- Causal analysis means determining the reason something happened or the consequences or effects of some event.

- Weigh the writer's arguments and explanations to be sure that he does not rush to judgment, assigning incorrect causes or pointing to effects that are no more than coincidences.

- If the writer presents a chain of events, determine whether they seem logical and how the events interlink to produce the result being analyzed.

- Identify ways the writer has suggested or asked about causes or effects, as opposed to stating them absolutely.

- From the details and patterns in the writing, speculate on your own about the causes and effects of issues presented by the writer.

- Ascertain whether the writer has stated clearly the causes and (or) effects she intends to explore in the paper.

Writing Causal Analysis

- Use prewriting to consider carefully the causes and effects of your chosen topic.

- Consider whether you want to stress causes or effects and determine the scope of your intended presentation.

- List the sequence of events or phenomena involved in the topic you're considering, and use the list as a rough outline.

- When you have decided on your focus—causes, effects, or both—produce a thesis statement that identifies the topic and your intended approach to it.

- Examine your drafts for appropriate logic, and beware of logical fallacies.

- Provide a sufficient number of causes or effects to make your point acceptable to your reader.

The Myth of Sisyphus

Albert Camus

Albert Camus was born in Algeria in 1913 and won the 1957 Nobel Prize for literature. He was tragically killed in a car accident in 1960. He worked in many genres and was first published during the Nazi occupation of France while he was a resistance fighter in the French underground. With the release, in 1942, of both *The Stranger* and *The Myth of Sisyphus* (the essay from which the following reading is taken), he instantly gained a reputation.

Camus found Sisyphus the prototypical absurd human being. The writer explores several issues surrounding the myth, but the unexplainable causes for Sisyphus's fate, and by extension humanity's, are his primary concern.

The gods had condemned Sisyphus to ceaselessly rolling a rock to   1
the top of a mountain, whence the stone would fall back of its own weight. They had thought with some reason that there is no more dreadful punishment than futile and hopeless labor.

If one believes Homer, Sisyphus was the wisest and most prudent of mor-   2
tals. According to another tradition, however, he was disposed to practice the profession of highwayman. I see no contradiction in this. Opinions differ as to the reasons why he became the futile laborer of the underworld. To begin with, he is accused of a certain levity in regard to the gods. He stole their secrets. Aegina, the daughter of Aesopus, was carried off by Jupiter. The father was shocked by that disappearance and complained to Sisyphus. He, who knew of the abduction, offered to tell about it on condition that Aesopus would give water to the citadel of Corinth. To the celestial thunderbolts he preferred the benediction of water. He was punished for this in the underworld. Homer tells us also that Sisyphus had put Death in chains. Pluto could not endure the sight of his deserted, silent empire. He dispatched the god of war, who liberated Death from the hands of her conqueror.

It is said also that Sisyphus, being near to death, rashly wanted to test his   3
wife's love. He ordered her to cast his unburied body into the middle of the public square. Sisyphus woke up in the underworld. And there, annoyed by an obedience so contrary to human love, he obtained from Pluto permission to return to earth in order to chastise his wife. But when he had seen again the face of this world, enjoyed water and sun, warm stones and the sea, he no longer wanted to go back to the infernal darkness. Recalls, signs of anger, warnings were of no avail. Many years more he lived facing the curve of the gulf, the sparkling sea, and the smiles of earth. A decree of the gods was necessary. Mercury came and seized the impudent man by the collar and, snatching him from his joys, led him forcibly back to the underworld, where his rock was ready for him.

You have already grasped that Sisyphus is the absurd hero. He *is,* as much   4
through his passions as through his torture. His scorn of the gods, his hatred of

death, and his passion for life won him that unspeakable penalty in which the whole being is exerted toward accomplishing nothing. This is the price that must be paid for the passions of this earth. Nothing is told us about Sisyphus in the underworld. Myths are made for the imagination to breathe life into them. As for this myth, one sees merely the whole effort of a body straining to raise the huge stone, to roll it and push it up a slope a hundred times over; one sees the face screwed up, the cheek tight against the stone, the shoulder bracing the clay-covered mass, the foot wedging it, the fresh start with arms outstretched, the wholly human security of two earth-clotted hands. At the very end of his long effort measured by skyless space and time without depth, the purpose is achieved. Then Sisyphus watches the stone rush down in a few moments toward that lower world whence he will have to push it up again toward the summit. He goes back down to the plain.

It is during that return, that pause, that Sisyphus interests me. A face that toils so close to stones is already stone itself! I see that man going back down with a heavy yet measured step toward the torment of which he will never know the end. That hour like a breathingspace which returns as surely as his suffering, that is the hour of consciousness. At each of those moments when he leaves the heights and gradually sinks toward the lairs of the gods, he is superior to his fate. He is stronger than his rock.

If this myth is tragic, that is because its hero is conscious. Where would his torture be, indeed, if at every step the hope of succeeding upheld him? The workman of today works every day in his life at the same tasks, and this fate is no less absurd. But it is tragic only at the rare moments when it becomes conscious. Sisyphus, proletarian of the gods, powerless and rebellious, knows the whole extent of his wretched condition: it is what he thinks of during his descent. The lucidity that was to constitute his torture at the same time crowns his victory. There is no fate that cannot be surmounted by scorn.

If the descent is thus sometimes performed in sorrow, it can also take place in joy. This word is not too much. Again I fancy Sisyphus returning toward his rock, and the sorrow was in the beginning. When the images of earth cling too tightly to memory, when the call of happiness becomes too insistent, it happens that melancholy rises in man's heart: this is the rock's victory, this is the rock itself. The boundless grief is too heavy to bear. These are our nights of Gethsemane. But crushing truths perish from being acknowledged. Thus, Oedipus at the outset obeys fate without knowing it. But from the moment he knows, his tragedy begins. Yet at the same moment, blind and desperate, he realizes that the only bond linking him to the world is the cool hand of a girl. Then a tremendous remark rings out: "Despite so many ordeals, my advanced age and the nobility of my soul make me conclude that all is well." Sophocles' Oedipus, like Dostoevsky's Kirilov, thus gives the recipe for the absurd victory. Ancient wisdom confirms modern heroism.

One does not discover the absurd without being tempted to write a manual ₈ of happiness. "What! by such narrow ways—?" There is but one world, however. Happiness and the absurd are two sons of the same earth. They are inseparable. It would be a mistake to say that happiness necessarily springs from the absurd discovery. It happens as well that the feeling of the absurd springs from happiness. "I conclude that all is well," says Oedipus, and that remark is sacred. It echoes in the wild and limited universe of man. It teaches that all is not, has not been, exhausted. It drives out of this world a god who had come into it with dissatisfaction and a preference for futile sufferings. It makes of fate a human matter, which must be settled among men.

All Sisyphus' silent joy is contained therein. His fate belongs to him. His ₉ rock is his thing. Likewise, the absurd man, when he contemplates his torment, silences all the idols. In the universe suddenly restored to its silence, the myriad wondering little voices of the earth rise up. Unconscious, secret calls, invitations from all the faces, they are the necessary reverse and price of victory. There is no sun without shadow, and it is essential to know the night. The absurd man says yes and his effort will henceforth be unceasing. If there is a personal fate, there is no higher destiny, or at least there is but one which he concludes is inevitable and despicable. For the rest, he knows himself to be the master of his days. At that subtle moment when man glances backward over his life, Sisyphus returning toward his rock, in that slight pivoting he contemplates that series of unrelated actions which becomes his fate, created by him, combined under his memory's eye and soon sealed by his death. Thus, convinced of the wholly human origin of all that is human, a blind man eager to see who knows that the night has no end, he is still on the go. The rock is still rolling.

I leave Sisyphus at the foot of the mountain! One always finds one's burden ₁₀ again. But Sisyphus teaches the higher fidelity that negates the gods and raises rocks. He too concludes that all is well. This universe henceforth without a master seems to him neither sterile nor futile. Each atom of that stone, each mineral flake of that nightfilled mountain, in itself forms a world. The struggle itself toward the heights is enough to fill a man's heart. One must imagine Sisyphus happy.

Meaning and Idea

1. What is Sisyphus's fate—how did the gods punish him? What is his guilt, and what is the severity of his crime? Is there justification for the severity of his punishment, do you think? Why? What does Camus note is the "breathingspace" for his hero.

2. Camus states that the rock has a victory, but which has the ultimate victory, the rock or Sisyphus? According to Camus, why is this so? What does he mean when he says "There is no fate that cannot be surmounted by scorn" and "But crushing truths perish from being acknowledged"?

3. What is an absurd hero, according to Camus? Why does he say that Sisyphus fits that category? What other heroes, either real or in literature, would you call absurd?

4. How does Sisyphus compare to the modern workman? What does Camus say that they have in common, and when does he note that each is the most tragic?

Language, Form, Structure

1. What is Camus's thesis here?

2. What is the essential cause-and-effect element that structures the essay? What other causes and effects do you note?

3. Why does Camus make a number of references to classical mythology? What do they contribute to the essay?

4. Comment on the final paragraph. What is the meaning of the sentence "One always finds one's burden again"? With what impression does Camus leave the reader at the end? Explain your answer.

5. Define the following words and use each in a sentence: futile; levity; citadel; benediction; dispatched; chastise; impudent; absurd; proletarian; lucidity; surmounted; Gethsemane; myriad; despicable.

Ideas for Writing

1. Write an essay about the cause-and-effect relation between an action you performed and a punishment that followed from it. Explain whether or not you felt the punishment was unjust.

2. Camus writes, "They [the gods] had thought with some reason that there is no more dreadful punishment than futile and hopeless labor." Write an essay in which you analyze that statement. Do you agree with it? Why? How do work programs in modern prison systems reflect Camus's beliefs?

3. Write an essay in which you examine the classical references in "The Myth of Sisyphus," particularly the references to the myths in paragraph 2 and the Oedipus story. How do these myths contribute to Camus's piece?

The Story of an Hour

Kate Chopin

Kate Chopin (1851–1904) was reared primarily by her Creole mother and great-grand-mother in St. Louis. In her late teens, Chopin married, and she moved to New Orleans with her cotton broker husband. After he died, following 14 years of marriage, Chopin started life again with her six children. She began her literary career with stories about Creole life, heavily influenced by Maupassant. Her short pieces were published in various magazines, establishing her reputation firmly. *The Awakening* (1899), a forward-thinking novel about the sexual awakening and need for self-fulfilment of a wife, is considered Chopin's masterpiece.

In this short, short narrative, Kate Chopin traces the ironic causal relationships of fate and its strange twists. As you read, look for various levels of meaning and how they affect the causal development of the story.

*K*nowing that Mrs. Mallard was afflicted with a heart trouble, great care was taken to break to her as gently as possible the news of her husband's death.   1

It was her sister Josephine who told her, in broken sentences, veiled hints that revealed in half concealing. Her husband's friend Richards was there, too, near her. It was he who had been in the newspaper office when intelligence of the railroad disaster was received, with Brently Mallard's name leading the list of "killed." He had only taken the time to assure himself of its truth by a second telegram, and had hastened to forestall any less careful, less tender friend in bearing the sad message.   2

She did not hear the story as many women have heard the same, with a paralyzed inability to accept its significance. She wept at once, with sudden, wild abandonment, in her sister's arms. When the storm of grief had spent itself she went away to her room alone. She would have no one follow her.   3

There stood, facing the open window, a comfortable, roomy armchair. Into this she sank, pressed down by a physical exhaustion that haunted her body and seemed to reach into her soul.   4

She could see in the open square before her house the tops of trees that were all aquiver with the new spring life. The delicious breath of rain was in the air. In the street below a peddler was crying his wares. The notes of a distant song which some one was signing reached her faintly, and countless sparrows were twittering in the eaves.   5

There were patches of blue sky showing here and there through the clouds that had met and piled above the other in the west facing her window.   6

She sat with her head thrown back upon the cushion of the chair quite motionless, except when a sob came up into her throat and shook her, as a child who has cried itself to sleep continues to sob in its dreams.   7

She was young, with a fair, calm face, whose lines bespoke repression and 8 even a certain strength. But now there was a dull stare in her eyes, whose gaze was fixed away off yonder on one of those patches of blue sky. It was not a glance of reflection, but rather indicated a suspension of intelligent thought.

There was something coming to her and she was waiting for it, fearfully. 9 What was it? She did not know; it was too subtle and elusive to name. But she felt it, creeping out of the sky, reaching toward her through the sounds, the scents, the color that filled the air.

Now her bosom rose and fell tumultuously. She was beginning to recognize 10 this thing that was approaching to possess her, and she was striving to beat it back with her will—as powerless as her two white slender hands would have been.

When she abandoned herself a little whispered word escaped her slightly 11 parted lips. She said it over and over under her breath. "Free, free, free!" The vacant stare and the look of terror that had followed it went from her eyes. They stayed keen and bright. Her pulses beat fast, and the coursing blood warmed and relaxed every inch of her body.

She did not stop to ask if it were not a monstrous joy that held her. A clear 12 and exalted perception enabled her to dismiss the suggestion as trivial.

She knew that she would weep again when she saw the kind, tender hands 13 folded in death; the face that had never looked save with love upon her, fixed and gray and dead. But she saw beyond that bitter moment a long procession of years to come that would belong to her absolutely. And she opened and spread her arms out to them in welcome.

There would be no one to live for during those coming years; she would live 14 for herself. There would be no powerful will bending her in that blind persistence with which men and women believe they have a right to impose a private will upon a fellow-creature. A kind intention or a cruel intention made the act seem no less a crime as she looked upon it in that brief moment of illumination.

And yet she had loved him—sometimes. Often she had not. What did it 15 matter! What could love, the unsolved mystery, count for in face of this posses- sion of self-assertion which she suddenly recognized as the strongest impulse of her being.

"Free! Body and soul free!" she kept whispering. 16

Josephine was kneeling before the closed door with her lips to the keyhole, 17 imploring for admission. "Louise, open the door! I beg; open the door—you will make yourself ill. What are you doing, Louise? For heaven's sake open the door."

"Go away, I am not making myself ill." No; she was drinking in a very elixir 18 of life through that open window.

Her fancy was running riot along those days ahead of her. Spring days, and 19 summer days, and all sorts of days that would be her own. She breathed a quick prayer that life might be long. It was only yesterday she had thought with a shud- der that life might be long.

She arose at length and opened the door to her sister's importunities. There 20 was a feverish triumph in her eyes, and she carried herself unwittingly like a goddess of Victory. She clasped her sister's waist, and together they descended the stairs. Richards stood waiting for them at the bottom.

Some one was opening the front door with a latchkey. It was Brently Mallard who entered, a little travel-stained, composedly carrying his grip-sack and umbrella. He had been far from the scene of accident, and did not even know there had been one. He stood amazed at Josephine's piercing cry; at Richards' quick motion to screen him from the view of his wife. 21

But Richards was too late. 22

When the doctors came they said she had died of heart disease—of joy that kills. 23

Meaning and Idea

1. What potential cause-and-effect sequence is averted by the action described in the opening sentence? Is it really averted after all?

2. How are Mrs. Mallard's immediate reactions to the news of her husband's death different from the norm according to the narrative? What are her subsequent reactions?

3. What is the "something" that was "coming to her and she was waiting for"? How is it possible to read that "something" on more than one level?

4. How does Mrs. Mallard's attitude change after she starts repeating the words—and emotions—"Free, free, free"? What is she free of?

5. What ultimately kills Mrs. Mallard?

Language, Form, Structure

1. Identify three distinct instances of cause and effect in this story. Explain how they relate to one another.

2. How does Chopin's physical description of Mrs. Mallard prepare readers for her exuberance at the sense of new freedom she experiences after her husband's "death"?

3. What are the ironies of this story? To what extent does any one take precedence over the others?

4. What view of marriage is expressed in this story? Whose view of marriage is it—Mrs. Mallard's or the narrator's? Explain your answer.

5. Explain the meanings of the following expressions in this story: veiled hints; hastened to forestall; all aquiver; crying his wares; coursing blood; exalted perception; blind persistence; moment of illumination.

Ideas for Writing

1. Write a causal analysis which explains a sudden change in attitude toward something that recently happened to you. Take into account both immediate and deep-seated causes.

2. Discuss the causation behind a recent joy or happiness you have experienced.

3. Stories are often reflections of the author's opinions about a certain aspect of life. How can you read "The Story of an Hour" as an expression of Chopin's opinion about something? What is that opinion? To what extent is it successfully developed in this story?

Why I Write

George Orwell

George Orwell (1903–1950) was the pseudonym for Eric Blair, the English essayist, novelist, and journalist who was perhaps best known for his scathing political fictions *Animal Farm* (1945) and *1984* (1949). His life was as fascinating as his works: He was born in India, educated at Eton, served in Burma from 1922 to 1927, and was wounded while fighting with the International Brigade during the Spanish Civil War.

Orwell was a master of the autobiographical essay. While his works and his life indicate a leaning toward political issues, in the following selection he states that such themes are not his own primary interests as a writer. Orwell's view of the cause-and-effect relations in his work reveals much about his craft.

*F*rom a very early age, perhaps the age of five or six, I knew that   1
when I grew up I should be a writer. Between the ages of about seventeen and twenty-four I tried to abandon this idea, but I did so with the consciousness that I was outraging my true nature and that sooner or later I should have to settle down and write books.

I was the middle child of three, but there was a gap of five years on either   2
side, and I barely saw my father before I was eight. For this and other reasons I was somewhat lonely, and I soon developed disagreeable mannerisms which made me unpopular throughout my schooldays. I had the lonely child's habit of making up stories and holding conversations with imaginary persons, and I think from the very start my literary ambitions were mixed up with the feeling of being isolated and undervalued. I knew that I had a facility with words and a power of facing unpleasant facts, and I felt that this created a sort of private world in which I could get my own back for my failure in everyday life. Nevertheless the volume of serious—i.e., seriously intended—writing which I produced all through my childhood and boyhood would not amount to half a dozen pages. I wrote my first poem at the age of four or five, my mother taking it down to dictation. I cannot remember anything about it except that it was about a tiger and the tiger had "chair-like teeth"—a good enough phrase, but I fancy the poem was a plagiarism of Blake's "Tiger, Tiger." At eleven, when the war of 1914–18 broke out, I wrote a patriotic poem which was printed in the local newspaper, as was another, two years later, on the death of Kitchener. From time to time, when I was a bit older, I wrote bad and usually unfinished "nature poems" in the Georgian style. I also, about twice, attempted a short story which was a ghastly failure. That was the total of the would-be serious work that I actually set down on paper during all those years.

However, throughout this time I did in a sense engage in literary activities. To   3
begin with there was the made-to-order stuff which I produced quickly, easily and without much pleasure to myself. Apart from school work, I wrote *vers d'occasion,*

semi-comic poems which I could turn out at what now seems to me astonishing speed—at fourteen I wrote a whole rhyming play, in imitation of Aristophanes, in about a week—and helped to edit school magazines, both printed and in manuscript. These magazines were the most pitiful burlesque stuff that you could imagine, and I took far less trouble with them than I now would with the cheapest journalism. But side by side with all this, for fifteen years or more, I was carrying out a literary exercise of a quite different kind: this was the making up of a continuous "story" about myself, a sort of diary existing only in the mind. I believe this is a common habit of children and adolescents. As a very small child I used to imagine that I was, say, Robin Hood, and picture myself as the hero of thrilling adventures, but quite soon my "story" ceased to be narcissistic in a crude way and became more and more a mere description of what I was doing and the things I saw. For minutes at a time this kind of thing would be running through my head: "He pushed the door open and entered the room. A yellow beam of sunlight, filtering through the muslin curtains, slanted on to the table, where a match-box, half open, lay beside the inkpot. With his right hand in his pocket he moved across to the window. Down in the street a tortoiseshell cat was chasing a dead leaf," etc., etc. This habit continued till I was about twenty-five, right through my non-literary years. Although I had to search, and did search, for the right words, I seemed to be making this descriptive effort almost against my will, under a kind of compulsion from outside. The "story" must, I suppose, have reflected the styles of the various writers I admired at different ages, but so far as I remember it always had the same meticulous descriptive quality.

When I was about sixteen I suddenly discovered the joy of mere words, i.e.,   4 the sounds and associations of words. The lines from *Paradise Lost*—

> So hee with difficulty and labour hard
> Moved on: with difficulty and labour hee.

which do not now seem to me so very wonderful, sent shivers down my backbone; and the spelling "hee" for "he" was an added pleasure. As for the need to describe things, I knew all about it already. So it is clear what kind of books I wanted to write, in so far as I could be said to want to write books at that time. I wanted to write enormous naturalistic novels with unhappy endings, full of detailed descriptions and arresting similes, and also full of purple passages in which words were used partly for the sake of their sound. And in fact my first completed novel, *Burmese Days,* which I wrote when I was thirty but projected much earlier, is rather that kind of book.

I give all this background information because I do not think one can assess   5 a writer's motives without knowing something of his early development. His subject matter will be determined by the age he lives in—at least this is true in tumultuous, revolutionary ages like our own—but before he ever begins to write he will have acquired an emotional attitude from which he will never completely escape. It is his job, no doubt, to discipline his temperament and avoid getting stuck at some immature stage, or in some perverse mood: but if he escapes from his early influences altogether, he will have killed his impulse to write. Putting aside the need to earn a living, I think there are four great motives for writing, at any rate for writing prose. They exist in different degrees in every writer, and in any one writer the proportions will vary from time to time, according to the atmosphere in which he is living. They are:

1. Sheer egoism. Desire to seem clever, to be talked about, to be remembered ⁶ after death, to get your own back on grown-ups who snubbed you in childhood, etc., etc. It is humbug to pretend that this is not a motive, and a strong one. Writers share this characteristic with scientists, artists, politicians, lawyers, soldiers, successful businessmen—in short, with the whole top crust of humanity. The great mass of human beings are not acutely selfish. After the age of about thirty they abandon individual ambition—in many cases, indeed, they almost abandon the sense of being individuals at all—and live chiefly for others, or are simply smothered under drudgery. But there is also the minority of gifted, willful people who are determined to live their own lives to the end, and writers belong in this class. Serious writers, I should say, are on the whole more vain and self-centered than journalists, though less interested in money.

2. Aesthetic enthusiasm. Perception of beauty in the external world, or, on the ⁷ other hand, in words and their right arrangement. Pleasure in the impact of one sound on another, in the firmness of good prose or the rhythm of a good story. Desire to share an experience which one feels is valuable and ought not to be missed. The aesthetic motive is very feeble in a lot of writers, but even a pamphleteer or a writer of textbooks will have pet words and phrases which appeal to him for non-utilitarian reasons; or he may feel strongly about typography, width of margins, etc. Above the level of a railway guide, no book is quite free from aesthetic considerations.

3. Historical impulse. Desire to see things as they are, to find out true facts ⁸ and store them up for the use of posterity.

4. Political purpose—using the word "political" in the widest possible sense. ⁹ Desire to push the world in a certain direction, to alter other people's ideas of the kind of society that they should strive after. Once again, no book is genuinely free from political bias. The opinion that art should have nothing to do with politics is itself a political attitude.

It can be seen how these various impulses must war against one another, and ¹⁰ how they must fluctuate from person to person and from time to time. By nature—taking your "nature" to be the state you have attained when you are first adult—I am a person in whom the first three motives would outweigh the fourth. In a peaceful age I might have written ornate or merely descriptive books, and might have remained almost unaware of my political loyalties. As it is I have been forced into becoming a sort of pamphleteer. First I spent five years in an unsuitable profession (the Indian Imperial Police, in Burma), and then I underwent poverty and the sense of failure. This increased my natural hatred of authority and made me for the first time fully aware of the existence of the working classes, and the job in Burma had given me some understanding of the nature of imperialism: but these experiences were not enough to give me an accurate political orientation. Then came Hitler, the Spanish civil war, etc. By the end of 1935 I had still failed to reach a firm decision. I remember a little poem that I wrote at that date, expressing my dilemma:

> A happy vicar I might have been
> Two hundred years ago,
> To preach upon eternal doom
> And watch my walnuts grow;
>
> But born, alas, in an evil time,
> I missed that pleasant haven,
> For the hair has grown on my upper lip
> And the clergy are all clean-shaven.
>
> And later still the times were good,
> We were so easy to please,
> We rocked our troubled thoughts to sleep
> On the bosoms of the trees.
>
> All ignorant we dared to own
> The joys we now dissemble;
> The greenfinch on the apple bough
> Could make my enemies tremble.
>
> But girls' bellies and apricots,
> Roach in a shaded stream,
> Horses, ducks in flight at dawn,
> All these are a dream.
>
> It is forbidden to dream again;
> We maim our joys or hide them;
> Horses are made of chromium steel
> And little fat men shall ride them.
>
> I am the worm who never turned,
> The eunuch without a harem;
> Between the priest and the commissar
> I walk like Eugene Aram;

And the commissar is telling my fortune
While the radio plays,
But the priest has promised an Austin Seven,
For Duggie always pays.

I dreamed I dwelt in marble halls,
And woke to find it true;
I wasn't born for an age like this;
Was Smith? Was Jones? Were you?

The Spanish war and other events in 1936–7 turned the scale and thereafter I knew where I stood. Every line of serious work that I have written since 1936 has been written, directly or indirectly, *against* totalitarianism and *for* democratic socialism, as I understand it. It seems to me nonsense, in a period like our own, to think that one can avoid writing of such subjects. Everyone writes of them in one guise or another. It is simply a question of which side one takes and what approach one follows. And the more one is conscious of one's political bias, the more chance one has of acting politically without sacrificing one's aesthetic and intellectual integrity.

What I have most wanted to do throughout the past ten years is to make $_{11}$ political writing into an art. My starting point is always a feeling of partisanship, a sense of injustice. When I sit down to write a book, I do not say to myself, "I am going to produce a work of art." I write it because there is some lie that I want to expose, some fact to which I want to draw attention, and my initial concern is to get a hearing. But I could not do the work of writing a book, or even a long magazine article, if it were not also an aesthetic experience. Anyone who cares to examine my work will see that even when it is downright propaganda it contains much that a full-time politician would consider irrelevant. I am not able, and I do not want, completely to abandon the world view that I acquired in childhood. So long as I remain alive and well I shall continue to feel strongly about prose style, to love the surface of the earth, and to take a pleasure in solid objects and scraps of useless information. It is no use trying to suppress that side of myself. The job is to reconcile my ingrained likes and dislikes with the essentially public, nonindividual activities that this age forces on all of us.

It is not easy. It raises problems of construction and of language, and it $_{12}$ raises in a new way the problem of truthfulness. Let me give just one example of the cruder kind of difficulty that arises. My book about the Spanish civil war, *Homage to Catalonia,* is, of course, a frankly political book, but in the main it is written with a certain detachment and regard for form. I did try very hard in it to tell the whole truth without violating my literary instincts. But among other things it contains a long chapter, full of newspaper quotations and the like, defending the Trotskyists who were accused of plotting with Franco. Clearly such a chapter, which after a year or two would lose its interest for any ordinary reader, must ruin the book. A critic whom I respect read me a lecture about it. "Why did you put in all that stuff?" he said. "You've turned what might have been a good book into journalism." What he said was true, but I could not have done otherwise. I happened to know, what very few people in England had been allowed to know, that innocent men were being falsely accused. If I had not been angry about that I should never have written the book.

In one form or another this problem comes up again. The problem of language is subtler and would take too long to discuss. I will only say that of late years I have tried to write less picturesquely and more exactly. In any case I find that by the time you have perfected any style of writing, you have always outgrown it. *Animal Farm* was the first book in which I tried, with full consciousness of what I was doing, to fuse political purpose and artistic purpose into one whole. I have not written a novel for seven years, but I hope to write another fairly soon. It is bound to be a failure, every book is a failure, but I do know with some clarity what kind of book I want to write. Looking back through the last page or two, I see that I have made it appear as though my motives in writing were wholly public-spirited. I don't want to leave that as the final impression. All writers are vain, selfish, and lazy, and at the very bottom of their motives there lies a mystery. Writing a book is a horrible, exhausting struggle, like a long bout of some painful illness. One would never undertake such a thing if one were not driven on by some demon whom one can neither resist nor understand. For all one knows that demon is simply the same instinct that makes a baby squall for attention. And yet it is also true that one can write nothing readable unless one constantly struggles to efface one's own personality. Good prose is like a windowpane. I cannot say with certainty which of my motives are the strongest, but I know which of them deserve to be followed. And looking back through my work, I see that it is invariably where I lacked a *political* purpose that I wrote lifeless books and was betrayed into purple passages, sentences without meaning, decorative adjectives, and humbug generally.

Meaning and Idea

1. What is Orwell's opinion of "purple passages"? What exactly does he mean? What has he always wished his own writing could be like? He says that "by the time you have perfected any style of writing, you have always outgrown it." What does he mean? When he wrote this essay, how long had it been since he last wrote a novel?

2. What, according to Orwell, are the four great motives for writing? How does he feel about paying excessive attention to any one category? What does he mean by the claim that, in terms of his own interests, "the first three motives would outweigh the fourth"? How does this self-analysis serve the cause and effect themes of the essay?

3. Orwell says, "The opinion that art should have nothing to do with politics is itself a political attitude." Do you agree? Why or why not? How in fact may art be seen as political?

Language, Form, Structure

1. What is Orwell's thesis here? State it in your own words. How does the essay fit the rhetorical category of causal analysis? What are the various causes and effects explored here?

2. What is the effect of Orwell's looking at his own work with a highly critical eye?

3. What is the effect of Orwell's long opening narrative? How does it contribute to the thesis? How does it engage the reader's attention?

4. What aspects of language, style, form, and structure in this piece explain to you Orwell's status as a brilliant essayist?

5. Define the following words and use each in a sentence: posterity; narcissistic; meticulous; arresting; snubbed; drudgery; aesthetic; typography; imperialism; dissemble; guise; integrity; reconcile; efface.

Ideas for Writing

1. Write an essay that explores the cause-and-effect relations that have led to your own choice of a career or that of someone close to you. Be sure to use an initial, framing narrative; then a listing of emphases you have decided upon; and, finally, further elaboration.

2. Orwell feels that everyone and everything is always political. Do you agree? Write a causation essay that considers why everyone is or is not political.

3. Reexamine Orwell's essay and write one of your own examining the relation between his statement that he is not inherently political and the fact that all his work is overtly political. See also the essay by Orwell in Chapter Six, "Politics and the English Language." How can Orwell assert one position and behave in an opposite way? Search the two essays and cite evidence to prove your point.

The Chain

Tobias Wolff

Tobias Wolff was born in Birmingham, Alabama, in 1945. He fought in Vietnam from 1964 to 1968. He attended Oxford University for his B.A. and Stanford University for his M.A. He is often published in the *Atlantic Monthly, Esquire,* and *The New Yorker,* among other venues, and is well respected for what Walter Kendricks has called his "boundless tolerance for the stupid sorrow of ordinary human entanglements."

Wolff does not editorialize in his stories. His ambivalent portrayals of ordinary people expose the flaws inherent in our value systems. The following story, written in his characteristically crisp style, relates an excessive but very imaginable series of events that have an inevitable conclusion.

*B*rian Gold was at the top of the hill when the dog attacked. A big   1
black wolflike dog attached to a chain, it came flying off a back porch and tore
through its yard into the park, moving easily in spite of the deep snow, making
for Gold's daughter. He waited for the chain to pull the dog up short, but the dog
kept coming. Gold plunged down the hill, shouting as he went. Snow and wind
deadened his voice. Anna's sled was almost at the bottom of the slope. Gold had
raised the hood of her parka against the needling gusts, and he knew that she
could not hear him or see the dog racing toward her. He was conscious of the
dog's speed and of his own dreamy progress, the weight of his gum boots, the
clinging trap of crust beneath the new snow. His overcoat flapped at his knees. He
screamed one last time as the dog made its lunge, and at that moment Anna
flinched away and the dog caught her shoulder instead of her face. Gold was
barely halfway down the hill, arms pumping, feet sliding in the boots. He seemed
to be running in place, held at a fixed, unbridgeable distance as the dog dragged
Anna backward off the sled, shaking her like a doll. Gold threw himself down the
hill helplessly, then the distance vanished and he was there.

The sled was overturned, the snow churned up; the dog had marked his   2
ground as its own. It still had Anna by the shoulder. Gold heard the rage boiling
in its gut. He saw the tensed hindquarters and the flattened ears and the red gleam
of gum under the wrinkled snout. Anna was on her back, her face bleached and
blank, staring at the sky. She had never looked so small. Gold seized the chain
and yanked at it but could get no purchase in the snow. The dog only snarled more
fiercely and started shaking Anna again. She didn't make a sound. Her silence
made Gold go hollow and cold. He flung himself onto the dog and hooked his arm
under its neck and pulled back hard. Still the dog wouldn't let go. Gold felt its
heat and the profound rumble of its will. With his other hand he tried to pry the
jaw loose. His gloves turned slippery with drool; he couldn't get a grip. Gold's
mouth was next to the dog's ear. He said, "Let go, damn you," and then he took
the ear between his teeth and bit down with everything he had. He heard a yelp

and something cracked against his nose, knocking him backward. When he pushed himself up, the dog was running for home, jerking its head from side to side, scattering flecks of blood on the snow.

"The whole thing took maybe sixty seconds," Gold said. "Maybe less. But it went on forever." He'd told the story many times now, and always mentioned this. He knew it was trite to marvel at the way time could stretch and stall, but he was unable not to. Nor could he stop himself from repeating that it was a "miracle"—the radiologist's word—that Anna hadn't been crippled or disfigured, or even killed; and that her doctor did not understand how she'd escaped damage to her bones and nerves. Though badly bruised, her skin hadn't even been broken. 3

Gold loved his daughter's face. He loved her face as a thing in itself, to be wondered at, studied. Yet after the attack he couldn't look at Anna in the same way. He kept seeing the dog lunge at her, and himself stuck forever on that hill; then his heart began to kick, and he grew taut and restless and angry. He didn't want to think about the dog anymore—he wanted it out of the picture. It should be put down. It was crazy, a menace, and it was still there, waiting to tear into some other kid, because the police refused to do anything. 4

"They won't do a thing," he said. "Nothing." 5

He was going through the whole story again with his cousin Tom Rourke on a Sunday afternoon, a week after the attack. Gold had called him the night it happened, but the part about the police was new, and Rourke got all worked up just as Gold expected. His cousin had an exacting, irritable sense of justice and a ready store of loyal outrage that Gold had drawn on ever since they were boys. He had been alone in his anger for a week now and wanted some company. Though his wife claimed to be angry too, she hadn't seen what he had seen. The dog was an abstraction to her, and she wasn't one to brood anyway. 6

What was their excuse? Rourke wanted to know. What reason did the cops give for their complete and utter worthlessness? 7

"The chain," Gold said. "They said—this is the really beautiful part—they said that since the dog was chained up, no law was broken." 8

"But the dog *wasn't* chained up, right?" 9

"He was, but the chain reaches into the park. I mean, way in—a good thirty, forty feet." 10

"By that logic, he could be on a chain ten miles long and legally chew up the whole fucking town." 11

"Exactly." 12

Rourke got up and went to the picture window. He stood close to the glass and glowered at the falling snow. "What is it with Nazis and dogs? They've got a real thing going, ever notice that?" Still looking out the window, he said, "Have you talked to a lawyer?" 13

"Day before yesterday." 14

"What'd he say?" 15

"She. Kate Stiller. Said the police were full of shit. Then she told me to forget it. According to her, the dog'll die of old age before we ever get near a courtroom." 16

"There's the legal system for you, Brian me boy. They'll give you all the ₁₇ justice you want, as long as it's up the ass."

There was a loud thump on the ceiling. Anna was playing upstairs with ₁₈ Rourke's boy, Michael. Both men raised their eyes and waited, and when no one screamed, Gold said, "I don't know why I even bothered to call her. I don't have the money to pay for a lawyer."

"You know what happened," Rourke said. "The cop who took the complaint ₁₉ fucked it up, and now the others are covering for him. So, you want to take him out?"

"The *cop*?"   ₂₀

"I was thinking of the dog."   ₂₁

"You mean kill the dog?"   ₂₂

Rourke just looked at Gold.   ₂₃

"Is that what you're saying? Kill the dog?"   ₂₄

Rourke grinned, but he still didn't say anything.   ₂₅

"How?"   ₂₆

"How do you want?"   ₂₇

"Christ, Tom, I can't believe I'm talking like this."   ₂₈

"But you are." Rourke shoved the naugahyde ottoman with his foot until it ₂₉ was facing Gold, then sat on it and leaned forward, so close their knees were touching. "No poison or glass. That's chickenshit, I wouldn't do that to my worst enemy. Take him out clean."

"Christ, Tom." Gold tried to laugh.   ₃₀

"You can use my Remington, scope him in from the hill. Or if you want, ₃₁ get up close with the 12-gauge or the .44 Magnum. You ever fired a pistol?"

"No."   ₃₂

"Better forget the Magnum, then."   ₃₃

"I can't do this."   ₃₄

"Sure you can."   ₃₅

"They'll know it was me. I've been raising hell about that dog all week. ₃₆ Who do you think they're going to come after when it suddenly shows up with a hole in its head?"

Rourke sucked in his cheeks. "Point taken," he said. "Okay, you can't do it. ₃₇ But I sure as hell can."

"No. Forget it, Tom."   ₃₈

"You and Mary go out for the night. Have dinner at Chez Nicole or Pauly's, ₃₉ someplace small where they'll remember you. By the time you get home it's all over and you're clean as a whistle."

Gold finished his beer.   ₄₀

"We've got to take care of business, Brian. If we don't, nobody will."   ₄₁

"Maybe if I did it. *Maybe*. Having you do it—that just doesn't feel right." ₄₂

"What about that dog still running wild after what it did to Anna? Does that ₄₃ feel right?" When Gold didn't answer, Rourke shook his knee. "Did you really bite the mutt's ear?"

"I didn't have any choice."   ₄₄

"Bite it off?"   45

"No."   46

"But you drew blood, right? You tasted blood."   47

"I got some in my mouth, yes. I couldn't help it."   48

"It tasted good, didn't it? Come on, Brian, don't bullshit me, it tasted good."   49

"There was a certain satisfaction," Gold said.   50

"You want to do what's right," Rourke said. "I appreciate that. I value that. It's your call, okay? But the offer stands."   51

Rourke produced the crack about Nazis and dogs not from deep reflection, Gold knew, but because to call people Nazis was his first response to any vexation or slight. Once he'd heard Rourke say it, though, Gold could not forget it. The picture that came to mind was one he'd pondered before: a line of frenzied dogs harrying Jews along a railway platform.   52

Gold was Jewish on his father's side, but his parents split up when he was young, and he'd been raised Catholic by his mother. His name didn't suit him; he sensed it made him seem ridiculous. When you heard Gold, what else could you think of but gold? With that name he should be a rich sharpie, not a mackerel-snapper with a dying business. The black kids who came into his video store were unmistakably of that opinion. They had a mock-formal way of saying "Mr. *Gold,*" drawing out the word as if it were the precious substance itself. Finding themselves a little short on the rental fee, some of them weren't above asking him to make up the difference out of his own deep pockets and acting amazed if he refused. The rusty Toyota he kept parked out front was a puzzle to them, a conversation piece; they couldn't figure out why, with all his money, he didn't get himself a decent set of wheels. One night, standing at the counter with her friends, a girl suggested that Gold kept his Cadillac at home because he was afraid the brothers would steal it. They'd been goofing on him, just messing around, but when she said this everyone went silent as if a hard truth had been spoken.   53

Cadillac. What else?   54

After years of estrangement, Gold had returned to the Catholic church, and went weekly to Mass to sustain his fragile faith, but he understood that in the eyes of the world he was a Jew. He had never known what to make of that. There were things he saw in himself that he thought of as Jewish, traits not conspicuous among the mostly Irish boys he'd grown up with, including his cousins. Bookishness, patience, a taste for classical music and complicated moralizing, aversion to alcohol and violence. All this he found acceptable. But he had certain other tendencies, less dear to him, that he also suspected of being Jewish. Corrosive self-mockery. Bouts of almost paralyzing skepticism. Physical awkwardness. A disposition toward passivity, even surrender, in the face of bullying people and oppressive circumstances. Gold knew that these ideas of Jewishness were also held by anti-Semites, and he resisted their influence, without much success.   55

In the already familiar picture that Rourke had conjured up, of Jews being herded by dogs, Gold sensed an instance of the resignation that he disliked in   56 himself. He knew it was unfair to blame people for not fighting an evil that their very innocence made them incapable of imagining, yet even while admitting that they were brutalized and starved and in shock, he couldn't help but wonder: Why didn't one of them hit a guard—grab his gun—take some of the bastards with him? *Do* something? Even in his awareness of the terrible injustice of this question, he'd never really laid it to rest.

And with that old image vivid in his thoughts, it seemed to Gold that the question had now been put to him. Why didn't he do something? His own daughter had been savaged by just such a dog, a flinch away from having her face torn off. He had seen its insanity, felt its furious will to hurt. And it was still out there, lying in wait, because no one, not even Gold himself, would do what needed to be done. He couldn't escape the consciousness of his own inaction. In the days following his conversation with Rourke, it became intolerable. No matter where else he was, at home or in the store, he was also on that hill, unable to move or speak, watching the dog come at Anna with murder in its heart and the chain gliding behind like an infinite black snake.

He drove by the park late one day and stopped across the street from the house where the dog's owners lived. It was a colonial with a line of dormer windows, a big expensive house like most of the others around the park. Gold thought he could guess why the police had been so docile. This wasn't a shooting gallery, a crib for perpetrators and scofflaws. The deep thunk of the brass knocker against the great green door, the glittering chandelier in the foyer, the Cinderella sweep of the staircase with its monumental newel post and gleaming rail—all this would tell you that the law was among friends here. Of course a dog needed room to roam. If people let their kids go tearing off every which way, they'd have to live with the consequences. Some folks were just natural-born whiners.

Though Gold despaired of the police, he believed he understood them. He did not understand the people who'd allowed this to happen. They had never called to apologize, or even to ask how Anna was. They seemed not to care that their dog was a killer. Gold had driven here with some notion of sitting down with them, helping them see what they ought to do—as if they'd even let him in the door. What a patsy!

He called Rourke that night and told him to go ahead.

Rourke was hot on the idea of Gold taking Mary out for dinner—his treat— on the big night. He had a theatrical conception of the event, which seemed to include the two of them toasting him with champagne while he did whatever he meant to do. Gold refused the offer. Mary didn't know what they were up to, and he couldn't sit across a table from her for three hours, even as the deed was being done, without telling. She wouldn't like it, but she wouldn't be able to stop it; the knowledge would only be a burden to her. Gold employed a graduate student named Simms who covered the store at night, except for Tuesdays, when he had a seminar. Though Rourke was disappointed by Gold's humdrum dramaturgy, he assented: Tuesday night it was.

   More snow fell that morning, followed by an ice storm. The streets and 62
sidewalks were still glazed by nightfall and business was slow. As always, Gold
had a new release playing in the monitor above the counter, but he couldn't follow the plot through the frantic cutting and ugly music, so he stopped it halfway
through and didn't bother to put in another. That left the store oddly quiet. Maybe
for this reason his customers didn't linger in the usual way, shooting the breeze
with Gold and one another. They made their selections, paid, and left. He tried to
read the paper. At 8:30, Anna called to say she'd won a poster contest at school.
After she hung up, Gold witnessed a fight in front of the Domino's across the
street. Two men, drunk or drugged, had a shouting match, and one of them took
a clumsy swing at the other. They grappled and fell down together on the ice. A
deliveryman and one of the cooks came outside and helped them up, then walked
them off in different directions. Gold microwaved the chili left over from Sunday
dinner. He ate slowly, watching the sluggish procession of cars and the hunched,
gingerly trudge of people past his window. Mary had laid on the cumin with a free
hand, which was just how Gold liked it. His forehead grew damp with sweat, and
he took off his sweater. The baseboard heaters ticked. The long fluorescent lights
buzzed overhead.

   Rourke called just before ten, when Gold was closing up. "Scooter has 63
buried his last bone," he said.
   "Scooter?"   64
   "That was his name."   65
   "I wish you hadn't told me."   66
   "I got his collar for you—a little memento."   67
   "For Christ's sake, Tom."   68
   "Don't worry, you're clear."   69
   "Just don't tell me any more," Gold said. "I'm afraid I'll say too much when 70
the police come by."
   "They're not gonna come by. The way I fixed things, they won't even know 71
what happened." He coughed. "It had to be done, Brian."
   "I guess."   72
   "No guessing about it. But I've gotta say, it wasn't anything I'd want to do 73
again."
   "I'm sorry, Tom. I should've done it myself."   74
   "It wasn't any fun, I'll tell you that." Rourke fell silent. Gold could hear him 75
breathing. "I about froze my ass off. I thought they'd never let the damned beast
out."
   "I won't forget it," Gold said.   76
   "*De nada*. It's over. Go in peace."   77

   In late March, Rourke called Gold with a story of his own. He'd been 78
gassing up on Erie Boulevard when a BMW backed away from the air hose and
put a crease in his door. He yelled at the driver, a black man wearing sunglasses
and a knit cap. The driver ignored him. He looked straight ahead and drove off

across the lot into the road, but not before Rourke got a good look at his license plate. It was a vanity tag, easy to remember—SCUSE ME. Rourke called the police, who tracked the driver down and ticketed him for leaving the scene of an accident.

So far, so good. Then it turned out the driver didn't have insurance. ₇₉ Rourke's company agreed to cover most of the bill—eight hundred bucks for a lousy dent!—but that still left him with the three-hundred-dollar deductible. Rourke figured Mr. SCUSE ME should make up the difference. His insurance agent gave him the man's name and particulars, and Rourke started calling him. He called twice at reasonable hours, after dinner, but both times the woman who answered said he wasn't in and gave Rourke the number of a club on Townsend, where he got an answering machine. Though he left clear messages, he heard nothing back. Finally Rourke called the first number at 7:00 A.M. and got the man himself, Mr. Vick Barnes.

"That's V-I-C-K," Rourke said. "Ever notice the way they do that with their ₈₀ names? You shorten Victor, you get Vic, right? V-I-C. So where does the fucking K come from? Or take Sean, S-E-A-N. Been spelled like that for about five hundred years. But not them, they've gotta spell it S-H-A-W-N. Like they have a right to that name in the first place."

"What did he say?" ₈₁

"Gave me a lot of mouth, natch. First he gets indignant that I woke him up, ₈₂ then he says he's already been through all this shit with the police, and he doesn't believe he hit anybody anyway. Then he hangs up on me."

Rourke said he knew better than to call back; he wasn't going to get any- ₈₃ where with this guy. Instead he went to the club, Jack's Shady Corner, where it turned out Mr. Vick Barnes worked as a deejay and no doubt retailed dope on the side. All the deejays did. Where else would he get the dough for a new Beamer? But Rourke had to admit he was quite the pro, our Mr. Barnes, nice mellow voice, good line of patter. Rourke had a couple beers and watched the dancers, then went looking for the car.

It wasn't in the lot. Rourke poked around and found it off by itself in a lit- ₈₄ tle nook behind the club, where it wouldn't get run into by drunks. He was going back tonight to give Mr. Vick Barnes a taste of his own medicine, plus a little extra for the vigorish.

"You can't," Gold said. "They'll know it was you." ₈₅

"Let 'em prove it." ₈₆

Gold had understood from the start where this story was taking him, even ₈₇ if Rourke hadn't. When he said, "I'll do it," he felt as if he were reading the words from a script.

"No need, Brian. I got it covered." ₈₈

"Wait a minute. Just hang on." Gold put the receiver down and took care of ₈₉ an old woman who was renting *The Sound of Music.* Then he picked it up and said, "They'll bust you for sure."

"Look, I can't let this guy fuck me over and just walk away. Next thing, ₉₀ everybody in town'll be lining up to give me the wood."

"I told you, I'll handle it. Not tonight—there's a talent show at school. 91
Thursday."

"You sure, Brian?"   92

"I said I'd do it. Didn't I just say I'd do it?"   93

"Only if you really want to. Okay? Don't feel like you have to."   94

Rourke stopped by the store Thursday afternoon with instructions and 95
equipment: two gallons of Olympic redwood stain to pour over the BMW, a hunting knife to slash the tires and score the paint, and a crowbar to break the wind-
shield. Gold was to exercise extreme caution. He should work fast. He should
leave his car running and pointed in the direction of a clear exit. If for any reason
things didn't look right he should leave immediately.

They loaded the stuff in the trunk of Gold's car.   96

"Where are you going to be?" Gold asked.   97

"Chez Nicole. Same place you'd have gone if you had any class."   98

"I had a good sole meunière last time I was there."   99

"Prime rib for this bad boy. Rare. Taste of blood, eh, Brian?"   100

Gold watched him drive off. It was a warm day, the third in a row. Last 101
week's snow had turned gray and was offering up its holdings of beer cans and
dog turds. The gutters overflowed with melt, and the sun shone on the wet pavement and the broken glass in front of Domino's, which had abruptly closed three
weeks earlier. Rourke's brake lights flashed. He stopped and backed up. Gold
waited while the electric window descended, then leaned toward the car.

"Careful, Brian, okay?"   102

"You know me."   103

"Don't get caught. I have to say, that's something you definitely want to 104
avoid."

Gold drove to the club at 11:30 with the idea that there wouldn't be much 105
coming and going at that hour on a weeknight. The casual drinkers would already
be home, the serious crowd settling in for the duration. A dozen or so cars were
scattered across the lot. Gold backed into a space as close to the rear of the building as he could get. He turned the engine off and looked around, then popped the
trunk, took the crowbar, and moved into the shadows around back. The BMW
was parked where Rourke said it would be, in the short driveway between the
alley and the dumpster.

Gold had no intention of using the stain or the knife. Rourke had suffered 106
a dent; that was no reason to destroy a man's car. One good dent in return would
even things up between Rourke and Barnes and settle his own debt in the bargain.
If Rourke wanted more, he was strictly on his own.

Gold walked around the car—a beautiful machine, a gleaming black 328 with 107
those special wheels that gang members were supposedly killing one another over.
The dealership where Gold took his Toyota for repairs also had the local BMW bou-
tique, and he always paid a visit to the showroom while he waited. He liked to open

and close the doors, sit in the leather seats and work the gears, compare options and prices. Fully loaded, this model ran in the neighborhood of forty grand. Gold couldn't imagine Mr. Vick Barnes qualifying for that kind of a loan on a deejay's salary, so he must have paid in cash. Rourke was right. He was dealing.

Gold hefted the crowbar. He felt the driving pulse of the music through the club walls, heard the vocalist—he wouldn't call him a singer—shouting along with menace and complaint. It was a strange thing. You sold drugs to your own people, ruined their neighborhoods, turned their children into prostitutes and thugs, and you became a big shot. A man of property and respect. But try to run a modest business, bring something good into their community, and you were a bloodsucking parasite and a Child of Satan. *Mr. Gold.* He smacked the bar against his palm. He was thinking maybe he'd do a little something with that knife after all. The stain, too. He could find uses for the stain.

A woman laughed in the parking lot and a man answered in a low voice. Gold crouched behind the dumpster and waited until their headlights raked the darkness and vanished. His hand was tight around the metal. He could feel his own rage, and distrusted it. Only a fool acted out of anger. No, he would do exactly what was fair, what he had decided on before coming here.

Gold walked around to the driver's side of the BMW. He held the crowbar with both hands and touched the curved end against the door at bumper height, where Rourke's car would have been hit. He adjusted his feet. He touched the door again, then cocked the crowbar like a bat and swung it with everything he had, knowing just as the act passed beyond recall how absolutely he had betrayed himself. The shock of the blow raced up his arms. He dropped the crowbar and left it where it fell.

Victor Emmanuel Barnes found it there three hours later. He knelt and ran his hand along the jagged cleft in the car door, flecks of paint curling away under his fingertips. He knew exactly who had done this. He picked up the crowbar, tossed it on the passenger seat and drove straight to the apartment building where Devereaux lived. As he sped through the empty streets he howled and pounded the dashboard. He stopped in a shriek of brakes and seized the crowbar and ran up the stairs to Devereaux's door. He pounded the door with his fist. *I told you next week, you motherfucker. I told you next week.* He demanded to be let in. He heard voices, but when no one answered him he cursed them and began working at the door with the crowbar. It creaked and strained. Then it gave and Barnes staggered into the apartment, yelling for Devereaux.

But Devereaux wasn't home. His sixteen-year-old nephew, Marcel, was spending the night on the couch after helping Devereaux's little girl write an essay. He stood facing the door while Barnes jimmied it, his aunt and cousins and grandmother gathered behind him at the end of the hall, shaking and clinging to one another. When Barnes stumbled bellowing inside, Marcel tried to push him back out. They struggled. Barnes shoved him away and swung the crowbar, catching Marcel right across the temple. The boy's eyes went wide. His mouth opened.

He sank to his knees and pitched facedown on the floor. Barnes looked at Marcel, then at the old woman coming toward him. "Oh, Jesus," he said, and dropped the crowbar and ran down the stairs and outside to his car. He drove to his grandmother's house and told her what had happened, and she held his head in her lap and rocked over him and wept and prayed. Then she called the police.

Marcel's death was on the morning news. Every half hour they ran the story, with pictures of both him and Barnes. Barnes was shown being hustled into a cruiser, Marcel standing before his exhibit at the All-County Science Fair. He had been an honors student at Morris Fields High, a volunteer in the school's Big Brother program, and a past president of the Christian Youth Association. There was no known motive for the attack. [113]

Camera crews from the TV stations followed students from their buses to the school doors, asking about Marcel and getting close-ups of the most distraught. At the beginning of second period, the principal came on the PA system and said that crisis counselors were available for those who wished to speak to them. Any students who felt unable to continue with their classes that day were to be excused. [114]

Garvey Banks looked over at his girlfriend, Tiffany. Neither of them had known Marcel, but it was nice out and there wasn't anything happening at school except people crying and carrying on. When he nodded toward the door, she smiled in that special way of hers and gathered her books and collected a pass from the teacher. Garvey waited a few minutes, then followed her outside. [115]

They walked up to Bickel Park and sat on a bench overlooking the pond. Two old white ladies were throwing bread to the ducks. The wet grass steamed in the sun. Tiffany put her head on Garvey's shoulder and hummed to herself. Garvey wanted to feel sad over that boy getting killed, but it was good being warm like this and close to Tiffany. [116]

They sat on the bench in the sun. They didn't talk. They hardly ever talked. Tiffany liked to look at things and be quiet in herself. Pretty soon they'd rent a movie and go over to Garvey's. They'd kiss. They wouldn't take any chances, but they'd make each other happy. All of that was going to happen, and Garvey was glad to wait for it. [117]

After a while, Tiffany stopped humming. "Ready, Gar?" [118]
"Ready." [119]

They stopped in at Gold's Video and Garvey took *Breakfast at Tiffany's* off the shelf. They rented it the first time because of the title, then it became their favorite movie. Someday, they were going to live in New York City and know all kinds of people—that was for sure. [120]

Mr. Gold was slow writing up the receipt. He looked sick. He counted out Garvey's change and said, "Why aren't you kids in school?" [121]

Garvey felt cornered and decided to blow a little smoke at the man. "Friend of mine got killed," he said. [122]

"You knew him? You knew Marcel Foley?" [123]
"Yes, sir. From way back." [124]

"What was he like?"   125

"Marcel? Hey, Marcel was the best. You got a problem, you took it to Mar-   126
cel. You know, trouble with your girlfriend or whatever. Trouble at home. Trouble with a friend. Marcel had this thing—right, Tiff?—he could bring people
together. He just had this easy way, and he talked to you like you were important,
like everybody's important. He could get people to come together, know what I'm
saying? Come together and get on with it. *Peacemaker.* Marcel was a peacemaker.
And that's the best thing you can be."

"Yes," Mr. Gold said. "It is." He put his hands on the counter and lowered   127
his head.

Then Garvey saw that he was grieving, and it came to him how unfair a   128
thing it was that Marcel Foley had been struck down with his life still before him,
all his sunny days stolen away. It was wrong, and Garvey knew that it would not
end there. He touched Mr. Gold's shoulder. "That man'll get his," he said. "Count
on it. He'll get what's coming to him."

Meaning and Idea

1. What is Wolff's story about? Are Gold's actions justified? Are his desires?
   Explain your opinions. What do you think should have happened to the
   dog?

2. Rourke refers to the taste of blood several times. What is Wolff pointing
   out by having a character like Rourke in the story? What role do the
   camera crews that follow Marcel's fellow students to class contribute to the
   story?

3. Who is Devereaux? When Vick Barnes came out of the club, saw the dent,
   and "knew exactly who had done this," whom did he suspect? What was
   Wolff's point in creating the character of Devereaux, do you think?

Language, Form, Structure

1. What are the various cause-and-effect relations in this story? What is the
   significance of the title "The Chain"? What do you think is Wolff's view of
   causality in people's lives?

2. Wolff's essay moves in time, but its last two sections reflect substantial
   shifts, even extending to shifts in point of view. What is the effect of the
   last section about Garvey and Tiffany?

3. Wolff often uses interesting turns of phrase and original images like "Gold
   heard the rage boiling in his gut" or "With that name he should be a rich
   sharpie, not a mackerel-snapper with a dying business." Comment on
   Wolff's use of language in "The Chain." Identify fresh images and phrases,
   explain them, and indicate how they contribute to the story.

4. Define the following words and use each in a sentence: trite; exacting; glowered; vexation; harrying; estrangement; bouts; conjured; resignation; flinch; dormer; scofflaws; dramaturgy; gingerly; indignant; hefted; distraught.

Ideas for Writing

1. Write an essay about how and why you did something you now wish or believe that you shouldn't have done.

2. Write a causation essay about a crime or scandal you know of and the series of events that led up to it.

3. If something is *justifiable,* it is defensible or warranted. *Just cause* is a legal term that refers to the reason someone does something and to whether the severity of that person's action was an appropriate and warranted response. Reread Wolff's story. Write an essay entitled "Just Cause," in which you discuss causation as a process and particularly how Wolff addresses it in this story.

Dream Deferred

Langston Hughes

Langston Hughes (1902–1967) was one of America's foremost poets, essayists, drama-tists, and fiction writers, whose self-proclaimed desire as a writer was "to explain and illu-minate the Negro condition in America." After being elected class poet in grammar school in Lincoln, Illinois, Hughes first gained adult notoriety as a poet when he was a busboy at a hotel in Washington, D.C. He left some poems by the plate of the poet Vachel Lindsay, who fortunately recognized his talent.

"Dream Deferred" has become one of Langston Hughes's best-known poems, especially during the racially turbulent 1960s. In this poem he asks—and perhaps answers—what the results of aspirations unfulfilled are.

W̶hat happens to a dream deferred?

Does it dry up
like a raisin in the sun?
Or fester like a sore—
And then run?   5
Does it stink like rotten meat?
Or crust and sugar over—
like a syrupy sweet?

Maybe it just sags
like a heavy load.   10

Or does it explode?

Meaning and Idea

1. What do you think is the "dream" in this poem? What cause-and-effect relationship is implied concerning this dream?

2. Remembering that Hughes was among the foremost writers about the modern black experience in America, how does this poem relate to that experience as you know it? What "message" is carried by the poem?

Language, Form, Structure

1. Identify the similes and metaphors in this poem. How effective are they? Do you see a logic to their placement in the poem? What effect does the

final metaphor have, coming where it does? Would a simile have been as powerful? Why?

2. The poem is a sequence of questions. What effect does this have on the reader? Would the poem be as effective were it built on a series of declarative statements? Why?

3. What is the effect of the rhymes in the poem—sun/run; meat/sweet; load/explode?

4. Make sure you know the meaning of *deferred* and *fester.*

Ideas for Writing

1. Write a short causal analysis about the effects of a time when you "put off" something. Were the results positive or negative? Did they occur naturally, or were they forced?

2. As we noted, Hughes arranges this poem as a series of questions. Write an essay in which you identify what in the writing—choice of language, tone, arrangement on the page, and so on—gives either an implicit or an explicit answer to these questions?

Richard Cory

Edwin Arlington Robinson

Edwin Arlington Robinson (1869–1935), described by critic Allen Tate in 1933 as "the most famous of living American poets," led a life of two greatly contrasting halves. Born and raised in a bleak Maine town, he had a depressing childhood. He later devoted himself to his writing, but was often penniless and alcoholic, relying on friends and, at one point, on President Theodore Roosevelt for subsistence. In 1921, his *Collected Poems* was unexpectedly well received, and in rather rapid succession, Robinson won the Pulitzer Prize three times, as well as an honorary degree from Yale University.

"Richard Cory" is one of the best-known of modern poems; Simon and Garfunkel's early song with the same title rephrases it and puts it to music. In the poem, Edwin Arlington Robinson surprises us with the result of a life seemingly headed in one direction, but taking a sharp turn in an opposite one.

*W*henever Richard Cory went down town,
We people on the pavement looked at him:
He was a gentleman from sole to crown,
Clean favored, and imperially slim.

And he was always quietly arrayed,   5
And he was always human when he talked;
But still he fluttered pulses when he said,
"Good-morning," and he glittered when he walked.

And he was rich—yes, richer than a king—
And admirably schooled in every grace: 10
In fine, we thought that he was everything
To make us wish that we were in his place.

So on we worked, and waited for the light,
And went without the meat, and cursed the bread;
And Richard Cory, one calm summer night,   15
Went home and put a bullet through his head.

Meaning and Idea

1. Before his suicide, what sort of person did Richard Cory appear to be? Was he a fair person? Arrogant? What was his social position? What were the townspeople's impressions of him?

2. Who is the narrator of this poem? What is his opinion of Richard Cory? To whom does he address the poem? What is the occasion of this poem?

3. What do you make of Richard Cory's act of suicide? Why do you think he did it? Was it to be expected from the preceding stanzas? Why or why not?

4. Explain the meaning of lines 13–14:

So on we worked, and waited for the light,
And went without the meat, and cursed the bread;

Who are the "we"? What is "the light"? Why do the "we" curse the bread?

Language, Form, Structure

1. *Situational irony* occurs when the results of a situation do not match our expectations of the outcome. How is "Richard Cory" an example of situational irony?

2. According to the poem, is there any cause-and-effect relationship between the townspeople's impressions of Richard Cory and his suicide? If so, what is it? Is it direct or indirect?

3. There are a number of descriptive words or phrases in this poem which suggest royalty or regal nature. Identify these and explain how each of them contributes to our understanding of Richard Cory and/or the speaker.

4. Define the following words as they are used in the poem: sole; crown; grace. Why do you think Robinson chose each of these words over possible synonyms?

Ideas for Writing

1. If you know personally of a suicide or a suicide attempt, try to write a causal analysis explaining it. If you have no direct knowledge of a suicide, choose another tragic event you know of and explain what caused it.

2. Choose someone in your school or social group who is greatly admired. Write a causal analysis of the reasons for this admiration.

3. The narrator tells of the events of this poem from a retrospective (after-the-fact) point of view. How does that point of view affect his descriptions of Richard Cory? How might the narrative have been different in its feeling and focus if this poem took place before the suicide or if there were no suicide? You may want to try your hand at writing a second version of the poem from either of those points of view. Your version may be prose if you wish.

When My Love Swears That She Is Made of Truth

William Shakespeare

Although William Shakespeare (1564–1616) is considered the world's greatest English-language playwright, some critics feel that his poetry alone would have brought him great fame. He began publishing poetry in 1593, around the same time as his earliest plays, and the 154 poems in his *Sonnets,* published in 1609, are considered his greatest poetic achievement. The sonnets, as do the plays, deal with love and death and with time's effects on each, but, of course, in much more compressed form. Shakespeare was born in Stratford-on-Avon, England, then spent a good deal of his time in London as a playwright-actor before retiring and eventually dying in his hometown.

The full range of Shakespeare's 154 sonnets, written in the 1590s, deals with the universals of change, time, and death, as well as the means by which art and love afford ways for us to face these universals. In "When My Love Swears That She Is Made of Truth," one of Shakespeare's 25 "Dark Lady" sonnets, he explores the cause-and-effect relationship between truth and love.

When my love swears that she is made of truth,
I do believe her, though I know she lies,
That she might think me some untutored youth,
Unlearned in the world's false subtleties.
Thus vainly thinking that she thinks me young, 5
Although she knows my days are past the best,
Simply I credit her false-speaking tongue;
On both sides thus is simple truth supprest.
But wherefore says she not she is unjust?
And wherefore say not I that I am old? 10
Oh, love's best habit is in seeming trust,
And age in love loves not to have years told:
Therefore I lie with her and she with me,
And in our faults by lies we flattered be.

Meaning and Idea

1. Is the speaker of this poem young or old? Is he younger or older than his beloved?

2. Lines 9 and 10 ask two questions about the main conditions analyzed in this poem. In more modern English, the questions are: "Why doesn't she

say she's unjust?" and "Why don't I say that I'm old?" Answer the two questions based on your reading of the poem.

3. What, according to the poem, are the causes for lying between lovers? What is the relationship between the causes and effects of lying?

Language, Form, Structure

1. Explain the meaning of the seeming contradiction of line 2. How else does Shakespeare use contradictions as an explanatory technique in this poem?

2. How is the word *lie* used as a *double entendre* (double meaning) in this poem?

3. What is the effect of Shakespeare's writing "When my love swears that she *is made of truth*" rather than ". . . that she *is telling the truth*"? How are the two wordings different? How does the actual wording contribute to the meaning of the poem?

Ideas for Writing

1. Tell about the last lie—or the most important lie—you told. Analyze the reasons for your lying and the effects of it.

2. Write a short causal analysis explaining the main basis of a love (or a close friendship) you have recently been involved in. Because of this basis, did the relationship work better or worse?

3. Shakespeare's sonnet deals with *lying* and *lovers*. In a short paper, identify the truths in the poem that seem to you most lasting and universal.

To Build a Fire

Jack London

Jack London (1876–1916), born to a poor family in San Francisco, built his reputation as an adventurer, as a journalist, and, most important, as a fiction writer. Many of his brutally realistic stories derive from his gold-seeking exploits in the Yukon Territory and reflect his socialist ideals. Among his novels are *The Call of the Wild* (1903), *The Sea-Wolf* (1904), *The Iron-Heel* (1907), and *Martin Eden* (1909). At the age of 40, London committed suicide through an overdose of narcotics.

By weaving a series of cause-and-effect relations, Jack London patterns an overall, very basic, and very frightening causal development. "To Build a Fire" is an analysis of imagination and survival, instinct and practicality.

Day had broken cold and gray, exceedingly cold and gray, when the ₁ man turned aside from the main Yukon trail and climbed the high earthbank, where a dim and little-travelled trail led eastward through the fat spruce timberland. It was a steep bank, and he paused for breath at the top, excusing the act to himself by looking at his watch. It was nine o'clock. There was no sun nor hint of sun, though there was not a cloud in the sky. It was a clear day, and yet there seemed an intangible pall over the face of things, a subtle gloom that made the day dark, and that was due to the absence of sun. This fact did not worry the man. He was used to the lack of sun. It had been days since he had seen the sun, and he knew that a few more days must pass before that cheerful orb, due south, should just peep above the sky line and dip immediately from view.

The man flung a look back along the way he had come. The Yukon lay a ₂ mile wide and hidden under three feet of ice. On top of this ice were as many feet of snow. It was all pure white, rolling in gentle undulations where the ice jams of the freeze-up had formed. North and south, as far as his eye could see, it was unbroken white, save for a dark hairline that curved and twisted from around the spruce-covered island to the south, and that curved and twisted away into the north, where it disappeared behind another spruce-covered island. This dark hairline was the trail—the main trail—that led south five hundred miles to the Chilcoot Pass, Dyea, and salt water; and that led north seventy miles to Dawson, and still on to the north a thousand miles to Nulato, and finally to St. Michael, on Bering Sea, a thousand miles and half a thousand more.

But all this—the mysterious, far-reaching hairline trail, the absence of sun ₃ from the sky, the tremendous cold, and the strangeness and weirdness of it all— made no impression on the man. It was not because he was long used to it. He was a newcomer in the land, a *chechaquo,* and this was his first winter. The trouble with him was that he was without imagination. He was quick and alert in the things of life, but only in the things, and not in the significances. Fifty degrees below zero meant eighty-odd degrees of frost. Such fact impressed him as being cold and uncomfortable, and that was all. It did not lead him to meditate upon his frailty as a creature of temperature, and upon man's frailty in general, able only to live within certain narrow limits of heat and cold; and from there on it did not lead him to the conjectural field of immortality and man's place in the universe. Fifty degrees below zero stood for a bite of frost that hurt and that must be guarded against by the use of mittens, ear flaps, warm moccasins, and thick socks. Fifty degrees below zero was to him just precisely fifty degrees below zero. That there should be anything more to it than that was a thought that never entered his head.

As he turned to go on, he spat speculatively. There was a sharp, explosive 4 crackle that startled him. He spat again. And again, in the air, before it could fall to the snow, the spittle crackled. He knew that at fifty below spittle crackled on the snow, but this spittle had crackled in the air. Undoubtedly it was colder than fifty below—how much colder he did not know. But the temperature did not matter. He was bound for the old claim on the left fork of Henderson Creek, where the boys were already. They had come over across the divide from the Indian Creek country, while he had come the roundabout way to take a look at the possibilities of getting out logs in the spring from the islands in the Yukon. He would be in to camp by six o'clock; a bit after dark, it was true, but the boys would be there, a fire would be going, and a hot supper would be ready. As for lunch, he pressed his hand against the protruding bundle under his jacket. It was also under his shirt, wrapped up in a handkerchief and lying against the naked skin. It was the only way to keep the biscuits from freezing. He smiled agreeably to himself as he thought of those biscuits, each cut open and sopped in bacon grease, and each enclosing a generous slice of fried bacon.

He plunged in among the big spruce trees. The trail was faint. A foot of 5 snow had fallen since the last sled had passed over, and he was glad he was without a sled, traveling light. In fact, he carried nothing but the lunch wrapped in the handkerchief. He was surprised, however, at the cold. It certainly was cold, he concluded, as he rubbed his numb nose and cheekbones with his mittened hand. He was a warm-whiskered man, but the hair on his face did not protect the high cheekbones and the eager nose that thrust itself aggressively into the frosty air.

At the man's heels trotted a dog, a big native husky, the proper wolf dog, 6 gray-coated and without any visible or temperamental difference from its brother, the wild wolf. The animal was depressed by the tremendous cold. It knew that it was no time for traveling. Its instinct told it a truer tale than was told to the man by the man's judgment. In reality, it was not merely colder than fifty below zero; it was colder than sixty below, than seventy below. It was seventy-five below zero. Since the freezing point is thirty-two above zero, it meant that one hundred and seven degrees of frost obtained. The dog did not know anything about thermometers. Possibly in its brain there was no sharp consciousness of a condition of very cold such as was in the man's brain. But the brute had its instinct. It experienced a vague but menacing apprehension that subdued it and made it slink along at the man's heels, and that made it question eagerly every unwonted movement of the man as if expecting him to go into camp or to seek shelter somewhere and build a fire. The dog had learned fire, and it wanted fire, or else to burrow under the snow and cuddle its warmth away from the air.

The frozen moisture of its breathing had settled on its fur in a fine powder 7
of frost, and especially were its jowls, muzzle, and eyelashes whitened by its crystalled breath. The man's red beard and mustache were likewise frosted, but more solidly, the deposit taking the form of ice and increasing with every warm, moist breath he exhaled. Also, the man was chewing tobacco, and the muzzle of ice held his lips so rigidly that he was unable to clear his chin when he expelled the juice. The result was that a crystal beard of the color and solidity of amber was increasing its length on his chin. If he fell down it would shatter itself, like glass, into brittle fragments. But he did not mind the appendage. It was the penalty all tobacco chewers paid in that country, and he had been out before in two cold snaps. They had not been so cold as this, he knew, but by the spirit thermometer at Sixty Mile he knew they had been registered at fifty below and at fifty-five.

He held on through the level stretch of woods for several miles, crossed a 8
wide flat of nigger heads, and dropped down a bank to the frozen bed of a small stream. This was Henderson Creek, and he knew he was ten miles from the forks. He looked at his watch. It was ten o'clock. He was making four miles an hour, and he calculated that he would arrive at the forks at half-past twelve. He decided to celebrate that event by eating his lunch here.

The dog dropped in again at his heels, with a tail drooping discouragement, 9
as the man swung along the creek bed. The furrow of the old sled trail was plainly visible, but a dozen inches of snow covered the marks of the last runners. In a month no man had come up or down that silent creek. The man held steadily on. He was not much given to thinking, and just then particularly he had nothing to think about save that he would eat lunch at the forks and that at six o'clock he would be in camp with the boys. There was nobody to talk to; and, had there been, speech would have been impossible because of the ice muzzle on his mouth. So he continued monotonously to chew tobacco and to increase the length of his amber beard.

Once in a while the thought reiterated itself that it was very cold and that he 10
had never experienced such cold. As he walked along he rubbed his cheekbones and nose with the back of his mittened hand. He did this automatically, now and again changing hands. But, rub as he would, the instant he stopped his cheekbones went numb, and the following instant the end of his nose went numb. He was sure to frost his cheeks; he knew that, and experienced a pang of regret that he had not devised a nose strap of the sort Bud wore in cold snaps. Such a strap passed across the cheeks, as well, and saved them. But it didn't matter much, after all. What were frosted cheeks? A bit painful, that was all; they were never serious.

Empty as the man's mind was of thoughts, he was keenly observant, and he 11
noticed the changes in the creek, the curves and bends and timber jams, and always he sharply noted where he placed his feet. Once, coming around a bend, he shied abruptly, like a startled horse, curved away from the place where he had been walking, and retreated several paces back along the trail. The creek he knew was frozen clear to the bottom—no creek could contain water in that arctic

winter—but he knew also that there were springs that bubbled out from the hill-sides and ran along under the snow and on top the ice of the creek. He knew that the coldest snaps never froze these springs, and he knew likewise their danger. They were traps. They hid pools of water under the snow that might be three inches deep, or three feet. Sometimes a skin of ice half an inch thick covered them, and in turn was covered by the snow. Sometimes there were alternate lay-ers of water and ice skin, so that when one broke through he kept on breaking through for a while, sometimes wetting himself to the waist.

That was why he had shied in such panic. He had felt the give under his feet 12
and heard the crackle of a snow-hidden ice skin. And to get his feet wet in such a temperature meant trouble and danger. At the very least it meant delay, for he would be forced to stop and build a fire, and under its protection to bare his feet while he dried his socks and moccasins. He stood and studied the creek bed and its banks, and decided that the flow of water came from the right. He reflected awhile, rubbing his nose and cheeks, then skirted to the left, stepping gingerly and testing the footing for each step. Once clear of the danger, he took a fresh chew of tobacco and swung along at his four-mile gait.

In the course of the next two hours he came upon several similar traps. Usu- 13
ally the snow above the hidden pools had a sunken, candied appearance that adver-tised the danger. Once again, however, he had a close call; and once, suspecting danger, he compelled the dog to go on in front. The dog did not want to go. It hung back until the man shoved it forward, and then it went quickly across the white, unbroken surface. Suddenly it broke through, floundered to one side, and got away to firmer footing. It had wet its forefeet and legs, and almost immediately the water that clung to it turned to ice. It made quick efforts to lick the ice off its legs, then dropped down in the snow and began to bite out the ice that had formed between the toes. This was a matter of instinct. To permit the ice to remain would mean sore feet. It did not know this. It merely obeyed the mysterious prompting that arose from the deep crypts of its being. But the man knew, having achieved a judgment on the subject, and he removed the mitten from his right hand and helped tear out the ice particles. He did not expose his fingers more than a minute, and was aston-ished at the swift numbness that smote them. It certainly was cold. He pulled on the mitten hastily, and beat the hand savagely across his chest.

At twelve o'clock the day was at its brightest. Yet the sun was too far south 14
on its winter journey to clear the horizon. The bulge of the earth intervened between it and Henderson Creek, where the man walked under a clear sky at noon and cast no shadow. At half-past twelve, to the minute, he arrived at the forks of the creek. He was pleased at the speed he had made. If he kept it up, he would certainly be with the boys by six. He unbuttoned his jacket and shirt and drew forth his lunch. The action consumed no more than a quarter of a minute, yet in that brief moment the numbness laid hold of the exposed fingers. He did not put the mitten on, but, instead, struck the fingers a dozen sharp smashes against his leg. Then he sat down on a snow-covered log to eat. The sting that followed upon the striking of his fingers against his leg ceased so quickly that he was startled. He had had no chance to take a bite of biscuit. He struck the fingers repeatedly

and returned them to the mitten, baring the other hand for the purpose of eating. He tried to take a mouthful, but the ice muzzle prevented. He had forgotten to build a fire and thaw out. He chuckled at his foolishness, and as he chuckled he noted the numbness creeping into the exposed fingers. Also, he noted that the stinging which had first come to his toes when he sat down was already passing away. He wondered whether the toes were warm or numb. He moved them inside the moccasins and decided that they were numb.

He pulled the mitten on hurriedly and stood up. He was a bit frightened. He 15 stamped up and down until the stinging returned into the feet. It certainly was cold, was his thought. That man from Sulphur Creek had spoken the truth when telling how cold it sometimes got in the country. And he had laughed at him at the time! That showed one must not be too sure of things. There was no mistake about it, it *was* cold. He strode up and down, stamping his feet and threshing his arms, until reassured by the returning warmth. Then he got out matches and proceeded to make a fire. From the undergrowth, where high water of the previous spring had lodged a supply of seasoned twigs, he got his firewood. Working carefully from a small beginning, he soon had a roaring fire, over which he thawed the ice from his face and in the protection of which he ate his biscuits. For the moment the cold of space was outwitted. The dog took satisfaction in the fire, stretching out close enough for warmth and far enough away to escape being singed.

When the man had finished, he filled his pipe and took his comfortable time 16 over a smoke. Then he pulled on his mittens, settled the ear flaps of his cap firmly about his ears, and took the creek trail up the left fork. The dog was disappointed and yearned back toward the fire. This man did not know cold. Possibly all the generations of his ancestry had been ignorant of cold, of real cold, of cold one hundred and seven degrees below freezing point. But the dog knew; all its ancestry knew, and it had inherited the knowledge. And it knew that it was not good to walk abroad in such fearful cold. It was the time to lie snug in a hole in the snow and wait for a curtain of cloud to be drawn across the face of outer space whence this cold came. On the other hand, there was no keen intimacy between the dog and the man. The one was the toil slave of the other, and the only caresses it had ever received were the caresses of the whip lash and of harsh and menacing throat sounds that threatened the whip lash. So the dog made no effort to communicate its apprehension to the man. It was not concerned in the welfare of the man; it was for its own sake that it yearned back toward the fire. But the man whistled, and spoke to it with the sound of whip lashes, and the dog swung in at the man's heels and followed after.

The man took a chew of tobacco and proceeded to start a new amber beard. 17 Also, his moist breath quickly powdered with white his mustache, eyebrows, and lashes. There did not seem to be so many springs on the left fork of the Henderson, and for half an hour the man saw no signs of any. And then it happened. At a place where there were no signs, where the soft, unbroken snow seemed to advertise solidity beneath, the man broke through. It was not deep. He wet himself halfway to the knees before he floundered out to the firm crust.

He was angry, and cursed his luck aloud. He had hoped to get into camp with 18 the boys at six o'clock, and this would delay him an hour, for he would have to build a fire and dry out his footgear. This was imperative at that low temperature— he knew that much; and he turned aside to the bank, which he climbed. On top, tangled in the underbrush about the trunks of several small spruce trees, was a highwater deposit of dry firewood—sticks and twigs, principally, but also larger portions of seasoned branches and fine dry last year's grasses. He threw down several large pieces on top of the snow. This served for a foundation and prevented the young flame from drowning itself in the snow it otherwise would melt. The flame he got by touching a match to a small shred of birch bark that he took from his pocket. This burned even more readily than paper. Placing it on the foundation, he fed the young flame with wisps of dry grass and with the tiniest dry twigs.

He worked slowly and carefully, keenly aware of his danger. Gradually, as 19 the flame grew stronger, he increased the size of the twigs with which he fed it. He squatted in the snow, pulling the twigs out from their entanglement in the brush and feeding directly to the flame. He knew there must be no failure. When it is seventy-five below zero, a man must not fail in his first attempt to build a fire—that is, if his feet are wet. If his feet are dry, and he fails, he can run along the trail for half a mile and restore his circulation. But the circulation of wet and freezing feet cannot be restored by running when it is seventy-five below. No matter how fast he runs, the wet feet will freeze the harder.

All this the man knew. The old-timer on Sulphur Creek had told him about 20 it the previous fall, and now he was appreciating the advice. Already all sensation had gone out of his feet. To build the fire he had been forced to remove his mittens, and the fingers had quickly gone numb. His pace of four miles an hour had kept his heart pumping blood to the surface of his body and to all the extremities. But the instant he stopped, the action of the pump eased down. The cold of space smote the unprotected tip of the planet, and he, being on that unprotected tip, received the full force of the blow. The blood of his body recoiled before it. The blood was alive, like the dog, and like the dog it wanted to hide away and cover itself up from the fearful cold. So long as he walked four miles an hour, he pumped that blood, willy-nilly, to the surface; but now it ebbed away and sank down into the recesses of his body. The extremities were the first to feel its absence. His wet feet froze the faster, and his exposed fingers numbed the faster, though they had not yet begun to freeze. Nose and cheeks were already freezing, while the skin of all his body chilled as it lost its blood.

But he was safe. Toes and nose and cheeks would be only touched by the 21 frost, for the fire was beginning to burn with strength. He was feeding it with twigs the size of his finger. In another minute he would be able to feed it with branches the size of his wrist, and then he could remove his wet footgear, and, while it dried, he could keep his naked feet warm by the fire, rubbing them at first, of course, with snow. The fire was a success. He was safe. He remembered the advice of the old-timer on Sulphur Creek, and smiled. The old-timer had been very serious in laying down the law that no man must travel alone in the Klondike after fifty below. Well, here he was; he had had the accident; he was alone; and he had saved himself. Those old-timers were rather womanish, some of them, he thought. All a man had to do was to keep his head, and he was all right. Any man who was a man could travel alone. But it was surprising, the rapidity with which his cheeks and nose were freezing. And he had not thought his fingers could go lifeless in so short a time. Lifeless they were, for he could scarcely make them move together to grip a twig, and they seemed remote from his body and from him. When he touched a twig, he had to look and see whether or not he had hold of it. The wires were pretty well down between him and his finger ends.

All of which counted for little. There was the fire, snapping and crackling 22 and promising life with every dancing flame. He started to untie his moccasins. They were coated with ice; the thick German socks were like sheaths of iron halfway to the knees; and the moccasin strings were like rods of steel all twisted and knotted as by some conflagration. For a moment he tugged with his numb fingers, then, realizing the folly of it, he drew his sheath knife.

But before he could cut the strings, it happened. It was his own fault or, 23 rather, his mistake. He should not have built the fire under the spruce tree. He should have built it in the open. But it had been easier to pull the twigs from the brush and drop them directly on the fire. Now the tree under which he had done this carried a weight of snow on its boughs. No wind had blown for weeks, and each bough was fully freighted. Each time he had pulled a twig he had communicated a slight agitation to the tree—an imperceptible agitation, so far as he was concerned, but an agitation sufficient to bring about the disaster. High up in the tree one bough capsized its load of snow. This fell on the boughs beneath, capsizing them. This process continued, spreading out and involving the whole tree. It grew like an avalanche, and it descended without warning upon the man and the fire, and the fire was blotted out! Where it had burned was a mantle of fresh and disordered snow.

The man was shocked. It was as though he had just heard his own sentence 24 of death. For a moment he sat and stared at the spot where the fire had been. Then he grew very calm. Perhaps the old-timer on Sulphur Creek was right. If he had only had a trail mate he would have been in no danger now. The trail mate could have built the fire. Well, it was up to him to build the fire over again, and this second time there must be no failure. Even if he succeeded, he would most likely lose some toes. His feet must be badly frozen by now, and there would be some time before the second fire was ready.

Such were his thoughts, but he did not sit and think them. He was busy all 25 the time they were passing through his mind. He made a new foundation for a fire, this time in the open, where no treacherous tree could blot it out. Next he gathered dry grasses and tiny twigs from the high-water flotsam. He could not bring his fingers together to pull them out, but he was able to gather them by the handful. In this way he got many rotten twigs and bits of green moss that were undesirable, but it was the best he could do. He worked methodically, even collecting an armful of the larger branches to be used later when the fire gathered strength. And all the while the dog sat and watched him, a certain yearning wistfulness in its eyes, for it looked upon him as the fire provider, and the fire was slow in coming.

When all was ready, the man reached in his pocket for a second piece of 26 birch bark. He knew the bark was there, and, though he could not feel it with his fingers, he could hear its crisp rustling as he fumbled for it. Try as he would, he could not clutch hold of it. And all the time, in his consciousness, was the knowledge that each instant his feet were freezing. This thought tended to put him in a panic, but he fought against it and kept calm. He pulled on his mittens with his teeth, and threshed his arms back and forth, beating his hands with all his might against his sides. He did this sitting down, and he stood up to do it; and all the while the dog sat in the snow, its wolf brush of a tail curled around warmly over its forefeet, its sharp wolf ears pricked forward intently as it watched the man. And the man, as he beat and threshed with his arms and hands, felt a great surge of envy as he regarded the creature that was warm and secure in its natural covering.

After a time he was aware of the first faraway signals of sensation in his 27 beaten fingers. The faint tingling grew stronger till it evolved into a stinging ache that was excruciating, but which the man hailed with satisfaction. He stripped the mitten from his right hand and fetched forth the birch bark. The exposed fingers were quickly going numb again. Next he brought out his bunch of sulphur matches. But the tremendous cold had already driven the life out of his fingers. In his effort to separate one match from the others, the whole bunch fell in the snow. He tried to pick it out of the snow, but failed. The dead fingers could neither touch nor clutch. He was very careful. He drove the thought of his freezing feet, and nose, and cheeks, out of his mind, devoting his whole soul to the matches. He watched, using the sense of vision in place of that of touch, and when he saw his fingers on each side of the bunch, he closed them—that is, he willed to close them, for the wires were down, and the fingers did not obey. He pulled the mitten on the right hand, and beat it fiercely against his knee. Then, with both mittened hands, he scooped the bunch of matches, along with much snow, into his lap. Yet he was no better off.

After some manipulation he managed to get the bunch between the heels of 28 his mittened hands. In this fashion he carried it to his mouth. The ice crackled and snapped when by a violent effort he opened his mouth. He drew the lower jaw in, curled the upper lip out of the way, scraped the bunch with his upper teeth in order to separate a match. He succeeded in getting one, which he dropped on his lap. He was no better off. He could not pick it up. Then he devised a way. He picked it up in his teeth and scratched it on his leg. Twenty times he scratched before he succeeded in lighting it. As it flamed he held it with his teeth to the birch bark. But the burning brimstone went up his nostrils and into his lungs, causing him to cough spasmodically. The match fell into the snow and went out.

The old-timer on Sulphur Creek was right, he thought in the moment of 29 controlled despair that ensued: after fifty below, a man should travel with a partner. He beat his hands, but failed in exciting any sensation. Suddenly he bared both hands, removing the mittens with his teeth. He caught the whole bunch between the heels of his hands. His arm muscles not being frozen enabled him to press the hand heels tightly against the matches. Then he scratched the bunch along his leg. It flared into flame, seventy sulphur matches at once! There was no wind to blow them out. He kept his head to one side to escape the strangling fumes, and held the blazing bunch to the birch bark. As he so held it, he became aware of sensation in his hand. His flesh was burning. He could smell it. Deep down below the surface he could feel it. The sensation developed into pain that grew acute. And still he endured it, holding the flame of the matches clumsily to the bark that would not light readily because his own burning hands were in the way, absorbing most of the flame.

At last, when he could endure no more, he jerked his hands apart. The blaz- 30 ing matches fell sizzling into the snow, but the birch bark was alight. He began laying dry grasses and the tiniest twigs on the flame. He could not pick and choose, for he had to lift the fuel between the heels of his hands. Small pieces of rotten wood and green moss clung to the twigs, and he bit them off as well as he could with his teeth. He cherished the flame carefully and awkwardly. It meant life, and it must not perish. The withdrawal of blood from the surface of his body now made him begin to shiver, and he grew more awkward. A large piece of green moss fell squarely on the little fire. He tried to poke it out with his fingers, but his shivering frame made him poke too far, and he disrupted the nucleus of the little fire, the burning grasses and tiny twigs separating and scattering. He tried to poke them together again, but in spite of the tenseness of the effort, his shivering got away with him, and the twigs were hopelessly scattered. Each twig gushed a puff of smoke and went out. The fire provider had failed. As he looked apathetically about him, his eyes chanced on the dog, sitting across the ruins of the fire from him, in the snow, making restless, hunching movements, slightly lifting one fore-foot and then the other, shifting its weight back and forth on them with wistful eagerness.

The sight of the dog put a wild idea into his head. He remembered the tale 31 of the man, caught in a blizzard, who killed a steer and crawled inside the carcass, and so was saved. He would kill the dog and bury his hands in the warm body until the numbness went out of them. Then he could build another fire. He spoke to the dog, calling it to him; but in his voice was a strange note of fear that frightened the animal, who had never known the man to speak in such way before. Something was the matter, and its suspicious nature sensed danger—it knew not what danger, but somewhere, somehow, in its brain arose an apprehension of the man. It flattened its ears down at the sound of the man's voice, and its restless, hunching movements and the liftings and shiftings of its forefeet became more pronounced; but it would not come to the man. He got on his hands and knees and crawled toward the dog. The unusual posture again excited suspicion, and the animal sidled mincingly away.

The man sat up in the snow for a moment and struggled for calmness. Then 32 he pulled on his mittens, by means of his teeth, and got upon his feet. He glanced down at first in order to assure himself that he was really standing up, for the absence of sensation in his feet left him unrelated to the earth. His erect position in itself started to drive the webs of suspicion from the dog's mind; and when he spoke peremptorily, with the sound of whip lashes in his voice, the dog rendered its customary allegiance and came to him. As it came within reaching distance the man lost his control. His arms flashed out to the dog, and he experienced genuine surprise when he discovered that his hands could not clutch, that there was neither bend nor feeling in the fingers. He had forgotten for the moment that they were frozen and that they were freezing more and more. All this happened quickly, and before the animal could get away, he encircled its body with his arms. He sat down in the snow, and in this fashion held the dog, while it snarled and whined and struggled.

But it was all he could do, hold its body encircled in his arms and sit there. 33 He realized that he could not kill the dog. There was no way to do it. With his helpless hands he could neither draw nor hold his sheath knife nor throttle the animal. He released it, and it plunged wildly away, with tail between its legs, and still snarling. It halted forty feet away and surveyed him curiously, with ears sharply pricked forward.

The man looked down at his hands in order to locate them, and found them 34 hanging on the ends of his arms. It struck him as curious that one should have to use his eyes in order to find out where his hands were. He began threshing his arms back and forth, beating the mittened hands against his sides. He did this for five minutes, violently, and his heart pumped enough blood up to the surface to put a stop to his shivering. But no sensation was aroused in the hands. He had an impression that they hung like weights on the ends of his arms, but when he tried to run the impression down, he could not find it.

A certain fear of death, dull and oppressive, came to him. This fear quickly 35 became poignant as he realized that it was no longer a mere matter of freezing his fingers and toes, or of losing his hands and feet, but that it was a matter of life and death with the chances against him. This threw him into a panic, and he turned and ran up the creek bed along the old, dim trail. The dog joined in behind and kept up with him. He ran blindly, without intention, in fear such as he had never known in his life. Slowly, as he plowed and floundered through the snow, he began to see things again—the banks of the creek, the old timber jams, the leafless aspens, and the sky. The running made him feel better. He did not shiver. Maybe, if he ran on, his feet would thaw out; and, anyway, if he ran far enough, he would reach camp and the boys. Without doubt he would lose some fingers and toes and some of his face; but the boys would take care of him, and save the rest of him when he got there. And at the same time there was another thought in his mind that said he would never get to the camp and the boys; that it was too many miles away, that the freezing had too great a start on him, and that he would soon be stiff and dead. This thought he kept in the background and refused to consider. Sometimes it pushed itself forward and demanded to be heard, but he thrust it back and strove to think of other things.

It struck him as curious that he could run at all on feet so frozen that he 36 could not feel them when they struck the earth and took the weight of his body. He seemed to himself to skim along above the surface, and to have no connection with the earth. Somewhere he had once seen a winged Mercury, and he wondered if Mercury felt as he felt when skimming over the earth.

His theory of running until he reached camp and the boys had one flaw in 37 it: he lacked the endurance. Several times he stumbled, and finally he tottered, crumpled up, and fell. When he tried to rise, he failed. He must sit and rest, he decided, and next time he would merely walk and keep on going. As he sat and regained his breath, he noted that he was feeling quite warm and comfortable. He was not shivering, and it even seemed that a warm glow had come to his chest and trunk. And yet, when he touched his nose or cheeks, there was no sensation. Running would not thaw them out. Nor would it thaw out his hands and feet. Then the thought came to him that the frozen portions of his body must be extending. He tried to keep this thought down, to forget it, to think of something else; he was aware of the panicky feeling that it caused, and he was afraid of the panic. But the thought asserted itself, and persisted, until it produced a vision of his body totally frozen. This was too much, and he made another wild run along the trail. Once he slowed down to a walk, but the thought of the freezing extending itself made him run again.

And all the time the dog ran with him, at his heels. When he fell down a 38 second time, it curled its tail over its forefeet and sat in front of him, facing him, curiously eager and intent. The warmth and security of the animal angered him, and he cursed it till it flattened down its ears appeasingly. This time the shivering came more quickly upon the man. He was losing in his battle with the frost. It was creeping into his body from all sides. The thought of it drove him on, but he ran no more than a hundred feet, when he staggered and pitched headlong. It was his last panic. When he had recovered his breath and control, he sat up and entertained in his mind the conception of meeting death with dignity. However, the conception did not come to him in such terms. His idea of it was that he had been making a fool of himself, running around like a chicken with its head cut off— such was the simile that occurred to him. Well, he was bound to freeze anyway, and he might as well take it decently. With this new-found peace of mind came the first glimmerings of drowsiness. A good idea, he thought, to sleep off to death. It was like taking an anesthetic. Freezing was not so bad as people thought. There were lots worse ways to die.

He pictured the boys finding his body next day. Suddenly he found himself 39 with them, coming along the trail and looking for himself. And, still with them, he came around a turn in the trail and found himself lying in the snow. He did not belong with himself any more, for even then he was out of himself, standing with the boys and looking at himself in the snow. It certainly was cold, was his thought. When he got back to the States he could tell the folks what real cold was. He drifted on from this to a vision of the old-timer on Sulphur Creek. He could see him quite clearly, warm and comfortable, and smoking a pipe.

"You were right, old hoss; you were right," the man mumbled to the old- 40 timer of Sulphur Creek.

Then the man drowsed off into what seemed to him the most comfortable 41 and satisfying sleep he had ever known. The dog sat facing him and waiting. The brief day drew to a close in a long, slow twilight. There were no signs of a fire to be made, and, besides, never in the dog's experience had it known a man to sit like that in the snow and make no fire. As the twilight drew on, its eager yearning for the fire mastered it, and with a great lifting and shifting of forefeet, it whined softly, then flattened its ears down in anticipation of being chidden by the man. But the man remained silent. Later the dog whined loudly. And still later it crept close to the man and caught the scent of death. This made the animal bristle and back away. A little longer it delayed, howling under the stars that leaped and danced and shone brightly in the cold sky. Then it turned and trotted up the trail in the direction of the camp it knew, where were the other food providers and fire providers.

Meaning and Idea

1. Where does this story take place? Briefly describe the physical environment. Where is the protagonist headed? What does he imagine awaits him at the end of his journey? What is the reality of that ending?

2. At a number of points in this story, the man welcomes pain. Identify three such instances. Why does he welcome the pain? What condition is he fighting off?

3. What is "the advice of the old-timer on Sulphur Creek"? What was the man's attitude toward this advice? Did it prove to be correct or incorrect advice?

4. What is the man's attitude toward the dog that's with him? How does it change within the story? What is the man's "last resort" use for the dog? Why is it impossible for him to follow through on this?

Language, Form, Structure

1. What is the overall cause-and-effect relationship in this story? This story is made up of many smaller causal relationships that contribute to the overall larger one. Identify ten of these smaller relationships.

2. Discuss the significance of the sentence, "The trouble with him was that he was without imagination." (See page 444.) How does the character flaw implied here become a cause for the man's death?

3. Throughout this story, London writes of both the man's and the dog's knowledge about the cold. Identify a few of those passages. How does London's comparison of the two different experiences (of the man and dog) advance the main point of the story? What is this main point?

4. Explain the final line of the story. Is the final line of this story really an expression of the dog's consciousness? How and what does it reveal about London's attitude about survival? What is the relation of that line to the earlier comment about the man's lack of imagination?

5. Write definitions for the following words: frailty; conjectural; appendage; reiterated; pang; conflagration; excrutiating; acute; nucleus; peremptorily; allegiance; drowsed.

Ideas for Writing

1. Write a causal analysis of an unfortunate result of someone's stubbornness. Attempt to build the overall causal relationship through a series of smaller ones.

2. Analyze the reasons behind a recent decision by the government with which you disagree. Make the effects the basis for your disagreement.

3. Throughout "To Build a Fire" the main character remains nameless; he is only "the man." Perhaps less important, the dog also remains simply "the dog." Write a short commentary about the causes and effects of namelessness in this story.

On Warts

Lewis Thomas

Dr. Lewis Thomas, born in 1913 in New York City, was president of the Memorial Sloan-Kettering Cancer Center in New York. He was educated at Princeton and Harvard, where he received his medical degree in 1937. He was well-respected for his seemingly tireless work in medical research, administration, and education. In 1970, he began writing a monthly, lay-oriented column for the *New England Journal of Medicine*. These articles have been collected in *The Lives of a Cell: Notes of a Biology Watcher* (published in 1974; recipient of the 1975 National Book Award for Arts and Letters) and *The Medusa and the Snail: More Notes of a Biology Watcher* (1979). He died in 1993 of Waldenstrom's disease.

In "On Warts," from the collection *The Medusa and the Snail*, Thomas explains what warts are, how they form, and how they may be removed. Perhaps most interesting is his explanation of how and why his attitudes have changed, as well as how he looks toward future results of increased knowledge about such misunderstood "wonderful structures."

*W*arts are wonderful structures. They can appear overnight on any 1 part of the skin, like mushrooms on a damp lawn, full grown and splendid in the complexity of their architecture. Viewed in stained sections under a microscope, they are the most specialized of cellular arrangements, constructed as though for a purpose. They sit there like turreted mounds of dense, impenetrable horn, impregnable, designed for defense against the world outside.

In a certain sense, warts are both useful and essential, but not for us. As it 2 turns out, the exuberant cells of a wart are the elaborate reproductive apparatus of a virus.

You might have thought from the looks of it that the cells infected by the 3 wart virus were using this response as a ponderous way of defending themselves against the virus, maybe even a way of becoming more distasteful, but it is not so. The wart is what the virus truly wants; it can flourish only in cells undergoing precisely that kind of overgrowth. It is not a defense at all; it is an overwhelming welcome, an enthusiastic accommodation meeting the needs of more and more virus.

The strangest thing about warts is that they tend to go away. Fully grown, 4 nothing in the body has so much the look of toughness and permanence as a wart, and yet, inexplicably and often very abruptly, they come to the end of their lives and vanish without a trace.

And they can be made to go away by something that can only be called 5 thinking, or something like thinking. This is a special property of warts which is absolutely astonishing, more of a surprise than cloning or recombinant DNA or endorphy or acupuncture or anything else currently attracting attention in the press. It is one of the great mystifications of science: warts can be ordered off the skin by hypnotic suggestion.

Not everyone believes this, but the evidence goes back a long way and is 6 persuasive. Generations of internists and dermatologists, and their grandmothers for that matter, have been convinced of the phenomenon. I was once told by a distinguished old professor of medicine, one of Sir William Osler's original bright young men, that it was his practice to paint gentian violet over a wart and then assure the patient firmly that it would be gone in a week, and he never saw it again. There have been several meticulous studies by good clinical investigators, with proper controls. In one of these, fourteen patients with seemingly intractable generalized warts on both sides of the body were hypnotized, and the suggestion was made that all the warts on one side of the body would begin to go away. Within several weeks the results were indisputably positive; in nine patients, all or nearly all the warts on the suggested side had vanished, while the control side had just as many as ever.

It is interesting that most of the warts vanished precisely as they were 7 instructed, but it is even more fascinating that mistakes were made. Just as you might expect in other affairs requiring a clear understanding of which is the right and which the left side, one of the subjects got mixed up and destroyed the warts on the wrong side. In a later study by a group at the Massachusetts General Hospital, the warts on both sides were rejected even though the instructions were to pay attention to just one side.

I have been trying to figure out the nature of the instructions issued by the 8 unconscious mind, whatever that is, under hypnosis. It seems to me hardly enough for the mind to say, simply, get off, eliminate yourselves, without providing something in the way of specifications as to how to go about it.

I used to believe, thinking about this experiment when it was just published, 9 that the instructions might be quite simple. Perhaps nothing more detailed than a command to shut down the flow through all the precapillary arterioles in and around the warts to the point of strangulation. Exactly how the mind would accomplish this with precision, cutting off the blood supply to one wart while leaving others intact, I couldn't figure out, but I was satisfied to leave it there anyhow. And I was glad to think that my unconscious mind would have to take the responsibility for this, for if I had been one of the subjects I would never have been able to do it myself.

But now the problem seems much more complicated by the information 10 concerning the viral etiology of warts, and even more so by the currently plausible notion that immunologic mechanisms are very likely implicated in the rejection of warts.

If my unconscious can figure out how to manipulate the mechanisms 11 needed for getting around that virus, and for deploying all the various cells in the correct order for tissue rejection, then all I have to say is that my unconscious is a lot further along than I am. I wish I had a wart right now, just to see if I am that talented.

There ought to be a better word than "Unconscious," even capitalized, for 12 what I have, so to speak, in mind. I was brought up to regard this aspect of thinking as a sort of private sanitarium, walled off somewhere in a suburb of my brain, capable only of producing such garbled information as to keep my mind, my proper Mind, always a little off balance.

But any mental apparatus that can reject a wart is something else again. 13 This is not the sort of confused, disordered process you'd expect at the hands of the kind of Unconscious you read about in books, out at the edge of things making up dreams or getting mixed up on words or having hysterics. Whatever, or whoever, is responsible for this has the accuracy and precision of a surgeon. There almost has to be a Person in charge, running matters of meticulous detail beyond anyone's comprehension, a skilled engineer and manager, a chief executive officer, the head of the whole place. I never thought before that I possessed such a tenant. Or perhaps more accurately, such a landlord, since I would be, if this is in fact the situation, nothing more than a lodger.

Among other accomplishments, he would be a cell biologist of world class, 14 capable of sorting through the various classes of one's lymphocytes, all with quite different functions which I do not understand, in order to mobilize the right ones and exclude the wrong ones for the task of tissue rejection. If it were left to me, and I were somehow empowered to call up lymphocytes and direct them to the vicinity of my wart (assuming that I could learn to do such a thing), mine would come tumbling in all unsorted, B cells and T cells, suppressor cells and killer cells, and no doubt other cells whose names I have not learned, incapable of getting anything useful done.

Even if immunology is not involved, and all that needs doing is to shut off 15 the blood supply locally, I haven't the faintest notion how to set that up. I assume that the selective turning off of arterioles can be done by one or another chemical mediator, and I know the names of some of them, but I wouldn't dare let things like these loose even if I knew how to do it.

Well, then, who does supervise this kind of operation? Someone's got to, 16 you know. You can't sit there under hypnosis, taking suggestions in and having them acted on with such accuracy and precision, without assuming the existence of something very like a controller. It wouldn't do to fob off the whole intricate business on lower centers without sending along a quite detailed set of specifications, way over my head.

Some intelligence or other knows how to get rid of warts, and this is a dis- 17 quieting thought.

It is also a wonderful problem, in need of solving. Just think what we would 18 know, if we had anything like a clear understanding of what goes on when a wart is hypnotized away. We would know the identity of the cellular and chemical participants in tissue rejection, conceivably with some added information about the ways that viruses create foreignness in cells. We would know how the traffic of these reactants is directed, and perhaps then be able to understand the nature of certain diseases in which the traffic is being conducted in wrong directions, aimed at the wrong cells. Best of all, we could be finding out about a kind of superintelligence that exists in each of us, infinitely smarter and possessed of technical know-how far beyond our present understanding. It would be worth a War on Warts, a Conquest of Warts, a National Institute of Warts and All.

Meaning and Idea

1. What is the cause of warts? What, according to Thomas, would most people think is the relationship between warts and virus by looking at a microscopic section of a wart? How is this impression different from the actuality?

2. Explain the causal relationship between wart removal and hypnotic suggestion. Why, in one experiment, was painting warts with gentian violet and then suggesting their imminent removal to patients a proof of the power of suggestion? On what basis does Thomas, a respected, responsible physician, believe in the power of hypnotic suggestion as it relates to warts?

3. What was Thomas's original opinion about the "Unconscious"? How did that opinion change? Why? How was that change of opinion a result of his investigations of warts?

4. What does Thomas hypothesize as the results of a fuller knowledge about how warts can be "hypnotized away"?

Language, Form, Structure

1. In this essay, does Thomas focus mainly on causes or effects? Explain your answer with specific references to the text.

2. What is Thomas's intended audience for this essay? What examples from the essay support your answer? How does his intended audience affect the level of diction in the writing? (*Diction* refers to word choice—among other things, to the level of language used—informal, specialized, colloquial, and so on.)

3. What is the effect of the opening sentence in this essay? What was your response to it? How did that response affect your reading of the essay? How would you characterize the overall tone of the writing? Support your answer with examples from the essay.

4. Identify descriptive sections in the essay. How does the description enhance the writing?

5. Write definitions for these words and then use each in a sentence: turreted; impregnable; exuberant; apparatus; ponderous; cloning; meticulous; intractable; plausible; disquieting.

Ideas for Writing

1. Write a causal analysis of your recent solution to a physical problem (even if that problem was only losing five pounds to look good in a bathing suit). Analyze both causes and effects.

2. Analyze why you recently changed an opinion about something that you had thought of as true for a long time. Why did you change your opinion? What resulted from this change of attitude?

3. The final paragraph strongly suggests a connection between understanding warts and cancer research. Yet Thomas uses a rather lighthearted tone— even humor at times—in this essay. How appropriate to his subject is the author's levity? Develop your answer with direct references to the text.

CROSSOVER

1. In this chapter, Kate Chopin, Langston Hughes, Edwin Arlington Robinson, Jack London, and Tobias Wolff all write of the tragic effects of particular situations. Choose two or three of these selections and write an essay that identifies and explains the major insight that each piece offers about the outcomes of conditions or actions. Draw on particular passages to develop your points. Which insight seems truest to you? Why?

2. Kate Chopin in "The Story of an Hour" and Langston Hughes in "Dream Deferred" bring thinking about gender and racial conditions respectively to bear on their works. What understanding about oppression do the two selections share? How does each piece develop the details of oppression and its effects to make its powerful point? How do the points differ? Write your views on these issues in a well-supported essay.

■

Chapter Eight

DEFINITION

William Kennedy's 1983 Pulitzer Prize–winning novel *Ironweed* opens with a definition that the author adapted from the Audubon Society's *Field Guide to North American Wildflowers.*

> Tall Ironweed is a member of the Sunflower Family (Asterasceae). It has a tall erect stem and bears deep purple-blue flower heads in loose terminal clusters. Its leaves are long and thin and pointed, their lower surfaces downy. Its fruit is seed-like, with a double set of purplish bristles. It flowers from August to October in damp, rich soil from New York south to Georgia, west to Louisiana, north to Missouri, Illinois and Michigan. The name refers to the toughness of the stem.

Ironweed is about Francis Phelan, a vagabond wino down on his luck who returns to Albany, where he had murdered a strikebreaker many years back and where he accidentally dropped and killed his infant son. The definition of ironweed helps explain the title of the book and establishes the metaphorical relation between the flower and the man. Like "Tall Ironweed," Francis Phelan shows up in lots of places starting with New York and is a lanky, tough-stemmed, off-season bloomer with a soft underbelly. Without the definition, many readers unfamiliar with this special sunflower would have little idea of what Kennedy had in mind in his title and could not make the connections that enrich our understanding of the novel. A dictionary would not have been much help either; *ironweed,* says *The American Heritage Dictionary,* is "Any plant of the genus *Vernonia,* having clusters of purple flowers." Period.

A researcher and scientist, Robert Ardrey, in an influential and controversial book of nonfiction called *The Territorial Imperative* (1966), opens his first chapter, "Of Men and Mockingbirds," with these two paragraphs:

> A territory is an area of space, whether of water or earth or air, which an animal or group of animals defends as an exclusive preserve. The word is also used to describe the inward compulsion in animate beings to possess and defend such a space. A territorial species of animals, therefore, is one in which all males, and sometimes females too, bear an inherent drive to gain and defend an exclusive property.
>
> In most but not all territorial species, defense is directed only against fellow members of the kind. A squirrel does not regard a mouse as a trespasser. In most but not all territorial species—not in chameleons, for example—the female is sexually unresponsive to an unpropertied male. As a general pattern of behavior, in territorial species the competition between males which we formerly believed was one for the possession of females is in truth for possession of property.

Understanding the main thesis of the book, the role of territory as an impulse in the human species, depends on our understanding of the word *territory* as Ardrey wishes us to understand its meaning; hence a clear definition of the word early in the text is essential.

William Shakespeare both pleases and jolts us with these humorous, unconventional musings on the word *honor* from Falstaff, the great comic character in *King Henry IV, Part 1* (bracketed information explains unfamiliar idioms):

Honor pricks me on. [Honor spurs my actions.] Yea, but if honor prick me off when I come on? [What if honor places me on the list of casualties?] How then? Can honor set a leg? No. Or an arm? No. Or take away the grief of a wound? No. Honor hath no skill in surgery then? No. What is honor? A word. What is in that word honor? What is that word honor? Air. A trim reckoning! Who hath it? He that died o'Wednesday. Doth he feel it? No. Doth he hear it? No. Tis insensible then? Yea, to the dead. But will it not live with the living? No. Why? Detraction will not suffer it. Therefore I'll none of it. Honor is a mere scutcheon. And so ends my catechism.

One of the main themes of *King Henry IV, Part 1* is honor, the honor human beings show to each other—child to parent, prince to subject, subject to prince, soldier to officer, friend to friend. In those famous lines from act V, scene ii, Shakespeare provides an illuminating, if eccentric, perspective on honor, one that is nonetheless perfectly consistent with Falstaff's nature as a likeable drunk and a coward. Men have killed for honor on the plains of Shrewsbury, and Falstaff's dismissive definition helps us wonder at the madness of war for so frail and yet so compelling a notion. Yet the actions of the male characters are chained to the notion of honor as the core of their existence.

Novelist, nonfiction writer, poet—and essayist, short story writer, biographer, news reporter, technical writer, textbook writer—anyone concerned with and committed to precision in language sooner or later will turn to definition as a strategy for clear writing.

READING DEFINITION

All definitions have as their unswerving purpose to bring meaning to a word, and readers should expect nothing less than to see a word or concept like a specimen under the best microscope—clear, sharply focused, unambiguous. At its most basic level, the definition aims at precise linguistic equivalence: This is that. Readers frequently encounter *lexical* (or dictionary) definitions, no matter what the larger purpose of the piece of writing; words that the writer thinks may be unfamiliar to the reading audience are accompanied by a statement of their meanings. Thus, you can expect to find definitions of foreign, complex, or technical words, or simply definitions of words whose lexical meanings writers wish to call attention to. Santha Rama Rau in her book *Home to India* neatly embeds some succinct yet necessary dictionary definitions as she explains Indian meal times: "*Chota hasari*—the little breakfast—consists of a cup of tea at five thirty or six in the morning, with possibly some fruit or toast served with it. At about eleven or at midday a heavier meal is eaten, *chapatis*—thin unleavened wheat cakes— and curry, with *dal*—a kind of lentil soup—and curds and sweets of some sort." Unaided by these definitions, readers would be pretty much in the dark about the italicized words in the selection. In each case, just a brief phrase identifies distinguishing characteristics of the word. Rama Rau uses dashes to set off these meanings. Experienced readers know to look for dashes, paired commas, parentheses, italics, quotation marks, the words "that is" or "means," and other language and punctuation clues as signals for definitions.

Sometimes a writer tries to clarify a complex word by providing a *restrictive* meaning, that is, a meaning considerably narrowed from a range of lexical possibilities. Here the writer peels away definitions that are extraneous to his or her purpose and directs readers only to those features of the word that bear upon the discussion at hand. A noted researcher in the acquisition of second languages, Stephen D. Krashen, offers a restrictive definition for *bilingual education* programs before he describes them in an essay written in 1981: "While we could use bilingual education as a cover term for practically all of the programs described below, it will be useful to limit it here. Bilingual education refers to situations in which students are able to study subject matter in their first language while their weaker language skills catch up." Many people who might challenge that as a general definition could accept it provisionally in the context of the essay.

In other cases, a writer will *redefine* a word entirely. The usual effect of this strategy is to make readers look critically at their fundamental assumptions about a word and see it from a new perspective. Ardrey's treatment of *territory* certainly redefines the word.

As you have seen, a simple phrase alone as a synonym is frequently insufficient in suggesting the possibilities of a word. As a result, writers often build to a carefully structured definition sentence with four parts: (1) The term is stated; (2) it is followed by the word *is* or *was;* (3) it is established in a general class or category; (4) and it is then distinguished from other members of its group. Ardrey follows the pattern quite precisely: (1) "A territory (2) is (3) an area of space, whether of water or earth or air, (4) which an animal or group of animals defends as an exclusive preserve." e. e. cummings's funny and ironical poem in this section is a perfect example of this type of formal definition, run wildly amuck with its startling metaphor.

In addition to occasional brief definitions of important terms—synonyms in a few words or phrases, more formal definitions in a few sentences—writers often turn to extended definitions. An *extended definition* is a rhetorical mode that defines a term in considerable detail. Extended definitions consider the spectrum of issues inherent in a word or concept. True to its name, an extended definition can take paragraphs or pages. It can address not only denotative meanings but also personal, highly subjective, even idiosyncratic views of words or ideas. Without any formal or predictable pattern, the extended definition advances through the use of other rhetorical strategies, alone or in combination, including description, narration, exemplification, process analysis, comparison and contrast, causal analysis, and classification. In this chapter, the essay by Joseph Epstein, "Your Basic Language Snob," draws upon many of the techniques you've studied up to this point. But all good definitions, like all good expository writing in any mode, come most alive when they advance a particular point of view or thesis. Exploring accrued meanings of words and terms, the writer advances a persistent point.

Writing Definition

This chapter provides opportunities for practice in the various kinds of definitions explained in the previous section, but for the most part you'll be concentrating here on writing the extended definition. It's a useful activity to practice; the extended definition has many applications, whether you're developing a laboratory report, a research paper, a short story or a poem, a business report, or an article for the school newspaper. In one sense, an extended definition is easy to write, for it allows you a great deal of freedom to choose from many different rhetorical patterns. In another sense, the task of defining can be rather complicated, especially if you are writing about an abstract term that is rich in connotative meanings. As usual, your purpose, thesis, and intended audience will help you shape the scope and direction of your definition.

Purpose and Audience

Choosing a word to define, like choosing any topic for any writing task, demands considerable thought and attention at the outset. How will you select a word or phrase from the hundreds of thousands available in our language? As you think about the various possibilities, as you choose and reject words in an effort to find the one you want to write about, be sure to consider what you intend to do with the term once you select it. Of course it should be one that interests you (for whatever reason)—*love,* perhaps, *heroism, sitcoms, machismo, literacy,* the term *media explosion* or *brotherhood of man* or *a good daughter,* the expression "Have a good day" or "Cool it!"—but unless you're clear on your reasons for writing, you risk a diffuse and fuzzy presentation.

An eye toward purpose will help you shape your topic as you consider some possibilities for your definition. If you selected an abstract term like *love,* for example, you'd soon be lost without some serious thought about why you were writing on this word. You might want to *indicate its particular characteristics* as a human emotion as opposed to other, related emotions, like *affection* or *passion.* Here you might choose to dwell on only one essential quality for the term. You might want to *teach* about the various psychological or philosophical definitions of love that key thinkers have used over the last century. You might want to write an *amusing* piece on the foibles of love or a piece that *argues* that love in the 1990s is a vanishing phenomenon. You might want to *explain* the meaning of Christian love.

Your topic is bound to sharpen as your own particular interest in the word interacts with your ideas about purpose. You might feel that the word *love* is too all-encompassing. Perhaps you want to zero in on some particular feature of love. Is your purpose to explore the nonromantic, nonphysical love that one human being, a stranger even, can show toward another? Are you interested in the sexual dimensions of love—man for woman, woman for man, man for man, woman for woman? Are you interested in love of country and its wrenching sacrifices in wartime? Are you interested in the sanctification of love through marriage and its connections to religious ritual? Any one of those approaches would lead you down a path quite different from any other. You might ultimately decide on a different but related term, one better suited to your purpose, like *brotherly love,* say, or *patriotism, fidelity, puppy love,* or *homosexuality.* Whatever your term and your purpose, a sharp thesis will enrich your writing. What is your position about your word or term and the thinking and associations surrounding it? Is romantic love, for example, a natural gift, or an invented trap? Is brotherly love a wondrous social ideal, or an impossible goal, or both? A clear and original thesis will help you expand your definition with direction and energy.

Consider, too, your audience's expectations as you shape your topic. Try to imagine the group of readers you want to aim for. A sense of audience will help you determine an appropriate level of language and idiom, of course, but it also will help you focus your definition so that your purpose matches your audience's needs and expectations. Suppose you wanted to define *puppy love,* the adolescent condition of infatuation. You'd take one approach if your intended audience were a group of teenagers you wanted to amuse. You'd use words and you'd present ideas familiar to this age group, and you'd explain any terms you thought your readers would not know, even, perhaps, one as basic to your definition as *infatuation.* Surely your jokes would be jokes that adolescents could appreciate. However, if your audience were a group of puzzled parents of junior high school–aged children whom you wanted to instruct about the value of puppy love in an adolescent's maturation, your approach would be quite different. In either case, readers would expect to know the distinguishing features of the concept so that they could recognize it easily.

It's a familiar point, the interaction of audience, purpose, and topic. You want to give these issues your careful attention every time you write.

PROCESS

In advance of writing, spend as much time as you can afford deciding on your topic, but don't be surprised if the process of limiting and shaping it continues beyond your early prewriting efforts and through a draft or two. You do have many options, and you want to explore them in depth before you finally decide on any one. A good place to start as a stimulus for ideas is an unabridged dictionary. The range of denotative meanings of a word certainly will simulate further thought. What has the dictionary excluded? How does the lexical meaning compare with connotative meanings? Depending on your topic, you might wish to consult one of the specialized dictionaries, like the 13-volume *Oxford English Dictionary* (OED), Eric Partridge's *Dictionary of Slang and Unconventional English,* or H. W. Fowler's *A Dictionary of Modern English Usage.* A dictionary of synonyms like *Roget's International Thesaurus* can show you a galaxy of words and concepts related to your topic.

We said earlier that for your extended definition you can use any of the various rhetorical strategies explained in other chapters of this book, and we want to examine that point a bit further by looking once again at the topic *puppy love.* You'll benefit greatly if you weigh you rhetorical options thoughtfully. You might investigate the meaning of the phrase by *describing* your kid sister's suffering in her most recent infatuation with the high school varsity quarterback. You might *narrate* a firsthand definition of puppy love, based on recollections of the moment your heart leapt at the sight of the green-eyed blonde who joined your tenth-grade algebra class at midsemester. You might build toward a definition as you *explain the process* of falling in love for an adolescent. To offer a specialized text-based definition, you might provide *examples* of characters drawn from children's literature who fall in love in their early teens. For some fun with word play you might develop *comparative* or *contrasting* definitions—puppy love with a person's love for puppies, say, or with puppies' love for each other; or, more seriously, you might contrast puppy love with mature love. You might *classify* the various types of puppy love you've observed and so create a multitextured definition. You might *argue* that puppy love is another manifestation of teenage hysteria or peer pressure or emotional immaturity or adult emulation. You might try to *persuade* what you perceive as a reluctant audience of health education teachers to cover puppy love in their courses of study for high school students. For any of these approaches you could draw upon your own personal experiences, your readings in fiction, periodicals, and reference books, or the films or television programs you have seen. The possibilities are far-reaching—we have presented only a few here, of course—and considered along with purpose and audience, the rhetorical strategies provide fruitful areas of exploration in this assignment.

No matter which approach you take, you should be prepared to make your definition clear and specific, to set it off from what may be related but, for your paper, extraneous meanings, and to provide adequate details to make your point comprehensible. You may have to rely upon *negation;* often a reader will best understand what your word means if you say what the word does not mean. When Emerson complains in his essay "Gifts" in this chapter that "Rings and other jewels are not gifts, but apologies for gifts," he startles us with a negative view that few of us hold. Negation, however, helps him move toward an equally surprising affirmation: "The only gift," he insists "is a portion of thyself. Thou must bleed for me."

Some writers of definition like to explore the *etymological features* of a term as a technique for developing meanings. Where did the word originate? How has its meaning changed historically? Yet another technique for constructing a concrete definition is to use an *analogy.* By showing your reader point by point how your topic is like something else, you can illustrate the unknown in terms of the known. Analogies can make concrete what may otherwise be hard to visualize. If you tried to define a *singles bar,* for example, by drawing a careful analogy between it and a supermarket or department store where people shop around before settling on a desirable product, you'd be helping readers who had never seen a singles bar to picture the scene with all its tensions, seriousness, and humor.

It seems altogether fitting to end here with a definition. According to *The American Heritage Dictionary,* to *define* means "to state the precise meaning of (a word or sense of a word, for example); to describe the nature or basic qualities of; to delineate the outline or form of; to specify distinctly; to serve to distinguish; characterize." Your emphasis should be precision, clarity, and specificity—all just challenges for practicing writers.

SUMMING UP—DEFINITION

Reading Definition

- As a sustained rhetorical strategy, definition—usually *extended definition*—means providing for a word or concept precise meanings beyond dictionary wording in order to produce clear and sharply focused ideas in a new or special context.

- As you read, identify the meanings of words and terms by looking for language and punctuation clues—such as paired commas, dashes, parentheses, italics, quotation marks, the words "that is" or "means."

- Be aware of any restrictive meanings the writer may produce, that is, meanings considerably narrowed from a range of dictionary definitions and determine whether you can accept the restrictive definition.

- Consider whether the writer has completely redefined the word or concept and whether you can accept the meaning for a new but valid perspective.

- Determine the elements of any carefully structured definitions.

- Explore the features of the extended definition, considering personal, subjective, even idiosyncratic meanings provided by the writer.

- Consider the various other rhetorical strategies the writer may have used to advance the extended definition. Find evidence of description, narration, exemplification, process analysis, comparison and contrast, causal analysis, and classification.

Writing Definitions

- Prepare to write an extended definition by choosing a word or concept that interests you and decide how you will explore it rhetorically in your paper. Use an unabridged dictionary as a good starting point for ideas.

- Give careful thought to the word you choose and be clear on your reasons for writing. For example, you might indicate a term's particular characteristics, teach something about its various and contradictory elements, argue some specialized quality of the term, or simply explain through examples a forgotten dimension of the word.

- Appraise your audience to determine the appropriate level of language and idiom and to focus your definition toward the audience's expectations.

- Use your prewriting to limit and shape your topic as much as you can, but expect the process of refining the definition to extend throughout the writing of your drafts.

- Weigh your rhetorical options carefully and consider which strategies—description perhaps, or comparison or classification, to name just three of the many explored in this book—can help you best develop your topic.
- Develop a well-focused thesis statement that names the term you wish to define and indicates your special focus.
- Present an appropriate kind and level of detail to support the elements of your definition; use sensory detail, statistics, cases, quotations, or paraphrases to build your definition.
- Consider the value of using one of these definition strategies to help you develop your paper:
  - negation
  - etymological features
  - analogy

Gifts

Ralph Waldo Emerson

Ralph Waldo Emerson (1803–1882), born into a family of Puritan clergy in Boston, was a Unitarian minister at Boston's Old North Church from 1829 to 1832. But he left the ministry because of his distrust of established creeds and his growing belief that an individual's intuition, drawn from nature, was the highest form of knowledge. With this personal philosophy already taking shape, Emerson traveled to Europe, where he met Thomas Carlyle, Samuel Taylor Coleridge, and William Wordsworth, all of whom greatly influenced Emerson and his contributions to the literary and philosophical movement of transcendentalism. Emerson was at the core of this movement—along with Thoreau, Alcott, and Fuller—which flourished in New England between 1836 and 1860.

Emerson was a noted lecturer as well as a poet and essayist. His writings include *Nature* (1836), his *Journals* (kept since his Harvard undergraduate days), his *Essays* (1841, 1844), and *Poems* (1847), as well as articles in the magazine *The Dial,* which he edited for two years.

In "Gifts" Emerson defines a term which is usually thought of as being a material object. Yet he skillfully combines the spiritual with the material in what is ultimately a prescription for allowing others to "feel you and delight in you all the time."

Gifts of one who loved me,—
'Twas high time they came;
When he ceased to love me,
Time they stopped for shame.

*I*t is said that the world is in a state of bankruptcy, that the world owes the world more than the world can pay, and ought to go into chancery, and be sold. I do not think this general insolvency, which involves in some sort all the population, to be the reason of the difficulty experienced at Christmas and New Year, and other times, in bestowing gifts; since it is always so pleasant to be generous, though very vexatious to pay debts. But the impediment lies in the choosing. If, at any time, it comes into my head, that a present is due from me to somebody, I am puzzled what to give, until the opportunity is gone. Flowers and fruits are always fit presents; flowers, because they are a proud assertion that a ray of beauty outvalues all the utilities of the world. These gay natures contrast with the somewhat stern countenance of ordinary nature: they are like music heard out of a workhouse. Nature does not cocker us: we are children, not pets: she is not fond: everything is dealt to us without fear or favor, after severe universal laws. Yet these delicate flowers look like the frolic and interference of love and beauty. Men used to tell us that we love flattery, even though we are not deceived by it, because it shows that we are of importance enough to be courted. Something like

1

that pleasure, the flowers give us: what am I to whom these sweet hints are addressed? Fruits are acceptable gifts, because they are the flower of commodities, and admit of fantastic values being attached to them. If a man should send to me to come a hundred miles to visit him, and should set before me a basket of fine summer-fruit, I should think there was some proportion between the labor and the rewards.

For common gifts, necessity makes pertinences and beauty every day, and one is glad when an imperative leaves him no option, since if the man at the door have no shoes, you have not to consider whether you could procure him a paint box. And as it is always pleasing to see a man eat bread, or drink water, in the house or out of doors, so it is always a great satisfaction to supply these first wants. Necessity does everything well. In our condition of universal dependence, it seems heroic to let the petitioner be the judge of his necessity, and to give all that is asked, though at great inconvenience. If it be a fantastic desire, it is better to leave to others the office of punishing him. I can think of many parts I should prefer playing to that of the Furies. Next to things of necessity, the rule for a gift, which one of my friends prescribed, is, that we might convey to some person that which properly belonged to his character, and was easily associated with him in thought. But our tokens of compliment and love are for the most part barbarous. Rings and other jewels are not gifts, but apologies for gifts. The only gift is a portion of thyself. Thou must bleed for me. Therefore the poet brings his poem; the shepherd, his lamb; the farmer, corn; the miner, a gem; the sailor, coral and shells; the painter, his picture; the girl, a handkerchief of her own sewing. This is right and pleasing, for it restores society in so far to its primary basis, when a man's biography is conveyed in his gifts, and every man's wealth is an index of his merit. But it is a cold, lifeless business when you go to the shops to buy me something, which does not represent your life and talent, but a goldsmith's. This is fit for kings, and rich men who represent kings, and a false state of property, to make presents of gold and silver stuffs, as a kind of symbolical sin-offering, or payment of black-mail.

The law of benefits is a difficult channel, which requires careful sailing, or rude boats. It is not the office of a man to receive gifts. How dare you give them? We wish to be self-sustained. We do not quite forgive a giver. The hand that feeds us is in some danger of being bitten. We can receive anything from love, for that is a way of receiving it from ourselves: but not from any one who assumes to bestow. We sometimes hate the meat which we eat, because there seems something of degrading dependence in living by it.

> Brother, if Jove to thee a present make,
> Take heed that from his hands thou nothing take.

We ask the whole. Nothing less will content us. We arraign society, if it do not give us besides earth, and fire, and water, opportunity, love, reverence, and objects of veneration.

He is a good man, who can receive a gift well. We are either glad or sorry at a gift, and both emotions are unbecoming. Some violence, I think, is done, some degradation borne, when I rejoice or grieve at a gift. I am sorry when my independence is invaded, or when a gift comes from such as do not know my spirit, and so the act is not supported; and if the gift pleases me overmuch, then I should be ashamed that the donor should read my heart, and see that I love his commodity and not him. The gift, to be true, must be the flowing of the giver unto me, correspondent to my flowing unto him. When the waters are at level, then my goods pass to him, and his to me. All his are mine, all mine his. I say to him, How can you give me this pot of oil, or this flagon of wine, when all your oil and wine is mine, which belief of mine this gift seems to deny? Hence the fitness of beautiful, not useful things for gifts. This giving is flat usurpation, and therefore when the beneficiary is ungrateful, as all beneficiaries hate all Timons, not at all considering the value of the gift, but looking back to the greater store it was taken from, I rather sympathize with the beneficiary, than with the anger of my lord Timon. For, the expectation of gratitude is mean, and is continually punished by the total insensibility of the obliged person. It is a great happiness to get off without injury and heart-burning, from one who has had the ill luck to be served by you. It is a very onerous business, this of being served, and the debtor naturally wishes to give you a slap. A golden text for these gentlemen is that which I so admire in the Buddhist, who never thanks, and who says, "Do not flatter your benefactors."

The reason of these discords I conceive to be, that there is no commensurability between a man and any gift. You cannot give anything to a magnanimous person. After you have served him, he at once puts you in debt by his magnanimity. The service a man renders his friend is trivial and selfish, compared with the service he knows his friend stood in readiness to yield him, alike before he had begun to serve his friend, and now also. Compared with that good-will I bear my friend, the benefit it is in my power to render him seems small. Besides, our action on each other, good as well as evil, is so incidental and at random, that we can seldom hear the acknowledgments of any person who would thank us for a benefit, without some shame and humiliation. We can rarely strike a direct stroke, but must be content with an oblique one; we seldom have the satisfaction of yielding a direct benefit, which is directly received. But rectitude scatters favors on every side without knowing it, and receives with wonder the thanks of all people. 5

I fear to breathe any treason against the majesty of love, which is the genius and god of gifts, and to whom we must not affect to prescribe. Let him give kingdoms or flower-leaves indifferently. There are persons, from whom we always expect fairy tokens; let us not cease to expect them. This is prerogative, and not to be limited by our municipal rules. For the rest, I like to see that we cannot be bought and sold. The best of hospitality and of generosity is also not in the will but in fate. I find that I am not much to you; you do not need me; you do not feel me; then am I thrust out of doors, though you proffer me house and lands. No services are of any value, but only likeness. When I have attempted to join myself to others by services, it proved an intellectual trick,—no more. They eat your service like apples, and leave you out. But love them, and they feel you, and delight in you all the time. 6

Meaning and Idea

1. According to Emerson, what is the greatest cause of difficulty in gift-giving? How can that difficulty be overcome?

2. What is Emerson's attitude about the best source for gifts? What does he mean by "The only gift is a portion of thyself"?

3. Why are beautiful things more "fit" as gifts than useful things?

4. According to Emerson, what is the greatest of all possible gifts? What is the most exalted basis for gift-giving? Why?

Language, Form, Structure

1. Throughout the essay, Emerson continually limits the scope of his definition of *gifts* until he arrives at one critical basis for all gift-choosing and -giving. Trace the process of limitation and identify the conclusion which derives from it.

2. What is the relation in this essay among gift-choosing, gift-giving, and gift-receiving? How do Emerson's discussions of these three categories amount to a definition of *gifts?*

3. What metaphor does Emerson create for gift-giving? How does it help define the term *gifts?*

4. Identify two sections where Emerson uses exemplification to limit the definition.

5. Write definitions for Emerson's use of the following words: chancery; vexations; impediment; countenance; imperative; veneration; onerous; commensurability; rectitude; prerogative.

Ideas for Writing

1. Choose a term that can have both spiritual and materialistic meanings (wealth, success, or marriage, for example), and write a definition which blends the two values and shows their relationship to one another.

2. Define the term *generosity.* Focus on either material or spiritual generosity—or both.

3. One critic writes of Emerson's contribution that the philosopher developed "the doctrine of self-reliance, a spirit of optimism, and defiance of tradition and authority: for to the extent that all men are godlike . . . they must trust themselves, can overcome evil, and should regard their fellow men as equal." Write a paper in which you explore the validity of this comment in regard to "Gifts."

A Tree. A Rock. A Cloud.

Carson McCullers

Carson McCullers (1917–1967), born in Columbus, Georgia, was an American fiction writer who often focused on an individual's sense of isolation and loneliness in the midst of a malevolent or uncaring society. Her stories were so finely wrought as to lend themselves easily to dramatizations; *The Member of the Wedding* (1946) was made into a play in 1950, and Edward Albee in 1963 dramatized McCullers's novella *The Ballad of the Sad Café* (1951). Her earlier well-known work is *The Heart Is a Lonely Hunter* (1940).

A tree, a rock, and a cloud are in this story both the end points of disillusionment and the starting points of love. McCullers's characterization and setting skillfully play against the ultimate happiness (or unhappiness?) she wants to define.

*I*t was raining that morning, and still very dark. When the boy   1
reached the streetcar café he had almost finished his route and he went in for a cup of coffee. The place was an all-night café owned by a bitter and stingy man called Leo. After the raw, empty street the café seemed friendly and bright: along the counter there were a couple of soldiers, three spinners from the cotton mill, and in a corner a man who sat hunched over with his nose and half his face down in a beer mug. The boy wore a helmet such as aviators wear. When he went into the café he unbuckled the chin strap and raised the right flap up over his pink little ear; often as he drank his coffee someone would speak to him in a friendly way. But this morning Leo did not look into his face and none of the men were talking. He paid and was leaving the café when a voice called out to him:

'Son! Hey Son!'   2

He turned back and the man in the corner was crooking his finger and nod-   3
ding to him. He had brought his face out of the beer mug and he seemed suddenly very happy. The man was long and pale, with a big nose and faded orange hair.

'Hey Son!'   4

The boy went toward him. He was an undersized boy of about twelve, with   5
one shoulder drawn higher than the other because of the weight of the paper sack. His face was shallow, freckled, and his eyes were round child eyes.

'Yeah Mister?'   6

The man laid one hand on the paper boy's shoulders, then grasped the boy's   7
chin and turned his face slowly from one side to the other. The boy shrank back uneasily.

'Say! What's the big idea?'   8

The boy's voice was shrill; inside the café it was suddenly very quiet.   9

The man said slowly: 'I love you.'   10

All along the counter the men laughed. The boy, who had scowled and   11
sidled away, did not know what to do. He looked over the counter at Leo, and Leo

watched him with a weary, brittle jeer. The boy tried to laugh also. But the man was serious and sad.

'I did not mean to tease you, Son,' he said. 'Sit down and have a beer with 12 me. There is something I have to explain.'

Cautiously, out of the corner of his eye, the paper boy questioned the men 13 along the counter to see what he should do. But they had gone back to their beer or their breakfast and did not notice him. Leo put a cup of coffee on the counter and a little jug of cream.

'He is a minor,' Leo said. 14

The paper boy slid himself up onto the stool. His ear beneath the upturned 15 flap of the helmet was very small and red. The man was nodding at him soberly. 'It is important,' he said. Then he reached in his hip pocket and brought out something which he held up in the palm of his hand for the boy to see.

'Look very carefully,' he said. 16

The boy stared, but there was nothing to look at very carefully. The man 17 held in his big, grimy palm a photograph. It was the face of a woman, but blurred, so that only the hat and the dress she was wearing stood out clearly.

'See?' the man asked. 18

The boy nodded and the man placed another picture in his palm. The 19 woman was standing on a beach in a bathing suit. The suit made her stomach very big, and that was the main thing you noticed.

'Got a good look?' He leaned over closer and finally asked: 'You ever seen 20 her before?'

The boy sat motionless, staring slantwise at the man. 'Not so I know of.' 21

'Very well.' The man blew on the photographs and put them back into his 22 pocket. 'That was my wife.'

'Dead?' the boy asked. 23

Slowly the man shook his head. He pursed his lips as though about to whis- 24 tle and answered in a long-drawn way: 'Nuuu—' he said. 'I will explain.'

The beer on the counter before the man was in a large brown mug. He did 25 not pick it up to drink. Instead he bent down and, putting his face over the rim, he rested there for a moment. Then with both hands he tilted the mug and sipped.

'Some night you'll go to sleep with your nose in a mug and drown,' said 26 Leo. 'Prominent transient drowns in beer. That would be a cute death.'

The paper boy tried to signal to Leo. While the man was not looking he 27 screwed up his face and worked his mouth to question soundlessly: 'Drunk?' But Leo only raised his eyebrows and turned away to put some pink strips of bacon on the grill. The man pushed the mug away from him, straightened himself, and folded his loose crooked hands on the counter. His face was sad as he looked at the paper boy. He did not blink, but from time to time the lids closed down with delicate gravity over his pale green eyes. It was nearing dawn and the boy shifted the weight of the paper sack.

'I am talking about love,' the man said. 'With me it is a science.' 28

The boy half slid down from the stool. But the man raised his forefinger, and 29 there was something about him that held the boy and would not let him go away.

'Twelve years ago I married the woman in the photograph. She was my   30
wife for one year, nine months, three days, and two nights. I loved her. Yes . . .'
He tightened his blurred, rambling voice and said again: 'I loved her. I thought
also that she loved me. I was a railroad engineer. She had all home comforts and
luxuries. It never crept into my brain that she was not satisfied. But do you know
what happened?'

'Mgneeow!' said Leo.   31

The man did not take his eyes from the boy's face. 'She left me. I came in   32
one night and the house was empty and she was gone. She left me.'

'With a fellow?' the boy asked.   33

Gently the man placed his palm down on the counter. 'Why naturally, Son.   34
A woman does not run off like that alone.'

The café was quiet, the soft rain black and endless in the street outside. Leo   35
pressed down the frying bacon with the prongs of his long fork. 'So you have
been chasing the floozie for eleven years. You frazzled old rascal!'

For the first time the man glanced at Leo. 'Please don't be vulgar. Besides,   36
I was not speaking to you.' He turned back to the boy and said in a trusting and
secretive undertone: 'Let's not pay any attention to him. O.K.?'

The paper boy nodded doubtfully.   37

'It was like this,' the man continued. 'I am a person who feels many things.   38
All my life one thing after another has impressed me. Moonlight. The leg of a
pretty girl. One thing after another. But the point is that when I had enjoyed anything there was a peculiar sensation as though it was laying around loose in me.
Nothing seemed to finish itself up or fit in with the other things. Women? I had
my portion of them. The same. Afterwards laying around loose in me. I was a man
who had never loved.'

Very slowly he closed his eyelids, and the gesture was like a curtain drawn   39
at the end of a scene in a play. When he spoke again his voice was excited and the
words came fast—the lobes of his large, loose ears seemed to tremble.

'Then I met this woman. I was fifty-one and she always said she was thirty.   40
I met her at a filling station and we were married within three days. And do you
know what it was like? I just can't tell you. All I had ever felt was gathered
together around this woman. Nothing lay loose in me any more but was finished
up by her.'

The man stopped suddenly and stroked his long nose. His voice sank down   41
to a steady and reproachful undertone: 'I'm not explaining this right. What happened was this. There were these beautiful feelings and loose little pleasures
inside me. And this woman was something like an assembly line for my soul. I
run these little pieces of myself through her and I come out complete. Now do
you follow me?'

'What was her name?' the boy asked.   42

'Oh,' he said. 'I called her Dodo. But that is immaterial.'   43

'Did you try to make her come back?'   44

The man did not seem to hear. 'Under the circumstances you can imagine   45
how I felt when she left me.'

Leo took the bacon from the grill and folded two strips of it between a bun. 46
He had a gray face, with slitted eyes, and a pinched nose saddled by faint blue
shadows. One of the mill workers signaled for more coffee and Leo poured it. He
did not give refills on coffee free. The spinner ate breakfast there every morning,
but the better Leo knew his customers the stingier he treated them. He nibbled his
own bun as though he grudged it to himself.

'And you never got hold of her again?' 47

The boy did not know what to think of the man, and his child's face was 48
uncertain with mingled curiosity and doubt. He was new on the paper route; it
was still strange to him to be out in the town in the black, queer early morning.

'Yes,' the man said. 'I took a number of steps to get her back. I went around 49
trying to locate her. I went to Tulsa where she had folks. And to Mobile. I went
to every town she had ever mentioned to me, and I hunted down every man she
had formerly been connected with. Tulsa, Atlanta, Chicago, Cheehaw, Mem-
phis . . . For the better part of two years I chased around the country trying to lay
hold of her.'

'But the pair of them had vanished from the face of the earth!' said Leo. 50

'Don't listen to him,' the man said confidentially. 'And also just forget those 51
two years. They are not important. What matters is that around the third year a
curious thing begun to happen to me.'

'What?' the boy asked. 52

The man leaned down and tilted his mug to take a sip of beer. But as he hov- 53
ered over the mug his nostrils fluttered slightly; he sniffed the staleness of the
beer and did not drink. 'Love is a curious thing to begin with. At first I thought
only of getting her back. It was a kind of mania. But then as time went on I tried
to remember her. But do you know what happened?'

'No,' the boy said. 54

'When I laid myself down on a bed and tried to think about her my mind 55
became a blank. I couldn't see her. I would take out her pictures and look. No
good. Nothing doing. A blank. Can you imagine it?'

'Say Mac!' Leo called down the counter. 'Can you imagine this bozo's 56
mind a blank!'

Slowly, as though fanning away flies, the man waved his hand. His green 57
eyes were concentrated and fixed on the shallow little face of the paper boy.

'But a sudden piece of glass on a sidewalk. Or a nickel tune in a music box. 58
A shadow on a wall at night. And I would remember. It might happen in a street
and I would cry or bang my head against a lamppost. You follow me?'

'A piece of glass . . .' the boy said. 59

'Anything. I would walk around and I had no power of how and when to 60
remember her. You think you can put up a kind of shield. But remembering don't
come to a man face forward—it corners around sideways. I was at the mercy of
everything I saw and heard. Suddenly instead of me combing the countryside to
find her she begun to chase me around in my very soul. *She* chasing *me,* mind
you! And in my soul.'

The boy asked finally: 'What part of the country were you in then?' 61

'Ooh,' the man groaned. 'I was a sick mortal. It was like smallpox. I con- 62
fess, Son, that I boozed. I fornicated. I committed any sin that suddenly appealed
to me. I am loath to confess it but I will do so. When I recall that period it is all
curdled in my mind, it was so terrible.'

The man leaned his head down and tapped his forehead on the counter. For 63
a few seconds he stayed bowed over in this position, the back of his stringy neck
covered with orange furze, his hands with their long warped fingers held palm to
palm in an attitude of prayer. Then the man straightened himself; he was smiling
and suddenly his face was bright and tremulous and old.

'It was in the fifth year that it happened,' he said. 'And with it I started my 64
science.'

Leo's mouth jerked with a pale, quick grin. 'Well none of we boys are get- 65
ting any younger,' he said. Then with sudden anger he balled up a dishcloth he
was holding and threw it down hard on the floor. 'You draggle-tailed old Romeo!'

'What happened?' the boy asked. 66

The old man's voice was high and clear: 'Peace,' he answered. 67

'Huh?' 68

'It is hard to explain scientifically, Son,' he said. 'I guess the logical expla- 69
nation is that she and I had fleed around from each other for so long that finally
we just got tangled up together and lay down and quit. Peace. A queer and beautiful blankness. It was spring in Portland and the rain came every afternoon. All
evening I just stayed there on my bed in the dark. And that is how the science
come to me.'

The windows in the streetcar were pale blue with light. The two soldiers 70
paid for their beers and opened the door—one of the soldiers combed his hair and
wiped off his muddy puttees before they went outside. The three mill workers
bent silently over their breakfasts. Leo's clock was ticking on the wall.

'It is this. And listen carefully. I meditated on love and reasoned it out. I rea- 71
soned it out. I realized what is wrong with us. Men fall in love for the first time.
And what do they fall in love with?'

The boy's soft mouth was partly open and he did not answer. 72

'A woman,' the old man said. 'Without science, with nothing to go by, they 73
undertake the most dangerous and sacred experience in God's earth. They fall in
love with a woman. Is that correct, Son?'

'Yeah,' the boy said faintly. 74

'They start at the wrong end of love. They begin at the climax. Can you 75
wonder it is so miserable? Do you know how men should love?'

The old man reached over and grasped the boy by the collar of his leather 76
jacket. He gave him a gentle little shake and his green eyes gazed down unblink-
ing and grave.

'Son, do you know how love should be begun?' 77

The boy sat small and listening and still. Slowly he shook his head. The old 78
man leaned closer and whispered:

'A tree. A rock. A cloud.' 79

It was still raining outside in the street: a mild, gray, endless rain. The mill whistle blew for the six o'clock shift and the three spinners paid and went away. There was no one in the café but Leo, the old man, and the little paper boy. [80]

'The weather was like this in Portland,' he said. 'At the time my science was begun. I meditated and I started very cautious. I would pick up something from the street and take it home with me. I bought a goldfish and I concentrated on the goldfish and I loved it. I graduated from one thing to another. Day by day I was getting this technique. On the road from Portland to San Diego———' [81]

'Aw shut up!' screamed Leo suddenly. 'Shut up! Shut up!' [82]

The old man still held the collar of the boy's jacket; he was trembling and his face was earnest and bright and wild. 'For six years now I have gone around by myself and built up my science. And now I am a master. Son, I can love anything. No longer do I have to think about it even. I see a street full of people and a beautiful light comes in me. I watch a bird in the sky. Or I meet a traveler on the road. Everything, Son. And anybody. All stranger and all loved! Do you realize what a science like mine can mean?' [83]

The boy held himself stiffly, his hands curled tight around the counter edge. Finally he asked: 'Did you ever really find that lady?' [84]

'What? What say, Son?' [85]

'I mean,' the boy asked timidly, 'have you fallen in love with a woman again?' [86]

The old man loosened his grasp on the boy's collar. He turned away and for the first time his green eyes had a vague and scattered look. He lifted the mug from the counter, drank down the yellow beer. His head was shaking slowly from side to side. Then finally he answered: 'No, Son. You see that is the last step in my science. I go cautious. And I am not quite ready yet.' [87]

'Well!' said Leo. 'Well well well!' [88]

The old man stood in the open doorway. 'Remember,' he said. Framed there in the gray damp light of the early morning he looked shrunken and seedy and frail. But his smile was bright. 'Remember I love you,' he said with a last nod. And the door closed quietly behind him. [89]

The boy did not speak for a long time. He pulled down the bangs on his forehead and slid his grimy little forefinger around the rim of his empty cup. Then without looking at Leo he finally asked: [90]

'Was he drunk?' [91]

'No,' said Leo shortly. [92]

The boy raised his clear voice higher. 'Then was he a dope fiend?' [93]

'No.' [94]

The boy looked up at Leo, and his flat little face was desperate, his voice urgent and shrill. 'Was he crazy? Do you think he was a lunatic?' The paper boy's voice dropped suddenly with doubt. 'Leo? Or not?' [95]

But Leo would not answer him. Leo had run a night café for fourteen years, and he held himself to be a critic of craziness. There were the town characters and also the transients who roamed in from the night. He knew the manias of all of [96] them. But he did not want to satisfy the questions of the waiting child. He tightened his pale face and was silent.

So the boy pulled down the right flap of his helmet and as he turned to leave 97
he made the only comment that seemed safe to him, the only remark that could
not be laughed down and despised:

'He sure has done a lot of traveling.'   98

Meaning and Idea

1. What is being defined in this story?

2. How old is the boy in this story? What does he do? Approximately what
   area of the country is the setting for this story? How do you know?

3. What is the man's "science"? Is it really an exact measure of things? Look
   at the line where he says the woman was his wife for "one year, nine
   months, three days, and two nights." Does that exactitude derive from
   scientific thought or from something else?

4. Has the man ever really given up his love for his wife? Where does he state
   a specific answer to that? Do you know the answer before he says it? How?

5. Why does the man choose to tell this story to the boy rather than to the
   other adult patrons in the café? Does he really "love" the boy? Why does
   he tell him he does?

Language, Form, Structure

1. How would you characterize the boy's attitude toward the man? How does
   it serve the definition being formulated?

2. Why is the name of the man's wife "immaterial"? If he loved her so, why
   wouldn't he say her name? What is the effect of that omission on the
   definition?

3. How is process analysis used at various points to develop the definition in
   this story? In the process of love, how is "A tree. A rock. A cloud." the
   correct starting point?

4. What is the purpose of Leo in this story? What is his attitude toward the
   man? How does it serve as a contrast to the man? How does that contrast
   contribute to the definition?

5. Look up and define the following words from the story; then use each in an
   original sentence: scowled; sidled; transient; floozie; undertone;
   immaterial; mania; tremulous.

Ideas for Writing

1. Write your own definition of *love,* arranging your definition in three stages: the beginning point of love; the point at which you know for sure; the point at which you are satisfied.

2. Write a definition for *loneliness.* Use experience as the main basis for your definition; in other words, try to avoid abstraction.

3. McCullers's great strength as a writer is her ability to evoke a rich human sensibility, to treat emotionally fragile people who are lonely and love-starved, and to honor individualism and sensitivity. To what degree does "A Tree. A Rock. A Cloud." support that judgment? In your essay response, make specific references to the text.

Femininity

Susan Brownmiller

Susan Brownmiller began her writing career as a journalist for the *Village Voice* and *Newsweek*. Born in 1935 in Brooklyn, New York, she was educated at Cornell and at the Jefferson School of Social Science. Her book *Against Our Will: Men, Women, & Rape* (1975) explores the women's movement and male-female relations. She founded Women Against Pornography in the late 1970s.

In this selection from *Femininity* (1984), Brownmiller examines the biological and cultural origins of her topic as she attempts to define the term and to provide a frame for understanding it. In so doing, she illuminates both her theme and her approach.

We had a game in our house called "setting the table" and I was   1
Mother's helper. Forks to the left of the plate, knives and spoons to the right. Placing the cutlery neatly, as I recall, was one of my first duties, and the event was alive with meaning. When a knife or a fork dropped to the floor, that meant a man was unexpectedly coming to dinner. A falling spoon announced the surprise arrival of a female guest. No matter that these visitors never arrived on cue, I had learned a rule of gender identification. Men were straight-edged, sharply pronged and formidable, women were softly curved and held the food in a rounded well. It made perfect sense, like the division of pink and blue that I saw in babies, an orderly way of viewing the world. Daddy, who was gone all day at work and who loved to putter at home with his pipe, tobacco and tool chest, was knife and fork. Mommy and Grandma, with their ample proportions and pots and pans, were grownup soup spoons, large and capacious. And I was a teaspoon, small and slender, easy to hold and just right for pudding, my favorite dessert.

Being good at what was expected of me was one of my earliest projects,   2
for not only was I rewarded, as most children are, for doing things right, but excellence gave pride and stability to my childhood existence. Girls were different from boys, and the expression of that difference seemed mine to make clear. Did my loving, anxious mother, who dressed me in white organdy pinafores and Mary Janes and who cried hot tears when I got them dirty, give me my first instruction? Of course. Did my doting aunts and uncles with their gifts of pretty dolls and miniature tea sets add to my education? Of course. But even without the appropriate toys and clothes, lessons in the art of being feminine lay all around me and I absorbed them all: the fairy tales that were read to me at night, the brightly colored advertisements I poured over in magazines before I learned to decipher the words, the movies I saw, the comic books I hoarded, the radio soap operas I happily followed whenever I had to stay in bed with a cold. I loved being a little girl, or rather I loved being a fairy princess, for that was who I thought I was.

As I passed through a stormy adolescence to a stormy maturity, femininity ₃ increasingly became an exasperation, a brilliant, subtle esthetic that was bafflingly inconsistent at the same time that it was minutely, demandingly concrete, a rigid code of appearance and behavior defined by do's and don't-do's that went against my rebellious grain. Femininity was a challenge thrown down to the female sex, a challenge no proud, self-respecting young woman could afford to ignore, particularly one with enormous ambition that she nursed in secret, alternately feeding or starving its inchoate life in tremendous confusion.

"Don't lose your femininity" and "Isn't it remarkable how she manages to ₄ retain her femininity?" had terrifying implications. They spoke of a bottom-line failure so irreversible that nothing else mattered. The pinball machine had registered "tilt," the game had been called. Disqualification was marked on the forehead of a woman whose femininity was lost. No records would be entered in her name, for she had destroyed her birthright in her wretched, ungainly effort to imitate a man. She walked in limbo, this hapless creature, and it occurred to me that one day I might see her when I looked in the mirror. If the danger was so palpable that warning notices were freely posted, wasn't it possible that the small bundle of resentments I carried around in secret might spill out and place the mark on my own forehead? Whatever quarrels with femininity I had I kept to myself; whatever handicaps femininity imposed, they were mine to deal with alone, for there was no women's movement to ask the tough questions, or to brazenly disregard the rules.

Femininity, in essence, is a romantic sentiment, a nostalgic tradition of ₅ imposed limitations. Even as it hurries forward in the 1980s, putting on lipstick and high heels to appear well dressed, it trips on the ruffled petticoats and hoopskirts of an era gone by. Invariably and necessarily, femininity is something that women had more of in the past, not only in the historic past of prior generations, but in each woman's personal past as well—in the virginal innocence that is replaced by knowledge, in the dewy cheek that is coarsened by age, in the "inherent nature" that a woman seems to misplace so forgetfully whenever she steps out of bounds. Why should this be so? The XX chromosomal message has not been scrambled, the estrogen-dominated hormonal balance is generally as biology intended, the reproductive organs, whatever use one has made of them, are usually in place, the breasts of whatever size are most often where they should be. But clearly, biological femaleness is not enough.

Femininity always demands more. It must constantly reassure its audience ₆ by a willing demonstration of difference, even when one does not exist in nature, or it must seize and embrace a natural variation and compose a rhapsodic symphony upon the notes. Suppose one doesn't care to, has other things on her mind, is clumsy or tone-deaf despite the best instruction and training? To fail at the feminine difference is to appear not to care about men, and to risk the loss of their attention and approval. To be insufficiently feminine is viewed as a failure in core sexual identity, or as a failure to care sufficiently about oneself, for a woman found wanting will be appraised (and will appraise herself) as mannish or neutered or simply unattractive, as men have defined these terms.

We are talking, admittedly, about an exquisite esthetic. Enormous pleasure   7
can be extracted from feminine pursuits as a creative outlet or purely as relax-
ation; indeed, indulgence for the sake of fun, or art, or attention, is among femininity's great joys. But the chief attraction (and the central paradox, as well) is the
competitive edge that femininity seems to promise in the unending struggle to
survive, and perhaps to triumph. The world smiles favorably on the feminine
woman: it extends little courtesies and minor privilege. Yet the nature of this competitive edge is ironic, at best, for one works at femininity by accepting restric-
tions, by limiting one's sights, by choosing an indirect route, by scattering concentration and not giving one's all as a man would to his own, certifiably
masculine, interests. It does not require a great leap of imagination for a woman
to understand the feminine principle as a grand collection of compromises, large
and small, that she simply must make in order to render herself a successful
woman. If she has difficulty in satisfying femininity's demands, if its illusions go
against her grain, or if she is criticized for her shortcomings and imperfections,
the more she will see femininity as a desperate strategy of appeasement, a strategy she may not have the wish or the courage to abandon, for failure looms in
either direction.

It is fashionable in some quarters to describe the feminine and masculine   8
principles as polar ends of the human continuum, and to sagely profess that both
polarities exist in all people. Sun and moon, yin and yang, soft and hard, active
and passive, etcetera, may indeed be opposites, but a linear continuum does not
illuminate the problem. (Femininity, in all its contrivances, is a very active
endeavor.)

What, then, is the basic distinction? The masculine principle is better   9
understood as a driving ethos of superiority designed to inspire straightforward,
confident success, while the feminine principle is composed of vulnerability, the
need for protection, the formalities of compliance and the avoidance of conflict—
in short, an appeal of dependence and good will that gives the masculine principle its romantic validity and its admiring applause.

Femininity pleases men because it makes them appear more masculine by   10
contrast; and, in truth, conferring an extra portion of unearned gender distinction
on men, and unchallenged space in which to breathe freely and feel stronger,
wiser, more competent, is femininity's special gift. One could say that masculinity is often an effort to please women, but masculinity is known to please by displays of mastery and competence while femininity pleases by suggesting that
these concerns, except in small matters, are beyond its intent. Whimsy, unpre-
dictability and patterns of thinking and behavior that are dominated by emotion,
such as tearful expressions of sentiment and fear, are thought to be feminine precisely because they lie outside the established route to success.

If in the beginnings of history the feminine woman was defined by her   11
physical dependency, her inability for reasons of reproductive biology to triumph
over the forces of nature that were the tests of masculine strength and power,
today she reflects both an economic and emotional dependency that is still considered "natural," romantic and attractive. After an unsettling fifteen years in

which many basic assumptions about the sexes were challenged, the economic disparity did not disappear. Large numbers of women—those with small children, those left high and dry after a mid-life divorce—need financial support. But even those who earn their own living share a universal need for connectedness (call it love, if you wish). As unprecedented numbers of men abandon their sexual interest in women, others, sensing opportunity, choose to demonstrate their interest through variety and a change in partners. A sociological fact of the 1980s is that female competition for two scarce resources—men and jobs—is especially fierce.

So it is not surprising that we are currently witnessing a renewed interest in 12 femininity and an unabashed indulgence in feminine pursuits. Femininity serves to reassure men that women need them and care about them enormously. By incorporating the decorative and the frivolous into its definition of style, femininity functions as an effective antidote to the unrelieved seriousness, the pressure of making one's way in a harsh, difficult world. In its mandate to avoid direct confrontation and to smooth over the fissures of conflict, femininity operates as a value system of niceness, a code of thoughtfulness and sensitivity that in modern society is sadly in short supply.

There is no reason to deny that indulgence in the art of feminine illusion can 13 be reassuring to a woman, if she happens to be good at it. As sexuality undergoes some dizzying revisions, evidence that one is a woman "at heart" (the inquisitor's question) is not without worth. Since an answer of sorts may be furnished by piling on additional documentation, affirmation can arise from such identifiable but trivial feminine activities as buying a new eyeliner, experimenting with the latest shade of nail color, or bursting into tears at the outcome of a popular romance novel. Is there anything destructive in this? Time and cost factors, a deflection of energy and an absorption in fakery spring quickly to mind, and they need to be balanced, as in a ledger book, against the affirming advantage.

Meaning and Idea

1. What is Brownmiller's definition of femininity? Discuss how she defines it.

2. How does Brownmiller use history to explore her subject? What bearing does that history have on today's quest for femininity?

3. What value does femininity have for men, according to the writer?

4. How does Brownmiller ultimately feel about femininity? What is her thesis? Is this thesis surprising? Why?

Language, Form, Structure

1. In the first part of the essay, Brownmiller often uses vivid description of her childhood to show how she was instructed in the ways of femininity. The table-setting game, the white organdy pinafores, the Mary Janes, and other elements lead up to her statement that it seems "biological femaleness

is not enough." What is the effect of drawing on these personal examples of behavior?

2. What rhetorical strategies does the writer use to build her definition?

3. Brownmiller's ultimate position in the essay is one of tolerance and even appreciation for femininity. How convincingly does she develop this view? What support does she offer? Cite particular passages.

4. Define the following words and use each in a sentence: formidable; capacious; esthetic; inchoate; palpable; rhapsodic; continuum; appeasement; ethos; whimsy; frivolous; fissures.

Ideas for Writing

1. Look back into your own past and think about the first memories you have of masculinity or femininity. Use these memories as an introduction to create an essay about where you stand on these issues today and why.

2. How should *they* act and why do you think so? Write a definition essay in which you clarify the parameters that you feel the opposite gender *should* fulfill, and in so doing build to a definition of the opposite sex.

3. Write an essay in which you weigh the success of Brownmiller's essay. How does Brownmiller use complexities and contradictions?

Primer Lesson

Carl Sandburg

Carl Sandburg (1878–1967) was born in Galesburg, Illinois, of Swedish immigrant parents. Many have considered him as a kind of bardic successor to Walt Whitman; both poets celebrated the common people and their activities and experiences. Sandburg himself never did well in school, but received his "education" as a laborer, soldier, wanderer, and journalist. In addition, he was active in the 1907–1908 presidential campaign of Eugene V. Debs, the candidate of the Social Democratic party; Sandburg himself maintained his socialist politics throughout his life. By his old age, he was well respected for collections such as *Chicago Poems* (1916), *The People, Yes* (1936), and the Pulitzer Prize–winning *Complete Poems* (1950). Between 1926 and 1939, he also wrote a six-volume biography of Abraham Lincoln. In 1964, President Lyndon Johnson awarded Sandburg the Presidential Medal of Freedom.

This poem is as simple as any primer book lesson, while its message carries much more complex meanings. Though Sandburg never actually defines the term *proud words,* we end up knowing its meaning.

---

*L*ook out how you use proud words.
When you let proud words go, it is
    not easy to call them back.
They wear long boots, hard boots; they
    walk off proud; they
    can't hear you calling—   5
Look out how you use proud words.

Meaning and Idea

1. Whom is the poet addressing in this poem? How do you know?

2. What is meant by "proud words"? Give examples of what might be considered "proud words." What might be an occasion to use them?

3. Why does Sandburg say that you can't call back proud words? Do your own personal experiences support that statement? Explain.

Language, Form, Structure

1. How does Sandburg use *personification* as a technique in this poem? How does it effectively serve the definition?

2. What is a *primer?* Why is the poem titled "Primer Lesson" and not "Proud Words"?

3. The first and last lines of this poem are the same, but how is their impact different? Why? How has implied definition changed their impact and value?

Ideas for Writing

1. Write a short definition of a *lie*. You may want to concentrate on the feelings that lies engender for both speaker and receiver.

2. Write a definition entitled "Famous Last Words." Use examples, but make sure you come to a clear definition of the term.

3. Sandburg never actually defines or gives examples of *proud words,* yet it is legitimate to say that the reader has a clear sense of the term by the end of the poem. How does Sandburg achieve that? Write a definition of *proud words* as you understand it from "Primer Lesson," and then explain how the poem brings you to that understanding.

The Naked and the Nude

Robert Graves

Robert Graves, born in 1895 near London, gained a reputation as a novelist, poet, and literary critic. Graves saw considerable action as a member of the Royal Welsh Fusiliers during World War I, during which time he befriended the poet Siegfried Sassoon. After the war, he studied at Oxford, where he later taught. Graves's novel *I, Claudius* (1934) is familiar to British and American television audiences as the basis for a critically acclaimed public television series. His war memoir *Good-bye to All That* (1929) is a haunting chronicle of the physical and social destruction of World War I. *The White Goddess* (1948), Graves's "historical grammar of poetic myth," delves into the matriarchal basis of history and artistic creation. Graves died in 1985.

In reading Graves's "The Naked and the Nude" pay special attention to the ways in which the poet separates, then synthesizes, the denotative and connotative values of two seemingly similar words.

*F*or me, the naked and the nude
(By lexicographers construed
As synonyms that should express
The same deficiency of dress
Or shelter) stand as wide apart   5
As love from lies, or truth from art.

Lovers without reproach will gaze
On bodies naked and ablaze;
The hippocratic eye will see
In nakedness, anatomy;   10
And naked shines the Goddess when
She mounts her lion among men.

The nude are bold, the nude are sly
To hold each treasonable eye.
While draping by a showman's trick   15
Their dishabille in rhetoric,
They grin a mock-religious grin
Of scorn at those of naked skin.

The naked, therefore, who compete
Against the nude may know defeat;   20
Yet when they both together tread
The briary pastures of the dead,

By Gorgons with long whips pursued,
How naked go the sometime nude!

Meaning and Idea

1. Check a dictionary to find the denotation of the word *naked*. What, according to Graves, does the word *naked* connote? What details does he offer to show what he means by the word? What do lines 11–12 mean?

2. What is the denotation of the word *nude?* What images support the connotation Graves is trying to present for the word?

3. How do the two compare? Explain the last stanza in your own words.

Language, Form, Structure

1. The first stanza of the poem establishes Graves's main point. What is that point? What is the purpose of the statement in parentheses in lines 2–5? Why is the language there so much more formal and scholarly than the language in the rest of the stanza? What in general is the tone of the poem?

2. Graves's definitions progress through a series of images. Which images are most vivid? Why does he use exemplification to define the words? How does the repetition of the words *naked* and *nude* serve as a transitional device? What other transitional devices are apparent?

3. In stanza two Graves explains what he means by *naked,* in stanza three what he means by *nude.* Then in stanza four he presents the two words together. How do you think this organizational pattern serves the meaning of the poem? Why does he choose comparison and contrast as a strategy for defining the words? What is the surprise in the last line?

4. What are the "briary pastures of the dead"? What is Graves's purpose in using the phrase "dishabille in rhetoric"? Check your dictionary for the meanings of the following words: lexicographers; deficiency; hippocratic; Gorgon.

Ideas for Writing

1. Write a paragraph in which you define the words *naked* and *nude* with images based upon your own connotations for the words.

2. Select any two synonyms that have similar denotations but different connotations and write an essay in which you explore the definitions of those words. Provide details in order to make your meanings of the words clear.

3. Write a paragraph in which you comment upon Graves's use of language in this poem. Consider, for example, his choice of words. Why does he select *deficiency* (line 4) instead of *lack? Gaze* (7) instead of *stare? Mount* (12) instead of *climb? Bold* instead of *daring* or *brave?* You might also comment on Graves's use of nouns and verbs, his use of classical references (lines 11–12 and 24), his use of rhyme, rhythm, and meter.

A Politician

e. e. cummings

Born in Cambridge, Massachusetts, in 1894, e. e. cummings took his B.A. and M.A. degrees at Harvard, lived in Paris in the 1920s, then settled in New York's bohemian Greenwich Village. His travels spurred him to write the semifictional, semisociological *The Enormous Room* (1922) and *Eimi* (1933). Cummings is best known, however, for his poetry, for his whimsical play with typography and syntax, as well as for his near abhorrence of capital letters (he did not use capitals even for his name). He died in New Hampshire in 1962.

Notice how in this very brief poem, Cummings manages to evoke various levels of meaning.

a politician is an arse upon
which everyone has sat except a man

Meaning and Idea

1. What is an *arse?* Why does cummings choose this spelling and pronunciation over the more common one?

2. What can you say about the poet's attitude toward politicians? Do his feelings seem to be general or specific? Explain.

Language, Form, Structure

1. What are the various meanings of the word *arse* in this poem? Explain how "everyone" can have sat on this arse, but not one man has. What various levels of meaning of *man* are implied?

2. Explain the metaphorical structure of this definition.

Ideas for Writing

1. Write an essay in which you define the word *politician.* Draw upon your personal experiences or upon what you have read or observed about politicians. Be specific.

2. Select a profession and write a series of two-line definitions of it, following cummings's plan.

3. Write a few paragraphs in which you respond to the seeming simplicity of cummings's statement. Do you think this definition is sufficient? Do you think it is a poem? Explain your responses.

Your Basic Language Snob

Joseph Epstein

I don't mean to make anyone tense or otherwise edgy, but perhaps it   1
is best you know at the outset that in me you are dealing with your basic language
snob. Mention to me that when you were young your parents were very "supportive," tell me that before "finalizing" your plans you would like my "input,"
remark that the job in which you are "presently" employed provides you with a
"nurturing environment"—say all or any of these things and you will not, I hope,
see a muscle in my face move. I shall appear to show a genial interest in all you
say, but beneath the geniality, make no mistake, I shall be judging you—and not
altogether kindly. "Hmm," I shall be thinking, "I see that I am dealing here with
someone who has a taste for psychobabble and trashy corporate and computer
talk and misuses the word *presently* into the bargain." I shall, of course, say nothing about it to you; I certainly won't attempt to reform you. In fact, I rather prefer you stay the way that you are, for in using language as you do you are a source
of real comfort to me. You allow me to feel that, in the realm of language at least,
I am vastly superior to you; and the feeling of superiority—need I say it?—is
what puts the lovely curl in the snob's smile.

As a language snob, one finds no shortage of playgrounds upon which to   2
exercise one's snobbery. Hegel reports that we learn from the study of history that
no one learns from the study of history. So, we learn from the careful study of language that not many people have ever used language very carefully. Permit me to
bring in an old adversary on this subject, that linguist of populist tendency, Professor Bernard Strawman.

"Arguably, you have a case," Strawman, trying to be polite, says.   3

"Wherever did you find so weak and weakly positioned an adverb as   4
arguably, Bernie?" I reply.

"Perhaps," he says, "you don't allow enough leeway for societal pressures   5
on language use."

"In the home of what woebegone sociologist did you ever find so ugly a   6
word as *societal?*" I inquire.

"At this point in time," he replies, "*societal* is a very popular word. What   7
do you have against it?"

"What I have against it, Bernie," I respond, "is that it tends to be used by so 8 many people who also use such phrases as 'at this point in time.'"

Even Bernie Strawman, normally a model of conversational good manners, 9 now sounds a touch petulant: "Wait a minute," he says. "Which are you against: the words or the people who use them? If the former, perhaps you are a man of principle; if the latter, it seems to me you are merely a snob."

To which I reply: "In this matter of language I view myself as a highly prin- 10 cipled snob. May I take a moment—an essay, in fact—to explain?"

Let us look more closely at the word *supportive*. (Here you must imagine 11 me picking up the word between my thumb and index finger, holding it as far from my body as possible, a disapproving pucker upon my lips.) At first glance, *supportive* seems harmless enough. At second glance, though, it strikes me as a fake. It is no more than the old words *supporting* or *supported* got up with a new suffix that gives it a psychological and hence high-flown air, rather like getting a letter from someone you used to know from the old neighborhood who, on his stationery, has had Ph.D. printed after his name. To use the word *supportive* is to take a sound enough old word and drag it from the solid ground of common usage into the marshlands of abstraction. The net result of this transfer, it seems to me, is not a gain in clarity but only an increase in pretension.

Richard Nixon has made it impossible ever again to say "Let me make one 12 thing perfectly clear," so let me instead be as clear as I can be here and announce that I am not against all new words. While I have the mike, let me also announce that I am of course aware that language is almost ceaselessly changing. Some changes—such as the word "breathalyzer" to measure the drunkenness of drivers—are necessary to accommodate new inventions. Some changes I like just for their rhythm and sound. *Rip-off,* which has been in the language for roughly fifteen years now, seems to me to have earned its way. *Shuck,* a rip-off with an element of bunko to it, seems to me a fine fresh minting. I am all for invention, asking only that it be useful, describe something that really exists, and, if possible (which it often isn't), be fun. For this reason I find myself partial to the recent neologism *wimp.* It seems to me a word in the family of those fine Yiddishisms *nebbish* and *nebbekle* and their spin-off *nerd.* I think of a wimp, in fact, as a Gentile nebbish.

I trust that by now I have established myself as not your run-of-the-mill 13 snob; I prefer, in fact, to think myself a custom-tailored snob. I like what I deem to be good new words. I like to toss in a neologism of my own every now and then, and I like what the linguistically prudish used to call Americanisms. One of the few things I have ever disagreed with Henry James about is his fear, set forth in *The American Scene,* that immigrant groups in the United States would pollute the pure stream of the English language. I think the current in this stream is stronger than James knew. It can carry a great deal before it and still remain fresh. It was, after all, the grandson of an immigrant, H. L. Mencken, who made the English language do one-and-a-half gainers, back flips, and triple somersaults. A. J. Liebling, another scion of the immigranti, as Mencken might have put it, for my money didn't do too shabbily either. But then I have a weakness for people who know how to play language for laughs. I have a taste for the concrete, the colorful, the comic (also, I see, for the alliterative). When the pro-basketball player Kareem Abdul-Jabbar, after dining at the home of a colleague, Julius Irving, was asked by the press if Mrs. Turquoise Irving was a good cook, Mr. Jabbar replied: "Yeah, man, Turquoise can burn." Henry James, I think, was too good-humored not to have enjoyed that.

As a snob, the people I like to lord it over are the quasi-semi-demi-ostensibly 14 educated, B.A., M.S., Ph.D. and degrees beyond. Few things please me more, for example, than to see the novelists Norman Mailer and Joan Didion misuse the word *disinterested.* Or to hear a noted scholar, George F. Kennan, use the word *transpire* as if it were nothing more than a high-toned synonym for *happen.* Or to hear more degreed people than I care to count use *intriguing* as if it meant nothing other than *fascinating.* (Take the verb *to intrigue* away from spies and you leave these fellows practically unemployed.) To give you some notion of how far gone I am, now that it has caught on with the putatively educated classes, I have stopped using the phrase "early on"; when I hear it from others, I think, "Whatsamatter, baby, *early* standing alone not good enough for a swell like you?" And of course I am death on people who use the term "bottom line."

Few things please me more than when to my language snobbery I can join 15 my economic jealousy—I am practically ecstatic, that is, when I hear a highly paid broadcasting journalist commit an egregious error. I watch television news ready to pounce; it is good exercise, for, as a language snob, I get to pounce rather a lot. One of the local anchormen hereabouts—about a $300,000-a-year man, I would estimate—made my day not long ago when, in connection with the Libyan embassy crisis in London, he asked a visiting expert whether this might spell the possibility of a *tête à tête* for Qaddafi. "Coup d'etat, you overpaid moron," I roared, leaping from my couch, "not tête à tête." Or when, during the NCAA basketball tournament, the former coach and current announcer Billy Packer referred to "three or four Achilles' heels" that De Paul University's team had. "Ah, dear boy," I whispered to myself, "one Achilles' heel was quite enough—even for Achilles." But I don't always require major screw-ups such as these. I am satisfied when one of the truly high-priced boys—Dan Rather, Tom Brokaw, or Peter Jennings—misuses *decimate,*which means to kill a tenth, or calls something "rather unique," which is akin to being rather pregnant. Do you take my point? Do you also think that what I have written thus far makes for "a good read"? If you do, please clean out your locker, for you're through—I hate the phrase "a good read."

One of the things a language snob learns early in his training is that there is 16 probably no word or phrase that someone of stature doesn't despise. Edward Shils has kept up a running attack against the phrase "check out," as in "check it out." I know many people who hate *authored* as a verb, but I recently read that E. B. White doesn't even like the word *author.* I can never hear or see the word *workshop,* referring to a management seminar or creative writing course, without thinking of Kingsley Amis's line, from his novel *Jake's Thing,* which runs: "If there's one word that sums up everything that's gone wrong since the war, it's Workshop." Legion are the people who loathe the phrase "pick your brain," and I am among their number. Whenever anyone says to me that they would, on a particular subject, like to pick my brain, I always think, "Yes, if I may kick your butt."

"I'd like to pick your brain," is a phrase my friend Dottie uses quite often. Dottie and I go way back. She is a good soul, large-hearted in so many ways. But Dottie is one of those people who seems to absorb whatever language is in the air, and the language that has been in the air in recent years has, I fear, driven my friend Dottie a bit, well, dotty. (Perfectly lovely people sometimes use the most awful language; that they do is, alas, the pebble in the caviar of language snobbery.) Because of language, Dottie's life reminds me of a man whom Keats, in his letters, records meeting at Robert Burns's cottage, whose life, Keats notes, is "fuz, fuzzy, fuzziest." ¹⁷

Dottie has been going through a rough patch in recent years. Among other crises in her life, she has had a painful divorce and two job changes. She explained her divorce to me in something like the following terms. Her husband, she feels, "seemed just to want to do his thing." She no longer knew quite "where he was coming from." He used to be so steady, but, suddenly, he was so "off the wall." She supposed it was in part "a question of life-style," or maybe a "mid-life crisis." When I pressed her for greater clarity, she said: "Whatever." On her last trip to my apartment to pick my brain, her subject was a new prospective boss. She had had three interviews with him and found him rather "flakey." ¹⁸

"What do you mean by 'flakey'?" I asked. ¹⁹

"You know," she said, "he's a bit spacey." ²⁰

"Spacey?" I asked. ²¹

"You know," she said, "like a real flake. I couldn't make out where exactly he was coming from." ²²

Dottie comes ostensibly to pick my brain, but in fact she usually succeeds in scrambling it. When I left her at the door of my apartment, I suggested that she try to get a clearer picture of this man for whom she might soon be working by asking other people in her industry about him. She kissed me on the cheek and, turning to leave, announced, "Whatever." ²³

Whatever! ²⁴

I have never seen what I think of as the all-purpose, flying "whatever" used as a transition before, as I have just used it above, but then that is what makes it all-purpose. "I love you, I need you, whatever," or so I imagine young men nowadays proposing to their wives-to-be. "Yes, darling, I love you too. I want to have your children, to live out my life with you, whatever," the young woman replies, at which point they fall into each other's arms while across the screen appears not The End but Whatever. Used in this way, *whatever* is simply the word *etcetera* carried to the highest power. But it can also be used in the following way: "I suppose what I really mean is that, given society's current setup, it appears unlikely that one can find fulfilling work as long as the structure of employment is likely to, you know, whatever." Here *whatever* really means "Oh, the hell with it; I can't formulate exactly what I wish to say, but you know what I mean." My problem is that I usually don't know what the person means. What I do know is the utility of a word such as *whatever* to a confused mind, or at any rate a mind that chooses ²⁵

not to struggle with its confusions. It is a very useful word, *whatever.* You can even end paragraphs with it. Whatever.

Whatever may also qualify for the category that the sainted H. W. Fowler, ₂₆ blessed be his name, called "meaningless words." Of meaningless words, Fowler wrote:

> Words and phrases are often used in conversation, especially by the young, not as significant terms but rather, so far as they have any purpose at all, as aids of the same kind as are given in writing by punctuation, inverted commas, and underlining. It is a phenomenon perhaps more suitable for the psychologist than for the philologist. Words and phrases so employed change frequently, for they are soon worn out by overwork. Between the wars the most popular were DEFINITELY and *sort of thing.* One may suppose that they originated in a subconscious feeling that there was a need in the one case to emphasize a right word and in the other to apologize for a possibly wrong one. But any meaning they ever had was soon rubbed off them, and they became noises automatically produced.

Fowler also mentions *actually* and *you know* among the crop of meaning- ₂₇ less words. (*Incidentally* is another meaningless word Fowler mentions, which, incidentally, reminds me that, a while back, I had a long bout of beginning most of my sentences, at least in conversation, with the phrase "By the way." Every-thing, in those days, seemed to me "by the way." It takes a big-hearted snob, don't you think, to admit to a small-gauge error. A few years ago, *basically* was having a good run. "Care for dessert?" "Basically, I don't think I do," is a ridiculous but not unreal example. *You know* has had very long innings, and flourishes today, particularly among athletes. Of Patrick Ewing, the fine center for the Georgetown University basketball team, it has been said that last year he led the nation in *you know*s. It was said, obviously, by someone like me, a language snob.

A language snob's work is never done. Natural feelings of superiority being ₂₈ fleeting, he must maintain his vigilance, staying almost perpetually on the look-out for fresh signs of solecisms and lapsed standards, if only to maintain his desired state of self-elevation. As infantrymen are sent out on missions known as search and destroy, so the language snob is regularly on missions to search and enjoy—to find and delight in the linguistic fatuities and faux pas of his fellows. While there is no shortage of these in the contemporary world, some of course are better than others and provide more profound delight. I wasn't there to hear it, but a friend informs me that he once heard a Chicago politician claim that he "wasn't one to cast asparagus at his opponent." It is not every day that one comes upon such treasure.

Still, the language snob must take his pleasures where he finds them. In ₂₉ bureaucratic prose, for example. Few samples of bureaucratic prose fail to include the verb *implement,* which generally causes me to want to reach for an implement to smash the person who has used it. *Guidelines,* too, has brought many a twin-kle to these crowfooted and pouchy eyes. "*Guidelines* is a bastardization," I cry out to the walls. "It comes from *guy lines,* you idiot." No question about it, bureaucratic prose writers need to prioritize, dichotomize, and finalize, at least if they are to be responsive and people-oriented. Is what I say here of any ongoing interest? If so, I shall keep on going.

A language snob must not fear descending to pedantry. I know this language snob doesn't. I have had a good deal of fun, in this regard, watching people misuse the word *whence,* turning it into a tautology by saying or writing "from whence." But I have suffered minor setbacks here. Recently I noted "from whence" in both Shakespeare and Edmund Burke. More recently still, I discovered T. S. Eliot—T. S. bloody Eliot, for God's sake—misusing *presently* to mean "now" or "currently." Shock and dismay is the language snob's lot. Believe me, I don't enjoy feeling superior to Shakespeare, Burke, and Eliot, yet what is a man of serious standards to do?

But a language snob need not confine himself to pedantry. Euphemism always yields a full crop for his scythe—and, like cauliflower, euphemism is available all year round. My very favorite euphemism over the past fifteen or so years has been, without doubt, "student unrest." It was used to refer to the attempt on the part of radical students in the late sixties and early seventies to destroy the universities. "Student unrest" implies a mild crankiness, the antidote for which was perhaps a few good afternoon naps. I like, too, "Due to mature theme viewer discretion advised," which I take to mean "simulated fornication, extreme violence, and filthy language follow—get the kids the hell out of the room." This may seem an idiosyncratic reading, but I understand the word *interdisciplinary,* used by academics, to mean "I deserve a grant." I recall reading a grant proposal for the National Endowment for the Humanities a few years back in which the author wanted a grant for a course that would not only be "cross-curricular" but "interdisciplinary" and "interuniversity" as well. I suggested that NEH turn it down because it wasn't interplanetary. None of this parochial stuff for me.

A language snob must also be ready to outlaw words because the wrong people use them. *Charisma* is such a word. It once had a significant meaning, but no longer. "He has charisma," I not long ago heard Bucky Walters, the basketball announcer, say of a player. "He's got that smile." *Gnostic,* at least as used by literary critics, is another word I should like to ban. I have never read a sentence by a literary critic with the word *Gnostic* in it that I have ever understood (except this one). *Syndrome,* too, must go. "This is a syndrome he had foisted on him," I recently heard one politician say of another. *Structure* is another gone goose. On television the other day I heard another politician, one of the zinc-throated orators of our day, affirm: "I have invested in activities that have gone to enhance this total city's overall structure." Does everyone out there know how to enhance a structure? You add a touch of tarragon and soak it in lime juice. While we are cleaning the linguistic closet, let's toss out *learning experience,* which was never any good to begin with. Besides, I have noticed that people who say "learning experience" tend never to learn from experience.

On the subject of experience, it was Walter Pater who invoked us to live intensely for the moment, to seek "not the fruit of experience, but experience itself." But Pater didn't live to see the word *experience* turned into a verb, lucky chap. What would he have made of recent advertisements that ask us to "Experience Yoplait Yogurt," "Experience the St. Regis," "Experience Our 9.6 Interest Rates"? Walter Pater was not notably—how to say it?—a fun person. I am not at all sure he could "wrap his mind around" what has happened to the word *experience*. Although in the passage of his I quoted above he seems to be inviting us to "get in touch with our feelings," he scarcely seems a man to whom one could say, as the people who use *experience* as a verb also tend to say, "Go for it!"

As a language snob, I judge a person less by the cut of his jib than by the 34 grab of his gab. Where the gab has no grab I see a certain mental—not moral— flab. When a prospective buyer of *The London Observer* remarks that he intends to make that paper's editor "toe the line of viability," I make a judgment that is not charitable to him. When I read the phrase, in a book by Alvin Toffler, "decisional environment," not one but both my eyebrows fly up just beyond my receding hairline. When I read, in *The New Yorker,* about a Harvard Law School professor who refers to "a societal role not perceived as particularly helpful," to myself I exclaim, "Et tu, Harvard!" Can you identify with or relate to this? If you can—"identify," "relate"—I want you to draw a final paycheck and be out of here by five o'clock this afternoon. I loathe those words and phrases. You're fired.

"I have never seen a word derive," says the heroine of Renata Adler's novel 35 *Speedboat.* I believe I have seen a word derive, and that word is *life-style.* I recall first coming across the word *life-style* (from the German *Lebensstil*) in Max Weber's essays on social class, some of which I read as an undergraduate. I was immensely impressed with it; on Max Weber, an authentic genius, all words looked good. In those days, I used it myself, slipping it into term papers and conversation whenever possible. (Those were also the days of *ambivalence* and *love-hate*—not the condition and the relationships but the cheap phrases.) Soon I saw *life-style* taken up by advertising agencies and low-grade sociologists. College students next took the word up in the most flyblown way: "Queen Victoria lived a very different life-style than most of her subjects." The word fell into more and more common—and more and more confused—use. Today the word carries something of a philosophical freight: implicit in it is the notion, which I, for one, don't believe, that life has an almost infinite plasticity—change your life-style, change your life, it's as easy as that.

I have come to feel a fine invigorating hatred for the word. Where I could 36 fight against it, I have done so. I have abused authors who use it when I have written about their books. My poor students always receive a slightly squinty-eyed query when the word pops up in their conversation: "*Life-style*—what do you suppose you mean when you say *life-style?*" I ask. But then a few years ago, in the course of editing a manuscript by the late Nobel-Prize–winning biologist Max Delbrück, who was a fluent and careful writer of English prose, I came across a reference to "the life-style of the cell." Over the telephone I explained to Professor Delbrück that *life-style* was a word that drove me beyond the confines of distraction and into the country of apoplexy and asked him if I couldn't persuade him to remove it from his manuscript. "I don't like it much myself," he replied, "but I am afraid that it is the word that scientists have given to the patterning of

certain cellular activity and that we are stuck with it." So there you have it—
living testimony of a word deriving.

Do I, I wonder, begin to seem to you—to put it ever so gently—a touch   37
crazed? Has the cheerful snob that I advertise myself as being begun to seem the
beady-eyed fanatic? There is something about caring for language that does not
allow for moderation. How can you tell if you care about language? You care, I
should say, if it grates upon you to hear the word *impact* used as a verb. Next you
begin to care if you see *impact* used to describe anything other than ballistics, car
crashes, and wisdom teeth. You care if you find yourself wishing to flee the company of anyone who uses such words as *parenting, coupling, cohabiting, hus-
banding,* or *wiving.* You care if it turns your stomach to see or hear a reference to
"the caring professions." You know for certain that you care if the last thing in the
world you care to be called is "a caring person."

In recent years language snobbery has suffered a real setback by having   38
become institutionalized. There have always been writers who worried and complained about the state of the English language. Swift, Hazlitt, and Orwell have
been among their number. But of late a great many books have been published on
the subject. Magazines—*The New York Times Magazine, Esquire, Gentlemen's
Quarterly*—have instituted regular columns on the state of the language. Such
journalists as Edwin Newman, John Simon, and William Safire—a bit of a falling
off here from Swift, Hazlitt, and Orwell—have set up shop as state-of-the-
language pundits. By now there are even reverse language snobs loose in the land.
Thus Professor Robert Pattison, in *On Literacy,* remarks upon "the dull, prag-
matic rationale of established literacy" and writes:

> The same students who resolutely remain in darkness about the niceties of correct
> English grammar are as capable of intelligence as any previous generation. . . .
> Months of exercises will not shake their nonchalance about commas, but few are
> likely to misspell the name Led Zeppelin.

What a shame that there isn't an antonym for the phrase "Right on!"

Mention of the state-of-the-language pundits brings to mind Lionel Trilling,   39
who once wrote: "I find righteous denunciations of the present state of language
no less dismaying than the present state of the language." Yet, I have to wonder,
is what I have been doing here not also righteous? Perhaps it is, but there does
remain the less than cheery state of the language. Then, too, I take some small
pride in the fact that I am for the most part attacking my own class. Nearly thirty
years ago, in *Noblesse Oblige* (1956), Nancy Mitford caused a great stir by pointing out the distinction in their use of language between U and non-U people—U
people being those who had gone to university. This distinction, as I recall, had
to do almost exclusively with social class, and spoke very little, if at all, to the
quality of language used by either group. Today, though, it is people who have
been to university who make the most gnawing depredations into the clarity and
cleanliness of language. I cannot, for example, imagine any supposedly uneducated person using the word *supportive,* except possibly about his jockstrap. Who

but a university student or graduate would refer to her mother as a "role model," or talk about "the gender gap," or say she wishes "to dialogue" with me? (I make it a rule never "to dialogue"; I find it gets in the way of serious conversation.) Who but a U person would fall back on so foggy a word as *values?* Wesleyan University, I note, has a course entitled "Touchstones of Western Values," and a current Democratic presidential candidate has said, "Values lead to values." See ya later, obfuscator.

With the possible exception of politicians, bureaucrats, professors with weak ideas, and those in other professions and trades where charlatanry is requisite, few are the people who have a real taste for obfuscatory language. Doubtless Nietzsche was correct when he said that "general is the need for new jingling words, which shall make life noisy and festive." Yet language is still far and away the best tool we have for deceiving ourselves. When a famous ecologist writes that, if we are to save the earth, "we must enter into a creative association with our environment," I don't think the man is a knave or even a liar; I do, though, think, perhaps unbeknownst to himself, that he is embarked on the mental equivalent of whistling Dixie. When a young mother takes an active hand in a political campaign because she wants "this country to be a positive experience for my son," I do not impugn her sincerity, only her clarity. Was Russia a positive experience for Tolstoy, Germany for Bismarck, France for Proust? Do countries supply "positive experience"? The thought makes one wonder whether this young mother isn't searching for something that is not available.

So the language snob persists, lorgnette held high. Sometimes he looks quite as much at the people who use them as at the words themselves. I have never, for instance, met a professor in the humanities who called himself or herself a "humanist," without irony, whom I didn't dislike. I am extremely wary of people who go in for botanical metaphors in a big way to describe psychological states. "I feel myself growing," they will say. Or: "It has been a growthful experience." To the basic botanical metaphor of growth, further metaphors are stitched in. Abra Anderson, a Rockefeller granddaughter and a millionairess who lives in Chicago, recently told a journalist:

> Right now I don't know where I am, except that I feel everything else is finished. The apartment's finished, I've got a wonderful man, my kids are fine, the bills are paid, the charities are OK. And I'm just repotting myself.

Repotting? Hmm. Sounds like a lot of fertilizer to me.

Certain words such as *growth* seem to have a built-in squishiness; they grow soft at the touch. But, as any language snob will be pleased to tell you, good solid words, if sedulously misused, can lose their solidity, too. The word *honest* applied to art—and for a long stretch it was the key word of praise for works of architecture—always merits suspicion. *Excellence* is nowadays all but drained of meaning, so often has it been applied to things that are scarcely mediocre. The word *complete,* when used to describe collections of one or another kind of writing, usually turns out to mean merely "quite a bit of." *Literally,* in so many current usages, doesn't mean "literally"; it's literally a scandal, so to speak. "Ballpark figure" is a nice fairly new phrase meaning "rough approximation" (such as the estimates of attendance at a ball game), but it sometimes seems, to this language snob at any rate, as if we are entering the era of ballpark language, where words are used approximately; they mean only roughly what we think they mean.

My biases ought by now to be clear; so, too, my snobbery. But I earlier 43 referred to myself as a principled snob. Wherein, you may about now be wondering, lie my principles? All right, turn down the houselights, boys, give me the strong spotlight and a drumroll, here they are: take out after all language that is pretentious and imprecise, under-educated and over-intellectualized. Question all language that says more than it means, that leaves the ground but does not really fly. Question authority only after you have first seriously consulted it; it isn't always as stupid as it looks. Never forget that today's hot new phrase becomes tomorrow's cold dead cliché. (What will we do, a writer in the *Chronicle of Higher Education* asks, "when the Baby Boomers get to Golden Pond?") Know in advance that the fight for careful language is probably a losing one, but at the same time don't allow this knowledge to take the edge off your appetite for battle. The war may be lost, yet the skirmishes are still worth waging. Recall the words of that grand snob, Proust's Baron de Charlus: "I have always honored the defenders of grammar and logic. We realize fifty years later that they have averted serious dangers."

Hey, you know, I guess that some of you think I'm doing a number on you. 44 If you do, check it out. C'mon over. I'd like your input. The old lady'll put out some peanuts, pretzels maybe—you know, fun food. We'll break out a few tall cool ones. See if you think I've really gone flakey on this language thing. I think you'll find I'm pretty viable and am playing well within myself. We'll do some zero-based thinking, look at it in terms of worst-case and in terms of best-case thinking—in terms of the process itself. Maybe, when you come right down to it, it's a policy question. It's an intriguing bit. Arguably, it's worth arguing about. I haven't gone so far beyond the wall as to be above a little insightful feedback. But I'd better knock off, you know, because I've come, as they used to say in the bad old days, to the bottom line—and when I say bottom line, daddy, I mean bottom line. Out of sight. Awesome. Really.

Meaning and Idea

1. What characteristics distinguish the language snob?

2. What is Epstein's attitude toward his snobbery? Where does this attitude show? Cite passages.

3. What are the different types of language misuse that Epstein lays out? Do they seem equally offensive to him? To you?

Language, Form, Structure

1. What is Epstein's thesis in this essay?

2. How does Epstein use humor about himself? How effective is this? Do you feel he is really laughing at himself? If so, in what ways?

3. The essay offers many references to great and less than perfect writers and speakers. What is the effect of this sampling of both good and bad? After reading the essay, do you think you will be more aware of the kinds of things Epstein writes about? Why?

4. Epstein uses many clichés—from the title to the end. How effective are these in advancing his point about language use and language snobs?

5. Define the following words and use each in a sentence: genial; petulant; neologism; scion; solecisms; faux pas; egregious; fatuities; obfuscator; lorgnette; sedulously.

Ideas for Writing

1. Write an essay in which you categorize and define a certain type of communication or way people communicate, say husbands with wives, boyfriends with girlfriends, students with teachers.

2. Write an essay in which you pick several of the language errors Epstein cites and define the context within which people use them. For instance, when do you dialogue with someone as opposed to talking with him or her? Is there a difference?

3. Write an essay to explore Epstein's definition of *language snob*. Are you a language snob? Why or why not?

Poetry

Marianne Moore

Marianne Moore (1887–1972) was born near St. Louis a year before another famous American poet, T. S. Eliot, was born there. Moore and her mother later moved to Carlisle, Pennsylvania, where she attended the Metzger Institute, then took her degree at Bryn Mawr College. She originally considered being a painter, but abandoned that pursuit to try writing poetry and to teach stenography at a U.S. Indian School from 1911 to 1915. In 1918, she moved to New York City, where she worked as a tutor and as an assistant in the New York Public Library, and where she became one of the most ardent Brooklyn Dodgers fans. For three years, Moore edited *The Dial,* an established literary review of the time.

"Poetry" is a classic example of Marianne Moore's straightforward style of poetry. She defines for us that most elusive of terms, effecting a synthesis of the abstract and the concrete, which she considered so vital.

I, too, dislike it: there are things that are important beyond
    all this fiddle.
Reading it, however, with a perfect contempt for it, one
    discovers in
it after all, a place for the genuine.
  Hands that can grasp, eyes
  that can dilate, hair that can rise   5
    if it must, these things are important not because a

high-sounding interpretation can be put upon them but
    because they are
  useful. When they become so derivative as to become
    unintelligible,
  the same thing may be said for all of us, that we
    do not admire what   10
    we cannot understand: the bat
      holding on upside down or in quest of something to

eat, elephants pushing, a wild horse taking a roll, a tireless
    wolf under
  a tree, the immovable critic twitching his skin like a
    horse that feels a flea, the base-   15
  ball fan, the statistician—
    nor is it valid
      to discriminate against 'business documents and

school-books'; all these phenomena are important. One
    must make a distinction   20
  however: when dragged into prominence by half poets,
    the result is not poetry,
  nor till the poets among us can be
    'literalists of
    the imagination'—above   25
    insolence and triviality and can present

for inspection, imaginary gardens with real toads in them,
    shall we have
  it. In the meantime, if you demand on the one hand,
  the raw material of poetry in
  all its rawness and   30
  that which is on the other hand
    genuine, then you are interested in poetry.

Meaning and Idea

1. What is the "it" of stanza one? What is "all this fiddle"? What is "the genuine"?

2. Summarize, in your own words, Marianne Moore's definition of poetry. What ideal combination of elements makes up genuine poetry? How is the image "imaginary gardens with real toads in them" an example of this ideal combination?

3. What do you suppose Moore meant by "half poets"?

4. What is Moore's attitude toward critics? Do you think that she was expressing her feelings about critics in general or about one specific critic? Why?

Language, Form, Structure

1. How would you characterize Moore's poem—as essentially concrete or abstract? Why? Which is more important to Moore?

2. How is the technique of exemplification important to stanzas two and three? What is exemplified in each? What examples are offered?

3. For whom did Moore intend this definition? How do you know? How does her audience affect her style here?

4. The phrases "business documents and school-books" and "literalists of the imagination" refer to writings by two of the world's greatest writers—Tolstoy and Yeats. What value do such references add to Moore's definition of poetry?

5. Be sure you understand how Moore uses the following words: dilate; derivative; quest; phenomena; insolence; triviality.

Ideas for Writing

1. Write a definition of the term *satisfaction.* Distinguish between abstract and concrete manifestations of the term, and integrate them to form your definition.

2. Write your own prose definition of *poetry.* You may use references to specific poems or poets, or you may make your definition more general in nature.

3. In the final edition of her *Collected Poems,* Moore ended this poem at the word *genuine* in line 3. What do you think of that version of the poem? Why do you think she might have first ended the poem at that point? Is it as effective as a definition (or as a poem) in that severely abridged version? Write an essay in which you compare the two versions.

The Tiger

William Blake

William Blake (1757–1827) was an English poet, artist, and mystic. Despite the fact that he was virtually unknown in his time, and only one early volume of his poetry, *Poetical Sketches* (1783), was published during his lifetime, Blake's written and visual works greatly influenced the English romantics and subsequent generations. His work expresses a mixture of naive lack of sentimentality (as in *Songs of Innocence*, 1789, and *Songs of Experience*, 1794) with mythological imagination (as in *The Marriage of Heaven and Hell*, 1790, and *Jerusalem*, 1804–1820).

Blake's well-known poem "The Tiger" perhaps on first sounding seems to be an innocent rhyme about an animal. But, on closer reading, "The Tiger" exposes the many levels of meaning that define this "fearful symmetry."

*T*iger! Tiger! burning bright
In the forests of the night,
What immortal hand or eye
Could frame thy fearful symmetry?

In what distant deeps or skies   5
Burnt the fire of thine eyes?
On what wings dare he aspire?
What the hand dare seize the fire?

And what shoulder, and what art,
Could twist the sinews of thy heart?   10
And when thy heart began to beat,
What dread hand forged thy dread feet?

What the hammer? what the chain?
In what furnace was thy brain?
What the anvil? what dread grasp   15
Dare its deadly terrors clasp?

When the stars threw down their spears,
And watered heaven with their tears,
Did he smile his work to see?
Did he who made the Lamb make thee?   20

Tiger! Tiger! burning bright
In the forests of the night,
What immortal hand or eye,
Dare frame thy fearful symmetry?

Meaning and Idea

1. Describe Blake's tiger in your own words.

2. What is meant by the tiger's "fearful symmetry"?

3. Who is the "he" of stanza five? Why does Blake question "his" work?

Language, Form, Structure

1. A *symbol* is a word that stands for something else so that its meaning reaches beyond the literal. Of what is the tiger a symbol in this poem? What animal expresses its opposite symbolic value in this poem? Explain how symbolism is used as a basis of definition in this poem. How is context important for symbolic value here?

2. Blake attempts to define the *tiger* through a series of questions. How does he organize those questions? How do they form the basis of a definition in this poem?

3. Why is the word and punctuation *Tiger!* repeated at the beginning of the poem? Why does the last stanza repeat the first? How? What is the purpose of the repetition in this poem?

4. What mood does the poem evoke? How does Blake accomplish the mood?

5. Briefly comment on the uses and types of metaphor in this poem.

6. Write definitions for: immortal; aspire; sinews; anvil.

Ideas for Writing

1. Write a definition of a particular animal or object. Try to introduce symbolic elements in your definition so that it reflects a feeling or condition.

2. Write a definition of *fear* or *bravery,* organizing your material in the framework of a series of questions. However, unlike Blake, you should use your questions as departure points for explicit answers that will aid your definition.

3. Earlier in this chapter, you read a poem by Marianne Moore, "Poetry," in which she refers to a criticism written about Blake by the poet W. B. Yeats. Yeats wrote:

> The limitation of his view was from the very intensity of his vision; he was a too literal realist of imagination as others are of nature; and because he believed that the figures seen by the mind's eye, when exalted by inspiration, were "eternal existences," symbols of divine essences, he hated grace of style that might obscure their lineaments.

Comment on "The Tiger" in light of Yeats's criticism. Specific to this poem, do you agree or disagree with Yeats?

Complexion

Richard Rodriguez

Richard Rodriguez was born in San Francisco in 1944 and held a variety of jobs, including janitor, before becoming a full-time writer in 1981, a transition which was facilitated by the publication and positive reception of *Hunger of Memory: The Education of Richard Rodriguez* in 1982. He has received a Fullbright Fellowship and a National Endowment for the Humanities Fellowship. Rodriguez's work often chronicles his (and others') alienation from his own culture; he has led a strong campaign against affirmative action, which he views as yet another form of cultural alienation. He claims George Orwell as his prose model.

In this selection from *Hunger of Memory: The Education of Richard Rodriguez*, the author defines for us what is essentially an objective, physical term. However, the nature of his personal definition of the physical takes us beneath the surface to the emotional roots of the term.

*C*omplexion. My first conscious experience of sexual excitement   1
concerns my complexion. One summer weekend, when I was around seven years old, I was at a public swimming pool with the whole family. I remember sitting on the damp pavement next to the pool and seeing my mother, in the spectators' bleachers, holding my younger sister on her lap. My mother, I noticed, was watching my father as he stood on a diving board, waving to her. I watched her wave back. Then saw her radiant, bashful, astonishing smile. In that second I sensed that my mother and father had a relationship I knew nothing about. A nervous excitement encircled my stomach as I saw my mother's eyes follow my father's figure curving into the water. A second or two later, he emerged. I heard him call out. Smiling, his voice sounded, buoyant, calling me to swim to him. But turning to see him, I caught my mother's eye. I heard her shout over to me. In Spanish she called through the crowd: 'Put a towel on over your shoulders.' In public, she didn't want to say why. I knew.

That incident anticipates the shame and sexual inferiority I was to feel in   2
later years because of my dark complexion. I was to grow up an ugly child. Or one who thought himself ugly. (*Feo.*) One night when I was eleven or twelve years old, I locked myself in the bathroom and carefully regarded my reflection in the mirror over the sink. Without any pleasure I studied my skin. I turned on the faucet. (In my mind I heard the swirling voices of aunts, and even my mother's voice, whispering, whispering incessantly about lemon juice solutions and dark, *feo* children.) With a bar of soap, I fashioned a thick ball of lather. I began soaping my arms, I took my father's straight razor out of the medicine cabinet. Slowly, with steady deliberateness, I put the blade against my flesh, pressed it as close as I could without cutting, and moved it up and down across my skin to see if I could get out, somehow lessen, the dark. All I succeeded in doing,

however, was in shaving my arms bare of their hair. For as I noted with disappointment, the dark would not come out. It remained. Trapped. Deep in the cells of my skin.

Throughout adolescence, I felt myself mysteriously marked. Nothing else about my appearance would concern me so much as the fact that my complexion was dark. My mother would say how sorry she was that there was not money enough to get braces to straighten my teeth. But I never bothered about my teeth. In three-way mirrors at department stores, I'd see my profile dramatically defined by a long nose, but it was really only the color of my skin that caught my attention.

I wasn't afraid that I would become a menial laborer because of my skin. Nor did my complexion make me feel especially vulnerable to racial abuse. (I didn't really consider my dark skin to be a racial characteristic. I would have been only too happy to look as Mexican as my light-skinned older brother.) Simply, I judged myself ugly. And, since the women in my family had been the ones who discussed it in such worried tones, I felt my dark skin made me unattractive to women.

Thirteen years old. Fourteen. In a grammar school art class, when the assignment was to draw a self-portrait, I tried and I tried but could not bring myself to shade in the face on the paper to anything like my actual tone. With disgust then I would come face to face with myself in mirrors. With disappointment I located myself in class photographs—my dark face undefined by the camera which had clearly described the white faces of classmates. Or I'd see my dark wrist against my long-sleeved white shirt.

I grew divorced from my body. Insecure, overweight, listless. On hot summer days when my rubber-soled shoes soaked up the heat from the sidewalk, I kept my head down. Or walked in the shade. My mother didn't need anymore to tell me to watch out for the sun. I denied myself a sensational life. The normal, extraordinary, animal excitement of feeling my body alive—riding shirtless on a bicycle in the warm wind created by furious self-propelled motion—the sensations that first had excited in me a sense of my maleness, I denied. I was too ashamed of my body. I wanted to forget that I had a body because I had a brown body. I was grateful that none of my classmates ever mentioned the fact.

I continued to see the *braceros,* those men I resembled in one way and, in another way, didn't resemble at all. On the watery horizon of a Valley afternoon, I'd see them. And though I feared looking like them, it was with silent envy that I regarded them still. I envied them their physical lives, their freedom to violate the taboo of the sun. Closer to home I would notice the shirtless construction workers, the roofers, the sweating men tarring the street in front of the house. And I'd see the Mexican gardeners. I was unwilling to admit the attraction of their lives. I tried to deny it by looking away. But what was denied became strongly desired.

In high school physical education classes, I withdrew, in the regular company of five or six classmates, to a distant corner of a football field where we smoked and talked. Our company was composed of bodies too short or too tall, all graceless and all—except mine—pale. Our conversation was usually witty. (In fact we were intelligent.) If we referred to the athletic contests around us, it was with sarcasm. With savage scorn I'd refer to the "animals" playing football or baseball. It would have been important for me to have joined them. Or for me to have taken off my shirt, to have let the sun burn dark on my skin, and to have run barefoot on the warm wet grass. It would have been very important. Too important. It would have been too telling a gesture—to admit the desire for sensation, the body, my body.

Fifteen, sixteen. I was a teenager shy in the presence of girls. Never dated. 9 Barely could talk to a girl without stammering. In high school I went to several dances, but I never managed to ask a girl to dance. So I stopped going. I cannot remember high school years now with the parade of typical images: bright drive-ins or gliding blue shadows of a Junior Prom. At home most weekend nights, I would pass evenings reading. Like those hidden, precocious adolescents who have no real-life sexual experiences, I read a great deal of romantic fiction. 'You won't find it in your books,' my brother would playfully taunt me as he prepared to go to a party by freezing the crest of the wave in his hair with sticky pomade. Through my reading, however, I developed a fabulous and sophisticated sexual imagination. At seventeen, I may not have known how to engage a girl in small talk, but I had read *Lady Chatterley's Lover.*

It annoyed me to hear my father's teasing: that I would never know what 'real 10 work' is; that my hands were so soft. I think I knew it was his way of admitting pleasure and pride in my academic success. But I didn't smile. My mother said she was glad her children were getting their educations and would not be pushed around like *los pobres.* I heard the remark ironically as a reminder of my separation from *los braceros.* At such times I suspected that education was making me effeminate. The odd thing, however, was that I did not judge my classmates so harshly. Nor did I consider my male teachers in high school effeminate. It was only myself I judged against some shadowy, mythical Mexican laborer—dark like me, yet very different.

Language was crucial. I knew that I had violated the ideal of the *macho* by 11 becoming such a dedicated student of language and literature. *Machismo* was a word never exactly defined by the persons who used it. (It was best described in the 'proper' behavior of men.) Women at home, nevertheless, would repeat the old Mexican dictum that a man should be *feo, fuerte, y formal.* 'The three F's,' my mother called them, smiling slyly. *Feo* I took to mean not literally ugly so much as ruggedly handsome. (When my mother and her sisters spent a loud, laughing afternoon determining ideal male good looks, they finally settled on the actor Gilbert Roland, who was neither too pretty nor ugly but had looks 'like a man.') *Fuerte,* 'strong,' seemed to mean not physical strength as much as inner strength, character. A dependable man is *fuerte. Fuerte* for that reason was a characteristic subsumed by the last of the three qualities, and the one I most often considered—*formal.* To be *formal* is to be steady. A man of responsibility, a good provider. Someone *formal* is also constant. A person to be relied upon in adversity. A sober man, a man of high seriousness.

I learned a great deal about being *formal* just by listening to the way my 12 father and other male relatives of his generation spoke. A man was not silent necessarily. Nor was he limited in the tones he could sound. For example, he could tell a long, involved, humorous story and laugh at his own humor with high-pitched giggling. But a man was not talkative the way a woman could be. It was permitted a woman to be gossipy and chatty. (When one heard many voices in a room, it was usually women who were talking.) Men spoke much less rapidly. And often men spoke in monologues. (When one voice sounded in a crowded room, it was most often a man's voice one heard.) More important than any of this was the fact that a man never verbally revealed his emotions. Men did not speak about their unease in moments of crisis or danger. It was the woman who worried aloud when her husband got laid off from work. At times of illness or death in the family, a man was usually quiet, even silent. Women spoke up to voice prayers. In distress, women always sounded quick ejaculations to God or the Virgin; women prayed in clearly audible voices at a wake held in a funeral parlor. And on the subject of love, a woman was verbally expansive. She spoke of her yearning and delight. A married man, if he spoke publicly about love, usually did so with playful, mischievous irony. Younger, unmarried men more often were quiet. (The *macho* is a silent suitor. *Formal.*)

At home I was quiet, so perhaps I seemed *formal* to my relations and other 13 Spanish-speaking visitors to the house. But outside the house—my God!—I talked. Particularly in class or alone with my teachers, I chattered. (Talking seemed to make teachers think I was bright.) I often was proud of my way with words. Though, on other occasions, for example, when I would hear my mother busily speaking to women, it would occur to me that my attachment to words made me like her. Her son. Not *formal* like my father. At such times I even suspected that my nostalgia for sounds—the noisy, intimate Spanish sounds of my past—was nothing more than effeminate yearning.

High school English teachers encouraged me to describe very personal feel- 14 ings in words. Poems and short stories I wrote, expressing sorrow and loneliness, were awarded high grades. In my bedroom were books by poets and novelists—books that I loved—in which male writers published feelings the men in my family never revealed or acknowledged in words. And it seemed to me that there was something unmanly about my attachment to literature. Even today, when so much about the myth of the *macho* no longer concerns me, I cannot altogether evade such notions. Writing these pages, admitting my embarrassment or my guilt, admitting my sexual anxieties and my physical insecurity, I have not been able to forget that I am not being *formal.*

So be it. 15

Meaning and Idea

1. In the incident by the swimming pool when the author is 12, why does his mother tell him to put a towel over his shoulders? Why does she say it in Spanish? What was the effect of the comment on Rodriguez?

2. What two expected results of his dark complexion did Rodriguez not fear? Why? What result did he fear most? How does he develop that fear?

3. What does Rodriguez mean when he says he was *feo?* What were the effects of the author's considering himself *feo* during his adolescence? What were the longer-lasting effects?

4. How does Rodriguez compare himself to the *braceros,* construction workers, and Mexican gardeners? Why does he envy them?

5. What is Rodriguez's definition of *machismo?* What were the "three F's"? How did Rodriguez arrive at his own definition of each? How did he see himself in relation to the "three F's"? What is his present view of himself in relation to them?

Language, Form, Structure

1. What is the main term defined in this essay? How does Rodriguez use various lesser definitions to build up support for the whole definition? Why does the author define both English and Spanish words? How does he connect them?

2. What is the connection between the use of language and the definition of character traits or feelings according to this essay? Explain fully at least two examples.

3. In the paragraph the begins "Thirteen years old. Fourteen." Rodriguez writes about his class photographs. He says: "I located myself . . . my dark face undefined by the camera." What is the meaning of the word *undefined* here? How does it relate to the overall definitional context of this essay?

4. How does Rodriguez use narration as an integral part of his definition? How does he arrange his narrations?

5. Write definitions for these words from the essay: buoyant; menial; vulnerable; precocious; pomade; effeminate; subsumed.

Ideas for Writing

1. Write an extended definition of the term *cultural* or *racial stereotype.* You may choose to focus on the stereotypes you know about your own cultural or racial group and develop your definition through personal narrative.

2. Write a definition of the term *ugly.* Use negation as your main development technique.

3. At the end of this essay, Rodriguez writes:

> Writing these pages, admitting my embarrassment or my guilt, admitting my sexual anxieties and my physical insecurity, I have not been able to forget that I am not being *formal.*

Do you feel that men exposing their emotions so publicly in writing is "unmanly," as Rodriguez fears it may be? Do you feel Rodriguez's writing in this essay is in any way effeminate? On a broader scale, do you feel there are appropriate differences in subject and tone in writing for male and female writers? Why? Explore these issues in an analytic essay.

CROSSOVER

1. Susan Brownmiller in "Femininity" and Richard Rodriguez in "Complexion" explore stereotypical thinking and its effect on individual development. Write an essay on the ways the two writers deal with stereotypes. What commonalities exist between the two pieces about how the culture transmits traditional gender ideas? What insights are unique to each piece?

2. Carl Sandburg's "Primer Lesson" and Robert Graves's "The Naked and the Nude" are both poems that take as a theme the power of language to alter human consciousness. How does each poem play with specific words to make its respective point about words? Which poem affects you more? What do you find most contributes to the poem's influence on you? Write an essay to explore these questions.

■

Chapter Nine

ARGUMENTATION AND PERSUASION

We devote a good deal of our daily thinking and talking time to reasoning, often reasoning with someone or other to convince the person to believe something that we ourselves believe, or to take some particular action we believe necessary. X is the best place to go; Y is the worst choice for mayor; plan B is the most reasonable solution to problem Z; course 1 is the only valid course to follow. In writing, too, we take positions and defend them, and this undertaking, stemming in the most formal sense from ancient Greek oratory, we call *argumentation.*

Although some logicians make a precise distinction between arguing and persuading, the two frequently work together. Strictly speaking, the essence of *argumentation* is a coolly rational presentation of statement and support, eschewing emotional appeals and prejudicial language and aiming instead for a person's intellectual faculty. The arguer's goal is to get you to agree. *Persuasion,* on the other hand, reaches for feelings; based in logic, too, it usually aims to arouse emotion, even passion, so that you act. The persuader's goal is to get you to agree—and then to do something about it. When you say "You're right" to a friend who marshals statistics—batting averages, win-loss records, runs batted in—to convince you that the Dodgers are a better team than the Cubs, he's won the argument. When you buy a new breakfast cereal because of a 30-second commercial spot on television, you're not only convinced, you're convinced strongly enough to take action.

Good written argumentation and persuasion, designed to appeal to reasonable readers, will be grounded in reason. The writer asserts something, takes a position (when stated formally, this is often called the *proposition*), and then advances this position point by point. But like effective argumentation in life, written argumentation usually provides more than direct logical proof. Readers and writers alike are complex creatures, feeling and thinking at once. No wonder, then, that throughout history, writers have developed argumentative approaches to convince readers both through reasoning and through emotional evocation.

READING ARGUMENTATION

From early literature to modern novels, stories, dramas, and essays, argumentation abounds. From Job's remonstrance to God to the polemics of Brecht, Lawrence, and Woolf in our century, we note lively evidence of the impulse to argue well so that others see important issues as we do.

Effective argumentation will not only move the reader through logic but will move the reader to "feel" the writer's position as well. In effective argumentative essays the writer may draw on a whole arsenal of strategies—comparison, classification, causation, description, narration, and so on. A sharp anecdote, a lambent sensory description, an explanation of ghastly or wonderful effects, an extended analogy, an apt comparison—all these can help persuade the reader to accept the writer's particular position or point of view. But fiction writers, poets, dramatists, and satirists also employ argumentation and persuasion. The essayist may dwell more on aspects of logic and the imaginative writer more on emotional appeals; but the good writer in any genre will draw on techniques that sway both intellect and emotions, yoking in the work both sense and sensibility. Indeed, writers from Aristotle to Austen to T. S. Eliot have recommended this joining in life and in literature.

In this chapter, Swift's satire, "A Modest Proposal," argues against popular policy and attitudes toward Ireland not by saying outright, "The British treatment of Ireland should be altered," but by using a variety of expository techniques that move us not only intellectually but emotionally. His comparison of babies to livestock, for example, to be bred, killed, "stewed, roasted, baked, or boiled," and put on the table for dinner alarms the reader, convincing us of the *narrator's* lunacy and of the *writer's* good sense. Point by point, Swift has his speaker argue for the wisdom of killing babies as a solution to "the Irish problem," and through well-chosen details, examples, facts and figures—"I compute that Dublin would take off annually about twenty thousand carcasses, and the rest of the kingdom (where they will be sold somewhat cheaper) the remaining eighty thousand"—makes readers see British proposals to maintain domination of impoverished Ireland as cruelty and madness in the name of reason and logic. Indeed the whole superlogical structure of Swift's satire encourages in the reader an *emotional* acceptance of the victims and an *emotional* aversion to the oppressor. The "Proposal" encourages the reader to say, "No more proposals, no more propositions. Just kindness, just love."

Good argumentation, then, can move not only our minds but also our hearts. Perhaps the most remarkable balance between logic and emotion in literature resides in Marvell's "To His Coy Mistress," one of the poems in this chapter. The poet appeals to his mistress's reason so that she'll accept his propositions; yet his language, fraught with subtle sensuality, aims for emotional appeal ("The grave's a fine and private place, / But none, I think, do there embrace"). The speaker's objective is to persuade his demure lady through reason and feeling to love him now, not later. He wants action, and he wants it today!

As we read argumentation, we can see, too, the choices of logical strategies. Will the writer start with a proposition and then support it point by point, or will the writer lay down points and let the proposition emerge? The former approach we call *deduction,* the latter, *induction.* Martin Luther King, in the "I Have a Dream" speech, works deductively; he comes right out with his proposition, which his entire speech then supports through example, analysis of causes and effects, and so on. Swift's essay, in contrast, works inductively. Readers, after experiencing the *speaker's* proposition, supporting details, and calculations, grasp on their own the *writer's* proposition—a rejection of the basic assumptions laid down in the "Proposal."

While reading argumentation, then, we can observe a rich play of the writer's options. Chekhov uses the principles of argumentation to achieve very funny effects in his play "A Marriage Proposal." But even in humorous writing, we can see the wide range of possibilities for argumentative ploys. To get us to embrace a proposition, writers will use a variety of dramatic and expository techniques. They may appeal to our reason and to our emotions, probably both. Writers may work deductively, guiding us from proposition to support, or inductively from detail and example until their handiwork frames the larger proposition. In short, reading argumentation provides a blueprint of strategies in logic that have already been used to win many readers and that remain useful as we ourselves write to argue or persuade.

WRITING ARGUMENTATION

The ancient Greeks developed certain rules that strictly governed formal argumentation and debate, and orators and writers followed these rules for centuries. Today we tend to approach argumentation with fewer rules. Still, it is useful to keep certain guidelines in mind as you develop your own argumentative essays, and to keep certain thoughts in mind even before you select your topic. Argumentation will require a good deal of you—your most careful reasoning, an energetic marshaling of support, extreme sensitivity to the emotional issues of your topic, and exact use of language. The first question you want to ask yourself is "What issue do I care strongly enough about to be able to take an emphatic position on?" This is no occasion for reticence; you must take a stand and stick by it. Also, before you choose your topic, you'll want to ask yourself, "What do I know about?" You don't necessarily want your first argumentation papers to end up being extensive research undertakings, and so a topic that you not only care about but also know something about will be a good place to start.

PURPOSE AND AUDIENCE

Argumentative essays have as their goal the logical presentation of ideas in order to convince the reader of a sound point of view. A further purpose may be to get their readers to act, once they accept the essay's proposition. In either case, you want to take readers with you from proposition to supporting points to conclusion. And to do so you must think carefully about *who* your readers are; what they know; and what information, data, illustrations, or other supporting details are likely to get them to think as you do. Your level of usage, your choice of vocabulary, and your tone and style all must serve your ultimate purpose. To argue against the excessive use of living animals for scientific experiments, you might present readers with a dispassionate paper that lays out statistics and cases drawn from reliable sources. Numbers have their own drama, and a careful, rational presentation could win over your readers. If your purpose were to recruit demonstrators for a march in Washington next month to support the Animal Protection League, you might spark your essay with your own bias, individualizing the cases, emphasizing the particular suffering of animals in selected examples, and exhorting your readers with emotionally charged language to meet you on the steps of the capitol.

One point to keep in mind is that readers are, more often than not, rational people. You will want, then, to build a sound argument and to avoid name-calling that might alienate your audience. As you develop your proposition, try for a statement that will respect your audience's diversity. If you say anyone who doesn't support school busing is "a Nazi and a right-wing hoodlum," you will prevent any readers inclined toward opposing busing from reading your essay with an open mind.

Of course, certain audiences tend to be in agreement on certain subjects. But, more often than not, an academic audience—generally your main readership—holds diverse views. As you write, try to imagine what a reader with opposing views might say. An excellent strategy is to include these opposing views somewhere in your essay and either acknowledge their viability before you go on to make your own points or refute them one by one. This *refutation,* a requirement in classical argumentation, is still useful for persuading readers on the other side or for convincing readers sitting on the fence. As for readers who agree with your position, the refutation and the good argumentation in general can help them to test their beliefs and to sharpen and strengthen their thinking.

As you prepare to write, think about the knowledge level of your readers. If they know very little about the subject, then your argument will have to cover some very basic point. What is *vivisection?* What is its history in the American scientific community? What are other options for researchers? If, on the other hand, your readers are specialists on your topic, then you will need to pitch your essay to their high level, avoid telling them what they already know, and include sophisticated thinking and information.

Think of your audience as you organize the points that support your proposition. If you put your strongest points first, most readers will lose interest as the essay moves on to weaker arguments. If you put all your strong points last, your readers may never be interested enough to get to them. A balanced strategy is to put your second strongest point first, then proceed to your less strong points, and end your argument with your strongest point—the point you most want your readers to remember.

Being especially clear about your own purpose and about your audience is critical as you develop essays designed to change minds.

PROCESS

Identify the issue you want to write about. Consider the matters raised in the selections in this chapter. If you have trouble identifying a strong belief or conviction, look at a news magazine or a newspaper. Study editorial pages; read a political column; listen to a commentator's opinion on radio or television. No doubt your thinking on different matters will perk up even if it's just to *oppose* what you read or hear. Once you've chosen a topic that you care about and perhaps even know a good deal about, you can turn to developing your argument.

First, you must shape your topic into a proposition, the thesis statement in argumentation. Whether the logical plan of your essay is deductive or inductive, you will need a clear statement of proposition to work with. As you know, not every essay states its thesis outright—writers sometimes leave you to figure it out on your own—but a clear statement of proposition helps a reader straight off to determine where the essay intends to go. Even an inductive essay can benefit from such a statement at the end so that readers can check their perceptions against the writer's. At any rate, a clear idea of the main position that the essay will assert directs you as you plan and as you write. An argumentative essay builds on a strong proposition (Y must be upheld; B should be abolished). Write your proposition and edit any language that could bait or alienate your audience.

Prewrite on your topic in order to generate the major points of your argument. Even the most fair-minded proposition needs strong supporting points in order for readers to accept it fully. Through jottings, lists, freewriting—whatever technique works for you—generate the points that will hold up your position. And before you write, generate examples, facts, figures, descriptions that make each point convincing and alive.

Also before you write, check your argument for logic. Logic, of course, plays a part in most writing, but in argumentation it plays an especially important role. If your logic is faulty, reasonable readers will reject your entire premise, however worthy it in itself may be. Look to see that your essay does not oversimplify complicated matters. Consider cautiously, for example, the value of calling for the end to all biological investigations that employ living animals. Many advances in human health care have followed such experimentation, and you might lose readers if you overlook the advantages stemming from such scientific research. Also, look to see that your conclusions logically follow the proposition and its supporting points. The Latin phrase *non sequitur,* meaning *doesn't follow,* refers to a statement that does not logically follow another statement, although we intend it to. "Opposing vivisection will improve the lot of helpless animals everywhere" risks being a *non sequitur* if you do not develop the issues in your paper carefully. What about the cruelty inflicted upon pets in some households? What about animals abandoned every September as resort areas close down all over America and families return home? Look as well to see that the authorities you invoke are truly authorities. Your brother's report of outrageous experiments with frogs in a summer camp nature program would not convince anyone that vivisection abuse is widespread throughout the scientific community. Another way to strengthen the logic of your position is to make sure that you've argued the issues and have not just attacked people connected with your "opposition." Such a personal attack is called *ad hominem,* from the Latin for "to the person." The *ad hominen* approach is easy to turn to in argumentation involving us emotionally, but readers can easily dismiss it as beside the point.

Good logic can work for you and so can good language. Solid argumentation relies on good writing. As you write and as you edit, try for the most alive language and the most alive examples and descriptions. The well-turned phrase will attract your readers' attention and incline them toward your position more than will dull phrases or repetitive syntax. Fresh figurative language, sensory description, lively comparisons, lively examples—all the rhetorical devices that you have at your command as a writer—will serve you well as you argue for your proposition, making logical and emotional appeals to your reader.

In arguing it's easy to overdo the use of transitions by linking ideas frequently with logical connectors—*therefore, thus, and so, as a result, then, consequently,* and many others like them. These transitions are useful certainly to connect points here and there; but the logic in a well-reasoned essay has its own flow that requires few guideposts. In most cases readers will know on their own when point A follows point B intelligently and will not need the added push of *therefore*.

Finally, the conclusion of your argumentative essay is particularly important. It's what readers "hear" last and it often can clinch or lose their support. There are no hard-and-fast rules for concluding argumentation. In a fairly long paper, a restatement of your proposition, one that presents your point with fresh language, will impress readers with what is most important to the essay without being boring. But you won't want to stop there in every case. Your conclusion might set a new frame of reference by generalizing from your stated proposal to an even larger, more relevant issue. Your conclusion can help readers apply your generalization in a broader context than the immediate concerns of your essay.

Throughout your college career and on the job, your skills at argumentation will serve you well. Spend time here in practicing these skills: presenting your points honestly, avoiding the overstatement of emotional appeals, and weighing the logic of your positions carefully.

SUMMING UP: ARGUMENTATION AND PERSUASION

Reading Argumentation and Persuasion

Argumentation is a rational presentation that takes a position and defends it without excessive emotional appeals and that is aimed at a person's intellectual faculty; *persuasion,* also based in logic, intends to arouse emotion to compel an action. Often argumentation and persuasion work together.

- Determine the elements in the selection that appeal to your intellect and your emotion.

- Determine the writer's assertion or position, often called the *proposition.*

- Consider how the writer advances her position point by point.

- Identify the various rhetorical strategies—narration, comparison, definition, causation, and others surely—that the writer uses to advance his argument.

- Weigh the uses of induction and deduction.

Writing Argumentation and Persuasion

- Choose a topic about which you can take a stand and stick by it; that is, determine an issue that you care strongly enough about to take an emphatic position on.

- Be prepared to use your most careful reasoning and exact language, to present your most convincing detail, and to show extreme sensitivity to the emotional issues of your topic.

- Take readers logically from your proposition to supporting points to your conclusion.

- Evaluate who your readers are; what they know about the topic; and what information, data, illustrations, or other supporting details are likely to get them to think as you do.

- Honor the diversity of your audience by considering what a reader with opposing views on your topic would say, and then address those views.

- Weigh the arrangement of the points in your arguments, ending with your strongest point.

- Develop your proposition, a thesis statement that indicates the main position of the essay and that directs you as you plan and write the essay.

- Use prewriting to help generate the major points in your argument: jottings, lists, freewriting—these activities can help you develop the early stages of your argument.

- Check your essay for adherence to logic; avoid *oversimplifying, non sequiturs,* and *ad hominem* arguments.

- As you edit, pay particular attention to language, aiming for clear, alive examples.

- Do not overdo the use of logical connectors as transitions.

- Produce a conclusion that clinches your argument.

I Have a Dream

Martin Luther King, Jr.

Martin Luther King, Jr. (1929–1968), was born in Atlanta, Georgia, the son of a Baptist minister. King followed his father's lead into the ministry and soon became known for his inspiring oratorical abilities. He became the most prominent leader of the early civil rights movement in the United States: In 1955, he organized the year-long, successful boycott of the segregated Montgomery, Alabama, bus system; he subsequently organized and led the Southern Christian Leadership Council, which promoted other boycotts, marches, and demonstrations in favor of civil rights for blacks. King was an instrumental organizer of the 1963 March on Washington and the 1965 voter-registration drive in Selma, Alabama. Staunchly devoted to Gandhian-style nonviolent resistance, the Reverend Dr. King received the 1968 Nobel Prize for Peace. In 1968, he was assassinated.

On August 28, 1963, nearly a quarter of a million people of all races converged on Washington, D.C., to take part in the historic March on Washington at the height of the American civil rights movement. In front of the Lincoln Memorial, on the one hundredth anniversary of the Emancipation Proclamation, the Reverend Dr. Martin Luther King, Jr., delivered the spellbinding "I Have a Dream" speech in which he outlined his vision of a better, more peaceful country.

Five score years ago, a great American, in *whose symbolic shadow* 1
we stand, signed the Emancipation Proclamation. This momentous decree came as a great beacon light of hope to millions of Negro slaves who had been seared in the flames of withering injustice. It came as a joyous daybreak to end the long light of captivity.

But one hundred years later, we must face the tragic fact that the Negro is still 2
not free. One hundred years later, the life of the Negro is still sadly crippled by the manacles of segregation and the chains of discrimination. One hundred years later, the Negro lives on a lonely island of poverty in the midst of a vast ocean of material prosperity. One hundred years later, the Negro is still languishing in the corners of American society and finds himself an exile in his own land. So we have come here today to dramatize an appalling condition.

In a sense we have come to our nation's capital to cash a check. When the 3
architects of our republic wrote the magnificent words of the Constitution and the Declaration of Independence, they were signing a promissory note to which every American was to fall heir. This note was a promise that all men would be guaranteed the unalienable rights of life, liberty, and the pursuit of happiness.

It is obvious today that America has defaulted on this promissory note inso- 4
far as her citizens of color are concerned. Instead of honoring this sacred obligation, America has given the Negro people a bad check; a check which has come back marked "insufficient funds." But we refuse to believe that the bank of justice is bankrupt. We refuse to believe that there are insufficient funds in the great

vaults of opportunity of this nation. So we have come to cash this check—a check that will give us upon demand the riches of freedom and the security of justice. We have also come to this hallowed spot to remind America of the fierce urgency of *now*. This is no time to engage in the luxury of cooling off or to take the tranquilizing drugs of gradualism. *Now* is the time to make real the promises of Democracy. *Now* is the time to rise from the dark and desolate valley of segregation to the sunlit path of racial justice. *Now* is the time to open the doors of opportunity to all of God's children. *Now* is the time to lift our nation from the quicksands of racial injustice to the solid rock of brotherhood.

It would be fatal for the nation to overlook the urgency of the moment and to   5 underestimate the determination of the Negro. This sweltering summer of the Negro's legitimate discontent will not pass until there is an invigorating autumn of freedom and equality. 1963 is not an end, but a beginning. Those who hope that the Negro needed to blow off steam and will now be content will have a rude awakening if the nation returns to business as usual. There will be neither rest nor tranquility in America until the Negro is granted his citizenship rights. The whirlwinds of revolt will continue to shake the foundations of our nation until the bright day of justice emerges.

But there is something that I must say to my people who stand on the warm   6 threshold which leads into the palace of justice. In the process of gaining our rightful place we must not be guilty of wrongful deeds. Let us not seek to satisfy our thirst for freedom by drinking from the cup of bitterness and hatred. We must forever conduct our struggle on the high plane of dignity and discipline. We must not allow our creative protest to degenerate into physical violence. Again and again we must rise to the majestic heights of meeting physical force with soul force. The marvelous new militancy which has engulfed the Negro community must not lead us to a distrust of all white people, for many of our white brothers, as evidenced by their presence here today, have come to realize that their destiny is tied up with our destiny and their freedom is inextricably bound to our freedom. We cannot walk alone.

And as we walk, we must make the pledge that we shall march ahead. We   7 cannot turn back. There are those who are asking the devotees of civil rights, "When will you be satisfied?" We can never be satisfied as long as the Negro is the victim of the unspeakable horrors of police brutality. We can never be satisfied as long as our bodies, heavy with the fatigue of travel, cannot gain lodging in the motels of the highways and the hotels of the cities. We cannot be satisfied as long as the Negro's basic mobility is from a smaller ghetto to a larger one. We can never be satisfied as long as a Negro in Mississippi cannot vote and a Negro in New York believes he has nothing for which to vote. No, no, we are not satisfied, and we will not be satisfied until justice rolls down like waters and righteousness like a mighty stream.

I am not unmindful that some of you have come here out of great trials and   8 tribulations. Some of you have come fresh from narrow jail cells. Some of you have come from areas where your quest for freedom left you battered by the storms of persecution and staggered by the winds of police brutality. You have been the veterans of creative suffering. Continue to work with the faith that unearned suffering is redemptive.

Go back to Mississippi, go back to Alabama, go back to South Carolina, go back to Georgia, go back to Louisiana, go back to the slums and ghettos of our northern cities, knowing that somehow this situation can and will be changed. Let us not wallow in the valley of despair. 9

I say to you today, my friends, that in spite of the difficulties and frustrations of the moment I still have a dream. It is a dream deeply rooted in the American dream. 10

I have a dream that one day this nation will rise up and live out the true meaning of its creed: "We hold these truths to be self-evident; that all men are created equal." 11

I have a dream that one day on the red hills of Georgia the sons of former slaves and the sons of former slaveowners will be able to sit down together at the table of brotherhood. 12

I have a dream that one day even the state of Mississippi, a desert state sweltering with the heat of injustice and oppression, will be transformed into an oasis of freedom and justice. 13

I have a dream that my four little children will one day live in a nation where they will not be judged by the color of their skin but by the content of their character. 14

I have a dream today. 15

I have a dream that one day the state of Alabama, whose governor's lips are presently dripping with the words of interposition and nullification, will be transformed into a situation where little black boys and black girls will be able to join hands with little white boys and white girls and walk together as sisters and brothers. 16

I have a dream today. 17

I have a dream that one day every valley shall be exalted, every hill and mountain shall be made low, the rough places will be made plain, and the crooked places will be made straight, and the glory of the Lord shall be revealed, and all flesh shall see it together. 18

This is our hope. This is the faith with which I return to the South. With this faith we will be able to hew out of the mountain of despair a stone of hope. With this faith we will be able to transform the jangling discords of our nation into a beautiful symphony of brotherhood. With this faith we will be able to work together, to pray together, to struggle together, to go to jail together, to stand up for freedom together, knowing that we will be free one day. 19

This will be the day when all of God's children will be able to sing with new meaning 20

> My country, 'tis of thee,
> Sweet land of liberty,
>   Of thee I sing:
> Land where my fathers died,
> Land of the pilgrims' pride,

> From every mountain-side
>   Let freedom ring.

And if America is to be a great nation this must become true. So let freedom ₂₁ ring from the prodigious hilltops of New Hampshire. Let freedom ring from the mighty mountains of New York. Let freedom ring from the heightening Alleghenies of Pennsylvania!

Let freedom ring from the snowcapped Rockies of Colorado!   ₂₂

Let freedom ring from the curvaceous peaks of California!   ₂₃

But not only that; let freedom ring from Stone Mountain of Georgia!   ₂₄

Let freedom ring from Lookout Mountain of Tennessee!   ₂₅

Let freedom ring from every hill and molehill of Mississippi. From every ₂₆ mountainside, let freedom ring.

When we let freedom ring, when we let it ring from every village and every ₂₇ hamlet, from every state and every city, we will be able to speed up that day when all of God's children, black men and white men, Jews and Gentiles, Protestants and Catholics, will be able to join hands and sing in the words of the old Negro spiritual, "Free at last! free at last! thank God almighty, we are free at last!"

Meaning and Idea

1. Who is the "great American" to whom King refers at the opening of his speech? What was the Emancipation Proclamation?

2. What comparisons does King make between the conditions of blacks in 1863 and 1963? Are these conditions always stated explicitly? What is the point of the comparison?

3. What examples does King offer of the daily conditions of blacks which lead him to the conclusion that satisfaction cannot be achieved "until justice rolls down like waters and righteousness like a mighty stream"? What does he mean by the term *satisfied* in this context?

4. What does King say of the relations between blacks and whites? What are the potential difficulties? What is his suggestion?

Language, Form, Structure

1. For what position is King arguing? Does he ever directly state a thesis for this speech? In a single sentence in your own words, state what his main proposition is. Is King's intention merely to convince the audience of his opinion, or does he also want to persuade them to action? Explain your answer.

2. King uses numerous metaphors in the development of his argument. Which do you find most impressive? Explain the extended metaphor (an *extended metaphor* sustains a figurative comparison through a number of related

images) that begins with the first sentence of paragraph 3: "In a sense we have come to our nation's capital to cash a check."

3. What is the role of repetition in this speech? How does King use repetition to compound his opinions? How does he use it to move his argument forward?

4. One of the most impressive features of this speech is the full range of vision and audience that King demonstrates. How does he cover descriptive, geographic, and social range? How does he make his words appeal to the widest possible audience?

5. Toward the end of the speech, King introduces the litany of "Let freedom ring." Analyze the meaning and use of the transitional phrase, "But not only that," in the middle of that section.

6. Make sure you know the meanings of the following words: manacles; languishing; degenerate; inextricably; wallow; interposition; nullification; exalted; prodigious. Select five for use in your own sentences.

Ideas for Writing

1. Write a speech in which you strongly argue a position and propose a plan for action concerning an important issue at your school. Try to use language as dramatically as possible.

2. Write your opinion of the present conditions of one aspect of black (or any other minority's) life in the country today.

3. As you know, Martin Luther King, Jr., like his father, was a Baptist minister. As such, he grew up on and practiced the art of stirring, emotional oratory. How is the language of this speech influenced by a "preacher style"? Do you feel it is effective as an essay alone, or is it written specifically to be orated? Explain your response.

A Modest Proposal

Jonathan Swift

Jonathan Swift (1667–1745) is rightfully afforded the title "greatest of English satirists." He was born in Dublin, Ireland, and was educated at Trinity College there. Swift was politically as well as literarily productive; originally a liberal Whig, he turned to Tory politics and wrote numerous political pamphlets. Appointed Dean of St. Patrick's Cathedral in Dublin in 1713, he remained at that post until 1736. His private life was secretive and somewhat complex. His *Journals to Stella* are a three-year series of letters to a young woman, Esther Johnson, whom he may or may not have secretly married. His early *Battle of the Books* and *Tale of a Tub* (1704) were satires on contemporary thought and religious excess. *Gulliver's Travels* (1726) and "A Modest Proposal" (1729) revealed the depth of Swift's social and political insights, along with his venomous satirical skills. He began experiencing terrifying bouts with metal illness around 1736, suffered a mental breakdown in 1741, and died four years later.

Next to *Gulliver's Travels,* "A Modest Proposal," written in 1729, is perhaps best known among Jonathan Swift's writings. It was directed at the British ruling class because of their oppressive treatment of the Irish. Clearly full of biting satire, this essay has its very serious side as well, easily discernible through careful reading of Swift's seemingly outlandish argument.

*I*t is a melancholy object to those who walk through this great town   1
or travel in the country, when they see the streets, the roads, and cabin doors, crowded with beggars of the female-sex, followed by three, four, or six children, all in rags and importuning every passenger for an alms. These mothers, instead of being able to work for their honest livelihood, are forced to employ all their time in strolling to beg sustenance for their helpless infants, who, as they grow up, either turn thieves for want of work, or leave their dear native country to fight for the Pretender in Spain, or sell themselves to the Barbadoes.

I think it is agreed by all parties that this prodigious number of children in   2
the arms, or on the backs, or at the heels of their mothers, and frequently of their fathers, is in the present deplorable state of the kingdom a very great additional grievance; and therefore whoever could find out a fair, cheap, and easy method of making these children sound, useful members of the commonwealth would deserve so well of the public as to have his statue set up for a preserver of the nation.

But my intention is very far from being confined to provide only for the chil-   3
dren of professed beggars; it is of a much greater extent, and shall take in the whole number of infants at a certain age who are born of parents in effect as little able to support them as those who demand our charity in the streets.

As to my own part, having turned my thoughts for many years upon this   4
important subject, and maturely weighed the several schemes of other projectors,

I have always found them grossly mistaken in their computation. It is true, a child just dropped from its dam may be supported by her milk for a solar year, with little other nourishment; at most not above the value of two shillings, which the mother may certainly get, or the value in scraps, by her lawful occupation of begging; and it is exactly at one year old that I propose to provide for them in such a manner as instead of being a charge upon their parents or the parish, or wanting food and raiment for the rest of their lives, they shall on the contrary contribute to the feeding, and partly to the clothing, of many thousands.

There is likewise another great advantage in my scheme, that it will prevent those voluntary abortions, and that horrid practice of women murdering their bastard children, alas, too frequent among us, sacrificing the poor innocent babes, I doubt, more to avoid the expense than the shame, which would move tears and pity in the most savage and inhuman breast.

The number of souls in this kingdom being usually reckoned one million and a half, of these I calculate there may be about two hundred thousand couples whose wives are breeders; from which number I subtract thirty thousand couples who are able to maintain their own children, although I apprehend there cannot be so many under the present distresses of the kingdom; but this being granted, there will remain an hundred and seventy thousand breeders. I again subtract fifty thousand for those women who miscarry, or whose children die by accident or disease within the year. There only remain an hundred and twenty thousand children of poor parents annually born. The question therefore is, how this number shall be reared and provided for, which, as I have already said, under the present situation of affairs, is utterly impossible by all the methods hitherto proposed. For we can neither employ them in handicraft or agriculture; we neither build houses (I mean in the country) nor cultivate land. They can very seldom pick up a livelihood by stealing till they arrive at six years old, except where they are of towardly parts; although I confess they learn the rudiments much earlier, during which time they can however be looked upon only as probationers, as I have been informed by a principal gentlemen in the county of Cavan, who protested to me that he never knew above one or two instances under the age of six, even in a part of the kingdom so renowned for the quickest proficiency in that art.

I am assured by our merchants that a boy or girl before twelve years old is no salable commodity; and even when they come to this age they will not yield above three pounds, or three pounds and half a crown at most on the Exchange; which cannot turn to account either to the parents or the kingdom, the charge of nutriment and rags having been at least four times that value.

I shall now therefore humbly propose my own thoughts, which I hope will not be liable to the least objection.

I have been assured by a very knowing American of my acquaintance in London, that a young healthy child well nursed is at a year old a most delicious, nourishing, and wholesome food, whether stewed, roasted, baked or boiled; and I make no doubt that it will equally serve in a fricassee or a ragout.

I do therefore humbly offer it to public consideration that of the hundred and twenty thousand children, already computed, twenty thousand may be reserved for breed, whereof only one fourth part to be males, which is more than we allow to sheep, black cattle, or swine; and my reason is that these children are seldom the fruits of marriage, a circumstance not much regarded by our savages, therefore one male will be sufficient to serve four females. That the remaining hundred thousand may at a year old be offered in sale to the persons of quality and fortune through the kingdom, always advising the mother to let them suck plentifully in the last month, so as to render them plump and fat for a good table. A child will make two dishes at an entertainment for friends; and when the family dines alone, the fore or hind quarter will make a reasonable dish, and seasoned with a little pepper or salt will be very good boiled on the fourth day, especially in winter.

I have reckoned upon a medium that a child just born will weigh twelve 11 pounds, and in a solar year if tolerably nursed increaseth to twenty-eight pounds.

I grant this food will be somewhat dear, and therefore very proper for land- 12 lords, who, as they have already devoured most of the parents, seem to have the best title to the children.

Infant's flesh will be in season throughout the year, but more plentiful in 13 March, and a little before and after. For we are told by a grave author, an eminent French physician, that fish being a prolific diet, there are more children born in Roman Catholic countries about nine months after Lent than at any other season: therefore, reckoning a year after Lent, the markets will be more glutted than usual, because the number of popish infants is at least three to one in this kingdom; and therefore it will have one other collateral advantage, by lessening the number of Papists among us.

I have already computed the charge of nursing a beggar's child (in which list 14 I reckon all cottagers, laborers, and four fifths of the farmers) to be about two shillings per annum, rags included: and I believe no gentleman would repine to give ten shillings for the carcass of a good fat child, which, as I have said, will make four dishes of excellent nutritive meat, when he hath only some particular friend or his own family to dine with him. Thus the squire will learn to be a good landlord, and grow popular among the tenants; the mother will have eight shillings net profit, and be fit for work till she produces another child.

Those who are more thrifty (as I must confess the times require) may flay the 15 carcass; the skin of which artificially dressed will make admirable gloves for ladies, and summer boots for fine gentlemen.

As to our city of Dublin, shambles may be appointed for this purpose in the 16 most convenient parts of it, and butchers we may be assured will not be wanting; although I rather recommend buying the children alive, and dressing them hot from the knife as we do roasting pigs.

A very worthy person, a true lover of his country, and whose virtues I highly 17 esteem, was lately pleased in discoursing on this matter to offer a refinement upon my scheme. He said that many gentlemen of this kingdom, having of late destroyed their deer, he conceived that the want of venison might be well supplied by the bodies of young lads and maidens, not exceeding fourteen years of age nor under twelve, so great a number of both sexes in every county being now ready to starve for want of work and service; and these to be disposed of by their parents, if alive, or otherwise by their nearest relations. But with due deference to so excellent a friend and so deserving a patriot, I cannot be altogether in his sentiments; for as to the males, my American acquaintance assured me from frequent experience that their flesh was generally tough and lean, like that of our schoolboys, by continual exercise, and their taste disagreeable; and to fatten them would not answer the charge. Then as to the females, it would, I think with humble submission, be a loss to the public, because they soon would become breeders themselves: and besides, it is not improbable that some scrupulous people might be apt to censure such a practice (although indeed very unjustly) as a little bordering upon cruelty; which, I confess, hath always been with me the strongest objection against any project, how well soever intended.

But in order to justify my friend, he confessed that this expedient was put into his head by the famous Psalmanazar, a native of the island Formosa, who came from thence to London above twenty years ago, and in conversation told my friend that in his country when any young person happened to be put to death, the executioner sold the carcass to persons of quality as a prime dainty; and that in his time the body of a plump girl of fifteen, who was crucified for an attempt to poison the emperor, was sold to his Imperial Majesty's prime minister of state, and other great mandarins of the court, in joints from the gibbet, at four hundred crowns. Neither indeed can I deny that if the same use were made of several plump young girls in this town, who without one single groat to their fortunes cannot stir abroad without a chair, and appear at the playhouse and assemblies in foreign fineries which they never will pay for, the kingdom would not be the worse. ₁₈

Some persons of a desponding spirit are in great concern about that vast number of poor people who are aged, diseased, or maimed, and I have been desired to employ my thoughts what course may be taken to ease the nation of so grievous an encumbrance. But I am not in the least pain upon that matter, because it is very well known that they are every day dying and rotting by cold and famine, and filth and vermin, as fast as can be reasonably expected. And as to the younger laborers, they are now in almost as hopeful a condition. They cannot get work, and consequently pine away for want of nourishment to a degree that if at any time they are accidentally hired to common labor, they have not strength to perform it; and thus the country and themselves are happily delivered from the evils to come. ₁₉

I have too long digressed, and therefore shall return to my subject. I think the advantages by the proposal which I have made are obvious and many, as well as of the highest importance. ₂₀

For first, as I have already observed, it would greatly lessen the number of Papists, with whom we are yearly overrun, being the principal breeders of the nation as well as our most dangerous enemies; and who stay at home on purpose to deliver the kingdom to the Pretender, hoping to take their advantage by the absence of so many good Protestants, who have chosen rather to leave their country than to stay at home and pay tithes against their conscience to an Episcopal curate. ₂₁

Secondly, the poorer tenants will have something valuable of their own, which by law may be made liable to distress, and help to pay their landlord's rent, their corn and cattle being already seized and money a thing unknown. ₂₂

Thirdly, whereas the maintenance of an hundred thousand children, from two ₂₃ years old and upwards, cannot be computed at less than ten shillings a piece per annum, the nation's stock will be thereby increased fifty thousand pounds per annum, besides the profit of a new dish introduced to the tables of all gentlemen of fortune in the kingdom who have any refinement in taste. And the money will circulate among ourselves, the goods being entirely of our own growth and manufacture.

Fourthly, the constant breeders, besides the gain of eight shillings sterling per ₂₄ annum by the sale of their children, will be rid of the charge of maintaining them after the first year.

Fifthly, this food would likewise bring great custom to taverns, where the ₂₅ vinters will certainly be so prudent as to procure the best receipts for dressing it to perfection, and consequently have their houses frequented by all the fine gentlemen, who justly value themselves upon their knowledge in good eating; and a skillful cook, who understands how to oblige his guests, will contrive to make it as expensive as they please.

Sixthly, this would be a great inducement to marriage, which all wise nations ₂₆ have either encouraged by rewards or enforced by laws and penalties. It would increase the care and tenderness of mothers toward their children, when they were sure of a settlement for life to the poor babes, provided in some sort by the public, to their annual profit instead of expense. We should see an honest emulation among the married women, which of them could bring the fattest child to the market. Men would become as fond of their wives during the time of their pregnancy as they are now of their mares in foal, their cows in calf, or sows when they are ready to farrow; nor offer to beat or kick them (as is too frequent a practice) for fear of a miscarriage.

Many other advantages might be enumerated. For instance, the addition of ₂₇ some thousand carcasses in our exportation of barreled beef, the propagation of swine's flesh, and improvement in the art of making good bacon, so much wanted among us by the great destruction of pigs, too frequent at our tables, which are no way comparable in taste or magnificence to a well-grown, fat yearling child, which roasted whole will make a considerable figure at a lord mayor's feast or any other public entertainment. But this and many others I omit, being studious of brevity.

Supposing that one thousand families in this city would be constant cus- ₂₈ tomers for infants' flesh, besides others who might have it at merry meetings, particularly weddings and christenings, I compute that Dublin would take off annually about twenty thousand carcasses, and the rest of the kingdom (where probably they will be sold somewhat cheaper) the remaining eighty thousand.

I can think of no one objection that will possibly be raised against this pro- ₂₉ posal, unless it should be urged that the number of people will be thereby much lessened in the kingdom. This I freely own, and it was indeed one principal design in offering it to the world. I desire the reader will observe, that I calculate my remedy for this one individual kingdom of Ireland and for no other that ever was, is, or I think ever can be upon earth. Therefore let no man talk to me of other expedients: of taxing our absentees at five shillings a pound: of using neither clothes nor household furniture except what is of our own growth and manufacture: of utterly rejecting the materials and instruments that promote foreign luxury: of curing the expensiveness of pride, vanity, idleness, and gaming in our women: of introducing a vein of parsimony, prudence, and temperance: of learning to love our country, in the want of which we differ even from Laplanders and the inhabitants of Topinamboo: of quitting our animosities and factions, nor acting any longer like the Jews, who were murdering one another at the very moment their city was taken: of being a little cautious not to sell our country and conscience for nothing: of teaching landlords to have at least one degree of mercy toward their tenants: lastly, of putting a spirit of honesty, industry, and skill into our shopkeepers; who, if a resolution could be now taken to buy only our native goods, would immediately unite to cheat and exact upon us in the price, the measure and the goodness, nor could ever yet be brought to make one fair proposal of just dealing, though often and earnestly invited to it.

Therefore I repeat, let no man talk to me of these and the like expedients, till 30 he hath at least some glimpse of hope that there will ever be some hearty and sincere attempt to put them in practice.

But as to myself, having been wearied out for many years with offering vain, 31 idle, visionary thoughts, and at length utterly despairing of success, I fortunately fell upon this proposal, which, as it is wholly new, so it hath something solid and real, of no expense and little trouble, full in our own power, and whereby we can incur no danger in disobliging England. For this kind of commodity will not bear exportation, the flesh being of too tender a consistence to admit a long continuance in salt, although perhaps I could name a country which would be glad to eat up our whole nation without it.

After all, I am not so violently bent upon my own opinion as to reject any offer 32 proposed by wise men, which shall be found equally innocent, cheap, easy, and effectual. But before something of that kind shall be advanced in contradiction to my scheme, and offering a better, I desire the author or authors will be pleased maturely to consider two points. First, as things now stand, how they will be able to find food and raiment for an hundred thousand useless mouths and backs. And secondly, there being a round million of creatures in human figure throughout this kingdom, whose sole subsistence put into a common stock would leave them in debt two millions of pounds sterling, adding those who are beggars by profession to the bulk of farmers, cottagers, and laborers, with their wives and children who are beggars in effect; I desire those politicians who dislike my overture, and may perhaps be so bold to attempt an answer, that they will first ask the parents of these mortals whether they would not at this day think it a great happiness to have been sold for food at a year old in the manner I prescribe, and thereby have avoided such a perpetual scene of misfortunes as they have since gone through by the oppression of landlords, the impossibility of paying rent without money or trade, the want of common sustenance, with neither house nor clothes to cover them from the inclemencies of the weather, and the most inevitable prospect of entailing the like or greater miseries upon their breed forever.

I profess, in the sincerity of my heart, that I have not the least personal inter- [33] est in endeavoring to promote this necessary work, having no other motive than the public good of my country, by advancing our trade, providing for infants, relieving the poor, and giving some pleasure to the rich. I have no children by which I can propose to get a single penny; the youngest being nine years old, and my wife past childbearing.

Meaning and Idea

1. Outline the six advantages Swift discusses as the results of enactment of his proposal. By what principle does he arrange them? What two types of "national profit" does he suggest?

2. How does the next to the last paragraph express Swift's genuine concern for the conditions of his native Ireland? What were some of those conditions?

3. What is the purpose of Swift's disclaimer at the end of the essay?

Language, Form, Structure

1. What is the main *proposition* of Swift's "modest proposal"? What are the *minor propositions?* (A *minor proposition* is a less generalized, though related, statement of opinion that supports the main proposition.)

2. The introduction in this essay spans a good many paragraphs. Identify the scope of the introduction. How does Swift begin establishing a fairly serious tone and purpose for his proposal? Where and how in the introduction does the reader begin to recognize the satire? (*Satire* is a literary form that uses wit, humor, irony, and sarcasm to criticize human behavior.) What satirical elements do you find in this essay?

3. Why does Swift repeatedly use words such as *modest, humbly,* and *sincerity?* Look up the etymology of the word *modest,* and check the *Oxford English Dictionary* for its various range of usages.

4. As in any well-written argumentation, Swift adequately deals with opposing arguments, although he does write: "I can think of no one objection that will possibly be raised against this proposal." What, in fact, is the purpose of his discussion of opposition arguments in this essay? What are some of the most important of these?

5. How does Swift use the "logic" of mathematics in support of his proposal?

6. *Logical fallacies* are errors in logical development of an argument. What major logical fallacies do you discern in Swift's argument? Was he aware of them as well? How do you know?

7. Define the following words from "A Modest Proposal": alms; rudiments; liable; prolific; repine; deference; prudent; contrive; emulation; parsimony; inclemencies.

Ideas for Writing

1. Write a "modest proposal" of your own in which you use satire to argue about an important issue in society today. Make sure to deal with potential opposition arguments.

2. Write an argumentative essay in which you propose specific means by which someone in your immediate family could make your family life better. Make your audience that particular person. Be sure to include some historical background to the present situation, as well as your vision of what future conditions will be if your proposal is adopted.

3. Check an unabridged dictionary or some other source for a complete definition of *satire*. Using the definition, comment upon Swift's use of satire. How is it an effective tool in Swift's argument? Do you feel that satire makes his discussion of the Irish condition more or less effective than, say, a straightforward causal analysis? Do you find the satire in any way detrimental to your understanding of the issue, or do you find it enhances your understanding? Explain with specific references to the text.

Professions for Women

Virginia Woolf

Virginia Woolf was born in London in 1882, a time when women rarely received an education or worked professionally. Without formal training, she went on to become one of the most respected and prolific writers of the twentieth century, and eventually she became an initial, clarion voice of the women's movement.

Woolf was a novelist, an essayist, a short story writer, and a critic, but the following selection was originally a speech delivered in 1931 to the aspiring professionals of a girls' school. She attempts to persuade her listeners that their lot will not be easy and to inform them of some of the "obstacles" they are likely to encounter.

When your secretary invited me to come here, she told me that your 1
Society is concerned with the employment of women and she suggested that I might tell you something about my own professional experiences. It is true I am a woman, it is true I am employed, but what professional experiences have I had? It is difficult to say. My profession is literature; and in that profession there are fewer experiences for women than in any other, with the exception of the stage—fewer, I mean, that are peculiar to women. For the road was cut many years ago—by Fanny Burney, by Aphra Behn, by Harriet Martineau, by Jane Austen, by George Eliot—many famous women, and many more unknown and forgotten, have been before me, making the path smooth, and regulating my steps. Thus, when I came to write, there were very few material obstacles in my way. Writing was a reputable and harmless occupation. The family peace was not broken by the scratching of a pen. No demand was made upon the family purse. For ten and sixpence one can buy paper enough to write all the plays of Shakespeare—if one has a mind that way. Pianos and models, Paris, Vienna and Berlin, masters and mistresses, are not needed by a writer. The cheapness of writing paper is, of course, the reason why women have succeeded as writers before they have succeeded in the other professions.

But to tell you my story—it is a simple one. You have only got to figure to 2
yourselves a girl in a bedroom with a pen in her hand. She had only to move that pen from left to right—from ten o'clock to one. Then it occurred to her to do what is simple and cheap enough after all—to slip a few of those pages into an envelope, fix a penny stamp in the corner, and drop the envelope into the red box at the corner. It was thus that I became a journalist; and my effort was rewarded on the first day of the following month—a very glorious day it was for me—by a letter from an editor containing a cheque for one pound ten shillings and sixpence. But to show you how little I deserve to be called a professional woman, how little I know of the struggles and difficulties of such lives, I have to admit that instead of spending that sum upon bread and butter, rent, shoes and stockings, or butcher's bills, I went out and bought a cat—a beautiful cat, a Persian cat, which very soon involved me in bitter disputes with my neighbours.

What could be easier than to write articles and to buy Persian cats with the ³ profits? But wait a moment. Articles have to be about something. Mine, I seem to remember, was about a novel by a famous man. And while I was writing this review, I discovered that if I were going to review books I should need to do battle with a certain phantom. And the phantom was a woman, and when I came to know her better I called her after the heroine of a famous poem, The Angel in the House. It was she who used to come between me and my paper when I was writing reviews. It was she who bothered me and wasted my time and so tormented me that at last I killed her. You who come of a younger and happier generation may not have heard of her—you may not know what I mean by the Angel in the House. I will describe her as shortly as I can. She was intensely sympathetic. She was immensely charming. She was utterly unselfish. She excelled in the difficult arts of family life. She sacrificed herself daily. If there was chicken, she took the leg; if there was a draught she sat in it—in short she was so constituted that she never had a mind or a wish of her own, but preferred to sympathize always with the minds and wishes of others. Above all—I need not say it—she was pure. Her purity was supposed to be her chief beauty—her blushes, her great grace. In those days—the last of Queen Victoria—every house had its Angel. And when I came to write I encountered her with the very first words. The shadow of her wings fell on my page; I heard the rustling of her skirts in the room. Directly, that is to say, I took my pen in hand to review that novel by a famous man, she slipped behind me and whispered: "My dear, you are a young woman. You are writing about a book that has been written by a man. Be sympathetic; be tender; flatter, deceive; use all the arts and wiles of our sex. Never let anybody guess that you have a mind of your own. Above all, be pure." And she made as if to guide my pen. I now record the one act for which I take some credit to myself, though the credit rightly belongs to some excellent ancestors of mine who left me a certain sum of money—shall we say five hundred pounds a year?—so that it was not necessary for me to depend solely on charm for my living. I turned upon her and caught her by the throat. I did my best to kill her. My excuse, if I were to be had up in a court of law, would be that I acted in self-defense. Had I not killed her she would have killed me. She would have plucked the heart out of my writing. For, as I found, directly I put pen to paper, you cannot review even a novel without having a mind of your own, without expressing what you think to be the truth about human relations, morality, sex. All these questions, according to the Angel in the House, cannot be dealt with freely and openly by women; they must charm, they must conciliate, they must—to put it bluntly—tell lies if they are to succeed. Thus, whenever I felt the shadow of her wings or the radiance of her halo upon my page, I took up the inkpot and flung it at her. She died hard. Her fictitious nature was of great assistance to her. It is far harder to kill a phantom than a reality. She was always creeping back when I thought I had despatched her. Though I flatter myself that I killed her in the end, the struggle was severe, it took much time that had better have been spent upon learning Greek grammar; or in roaming the world in search of adventures. But it was a real experience; it was an experience that was bound to befall all women writers at that time. Killing the Angel in the House was part of the occupation of a woman writer.

But to continue my story. The Angel was dead; what then remained? You may ₄ say that what remained was a simple and common object—a young woman in a bedroom with an inkpot. In other words, now that she had rid herself of falsehood, that young woman had only to be herself. Ah, but what is "herself"? I mean, what is a woman? I assure you, I do not know. I do not believe that you know. I do not believe that anybody can know until she has expressed herself in all the arts and professions open to human skill. That indeed is one of the reasons why I have come here—out of respect for you, who are in process of showing us by your experiments what a woman is, who are in process of providing us, by failures and successes, with that extremely important piece of information.

But to continue the story of my professional experiences. I made one pound ₅ ten and six by my first review; and I bought a Persian cat with the proceeds. Then I grew ambitious. A Persian cat is all very well, I said; but a Persian cat is not enough. I must have a motor car. And it was thus that I became a novelist—for it is a very strange thing that people will give you a motor car if you will tell them a story. It is a still stranger thing that there is nothing so delightful in the world as telling stories. It is far pleasanter than writing reviews of famous novels. And yet, if I am to obey your secretary and tell you my professional experiences as a novelist, I must tell you about a very strange experience that befell me as a novelist. And to understand it you must try first to imagine a novelist's state of mind. I hope I am not giving away professional secrets if I say that a novelist's chief desire is to be as unconscious as possible. He has to induce in himself a state of perpetual lethargy. He wants life to proceed with the utmost quiet and regularity. He wants to see the same faces, to read the same books, to do the same things day after day, month after month, while he is writing, so that nothing may disturb or disquiet the mysterious nosings about, feelings round, darts, dashes and sudden discoveries of that very shy and illusive spirit, the imagination. I suspect that this state is the same both for men and women. Be that as it may, I want you to imagine me writing a novel in a state of trance. I want you to figure to yourselves a girl sitting with a pen in her hand, which for minutes, and indeed for hours, she never dips into the inkpot. The image that comes to my mind when I think of this girl is the image of a fisherman lying sunk in dreams on the verge of a deep lake with a rod held out over the water. She was letting her imagination sweep unchecked round every rock and cranny of the world that lies submerged in the depths of our unconscious being. Now came the experience, the experience that I believe to be far commoner with women writers than with men. The line raced through the girl's fingers. Her imagination had rushed away. It had sought the pools, the depths, the dark places where the largest fish slumber. And then there was a smash. There was an explosion. There was foam and confusion. The imagination had dashed itself against something hard. The girl was roused from her dream. She was indeed in a state of the most acute and difficult distress. To speak without figure she had thought of something, something about the body, about the passions which it was unfitting for her as a woman to say. Men, her reason told her, would be shocked. The consciousness of what men will say of a woman who speaks the truth about her passions had roused her from her artist's state of unconsciousness. She could write no more. The trance was over. Her imagination could work no longer. This I believe to be a very common experience with women writers—they are impeded by the extreme conventionality of the other sex. For though men sensibly allow themselves great freedom in these respects, I doubt that they realize or can control the extreme severity with which they condemn such freedom in women.

These then were two very genuine experiences of my own. These were two 6 of the adventures of my professional life. The first—killing the Angel in the House—I think I solved. She died. But the second, telling the truth about my own experiences as a body, I do not think I solved. I doubt that any woman has solved it yet. The obstacles against her are still immensely powerful—and yet they are very difficult to define. Outwardly, what is simpler than to write books? Outwardly, what obstacles are there for a woman rather than for a man? Inwardly, I think, the case is very different; she has still many ghosts to fight, many prejudices to overcome. Indeed it will be a long time still, I think, before a woman can sit down to write a book without finding a phantom to be slain, a rock to be dashed against. And if this is so in literature, the freest of all professions for women, how is it in the new professions which you are now for the first time entering?

Those are the questions that I should like, had I time, to ask you. And indeed, 7 if I have laid stress upon these professional experiences of mine, it is because I believe that they are, though in different forms, yours also. Even when the path is nominally open—when there is nothing to prevent a woman from being a doctor, a lawyer, a civil servant—there are many phantoms and obstacles, as I believe, looming in her way. To discuss and define them is I think of great value and importance; for thus only can the labour be shared, the difficulties be solved. But besides this, it is necessary also to discuss the ends and the aims for which we are fighting, for which we are doing battle with these formidable obstacles. Those aims cannot be taken for granted; they must be perpetually questioned and examined. The whole position, as I see it—here in this hall surrounded by women practising for the first time in history I know not how many different professions—is one of extraordinary interest and importance. You have won rooms of your own in the house hitherto exclusively owned by men. You are able, though not without great labor and effort, to pay the rent. You are earning your five hundred pounds a year. But this freedom is only a beginning; the room is your own, but it is still bare. It has to be furnished; it has to be decorated; it has to be shared. How are you going to furnish it; how are you going to decorate it? With whom are you going to share it, and upon what terms? These, I think, are questions of the utmost importance and interest. For the first time in history you are able to ask them; for the first time you are able to decide for yourself what the answers should be. Willingly would I stay and discuss those questions and answers—but not tonight. My time is up, and I must cease.

Meaning and Idea

1. How, according to Woolf, did she become a journalist? Why did she become one?

2. To Woolf, what are the two problems women face, the two issues they must fight against? Are the two battles similar? How?

3. Consider Woolf's audience and what the "secretary" has asked her to talk about. Woolf does not deal with being a doctor, a lawyer, or even a writer for much of her speech. Why does she discuss what she discusses? What is her speech actually about?

4. What is Woolf alluding to when she notes "the extreme conventionality of the other sex"? When she discusses the impossibility of telling the truth about her own "experiences as a body," what does she mean?

Language, Form, Structure

1. What is Woolf's thesis? How does the introduction serve this thesis?

2. How does Woolf portray the struggle she has with the Angel? How does the Angel metaphor serve the essay? Find as many descriptions of the Angel as you can. Why does Woolf kill the Angel?

3. What elements of argumentation and persuasion do you identify here? Of what has she convinced her audience?

4. How does Woolf use transitions to create a coherent presentation?

5. Define the following words, and use each in a sentence: reputable; constituted; conciliate; lethargy; illusive; acute; impeded; nominally.

Ideas for Writing

1. Write an argumentative speech about some group you know of that has had to endure injustice.

2. Woolf writes here about women: "They must charm, they must conciliate, they must—to put it bluntly—tell lies if they are to succeed." Does the same judgment hold for women today, do you think? Write an argumentative essay to support or refute this position for the modern woman.

3. Reread Woolf's speech, taking note of her use of imagery and figurative language. Then write an essay in which you explore this use. How effective are the metaphors? How effective is the sensory language? Look again at the image of the Angel, but also at the imagery in the last paragraph.

To His Coy Mistress

Andrew Marvell

Andrew Marvell (1621–1678) is among the best known of the English metaphysical poets. He was a friend and assistant to John Milton, though he was somewhat more diplomatic and tolerant than his mentor. Marvell is best remembered for his biting wit and satire, some of it aimed directly at the Commonwealth, even though he remained a loyal member of Parliament until his death. Among his fine lyrical poetry are "The Garden," "Horatian Ode upon Cromwell's Return from Ireland," "The Nymph Complaining for the Death of her Faun," and "To His Coy Mistress."

Marvell makes an age-old argument the basis of this poem, but he gives it an energy and universality that have earned for him respect and admiration from readers for over three hundred years. As you read "To His Coy Mistress," pay special attention to Marvell's balance of subject, tone, and form in order to derive the full force of his argument.

*H*ad we but world enough, and time,
This coyness, lady, were no crime.
We would sit down, and think which way
To walk, and pass our long love's day.
Thou by the Indian Ganges' side   5
Shouldst rubies find; I by the tide
O Humber would complain. I would
Love you ten years before the Flood,
And you should, if you please, refuse
Till the conversion of the Jews.   10
My vegetable love should grow
Vaster than empires, and more slow;
An hundred years should go to praise
Thine eyes, and on thy forehead gaze;
Two hundred to adore each breast,   15
But thirty thousand to the rest;
An age at least to every part,
And the last age should show your heart.
For, lady, you deserve this state.
Nor would I love at lower rate.   20
        But at my back I always hear
Time's winged chariot hurrying near;
And yonder all before us lie
Deserts of vast eternity.
Thy beauty shall no more be found,   25
Nor, in thy marble vault, shall sound

My echoing song; then worms shall try
That long-preserved virginity,
And your quaint honor turn to dust,
And into ashes all my lust: 30
The grave's a fine and private place,
But none, I think, do there embrace.
        Now therefore, while the youthful hue
Sits on thy skin like morning dew,
And while thy willing soul transpires   35
At every pore with instant fires,
Now let us sport us while we may,
And now, like amorous birds of prey,
Rather at once our time devour
Than languish in his slow-chapped power.   40
Let us roll all our strength and all
Our sweetness up into one ball,
And tear our pleasures with rough strife
Thorough the iron gates of life.
Thus, though we cannot make our sun   45
Stand still, yet we will make him run.

Meaning and Idea

1. Why does the speaker call his mistress *coy?* How is her coyness a "crime" to him?

2. Of what is the speaker attempting to persuade his mistress? Approximately what age is the mistress?

3. How does the speaker use the element of time as a part of his argument?

4. The last two lines of the poem refer to a myth about Zeus, the Greek king of the gods: Zeus made the sun stand still so that his night of lovemaking with Alcmene would last all the longer. With that information, discuss the meaning of the last two lines of this poem.

Language, Form, Structure

1. What is the main point of the poem? Is it a poem about seduction, innocence, love, fleeting time, the mortality of the human race—any or all of these? Explain your answer.

2. Outline the three stages of the speaker's argument in his effort to convince his mistress. What transitions help Marvell connect the various argumentative strands?

3. What two contrasting views of seduction and sexuality does the speaker present? Which does he seem to prefer? Why?

4. Lines 29–32 form the end of the midpart of the speaker's argument. Would you say that his attitude has shifted from one of patience to one of slight sarcasm? Why? What words and phrases indicate his growing impatience? Do you feel he was *ever* really patient with his mistress? Why?

5. Marvell's use of language is extraordinary. Identify the most outstanding examples of original sensory images. Identify as many allusions as possible in the poem, especially in lines 5–20. Of what benefit to the argument are these allusions?

6. Identify and define at least five words that are new to you in this poem.

Ideas for Writing

1. Write an ironic argument in which you attempt to persuade a specific member of the opposite sex to do something. In the beginning of your argument, pay close attention to the other person's point of view, then refute it before proposing your own plan of action.

2. Write a narration of a time when you convinced *yourself* to do something you thought you didn't want to do. Arrange your narration/argumentation chronologically.

3. One critic calls some of the lines in this poem "as fine an example as English poetry can show of wit blended with imagination" and, referring to lines 31–32, says they are "the perfection of tragic whimsical." Write a paper in which you support this assessment of "To His Coy Mistress." Make specific references to the poem.

Dulce et Decorum Est

Wilfred Owen

Wilfred Owen (1893–1918) was among the English "war poets" of World War I, the most notable of whom was Siegfried Sassoon. Owen was born in Oswestry, England, and had a checkered education. He partially rejected Christianity in the midst of studying for the priesthood, then moved to Bordeaux, France. He returned to England in 1915 to enlist in the Manchester Regiment of the British Army. While recuperating in a hospital in Edinburgh, he met Sassoon, who encouraged Owen's poetry writing. Owen was killed a week before the Armistice in 1918, and his poems were published by Sassoon in 1920.

In "Dulce et Decorum Est" a young soldier pleads against the romanticization of war. The poet makes his case all the more convincing by the pointed contrast of his realistic description of a dying fellow soldier against an abstract and distant call to arms. The poem gains power from our knowledge that Owen himself died in that war. *Dulce et decorum est pro patria mori,* a line from Horace, the Roman poet who lived in the first century B.C., means "It is sweet and becoming to die for one's country."

*B*ent double, like old beggars under sacks,
Knock-kneed, coughing like hags, we cursed through sludge,
Till on the haunting flares we turned our backs,
And towards our distant rest began to trudge.
Men marched asleep. Many had lost their boots,   5
But limped on, blood-shod. All went lame, all blind;
Drunk with fatigue; deaf even to the hoots
Of gas-shells dropping softly behind.

Gas! GAS! Quick, boys!—An ecstasy of fumbling,
Fitting the clumsy helmets just in time,   10
But someone still was yelling out and stumbling
And flound'ring like a man in fire or lime.—
Dim through the misty panes and thick green light,
As under a green sea, I saw him drowning.

In all my dreams before my helpless sight   15
He plunges at me, guttering, choking, drowning.

If in some smothering dreams, you too could pace
Behind the wagon that we flung him in,
And watch the white eyes writhing in his face,
His hanging face, like a devil's sick of sin,   20
If you could hear, at every jolt, the blood

Come gargling from the froth-corrupted lungs
Bitter as the cud
Of vile, incurable sores on innocent tongues,—
My friend, you would not tell with such high zest   25
To children ardent for some desperate glory,
The old lie: *Dulce et decorum est*
Pro patria mori.

Meaning and Idea

1. Briefly describe, in your own words, the setting and action of this poem. How is the one soldier's experience different from the others'?

2. What are the "gas shells" and the "Gas!" that Owen writes about? What war do those references clearly place this poem in?

3. How does Owen use the quotation from Horace to establish his own idea? Why does he call Horace's opinion "The old lie"? What attitude does that description express?

4. Explain the double meaning of line 4. What is the "distant rest"?

Language, Form, Structure

1. What would you say is the position Owen is arguing here? Who is being addressed in this poem? What clue does the "you" of line 17 provide? Is the intended audience fighting in the war as the narrator is? How are the narrator and the audience linked by dreams in this poem?

2. Given the narrative context of the poem, does *ecstasy* seem like a strange word choice in line 9? Why? Why does Owen use that word?

3. What descriptive details are most powerful in making Owen's argument? Comment on Owen's use of similes in this poem. Identify each. How do they enhance the description of "Dulce et Decorum Est"?

4. Explain Owen's use of the following descriptions: blood-shod (line 6); helpless sight (line 15); desperate glory (line 26).

5. Make sure you know the meanings of the following words: hags; sludge; guttering; cud; vile; ardent.

Ideas for Writing

1. Write an essay in which you express your opinion of a current U.S. military involvement. Limit your argument to a specific part of the world rather than attempting to deal with U.S. military involvement generally. Try to make your argument as personalized as possible.

2. Write your own argumentation in response to the quotation from Horace.

3. Owen was only 25 years old when he died for his country. Referring to the language and style of this poem, do you think that Owen would have felt that his death was "sweet and becoming"? Does it seem possible, based on your interpretation of this poem, that Owen could have these antiwar sentiments yet still be proud of his fate? Explain your answer.

Myself in India

Ruth Prawer Jhabvala

Ruth Prawer Jhabvala was born in Cologne, Germany in 1927, emigrated to in England, later married an Indian architect, and moved to India, where she lived for many years. She won the Booker prize in 1975 for her novel *Heat and Dust* and wrote the screenplay adaptation for the film version. Her most consistent work in recent years has been on screenplays. She won the Academy Award for Best Adaptation for *Howard's End* in 1992.

In this essay she reveals her thoughts on living in India as a Westerner.

I have lived in India for most of my adult life. My husband is Indian 1 and so are my children. I am not, and less so every year.

India reacts very strongly on people. Some loathe it, some love it, most do 2 both. There is a special problem of adjustment for the sort of people who come today, who tend to be liberal in outlook and have been educated to be sensitive and receptive to other cultures. But it is not always easy to be sensitive and receptive to India: there comes a point where you have to close up in order to protect yourself. The place is very strong and often proves too strong for European nerves. There is a cycle that Europeans—by Europeans I mean all Westerners, including Americans—tend to pass through. It goes like this: first stage, tremendous enthusiasm—everything Indian is marvellous; second stage, everything Indian not so marvellous; third stage, everything Indian abominable. For some people it ends there, for others the cycle renews itself and goes on. I have been through it so many times that now I think of myself as strapped to a wheel that goes round and round and sometimes I'm up and sometimes I'm down. When I meet other Europeans, I can usually tell after a few moments conversation at what stage of the cycle they happen to be. Everyone likes to talk about India, whether they happen to be loving or loathing it. It is a topic on which a lot of things can be said, and on a variety of aspects—social, economic, political, philosophical: it makes fascinating viewing from every side.

However, I must admit that I am no longer interested in India. What I am 3 interested in now is myself in India—which sometimes, in moments of despondency, I tend to think of as my survival in India. I had better say straightaway that the reason why I live in India is because my strongest human ties are here. If I hadn't married an Indian, I don't think I would ever have come here for I am not attracted—or used not to be attracted—to the things that usually bring people to India. I know I am the wrong type of person to live here. To stay and endure, one should have a mission and a cause, to be patient, cheerful, unselfish, strong. I am a central European with an English education and a deplorable tendency to constant self-analysis. I am irritable and have weak nerves.

The most salient fact about India is that it is very poor and very backward. 4 There are so many other things to be said about it but this must remain the basis of all of them. We may praise Indian democracy, go into raptures over Indian music, admire Indian intellectuals—but whatever we say, not for one moment should we lose sight of the fact that a very great number of Indians never get enough to eat. Literally that: from birth to death they never for one day cease to suffer from hunger. *Can* one lose sight of that fact? God knows, I've tried. But after seeing what one has to see here every day, it is not really possible to go on living one's life the way one is used to. People dying of starvation in the streets, children kidnapped and maimed to be sent out as beggars—but there is no point in making a catalogue of the horrors with which one lives, *on* which one lives, as on the back of an animal. Obviously, there has to be some adjustment.

There are several ways. The first and best is to be a strong person who plunges in and does what he can as a doctor or social worker. I often think that perhaps this is the only condition under which Europeans have any right to be here. I know several people like that. They are usually attached to some mission. They work very hard and stay very cheerful. Every few years they are sent on home leave. Once I met such a person—a woman doctor—who had just returned from her first home leave after being out here for twelve years. I asked her: but what does it feel like to go back after such a long time? How do you manage to adapt yourself? She didn't understand. This question which was of such tremendous import to me—how to adapt oneself to the differences between Europe and India—didn't mean a thing to her. It simply didn't matter. And she was right, for in view of the things she sees and does every day, the delicate nuances of one's own sensibilities are best forgotten.

Another approach to India's basic conditions is to accept them. This seems to be the approach favoured by most Indians. Perhaps it has something to do with their belief in reincarnation. If things are not to your liking in this life, there is always the chance that in your next life everything will be different. It appears to be a consoling thought for both rich and poor. The rich man stuffing himself on pilao can do so with an easy conscience because he knows he has earned this privilege by his good conduct in previous lives; and the poor man can watch him with some degree of equanimity for he knows that next time round it may well be *he* who will be digging into that pilao while the other will be crouching outside the door with an empty stomach. However, this path of acceptance is not open to you if you don't have a belief in reincarnation ingrained within you. And if you don't accept, then what can you do? Sometimes one wants just to run away and go to a place where everyone has enough to eat and clothes to wear and a home fit to live in. But even when you get there, can you ever forget? Having once seen the sights in India, and the way it has been ordained that people must live out their lives, nowhere in the world can ever be all that good to be in again.

None of this is what I wanted to say. I wanted to concentrate only on myself in India. But I could not do so before indicating the basis on which everyone who comes here has to live. I have a nice house, I do my best to live in an agreeable way. I shut all my windows, I let down the blinds, I turn on the airconditioner; I read a lot of books, with a special preference for the great masters of the novel. All the time I know myself to be on the back of this great animal of poverty and backwardness. It is not possible to pretend otherwise. Or rather, one does pretend, but retribution follows. Even if one never rolls up the blinds and never turns off the airconditioner, something is bound to go wrong. People are not meant to shut themselves up in rooms and pretend there is nothing outside.

Now I think I am drawing nearer to what I want to be my subject. Yes, something is wrong: I am not happy this way. I feel lonely, shut in, shut off. It is my own fault. I should go out more and meet people and learn what is going on. All right, so I am not a doctor nor a social worker nor a saint nor at all a good person; then the only thing to do is to try and push that aspect of India out of sight and turn to others. There are many others. I live in the capital where so much is going on. The winter is one round of parties, art exhibitions, plays, music and dance recitals, visiting European artistes: there need never be a dull moment. Yet all my moments are dull. Why? It is my own fault, I know. I can't quite explain it to myself but somehow I have no heart for these things here. Is it because all the time underneath I feel the animal moving? But I have decided to ignore the animal. I wish to concentrate only on modern, Westernised India, and on modern, well-off, cultured Westernised Indians. 8

Let me try and describe a Westernised Indian woman with whom I ought to have a lot in common and whose company I ought to enjoy. She has been to Oxford or Cambridge or some smart American college. She speaks flawless, easy, colloquial English with a charming lilt of an accent. She has a degree in economics or political science or English literature. She comes from a good family. Her father may have been an I.C.S.[1] officer or some other high-ranking government official; he too was at Oxford or Cambridge, and he and her mother travelled in Europe in pre-war days. They have always lived a Western-style life, with Western food and an admiration for Western culture. The daughter now tends rather to frown on this. She feels one should be more deeply Indian, and with this end in view, she wears handloom saris and traditional jewellery and has painted an abnormally large vermilion mark on her forehead. She is interested in Indian classical music and dance. If she is rich enough—she may have married into one of the big Indian business houses—she will become a patroness of the arts and hold delicious parties on her lawn on summer nights. All her friends are there— and she has so many, both Indian and European, all interesting people—and trays of iced drinks are carried round by servants in uniform and there is intelligent conversation and then there is a superbly arranged buffet supper and more intelligent conversation, and then the crown of the evening: a famous Indian maestro performing on the sitar. The guests recline on carpets and cushions on the lawn. The sky sparkles with stars and the languid summer air is fragrant with jasmine. There are many pretty girls reclining against bolsters; their faces are melancholy for the music is stirring their hearts, and sometimes they sigh with yearning and happiness and look down at their pretty toes (adorned with a tiny silver toe-ring) peeping out from under the sari. Here is Indian life and culture at its highest and 9

[1]Indian Civil Service

best. Yet, with all that, it need not be thought that our hostess has forgotten her Western education. Not at all. In her one may see the best of East and West combined. She is interested in a great variety of topics and can hold her own in any discussion. She loves to exercise her emancipated mind, and whatever the subject of conversation—economics, or politics, or literature, or film—she has a well-formulated opinion on it and knows how to express herself. How lucky for me if I could have such a person for a friend! What enjoyable, lively times we two could have together!

In fact, my teeth are set on edge if I have to listen to her for more than five 10 minutes—yes, even though everything she says is so true and in line with the most advanced opinions of today. But when she says it, somehow, even though I know the words to be true, they ring completely false. It is merely lips moving and sounds coming out: it doesn't mean anything, nothing of what she says (though she says it with such conviction, skill, and charm) is of the least importance to her. She is only making conversation in the way she knows educated women have to make conversation. And so it is with all of them. Everything they say, all that lively conversation round the buffet table, is not prompted by anything they really feel strongly about but by what they think they ought to feel strongly about. This applies not only to subjects which are naturally alien to them—for instance, when they talk oh so solemnly! and with such profound intelligence! of Godard[2] and Becket and ecology—but when they talk about themselves too. They know Modern India to be an important subject and they have a lot to say about it: but though they themselves *are* Modern India, they don't look at themselves, they are not conditioned to look at themselves except with the eyes of foreign experts whom they have been taught to respect. And while they are fully aware of India's problems and are up on all the statistics and all the arguments for and against nationalization and a socialistic pattern of society, all the time it is as if they were talking about some *other* place—as if it were a subject for debate—an abstract subject—and not a live animal actually moving under their feet.

But if I have no taste for the company of these Westernised Indians, then 11 what else is there? Other Indians don't really have a social life, not in our terms; the whole conception of such a life is imported. It is true that Indians are gregarious in so far as they hate to be alone and always like to sit together in groups; but these groups are clan-units—it is the family, or clan-members, who gather together and enjoy each other's company. And again, their conception of enjoying each other's company is different from ours. For them it is enough just to *be* together; there are long stretches of silence in which everyone stares into space. From time to time there is a little spurt of conversation, usually on some commonplace everyday subject such as rising prices, a forthcoming marriage, or a troublesome neighbor. There is no attempt at exercising the mind or testing one's wits against those of others: the pleasure lies only in having other familiar people around and enjoying the air together and looking forward to the next meal. There

---

[2]The film director Jean-Luc Godard.

is actually something very restful about this mode of social intercourse and it certainly holds more pleasure than the synthetic social life led by Westernised Indians. It is also more adapted to the Indian climate which invites one to be absolutely relaxed in mind and body, to do nothing, to think nothing, just to feel, to *be.* I have in fact enjoyed sitting around like that for hours on end. But there is something in me that after some time revolts against such lassitude. I can't just *be!* Suddenly I jump up and rush away out of that contented circle. I want to do something terribly difficult like climbing a mountain or reading the *Critique of Pure Reason.*[3] I feel tempted to bang my head against the wall as if to wake myself up. Anything to prevent myself from being sucked down into that bog of passive, intuitive being. I feel I cannot, I must not allow myself to live this way.

Of course there are other Europeans more or less in the same situation as 12
myself. For instance, other women married to Indians. But I hesitate to seek them out. People suffering from the same disease do not usually make good company for one another. Who is to listen to whose complaints? On the other hand, with what enthusiasm I welcome visitors from abroad. Their physical presence alone is a pleasure to me. I love to see their fresh complexions, their red cheeks that speak of wind and rain; and I like to see their clothes and their shoes, to admire the texture of these solid European materials and the industrial skills that have gone into making them. I also like to hear the way in which these people speak. In some strange way their accents, their intonations are redolent to me of the places from which they have come, so that as voices rise and fall I hear in them the wind stirring in English trees or a mild brook murmuring through a summer wood. And apart from these sensuous pleasures, there is also the pleasure of hearing what they have to say. I listen avidly to what is said about people I know or have heard of and about new plays and restaurants and changes and fashions. However, neither the subject nor my interest in it is inexhaustible; and after that, it is my turn. What about India? Now they want to hear, but I don't want to say. I feel myself growing sullen. I don't want to talk about India. There is nothing I can tell them. There is nothing they would understand. However, I do begin to talk, and after a time even to talk with passion. But everything I say is wrong. I listen to myself with horror; they too listen with horror. I want to stop and reverse, but I can't. I want to cry out, this is not what I mean! You are listening to me in entirely the wrong context! But there is no way of explaining the context. It would take too long, and anyway what is the point? It's such a small personal thing. I fall silent. I have nothing more to say. I turn my face and want them to go away.

So I am back again alone in my room with the blinds drawn and the aircon- 13
ditioner on. Sometimes, when I think of my life, it seems to have contracted to this one point and to be concentrated in this one room, and it is always a very hot, very long afternoon when the airconditioner has failed. I cannot describe the *oppression* of such afternoons. It is a physical oppression—heat pressing down on me and pressing in the walls and the ceiling and congealing together with time which has stood still and will never move again. And it is not only those two—

[3]Work of Immanuel Kant, the eighteenth-century philosopher.

heat and time—that are laying their weight on me but behind them, or held within them, there is something more which I can only describe as the whole of India. This is hyperbole, but I need hyperbole to express my feelings about those countless afternoons spent over what now seem to me countless years in a country for which I was not born. India swallows me up and now it seems to me that I am no longer in my room but in the white-hot city streets under a white-hot sky; people cannot live in such heat so everything is deserted—no, not quite, for here comes a smiling leper in a cart being pushed by another leper; there is also the carcase of a dog and vultures have swooped down on it. The river has dried up and stretches in miles of flat cracked earth; it is not possible to make out where the river ceases and the land begins for this too is as flat, as cracked, as dry as the river-bed and stretches on for ever. Until we come to a jungle in which wild beasts live, and then there are ravines and here live outlaws with the hearts of wild beasts. Sometimes they make raids into the villages and they rob and burn and mutilate and kill for sport. More mountains and these are very, very high and now it is no longer hot but terribly cold, we are in snow and ice and here is Mount Kailash on which sits Siva the Destroyer wearing a necklace of human skulls. Down in the plains they are worshipping him. I can see them from here—they are doing something strange—what is it? I draw nearer. Now I can see. They are killing a boy. They hack him to pieces and now they bury the pieces into the foundations dug for a new bridge. There is a priest with them who is quite naked except for ash smeared all over him; he is reciting some holy verses over the foundations, to bless and propitiate.

I am using these exaggerated images in order to give some idea of how intolerable India—the idea, the sensation of it—can become. A point is reached where one must escape, and if one can't do so physically, then some other way must be found. And I think it is not only Europeans but Indians too who feel themselves compelled to seek refuge from their often unbearable environment. Here perhaps less than anywhere else is it possible to believe that this world, this life, is all there is for us, and the temptation to write it off and substitute something more satisfying becomes overwhelming. This brings up the question whether religion is such a potent force in India because life is so terrible, or is it the other way round—is life so terrible because, with the eyes of the spirit turned elsewhere, there is no incentive to improve its quality? Whichever it is, the fact remains that the eyes of the spirit *are* turned elsewhere, and it really is true that God seems more present in India than in other places. Every morning I wake up at 3 A.M. to the sound of someone pouring out his spirit in devotional song; and then at dawn the temple bells ring, and again at dusk, and conch-shells are blown, and there is the smell of incense and of the slightly overblown flowers that are placed at the feet of smiling, pink-cheeked idols. I read in the papers that the Lord Krishna has been reborn as the son of a weaver woman in a village somewhere in Madhya Pradesh. On the banks of the river there are figures in meditation and one of them may turn out to be the teller in your bank who cashed your cheque just a few days ago; now he is in the lotus pose and his eyes are turned up and he is in ecstasy. There are ashrams full of little old half-starved widows who skip and dance about, they giggle and play hide and seek because they are Krishna's milkmaids. And over all this there is a sky of enormous proportions—so much larger than the earth on which you live, and often so incredibly beautiful, an unflawed unearthly blue by day, all shining with stars at night, that it is difficult to believe that something grand and wonderful beyond the bounds of human comprehension does not emanate from there.

I love listening to Indian devotional songs. They seem pure like water drawn 15 from a well; and the emotions they express are both beautiful and easy to understand because the imagery employed is so human. The soul crying out for God is always shown as the beloved yearning for the lover in an easily recognisable way ('I wait for Him. Do you hear His step? He has come'). I feel soothed when I hear such songs and all my discontentment falls away. I see that everything I have been fretting about is of no importance at all because all that matters is this promise of eternal bliss in the Lover's arms. I become patient and good and feel that everything is good. Unfortunately this tranquil state does not last for long, and after a time it again seems to me that nothing is good and neither am I. Once somebody said to me: 'Just see, how sweet is the Indian soul that can see God in a cow!' But when I try to assume this sweetness, it turns sour: for, however much I may try and fool myself, whatever veils I may try, for the sake of peace of mind, to draw over my eyes, it is soon enough clear to me that the cow *is* a cow, and a very scrawny, underfed, diseased one at that. And then I feel that I want to keep this knowledge, however painful it is, and not exchange it for some other that may be true for an Indian but can never quite become that for me.

And here, it seems to me, I come to the heart of my problem. To live in India 16 and be at peace one must to a very considerable extent become Indian and adopt Indian attitudes, habits, beliefs, assume if possible an Indian personality. But how is this possible? And ever if it were possible—without cheating oneself—would it be desirable? Should one want to try and become something other than what one is? I don't always say no to this question. Sometimes it seems to me how pleasant it would be to say yes and give in and wear a sari and be meek and accepting and see God in a cow. Other times it seems worth while to be defiant and European and—all right, be crushed by one's environment, but all the same have made some attempt to remain standing. Of course, this can't go on indefinitely and in the end I'm bound to lose—if only at the point where my ashes are immersed in the Ganges to the accompaniment of Vedic hymns, and then who will say that I have not truly merged with India?

I do sometimes go back to Europe. But after a time I get bored there and want 17 to come back here. I also find it hard now to stand the European climate. I have got used to intense heat and seem to need it.

Meaning and Idea

1. What does Jhabvala mean when she says she is more interested in talking about herself in India than in talking about India? In paragraph 7, she notes that she could not write about herself in India before she explained something about what every newcomer to India experiences. What does she mean?

2. Do you agree with Jhabvala that "people suffering the same disease do not usually make good company for one another"? Why is or why isn't this so?

3. Why are the afternoons she mentions always long, and why is there always an oppressive heat and the air conditioner broken?

4. In paragraph 16, Jhabvala says, "To live in India and be at peace one must . . . become Indian." But how does she feel about this process? Has she become Indian? Can she? Does she want to? She admits to sometimes having the desire. Why?

Language, Form, Structure

1. What is the thesis of this essay? Where does Jhabvala come closest to stating it directly in the piece?

2. Identify the stages Jhabvala notes that Westerners who live in India pass through. Now, go through the essay to see whether she covers each one as she writes. Now examine the essay in the same way regarding the characteristics she says a person transplanted to India must have. Why does she give these lists and why or how does she follow or not follow them?

3. Jhabvala talks about the need to use hyperbole (exaggeration) in order to discuss "the whole of India." How well does she use exaggeration in this essay? Why does she use it?

4. How do the first two paragraphs serve as an effective introduction to the essay? Has the writer engaged you in her topic so that you want read on? How?

5. In what sense is this essay an argument? How does Jhabvala convince you of her position? What appeals to logic and reason does she provide?

6. Define the following words and use each in a sentence: despondency; salient; maimed; nuances; retribution; maestro; sitar; bolsters; gregarious; lassitude; redolent; sullen; congealing; hyperbole; propitiate; ashrams; emanate.

Ideas for Writing

1. Write an essay about a change in lifestyle that you or someone you know has experienced, and argue for or against one or the other aspect of that change. You might write about moving to a new country, about the difference between high school and college, or about the difference between living in a two-parent and a single-parent home.

2. Write an essay about world hunger or hunger in America, and argue for or against measures a society can take to end hunger.

3. Jhabvala identifies several ways to adjust to "the horrors with which one lives." Write an argumentative essay to detail the "horrors" you live with and how Jhabvala's methods of adjustment might or might not work for you.

Claiming an Education

Adrienne Rich

Adrienne Rich was born in 1929 in Baltimore. She graduated from Radcliffe College in 1951, the same year W. H. Auden chose her volume of poems, *A Change of World,* for the prestigious Yale Younger Poet series. Rich's later poetry concentrates quite a bit on feminist issues. *Diving into the Wreck* (1973) won the 1974 National Book Award, and *Of Woman Born: Motherhood as Experience and Institution* (1976) is a fascinating prose study of motherhood. The volume of poetry *The Dream of Common Language* (1978) delves into Rich's other major theme, the need for communication. In 1981, she published the volume of poems *A Wild Patience Has Taken Me This Far.*

Adrienne Rich delivered this speech to entering students at Douglass College, New Jersey, in 1977. The speech argues about the unfairness in our treatment of women in American higher education. More generally, the speech is about the intellectual subjugation of women and thus becomes her part of "our shared commitment toward . . . the inborn potentialities of so many women's minds."

*F*or this convocation, I planned to separate my remarks into two parts: some thoughts about you, the women students here, and some thoughts about us who teach in a women's college. But ultimately, those two parts are indivisible. If university education means anything beyond the processing of human beings into expected roles, through credit hours, tests, and grades (and I believe that in a women's college especially it *might* mean much more), it implies an ethical and intellectual contract between teacher and student. This contract must remain intuitive, dynamic, unwritten, but we must turn to it again and again if learning is to be reclaimed from the depersonalizing and cheapening pressures of the present-day academic scene. 1

The first thing I want to say to you who are students, is that you cannot afford to think of being here to *receive* an education, you will do much better to think of yourselves as being here to *claim* one. One of the dictionary definitions of the verb "to claim" is: *to take as the rightful owner, to assert in the face of possible contradiction.* "To receive" is *to come into possession of; to act as receptacle or container for; to accept as authoritative or true.* The difference is that between acting and being acted-upon, and for women it can literally mean the difference between life and death. 2

One of the devastating weaknesses of university learning, of the store of knowledge and opinion that has been handed down through academic training, has been its almost total erasure of women's experience and thought from the curriculum, and its exclusion of women as members of the academic community. Today, with increasing numbers of women students in nearly every branch of higher learning, we still see very few women in the upper levels of faculty and administration in most institutions. Douglass College itself is a women's college 3 in a university administered overwhelmingly by men, who in turn are answerable to the state legislature, again composed predominantly of men. But the most significant fact for you is that what you learn here, the very texts you read, the lectures you hear, the way your studies are divided into categories and fragmented one from the other—all this reflects, to a very large degree, neither objective reality, nor an accurate picture of the past, nor a group of rigorously tested observations about human behavior. What you can learn here (and I mean not only at Douglass but any college in any university) is how *men* have perceived and organized their experience, their history, their ideas of social relationships, good and evil, sickness and health, etc. When you read or hear about "great issues," "major texts," "the mainstream of Western thought," you are hearing about what men, above all white men, in their male subjectivity, have decided is important.

Black and other minority peoples have for some time recognized that their   4
racial and ethnic experience was not accounted for in the studies broadly labeled human; and that even the sciences can be racist. For many reasons, it has been more difficult for women to comprehend our exclusion, and to realize that even the sciences can be sexist. For one thing, it is only within the last hundred years that higher education has grudgingly been opened up to women at all, even to white, middle-class women. And many of us have found ourselves poring eagerly over books with titles like: *The Descent of Man; Man and His Symbols; Irrational Man; The Phenomenon of Man; The Future of Man; Man and the Machine; From Man to Man; May Man Prevail?; Man, Science and Society;* or *One-Dimensional Man*—books pretending to describe a "human" reality that does not include over one-half the human species.

Less than a decade ago, with the rebirth of a feminist movement in this coun-   5
try, women students and teachers in a number of universities began to demand and set up women's studies courses—to *claim* a woman-directed education. And, despite the inevitable accusations of "unscholarly," "group therapy," "faddism," etc., despite backlash and budget cuts, women's studies are still growing, offering to more and more women a new intellectual grasp on their lives, new understanding of our history, a fresh vision of the human experience, and also a critical basis for evaluating what they hear and read in other courses, and in the society at large.

But my talk is not really about women's studies, much as I believe in their   6
scholarly, scientific, and human necessity. While I think that any Douglass student has everything to gain by investigating and enrolling in women's studies courses, I want to suggest that there is a more essential experience that you owe yourselves, one which courses in women's studies can greatly enrich, but which finally depends on you, in all your interactions with yourself and your world. This is the experience of *taking responsibility toward yourselves.* Our upbringing as women has so often told us that this should come second to our relationships and responsibilities to other people. We have been offered ethical models of the self-denying wife and mother; intellectual models of the brilliant but slapdash dilettante who never commits herself to anything the whole way, or the intelligent woman who denies her intelligence in order to seem more "feminine," or who sits

in passive silence even when she disagrees inwardly with everything that is being said around her.

Responsibility to yourself means refusing to let others do your thinking, talk- 7 ing, and naming for you; it means learning to respect and use your own brains and instincts; hence, grappling with hard work. It means that you do not treat your body as a commodity with which to purchase superficial intimacy or economic security; for our bodies and minds are inseparable in this life, and when we allow our bodies to be treated as objects, our minds are in mortal danger. It means insisting that those to whom you give your friendship and love are able to respect your mind. It means being able to say, with Charlotte Brontë's *Jane Eyre:* "I have an inward treasure born with me, which can keep me alive if all the extraneous delights should be withheld or offered only at a price I cannot afford to give."

Responsibility to yourself means that you don't fall for shallow and easy 8 solutions—predigested books and ideas, weekend encounters guaranteed to change your life, taking "gut" courses instead of ones you know will challenge you, bluffing at school and life instead of doing solid work, marrying early as an escape from real decisions, getting pregnant as an evasion of already existing problems. It means that you refuse to sell your talents and aspirations short, simply to avoid conflict and confrontation. And this, in turn, means resisting the forces in society which say that women should be nice, play safe, have low professional expectations, drown in love and forget about work, live through others, and stay in the places assigned to us. It means that we insist on a life of meaningful work, insist that work be as meaningful as love and friendship in our lives. It means, therefore, the courage to be "different"; not to be continuously available to others when we need time for ourselves and our work; to be able to demand of others— parents, friends, roommates, teachers, lovers, husbands, children—that they respect our sense of purpose and our integrity as persons. Women everywhere are finding the courage to do this, more and more, and we are finding that courage both in our study of women in the past who possessed it, and in each other as we look to other women for comradeship, community, and challenge. The difference between a life lived actively, and a life of passive drifting and dispersal of energies, is an immense difference. Once we begin to feel committed to our lives, responsible to ourselves, we can never again be satisfied with the old, passive way.

Now comes the second part of the contract. I believe that in a women's col- 9 lege you have the right to expect your faculty to take you seriously. The education of women has been a matter of debate for centuries, and old, negative attitudes about women's role, women's ability to think and take leadership, are still rife both in and outside the university. Many male professors (and I don't mean only at Douglass) still feel that teaching in a women's college is a second-rate career. Many tend to eroticize their women students—to treat them as sexual objects—instead of demanding the best of their minds. (At Yale a legal suit [*Alexander v. Yale*] has been brought against the university by a group of women students demanding a stated policy against sexual advances toward female students by male professors.) Many teachers, both men and women, trained in the male-centered tradition, are still handing the ideas and texts of that tradition on to students without teaching them to criticize its antiwoman attitudes, its omission of women as part of the species. Too often, all of us fail to teach the most important thing, which is that clear thinking, active discussion, and excellent writing are all necessary for intellectual freedom, and that these require *hard work.* Sometimes, perhaps in discouragement with a culture which is both anti-intellectual and antiwoman, we may resign ourselves to low expectations for our students before we have given them half a chance to become more thoughtful, expressive human beings. We need to take to heart the words of Elizabeth Barrett Browning, a poet, a thinking woman, and a feminist, who wrote in 1845 of her impatience with studies which cultivate a "passive recipiency" in the mind, and asserted that "women want to be made to *think actively:* their apprehension is quicker than that of men, but their defect lies for the most part in the logical faculty and in the higher mental activities." Note that she implies a defect which can be remedied by intellectual training; *not* an inborn lack of ability.

I have said that the contract on the student's part involves that you demand to   10
be taken seriously so that you can also go on taking yourself seriously. This means seeking out criticism, recognizing that the most affirming thing anyone can do for you is demand that you push yourself further, show you the range of what you *can* do. It means rejecting attitudes of "take-it-easy," "why-be-so-serious," "why-worry-you'll-probably-get-married-anyway." It means assuming your share of responsibility for what happens in the classroom, because that affects the quality of your daily life here. It means that the student sees herself engaged *with* her teachers in an active, ongoing struggle for a real education. But for her to do this, her teachers must be committed to the belief that women's minds and experience are intrinsically valuable and indispensable to any civilization worthy the name; that there is no more exhilarating and intellectually fertile place in the academic world today than a women's college—*if* both students and teachers in large enough numbers are trying to fulfill this contract. The contract is really a pledge of mutual seriousness about women, about language, ideas, methods, and values. It is our shared commitment toward a world in which the inborn potentialities of so many women's minds will no longer be wasted, raveled-away, paralyzed, or denied.

Meaning and Idea

1. What is the occasion for Rich's speech? Where is she?

2. What is the "contract" that Rich proposes? What is the nature of that contract? What does she set forth in the very beginning as the potential benefits of fulfilling that contract?

3. State in your own words Rich's main proposition in this essay. Identify any *minor propositions* as well.

4. In this speech, what does Rich state or imply about the relation between men and women generally? Specifically, what does she say about that relation as it concerns higher education? As it concerns the shaping of history?

Language, Form, Structure

1. How does Rich announce that she will organize her speech? What does she indicate is the relation between the different parts of that organization? How well does she balance her discussion of the parts?

2. What, according to Rich, is the difference between *receiving* and *claiming* an education? How does she use lexical (dictionary) definition to support her own definitions? How does she use definition as a way to express opinion? Where else in the essay does she use definition as the basis for opinion?

3. Trace the way in which Rich refines her interpretation of the expression "taking responsibility toward yourselves." How does that refining process form a core for the argumentation in this essay?

4. What literary allusions does Rich use in this speech? What is their significance?

5. In many arguments, writers will combine both emotional and logical appeals to the reader. Where does Rich use logical appeal most effectively? Where does she use emotional appeal?

6. Check the definitions of the following words: poring; slapdash; dilettante; commodity; superficial; extraneous; dispersal; rife; intrinsically; raveled.

Ideas for Writing

1. Write an essay in which you argue for the necessity of a fresh approach to some aspect of the education you are receiving—or claiming. Give the background to the present situation as well as suggestions for improvements.

2. Write an argument concerning the portrayal of women in a film you have seen recently. Perhaps you have seen a 1950s film on television that can help you develop a thesis. What attitudes about women were expressed in the film? Would you categorize them as sexist or not? Did they confirm or deny any expectations you may have had about the film?

3. Clearly, Rich takes a feminist approach in this essay. First, develop for yourself (with lexical aids) a working definition of the adjective *feminist*. Then, read through Rich's essay once again and try to discern where specific word choice or logical connections can be termed *feminist*.

   Write a short essay in which you argue about the appropriateness of the word choice to the subject of Rich's essay.

The Judgment

Franz Kafka

Born in Prague in 1883, Franz Kafka posthumously became one of the most respected writers of this century. His works are steeped in the anxiety, alienation, and indifference of the modern world, especially as they pertain to the relation between the individual and society. The author himself lived in the shadow of a strong-willed, patriarchal father, and the social structure of family did not escape Kafka's eye.

He considered "The Judgment" (1913) an important story in his own work, though he saw few of his many, highly respected works published during his own lifetime. He died of tuberculosis at the age of 41.

*I*t was a Sunday morning in the very height of spring. Georg Bende-   1
mann, a young merchant, was sitting in his own room on the first floor of one of a long row of small, ramshackle houses stretching beside the river which were scarcely distinguishable from each other except in height and coloring. He had just finished a letter to an old friend of his who was now living abroad, had put it into its envelope in a slow and dreamy fashion, and with his elbows propped on the writing table was gazing out of the window at the river, the bridge and the hills on the farther bank with their tender green.

He was thinking about his friend, who had actually run away to Russia some   2
years before, being dissatisfied with his prospects at home. Now he was carrying on a business in St. Petersburg, which had flourished to begin with but had long been going downhill, as he always complained on his increasingly rare visits. So he was wearing himself out to no purpose in a foreign country, the unfamiliar full beard he wore did not quite conceal the face Georg had known so well since childhood, and his skin was growing so yellow as to indicate some latent disease. By his own account he had no regular connection with the colony of his fellow countrymen out there and almost no social intercourse with Russian families, so that he was resigning himself to becoming a permanent bachelor.

What could one write to such a man, who had obviously run off the rails, a   3
man one could be sorry for but could not help. Should one advise him to come home, to transplant himself and take up his old friendships again—there was nothing to hinder him—and in general to rely on the help of his friends? But that was as good as telling him, and the more kindly the more offensively, that all his efforts hitherto had miscarried, that he should finally give up, come back home, and be gaped at by everyone as a returned prodigal, that only his friends knew what was what and that he himself was just a big child who should do what his successful and home-keeping friends prescribed. And was it certain, besides, that all the pain one would have to inflict on him would achieve its object? Perhaps it would not even be possible to get him to come home at all—he said himself that he was now out of touch with commerce in his native country—and then he would

still be left an alien in a foreign land embittered by his friends' advice and more than ever estranged from them. But if he did follow their advice and then didn't fit in at home—not out of malice, of course, but through force of circumstances—couldn't get on with his friends or without them, felt humiliated, couldn't be said to have either friends or a country of his own any longer, wouldn't it have been better for him to stay abroad just as he was? Taking all this into account, how could one be sure that he would make a success of life at home?

For such reasons, supposing one wanted to keep up correspondence with   4
him, one could not send him any real news such as could frankly be told to the most distant acquaintance. It was more than three years since his last visit, and for this he offered the lame excuse that the political situation in Russia was too uncertain, which apparently would not permit even the briefest absence of a small businessman while it allowed hundreds of thousands of Russians to travel peace-fully abroad. But during these three years Georg's own position in life had changed a lot. Two years ago his mother had died, since when he and his father had shared the household together, and his friend had of course been informed of that and had expressed his sympathy in a letter phrased so dryly that the grief caused by such an event, one had to conclude, could not be realized in a distant country. Since that time, however, Georg had applied himself with greater deter-mination to the business as well as to everything else.

Perhaps during his mother's lifetime his father's insistence on having every-   5
thing his own way in the business had hindered him from developing any real activity of his own, perhaps since her death his father had become less aggressive, although he was still active in the business, perhaps it was mostly due to an acci-dental run of good fortune—which was very probable indeed—but at any rate during those two years the business had developed in a most unexpected way, the staff had had to be doubled, the turnover was five times as great, no doubt about it, farther progress lay just ahead.

But Georg's friend had no inkling of this improvement. In earlier years, per-   6
haps for the last time in that letter of condolence, he had tried to persuade Georg to emigrate to Russia and had enlarged upon the prospects of success for precisely Georg's branch of trade. The figures quoted were microscopic by comparison with the range of Georg's present operations. Yet he shrank from letting his friend know about his business success, and if he were to do it now retrospectively that certainly would look peculiar.

So Georg confined himself to giving his friend unimportant items of gossip   7
such as rise at random in the memory when one is idly thinking things over on a quiet Sunday. All he desired was to leave undisturbed the idea of the home town which his friend must have built up to his own content during the long interval. And so it happened to Georg that three times in three fairly widely separated let-ters he had told his friend about the engagement of an unimportant man to an equally unimportant girl, until indeed, quite contrary to his intentions, his friend began to show some interest in this notable event.

Yet Georg preferred to write about things like these rather than to confess that   8
he himself had got engaged a month ago to a Fräulein Frieda Brandenfeld, a girl

from a well-to-do family. He often discussed this friend of his with his fiancée and the peculiar relationship that had developed between them in their correspondence. "So he won't be coming to our wedding," said she, "and yet I have a right to get to know all your friends." "I don't want to trouble him," answered Georg, "don't misunderstand me, he would probably come, at least I think so, but he would feel that his hand had been forced and he would be hurt, perhaps he would envy me and certainly he'd be discontented and without being able to do anything about his discontent he'd have to go away again alone. Alone—do you know what that means?" "Yes, but may he not hear about our wedding in some other fashion?" "I can't prevent that, of course, but it's unlikely, considering the way he lives." "Since your friends are like that, Georg, you shouldn't ever have got engaged at all." "Well, we're both to blame for that; but I wouldn't have it any other way now." And when, breathing quickly under his kisses, she still brought out: "All the same, I do feel upset," he thought it could not really involve him in trouble were he to send the news to his friend. "That's the kind of man I am and he'll just have to take me as I am," he said to himself, "I can't cut myself to another pattern that might make a more suitable friend for him."

And in fact he did inform his friend, in the long letter he had been writing 9 that Sunday morning, about his engagement, with these words: "I have saved my best news to the end. I have got engaged to a Fräulein Frieda Brandenfeld, a girl from a well-to-do family, who only came to live here a long time after you went away, so that you're hardly likely to know her. There will be time to tell you more about her later, for today let me just say that I am very happy and as between you and me the only difference in our relationship is that instead of a quite ordinary kind of friend you will now have in me a happy friend. Besides that, you will acquire in my fiancée, who sends her warm greetings and will soon write you herself, a genuine friend of the opposite sex, which is not without importance to a bachelor. I know that there are many reasons why you can't come to see us, but would not my wedding be precisely the right occasion for giving all obstacles the go-by? Still, however that may be, do just as seems good to you without regarding any interests but your own."

With this letter in his hand Georg had been sitting a long time at the writing 10 table, his face turned towards the window. He had barely acknowledged, with an absent smile, a greeting waved to him from the street by a passing acquaintance.

At last he put the letter in his pocket and went out of his room across a small 11 lobby into his father's room, which he had not entered for months. There was in fact no need for him to enter it, since he saw his father daily at business and they took their midday meal together at an eating house; in the evening, it was true, each did as he pleased, yet even then, unless Georg—as mostly happened—went out with friends or, more recently, visited his fiancée, they always sat for a while, each with his newspaper, in their common sitting room.

It surprised Georg how dark his father's room was even on this sunny morn- 12 ing. So it was overshadowed as much as that by the high wall on the other side of the narrow courtyard. His father was sitting by the window in a corner hung with various mementoes of Georg's dead mother, reading a newspaper which he held to one side before his eyes in an attempt to overcome a defect of vision. On the table stood the remains of his breakfast, not much of which seemed to have been eaten.

"Ah, Georg," said his father, rising at once to meet him. His heavy dressing gown swung open as he walked and the skirts of it fluttered round him—"My father is still a giant of a man," said Georg to himself.

"It's unbearably dark here," he said aloud.

"Yes, it's dark enough," answered his father.

"And you've shut the window, too?"

"I prefer it like that."

"Well, it's quite warm outside," said Georg, as if continuing his previous remark, and sat down.

His father cleared away the breakfast dishes and set them on a chest.

"I really only wanted to tell you," went on Georg, who had been vacantly following the old man's movements, "that I am now sending the news of my engagement to St. Petersburg." He drew the letter a little way from his pocket and let it drop back again.

"To St. Petersburg?" asked his father.

"To my friend there," said Georg, trying to meet his father's eye.—In business hours he's quite different, he was thinking, how solidly he sits here with his arms crossed.

"Oh yes. To your friend," said his father, with peculiar emphasis.

"Well, you know, Father, that I wanted not to tell him about my engagement at first. Out of consideration for him, that was the only reason. You know yourself he's a difficult man. I said to myself that someone else might tell him about my engagement, although he's such a solitary creature that that was hardly likely—I couldn't prevent that—but I wasn't ever going to tell him myself."

"And now you've changed your mind?" asked his father, laying his enormous newspaper on the window sill and on top of it his spectacles, which he covered with one hand.

"Yes, I've been thinking it over. If he's a good friend of mine, I said to myself, my being happily engaged should make him happy too. And so I wouldn't put off telling him any longer. But before I posted the letter I wanted to let you know."

"Georg," said his father, lengthening his toothless mouth, "listen to me! You've come to me about this business, to talk it over with me. No doubt that does you honor. But it's nothing, it's worse than nothing, if you don't tell me the whole truth. I don't want to stir up matters that shouldn't be mentioned here. Since the death of our dear mother certain things have been done that aren't right. Maybe the time will come for mentioning them, and maybe sooner than we think. There's many a thing in the business I'm not aware of, maybe it's not done behind my back—I'm not going to say that it's done behind my back—I'm not equal to things any longer, my memory's failing, I haven't an eye for so many things any longer. That's the course of nature in the first place, and in the second place the death of our dear mother hit me harder than it did you.—But since we're talking about it, about this letter, I beg you, Georg, don't deceive me. It's a trivial affair, it's hardly worth mentioning, so don't deceive me. Do you really have this friend in St. Petersburg?"

Georg rose in embarrassment. "Never mind my friends. A thousand friends 28 wouldn't make up to me for my father. Do you know what I think? You're not taking enough care of yourself. But old age must be taken care of. I can't do without you in the business, you know that very well, but if the business is going to undermine your health, I'm ready to close it down tomorrow forever. And that won't do. We'll have to make a change in your way of living. But a radical change. You sit here in the dark, and in the sitting room you would have plenty of light. You just take a bite of breakfast instead of properly keeping up your strength. You sit by a closed window, and the air would be so good for you. No, Father! I'll get the doctor to come, and we'll follow his orders. We'll change your room, you can move into the front room and I'll move in here. You won't notice the change, all your things will be moved with you. But there's time for all that later, I'll put you to bed now for a little, I'm sure you need to rest. Come, I'll help you to take off your things, you'll see I can do it. Or if you would rather go into the front room at once, you can lie down in my bed for the present. That would be the most sensible thing."

Georg stood close beside his father, who had let his head with its unkempt 29 white hair sink on his chest.

"Georg," said his father in a low voice, without moving.   30

Georg knelt down at once beside his father, in the old man's weary face he 31 saw the pupils, over-large, fixedly looking at him from the corners of the eyes.

"You have no friend in St. Petersburg. You've always been a leg-puller and 32 you haven't even shrunk from pulling my leg. How could you have a friend out there! I can't believe it."

"Just think back a bit, Father," said Georg, lifting his father from the chair 33 and slipping off his dressing gown as he stood feebly enough, "it'll soon be three years since my friend came to see us last. I remember that you used not to like him very much. At least twice I kept you from seeing him, although he was actually sitting with me in my room. I could quite well understand your dislike of him, my friend has his peculiarities. But then, later, you got on with him very well. I was proud because you listened to him and nodded and asked him questions. If you think back you're bound to remember. He used to tell us the most incredible stories of the Russian Revolution. For instance, when he was on a business trip to Kiev and ran into a riot, and saw a priest on a balcony who cut a broad cross in blood on the palm of his hand and held the hand up and appealed to the mob. You've told that story yourself once or twice since."

Meanwhile Georg had succeeded in lowering his father down again and care- 34 fully taking off the woollen drawers he wore over his linen underpants and his socks. The not particularly clean appearance of this underwear made him reproach himself for having been neglectful. It should have certainly been his duty to see that his father had clean changes of underwear. He had not yet explicitly discussed with his bride-to-be what arrangements should be made for his father in the future, for they had both of them silently taken it for granted that the old man would go on living alone in the old house. But now he made a quick, firm decision to take him into his own future establishment. It almost looked, on closer inspection, as if the care he meant to lavish there on his father might come too late.

He carried his father to bed in his arms. It gave him a dreadful feeling to notice that while he took the few steps towards the bed the old man on his breast was playing with his watch chain. He could not lay him down on the bed for a moment, so firmly did he hang on to the watch chain. 35

But as soon as he was laid in bed, all seemed well. He covered himself up and even drew the blankets farther than usual over his shoulders. He looked up at Georg with a not unfriendly eye. 36

"You begin to remember my friend, don't you?" asked Georg, giving him an encouraging nod. 37

"Am I well covered up now?" asked his father, as if he were not able to see whether his feet were properly tucked in or not. 38

"So you find it snug in bed already," said Georg, and tucked the blankets more closely round him. 39

"Am I well covered up now?" asked the father once more, seeming to be strangely intent upon the answer. 40

"Don't worry, you're well covered up." 41

"No!" cried his father, cutting short the answer, threw the blankets off with a strength that sent them all flying in a moment and sprang erect in bed. Only one hand lightly touched the ceiling to steady him. 42

"You wanted to cover me up, I know, my young sprig, but I'm far from being covered up yet. And even if this is the last strength I have, it's enough for you, too much for you. Of course I know your friend. He would have been a son after my own heart. That's why you've been playing him false all these years. Why else? Do you think I haven't been sorry for him? And that's why you had to lock yourself up in your office—the Chief is busy, mustn't be disturbed—just so that you could write your lying little letters to Russia. But thank goodness a father doesn't need to be taught how to see through his son. And now that you thought you'd got him down, so far down that you could set your bottom on him and sit on him and he wouldn't move, then my fine son makes up his mind to get married!" 43

Georg stared at the bogey conjured up by his father. His friend in St. Petersburg, whom his father suddenly knew too well, touched his imagination as never before. Lost in the vastness of Russia he saw him. At the door of an empty, plundered warehouse he saw him. Among the wreckage of his showcases, the slashed remnants of his wares, the falling gas brackets, he was just standing up. Why did he have to go so far away! 44

"But attend to me!" cried his father, and Georg, almost distracted, ran towards the bed to take everything in, yet came to a stop halfway. 45

"Because she lifted up her skirts," his father began to flute, "because she lifted her skirts like this, the nasty creature," and mimicking her he lifted his shirt so high that one could see the scar on his thigh from his war wound, "because she 46 lifted her skirts like this and this you made up to her, and in order to make free with her undisturbed you have disgraced your mother's memory, betrayed your friend and stuck your father into bed so that he can't move. But he can move, or can't he?"

And he stood up quite unsupported and kicked his legs out. His insight made 47 him radiant.

Georg shrank into a corner, as far away from his father as possible. A long 48 time ago he had firmly made up his mind to watch closely every least movement so that he should not be surprised by any indirect attack, a pounce from behind or above. At this moment he recalled this long-forgotten resolve and forgot it again, like a man drawing a short thread through the eye of a needle.

"But your friend hasn't been betrayed after all!" cried his father, emphasiz- 49 ing the point with stabs of his forefinger. "I've been representing him here on the spot."

"You comedian!" Georg could not resist the retort, realized at once the harm 50 done and, his eyes starting in his head, bit his tongue back, only too late, till the pain made his knees give.

"Yes, of course I've been playing a comedy! A comedy! That's a good 51 expression! What other comfort was left to a poor old widower? Tell me—and while you're answering me be you still my living son—what else was left to me, in my back room plagued by a disloyal staff, old to the marrow of my bones? And my son strutting through the world, finishing off deals that I had prepared for him, bursting with triumphant glee and stalking away from his father with the closed face of a respectable businessman! Do you think I didn't love you, I, from whom you are sprung?"

Now he'll lean forward, thought Georg, what if he topples and smashes him- 52 self! These words went hissing through his mind.

His father leaned forward but did not topple. Since Georg did not come any 53 nearer, as he had expected, he straightened himself again.

"Stay where you are, I don't need you! You think you have strength enough 54 to come over here and that you're only hanging back of your own accord. Don't be too sure! I am still much the stronger of us two. All by myself I might have had to give way, but your mother has given me so much of her strength that I've established a fine connection with your friend and I have your customers here in my pocket!"

"He has pockets even in his shirt!" said Georg to himself, and believed that 55 with this remark he could make him an impossible figure for all the world. Only for a moment did he think so, since he kept on forgetting everything.

"Just take your bride on your arm and try getting in my way! I'll sweep her 56 from your very side, you don't know how!"

Georg made a grimace of disbelief. His father only nodded, confirming the 57 truth of his words, towards Georg's corner.

"How you amused me today, coming to ask me if you should tell your friend 58 about your engagement. He knows it already, you stupid boy, he knows it all! I've been writing to him, for you forgot to take my writing things away from me.

That's why he hasn't been here for years, he knows everything a hundred times better than you do yourself, in his left hand he crumples your letters unopened while in his right hand he holds up my letters to read through!"

In his enthusiasm he waved his arm over his head. "He knows everything a thousand times better!" he cried. 59

"Ten thousand times!" said Georg, to make fun of his father, but in his very mouth the words turned into deadly earnest. 60

"For years I've been waiting for you to come with some such question! Do you think I concern myself with anything else? Do you think I read my newspapers? Look!" and he threw Georg a newspaper sheet which he had somehow taken to bed with him. An old newspaper, with a name entirely unknown to Georg. 61

"How long a time you've taken to grow up! Your mother had to die, she couldn't see the happy day, your friend is going to pieces in Russia, even three years ago he was yellow enough to be thrown away, and as for me, you see what condition I'm in. You have eyes in your head for that!" 62

"So you've been lying in wait for me!" cried Georg. 63

His father said pityingly, in an offhand manner: "I suppose you wanted to say that sooner. But now it doesn't matter." And in a louder voice: "So now you know what else there was in the world besides yourself, till now you've known only about yourself! An innocent child, yes, that you were, truly, but still more truly have you been a devilish human being!—And therefore take note: I sentence you now to death by drowning!" 64

Georg felt himself urged from the room, the crash with which his father fell on the bed behind him was still in his ears as he fled. On the staircase, which he rushed down as if its steps were an inclined plane, he ran into his charwoman on her way up to do the morning cleaning of the room. "Jesus!" she cried, and covered her face with her apron, but he was already gone. Out of the front door he rushed, across the roadway, driven towards the water. Already he was grasping at the railings as a starving man clutches food. He swung himself over, like the distinguished gymnast he had once been in his youth, to his parents' pride. With weakening grip he was still holding on when he spied between the railings a motor-bus coming which would easily cover the noise of his fall, called in a low voice: "Dear parents, I have always loved you, all the same," and let himself drop. 65

At this moment an unending stream of traffic was just going over the bridge. 66

Meaning and Idea

1. Describe the relations between Georg and his father, Georg and his friend in Russia, and Georg and his fiancée. Which of these relations seem normal to you? Which seem odd, at best?

2. What is Georg's fate? How do you explain the end of the story? Would you say that Georg's fate reflects his guilt? His father's dominance over him? His own mental instability? Defend your response.

3. What would you say is the theme of the story, the main point Kafka is trying to make here?

4. Sanity and insanity never lie too far beneath the surface in Kafka's works. Who in this story is sane, do you think? Who is insane? Why do you think so?

5. Why did Kafka choose the title "The Judgment" for his story? What conditions or events does the title refer to? Exactly what is being judged here, do you think?

Language, Form, Structure

1. What are the various elements of argument and persuasion here? How, for example, do argument and persuasion play a role in Georg's thoughts about telling his friend of the engagement? What elements of argument do you observe in Georg's conversation with his father? What, do you think, ultimately persuades Georg to take his final action at the bridge?

2. Kafka uses the strategy of comparison and contrast here to intensify the theme of the story. For example, how does the comparison between Georg's friend in St. Petersburg and Georg himself enrich your understanding of Georg? What elements of Georg's analysis of his friend actually apply to Georg too? What other comparisons and contrasts do you note?

3. What elements of description, particularly of the father and his environment, contribute to your understanding of his mental and physical state?

4. Define these words and use each in an original sentence: ramshackle; latent; prodigal; estranged; mementos; plundered; remnants; grimace.

Ideas for Writing

1. Write an essay in which you present the arguments used by a family member to persuade you to do something you did not want to do.

2. What do you think are the obligations of a child to an aging parent? Write an essay in which you attempt to persuade the reader to take some course of action when it comes to dealing with a parent growing older, perhaps infirm, and unable fully to care for himself or herself.

3. Write an essay to convince your reader about the sanity of the characters in Kafka's story. Cite and analyze details from "The Judgment" to support your argument.

On Liberty

John Stuart Mill

John Stuart Mill (1806–1873), the Victorian British philosopher and economist, was one of the major influences on the direction of modern political, economic, and philosophical thought. Schooled in the utilitarianism of Jeremy Bentham and of his father, James Mill, John Stuart Mill liberalized that doctrine considerably. Mill's advocacy of *laissez-faire* economics is still highly touted, though Mill himself was an early advocate of such socialist movements as labor unions, women's rights, and farm cooperatives. His base of logic lay in induction and empiricism (the doctrine that all knowledge derives from experience) and can be found in such works as *Principles of Political Economy* (1848), *On Liberty* (1859), and *Utilitarianism* (1863).

"On Liberty" comes from Mill's *On Liberty; and Thoughts on Parliamentary Reform,* published in 1859. There are those who consider Mill's arguments in that collection the basis for liberal individualism, while others consider it the direct ancestor of the conservative *laissez-faire* doctrines of contemporary political leaders. In reading Mill's argument, postulate your own opinion about its contemporary importance, and pay close attention to the structure of his argumentative development.

The subject of this Essay is not the so-called Liberty of the Will, so   1
unfortunately opposed to the misnamed doctrine of Philosophical Necessity; but Civil, or Social Liberty: the nature and limits of the power which can be legitimately exercised by society over the individual. A question seldom stated, and hardly ever discussed, in general terms, but which profoundly influences the practical controversies of the age by its latent presence, and is likely soon to make itself recognized as the vital question of the future. It is so far from being new, that, in a certain sense, it has divided mankind, almost from the remotest ages; but in the stage of progress into which the more civilized portions of the species have now entered, it presents itself under new conditions, and requires a different and more fundamental treatment.

The struggle between Liberty and Authority is the most conspicuous feature   2
in the portions of history with which we are earliest familiar, particularly in that of Greece, Rome, and England. But in old times this contest was between subjects, or some classes of subjects, and the Government. By liberty, was meant protection against the tyranny of the political rulers. The rulers were conceived (except in some of the popular governments of Greece) as in a necessarily antagonistic position to the people whom they ruled. They consisted of a governing One, or a governing tribe or caste, who derived their authority from inheritance or conquest, who, at all events, did not hold it at the pleasure of the governed, and whose supremacy men did not venture, perhaps did not desire, to contest, whatever precautions might be taken against its oppressive exercise. Their power was regarded as necessary, but also as highly dangerous; as a weapon which they would attempt

to use against their subjects, no less than against external enemies. To prevent the weaker members of the community from being preyed upon by innumerable vultures, it was needful that there should be an animal of prey stronger than the rest, commissioned to keep them down. But as the king of the vultures would be no less bent upon preying on the flock than any of the minor harpies, it was indispensable to be in a perpetual attitude of defence against his beak and claws. The aim, therefore, of patriots was to set limits to the power which the ruler should be suffered to exercise over the community; and this limitation was what they meant by liberty. It was attempted in two ways. First, by obtaining a recognition of certain immunities, called political liberties or rights, which it was to be regarded as a breach of duty in the ruler to infringe, and which, if he did infringe, specific resistance, or general rebellion, was held to be justifiable. A second, and generally a later expedient, was the establishment of constitutional checks, by which the consent of the community, or of a body of some sort, supposed to represent its interest, was made a necessary condition to some of the more important acts of the governing power. To the first of these modes of limitation, the ruling power, in most European countries, was compelled, more or less, to submit. It was not so with the second; and, to attain this, or when already in some degree possessed, to attain it more completely, became everywhere the principal object of the lovers of liberty. And so long as mankind were content to combat one enemy by another, and to be ruled by a master, on condition of being guaranteed more or less efficaciously against his tyranny, they did not carry their aspirations beyond this point.

A time, however, came, in the progress of human affairs, when men ceased to think it a necessity of nature that their governors should be an independent power, opposed in interest to themselves. It appeared to them much better that the various magistrates of the State should be their tenants or delegates, revocable at their pleasure. In that way alone, it seemed, could they have complete security that the powers of government would never be abused to their disadvantage. By degrees this new demand for elective and temporary rulers became the prominent object of the exertions of the popular party, wherever any such party existed; and superseded, to a considerable extent, the previous efforts to limit the power of rulers. As the struggle proceeded for making the ruling power emanate from the periodical choice of the ruled, some persons began to think that too much importance had been attached to the limitation of the power itself. *That* (it might seem) was a resource against rulers whose interests were habitually opposed to those of the people. What was now wanted was, that the rulers should be identified with the people; that their interest and will should be the interest and will of the nation. The nation did not need to be protected against its own will. There was no fear of its tyrannizing over itself. Let the rulers be effectually responsible to it, promptly removable by it, and it could afford to trust them with power of which it could itself dictate the use to be made. Their power was but the nation's own power, concentrated, and in a form convenient for exercise. This mode of thought, or rather perhaps of feeling, was common among the last generation of European liberalism, in the Continental section of which it still apparently predominates. Those who admit any limit to what a government may do, except in the case of such governments as they think ought not to exist, stand out as brilliant exceptions among the political thinkers of the Continent. A similar tone of sentiment might by this time have been prevalent in our own country, if the circumstances which for a time encouraged it, had continued unaltered.

But, in political and philosophical theories, as well as in persons, success discloses faults and infirmities which failure might have concealed from observation. The notion, that the people have no need to limit their power over themselves, might seem axiomatic, when popular government was a thing only dreamed about, or read of as having existed at some distant period of the past. Neither was that notion necessarily disturbed by such temporary aberrations as those of the French Revolution, the worst of which were the work of an usurping few, and which, in any case, belonged, not to the permanent working of popular institutions, but to a sudden and convulsive outbreak against monarchical and aristocratic despotism. In time, however, a democratic republic came to occupy a large portion of the earth's surface, and made itself felt as one of the most powerful members of the community of nations; and elective and responsible government became subject to the observations and criticisms which wait upon a great existing fact. It was now perceived that such phrases as "self-government," and "the power of the people over themselves," do not express the true state of the case. The "people" who exercise the power are not always the same people with those over whom it is exercised; and the "self-government" spoken of is not the government of each by himself, but of each by all the rest. The will of the people, moreover, practically means the will of the most numerous or the most active *part* of the people; the majority, or those who succeed in making themselves accepted as the majority; the people, consequently, *may* desire to oppress a part of their number; and precautions are as much needed against this as against any other abuse of power. The limitation, therefore, of the power of government over individuals loses none of its importance when the holders of power are regularly accountable to the community, that is, to the strongest party therein. This view of things, recommending itself equally to the intelligence of thinkers and to the inclination of those important classes in European society to whose real or supposed interests democracy is adverse, has had no difficulty in establishing itself; and in political speculations "the tyranny of the majority" is now generally included among the evils against which society requires to be on its guard.

Like other tyrannies, the tyranny of the majority was at first, and is still vulgarly, held in dread, chiefly as operating through the acts of the public authorities. But reflecting persons perceived that when society is itself the tyrant—society collectively, over the separate individuals who compose it—its means of tyrannizing are not restricted to the acts which it may do by the hands of its political functionaries. Society can and does execute its own mandates: and if it issues wrong mandates instead of right, or any mandates at all in things with which it ought not to meddle, it practices a social tyranny more formidable than many kinds of political oppression, since, though not usually upheld by such extreme penalties, it leaves fewer means of escape, penetrating much more deeply into the details of life, and enslaving the soul itself. Protection, therefore, against the tyranny of the magistrate is not enough: there needs protection also against the tyranny of the prevailing opinion and feeling; against the tendency of society to impose, by other means than civil penalties, its own ideas and practices as rules of conduct on those who dissent from them; to fetter the development, and, if possible, prevent the formation, of any individuality not in harmony with its ways, and compel all characters to fashion themselves upon the model of its own. There is a limit to the legitimate interference of collective opinion with individual independence: and to find that limit, and maintain it against encroachment, is as indispensable to a good condition of human affairs, as protection against political despotism.

But though this proposition is not likely to be contested in general terms, the practical question, where to place the limit—how to make the fitting adjustment between individual independence and social control—is a subject on which nearly everything remains to be done. All that makes existence valuable to any one, depends on the enforcement of restraints upon the actions of other people. Some rules of conduct, therefore, must be imposed, by law in the first place, and by opinion on many things which are not fit subjects for the operation of law. What these rules should be, is the principal question in human affairs; but if we except a few of the most obvious cases, it is one of those which least progress has been made in resolving. No two ages, and scarcely any two countries, have decided it alike; and the decision of one age or country is a wonder to another. Yet the people of any given age and country no more suspect any difficulty in it, than if it were a subject on which mankind had always been agreed. The rules which obtain among themselves appear to them self-evident and self-justifying. This all but universal illusion is one of the examples of the magical influence of custom, which is not only, as the proverb says, a second nature, but is continually mistaken for the first. The effect of custom, in preventing any misgiving respecting the rules of conduct which mankind impose on one another, is all the more complete because the subject is one on which it is not generally considered necessary that reasons should be given, either by one person to others, or by each to himself. People are accustomed to believe, and have been encouraged in the belief by some who aspire to the character of philosophers, that their feelings, on subjects of this nature, are better than reasons, and render reasons unnecessary. The practical principle which guides them to their opinions on the regulation of human conduct, is the feeling in each person's mind that everybody should be required to act as he, and those with whom he sympathizes, would like them to act. No one, indeed, acknowledges to himself that his standard of judgement is his own liking; but an opinion on a point of conduct, not supported by reasons, can only count as one person's preference; and if the reasons, when given, are a mere appeal to a similar preference felt by other people, it is still only many people's liking instead of one. To an ordinary man, however, his own preference, thus supported, is not only a perfectly satisfactory reason, but the only one he generally has for any of his notions of morality, taste, or propriety, which are not expressly written in his religious creed; and his chief guide in the interpretation even of that. Men's opinions, accordingly, on what is laudable or blameable, are affected by all the multifarious causes which influence their wishes in regard to the conduct of others, and which are as numerous as those which determine their wishes on any other subject. Sometimes their reason—at other times their prejudices or super-stitions: often their social affections, not seldom their anti-social ones, their envy or jealousy, their arrogance or contemptuousness: but most commonly, their desires or fears for themselves—their legitimate or illegitimate self-interest. Wherever there is an ascendant class, a large portion of the morality of the coun-try emanates from its class interests, and its feelings of class superiority. The morality between Spartans and Helots, between planters and negroes, between princes and subjects, between nobles and roturiers, between men and women, has been for the most part the creation of these class interests and feelings: and the sentiments thus generated, react in turn upon the moral feelings of the members of the ascendent class, in their relations among themselves. Where, on the other hand, a class, formerly ascendant, has lost its ascendancy, or where its ascendancy is unpopular, the prevailing moral sentiments frequently bear the impress of an impatient dislike of superiority. Another grand determining principle of the rules of conduct, both in act and forbearance, which have been enforced by law or opinion, has been the servility of mankind towards the supposed preferences or aversions of their temporal masters, or of their gods. This servility, though essen-tially selfish, is not hypocrisy; it gives rise to perfectly genuine sentiments of abhorrence; it made men burn magicians and heretics. Among so many baser influences, the general and obvious interests of society have of course had a share, and a large one, in the direction of the moral sentiments: less, however, as a matter of reason, and on their own account, than as a consequence of the sym-pathies and antipathies which grew out of them: and sympathies and antipathies which had little or nothing to do with the interests of society, have made them-selves felt in the establishment of moralities with quite as great force.

The likings and dislikings of society, or of some powerful portion of it, are [7] thus the main thing which has practically determined the rules laid down for gen-eral observance, under the penalties of law or opinion. And in general, those who have been in advance of society in thought and feeling, have left this condition of things unassailed in principle, however they may have come into conflict with it in some of its details. They have occupied themselves rather in inquiring what things society ought to like or dislike, than in questioning whether its likings or dislikings should be a law to individuals. They preferred endeavouring to alter the feelings of mankind on the particular points on which they were themselves heretical, rather than make common cause in defence of freedom, with heretics generally. The only case in which the higher ground has been taken on principle and maintained with consistency, by any but an individual here and there, is that of religious belief: a case instructive in many ways, and not least so as forming a most striking instance of the fallibility of what is called the moral sense: for the *odium theologicum,* in a sincere bigot, is one of the most unequivocal cases of moral feeling. Those who first broke the yoke of what called itself the Universal Church, were in general as little willing to permit difference of religious opinion as that church itself. But when the heat of the conflict was over, without giving a complete victory to any party, and each church or sect was reduced to limit its hopes to retaining possession of the ground it already occupied; minorities, seeing that they had no chance of becoming majorities, were under the necessity of pleading to those whom they could not convert, for permission to differ. It is accordingly on this battlefield, almost solely, that the rights of the individual against society have been asserted on broad grounds of principle, and the claim of society to exercise authority over dissentients, openly controverted. The great writers to whom the world owes what religious liberty it possesses, have mostly asserted freedom of conscience as an indefeasible right, and denied absolutely that a human being is accountable to others for his religious belief. Yet so natural to mankind is intolerance in whatever they really care about, that religious freedom has hardly anywhere been practically realized, except where religious indifference, which dislikes to have its peace disturbed by theological quarrels, has added its weight to the scale. In the minds of almost all religious persons, even in the most tolerant countries, the duty of toleration is admitted with tacit reserves. One person will bear with dissent in matters of church government, but not of dogma; another can tolerate everybody, short of a Papist or a Unitarian; another, every one who believes in revealed religion; a few extend their charity a little further, but stop at the belief in a God and in a future state. Wherever the sentiment of the majority is still genuine and intense, it is found to have abated little of its claim to be obeyed.

In England, from the peculiar circumstances of our political history, though the yoke of opinion is perhaps heavier, that of law is lighter, than in most other countries of Europe; and there is considerable jealousy of direct interference, by the legislative or the executive power, with private conduct; not so much from any just regard for the independence of the individual, as from the still subsisting habit of looking on the government as representing an opposite interest to the public. The majority have not yet learnt to feel the power of the government their power, or its opinions their opinions. When they do so, individual liberty will probably be as much exposed to invasion from the government, as it already is from public opinion. But, as yet, there is a considerable amount of feeling ready to be called forth against any attempt of the law to control individuals in things in which they have not hitherto been accustomed to be controlled by it; and this with very little discrimination as to whether the matter is, or is not, within the legitimate sphere of legal control; insomuch that the feeling, highly salutary on the whole, is perhaps quite as often misplaced as well grounded in the particular instances of its application. There is, in fact, no recognized principle by which the propriety or impropriety of government interference is customarily tested. People decide according to their personal preferences. Some, whenever they see any good to be done, or evil to be remedied, would willingly instigate the government to undertake the business; while others prefer to bear almost any amount of social evil, rather than add one to the departments of human interests amenable to governmental control. And men range themselves on one or the other side in any particular case, according to this general direction of their sentiments; or according to the degree of interest which they feel in the particular thing which it is proposed that the government should do, or according to the belief they entertain that the government would, or would not, do it in the manner they prefer; but very rarely on account of any opinion to which they consistently adhere, as to what things are fit to be done by a government. And it seems to me that in consequence of this absence of rule or principle, one side is at present as often wrong as the other; the interference of government is, with about equal frequency, improperly invoked and improperly condemned.

The object of this Essay is to assert one very simple principle, as entitled to 9 govern absolutely the dealings of society with the individual in the way of compulsion and control, whether the means used be physical force in the form of legal penalties, or the moral coercion of public opinion. That principle is, that the sole end for which mankind are warranted, individually or collectively, in interfering with the liberty of action of any of their number, is self-protection. That the only purpose for which power can be rightfully exercised over any member of a civilized community, against his will, is to prevent harm to others. His own good, either physical or moral, is not a sufficient warrant. He cannot rightfully be compelled to do or forbear because it will be better for him to do so, because it will make him happier, because, in the opinions of others, to do so would be wise, or even right. These are good reasons for remonstrating with him, or reasoning with him, or persuading him, or entreating him, but not for compelling him, or visiting him with any evil in case he do otherwise. To justify that, the conduct from which it is desired to deter him, must be calculated to produce evil to some one else. The only part of the conduct of any one, for which he is amenable to society, is that which concerns others. In the part which merely concerns himself, his independence is, of right, absolute. Over himself, over his own body and mind, the individual is sovereign.

It is, perhaps, hardly necessary to say that this doctrine is meant to apply only 10 to human beings in the maturity of their faculties. We are not speaking of children, or of young persons below the age which the law may fix as that of manhood or womanhood. Those who are still in a state to require being taken care of by others, must be protected against their own actions as well as against external injury. For the same reason, we may leave out of consideration those backward states of society in which the race itself may be considered as in its nonage. The early difficulties in the way of spontaneous progress are so great, that there is seldom any choice of means for overcoming them; and a ruler full of the spirit of improvement is warranted in the use of any expedients that will attain an end, perhaps otherwise unattainable. Despotism is a legitimate mode of government in dealing with barbarians, provided the end be their improvement, and the means justified by actually effecting that end. Liberty, as a principle, has no application to any state of things anterior to the time when mankind have become capable of being improved by free and equal discussion. Until then, there is nothing for them but implicit obedience to an Akbar or a Charlemagne, if they are so fortunate as to find one. But as soon as mankind have attained the capacity of being guided to their own improvement by conviction or persuasion (a period long since reached in all nations with whom we need here concern ourselves), compulsion, either in the direct form or in that of pains and penalties for noncompliance, is no longer admissible as a means to their own good, and justifiable only for the security of others.

It is proper to state that I forgo any advantage which could be derived to my 11 argument from the idea of abstract right, as a thing independent of utility. I regard utility as the ultimate appeal on all ethical questions; but it must be ulitity in the largest sense, grounded on the permanent interests of man as a progressive being. Those interests, I contend, authorize the subjection of individual spontaneity to external control, only in respect to those actions of each, which concern the interest of other people. If any one does an act hurtful to others, there is a prima facie case for punishing him, by law, or, where legal penalties are not safely applicable, by general disapprobation. There are also many positive acts for the benefit of others, which he may rightfully be compelled to perform; such as, to give evidence in a court of justice; to bear his fair share in the common defence, or in any other joint work necessary to the interest of the society of which he enjoys the protection; and to perform certain acts of individual beneficence, such as saving a fellow creature's life, or interposing to protect the defenceless against ill-usage, things which whenever it is obviously a man's duty to do, he may rightfully be made responsible to society for not doing. A person may cause evil to others not only by his actions but by his inaction, and in either case he is justly accountable to them for the injury. The latter case, it is true, requires a much more cautious exercise of compulsion than the former. To make any one answerable for doing evil to others, is the rule; to make him answerable for not preventing evil, is, comparatively speaking, the exception. Yet there are many cases clear enough and grave enough to justify that exception. In all things which regard the external relations of the individual, he is *de jure* amenable to those whose interests are concerned, and if need be, to society as their protector. There are often good reasons for not holding him to the responsibility; but these reasons must arise from the special expediencies of the case: either because it is a kind of case in which he is on the whole likely to act better, when left to his own discretion, than when controlled in any way in which society have it in their power to control him; or because the attempt to exercise control would produce other evils, greater than those which it would prevent. When such reasons as these preclude the enforcement of responsibility, the conscience of the agent himself should step into the vacant judgement-seat; and protect those interests of others which have no external protection; judging himself all the more rigidly, because the case does not admit of his being made accountable to the judgement of his fellow creatures.

But there is a sphere of action in which society, as distinguished from the 12 individual, has, if any, only an indirect interest; comprehending all that portion of a person's life and conduct which affects only himself, or if it also affects others, only with their free, voluntary, and undeceived consent and participation. When I say only himself, I mean directly, and in the first instance: for whatever affects himself, may affect others through himself; and the objection which may be grounded on this contingency will receive consideration in the sequel. This, then, is the appropriate region of human liberty. It comprises, first, the inward domain of consciousness; demanding liberty of conscience, in the most comprehensive sense; liberty of thought and feeling; absolute freedom of opinion and sentiment on all subjects, practical or speculative, scientific, moral, or theological. The liberty of expressing and publishing opinions may seem to fall under a different principle, since it belongs to that part of the conduct of an individual which concerns other people; but, being almost of as much importance as the liberty of thought itself, and resting in great part on the same reasons, is practically inseparable from it. Secondly, the principle requires liberty of tastes and pursuits; of framing the plan of our life to suit our own character; of doing as we like, subject to such consequences as may follow: without impediment from our fellow creatures, so long as what we do does not harm them, even though they should think our conduct foolish, perverse, or wrong. Thirdly, from this liberty of each individual, follows the liberty, within the same limits, of combination among individuals; freedom to unite, for any purpose not involving harm to others: the persons combining being supposed to be of full age, and not forced or deceived.

No society in which these liberties are not, on the whole, respected, is free, whatever may be its form of government; and none is completely free in which they do not exist absolute and unqualified. The only freedom which deserves the name, is that of pursuing our own good in our own way, so long as we do not attempt to deprive others of theirs, or impede their efforts to obtain it. Each is the proper guardian of his own health, whether bodily, or mental and spiritual. Mankind are greater gainers by suffering each other to live as seems good to themselves, than by compelling each to live as seems good to the rest.   13

Meaning and Idea

1. What basic definition does Mill ascribe to the term *liberty?* How is that definition modified throughout the essay? On what "practical question" does Mill's argument about liberty hinge? What is the "principal question in human affairs"?

2. Trace the historical change in attitude toward rulers as outlined by Mill in this essay. Why did it occur?

3. According to Mill, why may it be necessary to limit the power of the majority opinion? What does he mean by "the tyranny of the majority"? What, according to Mill, is the difference between the rights of society to persuade and to compel its citizens to act in certain ways? Which is preferable? What acts *may* be compelled? On what basis?

4. What is Mill's attitude toward the connection between religion and liberty?

5. What, according to Mill, is the relation between personal preference and rules of conduct or propriety? Which class has usually determined morality? What examples of this does he offer? Can you offer a few more examples from present-day societies?

Language, Form, Structure

1. Mill's first paragraph is almost a model introduction to argument because of the elements it includes. Analyze how Mill: (a) identifies the focus of the

essay, (b) establishes a definition for his argument, (c) focuses on the contemporary importance of his discussion, (d) provides a historical context for his argument. Also, identify any other element of the first paragraph that you feel is especially important.

2. The introduction to this chapter discusses the difference between *inductive* and *deductive* reasoning (see page 519). You may want to clarify your understanding of these terms further by looking in a dictionary, an encyclopedia, or a basic philosophy textbook. Would you characterize Mill's logic in this essay as primarily inductive or deductive? Explain.

3. Where does Mill place his thesis statement in this essay? Identify it. Why is it placed where it is?

4. Analyze Mill's use of transitions in this essay. Is it significant to the logical development that three of the essay's thirteen paragraphs begin with the word *But?* How do the other transitions affect the development of Mill's argument?

5. What sentence signals the beginning of the essay's conclusion? How does Mill use *summary* as a part of his conclusion? What generalization does he derive from this summary?

6. Would you classify this piece more as an *argumentation* or a *persuasion* essay (see chapter introduction, page 518)? Where does Mill include specific suggestions for action?

7. Check the meanings of the following words from the essay: infringe; efficaciously; superseded; axiomatic; despotism; formidable; fetter; multifarious; fallibility; tacit.

Ideas for Writing

1. Select an aspect of life over which you feel the government exerts too much—or too little—control. Write an argument in favor of reversing the current trend. Be sure to include a blend of objective analysis and personal preference.

2. Write an argument for or against a greater voice by students in the shaping of curriculum at your school. Include a discussion of the relation between students' goals at your school and the present curriculum's ability to fulfill those goals.

3. John Stuart Mill is known for his advocacy of the doctrine of *laissez faire* both in economics and in personal life. Very basically, *laissez faire* is characterized by complete lack of, or at least minimal, government regulation. For further clarification, look up *laissez faire* in an encyclopedia and pay close attention to how it relates to ideas about individualism.

   How is Mill's argument in "On Liberty" a reflection of *laissez faire?* What do you think of this attitude? Is it applicable to the 1990s? How so?

A Marriage Proposal

TRANSLATED BY JOACHIM NEUGROSCHEL

Anton Chekhov

Anton Chekhov, born in 1860 and trained as a physician, is one of the most widely read and influential short story writers and dramatists of the twentieth century. Appreciative readers and audiences acknowledged and admired his innovations in both genres as a writer, during his lifetime, and many of today's writers reflect his influence.

Chekhov was concerned with the personal and the ordinary, which resulted in works about his characters' psychologies more than their actions. Early in his career he wrote farcical, lighthearted material like the following one-act play. Here, as in much of Chekhov's work, the characters' behaviors, idiosyncrasies, and agendas are what really drive the narrative forward.

CHARACTERS

STEPÁN STEPÁNOVICH CHOOBOOKÓV, *a landowner.*
NATÁLIA STEPÁNOVNA, *his twenty-five-year-old daughter.*
IVÁN VASSÍLIEVICH LÓMOV, CHOOBOOKÓV's *neighbor, a healthy and well-fed, but terribly hypochondriac landowner.*

*T*he action takes place in the drawing room of Choobookóv's country house.

SCENE I

(CHOOBOOKÓV *and* LÓMOV. *The latter enters, wearing tails and white gloves.*)

CHOOBOOKÓV (*going over to welcome his guest*): Why, of all people! My old friend, Iván Vassílievich! How nice to see you! (*Shakes his hand.*) This really is a surprise, old boy. . . . How *are* you?
LÓMOV: Very well, thank you. And may I ask how *you* are?
CHOOBOOKÓV: Not bad at all, old friend, with the help of your prayers and so on. . . . Please have a seat. . . . Now, really, it's not very nice of you to neglect your neighbors, my dear boy. And what are you all dressed up for? Morning coat, gloves, and so on! Are you off on a visit, old boy?
LÓMOV: No, I'm just calling on you, my esteemed neighbor.
CHOOBOOKÓV: But why the morning coat, old friend? This isn't New Year's Day!

LÓMOV: Well, you see, the fact of the matter is . . . (*Takes his arm.*) I've burst in on you like this, Stepán Stepánovich, my esteemed neighbor, in order to ask a favor of you. I've already had the honor more than once of turning to you for help and you've always, so to speak, uh! . . . But forgive me, my nerves . . . I must have a sip of water, dear Stepán Stepánovich.

(*Drinks some water.*)

CHOOBOOKÓV (*aside*): He's after money. Fat chance! (*To* LÓMOV) What is it, my dear fellow?

LÓMOV: Well, you see, my Stepán dearovich, uh! I mean dear Stepánovich . . . uh! I mean, my nerves are in a terrible condition, which you yourself are so kind as to see. In short, you're the only one who can help me, although, of course, I've done nothing to deserve it and . . . and I don't even have the right to count on your help. . . .

CHOOBOOKÓV: Now, now; don't beat about the bush, old friend. Out with it! . . . Well?

LÓMOV: All right, here you are. The fact of the matter is, I've come to ask for your daughter Natália's hand in marriage.

CHOOBOOKÓV (*overjoyed*): My *dearest* friend! Iván Vassílievich. Could you repeat that—I'm not sure I heard right!

LÓMOV: I have the honor of asking——

CHOOBOOKÓV (*breaking in*): My oldest and dearest friend . . . I'm *so* delighted and so on. . . . Yes really, and all that sort of thing. (*Hugging and kissing him.*) I've been yearning for this for ages. It's been my constant desire. (*Sheds a tear.*) And I've always loved you like a son, you wonderful person, you. May God grant you love and guidance and so on, it's been my most fervent wish. . . . But why am I standing hear like a blockhead? I'm dumbstruck by the sheer joy of it, completely dumbstruck. Oh, with all my heart and soul. . . . I'll go get Natasha, and so on.

LÓMOV (*deeply moved*): Stepán Stepánovich, my esteemed friend, do you think I may count on her accepting me?

CHOOBOOKÓV: A handsome devil like you? How could she possibly resist? She's *madly* in love with you, don't worry, *madly,* and so on. . . . I'll call her right away.

(*Exit.*)

SCENE II

LÓMOV (*alone*): It's so cold . . . I'm shaking all over, like before a final exam. The important thing is to make up your mind. If you think about it too long, or waver, talk about it too much, and wait for the ideal woman or for true love, you'll never marry. . . . Brr! It's cold! Natália Stepánovna is an excellent housekeeper, she's not bad-looking, and she's got some education. . . . What more could I ask for? Oh, I'm so nervous, I can hear a buzzing in my ears. (*Drinks some water.*) It would be best for me to get married. . . . First of all, I'm thirty-five years old already—and that, as they say, is a critical age. And then, I have to start leading a steady and regular life. . . . I've got a heart condition, with palpitations all the time. . . . I've got an awful temper and I'm always getting terribly wrought up. . . . Even now, my lips are trembling and my right eyelid is twitching. . . . But the worst thing is when I try to sleep. The instant I get to bed and start dropping off, something *stabs* me in my left side—ungh! And it cuts right through my shoulder straight into my head—ungh! I jump like a lunatic, walk about a little, and then I lie down again, but the moment I start to doze off, I feel it in my side again—ungh! And it keeps on and on for at least twenty times. . . .

SCENE III

(NATÁLIA STEPÁNOVNA *and* LÓMOV.)

NATÁLIA (*entering*): Ah, it's you. And Papa said a customer had come for the merchandise. How do you do, Iván Vassílievich!

LÓMOV: How do you do, my esteemed Natália Stepánovna!

NATÁLIA: I'm sorry about my apron and not being dressed. . . . We're shelling peas for drying. Where've you been keeping yourself? Have a seat. . . . (*They sit down.*) Would you like a bite of lunch?

LÓMOV: Thank you so much, but I've already eaten.

NATÁLIA: Well, then have a cigarette. . . . The matches are over here. . . . The weather's magnificent today, but yesterday it rained so hard that the men couldn't do a thing all day long. How much hay did *you* get done? Can you imagine, I was so greedy that I had the whole meadow mown, and now I regret it, I'm scared that all my hay may rot. I should have waited. But what's this? I do believe you're wearing a morning coat! How original! Are you going to a ball or something? Incidentally, you're getting quite handsome. . . . But honestly, why are you all dolled up?

LÓMOV (*nervously*): You see, my esteemed Natália Stepánovna . . . the fact is I've made up my mind to ask you to listen to me. . . . Naturally you'll be surprised and even angry, but I . . . (*Aside.*) God, it's cold!

NATÁLIA: What is it? (*Pause.*) Well?

LÓMOV: I'll try to be brief. You are well aware, my esteemed Natália Stepánovna, that for a long time now, in fact since my childhood, I have had the honor of knowing your family. My late aunt and her husband, whose estate as you know I inherited, always held your father and your late mother in utmost esteem. The Lómov family and the Choobookóv family have always maintained extremely friendly, one might even say, intimate relations. Furthermore, as you know, my property borders on yours. Perhaps you will be so kind as to recall that my Ox Meadows run along your birch forest.

NATÁLIA: Excuse me for interrupting you. You said *"my* Ox Meadows." . . . Are they *yours?*

LÓMOV: Of course. . . .

NATÁLIA: Oh, come now! The Ox Meadows belong to us, not you!

LÓMOV: Oh no! They're mine, dear Natália Stepánovna.

NATÁLIA: That's news to me. How did they ever get to be yours?

LÓMOV: What do you mean? I'm talking about the Ox Meadows that are wedged in between your birch forest and the Burnt Marsh.

NATÁLIA: Exactly. . . . They're ours.

LÓMOV: No, you're mistaken, dear Natália Stepánovna—they're mine.

NATÁLIA: Do be reasonable, Iván Vassílievich! Since when have they been yours?

LÓMOV: Since when? They've always been ours, as far back as I can remember.

NATÁLIA: Excuse me, but this is too much!

LÓMOV: You can look at the documents, dear Natália Stepánovna. At one time, there *were* some quarrels about the Ox Meadows, you're quite right. But now, everyone knows they're mine. Why argue about it? If you will permit me to explain: my aunt's grandmother lent them to your paternal great-grandfather's peasants for an indefinite period and free of charge in return for their firing her bricks. Your great-grandfather's peasants used the Meadows free of charge for some forty years and began thinking of them as their own . . . and then after the Emancipation, when a statute was passed——

NATÁLIA: You've got it all wrong! Both my grandfather and great-grandfather regarded their property as reaching all the way to the Burnt Swamp—which means that the Ox Meadows were ours. What's there to argue about?—I don't understand. How annoying!

LÓMOV: I'll show you the documents, Natália Stepánovna.

NATÁLIA: No; you're joking or trying to tease me. . . . What a surprise! We've owned the land for practically three hundred years and now suddenly we're told it's not ours! I'm sorry, Iván Vassílievich, but I just can't believe my ears. Those Meadows don't mean a thing to me. The whole area probably doesn't come to more than forty acres, it's worth about three hundred rubles; but I'm terribly upset by the injustice of it all. You can say what you like, but I simply can't stand injustice.

LÓMOV: Please listen to me, I beseech you. Your paternal great-grandfather's peasants, as I have already had the honor of telling you, fired bricks for my aunt's grandmother. Now, my aunt's grandmother, wishing to do them a favor in return——

NATÁLIA: Grandfather, grandmother, aunt . . . I don't know *what* you're talking about! The Meadows are *ours,* and that's that.

LÓMOV: They're *mine!*

NATÁLIA: They're ours! You can keep arguing for two days, you can put on fifteen morning coats if you like, but they're ours, ours, ours! . . . I don't desire *your* property, but I don't care to lose mine. . . . Do as you like!

LÓMOV: I don't need the Meadows, Natália Stepánovna, but it's the principle of the thing. If you want, I'll *give* them to you.

NATÁLIA: It would be *my* privilege to give them to *you,* they're mine! . . . All this is rather odd—to put it mildly, Iván Vassílievich. Up till now we've always considered you a good neighbor and friend. Last year we let you borrow our threshing machine, and as a result we couldn't finish our own grain until November, and now you're treating us like Gypsies. You're *giving* me my own land. Excuse me, but that's not a neighborly thing to do! To *my* mind, it's impertinent, if you care to——

LÓMOV: Are you trying to tell me that I'm a land-grabber? Madam, I've never seized anyone else's property, and I won't allow anyone to *say* I have. . . . (*Hurries over to the carafe and drinks some water.*) The Ox Meadows are mine!

NATÁLIA: That's not true, they're ours.

LÓMOV: They're mine.

NATÁLIA: That's not true. I'll prove it to you! I'll send my men over to mow them this afternoon.

LÓMOV: What?!

NATÁLIA: My men will be there this afternoon!

LÓMOV: I'll kick them out!

NATÁLIA: You wouldn't dare!

LÓMOV: (*clutching at his heart*): The Ox Meadows are mine! Do you hear! Mine!

NATÁLIA: Stop shouting! Please! You can shout your lungs out in your own place, but I must ask you to control yourself here.

LÓMOV: Madam, if it weren't for these awful, excruciating palpitations and the veins throbbing in my temples, I'd speak to you in a totally different way! (*Shouting.*) The Ox Meadows are mine.

NATÁLIA: Ours!

LÓMOV: Mine!

NATÁLIA: Ours!

LÓMOV: Mine!

SCENE IV

(*Enter* CHOOBOOKÓV.)

CHOOBOOKÓV: What's going on? What's all the shouting about?

NATÁLIA: Papa, please tell this gentleman whom the Ox Meadows belong to. Us or him.

CHOOBOOKÓV (*to* LÓMOV): Why, the Meadows belong to us, old friend.

LÓMOV: But for goodness' sake, Stepán Stepánovich, how can that be? Can't *you* be reasonable at least? My aunt's grandmother lent the Meadows to your grandfather's peasants for temporary use and free of charge. His peasants used the land for forty years and got in the habit of regarding it as their own, but after the Land Settlement——

CHOOBOOKÓV: Excuse me, old boy. . . . You're forgetting that our peasants didn't pay your grandmother and so on precisely *because* the Meadows were disputed and what not. . . . But now every child knows that they're ours. I guess you've never looked at the maps.

LÓMOV: I'll *prove* they're mine!

CHOOBOOKÓV: You won't prove a thing, my boy.

LÓMOV: I will *so* prove it!

CHOOBOOKÓV: My dear boy, why carry on like this? You won't prove a thing by shouting. I don't want anything of yours, but I don't intend to let go of what's mine. Why should I? If it comes to that, dear friend, if you mean to dispute my ownership of the Meadows, and so on, I'd sooner let my peasants have them than you. So there!

LÓMOV: I don't understand. What right do you have to give away other people's property?

CHOOBOOKÓV: Allow me to decide whether or not I've got the right. Really, young man, I'm not accustomed to being spoken to in that tone of voice, and what not. I'm old enough to be your father, and I must ask you to calm down when you speak to me, and so forth.

LÓMOV: No! You're treating me like an idiot, and laughing at me. You tell me that *my* property is yours, and then you expect me to remain calm and talk to you in a normal fashion. That's not a very neighborly thing to do, Stepán Stepánovich. You're no neighbor, you're a robber baron.

CHOOBOOKÓV: What?! What did you say, my good man?

NATÁLIA: Papa, have the men mow the Ox Meadows right now!

CHOOBOOKÓV (*to* LÓMOV): What did you say, sir?

NATÁLIA: The Ox Meadows are our property, and I won't let anyone else have them. I won't, I won't, I won't!

LÓMOV: We'll see about that! I'll prove to you in court that they're mine.

CHOOBOOKÓV: In court? My good man, you can take it to court, and what not. Go right ahead! I know you, you've just been waiting for a chance to litigate, and so on. You're a quibbler from the word go. Your whole family's nothing but a bunch of pettifoggers. All of them!

LÓMOV: I must ask you not to insult my family. The Lómovs have always been law-abiding folk. None of them was ever hauled into court for embezzlement the way your uncle was.

CHOOBOOKÓV: Every last one of them was insane.

NATÁLIA: Every last one of them, every last one!

CHOOBOOKÓV: Your grandfather drank like a fish, and the whole county knows that your youngest aunt, Nastasia, ran off with an architect, and what not——

LÓMOV: And your mother was a hunchback! (*Clutching at his heart.*) There's a twitching in my side. . . . My head's throbbing. . . . Oh, God. . . . Water!

CHOOBOOKÓV: And your father was a gambler and he ate like a pig!

NATÁLIA: And no one could beat your aunt at scandal-mongering.

LÓMOV: My left leg's paralyzed. . . . And you're a schemer. . . . Oooh! My heart! . . . And it's no secret to anyone that just before the elections you——There are stars bursting before my eyes. . . . Where's my hat?

NATÁLIA: Vermin! Liar! Brute!

CHOOBOOKÓV: You're a spiteful, double-dealing schemer! So there!

LÓMOV: Ah, my hat. . . . My heart. Where am I? Where's the door? Oooh! . . . I think I'm dying. . . . My foot's totally paralyzed.

(*Drags himself to the door.*)

CHOOBOOKÓV (*calling after him*): And don't ever set your foot in my home again!

NATÁLIA: Go to court! Sue us! Just wait and see!

(LÓMOV *staggers out.*)

SCENE V

(CHOOBOOKÓV *and* NATÁLIA STEPÁNOVNA.)

CHOOBOOKÓV: He can go straight to hell, damn him!

(*Walks about, all wrought up.*)

NATÁLIA: Isn't he the worst crook? Catch me trusting a good neighbor after this!

CHOOBOOKÓV: The chiseler! The scarecrow!

NATÁLIA: The monster! He not only grabs other people's property, he calls them names, to boot.

CHOOBOOKÓV: And that clown, that . . . freak had the colossal nerve to ask me for your hand in marriage, and so on. Can you imagine? He wanted to propose.

NATÁLIA: Propose?

CHOOBOOKÓV: Exactly! That's what he came for. To propose to you.

NATÁLIA: Propose? To me? Why didn't you *say* so?

CHOOBOOKÓV: And he got all dolled up in a morning coat. That pipsqueak. That upstart.

NATÁLIA: Propose? To me? Ohhh! (*Collapses into an armchair and wails.*) Bring him back. Get him. Ohh! Get him!

CHOOBOOKÓV: Get whom?

NATÁLIA: Hurry up, hurry! I feel sick. Bring him back. (*Hysterical.*)

CHOOBOOKÓV: What is it? What's wrong? (*Grabbing his head.*) This is awful! I'll shoot myself. I'll hang myself. They've worn me out.

NATÁLIA: I'm dying! Bring him back!

CHOOBOOKÓV: All right. Stop yelling!

(*Runs out.*)

NATÁLIA: (*alone, wailing*): What've we done? Bring him back! Bring him back!

CHOOBOOKÓV (*running in*): He's coming and all that, goddamn him. Ughh! *You* talk to him, alone, I really don't feel like. . . .

NATÁLIA (*wailing*): Bring him back!

CHOOBOOKÓV (*shouting*): He's coming, I tell you. Oh God! What did I ever do to deserve a grown-up daughter? I'll cut my throat. I swear, I'll cut my throat. We insulted and abused him, and it's all your fault!

NATÁLIA My fault? It was yours!

CHOOBOOKÓV Now *I'm* the culprit!

(LÓMOV *appears at the French doors.* CHOOBOOKÓV *exits.*)

SCENE VI

(NATÁLIA *and* LÓMOV.)

LÓMOV (*entering, exhausted*): What horrible palpitations . . . my foot's gone numb . . . there's a jabbing in my side. . . .

NATÁLIA: My apologies, Iván Vassílievich, we got so worked up. . . . I do recall now that the Ox Meadows are actually *your* property.

LÓMOV: My heart's palpitating. . . . The Meadows *are* mine. . . . There are stars bursting in both my eyes.

(*They sit down.*)

NATÁLIA: We were wrong.

LÓMOV: It's the principle of the thing. . . . I don't care about the land, it's the principle of the thing——

NATÁLIA: Exactly, the principle. . . . Let's talk about something else.

LÓMOV: Particularly since I have proof. My aunt's grandmother let your paternal great-grandfather's peasants——

NATÁLIA: All right, all right. . . . (*Aside.*) I don't know how to go about it. . . . (*To* LÓMOV) Will you start hunting soon?

LÓMOV: Yes, for grouse, Natália Stepánovna. I think I shall begin after the harvest. Oh, have you heard what bad luck I had? My hound Guess—you know the one—he's gone lame.

NATÁLIA: What a pity! How did it happen?

LÓMOV: I don't know. He must have twisted his leg, or else some other dog bit him. . . . (*Sighs.*) My very best hound, not to mention the money! Why, I paid Mirónov a hundred and twenty-five rubles for him.

NATÁLIA: You overpaid him, Iván Vassílievich.

LÓMOV: I don't think so. It was very little for a wonderful dog.

NATÁLIA: Papa bought his dog Leap for eighty-five rubles, and Leap is vastly superior to your Guess.

LÓMOV: Leap superior to Guess? Oh, come now. (*Laughs.*) Leap superior to Guess!

NATÁLIA: Of course he is! I know that Leap is still young, he's not a full-grown hound yet. But for points and action, not even Volchanietsky has a better dog.

LÓMOV: Excuse me, Natália Stepánovna, but you're forgetting that he's pug-jawed, which makes him a poor hunting dog.

NATÁLIA: Pug-jawed? That's news to me.

LÓMOV: I can assure you, his lower jaw is shorter than his upper jaw.

NATÁLIA: Have you measured it?

LÓMOV: Indeed, I have. He'll do for pointing, of course, but when it comes to retrieving, he can hardly hold a cand——

NATÁLIA: First of all, our Leap is a pedigreed greyhound—he's the son of Harness and Chisel, whereas your Guess is so piebald that not even Solomon could figure out his breed. . . . Furthermore, he's as old and ugly as a broken-down nag——

LÓMOV: He may be old, but I wouldn't trade him for five of your Leaps. . . . The very idea! Guess is a real hound, but Leap. . . . Why argue? It's ridiculous. . . . Every huntsman's assistant has a dog like your Leap. At twenty-five rubles he'd be overpriced.

NATÁLIA: You seem to be possessed by some demon of contradiction, Iván Vassílievich. First you fancy that the Ox Meadows are yours, then you pretend that Guess is a better hound than Leap. If there's one thing I don't like it's a person who says the opposite of what he thinks. You know perfectly well that Leap is a hundred times better than . . . than that stupid Guess of yours. Why do you insist on denying it?

LÓMOV: You obviously must think, Natália Stepánovna, that I'm either blind or mentally retarded. Can't you see that your Leap has a pug jaw?

NATÁLIA: That's not true.

LÓMOV: A pug jaw.

NATÁLIA (*screaming*): That's not true.

LÓMOV: Why are you screaming, Madam?

NATÁLIA: Why are you talking such rubbish? It's exasperating! Your Guess is just about ready to be put out of his misery, and you compare him to Leap.

LÓMOV: Excuse me, but I can't keep on arguing like this. My heart's palpitating.

NATÁLIA: I've noticed that the sportsmen who argue most don't understand the first thing about hunting.

LÓMOV: Madam, pleeeease, keep quiet. . . . My heart's bursting. . . . (*Shouts.*) Keep quiet!

NATÁLIA: I won't keep quiet until you admit that Leap is a hundred times superior to your Guess!

LÓMOV: He's a hundred times *in*ferior. Someone ought to shoot him. My temples . . . my eyes . . . my shoulder. . . .

NATÁLIA: No one has to wish that idiotic mutt of yours dead, because he's just skin and bones anyway.

LÓMOV: Keep quiet! I'm having heart failure!

NATÁLIA: I will *not* keep quiet!

SCENE VII

CHOOBOOKÓV (*entering*): What's going on now?

NATÁLIA: Papa, tell me, honestly and sincerely: which is the better dog— our Leap or his Guess?

LÓMOV: Stepán Stepánovich, I beseech you, just tell me one thing: is your Leap pug-jawed or isn't he? Yes or no?

CHOOBOOKÓV: So what! Who cares? He's still the best hound in the country, and what not.

LÓMOV: And my Guess isn't better? Tell me the truth.

CHOOBOOKÓV: Don't get all worked up, old boy. . . . Let me explain. . . . Your Guess *does* have a few good qualities. . . . He's pure-bred, he's got solid legs, he's well put together, and what not. But if you must know, my good man, your dog's got two basic faults: he's old, and his muzzle's too short.

LÓMOV: Excuse me, my heart's racing madly. . . . Let's examine the facts. . . . Please don't forget that when we were hunting in the Mapooskin Fields, my Guess ran neck and neck with the count's dog Waggy, while your Leap lagged behind by half a mile.

CHOOBOOKÓV: That was because the Count's assistant struck him with his riding crop.

LÓMOV: Naturally. All the other dogs were chasing the fox, but yours started running after sheep.

CHOOBOOKÓV: That's a lie! My dear boy, I fly off the handle easily, so please let's stop arguing. The man whipped him because people are always envious of everyone else's dogs. Yes, they're all filled with spite! And you, sir, are no exception. Why, the minute you notice that anyone else's dog is better than your Guess, you instantly start up something or other . . . and what not. I've got the memory of an elephant!

LÓMOV: And so do I.

CHOOBOOKÓV (*mimicking him*): "And so do I" . . . And what does your memory tell you?

LÓMOV: My heart's palpitating. . . . My foot's paralyzed. . . . I can't anymore. . . .

NATÁLIA (*mimicking*): "My heart's palpitating". . . . What kind of hunter are you anyway? You ought to be home in bed catching cockroaches instead of out hunting foxes. Palpitations! . . .

CHOOBOOKÓV: That's right, what kind of hunter are you? If you've got palpitations, stay home; don't go wobbling around the countryside on horseback. It wouldn't be so bad if you really hunted, but you only tag along in order to start arguments or meddle with other people's dogs, and what not. We'd better stop, I fly off the handle easily. You, sir, are not a hunter, and that's that.

LÓMOV: And you *are,* I suppose. The only reason *you* go hunting is to flatter the count and carry on your back-stabbing little intrigues. . . . Oh, my heart! . . . You schemer!

CHOOBOOKÓV: Me, a schemer. (*Shouting.*) Shut up!

LÓMOV: Schemer!

CHOOBOOKÓV: Upstart! Pipsqueak!

LÓMOV: You old fogy! You hypocrite!

CHOOBOOKÓV: Shut up, or I'll blast you with a shot gun like a partridge.

LÓMOV: The whole county knows that—Oh, my heart!—your late wife used to beat you. . . . My leg . . . my temples . . . I see stars . . . I'm falling, falling. . . .

CHOOBOOKÓV: And your housekeeper henpecks you all over the place!

LÓMOV: There, you see . . . my heart's burst! My shoulder's torn off. . . . Where's my shoulder? . . . I'm dying! (*Collapses into armchair.*) Get a doctor! (*Faints.*)

CHOOBOOKÓV: Pipsqueak. Weakling. Windbag. I feel sick. (*Drinks some water.*) I feel sick.

NATÁLIA: What kind of hunter are you anyway? You don't even know how to sit in a saddle! (*To her father.*) Papa! What's the matter with him? Papa! Look, Papa! (*Screams.*) Iván Vassílievich! He's dead!

CHOOBOOKÓV: I feel sick! . . . I can't breathe! . . . Air!

NATÁLIA: He's dead! (*Tugs at* LÓMOV'S *sleeve.*) Iván Vassílievich! Iván Vassílievich! What've we done? He's dead. (*Collapses into easy chair.*) Get a doctor. (*She becomes hysterical.*)

CHOOBOOKÓV: Oh! . . . What is it? What's wrong?

NATÁLIA (*moaning*): He's dead . . . he's dead!

CHOOBOOKÓV: Who's dead? (*Glancing at* LÓMOV.) He really is dead! Oh, my God! Get some water! Get a doctor! (*Holds a glass to* LÓMOV'S *mouth.*) Go ahead and drink! . . . He won't drink. . . . I guess he's dead and so on. . . . Why does everything have to happen to me? Why didn't I put a bullet through my head long ago? Why didn't I cut my throat? What am I waiting for? Give me a knife! Give me a gun!

(LÓMOV *stirs.*)

He's reviving, I think. . . . Drink some water! . . . That's right.

LÓMOV: Stars . . . fog . . . where am I?

CHOOBOOKÓV: You two'd better hurry up and get married. . . . Dammit! She accepts. . . . (*Joins* LÓMOV'S *hand with* NATÁLIA'S.) She accepts. . . . My blessings and so forth. . . . Just do me a favor and leave me in peace.

LÓMOV: What? (*Getting up.*) Who?

CHOOBOOKÓV: She accepts. Well? Kiss her and . . . the two of you can go straight to hell.

NATÁLIA: (*moaning*): He's alive . . . I accept, I accept. . . .

CHOOBOOKÓV: Kiss and make up.

LÓMOV: What? Who? (*Kisses* NATÁLIA.) *Enchanté.* . . . Excuse me, but what's going on? Oh yes, I remember. . . . My heart . . . stars . . . I'm very happy, Natália Stepánovna. (*Kisses her hands.*) My leg's paralyzed. . . .

NATÁLIA: I . . . I'm very happy, too. . . .

CHOOBOOKÓV: That's a load off my back. . . . Whew!

NATÁLIA: But. . . . all the same, why don't you finally admit that Guess isn't as good as Leap.

LÓMOV: He's much better.

NATÁLIA: He's worse.

CHOOBOOKÓV: The launching of marital bliss! Champagne!

LÓMOV: He's better.

NATÁLIA: Worse! Worse! Worse!

CHOOBOOKÓV (*trying to outshout them*): Champagne! Champagne!

Meaning and Idea

1. How does Choobookóv respond to the idea of Lómov's marrying Natalia? How does Lómov himself feel? Why does he feel that way?

2. What interferes with Lómov's plans to propose marriage? Explain the issue of the Ox Meadows.

3. How does Natalia react when she learns Lómov's intentions from her father? What is Chekhov saying about marriage here? What happens when Lómov is summoned back? Where does the conversation about Leap and Guess take Lómov and Natalia?

4. How do Natalia and Choobookóv react when Lómov collapses?

5. Explain the irony in Choobookóv's line "The launching of marital bliss!" Why does he call for champagne? How is that also ironic?

Language, Form, Structure

1. What elements of argument do you find in the play? Where do the arguments seem logical and rational? Where do they defy logic and rationality and turn into shouting matches?

2. What are the propositions about the Ox Meadows and the two dogs?

3. Identify lines of dialogue that seem highly typical of each character.

4. Where do the characters use narration? Exemplification? Comparison and contrast?

5. How does Chekhov achieve humor in this play?

6. Define the following words and use each in a sentence: esteemed; fervent; palpitations; statute; beseech; threshing; impertinent; quibbler; pettifoggers; scandal-mongering; piebald; intrigues.

Ideas for Writing

1. Write a scene for a modern-day play version of "A Marriage Proposal." Draw your characters from people you know. Show a typical argument and how the two parties deal with it.

2. Write an essay in which you argue a position about marriage.

3. Write an essay in which you examine Chekhov's play as a farcical example of human behavior.

CROSSOVER

1. Virginia Woolf in "Professions for Women" and Adrienne Rich in "Claiming an Education" consider women's education and training and lay out what they see as old hardships as well as new hopes. What thesis does each essay advance? What examples does each author use to develop her point? How valid do you think these points are for current times? Why?

2. Jonathan Swift in "A Modest Proposal" and John Stuart Mill in "On Liberty" explore freedom and oppression in specific historical instances. In an essay, identify the basic social beliefs that the two selections reflect. What unique point does each selection make? Which selection rallies you the most? Why?

Acknowledgments

Brooks, Gwendolyn. "We Real Cool" from *Blacks* by Gwendolyn Brooks. Copyright © 1991 by Gwendolyn Brooks. Reprinted by permission of the author.

Brownmiller, Susan. Reprinted with the permission of Simon & Schuster from *Femininity* by Susan Brownmiller. Copyright © 1983 by Susan Brownmiller.

Camus, Albert. "The Myth of Sisyphus" from *The Myth of Sisyphus and Other Essays* by Albert Camus, translated by Justin O'Brien. Copyright © 1955 by Alfred A. Knopf, Inc. Reprinted by permission of publisher.

Cane, Melville. "Snow toward Evening" from *January Garden* by Melville Cane. Copyright 1926 by Harcourt Brace & Company and renewed 1954 by Melville Cane. Reprinted by permission of the publisher.

Carver, Raymond. "My Father's Life" by Raymond Carver. Reprinted by permission of International Creative Management, Inc. Copyright © 1984 by Raymond Carver.

Cather, Willa. Reprinted from *Willa Cather's Collected Short Fiction, 1892–1912* by permission of the University of Nebraska Press. Copyright ©1965, 1970 by the University of Nebraska Press. Copyright © renewed 1993 by the University of Nebraska Press.

Clifton, Lucille. "Good Times" copyrights 1987 by Lucille Clifton. Reprinted from *Good Woman: Poems and a Memoir 1969–1980*, with the permission of BOA Editions, Ltd. Rochester NY.

Cofer, Judith Ortiz. "The Witch's Husband" from *The Latin Deli: Prose & Poetry* by Judith Ortiz Cofer. Reprinted by permission of The University of Georgia Press.

Cowley, Malcolm."The National Heartbeat 'We-Ness' and 'Me-Ness'" by Malcolm Cowley. Reprinted by permission of the Literary Estate of Malcolm Cowley.

Cullen, Countee. Reprinted by permission of GRM Associates, agents for the estate of Ida M. Cullen. From the book *Color* by Countee Cullen. Copyright © 1925 by Harper & Brothers; copyright renewed 1953 by Ida M. Cullen.

cummings, e. e. "A Politician Is an Arse Upon" copyright 1944, © 1972, 1991 by the Trustees for the e. e. cummings Trust. Copyright © 1985 by George James Firmage, from *Complete Poems: 1904–1962* by e. e. cummings. Edited by George J. Firmage. Reprinted by permission of Liveright Publishing Corporation

cummings, e. e. "Nobody Loses All the Time" copyright 1926, 1954, © 1991 by the Trustees for the e. e. cummings Trust. Copyright © 1985 by George James Firmage, from *Complete Poems: 1904–1962* by e. e. cummings. Edited by George J. Firmage. Reprinted by permission of Liveright Publishing Corporation.

Dickinson, Emily. "There's Been a Death in the Opposite House" by Emily Dickinson. Reprinted by permission of the publishers and the Trustees of Amherst College from *The Poems of Emily Dickinson*, Thomas H. Johnson, ed., Cambridge, Mass: The Belknap Press of Harvard University Press. Copyright © 1951, 1955, 1979, 1983 by the President and Fellows of Harvard College.

Didion, Joan. "On Keeping a Notebook" from *Slouching Towards Bethlehem* by Joan Didion. Copyright © 1968 and copyright renewed © 1996 by Joan Didion. Reprinted by permission of Farrar, Straus & Giroux, Inc.

Epstein, Joseph. "Your Basic Language Snob" by Joseph Epstein, pen name "Aristedes" originally published in *The American Scholar*, Volume 53 Number 3, Summer, 1984. Copyright © 1984 by author. Reprinted by permission of the publisher.

Erdrich, Louise. From *Jacklight* by Louise Erdrich. Copyright © 1984 by Louise Erdrich. Reprinted by permission of Henry Holt and Company.

Frost, Robert. "Fire and Ice" from *The Poetry of Robert Frost* by Robert Frost edited by Edward Connery Lathem. Copyright 1951 by Robert Frost, copyright 1923, © 1969 by Henry Holt & Co., Inc. Reprinted by permission of Henry Holt & Co., Inc.

Gould, Stephen Jay. "The Geometer of Race" by Stephen Jay Gould, *Discover* magazine, 1993. Printed by permission of the author.

Graves, Robert. "The Naked and the Nude" from *Five Pens in Hand* by Robert Graves. Copyright © 1958 by Robert Graves. Used by permission of Oxford University Press, Inc.

Heaney, Seamus. "Digging" from *Death of a Naturalist and Poems 1965–1975* by Seamus Heaney. Copyright © 1980 by Seamus Heaney. Reprinted by permission of Farrar, Straus & Giroux, Inc. and Faber & Faber Ltd.

Hemingway, Ernest. "Camping Out" by Ernest Hemingway. Reprinted with permission of Scribner, a Division of Simon & Schuster, from Ernest *Hemingway: Dateline Toronto*, edited by William White. Copyright © 1985 by Mary Hemingway, John Hemingway, Patrick Hemingway and Gregory Hemingway.

Hughes, Langston. "Dream Deferred" from *The Panther and the Lash* by Langston Hughes. Copyright © 1951 by Langston Hughes. Reprinted by permission of Alfred A. Knopf, Inc.

Hughes, Langston. "Salvation" from *The Big Sea* by Langston Hughes. Copyright © 1940 by Langston Hughes. Copyright renewed © 1968 by Arna Bontemps and George Houston Bass. Reprinted by permission of Hill and Wang, a Division of Farrar, Straus & Giroux, Inc.

Jhabvala, Ruth Prawer. "Myself in India" from *Out of India by* Ruth Prawer Jhabvala. Copyright © 1976, 1986 by Ruth Prawer Jhabvala. By permission of William Morrow & Company, Inc.

Joyce, James. "Araby" from *Dubliners* by James Joyce. Copyright © 1916 by B. W. Heubsch. Definitive text Copyright © 1967 by the Estate of James Joyce. Used by permission of Viking Penguin, a Division of Penguin Books USA Inc.

Kazin, Alfred. "The Kitchen" from *A Walker in the City* by Alfred Kazin. Copyright © 1951 and renewed 1979 by Alfred Kazin, reprinted by permission of Harcourt Brace & Company.

Kingston, Maxine Hong. From *The Woman Warrior* by Maxine Hong Kingston. Copyright © 1975, 1976 by Maxine Hong Kingston. Reprinted by permission of the publisher.

Lawrence, D. H. "The Rocking-Horse Winner" by D. H. Lawrence, copyright 1933 by the Estate of D. H. Lawrence, renewed © 1961 by Angelo Ravagli and C. M. Weekley, executors of the estate of Frieda Lawrence, from *Complete Short Stories of D. H. Lawrence* by D. H. Lawrence. Used by permission of Viking Penguin, a Division of Penguin Books USA Inc.

Laye, Camara. Excerpt from *The Dark Child by* Camara Laye, translated by James Kirkup, Ernest Jones, and Elaine Gottlieb. Copyright © 1954 and renewed © 1982 by Camara Laye. Reprinted by permission of Hill and Wang, a Division of Farrar, Straus & Giroux, Inc.

Lopate, Phillip. Reprinted with the permission of Simon & Schuster from *Against Joie De Vivre* by Phillip Lopate. Copyright © 1989 by Phillip Lopate.

Lowell, Arny. "Wind and Silver" from *The Complete Poetical Works of Amy Lowell* by Amy Lowell. Copyrights 1955 by Houghton Mifflin Company, © renewed 1983 by Houghton Mifflin Company, Brinton P. Roberts, and G. D'Andelot Belin, Esq. Reprinted by permission of Houghton Mifflin Co. All rights reserved.

McCullers, Carson. "A Tree. A Rock. A Cloud" from *The Ballad of the Sad Cafe and Collected Short Stories* by Carson McCullers. Copyright 1936, 1941, 1942, 1950, © 1955 by Carson McCullers, © renewed 1979 by Floria V. Lasky. Reprinted by permission of Houghton Mifflin Co. All rights reserved.

Mehta, Ved. "The Baby Myna" from *Vedi* by Ved Mehta. Copyright © 1982 by Ved Mehta. Reprinted with the permission of The Wylie Agency, Inc.

Momaday, N. Scott. From *The Way to Rainy Mountain* by N. Scott Momaday, 1969, first published in *The Reporter*, January 26, 1967. Copyright © 1969 University of New Mexico Press. Reprinted by permission.

Moore, Lorrie. "How to Become a Better Writer" from *Self-Help* by Lorrie Moore. Copyright © 1985 by M. L. Moore. Reprinted by permission of Alfred A. Knopf, Inc.

Moore, Marianne. "Poetry" by Marianne Moore. Reprinted with the permission of Simon & Schuster from *Collected Poems of Marianne Moore*. Copyright 1935 by Marianne Moore; copyright renewed © 1963 by Marianne Moore and T. S. Eliot.

Morrison, Toni. "A Slow Walk of Trees" by Toni Morrison. Copyright © 1976 by Toni Morrison. Reprinted by permission of International Creative Management, Inc.

O'Brien, Edna. "My Mother's Mother" from *A Fanatic Heart* by Edna O'Brien. Copyright © 1984 by Edna O'Brien. Reprinted by permission of Farrar, Straus & Giroux, Inc. and The Wylie Agency.

Orwell, George. "Politics and the English Language" by George Orwell, copyright 1946 by Sonia Brownell Orwell and renewed 1974 by Sonia Orwell, reprinted from his volume *Shooting an Elephant and Other Essays* by permission of Harcourt Brace & Company and A. M. Heath & Company Ltd. Copyright © Mark Hamilton as literary executor of the estate of the late Sonia Brownell Orwell and Martin Secker and Warburg, Ltd.

Orwell, George. "Why I Write" from *Such, Such Were the Joys* by George Orwell, copyright 1953 by Sonia Brownell Orwell and renewed 1981 by Mrs. George K. Perutz, Mrs. Miriam Gross and Dr. Michael Dickson, executors of the estate of Sonia Brownell Orwell, reprinted by permission of Harcourt Brace & Company and A. M. Heath & Company Ltd. Copyright © Mark Hamilton as literary executor of the estate of the late Sonia Brownell Orwell and Martin Secker and Warburg, Ltd.

Owen, Wilfred "Dulce et Decorum Est" by Wilfred Owen from *The Collected Poems of Wilfred Owen*. Copyright © 1963 by Chatto & Windus, Ltd. Reprinted by permission of New Directions Publishing Corp.

Plath, Sylvia. Excerpt from *Johnny Panic and the Bible of Dreams* by Sylvia Plath. Copyright 1952, 1953, 1954, 1955, 1956, 1957, 1960, 1961, 1962, 1963 by Sylvia Plath. Copyright 1977, 1979 by Ted Hughes. Reprinted by permission of HarperCollins Publishers, Inc. and Faber & Faber Ltd.

Reed, Henry. "Naming of Parts" by Henry Reed. Reprinted from *Henry Reed: Collected Poems* edited by Jon Stallworthy (1991) by permission of Oxford University Press.

Rich, Adrienne. "Claiming an Education" from *On Lies, Secrets, and Silence: Selected Prose 1966–1978* by Adrienne Rich. Copyright © 1979 by W. W. Norton & Company, Inc. Reprinted by permission of the author and W. W. Norton & Company, Inc.

Robinson,.Edwin Arlington. "Richard Cory" by Edwin Arlington Robinson. Reprinted with the permission of Simon & Schuster from *The Collected Poems of Edwin Arlington Robinson* (New York: Macmillan, 1937).

Rodriguez, Richard. "Complexion" from *Hunger of Memory* by Richard Rodriguez. Reprinted by permission of David R. Godine, Publisher, Inc. Copyright © 1982 by Richard Rodriguez.

Shaw, Irwin. "The Girls in Their Summer Dresses" by Irwin Shaw. Reprinted with permission of Arthur B. Greene, Atty. for Marian Shaw, executrix of the estate of Irwin Shaw. Copyright © Irwin Shaw.

Sontag, Susan. Excerpt from *Illness as Metaphor* by Susan Sontag. Copyright © 1977, 1978 by Susan Sontag. Reprinted by permission of Farrar, Straus & Giroux, Inc.

Tan, Amy. Reprinted by permission of G. P. Putnam's Sons from *The Joy Luck Club* by Amy Tan. Copyright © 1989 by Amy Tan.

Thomas, Dylan. "Do Not Go Gentle into That Good Night" by Dylan Thomas from *The Poems of Dylan Thomas*. Copyright © 1952 by Dylan Thomas. Reprinted by permission of New Directions Publishing Corp. and David Higham Associates Ltd.

Thomas, Lewis. "On Warts", copyright © 1979 by *The New England Journal of Medicine*, from *The Medusa and the Snail* by Lewis Thomas. Used by permission of Viking Penguin USA, a Division of Penguin Books USA Inc.

Thurber, James. "Courtship through the Ages" from *My World and Welcome to It* by James Thurber. Copyright © 1942 James Thurber. Copyright © renewed 1970 Helen Thurber and Rosemary A. Thurber. Reprinted by arrangement with Rosemary A. Thurber and The Barbara Hogenson Agency.

Tuchman, Barbara W. "The Black Death" from *A Distant Mirror* by Barbara W. Tuchman. Copyright © 1978 by Barbara W. Tuchman. Reprinted by permission of Alfred A. Knopf, Inc.

Walker, Alice. "Everyday Use" from *In Love and Trouble: Stories of Black Women* by Alice Walker, copyright © 1973 by Alice Walker, reprinted by permission of Harcourt Brace & Company.

White, E. B. All pages from "Once More to the Lake" from *One Man's Meat* by E. B. White. Copyright © 1941 by E. B. White. Copyright renewed. Reprinted by permission of HarperCollins Publishers, Inc.

Wolff, Tobias. "The Chain" from *The Night in Question* by Tobias Wolff. Copyright © 1996 by Tobias Wolff. Reprinted by permission of Alfred A. Knopf, Inc.

Woolf, Virginia. Excerpt from *Mrs. Dalloway* by Virginia Woolf, copyright 1925 by Harcourt Brace & Company and renewed 1953 by Leonard Woolf, reprinted by permission of the publisher.

Woolf, Virginia. Excerpts from *A Room of One's Own* by Virginia Woolf, copyright 1929 by Harcourt Brace & Company and renewed 1957 by Leonard Woolf, reprinted by permission of the publisher.

Woolf, Virginia. "Professions for Women" from *The Death of the Moth and Other Essays* by Virginia Woolf, copyright 1942 by Harcourt Brace & Company and renewed 1970 by Marjorie T. Parsons, executrix. Reprinted by permission of Harcourt Brace & Company.

Wright, Richard. Chapter 1 from *Native Son* by Richard Wright. Copyright ©1940 by Richard Wright. Copyright © renewed 1968 by Ellen Wright. Reprinted by permission of HarperCollins Publishers, Inc.

Zinsser, William K. Chapter 3, "Clutter" from *On Writing Well*, Fifth edition by William K. Zinsser. Copyright © 1976, 1980, 1985, 1988, 1990, 1994 by William K. Zinsser